Women and their Moon Signs

Women and their Moon Signs

Jacqueline Bigar

AVON BOOKS ◆ NEW YORK

AVON BOOKS, INC.
1350 Avenue of the Americas
New York, New York 10019

Copyright © 1998 by Jacqueline Bigar
Interior design by Kellan Peck
Published by arrangement with the author
Visit our website at **http://www.AvonBooks.com**
ISBN: 0-380-79779-8

Library of Congress Cataloging in Publication Data:
Bigar, Jacqueline.
  Women and their moon signs / Jacqueline Bigar.
    p. cm.
  1. Astrology. 2. Moon—Miscellanea. 3. Women—Psychology—Miscellanea. 4.
Man-women relationships—Miscellanea. I. Title.
BF1723.B54 1998   98-23587
133.5'32'082—dc21   CIP

First Avon Books Trade Paperback Printing: August 1998

AVON TRADEMARK REG. U.S. PAT. OFF. AND IN OTHER COUNTRIES, MARCA REGISTRADA, HECHO
EN U.S.A.

Printed in the U.S.A.

OPM   10 9 8 7 6 5 4 3 2 1

CONTENTS

MOON IN GEMINI · 61

MOON IN CANCER · 89

MOON IN LEO · 118

MOON IN VIRGO · 142

MOON IN LIBRA · 171

MOON IN SCORPIO · 200

MOON IN SAGITTARIUS · 230

MOON IN CAPRICORN · 259

MOON IN AQUARIUS · 287

MOON IN PISCES · 315

INTRODUCTION

"We don't see things as they are, we see them as we are."
—ANAIS NIN
from *Quotable Women*, Running Press, Philadelphia

Millions of readers scoop up newspapers and magazines to read their horoscope. But what they are actually reading are their "Sun" signs. There is much more to an individual's astrological chart than the Sun, but this is the one piece of information most people know, since it is determined by one's birth date alone.

Did you know you not only have a Sun sign, but another sign for the Moon and planets, such as Venus, Mars, and Mercury? It's true. You have many signs, not just your Sun sign. Together, they make up your complete chart. To learn all your signs, you need more information about the position of the planets at the time of your birth.

This book will teach you about your Moon sign, describing the essential qualities that the Moon gives you. These qualities often make up the very core of your femininity and are vital to the success you hope to find in love relationships.

Astrologers, as well as psychiatrists, have always know that each person, regardless of gender or sexual orientation, has a masculine side and a feminine side that combine to make the whole person. The psychologist Carl Jung described these two sides as the animus, for the masculine nature, and anima, for the feminine. Astrologers define this psychological difference by using the Moon to define the feminine and the Sun to define the masculine. That's the reason we have used the combination of Sun and Moon to best describe relationships between men and women.

Astrologers have always known that women are not fully represented by their Sun signs. Ironically, what women fought to communicate to the world in the 1970s, their ability to function in a society dominated by masculine values, is that aspect of their nature described by the Sun. Their Sun qualities are what let women compete in the business world, enjoy sports, and analyze. But it is the Moon that endows a woman with her feminine virtues, inclinations, and emotional needs. It is the Moon that calls for a particular type of man to fulfill her as a woman.

The Moon gives a woman her very essence, her feminine essence, her feminine core; her sensual, tender, nurturing, caring side. A woman's aura is bathed in moonlight and it is hers alone. The Moon compels a woman, regardless of worldly success, to satisfy her emotional hunger for love, home, children, and romance.

The purpose of this book is to give women a tour of their very private Moonscopes. If you are a woman, you'll discover the Moon's map of your nature, your partnerships, and how you project your image in the world. That image might be very different from the person you really are and what you want from a relationship. If you are a man, you'll learn secrets about the women in your life and what makes them tick, as revealed by their Moon signs. By studying his own Moon sign, a man can learn about that part of his nature, that anima, that traditional society has taught him to repress.

You know what your Sun sign is, the sign determined by your birth date. But what is your Moon sign? At the back of the book [page 343)] you'll find charts that locate both your Sun and Moon signs, according to the date and time of your birth. Start by using the charts. Identify your Moon sign and verify your Sun sign—the one you check in the daily horoscope column.

Once you know your Moon sign, find the chapter that describes your Moon nature. Read about yourself, specifically your emotional disposition and outlook on life, your expectations, your dreams and hopes.

Following the general description of your Moon sign, the book gives even more information, based on the combination of your Moon and Sun signs. For while each Moon sign endows specific feminine traits to those born under it, these qualities are shaded by the Sun. By reading your Moon description with its companion Sun sign, you'll learn even more about your total nature.

Under each Moon-Sun combination, you'll discover relationship options with men, based on their Sun signs. These descriptions reveal which men are most likely to be compatible with you. Whatever your current relationship status, this book promises you new insights into past, present, and possible future relationships. It can change your life. You will gain a better understanding of why you repeat patterns—positive or negative. You could get a good look at "Mr. Right"!

Women can also use this book to learn a powerful secret: A man's Moon sign can tell you not only about his hidden emotional nature; it can describe the type of woman he wants and needs. So after you finish reading about yourself, you can use the book to gain extra insights about the men in your life.

The book charts a long-needed map of women's special needs. So pick up a pen and paper and get ready for an emotional adventure no horoscope book has ever provided. It was written to give you pleasure, new perspective, and an enthusiasm for fun, love, and life.

Moon in Aries

*"I can promise to be frank, but I can't promise to be
impartial."*

—GOETHE

Yorou blaze into a room, promising energy and vitality. You make a
statement: I am. You are a presence. You project honesty, clarity,
and directness. The color red is associated with you. It can be your ruddy
complexion, your reddish hair, or maybe just a color you like to wear.

This is not an easy position for the Moon. The Moon in Aries encourages independence, acting out, and impulsiveness. Sometimes you might
not even recognize your feelings, though you think you do. Confusion
between impulses and feelings is common for this spirited Moon position.
Action always feels better to an Aries Moon than flowing along with
feelings.

You are loving, yet might react in ways that counteract closeness and
intimacy. You could deflect feelings into your sexuality. Partners might
not mind this defense at all, though you are avoiding feeling dependent
or needy. This trait could work with the right partner, but some suitors,
seeking true intimacy, could be turned off.

A hot temper is associated with Moon in Aries. The old saying that
the best defense is a strong offense works for you, especially when you
feel vulnerable. Your frequent eruptions of anger shield the vulnerable,
tender human being within. If you stop and think before you explode,
or even after, you'll discover that frightening, deep feelings are involved.

As a Moon in Aries, you must be busy and active. A full schedule
is a given, possibly connected to a cause. Maintaining a busy schedule
prevents you from experiencing your deep, scary feelings; you are simply
too busy.

Life breathes through you. You are always ready to participate. You enjoy movement and need it. Through action, you discharge your tension, anger, and frustration.

In a relationship, you will not want to be saddled with the housekeeping, cooking, or other traditional roles. You want duties to be equally shared. When you find a partner who meets you halfway, you will open up to your hidden passions.

You offer loyalty and dependability. To the outside world, you will always defend your inner circle. You will tell off a loved one you think is wrong, but the world will never know.

To many men, your independence, free spirit, and open thinking make you a highly desirable companion and lover. They can count on adventure, excitement, and fairness.

MOON IN ARIES, SUN IN ARIES

You are hot, energetic, and impulsive. You go for whatever you want with direction and determination. You're like a full-throttle freight train. You are committed and active, attractive and athletic. You are movement—alive, sexy, and dynamic.

You seek a man much like you. You want him to be fiery, manifesting his caring in service and commitment. You expect strong ethics, loyalty, and determination. You want to count on him to come through for you, in good times and bad. You expect to be an equal partner. He must want you to be that way, because you will not tolerate fighting turf wars. The two of you will need joint interests because both of you are so committed to your activities.

Sometimes you judge love by the heat of the passionate flares you shoot up. Because you are hot-tempered and impulsive, there will be arguments with any man you choose.

Sometimes in relationships you have difficulty understanding where your partner is coming from. You see life from your own perspective. You get behind your ideas and push them because you know they are right, at least for you.

You offer much in a relationship—caring, depth, commitment. You want the same in return. Expect a whirlwind romance in which impulse rules. You are likely a one-marriage woman and will do all you can to keep in that way.

With Aries SUN man: Both of you are pistols, ready to trigger at the drop of a hat. To have this match work, someone has to be the bullet and someone, the gun. You are both headstrong, independent, and willful.

Pick your roles in this relationship and you'll both win. This combo is like a volcano, seething and occasionally erupting.

With Taurus SUN man: The day you meet this man might be interesting, but it will be inconsequential in the long run unless you are looking for a banker or an investment counselor. He is great with money, even-tempered, and sensuous. However, he doesn't like histrionics and displays of tempers. Relating to him will make you want to scream.

With Gemini SUN man: You are active, and he is rambunctious. He is mental energy and inquisitiveness. He's got the art of flirtation down pat. You could find him exciting, funny, and delightful. You won't like it, though, when he tries to be helpful and he analyzes the pros and cons of an idea you love. This match can be wickedly naughty, but don't expect him to be like you.

With Cancer SUN man: You are a fire sign; he is a water sign. Mix the two of you and you get a lot of steam. You might not mind the fights because of the attraction, but he can't do it for you. He will withdraw into his cocoon. Once he withdraws, he might never come out. He needs a nurturing partner, and that isn't you!

With Leo SUN man: Passions swell between you. You love his energy and style. Above all, you adore how you feel with him. Whether this pairing can last long term depends on two factors. Can you accept his values? Can you deal with his tendency to meander? You are hot stuff together, but remember, to make this work you also have to stroke this big lion's ego.

With Virgo SUN man: He is logical, detached, and caring. He might get involved with one of your pet projects, but he has a problem with emotional displays, which are as natural to you as swimming is to a fish. He could be bitter, sarcastic, and critical. Do you want this?

With Libra SUN man: He is your opposite. He avoids confrontation and has trouble making decisions. You both need people, though in very different ways. He thinks in terms of "we." You think in terms of "I." This relationship can offer tremendous growth, excitement, and passion, but it also requires mutual respect and maturity.

With Scorpio SUN man: You are both Mars-ruled, and your passions could blend. He can enjoy your fiery nature and draw from its heat. As much as you act on your commitments and ideas, he feels them. He is deep, intense, and emotional. You will need to understand these aspects of his nature.

With Sagittarius SUN man: This man is impulsive, fiery, and dynamic. Both of you enjoy grand passion, yet value your independence. While he longs for the grass on the other side of the fence, you act in pursuit of challenges. This romp could last a lifetime, though you must understand his values aren't yours. Love, heat, and romance mark this pairing.

With Capricorn SUN man: He is committed to his work, accumulating wealth, and building security. This match might work if you have similar commitments. He has the energy to meet yours. However, you'll have battles royal. You are both strong enough to deal with them, and the clashes only add to the passion of the moment. You'll enjoy kissing and making up.

With Aquarius SUN man: He is thoughtful, yet wild. He is as independent as you. You'll love his humor, wicked ways, and delightful flirtation. You make quite the team, especially when you have a cause to share. He thinks of things you don't. Your love is fun, dynamic, and sexy.

With Pisces SUN man: You might want to skip this one. He is very sentimental and caring. But he is needy; and you are independent. His neediness could burn you out if you stick around too long. Neither of you will be happy. Keep on walking.

MOON IN ARIES, SUN IN TAURUS

You are fiery, yet grounded. You have one of the most powerful Moon in Aries combinations. Your enthusiasm and energy propel your crusades. Even if your vitality fails, you put enough forethought into your campaigns to guarantee success. You're a strong leader, a wonderfully loyal person to have on one's side.

You're sensual and attractive. Though energetic, you might think you need to lose weight as you may be somewhat pear shaped. Remember, skinny isn't always sexy. Your love of movement and sensual ways make you one of the zodiac's most desirable women. Though you are a delight to court and a loyal partner, you can be stubborn.

You crave security, emotional and material. You can be difficult if your security is threatened. You need a very strong man, one who offers the stability you need to emotionally dedicate yourself to your interests.

You expect sensuality, an appreciation of the good life, and financial savvy.

You are romantic and passionate and appreciate a romantic courtship with cards and tokens of affection. Although you're open to novelty, you like solid expressions of caring. Trips, jewelry, and memorable meals are all part of the scenario.

You will tend to marry once. Quite possibly, you'll wed your first love. You seem to have it all—balance and hot energy, yet a conservative bent that prevents you from doing anything too wild.

With Aries SUN man: He heats you up and makes your life even more passionate. You are two flames merging. You might feel as if you have known each other forever. You understand what to do to make each other happy. You will be the conservative here, the one who demands traditional tokens of caring.

With Taurus SUN man: He is your image of the perfect man. He knows how to make you happy and secure. Your love affair will be slow-moving, steady, and sensual. Expect to be tantalized and delighted. You can find a lifetime commitment here. You will be the light of his life.

With Gemini SUN man: He is a delightful charmer who makes you want to play. He will feed your fire and crusades with ideas. He'll stroke your passion with love letters. However, if you are looking for Mr. Stability and Consistency, keep looking. He won't be your anchor. He lives in the world of ideas.

With Cancer SUN man: He is sensitive and values security as much as you. You'll enjoy many romantic, sentimental moments. However, he is needy and gets crabby if he can't find you. Can you be at his beck and call? This relationship's exquisite tenderness and seductive sensuality might just make you say yes.

With Leo SUN man: You want romance? You just ran into Clark Gable. He knows how to wine and dine you to the umpteenth degree. The love temperature will always run high, even years later. He can provide you with security, but you must fawn over him to keep him content. A water bed might help counteract the hot temperatures you two generate.

With Virgo SUN man: He adores and nurtures you. You can thrive on his logic, and he delights in your easy, natural sensuality. There is trust. When you erupt into flames over a key issue, he will understand, as he too values service and commitment. You must accept his snappy criticisms, and he must deal with your hot tamale temper.

With Libra SUN man: The attraction is undeniable. He offers you romance, understanding, and room to express your dynamic energy. You will need to run the budget and be the practical one. He won't challenge you, but you can learn much from his diplomatic, gentle ways. You both like peace. There's enough here to last a lifetime.

With Scorpio SUN man: He might be quiet, but he is a powerhouse. He is his own person and will let you know when he doesn't agree with you. However, as strong as the passion is, the standoffs are just as difficult. If you can figure out how to resolve them, this can be a lifetime delight.

With Sagittarius SUN man: Both of you are interested in money and its creative uses. Only, his creativity might be much more risk-oriented than yours. He is fiery and enthusiastic, and together, you can experience the finest of life. Go for it.

With Capricorn SUN man: He is stable, earthy, and materialistic. This match clicks, sensually as well as intellectually. You like how he establishes and builds his power base. Security is a plus here. The minus is that sometimes he seems like a stick-in-the-mud. If you two can resolve this difference, you could be heading down the aisle.

With Aquarius SUN man: He is a wonderful friend and an eccentric freethinker. On one level, you absolutely adore that. However, the hairs on the back of your neck stand straight up at some of the risks he takes. He won't be your anchor, but he could be good for a wild romp and a great pal. Leave it there.

With Pisces SUN man: You seem to understand this emotional and sensitive man. You give him security. If you decide to accept him as your crusade and help stabilize him, this match might work. You could be the best thing that ever happens to him. Be sure you want this burden, because he can weigh you down. Think before you leap!

MOON IN ARIES, SUN IN GEMINI

Others seek your company. There is seldom a dull moment with you. You are vibrant, passionately determined, witty, and as naughty as one can get! You are everyone's friend, the life of the party.

You have the right answer for any situation and can do two or three things at once. No matter how charming you are, you are highly competitive. It is important not to bring this attitude into your relationships.

You can get along with many men, but finding a partner who complements your multiple facets is your challenge. Unless you do, you could feel as if you are selling yourself out.

The real issue is what kind of partnership you want. Do you visualize always being together, or leading highly independent lives outside your bonding? The better you define the roles of the relationship, the more likely you are to hit bingo. If you don't, never fear; there are always other fish in the sea.

Your desirability is strong, giving you choices. You do have a difficult time with intense feelings. Though you are one hot, sometimes volatile woman, clinging neediness and self-pity send you up the wall. So beware of men with those traits.

You thrive on social interaction and want a relationship that allows you to continue the social whirl. Above all, you need to express your passionate nature. You live your life 100 percent, as long as your interest endures. You are an all-or-nothing lady!

With Aries SUN man: You can stop looking right now. His energy meets yours, and he delights you. You both love a hardy game of tennis or chess, enjoying competition. The passion can surge out of control! Though there could be a domestic fracas or two, you always seem to be in synch. Your wit and charm amuses him; his manliness has you swooning. Need we say any more?

With Taurus SUN man: Go right past this man and keep on moving. He is stable and anchored, but that isn't the problem. The issue is how bored you will get and how quickly at that! Keep on trucking!

With Gemini SUN man: You have met someone nearly as versatile, naughty, and charming as you. You might like this match, although endurance isn't his strong suit. He might take off at the drop of a hat. However, embers burn brightly between you, so he will probably come home in due time.

With Cancer SUN man: The odds of an attraction aren't strong here, though you could meet at the gym, jogging to the bank, or checking out a favorite resort. You are so easily distracted that you will be long gone before he even turns his head. I don't think so!

With Leo SUN man: He is like a blaze of passion as he enters your life. Your fast, witty responses draw him in, and once he meets the animal in you, neither of you will want to pull away. You actually might love living in his lair. The common bond is simple: You both love living and demonstrating it!

With Virgo SUN man: He is a detail man, with unusual precision. Though you might enjoy a chat with him, you won't like it a bit when he starts scrutinizing you. Don't get carried away with this one. Be realistic.

With Libra SUN man: He is even more charming and delightful than you. Is that possible? You are like two magnets, the attracting force is so strong. This is unlikely to diminish over time. Your differences are complementary. You are active and demanding; he is passive and adoring. You can work nearly anything out.

With Scorpio SUN man: This combination is enough to put anyone in a sweat. The high energy and intensity could scare mere mortals! You can handle this man. Though he has a deep reservoir of feeling and strength you have the passion to meet his and the intellect to turn his interest to fascination. He won't be able to figure you out, but he'll never quit trying. Hot, hot, hot!

With Sagittarius SUN man: He is fiery, and like you, ready to act on ideas. You team up easily and could keep it going for a lifetime marathon. You will challenge him mentally and provoke him physically. Your passions make his boil. Excitement, adventure, and laughter mark this match.

With Capricorn SUN man: There is an innate tension here. He might admire your ideas and enjoy your blasts of energy, but he really finds you way too flaky. There is fight after fight here. Why do it? If you feel the need to play it out, poor you, poor him.

With Aquarius SUN man: He is naughty, eccentric, and fun. You'll have lots of laughs. The two of your will giggle about things others don't understand. Your passion will intrigue this offbeat man. There is nothing stopping you here. This is the merger of two free spirits who can be friends and lovers.

With Pisces SUN man: This a mismatch in every sense. There could be an attraction, but his sensitive, gooey ways give you the creeps. This is most definitely a "no." Just being yourself will hurt his feelings.

MOON IN ARIES, SUN IN CANCER

You feel deeply and sometimes emote a seething intensity that only the strong can take and only the wise will understand. You can be quiet and understanding at one moment, only to explode in a fireball of emotion the next.

You intuitively give those you love what they need; you are a natural nurturer. Because you fulfill so many needs, you become indispensable. Defending loved ones, or your favorite cause, you can summon lightning bolts. You will do all that is possible to further their rights and wants. You are clearly an asset on anyone's team.

You are very attractive, possibly with an ethereal quality. You draw men with your delightful femininity and emotional sensitivity. You seem to know what they want before they do. You are also passionate, physical, active, and competitive.

As a natural giver and protector, it is important to not sell your own emotional needs short. Never forget it is your responsibility to establish your own boundaries and expectations. If you don't, you could sometimes feel as if others walk on you. They might, but you permit it.

You will seek a man who is sensitive, perhaps moody, and who obviously needs a woman like you. Emotional and financial security are very important to you. If that need is taken care of, you are likely to become a crusader, perhaps campaigning for women's or family rights. Your caring is well anchored and deep. You will want one marriage into which you can pour your heart and soul. Your challenge in making that happen will be to pull together your diverse nature into a unified whole.

With Aries SUN man: This is a winner. You might have different desires, but there is enough similarity that you can live well together. You can crusade and love together. Though there is explosive passion, he might not be as sensitive as you'd like. Perhaps he doesn't understand your emotionalism. Accept this, and the world is your oyster.

With Taurus SUN man: This man will make a very clear impression on you. Will it be pure sensuality or boredom? That depends on chemistry. Though he can provide everything you want, your sometimes rash ways will irk and perhaps hurt him. Be sure commitment isn't a prison sentence here.

With Gemini SUN man: You just met a spark plug who can help keep your motor humming. He will encourage your passions and cheer on your crusades, but he is not emotionally sensitive. You need to build your own security and structure here. The good news is that there will never be a boring moment.

With Cancer SUN man: This man is emotional and intense. He will court you, and you will purr. This is a courtship full of romance, wonderful meals, and exciting trips. Security is a natural element here, as you have similar needs. Just don't take your crusades too far from the home and he will be happy.

With Leo SUN man: You are a romantic at heart, and this man knows romance. There are sultry moments, heated exchanges, and much conversation. You know how to light each other's fire. He can be very sensitive when he chooses, but not at your calling. He is his own person. Team up with him and you have a life of adventure.

With Virgo SUN man: You can count on this man. He comes through and is dedicated. You will feel secure. Just don't be surprised by his quizzical look when you cry at the drop of a hat. He might join you in your crusades, as he too values service. However, it is you who ignites his passion.

With Libra SUN man: Though this man certainly doesn't mean to be, he is at odds with your very nature. He is passive; you are assertive. You have deep commitments; he wants a happy life without challenges. You wouldn't spend a second with him except that there is a heavy physical attraction. Be smart. Turn away before disaster strikes.

With Scorpio SUN man: His reserve hides a deep dedication. He feels as much as you do. There is a true soul union here. He is committed in life and love. Trust builds, though hot sparks begin from the first moment. Count on his wanting to possess you forever. Trust me, you will succumb!

With Sagittarius SUN man: You make an odd couple. You understand his passionate need to explore, and you love exploring each other. However, you might become unhappy when you can't settle him down to a traditional life. To be with him, you might need to sell out part of yourself. It could be tempting, but you can do better.

With Capricorn SUN man: Though he's a good provider and grounds you, underlying tensions exist. You both want a family and home. However, you might be offended by his values. You seek reform, while he backs the status quo. Arguments will erupt. Yet other times, you like the soaring temperatures. This is a hard one to call.

With Aquarius SUN man: No question, he will amuse you and delight you. You think his eccentric love offerings are fun. The friendship builds, the flirtation increases. Unfortunately, Aquarians don't like to be tied down. You need to give him oodles of space. The constant excitement just might be worth reconciling your differences.

With Pisces SUN man: He wants to heal others. Merged with your need to reform and crusade, this could be an interesting coupling. Remember, though, he really needs you, so don't be surprised if he balks at your independent moments. You need a lot of togetherness here.

MOON IN ARIES, SUN IN LEO

You are all fire and flames. Your warmth draws others, and your sparkle is never missed when you walk into a room. You are the essence of passion and energy. Once you determine a course of action, little can stop you. You have strong follow-through. You sometimes might be impulsive rather than sorting through your feelings. You get more done than most, and you're always ready for a new challenge.

To men you project magic and mystery. They want to get to know you better. They can't help themselves. However, like everyone, you need the right man, the right personality. You probably will have many choices.

Though you certainly have a penchant for the good life, under your beautiful exterior is a reformer, a crusader, an independent thinker. You have a set of firm beliefs and you will stand up for them. It is important to you that you are valued not just for your beauty, but for your deep caring. If you meet a man who teams up with you on this level, it is a go.

Because you have so many possibilities, you tend to be demanding with men. And why not? You want security, personality, charm, and a fabulous lover. Though this might seem like a lot, you will tend to fulfill your expectations, most likely in your first marriage.

You offer a partner romance, passion, and commitment. You are loyal and courageous. Even after many years, you tend your relationship with care. Time breeds even more loving and caring. You rarely say no to those you love.

With Aries SUN man: Everyone will be looking for a fire extinguisher when the two of you meet. Of course, you can handle the combustion you create. You fit together perfectly. You have the same cycles, needs, and energy. This is a primo match!

With Taurus SUN man: You like the way he wines and dines you. The courtship is delightful, romantic, and slow—nearly tedious. That's where the problem begins. You are a forest fire, and he is a slow-building campfire. You will always be egging him on, and he will never change his pace. One date is nice; a lifetime together could be very frustrating!

With Gemini SUN man: Once you meet, the flirting and witty exchanges will never end. He is funny and romantic. He is a wind blowing on your fires. His ideas and observations will encourage you. He plays devil's advocate to your plans and helps you succeed. This match has many plusses and few negatives.

With Cancer SUN man: You are emotional and impulsive, you thought, until you met this man. He is so very feeling and emotional, you seem like a stoic next to him. You act on your passions, he lives in his. This is a case of two very nice people who will clash harder the longer they are together.

With Leo SUN man: Your knight in shining armor just knocked on your door. This can happen with great force and dynamic magnetism. You might have little choice as you tumble into each other's arms, and go from your lair to his. However, you are both very proud and need, excuse me, your egos stroked. Learn to do his, he will do yours!

With Virgo SUN man: He is very sensible, logical, and clear. You are too, but don't manifest it the same way. You act on your passions and feelings. He thinks everything through. You could be team players at work on a project, but as lovers? I think not.

With Libra SUN man: There is a link here that is like iron. The magic is undeniable, long term, and irresistible. You are very different people. You are action, he is charm. Courtship is his specialty, and he will make you smile and feel special. Love grows if you appreciate each other for your differences rather than similarities.

With Scorpio SUN man: He has energy, seething passion, and precise insights. He seeks answers to universal mysteries. He won't flatter you; he will tell you the truth. You will need to appreciate his honesty and directness. This acceptance could be helped along by his intense sensuality in private times. You might be jumping into the fire—careful!

With Sagittarius SUN man: He is the zodiac's wanderer and adventurer. He likes to risk as much as he likes to spend money. His life is like a roulette wheel. You might decide to take a spin, because together you will lovingly pioneer new frontiers. Don't expect this man to settle in for a long time. Life is torrid and searing, and every day together is a new adventure.

With Capricorn SUN man: You find him steady, powerful, and intense. His animal ways draw you. You like his style. Sexuality is a key tie here. You work to be powers in each other's life. Eventually, you will get bored with his materialistic values and risk-avoiding nature. But until then, it is a great ride.

With Aquarius SUN man: Expect an endless celebration of life here. He loves humanity and friends. You love people. He provides perspective while you take action. He adds quirky ideas to your hot, intimate ways. The bonding can last forever if you are willing to acknowledge you have something to learn from each other. And you do.

With Pisces SUN man: You will adore his poetry and sentimentality. When he serenades you under your window or throws rose petals on the bed, your goose is cooked. You have little resistance. Your cheery personality and get-up-and-go can help him when he gets depressed. He needs you very much.

MOON IN ARIES, SUN IN VIRGO

You are committed, determined, and caring, yet there is flashing passion, a potential rainbow display of emotions. However, as emotional as you are, you are also clear and logical about your life choices and decisions. You have a tremendous need to serve.

You expect devotion and loyalty. You want a traditional marriage and family. You will tend to marry once, though there will be no lack of partners.

It is best if you choose a partner who is cool, not reactive like you. You want someone who can help you calm down and see the whole picture. Your partner should have a strong emotional constitution. You are well intentioned, but your precision with words can cut to the quick. You have a wry sense of humor.

You are very attractive and probably diminutive if your gene pool allows it. You might dress in a sedate, conservative manner, but your flaming personality comes through anyway, perhaps in your choice of colors or your intense, lively expression. Because of your personality and occasional shyness, you draw a very special man who values those qualities. The right man will value your devotion.

With Aries SUN man: You meet each other and have a sense that you have known each other forever. He too has a volcanic temper. You each will understand when the other erupts. Physically, expect intense and loving situations. You will want marriage; he might go along because he needs your torch in life.

With Taurus SUN man: He appeals to your logical, sensible side. He understands your need for order. This man's extraordinary sensuality leaves you ecstatic. This relationship is steady and can keep you grounded when you decide to be a powder keg. This can be a lasting match.

With Gemini SUN man: His mind is delightful and appealing. You will spark his intellect while the embers of flirtation can ignite. He is logical and will help you think through situations that trigger you. If you are looking for a calm, conservative, grounded force in your life, it isn't this man. But don't nix this sizzle without trying it.

With Cancer SUN man: He is moody and sensitive. Though you might like his values, he will shut down when confronted by your temper. He will become a hard-shelled crab and be no fun to deal with. Don't try, please, unless he is less crusty than most of his sign.

With Leo SUN man: You might like your guys coy, but his man is downright seductive and alluring. You react impulsively and passionately. He can burn you out, so do be careful. A couple of your sharp comments and impulsive displays, and he could be off chasing another tasty morsel.

With Virgo SUN man: He is noble in your book. He seems caring because he is patient with you. When you get caustic or a bit wild, he understands. He loves your displays; he finds them as beautiful as the northern lights. This can work, but never expect him to be a hot bed of passion. He's a cool cookie.

With Libra SUN man: You are like night and day. He is charming and easygoing, and runs from commitment. He responds to your rash behavior by heading for the hills. Your sarcastic comments make him as uncomfortable. Yet, the feverish chemistry could make you blush.

With Scorpio SUN man: He is the match that can ignite you. He can match your temperament with deep, seething emotions. Forget sarcasm, he can outdo you. He likes your practical mind, and you adore his incendiary effect on your calm exterior. Together, you cook.

With Sagittarius SUN man: This man is a gambler in life and love, which is nearly offensive to you. Yet there is a longing when you see each other. Take a romp with him, but get any long-term ideas out of your head. Enjoy the fever. That is the *practical* thing to do here.

With Capricorn SUN man: He is a power who is grounded and very practical. Together you can build empires, particularly if he is okay with your drive and dedication. You both need exercise to work off stresses. You will find him a dynamo in both life and love. There could be a row or two, but the love here melts any resistance.

With Aquarius SUN man: You like his humanitarianism. You can identify with it. You find him amusing and a little ditzy. Ah, practical he is not. Ultimately you share a wonderful friendship and a lot of naughtiness. You will adore the far-reaching spins of his fantasies. However, endurance and commitment isn't his thing. Be careful about going beyond being buddies.

With Pisces SUN man: As hard as it might be to believe, he is more emotional than you ever could be. You are impulsive. He feels, fathoms deep. You want to stabilize and help him. He could be your private cause! This can work, but be aware of the possible codependency. You might not ever find your way out; but, then, you might not want to!

MOON IN ARIES, SUN IN LIBRA

You are a beautiful mix, inside and out. Others see you as highly desirable, very alive, and essential. You are a romantic, soft and feminine in appearance. Men turn their heads as you walk by.

But under your serene exterior seeths a bubbling geyser. You erupt periodically, surprising people. You can be direct, nearly abusive when you speak from your feelings. Those who don't understand you could wonder which is the real you. (It's all you.)

With maturity, you will find balance between your soft, feminine side and your fiery emotional surges.

To romance, you add burning sensual knowledge. You instinctively know how to please, and do so until it no longer suits you. Your femininity brings out "the man" in any suitor. You can be trusted to be honest and loyal, once committed, even if you are one of the world's biggest flirts.

You might not be sure what you want from a relationship or how to interact with men. Don't worry, you will have plenty of opportunity to find out. You might make several stabs at marriage, though, before you get it right.

You ultimately will seek an easygoing partner who can contend with your tempestuous temperament. Ideally, he considers your swings an exciting plus. If he knows how to demonstrate his imagination and dedication, you're hooked. You want roses, soft-candlelight dinners, cards, tokens of affection—the whole ball of wax!

With Aries SUN man: You lock into each other the first time you meet. Your feminine ways draw in this masculine, strong man. When he discovers that under the lacy exterior lies a passionate, direct woman, he will be delighted. You add a softness to this relationship, which is as direct as can be. There could be a squabble or two. Who cares!

With Taurus SUN man: Both of you delight in the best and most luxurious. He might not understand your outbursts, but he will offer stability to ground you. Eventually you will impulsively react to that. Think about this relationship. It might not always be exciting, but it could prove to be what you want when you finally decide to settle in.

With Gemini SUN man: He is known as the twin, the Dr. Jekyll/Mr. Hyde of the zodiac. He is even more subject to mood changes than you. You will never know who is meeting whom. Expect wit, diversity, and charm from this man. He will court your mind, enchant your soul, and bewitch your body. This could be a happily ever after story.

With Cancer SUN man: He can enchant you and delight you for a night or two. But a lifetime partner? I don't think so. He wants an anchor. How can you anchor him when you can't do it for yourself?

With Leo SUN man: You might feel this man is every great lover you have ever met rolled into one. Your energy charges him, yet your femininity lulls him into a mesmerized state. He is a player, but with your diversity, he will feel like he has many women in one. The two of you could tantalize each other for a lifetime.

With Virgo SUN man: Like many others, he could be attracted to you physically. You will fascinate him, but he will eventually turn away. He isn't up for loving and living with a hurricane. He is simply too grounded. You won't care either. Though you like him, you don't appreciate his criticisms.

With Libra SUN man: This man weaves a web of enchantment, and you will get caught in it. Outwardly this could seem to be a superficial tie. But what the world doesn't see is how he pours gasoline on your flaming passions. You might burn each other out, but that is unlikely. Expect uncontrollable fires, forever.

With Scorpio SUN man: His passion rages within and his eyes penetrate through you. You are desperately attracted to his extraordinary depth. Your charm and femininity are like an erotic perfume, and your impulsive, searing feelings intrigue him. Though he might dally with you, he is looking for a soul mate and could desert you.

With Sagittarius SUN man: You may have a hard time keeping up with this man. He is a risk-taker and has no problem with your fiery nature and direct ways. The coquette in you intrigues him, and he might want to stay for a long while. When boredom hits, the two of you will pull up stakes together. Stick with this man.

With Capricorn SUN man: Your femininity graces his masculinity well, and he is strongly attracted. When you decide to wear the pants and make some strong decisions, the wars begin. If you like roller-coaster rides, continue. Otherwise get off now.

With Aquarius SUN man: He tweaks the conventional in you. You will shake your head, giggle, and probably go for it. He will be your friend and very eccentric lover. You won't judge each other. When you decide to take action and demonstrate the passions you feel, he is yours.

With Pisces SUN man: You could find this endurable romantic to be a sensual treat. He will assault your imagination. The problem is that you cannot live in his fairy-tale, rainbow-bannered world. You need and want much more.

MOON IN ARIES, SUN IN SCORPIO

Your sensual magnetism speaks through your penetrating looks and comes out no matter what you wear, do, or feel. It is simply part of you. You won't hesitate to stand up for what you think is right. You have a strong knack for confrontation that could have meeker souls running for the hills. You are direct, incisive, and sometimes very bold.

There is part of you that others might never know. You have deep emotional caverns. Many of your actions come from this wellspring of feeling, yet they may remain unfathomable, perhaps even to you.

You question the world and your own desires. You have a difficult time tolerating injustice on any level, and could become a crusader or troubleshooter. You expect ethics and quality.

You are only interested in those who understand you and take you as you are. You are picky about partners. You want a man who cares about what he does, and does it with excellence. It is important that he seeks the real meaning in life, not its superficialities.

You make a very special partner who will not settle for anything less than equality. You will provide for your partner emotionally, ethically, and spiritually, supporting him in what you view as life's battle. Together you expect to be a team, friends and lovers charging and creating.

With Aries SUN man: Neither of you will be bored! He will find you a seething volcano, and you will turn him to lava. Your passions will singe a trail of true loving. Since both of you are impulsive and direct, you could lock horns. You won't be able to leave each other, but you will need to communicate and compromise to be happy.

With Taurus SUN man: The dynamic attraction is clear to both of you. He is a peacemaker, a lover, a sensualist. He is driven to explore your reservoirs of feelings and fathomless passions. He won't fight if you chip at him, but once he has enough he will get stubborn and let you know it. There are many lessons here, and very little boredom.

With Gemini SUN man: He knows how to toy with you and make you laugh, teaching you the value of humor. There is an unusual, sensual draw. He is dexterous, inventive, and naughty. You are deep, passionate, and delighted with his energy. He's a breath of fresh air. Smile, lighten up, and say yes.

With Cancer SUN man: You could feel tormented by this gentleman. You pick up on his sensitivity and depth and want to merge forces with him. He is possessive and will try to restrict you. You will never know freedom, though you will find closeness. This portends slow emotional death or a hardy rebellion on your part! Bet on the rebellion.

With Leo SUN man: The two of you form a love knot that will not easily be untangled. This man makes you steamy and wild with his courteous, yet knowing pursuit. His sensual knowledge will undo you. You are both stubborn, so expect battles. Try deferring to him once in a while. He needs loving, praise, and acceptance, not retaliation!

With Virgo SUN man: He is ice to your fire. Nevertheless, you may be curious and decide to stop to take a gander. Should you melt him and heat him up, he will never leave you. Otherwise, it might be best to simply leave him as a fellow crusader and pal. He will always be rational and analytical. Can you stand it?

With Libra SUN man: You have encountered one of the gentler creatures in the zodiac. He is charming, affable, and romantic. You are the bee and he is your honey. Should you decide to use your stinger, you could do much damage. He might not leave you, but he could look elsewhere. Be careful and tame yourself if you want him! He will allow you to make all the decisions.

With Scorpio SUN man: You have just met the other pea in your pod. You both feel so deeply, there are no words for the emotions. He will love the magic trails you wind through his life. He admires your get-up-and-go. You're both stubborn and could clash. Learn to give in and you will be well rewarded!

With Sagittarius SUN man: He is a ball of fire as he whirls past you. He philosophizes and thinks about life. There is energy here, but no deep feelings. You might want to join him on his merry-go-round for a while. You might even decide to stay, but don't criticize him for not being deeper. You knew that from the get-go.

With Capricorn SUN man: He is an empire-builder and uses his strength to create material wonders. There is a sense of comfort and knowledge, as well as a steamy attraction here. Eventually you could decide to attack his values. It might be wise before you leap into his life to decide if you can live with what he stands for.

With Aquarius SUN man: He makes you laugh and wants to ease your worries with merrymaking. He appreciates your commitments and might decide to pitch in and make them happen. He will never feel deeply, but because you like each other, this match could work out.

With Pisces SUN man: This is a merger of emotional spirits. As waves of feelings cascade over you, you could have some fear of drowning in his outpourings. Careful here, as it is quite possible you might lose some of your spirit and fire. He won't like your independence *at all!*

Moon in Aries, Sun in Sagittarius

You are enthusiastic, passionate, and ready to leap on any bandwagon that might interest you. A woman of action, not words, you certainly will speak your mind. You love life and want to make the most of it, and that includes loving. You have tremendous commitment and a good sense of ethics. You feel as if you are in control of your universe and you have the energy to change what isn't to your liking. For the most part, you create your destiny.

You are athletic, interested in life, and ready for fun and romping. Because you like people so much, you might want many men, even desire more than one at one time. Taming your choices and becoming more discriminating will serve you best in the long run. You will always be a flirt.

You want a relationship that is dynamic, in which you can count on your partner. Loyalty, joy, and dynamic interaction are necessary to keep you happy. It probably is a good thing that you have so many admirers, because few men will be able to provide all you want. But to a man who can meet you as an equal, you are a joy and pleasure.

There is a possibility of two marriages. You are a complex person who changes and transforms, so you could outgrow a relationship. With luck you will choose a partner who also has the ability to grow.

With Aries SUN man: Someone with as much energy as you? You have met your match in commitment, loyalty, and vitality. The two of you charge your batteries together. To others, the heat is overwhelming. To you, it is great. Impulse, passion, and pleasure are naturals here. No wonder you are beaming!

With Taurus SUN man: Money and its workings interest you, but this man lives and breathes it. He likes the security money provides and he loves quality living. Together, you are likely to relish life's luxuries. Problems come if your values change. You might not want a long-term commitment.

With Gemini SUN man: You are intrigued by your zodiac opposite. He will provoke you mentally, physically, and emotionally. You discover life is a picnic with him as he makes you giggle at what would normally irritate you. You will gain by knowing this man, and you will learn much about other styles of loving.

With Cancer SUN man: He is a nice man, but not for you beyond a gourmet date or trip to your favorite water resort. He can't take your snap, crackle, and pop. He needs someone a little less exciting and dynamic. You would be a tidal wave in his still waters.

With Leo SUN man: He too is a fire sign. The blaze you two create will be beautiful and hot, yes, very hot. You might have to make a minor adjustment to your style to keep the zodiac's lover close to you. He needs to be fawned over, appreciated, and adored. You can do this. Just consider all the joy you have with this man.

With Virgo SUN man: He is practical and earthy. Though you aren't his antithesis, you have nothing in common. You will scare him to death as you, in his opinion, blindly take risks, spend money, and encourage change. You will think the way he lives his life is a real drag. I don't think so.

With Libra SUN man: He is as gentle as you are impulsive. He will court you, but you are likely to jump in and pull him into an abyss of passion. This could be a long-term game for the two of you. You won't care if he is indecisive; you are quite capable of asking him to meet you at the altar. His kindness and gentleness will melt your resistance.

With Scorpio SUN man: This man is moody and seems hidden from you. You might be intrigued, but you won't have the patience to wait for him to reveal himself. You know it might never happen. You race by him as he tries to emote about what happened here.

With Sagittarius SUN man: He is like you, ready for the next challenge, the next adventure or risk. You find each other fun and could take a wild romp. To no one's surprise, this could be a long-term match. You discover love in the midst of these fun times. You will travel, explore, and live well together.

With Capricorn SUN man: He is a fan of the status quo. You, on the other hand, will not hesitate to rip down structures. This is a no way, José. You're more likely to become lethal enemies on the opposite side of intellectual and emotional fences. Neither of you is right or wrong. You are simply different.

With Aquarius SUN man: You like him. He touches you and is full of wild schemes. There is a strong friendship here that lays the groundwork for a fabulous relationship. You will like all that he offers and his naughty imagination is the icing on the cake. He will burn off your worries, help you relax, and make you laugh.

With Pisces SUN man: He might be a dreamer and you might be inspired by one of his suggestions, but a relationship? The result would be a pile of problems. You would feel burdened, and he would feel unappreciated. Puh-leez!

MOON IN ARIES, SUN IN CAPRICORN

You can be a powerful combination of strengths or an odd dichotomy, depending on how you blend your talents. You are brash and full of energy. You care about others and try to make their lives better. You tend to work within the status quo because you respect structure and the system.

Your energy is hot and dynamic. Men feel it and are drawn to you. You might not always be coy or the epitome of femininity, but you evoke desire from the gentlemen around you. And you will demand that they be gentlemen. Your partner will know where he stands with you and what to expect.

You need a powerful man who can meet your needs, handle your hot temperament, and know when to put his foot down and say "enough." You will want to respect him, put him on a pedestal, and admire his values. The man you choose could be a bit solemn or remote, but he will have you to perk up his life. It will be very important to you that he is a good breadwinner.

It would be surprising if you had more than one marriage. Everything about you is committed—even if at times you have a hard time making your message clear. You will offer a man a traditional marriage, supporting his career and his endeavors in any way possible. You might opt to work as well, because of your concern for material security. You will be very much in control. You have the energy to fulfill your desires, and the desire to fulfill your partner.

With Aries SUN man: This is a merger of like spirits. He knows how to please you, love you, and raise your temperature a few degrees. Yes, this is a go. You might be a little demanding with him if he doesn't bring in the bucks you want; but you'll sure enjoy the private times.

With Taurus SUN man: You just might have it all here, if you can be patient with this man. He never does anything quickly, but he moves with a sturdiness and commitment that could delight you. His specialty is teasing and luring. You will have to waltz to his beat. He can tolerate your impulsiveness if it is expressed with him, behind closed doors.

With Gemini SUN man: This man excites your mind, soul, and body. He is a dynamic thinker, and with your incredible strength, you could make a mint together. His imagination knows no boundaries, and you could stimulate his inventiveness. He might be moody, but he won't be solemn. You make an interesting couple.

With Cancer SUN man: This man appeals to you. He cares about home, family, and traditional values. You are proud to have him on your arm. Your wild streak could profoundly upset him. When you become vocal about what you think is wrong, he could take it personally. This man is gentle. He needs to be treated accordingly.

With Leo SUN man: He represents romance, security, and the good life. There is a lot here. He will keep your fires stoked, yet he can give you the financial security you crave. Best of all, there will be laughter, good times, and wonderful friends. Just remember to stroke his very strong ego. That is the exchange.

With Virgo SUN man: You have your calm, cool man here. He is practical. You are the schemer. Together, security and service merge. You will feel good about what you can create together. He can take a sarcastic comment or two. He might fire one at you when you leap into the air to express a point poignantly. Laughter and respect are a must here.

With Libra SUN man: The attraction could be lethal, as you cannot stay away from each other, yet you could have a difficult time making this more than a heavy flirtation. He isn't an empire builder, he is into being fair. On some level, that really appeals to you. Work on not criticizing him and changing him, and he might stick around.

With Scorpio SUN man: His depth and reserve appeal to you. He could be the type of man you have dreamed about. He is a private person and is drawn to the mysteries of life, one of which is you. He cannot believe how you can excite him, and vice versa. It is hard to determine who is hotter here, and frankly, you won't care.

With Sagittarius SUN man: This man will put a smile on your face; his love of life is contagious and effusive. He could be excellent with money, though he will take risks with it, as he does in other aspects of his life. In the fiery world of love and romance, you'll enjoy his style. The question is whether you can tolerate his wildness in other areas of your life.

With Capricorn SUN man: He is determined to create a strong future for himself and his loved ones. Yet, he sometimes complains about your wild impulsiveness, and you might attack his stick-in-the-mud mentality. The fighting could be volcanic, as could other emotions. You might consider sticking around, if this kind of caring appeals to you.

With Aquarius SUN man: He is your friend and could be your lover. However, unless he is a very unusual Aquarius, he will not give a hoot about financial security. He marches to a different drummer. Admire his independence and freedom of thought, but be honest with yourself. Can you live with it?

With Pisces SUN man: You stabilize his emotional upheavals. He feels all, even others' feelings that he picks up. The problem is your bursts of anger and emotionalism could be a little tough on him. If he can take it, and you can manage his money, this could be an equitable arrangement. You will be romanced for the rest of your life.

MOON IN ARIES, SUN IN AQUARIUS

Conventional behavior is not your style. Your hairstyle, the colors you choose, and the way you approach life all speak of your independence. You like this distinction, which is natural. You make choices that feel right, not based on what is appropriate according to others' judgments.

Courage defines you. You go your own way, believing in your convictions. You offer loyalty, novelty, excitement, and passion in a relationship. You listen to your partner and respond from the heart. You tend to move fairly quickly through issues and flex with situations. You have a somewhat explosive temper. You want one marriage, but won't hesitate to move on if that marriage isn't to your liking.

The right man needs to be able to provide you with the space to make your own decisions and be yourself. You need his support in your life choices rather than his judgments. You want a like-spirit, a friend who can be there for you.

Loyalty, sage comments, and romance are all qualities you seek. You also expect romance and play. You might not always be comfortable with emotional, heart-to-heart discussions, though you will support your partner through life's passages. You believe in growth and commitment to change. You won't tolerate a partner who feels sorry for himself.

You see humor where many can't, and can laugh in grim circumstances. That sense of humor helps you grow. And if your partner doesn't have a good one, it won't be funny.

With Aries SUN man: Two Bohemians meet here and are off on their personal crusades. You blow hot air on his already hot triggered nature, sometimes adding to his explosiveness. The flames you create flow from one area of your life to another. Desire and friendship merge. You make quite the team.

With Taurus SUN man: This is a very nice man. He is simply too traditional and maybe a little too boring for you. You might enjoy breaking bread with him, but past that, no chance. He is too slow, you say, as you whiz by.

With Gemini SUN man: This man is naughty and brilliant. Your mischievous spirits merge, and there is no lack of merriment. His ideas will trigger your impulsiveness and off you'll go, laughing all the way. The fires burn steadily. The problem is, you will have to work on being practical and handling life's mundane chores.

With Cancer SUN man: He isn't what you want. He is moody and somewhat dependent. This doesn't work, and you and he know it. However, you still might decide to romp a little. Remember, he will take the relationship far more seriously than you will.

With Leo SUN man: You find him steamy, romantic, and full of joy. You have very different styles and values, but there is a magnetism that forces you to work it through. You both love to party and could rock away for the rest of your lives. He needs more attention than you, so remember to let him know he is wonderful.

With Virgo SUN man: He loves to take care of others, but he is cool by nature and not in tune with your impulsiveness. Though you could be attracted and have some fun, you'll face a war of recriminations if you let this courtship go too far. You simply aren't right for each other. And nothing can change that.

With Libra SUN man: You are deeply attracted. So is he. Even if he is traditional, he is wonderful and he accepts and loves your uniqueness. He too has a naughty streak that widens once he gets to know you. Romance is his specialty. The magnetic bond is so heavy, you cannot break away. Worse things have happened!

With Scorpio SUN man: This man is attractive and thoughtful. He likes your fire and energy, and you turn him on. You both are independent and clear, but stubbornness can wreck this relationship. There must be negotiating, transformation, and dynamic processing if this match is to work.

With Sagittarius SUN man: He is a mirthful explorer. Of course, that isn't out of whack with your independent streak. You will hook up for the adventure, which will feed both of your passions, and he will adore the friendship you offer. You make a hot, unconventional match, capable of creating interesting twists.

With Capricorn SUN man: There's a strong sensual attraction, but it doesn't take much to see that the match isn't going to work. This man is dynamic and energetic, but an advocate of the status quo. That's a no-no for you.

With Aquarius SUN man: You are similar spirits, full of ideas, sharing a quirky wildness. Others will never understand your naughty glints and knowing looks. You understand his need for variety and add your own perky touch to the recipe of love you brew together. Yesss.

With Pisces SUN man: He is romantic and empathetic on some level. However, you will not be able to deal with his emotional diatribes and needs. You are independent; he is a clinger. Unhook this one and toss him back.

MOON IN ARIES, SUN IN PISCES

You have heavy, steamy energy. You could have an explosive temper. You're so intense that sometimes you can't handle it and need release. You can seem tough and independent, like a woman who can make her goals happen. But you can also come off as a frail flower who could easily be crushed.

The right man must be sensitive and compassionate. He will support you and help you understand yourself. A warning: You want to help others and make this a better world. That need might cause you to choose partners who are addictive or problem-prone. That could describe you as well. But that doesn't have to happen. You have control.

You are very attractive, with a tendency to have a wanton or promising look of what could be. Though you have flash and spark, you still leave a watery, ethereal impression. You seem to promise unspoken dreams, yet impel action. You can be meditative or very active as a result of your swings.

You will fight for your partner as if there is no tomorrow. You will be loyal, faithful, and determined. Yet within the privacy of your home, there will never be anyone more loving, caring, and emotional than you. Should you become angry or feel deprived, you won't hesitate to go on the warpath. For this reason, you need to work through problems in your relationships quickly. Otherwise the issues might never get resolved.

With Aries SUN man: Your amorous side emerges when you meet this man. You both seem to move and make choices at the same time. You intuitively know what to do to make him comfortable. He might not understand your sensitive ways, but he will want to know more. Once you get into the swing together, you'll be like Tarzan and Jane.

With Taurus SUN man: He is sensitive and wants to understand more about you. He is as stable as a rock; he will enjoy the variety you bring into his life. You won't always see eye-to-eye. He can take your impulsive moments, but eventually they could become a sore spot. Be as sensitive to him as he is to you. Then this is a go.

With Gemini SUN man: He is chatty, charming, and naughty. You are attracted, and he is too. However, your styles are very different. He lives in his mind and is uncomfortable with passionate displays. This match is probably no more than a fling, but could result in a lasting friendship.

With Cancer SUN man: You could become lovers, empathetic to each other, sharing sensual delights. You won't say no to this type of bonding. But when you become hot-tempered and impulsive, he might get very upset, curl up in a ball, and become a hard-shelled Crab, impossible to penetrate.

With Leo SUN man: There is a strong bonding. He likes your romantic dreams. They inspire him to be the love of your life. Your energies feed each other, and you burn hot. You both are committed to love and could easily hook up forever. Enchantment, energy, and enthusiasm—what more could you want?

With Virgo SUN man: He can help you think through your emotionalism and make sense of it. Like you, he cares, and when you take off on a crusade, he might join you, contributing his logic. If you want a cool cucumber, for whom you will provide the passion, go for it. But do think twice here.

With Libra SUN man: Love and attraction bind so tightly, you might have difficulty sorting one from the other. And you might not care. The glue between you is powerful enough that this is a lasting tie. When you take off, full of energy, you will invigorate him. He loves your drive and passion.

With Scorpio SUN man: He has depth, power, and understanding to indulge all your beautiful facets. There are parts of him that can relate to all of them. He reads your depth and senses the wild riptides in you. He will reach out and calm your waters with his sensual magic. Your heat and impulsiveness only add to the passion.

With Sagittarius SUN man: He is on a roll whenever you meet him. You can tag along and have a flash affair that is a lot of fun. You could play together, even tour the world, but if you expect understanding when you become sad or deeply emotional, think again. You might not be able to tolerate this man forever. Nor should you.

With Capricorn SUN man: He is earthy, yet emotional; mental, yet sensual. You will find his touch makes you feel secure. There is strong attraction. At times your lively ways and impulsive ideas will cause this man to shake his head. If you respect your differences, this can be a wonderful pairing.

With Aquarius SUN man: He is your friend and can be your playmate. His eccentricities make him independent. He accepts your cascading feelings, though he can't relate. Actually, you love being together and swinging to each other's beat. Strike up the band!

With Pisces SUN man: You touch each other on a deeply sentimental and sensual level. You will nurture each other as you go through vulnerable moments. You find the magic happens naturally. He will understand, but might not like it, when you decide to be Ms. Independent. This will be your biggest problem, but much love is available here.

Moon in Taurus

"The rule of my life is to make business a pleasure, and pleasure my business."
—AARON BURR

When you enter a room, you are sure of yourself, poised and grounded. You can be friendly, or reserved. Either way, you are determined and directed. The Taurus symbol, the bull, is not an accident. Yes, you, my dear Taurus, are stubborn as a bull. Security is a prime issue for you.

For Taureans, security often means having important things, such as a big bank account, or being able to buy what they need. Often young Taureans can be a bit tight with money as they learn what role generosity plays in their lives. Older Taurus Moons find security through creativity, self-esteem, and a sharing spirit. They find security from the loving people they will draw into their lives, people who appreciate the Taurus gentleness and evenness.

The gift of Moon in Taurus is its connection to the earth. The outdoors has special significance to you. So do the stones and crystals that come from the earth. You might have an unusual attraction to jewelry or silver.

Any insecure Moon in Taurus can have a difficult time tempering eating, drinking, and spending habits. Some of you could react to this proclivity by becoming rigid self-disciplinarians.

Moon bequeaths sensuality in this sign and magnetically draws many potential lovers. Also Moons in Taurus have excellent taste. They know quality and will not settle for less. One of their favorite words is comfort.

Moon in Taurus breeds successful relationships and gives others security just by being in their lives.

Emotionally, you offer understanding, grounding, and security. Others feel they can trust you with their secrets and you will honor them. Actually, you can be quite judgmental, but you are loving and walk in another's shoes with ease. You have a strong sense of values. You expect the same of those close to you.

Your magnetism is endless. It is in the way you walk, your manner when you talk or look at someone. Your body language announces that you love touching and being touched. Though you tend to have eyes only for the love in your life, don't kid yourself. There will be many members of the opposite sex who would like to be your significant other.

It's important to you to provide a wonderful home life for your loved ones. You care about quality food, loving, and living. Seeing the world is important to you, as well. Childhood lifetime romances are not uncommon for Moons in Taurus. Happily ever after stories have a great chance to happen under your wise Moon sign.

MOON IN TAURUS, SUN IN ARIES

You are sedate, yet you have more get-up-and-go. You are vivacious, energetic, and strong. When opposed, you can be a formidable opponent. You have bursts of impulsiveness and strength. Though some people think you've gone off the deep end, your actions are usually planned. It could be subliminal, but there is organization to your ways.

Your balance between male and female traits makes you interesting to men. You lay back, then take action. You are the seductress, then become the seducer. You are earthy and receptive, then become passionate and active. You've got quite a personality package and you need a solid, integrated, balanced partner. He needs to relish your variety, rather than be threatened by your unpredictability.

The right man needs to be direct, animated, and committed. He must be his own person, independent, and willing to go for what he wants. It is okay with you if he isn't as grounded as you. You would prefer flash, fire, and energy, a vital playmate. It is best that he doesn't have a preconceived ideal woman, as you break the mold. You are intent on one marriage and will sort through your choices carefully. You have courage and loyalty, which always make you a highly sought-after friend and companion.

With Aries SUN man: Heat meets energy here. You will be off together making a difference to humanity and you'll have a hot time doing it. Your sensuality will rope him in as you teach new ways and styles. You delight in making his eyes pop and his mouth water. He'll probably want to sign on for the long haul. Want him?

With Taurus SUN man: You resonate well. As a couple, you're mellow and sensitive to each other. This is as good as it gets. Sensuality constantly simmers in the background. You have the same values. However, if there is going to be action, you will have to set it off. He finds you exciting, and you feel accepted to be yourself. Excellent.

With Gemini SUN man: You instantly connect. His words stimulate your imagination, you swap jokes, share social amenities, and fantasize about each other. He is a spirit, moving freely and experiencing life intellectually. He might be drawn to your sensuality, but don't count on ever anchoring him. He is the ultimate free spirit!

With Cancer SUN man: He is emotional and feeling. Your constant activity and movement might irritate him, even anger him, yet he senses your stability. Without trying, you evoke myriad feelings in him, from defensiveness to neediness. There will always be an element of frustration. You can do this if you want. You can probably do better.

With Leo SUN man: This man wrote the book on romance and love, and you know it when he crosses your threshold. When he touches your sensuality and learns of your magic, both of you are bewitched. For this to work long term, you will need to know when to back down. He is stubborn too! Together you will create a beautiful home and a comfortable life.

With Virgo SUN man: You feel at ease with this man. He too is grounded and practical. Sometimes you might need to nudge him to see the big picture, but he will. You both care about others and could team up in social endeavors. You will show him new ways of living and loving life. He thinks you are his magic charm. Don't tell him otherwise!

With Libra SUN man: No one will question the draw here, but often your timing as a couple is off. You both value living and loving. He knows how to romance you out of your defenses and into his arms. You are his inspiration and energizer, and he is your fuse. You will have much to work through, but the good times are great and worth the effort.

With Scorpio SUN man: Sparks fly when the two of you meet. Thermal chemistry is at work here. Both of you are primitive in your passions, yet have very different styles. He is jealous; you are possessive. You create with your ideas, and he effects change in a decisive way. Making this match last means understanding each other, not conquering the other.

With Sagittarius SUN man: He flies by, and you turn your head. You like his spirit of adventure and his willingness to gamble. You both love money and what it can buy. He will take risks with security and that might make you nervous. Yet there will be traveling, indulging, and enjoying the best places together. Hands down, though, the best times will be spent alone together.

With Capricorn SUN man: You could drive this controlled man up a tree. He is very masculine and directed, and he likes his women passive and feminine. If you get past the initial shock, you find there are many sensual treats to share. Much can be worked out in private moments as he tames the ram in you. You might like this a lot.

With Aquarius SUN man: He loves his friends nearly more than he loves his partner. You naturally become his friend, admire his eccentricities, and are amused by his ventures—a nice start. However, he isn't cut out for the domestic life; you definitely are. Commitment is not his strong suit; it is yours. Play this as a fling, and then move on.

With Pisces SUN man: You might find his neediness restricting. However, he knows how to please and delight you. The grounding you offer brings him to his true potential, and the creative, artistic man emerges. His imagination and sense of touch are powerful aphrodisiacs for you. You might want to work this out.

MOON IN TAURUS, SUN IN TAURUS

You are beautiful, sensual, and quite magnificent for men to behold. You'll have no shortage of suitors. It is obvious how much you offer. You are anchored and direct, and know what you want. Your ability to motivate others is key to completing projects, making you a leader.

As magical as you are, you still have difficulty with the meat and potatoes of relationships. You don't see issues or life from any point of view other than your own. You can be the proverbial bull, determined to have it your way. You will use charm, sensuality, and any other manipulation that works. However, to really come into your own, you need to rise above problems, issues, and confrontations to see what is truly going on. Detach, my bull, and try to see the big picture.

Learning to walk in others' shoes is a hard task for you, but once you learn this skill you will relate more easily and feel less threatened by unexpected behavior. Unlike your Taurus Moon sisters, you could easily have more than one marriage, mainly because of your inability to empathize and negotiate.

You are skilled with finances and are able to live a quality life. You'd like the right man to add financial soundness and provide those special touches that add to your life. You will want him cut from a similar mold as you. He should be conservative, with a strong sense of values to make you happy forever. He needs to remember all the holidays and sentimental occasions.

With Aries SUN man: No, he isn't your cup of tea no matter how or when you meet each other. He will be frustrated with your strong ways and seemingly irrevocable opinions. You will just turn on your heel and walk away.

With Taurus SUN man: You find your match, at least in personality, values, and stubbornness. If you always agree, there will be no collision. Should you lock horns, the holdouts could be serious, irrational, and long-lasting! You have a lot going here—sensuality and security. Both of you need to learn how to give in once in a while.

With Gemini SUN man: As stable as you are, he is flaky. He is an intellectual, capable of changing his mind at the drop of a hat. He is flexible, open, and appealing. His sensuality doesn't escape you, though it is very different from yours. Considering you have nothing in common, you might be well advised to keep on trucking.

With Cancer SUN man: He is sentimental and romantic, and has admirable values. You will love his emotional flair. His touch will send shivers down your back. You feel like this is it. He is most likely a good earner. Security and money are important to him too. You can have beauty, romance, and a partner who is happy to let you have it your way. You stabilize him. He will water and groom your love.

With Leo SUN man: He is romantic, sparkling, and full of laughter. His joie de vivre comes out at every twist of the road. You're drawn to each other. The problem is stubbornness. You both are willful. Yet there is so much that is positive. He feels soothed by your voice and loves your touch. You brighten up whenever he is around. Give it a shot, but only if you can flex sometimes.

With Virgo SUN man: He is able and quiet, and appreciates your assets and manner. If you want it your way, that's fine with him. Your warm style makes him want to give you all. You will adore his devotion, practical ways, and nurturing. This is a quiet, but very strong relationship.

With Libra SUN man: You both have highly aesthetic values. You appreciate the quality of life, as does he. Though there is a match here, you might find him superficial and impractical at times. This might be perfect, though, because then you get to rule the roost. No matter what he says, he knows you are more grounded. Sensuality abounds as two children of Venus express their love.

With Scorpio SUN man: You are both motivated by a strong drive for security. He looks to the mysteries of life for answers, while you eye the bank account. He is instinctive, knows where to touch, and will brush the recesses of your heart. He will love guiding you beyond the practical realm, and you will thank him, possibly forever.

With Sagittarius SUN man: Knowing him could turn you from sweet and earthy to a fuming volcano. He is an adventurer, and though you both like to travel, this pairing could blow to kingdom come. He might even have financial security, but you will still shake your head when it is obvious he would prefer never to have a home.

With Capricorn SUN man: Yes, there is someone as stable and strong as you and he has just sailed across your bow. Understanding seems to flow. You have similar goals, though you will have to coax this man to take time off. Making money is fun to him, and you love having it. The chemistry is great here.

With Aquarius SUN man: He seems to come from another planet. He walks off the beaten track, cares little about money and conventional pleasure. There is a surprise here for you. He loves life as much as you do. Just check out the mischievous glint in his eyes. You make wonderful friends with a touch of naughtiness here and there. Stop at that.

With Pisces SUN man: This man is touched by your consideration, empathy, and understanding. He is easy for you to understand. You help him put form to his feelings and unleash his creativity. He will be thrilled with your money management and practical ways. You are the salt of the earth to him. His love touches you on many levels. Being with him is being adored.

MOON IN TAURUS, SUN IN GEMINI

You are lighter, easier going, and more mischievous than your Taurus Moon sisters. Your wit and humor make you very desirable. You seem to offer a little of everything, not locking into any one point of view.

You are active and probably slender, if you are genetically so disposed. You seem to have a lot of nervous energy that needs direction. You are vivacious, capable of doing two things at once. You are quick to respond to a question, idea, or proposition.

It is through your love of movement that your sensuality speaks. You enjoy the caress of air blowing through your hair, the earth between your toes, and the feeling of moving and stretching. Others notice this, your body language.

You need a man who can meet your mental dexterity with a strong sense of humor and a willingness to change plans or objectives at the drop of a hat. The more versatile he is, the happier you will be. Travel and mental explorations are very important. You want to grow and exchange ideas. You might have to look awhile to find the right man. There could be two marriages as you seek your life-mate!

You make a loyal, loving partner who can laugh through the hard times, understand, nurture, and find answers to life's hassles. You're a true people-person.

With Aries SUN man: He is as masculine as you are feminine. He responds strongly to your coquetry and sensuality. Witty exchanges and charming flirtations mark this relationship. You are his anchor. And when he comes home to port, he wants you. You are versatile enough to join him in his explorations as well.

With Taurus SUN man: This union is a mystical experience. You feel as if you have known his presence forever. You can dance a tight tango together, but when you start whirling, he is at a loss for words. However, the good times are so great, it makes up for these minor interruptions. The issue is whether you want this man, with his limitations, for the rest of your life.

With Gemini SUN man: The two of you can be unconventional together, write love sonnets, and play endlessly. The difference is that you can anchor when you need to. He, on the other hand, will skip through life happily, intellectually, and with wonder. You are a gift to him. You introduce him to the deeper side of life and its forces. The sensual tie is what binds this relationship.

With Cancer SUN man: He is sweet, emotional, and tender. He offers security, family values, and love. You feel secure together. He can be quite hurt if you aren't there for him when he wants you. You will need to explain your meandering. Otherwise you could get nipped by the Crab's pincers. He is instinctive on a physical level, and you meld there.

With Leo SUN man: You have never experienced a romantic moment like those with this man. He courts, wines and dines you, and leaves you speechless, admiring his grace, and then his sensual ways. You want the same things: a good life, social interchanges, and a loving, growing relationship. Remember, if you don't stroke his ego, he could wander.

With Virgo SUN man: Your earthy ways appeal to this practical man. There is common ground and a special type of touching, through which you connect. There is an inner understanding. However, you have an intrinsic difference in how you think and what you want. The problems come with your illusions rather than your realities. Remember, don't blame him—you chose him.

With Libra SUN man: Charm and romance are his specialties. He appeals to your most feminine, romantic instincts. You both specialize in indulgences, and share your knowledge with each other. Expect a full menu when it comes to romance—roses, candlelight dinners, and intimate conversations. He will be egged on by your wit, humor, and loving ways. Definitely.

With Scorpio SUN man: He is deep and profound. You sense his reserves of sensuality, energy, and creativity. Merging with this mysterious man will lock you to him. He needs your softness and endurance. His deep waters feel directed by your earthy ways. Mentally, you meet each other. In your pairing you'll find depth and long-term possibilities.

With Sagittarius SUN man: You charge his batteries with your ideas. He is a spark plug that you can't resist. You have very different styles, but there is common ground if there is respect. Your sensual magnetism draws in this adventurer. He might not lose his wanderlust, but he will ask you to join him for a lifetime of adventure. Be sure you want this.

With Capricorn SUN man: There is much that is sensual and passionate here. Your imagination and ardor lure him in, and he might never want to leave after the first night together. You are empire builders. You both love playing in the world of money, power, and ideas. Make it your job to schedule the vacations.

With Aquarius SUN man: The two of you meet, and there is a sense that you have met a kindred spirit. Together you act on your ideas and silliness. From the hot tub to a concert, you never stop enjoying each other. However, as excellent as this relationship is, you and he ultimately want different things. He might not settle down easily. You want a home life. Be warned!

With Pisces SUN man: His dramatic, imaginative scenarios lure you into his pond, and you might pop in for a swim or two. He could be devoted, but you need to make a decision here. When you decide to spread your wings and fly, he transforms into quicksand. Be sure you want his neediness. On the other hand, there are all those wild fantasies he plays out.

MOON IN TAURUS, SUN IN CANCER

Your sensitivity reaches out to the world. You feel others' pain, empathize with them, yet can teach them to process their feelings. The reason you know so much about handling and moving with emotions is that you experience intense emotional vibrations too. You mix your earthy sensuality with intuitive feeling. You have an uncanny ability to touch the right spot, move in the right direction, sense which way is right. The practical, mixed with soft, receptive emotional qualities, creates a sensitive friend, lover, and parent. Your combination of finesse, caring, compassion, and excellence is unbeatable.

Be exact about what you want, and do not settle. The right man needs to be as sensitive, feeling, and intuitive as you. You expect a man who wants a family and home and is a good provider. You want to work together as a team.

Romance and courtship are important to you always. Your souls must meet. Nurturing needs to be mutual. Your search for someone with a similar sense of commitment makes it likely you will have only one marriage.

You love the good life and, as a result, might need to diet frequently and maintain strict self-discipline. For you, sharing bread is like extending love and nurturing. Water also plays a significant role in your life. Nothing beats walks along a river or the ocean with your significant other.

With Aries SUN man: He is direct, confrontational, and energizing. You admire his energy and want a sample. Make it no more than that, because in the long run he can't give you the kind of nurturing you want, unless he is a special breed of ram.

With Taurus SUN man: You are strongly connected. In fact, you have a sense of having known each other before. You can't question what is happening here; there is an unexplainable sense of timing and rhythm. Your private life reflects this incredible connection. There's a psychic, intuitive touch to this relationship that keeps it fluid.

With Gemini SUN man: You might feel a bit uneasy when you meet this witty, charming man. You sense you might get in too deep for your own good if you flirt with him. He seems to be able to draw nearly anyone in. You know he is trouble in the long run, as he is a roaming free spirit by nature. Yet there is so much appeal. Trust your intuition.

With Cancer SUN man: He is emotional, moody, and very tender. You like his values and his profound nature. This could be a close-to-perfect romance, though be warned: You two go through the same cycles simultaneously. You can be up together or down together. If there are problems, they come when you both need the other and are down. Otherwise, this is a go.

With Leo SUN man: He makes a dashing figure: lovable, attractive, full of life and romance. Can you say no? Few can to this man, you included. You enjoy the passion, but eventually the fur will fly. He offers security, needs adoration, and provides delicious seduction. The problem is you both are stubborn and have very different values. Go ahead if you must, but you were warned.

With Virgo SUN man: You won't have to worry about the budget or other practical matters with this man in your life. This latitude allows your creative energies to flow. He benefits and adores your heated, passionate responses. You love the freedom to create and live. The thank-you's for what you add to each other's life could go on forever.

With Libra SUN man: He is romantic, enticing, and certainly easy to like. However, though you both value the quality life, you could irritate each other. The odd thing is both of you have the same motto: Make love, not war. Still, it is a rough match for the long run. He isn't as deep as you, and what he cares about is quite different.

With Scorpio SUN man: This is as close to perfect as perfect gets. He is a wellspring of feelings, knowledge, and wisdom. His sensuality is a delight to nearly any woman, but you are a tremendous turn-on to him. To him, you're a match that can't be blown out. Your depth and inner reservoir intrigue him. Touch meets touch, and water runs over quiet earth. This combo is very nice for the now as well as the future.

With Sagittarius SUN man: He is exciting, full of hot sparks. The attraction is awesome. Money and travel seem to bring you two together. The problems start when you realize you have very different values and the steam burns both of you. Careful, please.

With Capricorn SUN man: He is your life-treat, even if he is focused on making his way in the world. You have superglue holding you together, as the passion will always be hardy. You have everything you want here: security and a dedicated lover and family man, even if he isn't home and is off providing. Bank on this tie.

With Aquarius SUN man: Nice idea; however, continue on. At best, there is a friendship. At worst, there could be animosity. He is liberal. You are conservative. His friends are his family; your family is your highest priority. And on it goes. You're peas in different pods.

With Pisces SUN man: There is poetry in this man. He could be extremely needy or very inspirational, depending on his development. He will adore your feeling, sensual ways. Your touch will melt him and anchor him simultaneously. With you managing the budget or finding solutions, he can unleash his dynamic creativity. He will make you feel like his queen.

MOON IN TAURUS, SUN IN LEO

You are strong, magnetic, and willful. Drama surrounds you, with your mane of hair and expressive, woeful eyes. People notice you, envy you, want to be with you.

You seek a solid relationship and are likely to decide that your first love is the love of your life. It is the old-fashioned girl in you. You want a traditional relationship with security, commitment, and loyalty. It's important for you to have a beautiful home with plants and good entertainment space. You are very social and want to share your life with family and friends.

Men find you not only a wonderful person, but also a very attractive woman. However, you are very determined about what you want, and can be quite a handful as a result.

Problems come because you love adoration and are a born flirt. This behavior can belie your serious, earnest nature and the way you truly value commitment. Men have problems reading you. You can be quite the party girl and coquette. This seem contrary to the solid emotional life you desire.

The man you choose could be dramatic, fun-loving, and highly personable. He needs to understand your flirting and may do his own share. You will expect romance, security, and all the baubles that come with a significant relationship. You want someone who loves life and the good times as much as you.

With Aries SUN man: You are drawn by his energy, values, and masculinity. You find him passionate when he focuses on you. He provides fun, adventure, and true loving. He might be too much on the run for your family orientation, but never fear, he will eventually make it home. Love abounds here. Just don't interfere with his crusades and hobbies.

With Taurus SUN man: Your souls, needs, and sensuality connect. You will share many pleasures and can live in synch. You might be a bit too much of a flirt for him, which could cause a hassle. Stop and look at what you have. This man fulfills your dreams. Flirt only with him!

With Gemini SUN man: He tweaks your soul and excites your imagination. Despite yourself, you will be waiting for his next call. He is animated, dexterous, and a live wire. This can only get hotter. He might not be able to resist you, and might even settle down, but realize he is much more airy and light than you. He too is a born flirt, yet the fun and playtime are worth it.

With Cancer SUN man: He is emotional and sometimes drippy, but you know how to lighten him up. He senses the deeper you and connects with your earthy, anchored side. There is a merger here in which touch, caring, and need mix. He loves his home and will go along when you want to entertain. Cut the wild flirting. You are his. And he wants you to remember that.

With Leo SUN man: Two flirting romantics meet. Your hands join, symbolic of the potential union. Both of you insist on having your egos stroked. If that need isn't met, the offended party will head for the hills and find another human delight. Taking that in consideration, if you both follow the rules, this is a union of passion, love, and extravagance.

With Virgo SUN man: This could be a love/hate relationship. You tough each other's core and know there is a connection. There is a sweetness, depth, and caring. However, you might get on his case for being too practical, not the fun-loving flamboyant man you want. He might not take kindly to your lifestyle. Once the recriminations begin, they probably won't stop.

With Libra SUN man: He loves the good life as much as you do. He is hard to pin down, even if your flirtatious ways delight him. The passion is extremely heated. He seems to know how and where to take you. The flowers, champagne, and romantic dancing melt you. This can be a lifetime match, offering laughter, good times, and a quality life. You need to be the practical one here.

With Scorpio SUN man: Your depth, laughter, and love of life attract him. Count on the heat overwhelming both of you. As hot as the passions fan, so are the problems dramatic. You both are determined and rigidly fixed. He has seething emotions and a very possessive streak. You will both need great skill in negotiation and compromise if this coupling is to work.

With Sagittarius SUN man: You might need to call out the fire department when the two of you start playing. Just remember, the operative word is play. You are both flirts and love to exercise your magnetism. You are interested in his adventuresome ways with money. This can only work if he remembers to adore you, putting you ahead of his other ladies.

With Capricorn SUN man: Your flash makes him feel even more masculine. He will try to make you part of his empire. If you want courtship and adoration, let him know from the very beginning. He wants an earthy, long-term merger. You have a decision to make. Remember, he is a workaholic. It will be your job to remind him there is more to living.

With Aquarius SUN man: He is about friendship; you are about loving. You both love parties and are wicked flirts. Your need for anchoring and the conventional life might give him the creepy-crawlies. He is an eccentric through and through. If you can take his comings and goings, you could have a lifetime party.

With Pisces SUN man: You make a romantic, loving couple. You know the type: They walk down the street hand in hand. You have a special magic that keeps the enchantment going forever. His emotions weave

around you and give your love even more form. This match can be
everything you always wanted.

Moon in Taurus, Sun in Virgo

You know who you are and where you are going. It is with precision
that you make your choices in life, even relationship decisions. You are
clear, exact, and grounded, as together as it gets.

You like working as a duo; this is how life is supposed to be. You
have empathy for women's rights, yet ultimately you opt for marriage,
and perhaps a traditional home.

You express all that is beautiful about a Moon in Taurus. You are a
born nurturer and caretaker, wanting to help others and create a whole
life for your loved ones. You have a strong sense of money management
and you build stability. You will buy quality—at the best price possible.

Though you love wonderful meals and the finest champagne, you
know clean living, good dieting, and exercise are the stepping-stones to
a quality life.

You have a calm exterior that hides a deeply seductive woman who
loves and adores her sensuality. Any man on whom you choose to unleash this passion will experience your vast emotional range, from cold
to boiling. You challenge, entice, and adore your physicality. You want
a man who can delight in it as well. The right man will help you build
a home and family that allows your inner joy to shine through.

With Aries SUN man: He adds fire to your earthy qualities. If you are
enticed, being with this man will be like living on a volcano, never
knowing when the next eruption will hit. It is doubtful you can sustain,
much less tolerate, a relationship like this. It is a bad mix.

With Taurus SUN man: Do stop and take some time with this gentleman, though it is doubtful you will need the suggestion. Your pace
together is like a well-practiced rhythm. Neither of you lose a beat. You
are both sensualists, yet know when to stop the indulgence. You make
a wise and mellow couple. The Cheshire cat smiles on your faces tell
it all!

With Gemini SUN man: You need a partner who is anchored, reserved,
and practical. What are you doing here? He is a very enticing man, alive
with mental energy, but to expose yourself to this is akin to torturing
each other. Please, be practical.

With Cancer SUN man: He will lavish you with feelings, sentimental offerings, and wonderful meals. There isn't anything to not like. He adds dimension to your practicality, and his sensuality touches you. He is intuitive and receptive with a touch that will unearth you. Love is well taken care of here. He will provide it all, whatever you dream of.

With Leo SUN man: He is the magician of romance. There is passion between you, but also plenty of problems. You don't put your significant other on a pedestal to be fawned over. He needs that. Otherwise this lion will meander to where there is more fondling and purring. You still might not be able to help yourself.

With Virgo SUN man: You have met Mr. Right. You will like his ways and style. Together you can create the stable, nurturing life you want. This man might not always be as romantic as you desire, but he will take good care of you and your relationship. He is not one for grandiose displays, yet his actions are clear and loving.

With Libra SUN man: This man specializes in enchantment, and you can feel yourself being slowly drawn in. Love heats up, even as disaster impends. He doesn't understand the word practical, and you can't teach him. In your book, he is all words and no actions. But he is sooo nice, loving. Too bad.

With Scorpio SUN man: You have found someone who is more magnetic than you. Desire steams between you and neither of you can say no. There is a long-term dance in which you will tempt, lure, treat, and cajole, always with the same ending. He is interested in what makes the world work, and will delve into the mysteries of life while you will be the practical one.

With Sagittarius SUN man: This is a hot flash in the pan. No more. He is interesting, but irritating. And as far as your dreams of a solid, grounded life, it won't happen riding this roulette wheel. His specialty is risk. Yours is security.

With Capricorn SUN man: You are sedate. He is strong. You compliment each other when you don't have common ground. Both of you want a solid bank account and lives that grow. With your excellent interchange, how can your love life be anything but the same? You will find out how good good can be!

With Aquarius SUN man: As eccentric as he is, you are conservative, yet you do have something in common: your need to be of service to others. He cares, and so do you. Unfortunately, that is where the similarity ends. Keep this match platonic and your causes will benefit. You might, too.

With Pisces SUN man: You might not have been looking for this much romance, but you've found it. He is very different from you, but he can add much to your life. He is like music, flowers, and candy. Your home might be a bit more lavish or arty than you think is necessary, but you are walking into a wonderfully special relationship. Respect and enjoy your differences.

Moon in Taurus, Sun in Libra

You are an artist in feeling, if not in practice. In some form, you express a strong sense of intuitive knowledge. You work from soft energy, always preferring the good in life, the quality experience. You spend to enjoy life. Life is for living, isn't it?

You want grand passion, hot passion, and lots of romantic moments. You simply will not understand or tolerate anything short of your romantic visions. Once the candlelight dinners are replaced with, "Hurry, I've got to meet the guys for bowling," you're out of there. Your challenge is to find a romantic man, buy a pair of rose-colored glasses, or bite the bullet and accept reality. You are about love, illusions, and starry-eyed moments.

You offer much caring, romance, and nurturing. What you give is what you want in return. You will make an excellent partner, not particularly possessive or demanding. You are fair with your chosen man. You can see him as a human being and not as a paycheck. You do want a classic courtship and marriage.

Your femininity draws men. You know what to say to make them feel better, to open them up. Your smile is contagious; others want to be close to you. You won't lack for romantic possibilities, but you need to really think about your choices, especially as you are likely to fall for the most romantic figure.

With Aries SUN man: This man is intriguing. As feminine as you are, he is masculine. It feels as if you are connected by an invisible rubber band that, no matter how far away you move from each other, snaps you back together. He is basic, sometimes blunt. His fervor more than makes up for it. Is passion romance? Expect to ponder this for many years.

With Taurus SUN man: His pulse is your pulse. You share common ground and can live well together. There is a slow pace here that breeds trust, fervor, and sensual times. You can expect longevity, but the pace could be nerve-racking, even for you. He will think your manipulations to speed the relationship are adorable. You have to decide how patient you really can be.

With Gemini SUN man: He is a tease and he finds you a pretty bauble to tantalize and seduce. There is laughter and joy here. He is intellectual, courteous, and very physical. He is moody, though, and sometimes needs space. He might like your stability, but can you give him his freedom? This answer can make or break the relationship.

With Cancer SUN man: He gravitates to your earthy, womanly ways. His romantic style, depth, and special touch thrill you. But don't kid yourself about this man: He needs lots of nurturing and care in return. You might feel like you need to invest in Kleenex stock, he is so emotional at times. This could irritate you, but this is the source of his sensitivity.

With Leo SUN man: You will know passion and romance with this man. The chemistry and just plain liking link you. You can tease and flirt him into a lather. Yet he will see the humor in what's happening. Like you, he loves to spend to add to the quality of life. There is a lot going here, but don't think it is going to go your way. Remember, he is the Lion. He rules his jungle.

With Virgo SUN man: There is a deep connection between your two earthy souls. However, as much as he digs you, he can never meet your standards for love and romance. He is simply too practical for your taste, but he is very sweet and promises fidelity. Think before you totally nix him.

With Libra SUN man: You both have a naughty, flirtatious streak. He wants to romance you as if there is no tomorrow. He lives in the here and now, so making commitments is hard for him. The loving is so good that you might decide this is okay. You never lose the spark here, unless you decide to be hard on him. He wants only gentleness.

With Scorpio SUN man: Expect to be knocked off your feet by his sizzling, quiet, yet formidable seduction. A side of you wants to run, as you know this is no light acquaintance. Yet you, the earthbound, grounded woman, know it is worthwhile to explore what is here. Romance will be replaced by true passion. You will grow and learn from this man.

With Sagittarius SUN man: He is active, physically enticing, and knows how to spark your interest. There is much going on here. Your teasing puts him in a frenzy, yet your earthy ways stop him in his tracks. This man really has a hard time settling down, but your feminine, party ways certainly motivate him. This is a definite maybe!

With Capricorn SUN man: You have met up with life's power broker. He is the prince of wheeling and dealing. He loves business and work. That's all nice and good, and he might appeal to you as a "grounded" choice. But, come on, unless you count money as romance, you can forget it here. He will be annoyed when you try to flirt him into having a good time.

With Aquarius SUN man: He is his own man, quite eccentric, yet there is so much chemistry with you that it can get out of control. His naughtiness follows him everywhere, even into the bedroom. However, you need more to sink your teeth into, though it might take a long time for you to realize it. You are having such a good time!

With Pisces SUN man: There is an invisible link here that, once formed, won't break. You will be loved and romanced from past to beyond. Expect to be astounded by his imagination and his bag of endless treats. You will provide the banks for his steamy emotional waters and it will be your pleasure, and his. Wow, what a pair!

MOON IN TAURUS, SUN IN SCORPIO

You are provocative, deep, and born with a charisma that is both a gift and a burden. With your intelligence, bewitching sex appeal, and perceptive ways, how could life be anything but easy? Ultimately, you probably endure more ups and downs than most people. It is simply your courageous spirit that makes it look like a snap.

You find relationships particularly difficult. You aren't exactly sure what to say or how to answer. You are proud, stubborn, fixed. Few can break past your barriers. You might not want to let anyone know you deeply. You fear vulnerability and the hurt that you associate with it. Often you equate money and comfort with security.

At some point, having a viable relationship might become more important to you because, like your Taurus Moon sisters, you really crave a good partnership. When you find the right man, you could open up like a rosebud, though often you commit to your first great love.

The right man must be wise and loving. You will find him more intriguing if he is reserved, saying little but understanding much. If he is quietly loving, passionately expressive, and deeply insightful, all the better. Yet, you also need someone who can provide you with the quality lifestyle that is so instrumental to your security.

With Aries SUN man: You like his clarity, direction, and energized ways. He is out there risking. Though you will attract him, he might not have the patience to break down your defenses. Nevertheless, don't dismiss him as a lightweight. If you are ready to be clear and open, this match might just work.

With Taurus SUN man: Here are soul mates who can understand and love each other beyond the moment. You share sensuality and similar needs. You might be defensive, but he won't care. He will guide you past your fears until you know the comforts he offers. This shield will cover every realm of your life. You can find security with this man.

With Gemini SUN man: This can't happen, or could it? No! You don't want to tangle with this man. He loves to toy with the mind, can flip personalities and drive you wiggy. Though he understands your heated ways, he knows you are no more than a fling. Be realistic.

With Cancer SUN man: This man is tender, sensitive, and understands you. He provides the same kind of healing touch as you. Together, you can turn calm waters into a heated geyser. Be careful, though. If you become too critical or difficult, he could turn inward. He loves to love; he needs to be loved. Don't turn away from him.

With Leo SUN man: He is the personality kid of the zodiac and has great skills as a Romeo. You can't stay away, but the battle here could be a war. On one level, you know he offers you passion, security, and a quality life. Though you will laugh many hours away, on some level you judge him as superficial. Your criticism could throw him into another's arms.

With Virgo SUN man: Here, sweet earth kisses sweet earth. His quiet, methodical ways put away many fears as you seem to naturally know what is next. Your intuition helps him break past his cold barriers, something that is quite familiar to you. You make each other feel safe, permitting emotional magic and intimacy. You can count on him.

With Libra SUN man: He is charming, attractive, and gentle. You are drawn, but though there is an attraction, he can't penetrate through your barriers. In fact, he might not even realize there are any! It is in that lack of understanding that the problems lie. He's hot, you're hot, but that's where it ends.

With Scorpio SUN man: You have met a force, a power. He can stand up to you, see through your games, and at the same time lure you into his cave. He's a sensual animal, though you will be one of the few to see him go wild. Your styles are different, yet there is understanding. You will teach him about the quality life while he heats your passion and warms your home.

With Sagittarius SUN man: He is fun, lively, and an adventurer. He might be nice to meet or have a drink with. You could be intrigued by his ideas, but you know better than to throw yourself on his merry-go-round. Stay away.

With Capricorn SUN man: His strength draws you. You see a man who is what he says he is. You are drawn to the potential of security with him. He might not try to break down your defenses; however, you find there is little reason to shield yourself with this man. When you can distract him, there are torrid, memorable scenes.

With Aquarius SUN man: Keep skipping along. He could make an interesting friend, but even the first sign of wildness demonstrates different styles. Unless he is very unusual, he just sees things completely differently than you do. You could spend a lifetime trying to convince the other you are right. Give it up. This is a no win.

With Pisces SUN man: He is poetry in motion and flows right to you. You are at ease with his romantic ways, his sweetness, and his willingness to reveal his insecurities and vulnerabilities. His creativity meets yours. Together you could indulge your lives away. You will feel secure with him. He clearly needs you. The rest falls into place.

MOON IN TAURUS, SUN IN SAGITTARIUS

Your energy could awe others, you have so much get-up-and-go. You have stable, strong values, an interest in making and spending money, and a determination to make it happen. Your ability to get others involved in your ideas reflects your energy and charisma.

You also unconsciously draw others to you, especially men. You might find yourself with a suitor when you least expect it. You aren't out there to be a seductress, but to live. Yet you find you always have an admirer or two around.

You offer enthusiasm, fun, and an ability to risk, in addition to your solid fundamentals. You rarely go too far in your adventures, yet you will take a well-considered chance. As you have good taste, a love of luxury, and an endless yearning to travel, you will need plenty of money.

You seem to know what to say and have a social sense that makes others feel at ease. You are passionate about your partner. You could run through quite a few possibilities and could have more than one marriage. You could burn out a lover.

Mr. Right is a dynamic, enthusiastic man with energy to meet yours. You want someone whose vitality meets yours and enjoys adventure. You want a partner in life, not an anchor. As you enjoy the good life, it will help if he has strong earning power.

With Aries SUN man: He goes yippee when he meets you and hops on your bandwagon. In his eyes, you offer everything: enthusiasm, practicality, and wit. You bring out flaming passions in each other. Expect this to be a sizzler of a romance and a lifetime tie. You'll love the adventures.

With Taurus SUN man: This is a fine combination. There is rhythm here. The two of you can make poetry for the rest of your lives. It seems that you naturally fill each other's needs. Your sparkly ways add flourishes to the relationship, making this union even more exciting. Go for it.

With Gemini SUN man: This man makes you laugh, yet could pose quite a challenge. He is full of mental energy and feeds your impulsiveness with even wilder ideas than you can cook up. He thinks; you act. The lusty attraction makes you want to stay with him. You can, as long as you remain open to the other's style.

With Cancer SUN man: He might have trouble with your freewheeling, adventuresome travel. He can be threatened by changes. Never take off without him or you will discover what a true Crab is like. He loves your seductive, earthy ways. He would like to mellow out on that level forever. Can you take being reined in?

With Leo SUN man: Expect to be tossed into turmoil for a moment when this daring man enters your life. You thought you always knew what to say. He will charm you. He has the same appetite as you do for quality living. His romantic style reminds you of a dream and not reality. The two of you greatly enjoy each other. There is much to say yes to.

With Virgo SUN man: He is grounded and practical, but he is no fun to play with. He isn't a risk-taker, even the most considered risk. Expect him to criticize your vitality and adventuresome ways. You might be a lot happier not letting this relationship develop too far. He puts down important aspects of your essence. Why would you want that?

With Libra SUN man: He is a delight and a charmer. He ignites you. You will want each other. Times can be exciting, yet he also has the same need as you to languish hours away together. His gentleness brushes your heart, while your earthy ways make him yours. The love and passion will last.

With Scorpio SUN man: He is a reservoir of passion, insight, and intensity. You could get singed when you reach out for his magic. It will be his terms the whole way. Both of you know chemistry is at work. He might long for you, but on some level he doesn't approve of you. Your need for adventure seems, to him, the wrong answer to the mysteries of life. Proceed with care.

With Sagittarius SUN man: He is as spirited as you, perhaps even more. The problem is that the two of you are so busy experiencing life, there might not be enough commitment to hold the relationship together. He could wander off, leaving you sad and lonely. The grass is always greener on the other side of the fence for him.

With Capricorn SUN man: Your earthy ways draw this man, though he could cringe at your ability to spend. You like money as much as he does. You see it as a vehicle for pleasure; he sees it as a vehicle for power. If you get over this hump, there could be many great moments ahead. Your femininity ignites his passions. You will be able to lure him from work into your luxurious, sensual lair with ease.

With Aquarius SUN man: He is your friend first and your partner-in-mischief second. It will take all the grounding you have not to be swept off your feet. He will do nearly anything for an adventure, though he does have some pet causes. He might want you to join in. Beyond the sensual sparks, to make this match work will take some magic. Play this light and easy.

With Pisces SUN man: The tension between you is very strong. You might want to reach out and help him make more of his life. He certainly is a romantic and knows how to enchant you. However, his magic still will not prevent you from wanting to take off every so often. That is where the friction begins. And it probably doesn't end.

MOON IN TAURUS, SUN IN CAPRICORN

Established values and institutions are a key force in making your life run. You believe in structure and the status quo.

You offer stability, understanding, and compassion. You have the discretion to know when to pull back and say no to another, because you have strong boundaries and honor them. Others hear you loud and clear when you let them know where you stand.

You have a very appealing nature, even though you might not choose bright colors or be splashy. Others gravitate to your poise, self-confidence, and nurturing style. You seem to reflect what is good in life, what can happen if you are together.

Your sensuality speaks subtly through your body language, smile, and movement. You might appear much more sedate than the real you— a secret sizzler, someone who puts a man in awe with the response and heat you can generate.

You might marry late in life, though you are sure of what you want. You might simply take your time being sure that you have it. That's why a long courtship could suit you.

You are willing to be there for the bad times, but you aren't interested in putting someone together. You will expect an even, sensitive dating ritual with tokens of his caring.

With Aries SUN man: Nice man, but he's not for you. He is a pioneer, a crusader, someone who is into changing the status quo when it doesn't function in his terms. You and he will be at odds because your values are so different. Try again.

With Taurus SUN man: You will delight him because you understand him so thoroughly and know what to do to make him comfortable. He will seduce, cajole, and adore you. Pinch yourself. This is the way it is—terrific! You can count on him for long term.

With Gemini SUN man: He is witty, moody, and tantalizing. His raw sensuality awakens yours. Yet, he really isn't what you want. He doesn't offer the solid life you demand. He can be brilliant. He can be a good friend. But he isn't Mr. Right.

With Cancer SUN man: He is emotional, a lover, and a sensitive man. He values the past and his traditions. You mix well with this romantic man. You allow him to be who he is, yet give form to his feeling. You are his anchor. In return he adds magic, feelings, and romance to your life. You and your family will always be his highest priority. This is an exciting life commitment for you.

With Leo SUN man: He is a class A lover and adores women. You might catch his eye. He likes how sturdy you are, your sense of direction. However, you will never put up with his wanderlust and flirtation. He might be fun to wink at, but past that, I don't think so, nor will you.

With Virgo SUN man: He has precision and a sense of who he is similar to yours. There is a sweet receptivity between you. You both nurture and care about each other in a quiet, steady way. Though you might not be dynamic, this can be a strong life-tie for you. You can trust one another when it counts. Years build a special intimacy between you.

With Libra SUN man: He is gentle and charming. There is strong attraction, even a bond. You might like to toy with him, but ultimately he will take off. He likes to be free and easy. He doesn't want commitment. No, thank you.

With Scorpio SUN man: You have stepped into fathoms of emotions and feelings. He is bright, insightful, and penetrating. The attraction is undeniable. He will take you into uncharted waters, emotionally and physically. You might feel overwhelmed, but take the dive and go for it. You will know passion with him like with no other.

With Sagittarius SUN man: He is a fountain of energy, not to be stopped. You might think he is enticing, but forget it, he isn't the settling-down type. He isn't looking for stability; he is pursuing adventure.

With Capricorn SUN man: You have met someone who can fulfill your desires. He has charisma in all realms, a true success. You will find that you want to be part of his life. The two of you find you are even luckier together. Desire on many levels—for money, security, and each other—mark this love-tie.

With Aquarius SUN man: As conventional as you are, he is as eccentric. There is no middle ground here, though you might learn a lot from his outlook. He really isn't making mincemeat of your beliefs. He simply is a free spirit. If you are lucky, you might become his friend. You can't have a better pal.

With Pisces SUN man: He adds dimension to your life. He doesn't negate what is important to you. In fact, on some level he craves it. You are the sweet receptacle for his overflowing feelings. You help bring him stability and give his creativity direction. He is a dramatic, romantic plus in your life. He will teach you much about emotions and loving. This is a fluffy pink cloud.

MOON IN TAURUS; SUN IN AQUARIUS

You are an interesting dichotomy of conservative and liberal. You seem to bounce from one side to another, unaware of the confusion you can create. You give off wild and lively vibrations, dressing eccentrically and doing the unexpected. Your physical presence is unusual, mystical, and magnetic, drawing men. You like people who are offbeat, and often choose those who walk a different path. However, down deep is a conservative woman who wants all the beauty of love and marriage. You have a lot to give and offer.

You are very loving, nurturing, and surprisingly stable, making an exceptional friend, lover, and partner. Your first love is the focus of your attention, and it is quite likely you could marry him. Your loyalty seems to know no limits, but you want others to agree with you. In fact, you get difficult and contrary when life doesn't fall the way you want it to.

You might protect your beautiful and sensitive nature through unpredictable behavior or a cool, but friendly, exterior. Though this can intrigue men, it might make it hard to get through to your essence.

The right man will be able to read through you, though you are likely to be attracted to a wild and carefree man, much like one of the images you project. It is possible you will have two marriages before you find exactly what you want. Part of this proclivity comes from the mixed message you project. You will want a man who can relate to and love the core of you, yet will delight in your eccentric quirks.

With Aries SUN man: He is a pistol, a vibrant man who does his own thing. You like him, and he is a loyal, excellent friend. However, he senses there are deeper curves to your personality. He will explore the pluses of your varied nature and come to know you more deeply. There is a union here. He will appreciate all you offer.

With Taurus SUN man: There is a merger, a perfect balance of male and female here. He responds to your yin and you to his yang. Your friendship and loyalty touch him on a deep level. If you don't know it now, you will know soon. He is yours forever.

With Gemini SUN man: You respond to his multifaceted personality, high level of mischief, and distinct wit. The two of you might laugh so hard, others wonder whatever could be so funny. There is a teasing level between you that adds to the smoky flames that arise. You might be able to laugh with him down the aisle, but be sure this is what you want.

With Cancer SUN man: Though he isn't your type, he could be a delight to live with. He adores your loving style and earthiness. With you he feels secure and will show you true sensitivity and caring. There will be exquisite, romantic moments. He won't understand your some-times remote ways. Be open with him and don't hurt him. He is a truly gentle man.

With Leo SUN man: There will always be a dynamic attraction between you. He will set you on fire, and you only fan his flames with your airy ways. Your sensuality tells him worlds about you. Your love of the good life plus your caring of others make this merger a strong, long-term possibility. He loves to be adored. Do some fawning if you want to keep him.

With Virgo SUN man: You will find his concern nice and might decide to join forces with him. You are both detached at first, but you will have to be the one who sends out sparks. He is very cool, reasonable, and together. Be sure you want this kind of man before you teach him what it means to sizzle.

With Libra SUN man: This is a close bonding where love and affection bloom. You are drawn by his gentleness; he likes your friendship and indulgent ways. The mutuality, sharing, and intimacy become better as the years go on. He likes your stability, though don't try to weigh him down. He is a free spirit, who adores and loves you.

With Scorpio SUN man: There is a deep connection between you. When you tumble into his world of sensuality, you might feel like you are riding a tidal wave. The feelings run deep with this man. He is very possessive. When you become remote and distant, he might flip out. He will either understand you, or his vindictive attacks might make you leave.

With Sagittarius SUN man: He grabs your interest the second he appears on the scene. You want a merger. Together you breed friendship, inspiring each other to new heights, mischief, and loving. The added luster to being with this man is that together, you can create a financial empire. Don't worry, in his book, you have it all—sensuality, stability, and spirit. He likes your thinking.

With Capricorn SUN man: You have run into the zodiac's power broker. He can provide nearly anything a woman could wish for: commitment, seething sensuality, and security. Only you might decide he is just too much of a stick-in-the-mud. Whether this is a go depends on your clarity about your priorities. Funny, here you are the power broker! (But don't bust his bubble!)

With Aquarius SUN man: You might have split town together before you even have a chance to read this. Here we have two very wild spirits who don't understand limits or constraints. What goes on between the two of you might be unmentionable; but boy, do you have a good time! Warning: You will have to take care of your practical needs, because he sure won't. Have fun!

With Pisces SUN man: He is emotional, deep, and caring. His imagination allows him to take you on a magical mystery tour of romance and sensuality. You can help him anchor and feel good. There is a lot of give-and-take in this match. You might have a problem should he get clingy or have an attack of the poor me's. Remember, he needs you.

MOON IN TAURUS, SUN IN PISCES

You are poetry in motion. Others turn around when you glide by. You have a superb imagination and intuitive knowledge. You mix your strong base of feelings well with your anchored earthiness. You know how to use your feelings to empower yourself, to choose a direction.

You are sensual and an unusually attractive woman. Both men and women notice you. You have a strong sense of who you are and what you are like as a woman. Your walk, your glances reveal your sensuality. You have a tendency to pick up on your environment and reflect it in some way. Your sense of whether things are right or wrong for others makes you particularly empathetic and sought after.

You will make an excellent wife, supporter, and friend to your chosen partner. You will provide balance in the relationship. You know when to communicate, when to change directions.

You seek a man who is very sensitive and creative. You want imagination, passion, and gentleness. You want to be needed, and if your significant other is needy or dependent, that is okay with you. For that reason, you could tend to get into codependent relationships. You might be more comfortable than most in one. Be careful, as this could create the likelihood of two marriages.

With Aries SUN man: You might like him; you could admire him. However, your temperament and his don't match. You want someone who is more self-indulgent and less preoccupied. Leave him alone.

With Taurus SUN man: He bonds with the stable, beautiful, emotional woman that exists within you. The two of you will build a wonderful, anchored life in which beauty, travel, and sensuality blend. That you are so artistic and dynamic only adds to his fervor. He will put you on a pedestal. Your touch will send him to Never-Never-Land.

With Gemini SUN man: He is happy and witty. You might appreciate his fast answers, his jokes, and his great style of flirtation. Creatively, you are interesting together but as a tandem, you flop. He seems to always be off on another conquest. You'll feel like dust in his boots. Don't do this to yourself.

With Cancer SUN man: You swirl together, losing your sense of identity to the oneness that forms. Intuitive touch and emotion make words unnecessary. The connection only deepens with time. You soothe his soul; he provides you with family and financial security. You seem to have the best of all worlds.

With Leo SUN man: He is the zodiac playboy and is tantalized by your imagination, subtlety, and fluid sensuality. You make an interesting couple, able to establish security, a strong life, a beautiful home. He too appreciates the quality life. You will travel the world, reinventing romantic moments.

With Virgo SUN man: He adds some new ideas and helps you channel your creativity and artistic ability to benefit others. He is anchored and allows you to enjoy your whims while he holds the fort. Being with him stabilizes you, and the attraction never fades.

With Libra SUN man: He is artistic and loving. You respond to him in a big way, wanting to know him better. You both are creative, and express it in your lifestyle and luxuries. There is chemistry, adoration, and a link of souls that cannot be broken. You will anchor him. Count on you being the practical one.

With Scorpio SUN man: He communicates on a telepathic level, and you know what he wants. You read each other clearly. Often a touch says it all. He finds security in loving and within himself. You find security in the material world. You are challenged to evolve past liking "things." This is a deep love with physical harmony.

With Sagittarius SUN man: This man is an exciting adventurer. However, you are too stable and sensitive for the zodiac wanderer. Quickly, you get on each others nerves. Call this quits while you are still ahead. This match can only hurt you.

With Capricorn SUN man: He molds into your earthy side, and you make a strong, hot union. Your ingenuity delights him, and he provides you the foundation to give free rein to your creativity and high energy. You can follow your whims in every area. He will adore your sensual ideas.

With Aquarius SUN man: He is an eccentric. You like his ideas, his values, and his respect for friendship and humanity. However, that is where the affinity ends. He is too airy and free for the intimate requests and demands you will make.

With Pisces SUN man: His ideas are as romantic and inspirational as yours. You two are natural bon vivants who let go and live life. You have an uncanny sense of timing together. In practical matters, you will need to be the anchor. He will always trust in your judgment and your love. Your mutual love only deepens with time.

Moon in Gemini

"The time has come," the Walrus said, "To talk of many things:
   Of shoes—and ships—and sealing wax—
   Of cabbages—and kings—"
      —LEWIS CARROLL, *Through the Looking-Glass*

You have a gift for gab. You're always the one at the party making conversation, sharing jokes, swapping information. Not only are you a walking encyclopedia of information, you have charm and wit. You're extremely social, quick, dexterous.

Always thinking, you maintain an intense inner dialogue, weighing the right way to go, the correct solution. You are a fountain of trivia and information. It is instinctive to you to gather facts and share them. You believe profoundly that mental acumen can make your life work, and it can, in a way.

Yet on some level, this gift for gab is a defense to avoid your feelings and emotions. You might be uncomfortable with feelings and your body. So to compensate, you develop your mind. Though you can relate to others mentally, the challenge for you comes in learning how to relate on a feeling and physical level.

Do you explore life and knowledge with your friends, relating to them on a feeling level? Or are they merely friends because they pique your interests at the moment? If you have a changing palate of Byzantine, unusual, but exciting friends, they might represent your defense against getting to know anyone well. Instead, you collect unusual people, and live in a whirlwind of trivia.

If you use your intelligence to sort through the many feelings you experience, and seek dialogue on a feelings level with others, your relationships become much richer and deeper. You will discover commonality with others if you listen and help them find solutions to their problems. Use your people skills to draw others closer to you.

You will tend to move and be physically active. You move your hands and often gesture. Sometimes you do two things at once. Your high nervous energy keeps you rambling from subject to subject. On the plus side, your high energy level can keep you feeling young.

It's likely you will have two marriages, as you are so changeable. What might appeal to you this year could be utter dread in ten years. To make solid choices, you need to know yourself well. You do not work well in possessive relationships. Your partner should be flexible, willing to be spontaneous. Like a chameleon, you can change tone, even style, depending on where you are and what you are doing. Your partner needs to deal with that.

You offer excitement, intelligence, and variety. You show your caring in a verbal, insightful way and have talent in the sensual realm. You're more likely than most to check out the Kama Sutra. Another contributor is your physical dexterity, which can border on acrobatic. Men consider themselves lucky to be your sweetie. You keep things lively and provide a life passport to excitement, dimension, and fun.

MOON IN GEMINI, SUN IN ARIES

You seem to mix words with actions, making you an unbeatable combination. Because you live your words, you make a very clear and direct friend, partner, or associate. Your passion and commitment mix delightfully with your cynicism and mental gyrations.

Your vitality, brightness, and quickness attract men. You never do anything halfway, though you tend toward explosions of energy and emotions. In between, you think a lot, keeping your inner hotbed quiet.

You exude sparks of life that promise sensual magic and a mind that declares excitement. The good news is that you promise and you deliver. When a man decides to get to know you, he might feel as if he has opened Pandoras's box. He will find you bewitching, invigorating, and unusual. You will commit only to that which you believe in, and that includes him.

You will want a man with energy, spirit, and vivaciousness to keep up with you physically and be your mental playmate. After all, if you can't flirt, discuss, and swap ideas, what purpose is there to communication? You want your partner to be your match in the pure sense of the word. You want him to kindle your desire and provoke your mind. You won't hesitate to move on if he doesn't fulfill your needs. You are in control of your mind, and once you make a decision, you have no problem following through. Remember, you have the fire to make your ideas live.

With Aries SUN man: You are full of hot air, and he is flaming energy. You two explode into passion. He can meet you at every turn. This man has the energy to blast right by you. He might not be as much of a thinker as you, and that is okay. Your ideas stoke his fires. This match can sizzle for a lifetime.

With Taurus SUN man: Say hello, be polite, and do whatever you have to. However, do not think in terms of a long-term relationship. You are barking up the wrong tree! He'll bury your passion.

With Gemini SUN man: When he asks you out on the first date, you could already be thinking of a life together. What is going on here? You are meant to be together, and both of you know it. Your extra pep is a big plus. He will feel loved by your willingness to act on his ideas and on his behalf. Your energy guarantees that an already loving tie will become a scorcher.

With Cancer SUN man: He is weepy and emotional. You will get heated when you try to cheer him up. Don't waste your steam here. You can do better.

With Leo SUN man: Your wit will catch his attention. Your repartee is only a reflection of what lies past the words. Together, you blaze. You love his imagination. You are a handful, he knows it. It will be all he can do to stay with you. He might be a player, but he will be too tired chasing after you to think of anyone but you! He'll recharge you, and off you go again.

With Virgo SUN man: You need to think carefully before you toy with him. He might be full of chatter, talk, and wit but to you, he is a drag. Don't go here.

With Libra SUN man: He is gentle, soft, and airy. You adore his charm and repartee. He likes your action. You can write him poetry, he will bring you roses, and there you go down the aisle. He isn't the type to make decisions, so be spontaneous with him. He will want you forever and will indulge whatever's in your head.

With Scorpio SUN man: He is steamy, sensual, and wise. Your adoration might flatter him. But there is a sensual attraction that makes both of you want to explore. You feel like you are visiting Pompeii, just as Mount Vesuvius blew. You will need to reach out to him, but he wants you. He can get possessive if he gets scared.

With Sagittarius SUN man: He always feels the grass is greener where he isn't, until he has the pleasure of meeting you. Your wit and ideas draw him in. You will be flattered when he decides to follow through on one of your ideas. You both find passion in each other's touch. He might feel like he just hit the million-dollar jackpot and he did. He found you!

With Capricorn SUN man: There is a quirky attraction that seems like it must be explored. Your ideas stop him in his tracks. He is a power broker, someone who supports the system. As long as your crusades don't go against him, he can have a good time with you. You pique his interest; don't count on this for the long term.

With Aquarius SUN man: He's fun. You are naughty spirits together, one's ingenuity egging on the other's mischief. Friendship and love are the natural outcome. You will have so much fun, others will be jealous. But they don't know the half of it, and we won't tell here. This match will provide long-term happiness.

With Pisces SUN man: He is emotional and appreciates some of your romantic ideas and gestures. However, you will feel suffocated with this man: You need space; he needs closeness. There is very little chance of even finding a midpoint. Move right along.

MOON IN GEMINI, SUN IN TAURUS

You want things predictable, yet you crave change, variety, and diversity. You seem to flip back and forth. However, you express yourself in a determined, steady fashion unless you feel insecure or there is a change you don't anticipate.

Eyes turn toward you when you walk into a room. You have a sultry walk and strong eyes. You gesture and tell a heartfelt story with your eyes, face, and expressions. Your style draws suitors who want to feel your energy and vitality.

You are determined, and your ingenuity makes things happen. You offer a lot—friendship, loyalty, resourcefulness, and an endless source of ideas. You can also be more flexible than most people imagine.

You will make an exciting, yet loyal partner. You want the stability and security of a marriage. But within those constraints, you can take a lot of change, humor, and upheaval. That is part of life, isn't it?

You aren't always comfortable with togetherness. For that reason, you could choose a man who is emotionally unavailable if you aren't sure of your ability to maintain distance. This choice might not be conscious. Being aware of this tendency can help you in the long run. The right man will offer you the love, family, and home life you want. He will give you freedom to do the unusual, to follow extremes, to pursue some of your ideas.

With Aries SUN man: You say something to him, and he reacts right away. He responds big time, and you like it, but he might not be the stable, sedate gentleman you are looking for. Count on action with this man. You will have a decision here. Can you do without an anchor?

With Taurus SUN man: He is what you always wanted, but now that you can have him, you have mixed feelings. He pulls in close and is there for you, and you will want to take off. If you understand your conflict, you can make this work. You need to be open about your dichotomy—wanting security, yet needing freedom.

With Gemini SUN man: You want to take off on an adventure with him as soon as you meet him. There is soulful rapport and understanding that seems unearthly. You seem to match wit, humor, and dexterity where it counts. You live and love well together. Don't mope if he isn't Mr. Conservative. Ultimately you will have great rapport with him. The flame burns bright.

With Cancer SUN man: He is emotional and offers strong family values. You like this quality in him. However, when he ropes you down to be his significant other, you might feel uneasy. Though there is a sweetness and intuitive sensuality between you, the discomfort could become overwhelming. Your freedom-loving side could put the kibosh on this one.

With Leo SUN man: He is forceful, commanding, and romantic. You love the flirting and mental exchanges. He will provide for you and make you comfortable. Better news yet, he isn't the clinging type. There will always be money here, as he adores the good life, like you do. The chemistry is undeniable. Just remember to tell him how wonderful he is. He needs to hear that every day!

With Virgo SUN man: There is a lot of tension between you. An earthy understanding gives way to annoyance. He will find your spinning of ideas and impulsiveness impractical. He becomes critical, you get stubborn, and the problems begin. He isn't a big enough thinker for you.

With Libra SUN man: This man hooks your heart with his gentleness and romantic ways. With him you find humor and lightness. The courtship is all hearts, roses, and love. You both have a similar indulgent side. However, if you think he is practical, think again. You are going to have to be the responsible one. But the pleasure is worth it.

With Scorpio SUN man: There is an unspoken connection here. You might be very different, but the passion more than makes up for it. He has great reserves of feeling and wisdom. Though your styles are quite different, the sparks draw you together. Your verbal gifts delight him. He loves brainstorming and sharing ideas.

With Sagittarius SUN man: You might be set back by this fervent man, who bubbles with enthusiasm and spirit. You make one of your witty, sparkling comments, and he stops. He likes your financial sixth sense and might ask your opinions often. He can be a wild card financially and emotionally. Yes, he's hot and he's dangerous.

With Capricorn SUN man: He is earthy and stable—just what you want. He provides you with strong financial backing to be free and whimsical. You can have a great time here and feel safe, as he is the perpetual workaholic and won't get too close. Better yet, this tie sizzles. You will enjoy the sparks, the anchor, and the stability. He will like your mind and will always appreciate your feedback.

With Aquarius SUN man: He is eccentric and mental, and spins wild ideas. The two of you seem to trigger each other's wildness. It is a good thing that sometimes you can pull back and be rational, or the trouble that spins out of this match could be a problem. You can count on him for mischief, but not to be the stable, earthy man you want. The good times might make it worth the ride.

With Pisces SUN man: You can almost cut the stress with a knife. You want to talk ideas, he wants to emote feelings—already a hassle. He isn't stable, but you do like his imagination, love of life, and ability to let go. Think about the pros and cons before you leap into a perpetually difficult situation.

MOON IN GEMINI, SUN IN GEMINI

You are creative and lively, full of wild ideas, and willing to risk. You have many facets. Some think you have multiple personalities. Not so. You respond to each situation differently.

You are able to talk on the phone, cook, and perhaps make a grocery list simultaneously. Your versatility makes you a tremendous asset, though those talking to you might be thrown off by your thoughts, which do not necessarily follow sequence or logic—except to you.

You probably have a slim build, are a bundle of energy, and tend to spark others to think and take action. Your laughter, humor, and detachment draw people. You might have a difficult time just feeling sometimes, not acting or talking. You might feel uncomfortable with intimacy and might do or say things to distance a suitor or partner. Yet you sparkle with sensuality and a willingness to try all.

Your jovial personality draws men. You are likely to choose a man who is witty and full of ideas, and is up for play. He might also have a difficult time with a close relationship in the traditional context.

You sometimes have difficulty seeing situations from any point of view but yours, especially if you are emotionally involved. Learning to see life from another's viewpoint is important. With this skill, you'll increase your ability to relate and love.

You are likely to have several major relationships or marriages. You tend to get bored easily, so when you say "yes," please be sure.

With Aries SUN man: He is the spark and you are the gasoline. Together you will detonate. He loves your versatility, dexterity, and playfulness. You will give him feedback on his projects and inspire him with ideas and your ability to move quickly. There is impulsiveness on all levels here, enough to enjoy for the rest of your lives.

With Taurus SUN man: He is earthy, stable, and conventional. What are you doing here? There isn't a chance this will work. He wants someone who is there, who will spend hours in sensual play and talking money. Is that you?

With Gemini SUN man: If you don't have enough diversity in your life, you just let more in. There will be fragmented conversations that only the two of you can understand. You are the couple who will try anything and do anything. Ideas are the world for both of you. However, you are both players, so if one of you gets bored, there could be trouble.

With Cancer SUN man: You will feel as if you are drowning with this man. He is emotional and feeling, and doesn't like giving space. He wants home and family, while you need to crow about life and living. Forget it, unless you are willing to have your wings clipped forever.

With Leo SUN man: You have met the zodiac's all-time lover. Enjoy the cheery words, flirtation, and flashing sensuality. He will be amazed by your physical prowess, and you will make him feel adored. You won't easily forget his heated animal responses. Be careful; he can play around, just like you. Stay focused on this lion if you want to keep him.

With Virgo SUN man: He is about practicality and grounded behavior. He won't mean to, but inevitably he will put you down. There is only frustration and irritation here in the long run, even if you bond on some level. Take a hike, or tell him to.

With Libra SUN man: He is a delight, and you know it. He loves your mind; you love his charm. There is more going on than mutual admiration here. You find romance on intellectual, emotional, and physical levels. This is likely to be a lifetime passion. You both have problems committing, but you can't say no to each other.

With Scorpio SUN man: There is chemistry here that you will want to explore. He is emotional, deep, and loving. Meeting him might trigger an endless series of games, as you avoid getting too heavily involved. You love the play, not the commitment. Be clear with him about what you want, or someone could get hurt.

With Sagittarius SUN man: You are different sides of the same coin. You both disseminate ideas. You do it through your mind and sharing. He does it through actions and living. As long as you don't criticize each other, there is long-term chemistry and bonding. Evolving the relationship into a marriage might take a lot of work, as neither of you seeks commitment.

With Capricorn SUN man: He is earthy, stable, and hot for you! Though this is unlikely to be a long-term combination unless he has a very unusual chart, it sure can be a sizzling fling. You both like what the other brings to the bunk. Let it burn out and don't push your luck.

With Aquarius SUN man: You are a live wire, and he is an independent eccentric. You are both free spirits ready to take off at the drop of a hat. Love and life seem to mix well here. You are guaranteed a lifetime of fun, laughter, and happiness. You feed each other on many levels. Let it happen. You will love hanging out together.

With Pisces SUN man: Tension is high with this man. He wants someone who is always there for him, and that isn't you. Be open to a conversation, maybe even a date, but nothing more.

MOON IN GEMINI, SUN IN CANCER

You have a fluid sensuality that draws men. You seem to understand problems intuitively and can sense what is going on with others. You are a valuable friend, loving and understanding.

You expect commitment, family orientation, and a sense of direction. Because you are so romantic, you will seek someone who loves candlelight dinners, intimate moments, and conversation.

You offer strong responsiveness, availability, and concern with traditional values. You are always there with feedback and bright ideas. You are a person who can be very present, aware of the moment and your desires. You need to talk about what you feel, but you also want to hear from others about their feelings. Your liberality opens many doors and possibilities. People feel as if they can share nearly anything with you.

You will do your best to make a relationship work, pulling out all the stops as needed. You know when to give it up or move on. You are destined to find a rewarding, special partnership, as long as you approach it centered in your own feelings.

With Aries SUN man: This match has its pros and cons. He excites your mind, stimulates your energy levels, and makes you want to leap on his bandwagon. But though he is caring, he might not be the sensitive man you need. There is a lot of action, passion, and caring here. Is it enough?

With Taurus SUN man: You discover that he is mellow and anchored, and gives of himself. You love the candlelight dinners. But you like excitement and change. You'll have to trade that in for comfort. If you think you can roust him out of his patterns, forget it.

With Gemini SUN man: He might not be practical, but he does understand you and knows how to respond to you. You have similar needs and patterns. Your bonding includes a deep, seething sensuality, seasoned with variety. You decide you have the best of all worlds here.

With Cancer SUN man: You have met a like soul who feels as deeply as you. Both of you can be defensive because you're so tender and vulnerable. If you hit a wall, this sensitive man is probably feeling hurt. Reaching out will be more your job here. He will love your solutions. You get to play doctor, nurse, and whatever games please you.

With Leo SUN man: This man is drawn to your femininity and soft ways. You will keep him guessing about what you are up to, yet he'll feel nurtured. He will want you to never leave. He will try to impress you with his romantic skills. You love that in him, as well as his love of the good life. You'll enjoy moment after moment with him.

With Virgo SUN man: Though you like his logic, when you are in an emotional fuddle, you might be exasperated by his conservative, practical ways. He doesn't see life as you do, nor is he likely to. Your different outlooks could cause many a grouchy moment. Phooey.

With Libra SUN man: He makes your heart skip a beat with his soft, gentle manner. He understands romance, loves repartee and flirtation. However, he doesn't deal well with heavy feelings. So when he senses your emotional plunges, he could get mighty uncomfortable despite the good loving. This isn't a man made for heavy commitments either.

With Scorpio SUN man: There is a union that is unspoken, sensual, and deep. Though you are the princess of words, they aren't needed here. You touch, you see, you know each other. The rhythm never misses a beat. He will love your endless ideas, especially when you plug them into his areas of interest. It will be your pleasure.

With Sagittarius SUN man: You two are attracted; this is a case of chemistry without compatibility. You will boil with fury when he takes off without a thought after making mad passionate love to you. You like your space, but not the way he gives it. He won't be a family man either. Don't torture yourself.

With Capricorn SUN man: You will find comfort, security, and intense sensuality in this man. You are very different, though you both want security. Learn from each other, rather than fighting the other's style. Your interesting mind will always keep this man at a peak, wondering what is next.

With Aquarius SUN man: He entices you, and you want to play with him. The fun is great, but he walks an untraveled path. You might have

problems with a man as untraditional as he. You want family, commitment, and a classic romance. You might want to play in these waters.
Just don't try to make him into something he isn't.

With Pisces SUN man: He stirs deep feelings when you meet. It is as
if there's an invisible string between you, as you feel him, experience
him, and know him. You love the same things—water, romance, and the
good life. However, he wants you close always, and you need freedom.
Can you harness your spirit? Doubtful, but he might understand your
needs if you explain them.

MOON IN GEMINI, SUN IN LEO

You respond with lightning swiftness. You act on your ideas before
others can even consider the pros and cons. It is clear you know what
you want and will pursue it.

You are flamboyant, vibrant, sensual, extremely attractive, and desirable. You love life, and others sense this vitality in you. Your eyes are
probably big with wonder. You gesture wildly to express your enthusiasm. You have a strong mane of hair that you might toss around. Despite
your love of food, you are unlikely to have much of a weight problem.
Your vanity forces you to keep yourself in peak shape, and your high
activity level helps too.

Men find you romantic and sexy, a real catch. You project strong
magnetism and raw energy. You promise excitement as a lover. In fact,
a boring moment seems hard to imagine with you. Your drama, presence,
and vibrant love of life all draw men.

You love the opposite sex. It is quite apparent. You will have your
choice of suitors. Mr. Right needs to love life as much as you do. You
will expect a full courtship with loving tokens, special nights together,
and many heated, moonlit moments. You thrive on flirtation and animated
exchanges, and expect wit. You will put the right man on a pedestal and
make him king of your world.

You are likely to date often until you find the right relationship, but
you will give 100 percent when you finally find the right man.

With Aries SUN man: Bingo. This is an instant fit. He sets you on fire
with his sheer masculinity and high energy. You turn him on with your
feline coyness and bright conversation. You link, and it is wonderful and
passionate. He makes up for any lacks with his hot, sensual ways. This
is a scorcher.

With Taurus SUN man: You might like what he offers, especially his languid, steamy courtship style. Though there is chemistry here, there are also problems. He isn't as quick as you, or as trendy. He is likely to be comforting, demanding, and rigid. You can't be appreciated for your witty self. Expect control games and power plays.

With Gemini SUN man: You dance to the same tune, follow the same schedule, and are happy and blue together. Your flair has this normally witty playboy hot on your tracks. He wants you with passion and will go out on a limb for you. This only gets better as it gets older.

With Cancer SUN man: He is a romantic, sensitive man. Though he can appreciate your feminine drama, he is unlikely to meet your needs. Be sensitive and don't play with him. Just when he starts caring, you will notice another interesting catch go by.

With Leo SUN man: Your egos will either kiss or crash, depending on how evolved the two of you are. You both need to be appreciated and you could become competitive. You will delight him with your easy spirit and flexibility. You always seem to cast a different slant on a situation. Stay fluid and he is yours. You find the romance is the stuff of dreams.

With Virgo SUN man: He is picky, demanding, and practical. He won't hesitate to tell you what he thinks, even if you don't want to hear it. Your ego gets dented, and your logic doesn't work on him. If you continue down this path, don't say you weren't warned. Promise, you won't like it.

With Libra SUN man: Plan on falling hard over this man. He is delightfully charming and easygoing, and offers plenty of romantic touches. You like his style and you catch his attention with your feminine ways. It is your passion that he can't resist, though, and that is what will encourage this man to make a commitment. He won't have much choice.

With Scorpio SUN man: There is a raw, hot attraction at work here. The chemistry will throw you into each other's arms, but past that you might have a hard time finding common ground unless it is over what to fight about. There will always be flames, but not necessarily the type you want. You could get burned.

With Sagittarius SUN man: Don't expect to say no to anything he suggests. You will love this man. His magic is undeniable. He acts on your ideas, making you feel valued. He invites you on each adventure, as he wants your joie de vivre as part of his life. The enchantment is mutual and showers every area of your life. Don't let anything stop you.

With Capricorn SUN man: You provoke each other in many ways. He might be desperately attracted, but you need to think here. He is into work, power, and money, all very nice but there is much more to living in your book. Such delicious chemistry might be tough to resist, but you could be hungry later.

With Aquarius SUN man: He is friendly and a tease. He loves your femininity. You like his loyalty and freewheeling thinking. This man is a fountain of wild ideas, and you want to pursue them with him. The romance is offbeat, but you like his spirit. The attraction is long term, though you do accept your differences. There is little that the two of you can't talk through.

With Pisces SUN man: You might be touched by his romantic entry and gestures. You might fantasize about what could be. However, your need for space might irk him. The chemistry will keep this match burning for a long time. You both need to think about this. Can he give you the space you need?

MOON IN GEMINI, SUN IN VIRGO

You are coy sometimes; other times you can speak incisively. Those dealing with you might sometimes worry about your reactions because you are unpredictable. Your responses depend on your mood and thoughts. Because you appear so coquettish, you draw men. You're shy and probably diminutive, yet you effervesce with opinions and ideas.

You actually are quite thoughtful, though your opinions can change at the drop of a hat. If people disagree with you, they know if they try another day, you could have a different opinion.

You are a caring partner and friend. People can count on your planning and following through. However, you can become sarcastic and demanding if you don't see others do their parts the way you think they should.

One side of you seems to sabotage the other, one part easygoing and the other perhaps uptight. Your occasional ambivalence could complicate your relationships. Balancing these two sides isn't easy, but it's important for you to understand they're both part of you.

The man you choose will help furnish the details, that precision and order you seek. You want him to be level, allowing you to indulge your whims. Yet at times, you might attack his inability to float and be more flexible. Remember, you chose him and he reflects part of you. You might go through more than one marriage as you evolve to a clearer self-understanding.

With Aries SUN man: He cares about others, and you have similar needs for structure and order. You will like his crusading flair. You make excellent work and late-night buddies. He can take a sarcastic comment or two, if he enjoys you otherwise. You add to his passion, and he is willing to cater to you. This could work.

With Taurus SUN man: You seem to like his earthy, logical ways. To him, you're a flirt and a bundle of surprises. He finds your whimsical nature delightful, exciting, and provocative. However, he needs depth and feelings. He will help you ground and center. Be sure you want to dig in with him, or later you'll think he's a stick-in-the-mud.

With Gemini SUN man: You adore him, yet he could give you fits. On one level, he reads you cold, and you live well together. Yet you could fuss because he isn't practical or detailed. You will be forced to take care of that side of life if it is important to you. Let your intuition flow here, and the sultry moments will carry you over the humps.

With Cancer SUN man: This man adores your order and precision. He wants you to fuss and take care of him. To him, this is loving. Your sweet ways seem to give his emotions form. Before you know it, he'll want to walk you down the aisle. However, when your need for freedom comes into play, he could be deeply hurt because he won't understand.

With Leo SUN man: He is a live wire and will have you tumbling into his arms. He likes your lithe style and quick wit. Money is important to him. He wants to live the good life. When you search for space and freedom, he will find you enticing and worth the chase. A word of caution: Don't criticize him too much. He will run. He wants you to adore him.

With Virgo SUN man: He is practical and dependable. With him, you can be easygoing and less fussy. Realize he manifests a side of you, so if you decide to attack him for not being a risk-taker, or for not liking wild romps, you are attacking an aspect of yourself. To make this relationship work, you must resolve your own conflicts.

With Libra SUN man: This man is certainly enticing. You feel as if you can openly be yourself with him. He needs your practical earthbound ways, but he delights when you spread your wings. The fervor is intense here, and the romance dreamy. Just don't criticize him for not being the man you want. He will always be his sweet self.

With Scorpio SUN man: He relates so well to you. The embers spark when the two of you are in the same room. The attraction never seems to ebb. He loves your practical, grounded streak and feels safe to share some of his many highs and lows. Both of you can let it all hang out. Perfect!

With Sagittarius SUN man: Opposites attract in a dynamic way here. You like this fiery, exciting man, though he is not the image of what you THINK a man should be. He is a risk-taker and seeks adventure, travel, and good times. You can't deny what a good time you have together. It is your pictures of what should be that could interfere.

With Capricorn SUN man: He intrigues you because he is grounded, stable and, if nothing else, practical. He fits your image of a partner. You find there are strong, sensual ties here that you want to explore. He is a workaholic, so you can indulge your whimsical, carefree side and he won't care. Let this happen.

With Aquarius SUN man: This man follows his own path. Above all he is whimsical, naughty, and free. You want to join in and become a player on his team. He exposes you to tantalizing sensuality, but also to a special friendship. If you insist upon looking for the practical in him, forget it. Being with him is like attending the Mad Hatter's Tea-Party.

With Pisces SUN man: You are drawn to each other, but the difference might be too radical to overcome. He is a dreamer who lives and loves in imagination and fantasy. You, on the other hand, are practical or whimsical, which really doesn't flow with him. There is an undeniable raw attraction. Have fun, but then call it a night.

MOON IN GEMINI, SUN IN LIBRA

Your femininity, savoir faire, and verbal acumen make you very appealing. Your gift with words includes fine timing and the charm to carry through your message. When dealing with other people's feelings, you are sensitive, allowing you to make very strong statements in your sugar-coated style.

You love courtship and its rituals. If a suitor brings you traditional tokens of affection, you enjoy it. The thought is what's important to you. You love your roses, champagne, and candlelight dinners, the step-by-step process of knowing another.

You are social to the core. You love your friends, your family, and your suitors—and there could be many. Even when you are having problems, you never lose that sense of caring. In fact, you could choose a cause involving fairness and equal expression or champion the underdog. You might somehow channel your artistic talents into your daily life.

You need a special type of man who can appreciate your airiness. He too needs to appreciate the good life, but most of all, he needs to know how to court and love you. You expect spontaneity, liveliness, and joy. You love the process of dating and will have many loves until you decide you have met Mr. Right.

With Aries SUN man: Your meeting is like a solar flare. His masculinity feeds off your femininity. He thinks in terms of "I," and you in terms of "we." He has the energy to follow through on your many concerns. Your ability to add ideas to his energy makes you a big plus in his life, and your social skills make you the other half that he lacks.

With Taurus SUN man: He loves the good life. He expresses himself artistically or creatively in a similar way to you, and you both enjoy the dating game. You will be charmed by his loving dance, though he might be somewhat put off by your whimsical, carefree nature. You will let him lure you to his side every time. You love his skills.

With Gemini SUN man: You belong in the same pea pod. He knows it, you know it. The bonding is undeniable. You seem to know what the other desires. Your willingness to feed his needs makes for good will. He will love you forever, drawn by your wit, beauty, and loving ways. Say yes.

With Cancer SUN man: This man is compassionate and appealing. You love others and are drawn to his feeling nature. However, he can never hop on the merry-go-round of life the way you can. You will leave him miles behind.

With Leo SUN man: He is the genius of courtship and can't help but notice a pretty, fun treat like you. You tease his mind, play with his heart, and draw this playboy. He will be so busy chasing and loving you that he'll forget the other women in his life. Let him know how special he is if you want to keep him.

With Virgo SUN man: You might appreciate his precision and caring. Yet he is picky and difficult, not someone you want to know intimately. Neither of you could be happy so close. Try friendship.

With Libra SUN man: Both of you complement the other. Your whimsical nature and the naughty twinkle in your eye make him want to hasten the love ritual. There is fun, an unspoken bonding, and lots of understanding with this man. You will always be turning up the other's temperature. The rituals between you will be endless.

With Scorpio SUN man: You realize you might be diving into waters that you can't swim when you meet this man. You are right, but that won't stop the boy-meets-girl magic. You are both lively, sensual people. You can't stop the electricity between you. This could be a memorable romp.

With Sagittarius SUN man: You are drawn to this man of action. You like to wander too, but more in your mind than in reality. With this man, you will have the chance for real adventure. He loves your feminine style and romantic gestures. You alone might know how really soft and caring this man is. You bring out the best in him, and he will give you a lot to smile about.

With Capricorn SUN man: You like the fact that he is so secure. You admire him for his goals and his ability to accomplish them. Underneath this admiration is a sizzling desire that he provokes. He can be nice for a while, but eventually you could turn up your nose and move on. You'll find a kind way to say he wasn't attentive enough.

With Aquarius SUN man: This man is everyone's friend, including yours. You will need to take this relationship past friendship. This should be a snap, considering his yen to explore your sensual world. You feel more complete together. You like his naughtiness and independence. He adores your whimsy and silky feminine ways. This match is good the whole way.

With Pisces SUN man: Though there are gentlemen that you could be more in synch with, once the two of you start dancing, you are both hooked. He weaves enchantment, romance, and love around you. He can go overboard emotionally. He will want you as his anchor; this won't happen. That is the problem in a nutshell and you can't crack it.

MOON IN GEMINI, SUN IN SCORPIO

You project intrigue and mystery, and can set others' imagination afire. You have deep reserve, yet you are a bundle of action and movement. You are quick to respond, but can be thoughtful, deep, and considerate.

With your intense looks and the love of movement, men can only imagine what you might be like as a lover. Sultry and experimental describe you to a tee.

You offer a man understanding, a willingness to pitch in, and yet a strong sense of boundaries. You are fun, vivacious, and always good for a witty comment. Your understanding and insights are a gift to others, especially to a partner. You help them see why things happen, what motivates others.

You are likely to choose a man who is intense, reserved, and reads people well. There might be a smoky sensuality that marks him. It is important for him to value living rather than collecting the symbols of what life and money offer.

You might date a lot, reflecting your love of living and people, until you find the right man. You could even wade through a difficult marriage until you find him, but you are clear about what you want. A good relationship doesn't have to be easy, but you want mutuality, love, and a willingness to work out problems.

With Aries SUN man: You are both strong and direct. As if you aren't hot enough, he brings you to the boiling point. Expect to be singed at times, but usually you'll love bubbling along. He likes your mind, precision, and whimsical energy. If you two have similar interests, this is a strong yes.

With Taurus SUN man: He is even and sensual, and loves the good life. He will draw your mind, body, and soul until you are his. Your heated ways and spontaneity delight him. You are very different, and you must value the differences, not fight about them if this match is to work. There is much to learn, give, and enjoy together.

With Gemini SUN man: He senses your energy and knows how to move you. His high-voltage dash, dexterity, and ingenuity are his strong suit. The mix is bound to delight you. You feel at home. He adores your sultry ways. You two love to chat like two magpies—all day and all night long.

With Cancer SUN man: There is an unspoken connection here that binds the two of you. This is an emotional tie. You sense and feel each other. You find depth of an unusual nature. He might get confused when you go into pixie mode and become capricious, yet he loves it. This pairing can work as long as you are both secure with each other.

With Leo SUN man: This man adores women. He finds you exciting, sexy, and a wondrous mix. You both truly believe in yourselves, and when there is a conflict, neither will back down. To keep your nest toasty, you need to give in once in a while. This man makes love a magical mystery tour.

With Virgo SUN man: You find him practical, sweet, and earthy. However, he is not as exciting as you might like. You can count on being well taken care of, and you will make him yours forever when you teach him what hot really means. Don't expect grand displays of emotions. Do expect a little criticism here and there.

With Libra SUN man: He is generous and easygoing, and can charm the socks right off you. He knows how to love women and keep them hot in pursuit. However, you mystify him and pique his interest. Your insight adds to the relationship, though you still might walk from this man. He could be too superficial for your taste.

With Scorpio SUN man: You bond on a deep level. This can work if you have similar interests and viewpoints. Otherwise, the quarreling could end it. He finds you magical and alluring, even if you decide to disagree. This can be like a hot tango and will take maturity and perhaps old age to get under control.

With Sagittarius SUN man: He is drawn to your coquette style. He likes your mind, but your heated ways stir his fires. However, he has wanderlust, and you want someone who has more depth and feeling. You might decide to give him a spin, but in the long run, you might get off the bus.

With Capricorn SUN man: He is earthy, powerful, and intense. His touch can make you shiver. You find him interesting and a great playmate. He loves your mind and appreciates feedback from you about his career and life. There is respect, high energy, and heat. This match is long term and exciting.

With Aquarius SUN man: He is stubborn, eccentric, and bright. This is a natural party for two. You take off spontaneously on one adventure after another. He is as whimsical as you are. He values friendship, perhaps more than love. He will be there for you, but he might not be your life mate.

With Pisces SUN man: His web is enchanted, and you will feel him weave his way around your defenses. You are likely to succumb. There is a sense of knowing each other deeply. However, he wants you to stay put. He needs to know you are there. That might be close to impossible for high-spirited you.

MOON IN GEMINI, SUN IN SAGITTARIUS

There is no stopping you once you focus on an idea. You will be off making it a reality. You are a jolt of energy and are enthusiastic about nearly everything.

You have many friends and acquaintances, and lots of potential suitors. There is a strong possibility of multiple marriages. You are so versatile and changeable, the résumé of Mr. Right could change from year to year.

You were born on a full moon. This position gives you an unusual awareness of others, but it usually denies you strong relationship models. Critical to your relationships is having a clear concept of yourself and your desires, then gaining the ability to express them.

You offer men brightness, high energy, and a sense of humor. Your sensuality is expressed through your love of movement. You can flirt with words. You like to move, feel, and touch. As you mature, you will be able to verbalize your feelings and relate more easily.

You will seek a man who is passionate, fiery, and somewhat of an adventurer. You tend to choose men with a roving eye. Perhaps your biggest issue will be commitment. You choose men who won't give you one. By doing so, you are also stating your own need for freedom. By understanding your own need for space and freedom, you can choose a partnership more on your terms.

With Aries SUN man: He lights your fire and ignites your passion. He adores your style, friendliness, and endless wit. You are like a hot desert wind fanning his fire. Together you will crusade, disseminate ideas, and see the world. You both want to know more about life. You will always swap, share, and experience together.

With Taurus SUN man: You could spook this stable, grounded man. He likes you, he might even want to get to know you better, but your carefree energy and capriciousness throw him into a tizzy. He wants someone he can find, and your address is here today, gone tomorrow! You might be too much for him to handle.

With Gemini SUN man: He brushes your heart, touches your soul, and adds to your life. The two of you can chatter like birds in the morning. There seems to be so much to share. In this action-packed match, you follow a similar beat. He loves your ability to take off and act on his ideas! Promise: Neither of you will be bored.

With Cancer SUN man: You find he is mellow and sensitive. That might be nice for a date, but you get the creepy-crawlies when someone emotes on a regular basis. Needless to say, this isn't going to work.

With Leo SUN man: He comes out of the dark on his white charger and seems like a dream fulfilled. There is chemistry, chase, and loving. He is a player, be forewarned. You are likely to give him such a run for his money that he won't have time to flirt with other women. The two of you will experience life to the max together.

With Virgo SUN man: There is a basic incompatibility here. He is practical, into basics, wanting to take care of needs. This match might be nice for a week or two, but you will quickly hop along. You'll find him oh, so boring.

With Libra SUN man: You might overwhelm him with your energy, spark, and wit. Yet you will entice him. This man is great for you. He is willing to take his time. You will slow down and enjoy being courted. He has a hard time making a decision, so commitments, at least formal ones, don't come easily. That will be okay as long as he sticks around. Love will grow.

With Scorpio SUN man: You will need to tread water with this man. His emotions run fathoms deep, and you sense you are out of your league. You are right. Swim along, if you are smart. He can drown you.

With Sagittarius SUN man: It is hard to believe there could be anyone with as much get-up-and-go as you, but here he is. The two of you will pack your knapsacks and see new worlds, and that includes exploring each other. He loves your verbal facility and brightness. You dig his passion. You're likely to be on the move for quite a while, together.

With Capricorn SUN man: He is earthy and grounded. You and he are like fire and ice. You don't belong together and could be hard on each other. He wants someone who is there, not here today, gone tomorrow.

With Aquarius SUN man: He is refreshing, a freethinker. Being with him is like hanging out at the amusement park. He's an adventure. No matter how much mischief you get into, he will always be your friend. He is able to let go and give you space, but welcomes you with open arms when you return. This can be an open-ended, long-term relationship.

With Pisces SUN man: He is so imaginative about his compliments and wooing ways. Be kind to this man and let him move on. He needs someone who will always be around to hold his hand.

MOON IN GEMINI, SUN IN CAPRICORN

You are bright, logical, fast, and practical. You understand how society works and are content to work within its framework. You do what is wise as often as you do what is impulsive.

Like rare wine, aging seems to make you better. You will always have a youthful quality. Because you grow and change so much, there is a strong likelihood of two marriages. The second could be very different, perhaps occurring late in life.

Your charm comes from a groundedness seasoned with sparking humor. Your liberal nature allows you the freedom to try new things, yet your practicality tells you when to say enough, keeping you out of deep trouble.

You are strong and want a relationship on your terms. Though you have a need for movement, travel, and freedom, you demand a strong commitment. You will test, twist, and question a relationship. Sometimes you will talk out rather than feel. Other times, you could be demanding.

Your partner needs to be flexible and able to handle your mental and emotional intensity. You could flunk out a fair number of suitors looking for Mr. Right. You will want a tried-and-true lover and partner. After all, you are 100 percent there for your loved one and expect the same back.

With Aries SUN man: He is passionate and direct. You like this quality, but remember, you are strong and want things your way. There could be a war of wills here, and who knows who will win? Be smart. Be his friend, have a good time with him, but don't try to make more out of this. He is fun to play with, isn't he?

With Taurus SUN man: You like his multiple skills. He is great handling money and great handling you. You tweak his mind and sometimes run circles around him mentally. It is at this point that the problems begin. If you don't respect this man in all walks of life, forget it. This could be a sizzling fling and perhaps can go farther.

With Gemini SUN man: He can leap in the air, higher than you and with as much spirit and spontaneity. You find him a treat in all regards. He will question you, tease you, and seduce you. However, he might not have the longevity and constancy to take all your testing. There is love here, if you can forgive his not being as perfect as you!

With Cancer SUN man: How this relationship goes depends on the strength of your Crab. You both crave security, but he needs it emotionally, and you need it financially. Your testing reveals he has stronger needs than you might want to address. Be careful with your jesting. He is sensitive. You will want this to work, as there is superglue between you.

With Leo SUN man: He certainly is debonair and charming as he appears on the scene. Your wit will make him laugh. You like him and the way he handles his money. You need to admire this lion of a man if you want to make him yours forever. He expects to be appreciated for his special ways, especially in dealing with women.

With Virgo SUN man: He might be too picky and uptight for your style. He might not even get it when you become playful and tease him. You could respond to him and want to hold hands. Past that, let go.

With Libra SUN man: He delights the imp in you. Together there is touching, flirting, and perhaps much more. However, he's impractical and can't make a decision. You might find yourself putting him down at the worst time. He is who he is. He might be a playmate, but don't try to make this into something it isn't.

With Scorpio SUN man: This odd combination can work. Should you decide to put him down, he can counter with a sarcastic comment that could have you gasping for breath. You share a tantalizing dance and sense the sizzling possibilities. Both of you hold the key to open up the other to a vast range of love experiences.

With Sagittarius SUN man: He tweaks your soul, invites you to put fire in your life, to take a chance and risk on a profound level. You are likely to play ball and just be the saner one. He is strong, and if you push hard, he will go where the grass is greener. Careful. You'll miss him.

With Capricorn SUN man: He is even more serious than you. You will be able to play, tweak, and tease this man to your heart's delight and know everything is okay. You find peace in him, yet plenty of naughtiness. The heated tie is likely to stand the test of time.

With Aquarius SUN man: You like him. He is adventuresome. You could be off on a wild safari before you know it, only you'll be the hunted one. You will laugh, you will smile. He can be your friend and lover, but he won't take kindly to your tests and status quo thinking.

With Pisces SUN man: You might want to go on an adventure with him, and you'll scarcely believe what you experience. You ground him, and he makes you want him. However, your whimsical, flirtatious ways could make him nervous. If you are to stay together, you need to understand each other's needs as well as your own.

MOON IN GEMINI, SUN IN AQUARIUS

Spontaneous and vivacious, you are a live wire, an independent spirit who does her own thing. Where there is laughter, you are there. Where there are odd goings-on, you are in the vicinity. You are intellectual, using thought to clarify situations and determine your path.

Men are drawn to your open, friendly ways, your charm and flirtation. You have big eyes, gesture wildly, and have unusual hair. You tend to be social, popular, and personable. Everyone wants to be your friend, or more.

Having your space is very important to you. You also give loved ones a lot of freedom. You rarely manipulate someone into making the decision you want. You will state your case and let the final chips fall where they may.

You are very open and, because of that, you could have more than one marriage. You will be the first to state that a relationship isn't working after you have given it your best shot. You believe in fulfillment

and creative self-expression rather than commitment to years of pain.
You stay friends with your past lovers.

The right man will need to be somewhat an eccentric in his own
right. Rather than a traditional man, you want one who listens to his
inner voice. You will look for a quality friendship.

With Aries SUN man: You like his determination and fiery spirit. You
want to hop on his bandwagon. Though you are likely to turn his crusade
into a party, this man will appreciate your enthusiasm and ideas. You've
got a lot going for you two. You love each other's mind, and the passion grows.

With Taurus SUN man: He is the epitome of balance and conservatism.
He would be great for a lot of people but, I am sorry, not for you. You
will quickly be bored and go skipping along.

With Gemini SUN man: He meets you halfway. He is enthusiastic and
a deep thinker, and knows how to make you shine. You have harmony
here, a treasury of ideas and natural laughter. You have similar needs.
As long as he can keep you charged and bright, this is a go.

With Cancer SUN man: He is a family man who is deeply caring and
possessive. You might like and enjoy sharing with him, but there will
be problems. He will grab on to you with his pincers and you will head
for the hills. He doesn't understand your type of needs.

With Leo SUN man: Your laughter draws him as he senses he has met
a similar soul, someone who loves life as much as he does. If you
twinkle now, you will be a brilliant star after meeting him. He romances
you and delights in your spirit, energy, and ideas. Always let him know
how wonderful he is. Say thank you often in his favorite way.

With Virgo SUN man: You might get involved in a common cause and
work together to make it happen. However, he will judge your style as
flighty, and you could decide to take off. This is better as a work
friendship.

With Libra SUN man: As a couple, you are phobic about commitment,
yet you will commit through your presence in each other's life. You will
flirt, spar, and play together. Many good ideas come from you together,
but alone you have enough imagination to take you both into a lifetime
of adventure. You are like a summer storm together.

With Scorpio SUN man: He is an animal with an ability to cut to the quick, at least in your book. Actually, he is deep and incisive. You receive so many sexual sparks from him, you might want more. Yet he often hurts your feelings. The truth is, he wants someone very different from you. Still, you might spring for a fling.

With Sagittarius SUN man: Meeting him is like walking into a firestorm. You like his hot energy and want to play. The friendship you offer will stop him in his tracks. You present each other different points of view. As passion grows, you will want to pack your bags and join him in life's adventures. This match turns out to be a sizzler.

With Capricorn SUN man: He is so practical. He will think you are coming from another planet. You might judge him as downright stuffy and boring. Yet there is some chemistry here. This won't work, but it might be fun to try—briefly.

With Aquarius SUN man: Here is a man with some of your values. He is eccentric, but his own man. You could butt heads, as you both have strong views, but you both value friendship and have lots of fun exploring each other. You will fall in love when he does something daffy like give you dandelions as a token of caring. Your elflike naughtiness keeps his interest piqued. Oh, yeah.

With Pisces SUN man: He is interesting and imaginative. You will want to brainstorm with him, but he fails to enchant you for long. You might like to party together, as both of you go to extremes, but past that, two thumbs down.

MOON IN GEMINI, SUN IN PISCES

You appear ethereal and distant at times, yet are capable of discussing nearly anything. You have a yen for gathering information. The collected facts could seem disjointed, but somehow in your mind they are all connected. Others find you fascinating as you flip from intellectual to emotional. You can cry at a sad story, become logical, and then move to the next item in the agenda within a short span.

Men find you enchanting, but hard to get to know. You are like a glowing, constantly altering gem. Your compulsive, creative energy needs expression.

You have a love of debate, talking, and sharing ideas. Sometimes you can argue another into exhaustion. Yet you could still have problems discussing feelings, especially if you think expressing yourself can hurt another.

You offer nurturing and solutions. A relationship is very important to you. You need someone to communicate with, to share your adventures. The romantic in you demands an outlet for your imagination and creativity. In some ways you are in love with love. You can go from suitor to suitor, each being the love of your life. You'll probably have several major relationships, if not marriages.

You will seek men who inspire you, who open doors for you. You want them to present different points of views and expose you to new outlooks. It is important for you that they dote on you and court you to the fullest. You also want what you give: nurturing and solutions.

With Aries SUN man: Should you decide you want a hot argument, find this man. He might be able to outdebate you. He is direct, lively, and responsive. He enjoys your mind and tries to be supportive, but in the long run, there isn't enough glue here to hold it together. He is nice to know, though.

With Taurus SUN man: He will slowly reel you in with a delightful courtship. You find he sweetly supports you as you switch gears from one mood to another. Your chattering, however, could get to him. He is a mood man. Let him control and create the loving scenario you want. You will always find stability and caring here.

With Gemini SUN man: The two of you merge as if there is no tomorrow. It feels as if you have always known each other. You instinctively say and do the right things for each other. You share a capriciousness and both of you are teases. He might have a hard time with your intense emotions, but you can work it through.

With Cancer SUN man: There is an inundation of feelings between you. His touch evokes fantasies and sets off sparks. There is a sense of dedication and caring here. You might need to be careful choosing your words, as he is very sensitive. Yet there are endless good times as long as you are sensitive to this man.

With Leo SUN man: In your book, this man is a prince. He could knock you off your feet. His sensuality and loving ways enflame your imagination and sense of romance. Your mental gyrations and teasing keep his interest. He feels appreciated by you; he feels excited by you. He will want to stick around for a long time. You are likely to say yes.

With Virgo SUN man: Opposites attract here, hard and heavy. You like his logic. He defines your emotions and helps find solutions to your woes. You will appreciate his clarity and practicality. When you become spirited and lively, he will just shake his head, but your capriciousness could make him nervous.

With Libra SUN man: This romantic man spells magic. You are hooked. His special ways have you blazing a trail toward him. Your mind and ever-changing nature keep him interested. He isn't the clinging type, which you can be. He might need distance every so often. You will snap until you learn to understand what is happening. There are ups and downs here.

With Scorpio SUN man: He makes your heart pitter-patter. His sensuality and feelings plunge you into love. You might feel caught in a riptide, out of control. You can come up for air, but you will willingly dive in again. Your airy ways and mind provoke him. He will want to possess you totally. Be sure you want this intensity.

With Sagittarius SUN man: There's action where this man is. Your curiosity will make him hard to resist. Don't try. There is a lot to be learned here for both of you. You need to handle your neediness. He isn't a nurturer, though he is exciting. Go ahead. Jump off the cliff of love.

With Capricorn SUN man: His groundedness is a relief to you, and he seems to help you contain your emotionalism. You will always be secure with him. He will like your sweet ways and high-strung mind. You'll make him feel needed and cared about. Your opinions mean a lot to him. There is electricity here, the kind that sends you to Nirvana.

With Aquarius SUN man: There is magic, enchantment, and endless laughter. You two will find things funny that no one else would. One idea triggers another, and before you know it, there is wildness beyond control. He will be a friend and try to understand your emotional ways. Actually, you might enjoy being with him so much, you'll seldom become upset.

With Pisces SUN man: Your eyes meet, and you know there is much to explore. He has an uncanny sense of touch, like you. Before you know it, you are in the throes of passion. Your airy comments make him laugh and add dimension to your relationship. Occasionally, you ask for space, because being Siamese twins can be a bit much for you.

Moon in Cancer

"There's no place like home."
—Dorothy, in *The Wizard of Oz*

You change with the flow of the Moon, perhaps as much as ten times a day. Others call you moody; the Moon rules you, and you are clearly responsive. Ultimately, a Cancer Moon bestows many feelings, great inner beauty, and a love of all that is related to home and family. At an early age you understood the importance of home and family.

You have a flowing projection, flowing with the momentary mood and the Moon's phases. Frequently, Moon in Cancer women have big eyes, clear skin, round faces, and full chests. Pearls, opals, and watery colors draw you. It is likely you will have a weight problem, as Cancer Moons tend to love food and the good life.

Your femininity speaks for itself, and men are drawn to you. You often choose flowing clothes that drape. Your ability to nurture and be nurtured, if your astrological chart is free of difficult aspects, far surpasses other Moon signs. You are often maternal in your caring, extremely protective of those who are close to you. Yet you have a coy, girlish side as well.

You have extreme sensitivity. You can easily be brought to tears. Often when you are unhappy, you overeat, spend, or indulge in other forms of self-abuse. You act on your feelings if you don't process them. You might have developed refined defense mechanisms. These can include clinging to your past, to possessions, to others, or to "what was." Other ways Cancer Moons handle this sensitivity is to withdraw into a dream world, far away from reality, or perhaps to be so sad, others feel as if they must help. Eventually, you will realize these defenses don't bring quality or satisfaction into your life.

You mature and embrace the hurts of the past, and are able to declare a new wave. You learn to communicate and nurture. When you feel hurt, you will learn how to explore your response with the offending party. This will curb your tendency to overreact. You will also learn not to "smother" others in your need to care, but will allow them to stand on their own. You will love and heal your inner child rather than look to others for this healing. Once you develop your own security system, your Cancer Moon influence will strengthen to its highest level, allowing you to experience the full depth of love.

You are likely to marry just once. This is not to say that relationships will be easy for you. However, you will work, grow, and change with your significant other. You believe in commitment and you honor that ideal. You will fare well through good and hard times, believing that there is a better future. You need to be careful of a tendency in your relationships to fall into unhealthy dependencies, and it is quite possible that you will see nothing wrong with them.

You might date extensively, because you love relating so much. This is a very healthy process as you grow and mature until you make your ultimate marital commitment.

MOON IN CANCER, SUN IN ARIES

You are constantly in action, and in fact have a hard time stopping. It is through constant movement that you often process your feelings, though you might not be aware of it.

Your femininity is spiced with a strong sense of direction. At times, you could do things that seem out of character: acting very assertive and direct, perhaps even bullish.

You have a broader commitment than marriage and nesting. You want to heal and nurture the universe. It would not be surprising to see you working for Greenpeace or fighting world hunger. You display caring on many levels.

You want to compete and win. This side comes out often in your dealings with men. You might be very proud of outdoing the man in your life, beating him at a game of tennis, or outrunning him. Is this what you want in a relationship?

You want a loving relationship in which you can build a home and feel secure. You will learn much about intimacy and caring. They are very important to you. You can manage the household, run the budget, work, and have plenty of spare time for your significant other.

Men sense your sensual, vigorous, physical nature. You probably have a quality of fire in your looks, whether it is reddish hair or ruddy skin. You express both vitality and softness, once you get past your innate defenses and competitiveness. No one loves intimate moments more than you. Here you merge your extremely physical nature as well as your need to love and be loved. You are truly a passionate lover.

With Aries SUN man: You are both active, competitive, and crusaders. Together, no one can stop you. No one is likely to try! You fire each other's furnaces in all respects of your life. With him, you seesaw, though, between fiery and emotional moments. Let this grand passion happen.

With Taurus SUN man: He soothes your soul, makes music to your body, and plucks your heartstrings. His nurturing and passion need to be treasured. When you blaze, he will stand back, not knowing how to handle the situation. But then neither do you. Try joining the gym if you want to stay with this man.

With Gemini SUN man: There is genuine friendship and mischief here. You two can dance together until all hours, sit on the beach solving the problems of the world, and spend hours flirting with each other. However, he doesn't know what to do with your moody side. You must establish your wholeness for this to work. Sorry, he isn't into weeping willows.

With Cancer SUN man: This is an incredible psychic, sensual, magnetic merger. You sense each other, falling prey to each other's uncanny touch. Expect similar needs. You naturally do the right thing for each other. There's romance aplenty here, though expect stormy moments, especially when you decide to tell it like it is. Remember, be nice, he is as sensitive as you are. This will work.

With Leo SUN man: Together you redefine passion, masculinity, and femininity. He is romantic and dashing, and has a look that will warm your insides until you burn. You find that you want to succumb to his beckon and command. He likes your energy, but your soft, feminine, loving ways make him a fly on your flypaper. He isn't going anywhere. Believe me.

With Virgo SUN man: He is logical when you are irrational. He is practical when you cook up wild ideas. He is anchored while you fly off the wall. Do you want such contrast? He will think yes, especially when you stir his embers. He will never forget how you turned him on, like a switch.

With Libra SUN man: Opposites merge here. His soft ways touch your soul and heat your body. It is mutual. He loves your ethereal, soft ways and your animated, lively style. However, there is built-in tension with this combination, especially if you get clingy. He needs his space. Count on your share of arguments, though you will love the peacemaking ceremonies.

With Scorpio SUN man: He understands your energy, is proud of your commitment, and adores your intuitive sensuality. There is a profound union of raw energies, touch, and caring. You will feel secure with him. He is possessive; you are clinging. What could be more perfect? You naturally take care of each other's needs. This is the bonding of a lifetime.

With Sagittarius SUN man: You two have a raw attraction, and you charge each other's batteries. But his risk-taking ways, both emotional and financial, will have you racing in another direction. You need much more security than this. Do stay realistic on some level, for your own sake. Forget any thoughts of changing him.

With Capricorn SUN man: Security reigns here. He will provide for you in every way. He might not understand your emotionality, but he will wipe away the tears. He doesn't get the side of your nature that needs to go crusading. He wonders why change what obviously works? There could be an argument or two. He wants the real, emotional, loving woman he sees within.

With Aquarius SUN man: He is your friend and could be fun to take a whirl with. The long-run odds of this holding together aren't good. He isn't into providing a traditional base or family. He is his own person and can't stand to be hemmed in. This is strictly playtime.

With Pisces SUN man: He touches your depth and strokes your soul. Let loose; the two of you could get out of control. Everything seems to happen to excess. There may be nothing wrong with any one escapade, but eventually you will need to look at the cumulative toll these extremes take on you. But you might not care.

MOON IN CANCER, SUN IN TAURUS

You handle life's ups and downs well. Your earthy logic carries you through them. Sometimes you might whine or feel sorry for yourself, but ultimately you are strong, together, and sensitive. This combination is unbeatable. You make strong choices for yourself, though you might take a long while to come to terms with a decision. You hate, really hate, change. It is one thing to go through mood swings; it is quite another to make major changes in your status quo. You are conservative at heart.

You are voluptuous, the essence of femininity. Men cannot resist. You can live life to the utmost. You appreciate a good meal at home or out, more than most. You can lose yourself for days walking on a beach with a loved one. You count the intimate moments. The other times don't matter.

You provide a strong home life, anchoring and centering your significant other. You want to be 100 percent involved in your partner's life. None of this distance thing for you. You won't cramp a mate's style, but you want him to be yours, to be open to you.

You are the best of loyal friends. You understand what makes people tick and accept others generously. However, you have strong boundaries and you maintain them. Under no circumstances are others to cross the line. You let people know your expectations.

You will seek a partner who has many of your characteristics. You want him to be secure, wise in money-handling and emotional issues. It is key his sensuality mold to yours and that he is willing to court you forever.

With Aries SUN man: You might wonder what motivates him, but you won't be able to stop him in his tracks. A fun discussion is about all that can happen here.

With Taurus SUN man: He seems to see into your core, fulfilling your dreams and desires. He performs a slow courtship ritual that makes you feel secure and loved. The heat pulses sweetly between you. He finds your feminine sensuality and ever-changing moods delightful. Let it happen. Both of you want the same things.

With Gemini SUN man: Think before you leap here. Yes, he is charming, but he hardly is your stay-at-home man. He likes action, movement, and variety. Your mind fascinates him for a while, but he wants a different type of relationship than you can provide.

With Cancer SUN man: He knows what you need, because his needs are similar. You are both deeply feeling people who want nurturing and caring. You weave intuitive magic around each other. Expect many journeys and much amour in the style that you dream of. You know how and when to touch each other. Just listen to your intuition: This will last.

With Leo SUN man: This man is considered the romancer of the zodiac. You see his fireworks, but you also read right through him. He loves a good time and could play around. Unless he has a special chart, he doesn't have the depth you need. But he could be fun to toy with!

With Virgo SUN man: There is a bond here. You both are extremely rational in dealing with problems. Your emotional depth pleases him. You read him so clearly, you can make his toes curl. However, he won't understand your moodiness. He will encourage you to get a grip on yourself. You will learn to center with him.

With Libra SUN man: Both of you enjoy candlelight dinners and affectionate moments. You care about the artistry of the courtship, but you realize this isn't the right man. He doesn't have depth as you know it. Be smart. Enjoy him as one of your many suitors, but don't let it get past that.

With Scorpio SUN man: You dance to the same tune. You are basic and practical. He is deep and reserved. There is a special tie that binds you on many levels. You will succumb to his sensual magic and want more. He is strong, yet feels deeply. Yes, you could swim his waters for the rest of your life.

With Sagittarius SUN man: A love of money and quality living could bring you together. However, you amass money; he spends it. You are unlikely to take risks; he is king of adventure. Though you can enjoy some lively conversation, to consider more is frankly a bit ludicrous.

With Capricorn SUN man: Consider this a close-to-perfect match. You bind in an earthy way. You like how he handles his power and makes money; you want to be part of it. He adores the way your sweet emotional waters spill over on him. You make him feel alive, passionate, and happy. Together, you will build love, family, and a good life.

With Aquarius SUN man: A bit eccentric, he is a great friend and makes you laugh. You each view life very differently. Let this stay a friendship. You will appreciate each other more that way.

With Pisces SUN man: The two of you flow like a river into the sea. You belong together. You know it from the first moment you see each other. This is magic. You can be wild and sometimes naughty together. You will be the sane one, and remember, that can take work. But in between those necessary times, this party could go on forever.

MOON IN CANCER, SUN IN GEMINI

Sensual, active, and vivacious, you are able to understand and empathize where many cannot. You are a sensitive partner. Once you work through your issues, you can enjoy a flowing, loving relationship. Because of your youthful need to repress your feelings, you might find it takes two major relationships or marriages for your potential to flower.

You will experience many highs and lows. Your mood can change, and at the drop of a hat. You will let your mind flow comfortably once you trust your emotional process.

Your many facets make you an interesting partner. A man will never be bored with you. He might get tired of the emotional peaks and valleys, but bored? No way. You are extremely feminine, physical, and loving. Often, you stabilize through physical intimacy. This leads to an eagerness that will delight your partner.

You make a sensual, exciting partner. You will seek a man who is interesting, bright, and also a little changeable. He might not verbalize as much as you would like, though you will sense him and know what is going on. It's possible there is a side of him that is the eternal child. If you have worked through your issues, you'll accept his periods of retreat, when he goes into his cave to work through his problems. You will understand that is important for both of you. You'll be generous of spirit and affection, and besides, you like a change of pace.

With Aries SUN man: He gallops by you like a wild stallion. How can you help but notice him? He will tweak your fantasies, and you will race after him. But he'll be busy on his crusades, so to have the love storm rage, you'll want to join him. You both are extremely caring—to the world and to each other.

With Taurus SUN man: Your emotional waters feel secure within his earthy banks. He will help you stabilize while treating you to a dreamy sensuality. You will know quality, stability, and nurturing. You'll need to work through your issues and let him stay close. Can you do it? Sure you can!

With Gemini SUN man: He fits your dating portfolio, yet you will feel somehow he is distant. In fact, he doesn't feel as deeply as you. Don't try to project your feelings on him, because he isn't good at dealing with them. Yet he will romance you and excite you sensually, and with his multifaceted personality. This can work if you accept him.

With Cancer SUN man: You melt into him and he into you. You will float together, feel together, and think together. Don't complain about his closeness. You want it, though his nearness doesn't fit your old images of the ideal relationship. Give up the past and look only to the future.

With Leo SUN man: Your mischievous, childlike side warms when this man walks across your threshold. He likes your femininity. However, once you let your feelings flow, he might take off for the hills. He gets worried at needy displays. You could be hurt if you aren't careful. It is only through mystery and adoration that you will keep him.

With Virgo SUN man: He is practical and sometimes critical, yet he helps you work through your feelings. He is of the mind, earthy and present. If you want someone who is fun, lively, and exciting, you are barking up the wrong tree. Think before you nix. You can count on him.

With Libra SUN man: This man gives you wonderful experiences that you might want to repeat. He delights in your youthfulness, free spirit, and lightness. Your moods give him a basis for becoming physically close to you, always making you feel better. You actually could blend well together, as long as you don't get too needy.

With Scorpio SUN man: Together, you are like an underwater volcano erupting, causing tidal waves in both of your lives. When you're in synch, the closeness is wonderful. Love is present as well as security. Should you need to distance, he might become more reserved. You will need to draw him back into openness to restart the cycle.

With Sagittarius SUN man: He brings out all your fears and issues. You have a wonderful opportunity with this man to confront them, and you will if you hang in there. The attraction is strong and enduring. You won't find him a nurturer—quite the opposite. But he is exciting. You'll thank him for helping you find your core.

With Capricorn SUN man: He is stable, a moneymaker, and earthy. He quells your fears. You feel comfortable here. There is a sizzling attraction that you fire up. When he isn't working, you'll spend many hours lavishing affection on each other. You will like this.

With Aquarius SUN man: You could start one of your life's great adventures with this man. Each of you build on the other's ideas and naughtiness. He will be a friend and try to support you through your moods. However, if you get emotionally reliant, he could be long gone. He isn't the type to settle down, and if he does, it isn't for long.

With Pisces SUN man: He loves to overindulge. You will find that being with him can be the fastest road to gaining weight and going overboard. There is a sensual connection that adds to the romantic games you play. He is emotional, sometimes clinging. You'll need space. He might not like it. Then the grumbling begins.

Moon in Cancer, Sun in Cancer

You have been gifted with unusual creativity and magic. You radiate charisma like moonbeams and have a pearly look to your complexion, clothes, or jewelry. You've been given psychic sensitivity and a sense of knowing. Your tremendous drive for security can play out in many ways.

Sometimes you feel like a mass of feelings, unsure which way to go. You have great depth, and your ability to process your feelings will develop to a high level. You understand much, yet you can have a difficult time understanding boundaries and others' viewpoints.

You are extremely alluring and sensual. Your charisma seems to bring you breaks, and you are able to get what you want with a smile. Men seek you out. If you have a weight problem, it doesn't seem to stop you in the social world. Quite possibly, you will have a succession of relationships, if not more than one marriage.

You will seek a man much like you—sensitive, psychic, and receptive. Sometimes he might present himself as hostile, but you will read through it, knowing he has been hurt a lot. You will deal with feelings, ideas, and thoughts together. You will have a close, bonded relationship. You'll always want to spend time together.

With Aries SUN man: He will stir up your waters until they boil. He is fiery and confrontational, and cares about others. However, he isn't used to dealing with someone as gentle and sensitive as you. You will be unhappy with him. You'll be angry, and he will feel as if he is drowning. Say no.

With Taurus SUN man: He is sweet, earthy, and receptive to your undercurrents. He doesn't get upset when your waters spill over him, nor does he mind being the source of your psychic vibes. You will find him a steady, supportive romantic who can make you jump for glee. His touch pacifies and ignites you. For sure.

With Gemini SUN man: He is full of ideas, frequently takes off, and tends to talk out his feelings. He has none of the centering and stillness that you do. He meditates while jogging. You meditate staring at a candle. You are very different people; don't even try. Even if he lingers for a while, he will eventually hit the road. He wants to see and experience all.

With Cancer SUN man: Your moods play into each other. If you aren't always there for him, he could become disgruntled and pull back. You could be dealing with the proverbial Crab—he could. What must happen for this to work is for both of you to become solid and centered. If you manage it, the sensuality will be exquisite.

With Leo SUN man: Meet the zodiac's romantic. You might find him quite dapper, but you know better than to take a dip in his waters. You're likely to head the other way. Smart.

With Virgo SUN man: You will appreciate his practical ways and caring. He will be your devoted fan and supporter. Unless he is unusual, no way can he identify with your moods, feelings, or psychic vibes, though he certainly will always be interested in your feedback. You will appreciate his sturdiness, and he will adore your touching, nurturing ways.

With Libra SUN man: Trouble just happened. You sense his softness and loving nature. However, he is superficial compared to you and has little inclination to deal with your type of self-expression. You might enjoy a romp with him, but past that, you will back out, or he will. He will feel inundated by you.

With Scorpio SUN man: Expect passion, understanding, and swirling feelings when you meet. He feels as deeply as you and can be as defensive. He seeks to understand the world's mysteries and what makes others tick. Count on him to explore you completely, to your joy and his delight. You will feel loved, secure, and cared for. Don't say no.

With Sagittarius SUN man: You don't mix. Somehow the coupling feels like oil and water. You will be left standing with your arms open; he will take off for his next adventure.

With Capricorn SUN man: He is your opposite. He seeks security and finds it through power and money; you seek security and find it within. However, when you meet each other, the attraction is as profound as the lessons you will learn from each other. He will provide the boundaries of your feelings. You will be the gateway to his self-knowledge. You will passionately seek each other throughout your lives.

With Aquarius SUN man: You might wonder what is behind this Bohemian man. Unfortunately, you will not be able to identify with him and his lifestyle. He might want to be a friend, but anything more is unlikely. Move on.

With Pisces SUN man: He is an artist—creative, feeling, and loving. You will want to be together forever. You flow with him, are inspired by his insights and quest for spirituality. When you two let loose, there is nothing like it. You might never want to come home. A mere touch can ignite you. Phew!!

MOON IN CANCER, SUN IN LEO

Your sunny personality makes others want to know you, especially men. You emanate a sense of drama. Your strong charisma makes it impossible not to notice you. You are generous, forgiving, and loving. However, if you become angry or hurt, you might shut down.

Often you are mysterious, even to yourself. Sometimes your feelings come out of left field and whack you. You try to be logical about what you are experiencing, yet there is so much moodiness, you know more is going on. You are capable of talking incessantly about a problem or acting out.

You have sensitivity, sensuality, and a love of life that draws others. You might come off strong or egotistical, but those who know you experience a gentle, fragile woman. You can cry easily and feel others' pain. You will make a receptive partner, wanting to be part of a man's life, a willing nurturer and lover. You have an uncanny sense of touch, a love for drama and romance that makes a man feel alive. You know what to do in social situations, yet are a tender lover in intimate times. Family and home are important to you.

You will seek a man with a strong personality who perhaps gives you a sense of direction. You want glamour, excitement, and a love of life. If there is one thing you love to do, it is to live and spend, so you'll look for a good breadwinner. You will want to experience the best—

whether in restaurants or suitors. You'll expect a lot of loving and romancing.

With Aries SUN man: A blaze of heat and energy goes by, and you turn your head. This man seems worth taking some time with. He lives with a passion, and you discover his passion extends to his love life. He is clear, direct, and open. However, your Moon in Cancer could go ouch with some of his revelations. This is the liability. Can you handle his directness and stay loving?

With Taurus SUN man: This man can make you jump for glee because of his easy, loving style. Once you start dating, you might feel as if chivalry is still in style. He treats you like the beautiful, loving woman you are. He possesses a delicacy that emerges as you relate to him. You'll be sure you are in love. Great choice. Just remember, he expects to call the shots.

With Gemini SUN man: Flirting seems as natural as laughter with this man. Your coy statements are returned quickly and delightfully. He is a mental person and might feel ill at ease with heavy displays of emotions. He'll dissect your feelings, but he can't relate to them. You might feel quite isolated with this man. You will become angry and see him as a lightweight.

With Cancer SUN man: There is a clandestine, enchanting side to this relationship. The two of you share on a special level and love to be behind closed doors. You have met a fellow empath, someone who can appreciate your depth and longing. He knows what you need and when you need it, and is happy to provide. You seem to breathe as one, think and feel as one.

With Leo SUN man: You discover magic, old-fashioned courtship, and laughter with this man. He is a live wire and wants to live life well. That includes loving with compassion and style. Both of you are strong-willed and want your own way. Know when to back off to keep him around. Your femininity will be a constant draw. Now, let the good times happen.

With Virgo SUN man: He might not have the flair you crave, but he is level and good to you, and tends to your needs. He is tight with his money, and you might not appreciate his attitude toward candlelight dinners or romantic getaways. You need them; he thinks they are a silly waste of money. Think twice here!

With Libra SUN man: This seems to be your knight in shining armor. Realistically, he doesn't understand the empathy and emotions that you experience. Yet you are drawn to each other. He finds you a magnificent woman and wants to know you more. The question for you here is what type of relationship you want.

With Scorpio SUN man: He is an endless resource of wisdom, feelings, and instincts. He meets you on a deep level, and you know you have met your match. Your flair and drama draw him in. You are both willful and think you're always right. Unless you want to replay WWII, you'll have to learn to compromise. Yet it's hard to be rational when you're so head over heels.

With Sagittarius SUN man: He is a risk-taker, willing to try everything. With him you will find the adventure of your life, with lots of fireworks and passion. However, if you want to nest and create for the white picket fence scene, take another look. Explore what he wants before you totally nix this celebration of life.

With Capricorn SUN man: Opposites attract here. He offers financial and emotional security. He will tease, court, and tantalize you until he has the ring on your finger. You both love living in grand style. You have a good chance at it together. He might sense your emotions and work with you to quell them. He is 100 percent there for you—when he isn't working.

With Aquarius SUN man: He tweaks your heartstrings. He loves your manner, your drama and joy. He will be your friend and love your friendly lessons about how to make love simmer. You always need to respect each other. He might be astounded at how deeply you feel. He will want some of that intuitive knowledge.

With Pisces SUN man: He is the ultimate romantic. He idolizes love and loving. He'll play any love role to make you his. You'll be amused and tantalized, and become his. The earth seems to move when you are together. Together you feel and live life to the utmost. What's to say no?

MOON IN CANCER, SUN IN VIRGO

You're deep, precise, and earthy. You use your feelings to make the world a better place, especially for you and yours. Good times last with you, and your enjoyment of life draws a wide, diverse array of friends.

Emotions empower you and send you in the right direction. Your tightly focused instincts give you knowledge from within. You tend to make the right decisions for yourself.

Emotions can be your allies as you harness them to your ends and use your feelings professionally to make things tick. You are a natural healer or nurturer at home and in the world.

As a partner, you offer loyalty and an unusual sense of nurturing. You can use logic when it is appropriate and sense which way to go to help your partner if he has a problem. You can help another process through your fine mind or your gentle touch. Your partner will appreciate both. It is quite possible you do some sort of physical work. You instinctively know where to touch. As a lover you have a very special quality.

The man you seek needs to be direct, nurturing, and practical. In addition to being emotionally attuned, you are logical. You seek dependability and emotional comfort. You understand your depth and caring, and know you need to be with someone in whom you can trust this sensitivity.

With Aries SUN man: His natural masculine, energetic ways are appealing, you will give him that. You probably will choose to let him go, because you understand he is a risk-taker and not meant for you. You want someone more tried and proven.

With Taurus SUN man: You might have it all here. He is seductive, appealing, even, and sweet. He is receptive to your touch and gentle ways. You will be wooed in style for the remainder of your life. There is security, stability, and grounding. You know he's right for you.

With Gemini SUN man: You certainly can have an animated conversation with him. He has ideas, opinions, and a gift for gab. You won't agree, but he will find that provocative and exciting. Your instincts say move on. Listen to your intuition.

With Cancer SUN man: This is the match of a lifetime. You sense that you belong together, and so does he. You don't need to talk, you simply exchange feelings through touch or a look. There might be a sense of déja vù. According to karmic astrology, you have been married in a past lifetime. This time around, you get to work through what you didn't before.

With Leo SUN man: You aren't interested in being part of a harem, are you? Well, then, move over and let him go by. He loves love and good living. You like all of that, but you demand an exclusive relationship.

With Virgo SUN man: He is every bit as practical as you, if not more. He runs a tight budget, understands what is practical, and isn't overindulgent. You can be very comfortable here, but if you seek romance, well, try again. The only reason he wants to burn a candle is to save on the electricity!

With Libra SUN man: This man has no idea how to save a penny, and can be frivolous. He is romantic, sweet, and gentle. You might be drawn to him, but you will eventually push him away. You'll start criticizing him for his wild schemes and imagination when your more rational ways don't prevail. You can't change his stripes.

With Scorpio SUN man: There is something so alluring and mysterious about this man that you lose all control, not that he minds! He likes who you are, your natural way of healing. You seem to have otherworldly knowledge, and this man is always seeking to learn more. With him beside you, you are in life's hot tub.

With Sagittarius SUN man: Did you say you were seeking practical? Oops, wrong turn! Did you say you want romance? Perhaps you might want to play in these waters for a while, but emotionally, it is like you are a dolphin and he is a killer shark. He's an adventurer, loves to experience and move on. Not your style.

With Capricorn SUN man: You sense his power and protection when he's near. He can't help but appreciate your practical ways, and will be delighted with your knowing hands. You rub his back, instinctively finding the right places. The strength of his feelings will have him courting you forever. He finds you magical. A good choice.

With Aquarius SUN man: You will feel as if you just stepped into the future. He has a sense of what is going to happen. He's a trend-setter. You might like the way he works on his friendship with you. Past that, though, forget it.

With Pisces SUN man: You will know his loving style, feel his depth of emotions, and understand his needs. Your centering makes you an excellent choice for him. You feel as deeply as he does, opening up a whirlwind of emotion. There is intuitive touch and understanding. Much will go unsaid.

MOON IN CANCER, SUN IN LIBRA

Men find you absolutely lovely. Your femininity comes through, even when you don't try. You flow with the tides of the Moon. Though you might attempt to make light of your depth, you have intense emotionality. You like to present your charming, flirtatious side. It is superficial, yet still extremely feminine.

You want love and affection. You have visions of wonderful dates, a fairy-tale romance, and a happily ever after home with a white picket fence. You can have it all, though it might take more than one try.

Your currents of strong feelings often overwhelm you. To empower yourself, to let others understand how profound your emotions are, you need to learn how to handle these feelings. It is very hard to hurt someone you know is fragile and gentle. But if you only reveal your lighter, superficial side, it can happen inadvertently.

You project as a happy, flirty, feminine lady who loves life. That is part of you, but not all of you. You need a man who can balance both sides of your nature.

You live for partnership, think in terms of "we," and want to be partnered forever. This desire makes you not only susceptible but easily taken in. If you learn to center in your feelings, you will know when you are barking up the wrong tree. Trust your intuition.

With Aries SUN man: Both of you use movement to ease the soul, yet you find it hard to pull in the same direction. He thinks in terms of I, you in we. He can be a bull in a China shop. Physically, there is great ardor, but otherwise, to make it you both must lovingly accept your differences.

With Taurus SUN man: You both love indulgence, even more so together. You take loving as a zealous pursuit, one that requires the finest of taste and skill. He has the depth and understanding to negotiate your emotional waters. You'll enjoy wonderful meals, romantic moments, and yes, that white picket fence! You will both feel lucky to have the other.

With Gemini SUN man: He is like a wonderful elf, full of merriment, whimsical, bright and witty. You can't help but smile when you are with him. The two of you have a great time, loving seduction, teasing, and tantalizing. You fall prey to each other. Watch out, though. He doesn't handle heavy, overwhelming feelings.

With Cancer SUN man: He melts into you emotionally, spiritually, and any other way you want. He is nourished by your presence. You feed each other on all levels. You are soul mates. You know how to bring each other to the boiling point. When you get light and giggly, he reads through it. Thank goodness, you say.

With Leo SUN man: He lusts for your femininity. You will become silly, airy, and coquettish. The chase becomes more fervent, as he is the zodiac's king of lovers. Be very careful here, and be sure you can handle this man. He needs to be unusual if you are to reveal your profound emotions.

With Virgo SUN man: You will be drawn to his earthiness, yet he might not be as flirtatious or romantic as you want. Think twice before leaping onto his bandwagon. Intuitively you feel you can gush your feelings and find stability with him. But don't expect him to understand your tidal moods.

With Libra SUN man: You merge on a fun, lively plane. Both of you have mastered your styles of flirtation. The seduction could be delightful, romantic, and gentle. He has a difficult time committing, but should he fall in love, he won't ever leave you. Unless he is a special Libra, he might run at any ranting or emotionally heavy displays. Watch out.

With Scorpio SUN man: It doesn't get more seething and sultry than with this man. Your souls, bodies, and hearts join. You have met your equal in feelings. Together you will wait feverishly to be alone, where you touch, feel, and share your essence. When you become light, he laughs. He finds you loving, charming, and hot. The feeling is mutual.

With Sagittarius SUN man: He is attracted to your airy ways. Flirtation is natural between you. This man is so busy, he hardly has time to stop and explore your depth. He is intrigued. Hopefully, you're not. You need more meat-and-potatoes loving, someone who truly wants to know you.

With Capricorn SUN man: With this man, you can dwell in the world of deep feelings. However, your flirtation could irritate him if it isn't directed at him. He is interested in the basics of life and the power that puts him in control. You will feel secure with him if you decide he's the guy. Your sensuality delights him, especially your keen sense of touch. He thinks your touch was made just for him!

With Aquarius SUN man: Being with him will make you laugh. There is a natural rapport and sense of delight here. He can put a smile on your face when no one else can, and vice versa. He is a wild man in all walks of life, and a romp with him is unique. Be sure before making any commitments that he is aware of your multifaceted personality and can relate.

With Pisces SUN man: He matches your love of feeling, sensuality, and indulgence. Without words, you touch each other, understand what the other needs. Let it happen. You'll share long-term love and indulgence. Don't plan on separating once this begins. Your bond is like steel.

MOON IN CANCER, SUN IN SCORPIO

If you follow your inner knowledge, you'll always land on your feet. Your psychic receptivity is very strong, allowing you to simply know, feel, or understand the right way to go. You are compassionate, yet you don't hesitate to establish your limits.

You don't have time for flighty pursuits. Emotion and real-life situations interest you. You seek answers.

You are sensual and clear about it. To you, sexuality is a testimony to living. Your strong libido takes form in many interests. However, your favorite is probably men.

You offer understanding, sensuality, depth, and perception. Though you can be extremely nurturing, you know when to say there is a problem. Sometimes you can be blunt about your ideas, and generally you are right. The man who chooses you needs be strong enough to admit when he is wrong.

You will want a family, though you might not always accept traditional roles. You'll choose the path that works.

You want one marriage, but if hurt or disappointment occurs in a relationship, you could become hard, sarcastic, and contrary. Learning how to clear out those overwhelming feelings so they don't eat at you can be important to your well being.

With Aries SUN man: He has the strength and power to meet you on all your different levels. He is energetic, clear, and direct. However, he will feel as if he is in uncomfortably hot waters with you. He might take off. But then, you liked meeting him, even if you knew it wasn't long term, didn't you?

With Taurus SUN man: You can spin your charms around this man, but you still cannot throw him off. He is stable, secure, and knows he offers a lot. With his slow and easy pace, he will have you trembling with ardor. You will find security and stability with this man. He will love your emotional outpourings.

With Gemini SUN man: He knows how to calm and tantalize you. But you know right off where this is going—nowhere. Both of you could have a bad case of hot pants, but if you think you can breathe more into this, well, good luck.

With Cancer SUN man: He meets she. There is a natural merger here. You are connected on deep levels, and nothing can separate you. The magnetic field between you is too strong to break. You will explore uncharted ground with this man. You'll linger in each other's caring, possibly for life. This is love and sensuality as few will experience it.

With Leo SUN man: He certainly is a flashy, debonair man. Though you know better, you can't help it. You need to check out his etchings. And you will. The passion here is mind-boggling, for both of you. Both of you want it your way. This is a two-powers meeting. There will be a lot of snap, crackle, and pop.

With Virgo SUN man: He is quiet, earthy, and stable, though your grand, tumultuous passion could leave him frayed at the ends. Your feline powers can work here. Do realize, though, he will never be the hot tamale that you are. But he will always be ready and willing to learn.

With Libra SUN man: This is like a funny joke. You are nearly like night and day. You can see him in his totality and can admire his gentleness and beauty. You will adore his charm and seduction, but once he gets a sense of how deep your still waters are, he will fear drowning. He might not even say bye!

With Scorpio SUN man: He is a sizzler. You have met your match. Together you become bestial. Each of your touch tells the other there is much more here. You will explore the profound depths of your bonding. Your sensitivity is strong; you read him clearer than he reads himself. He needs your love and nurturing.

With Sagittarius SUN man: He is fiery and on the move, though he certainly will stop and have a look at you. There might be a fire here to stoke, but really, you can't slow him down. Before you know it, he will be off on his next adventure.

With Capricorn SUN man: He will gravitate toward you. He understands raw power when he sees it. Your femininity might cloak that strength from others, but not him. He too is a power, and the merger seems destined. You will dance into his arms, and he will always be able to count on a sultry escape with you from life's trials. You find he wants your mind and intuition as well.

With Aquarius SUN man: He is stubborn and eccentric, and likes to do his own thing. Just as you specialize in passions, power, and perception, he specializes in friendship, detachment, and experiencing life. There is a natural clash here. If you must find out, well, go ahead.

With Pisces SUN man: From the moment you meet him, you sense a completeness. You connect in an unearthly fashion. There are voluptuousness and passionate moments marked by soul-stirring feelings. You have a bit more self-discipline. He will need your mind and perceptions to keep him from total debauchery, otherwise both of you might forget your worldly commitments.

MOON IN CANCER, SUN IN SAGITTARIUS

You swing from laughter and energy to deep feelings, depending on the situation, choices, and objectives. Your vitality is particularly attractive. You love sports, possibly more than the men in your life do. Ungirlish things attract you.

You have a deep sensuality that you can't hide, as well as a strong sense of intuition that helps guide you through various risks. You simply know things and have learned to follow this knowledge, giving you great timing and decision-making skills. You are much deeper than you let on. In a way, you play the game of life that way—never showing all your cards.

Quite fragile, you are sensitive to an extreme. No one is harder on herself than you. You can be your own best friend or worst enemy. Self-discipline isn't easy for you, but it is a quality you need to develop.

You have deep feelings and a sensitive touch. You might try to hide from the world by putting your wild side forward. Because of this, you are likely to attract a man who likes your fiery spirit, risk-taking, and seemingly wild ways. However, if your relationship is to work, you need to clue him in to your oceans of feelings and see if he can deal with them. It takes skill and sensitivity to be able to relate on this feeling level.

You draw men easily. Your challenge is choosing the right one.

With Aries SUN man: He sets you ablaze with his passion and energy. He wants a life partner. The two of you will have such a wonderful, heated relationship, you might not find time to make a nest and family. Eventually, you will need to let him know what it takes to keep you. He will do it, never fear.

With Taurus SUN man: He reaches out to the gentle lover in you. He reads you and understands the total package. He loves travel and adventure. When he discovers just how intuitive you are, he might try an educated gamble based on your call. You find comfort in his acceptance and become fevered in his arms. This is a yes.

With Gemini SUN man: He tingles with excitement when he meets you in adventure. He is passionate, a tease who can charm your socks off. The problem is that he needs to be free and loves to meander through the world of ideas. There is passion here, but deep compatibility is unlikely. He will be overwhelmed by your emotionality.

With Cancer SUN man: You feel you have met a soul mate here and you have. You want what he wants on a deep level. However, you need to get real, because he will be turned off by your wildness and need to wander. You have played the game so long, this could be quite the challenge, but a worthy one. This match can be very good.

With Leo SUN man: You will feel that you have met one of the dreamiest men around. His approach is romantic and exciting. Your adventurous and fiery ways make him run all the faster after you. When you express your deeply sensual side, he is a goner. Expect good times with this man. He believes that life is for living and loving.

With Virgo SUN man: He is practical and will be offended by your risk-taking, no matter how positive the results are. You will think he is a dud with no sense of fun. He might be able to understand your emotional needs, but he can't relate on this level. There are so many no's here, why try?

With Libra SUN man: You are attracted to this soft gentleman who really understands women and loves femininity. He will have a glint in his eye even when you are playing softball together. He doesn't miss one of your movements. If the magnetism holds, you might stick around.

With Scorpio SUN man: He bypasses your exterior, homing in on your deeply sensitive side. You might be a bit frightened at meeting someone so intense, especially as he reads you loud and clear. One caustic comment from him could rattle your feelings. This relationship is strongly physical and emotional. Be sure you want this kind of partner.

With Sagittarius SUN man: He likes your wildness. It matches his. However, he could draw back when he discovers how sentimental and dear you are. He might very well want to become more to you, but that needs to be his choice. You don't want to chase him, you want him to chase you. Remember that if this is to work.

With Capricorn SUN man: You dance to different tunes, though you both need a lot of security and loving. He is powerful, which you want. Your adventuresome, risk-taking ways don't go down well with him but when he sees how intuitive you are, he becomes fascinated. You bewitch each other with your high sensuality. Your touch is the glue that makes this relationship stick.

With Aquarius SUN man: The two of you are natural partners in mischief. You could both grab your knapsacks and travel the world. You are great friends, and his unusual style piques your interest. He doesn't do well with emotional drama, but he appreciates your strong intuition. This might not be a lasting partnership, but it could be a barrel of fun.

With Pisces SUN man: There is a link that goes way past the immediate bond. He sees you on your true level, as a loving, caring woman. He prizes your feelings, sensuality, and caring. However, if you want to get wild or take an outrageous gamble, it better be with him unless you want sorely damaged feelings. How this relationship develops is your call.

MOON IN CANCER, SUN IN CAPRICORN

You are unpredictable and exciting. You sometimes are logical and practical, building a strong security base. Other times you toss caution to the wind and act in a deeply emotional way. Those around you wonder what happened!

From either your earthy, practical side or its feeling, emotional counterpoint, you seek security. You might decide that security comes from having money. You want to build your power base and have the money to enable your life decisions. You will seek a man who agrees, someone who is secure in the material realm, who can take good care of you.

Through your deeply emotional side, you are empathetic and understanding. But you are also extremely fragile and sensitive. Your feelings get hurt easily, and you can overreact. When you are insecure, you have a tendency to be self-destructive. You will discover that making yourself emotionally whole will bring the security you crave. When you become whole, you will discover self-esteem is the way to security and you'll stop seeking security in other people and things, finding it within yourself.

Your love of touch and need for physical closeness delight any man in your life. You will open up like a beautiful flower when you meet the right man. You'll demonstrate a deep love, loyalty, and nurturing nature.

With Aries SUN man: Oh dear, you just blundered up the wrong lane, and it won't take long to realize it. He is dynamic and powerful, but security isn't his primary motive. Rather he seeks to create and energize. You two are like fire and water. No way.

With Taurus SUN man: He is earthy, direct, and on his way to affluence. He's at least as sensual as you are, if not more. You have quite the treat here as he nibbles away at your defenses and leaves you a raw mass of desire. Believe me, it's mutual. You find that there is nothing you can't talk about or share, as silly as it might seem to others.

With Gemini SUN man: He is a mental giant. He loves ideas, brainstorming, and problem-solving. You might like to keep him as a friend because that's the only way you'll keep him around.

With Cancer SUN man: He is the same; he is the opposite. How like you! You will feel an instant bond with this delightful man, who feels as much as you. You want the same things. You are both intuitive with touch and feeling. However, it is you who will be the anchor here, the practical one. Nevertheless, this is the path to Nirvana.

With Leo SUN man: He is hot, toasty, and humorous. He is a lover above all. You will have the experience of living life to the max. He doesn't have the same drive as you for security. His focus is on living and experiencing. This is a nice happening, not a relationship.

With Virgo SUN man: He is drawn to you and likes your power and magic. Your many facets will enchant him. You'll understand how wonderful he is as he nurtures you and helps you experience good living. He has none of your passion and drive, but he is a worthy partner. You will melt him to the core with your charm and loving ways.

With Libra SUN man: This man is extremely attractive and gentle. But let's not confuse gentle with emotional. He isn't one for grand feelings or overwhelming emotions. He admires your business savvy, though he intuitively steers his ship in another direction when it comes to personal matters. Don't take his flirting too seriously.

With Scorpio SUN man: You have met someone here who can set off fireworks with his sheer gaze. You will be heated to boiling by this sultry, sensual man. He has the mind to appreciate your dimensions and the sensitivity to touch your depths. You will have a very special, deep bond.

With Sagittarius SUN man: He is a risk-taker and adventurer. You need to walk in the other direction. His wanderings will leave you in tears, because you will want him as your own. This is trouble for you.

With Capricorn SUN man: With him, you will never have to worry about security. You will have the space and freedom to indulge your deeply creative mind and emotions. If there is an artist or writer within you, it will emerge in the safety of his care. You can't ask for a better protector or a more fervent lover. He adores your ways, ethereal manner, and fine femininity.

With Aquarius SUN man: This man might cross your path, and you share a mutual interest in business. A rewarding friendship is possible. You will not like his detachment as a lover. He needs space—a lot of it.

With Pisces SUN man: This is a fairy-tale romance. You turn him from a frog into a prince. Well, not exactly, but your existence in his life stabilizes him and gives him direction. You join in love at a deep level, flowing into each other, feeling and sensing. Sweet waters churn between you. There is security. Your creativity flowers. You are his muse. He is yours.

MOON IN CANCER, SUN IN AQUARIUS

You find direction through your feelings, although you seem quite intellectual and thoughtful. Because emotions are your engine, others can view you as erratic. Sometimes you are in high gear, other times you go in reverse. You are considered unpredictable, but in reality, you simply are acting on your feelings.

Because of this intuitive approach, you often make the right choices. You do not have conventional restraints.

You reflect your independence in your looks, taste, and mannerisms. Your hair is probably a little unconventional, as is your dress.

It takes a special man to appreciate your spirit and energy. Especially as you mature, you are delightful, refreshing, and free. You are a special friend, seeing your partner and loved ones for who they are. People don't know how you come up with such novel solutions.

You tend to hook up with an unusual man, one many would consider strange. He could be brilliant or walk a very unusual road in life. The man you choose is likely to reflect your disregard for the conventional as much as your clothes. Most of all, you need a man who is true to himself.

It might take you several attempts to find the right man. You will find a match that works for you, especially as you offer integrity and a unique blend of friendship. Your sensuality is also quite enticing. There is a quirkiness here.

With Aries SUN man: This man is a bundle of energy you would love to be with. He is invigorating and recharges your battery. There is a deep friendship here and unusual understanding. You might not be able to deal with him on a deeply emotional level because his confronting style could hurt your gentle feelings. He doesn't mean to, though.

With Taurus SUN man: At best, this is an odd hookup. You will find that he is genuine, but also genuinely conservative. Before you know it, you will be attacking his belief system. Oh, dear. His sensuality is a delight, but in the long run you will nix this. You don't like to feel tied up in this relationship.

With Gemini SUN man: You seem to be able to toy with each other's minds endlessly. You do a tantalizing tango, and he loves it. He is baffled and intrigued by your erratic behavior. However, he will never be able to touch your deeply sensitive side, unless he has a special chart. He likes mental, airy interactions and your ability to be a freethinker.

With Cancer SUN man: There is a deep meeting of the souls here. He responds to your sensitivity and ethereal ways. You will find his touch exquisite, and his feelings very special. You'll give this a shot because of the deep waves that roll through both of you. However, you might eventually decide he is too conventional for your style. Remember, he always was like this.

With Leo SUN man: ''Yes!'' you say. There is nothing wrong with this man. He has the humor to enjoy your spirited decisions and actions. The profound attraction could have lesser people trembling in fear, but not you two! You both love people and could have a ball together. Your quirky behavior intrigues him, though be careful to adore him. He needs that! He is worth it.

With Virgo SUN man: You like his logic and you could hook up working on a favorite crusade or cause. However, he might not be able to take your jolts and unexpected ways. He wants everything predictable and spelled out in his little guide to women. There will never be a guide to you!

With Libra SUN man: He might not have the shock system to ride your bumpy road, though he will be intrigued. He is quite conventional in his courtship, yet you still seem to fall under his spell. His choices clearly reflect who he is. This match is not impossible, but it's sure no snap.

With Scorpio SUN man: Together you stir each other's cauldrons. You boil together and blend with sensuality and understanding. Both of your touches are intuitive. He is perceptive, direct, and knows who he is. Together you will learn about life's mysteries.

With Sagittarius SUN man: He is an adventurer. You adore his get-up-and-go and you might jump along for the ride. Friendship and passion result in this bonding. He might enjoy your quirkiness, but careful, he doesn't go for overwhelming emotions. He does like your Bohemian ways.

With Capricorn SUN man: There is interest here, but you are quite different people. You find he wants more than you want to give, but he could be fun for a date or two. You discover he is a power broker and very conventional. He often is away working, giving you space, and you do like the lifestyle he offers. Think, though. Are you settling?

With Aquarius SUN man: He is as eccentric as you, though he might not have as deep a connection with his feelings. You will delight in the freedom you have with him and with the way you respond to each other. One caution: You might not always be able to deal with his mental ways.

Sometimes you demand passion. That might be like squeezing a turnip. Yet otherwise, he seems nearly perfect.

With Pisces SUN man: You touch each other on a psychic, feeling level. You love his creativity and imagination. If he gets off-kilter, all the more power to him. You'll like that. You will try to help him anchor, though you simply adore him for who he is. His wooing style sends you to Never-Never Land.

Moon in Cancer, Sun in Pisces

You are emotional, deep, and feeling. Your sensitivity is strong. You pick up on vibrations that few know exist. It is hard to get centered, as feelings constantly swirl through you. In fact, you would feel dead if you didn't have the continual ups and downs. You walk to another beat, following something quite unworldly.

Many would love to possess your sensuality. Men see it in the way you move your mouth or touch your cat. You instinctively reach out for others in pain on a psychic or physical level, knowing that a touch or expression from you could help.

You like the good life, and are prone to overindulgence. If it feels good or tastes good, you'll probably do it. Self-discipline is like a foreign word. Yet when you see the result and how bad you feel, you could decide it's preferable to discipline yourself.

However, you probably will never feel stable or at rest until you create a home or family for yourself. You have a strong maternal instinct that needs to be satisfied.

You will choose a man who is gentle, loving, and has similar emotional currents to yours. He might be an artist or a man who uses his imagination to create. You will appreciate his gift for romance, which to him is an art form. He will touch you in many ways, not just physically.

With Aries SUN man: He is not your type, though he certainly could have a strong role in your life. He is your energizer, always getting you going, never letting you bemoan the whims of fate. He's an excellent choice for a friend.

With Taurus SUN man: He is sweet earth receiving your gentle waters and emotions as a gift. In a way he is your conduit. He will pursue you steadily until the two of you are ready for a deeper commitment. This man can be artistic, yet he is always grounded. This allows you the space to imagine and create. You can have it all with this sensible choice.

With Gemini SUN man: This man is a mental giant who loves to twist and play with ideas. Your feeling levels are foreign to him, so much so that he will opt to split rather than explore. You simply are too heavy for him.

With Cancer SUN man: This is an all-out go. Your relationship seems written in the stars. You both know from the moment you first met that this is forever. Ties exist that have you longing to know each other better. Your gentleness delights him. You make a very special, caring couple. Your choices together reflect that special quality.

With Leo SUN man: You think he might be a romantic like you. You're right. Your looks and glances set him ablaze. You might like his hunt, and adore being his prey, but ultimately he will hurt you. He can't help it; he isn't as sensitive as you. He wants love, life, and experience. He blazes trails from one experience to another.

With Virgo SUN man: Opposites attract, and there is a gluelike attraction here. The problem is, though he means well, he is always logical and grounded. This might be refreshing for you, but not being known in the fullest sense could ultimately be extremely frustrating.

With Libra SUN man: There is a love here that isn't grounded or easy, but somehow you work it out. You find him affectionate, gentle, and wonderful to be with. However, he doesn't have the depth you need. Yet the connection is so strong, and the attraction so undeniable, you could have trouble getting out.

With Scorpio SUN man: You feel union and completeness with him. He fills a dimension you weren't aware you lacked. Intuitively, he gives structure to life's mysteries. He delights you. Your exquisite sense of touch sends him flying. He wants and will know you completely. He's an excellent choice to settle down with.

With Sagittarius SUN man: His spirit of adventure brings out the gambler in you, but no good is likely to come from a loving relationship here. Both of you will feel very uncomfortable and unable to provide for each other's needs. Yet you can learn to risk from him.

With Capricorn SUN man: He will give you structure and comfort. You like his earthy, intuitive approach and his raw sensuality. This man will delight in your soothing touch. He will appreciate your intuitive knowledge and use it to empower himself and your life together. You can have a traditional household and more.

With Aquarius SUN man: You can see right from the beginning that this is a no-no. He is a wonderfully caring friend. He will try to help you scale your emotional pinnacles and seek to understand what makes you tick. He won't get it, but he will always be intrigued. Don't be surprised if your mutual admiration leads to a fun romp.

With Pisces SUN man: Like you, he is inspired by his feelings. His swings are stunning, but something you can understand. You both need to help the other to process and clear feelings. Your nurturing makes him feel whole; his tenderness helps you stay open. Count on little structure here.

Moon in Leo

"Life is short; live it up."
—NIKITA KHRUSHCHEV

You enter the room. People notice you and drift toward you. You impress some as a snob. They don't understand the Leo Moon. It gives you charisma and a regal flair. Perhaps you were royalty in a past life. That might explain your queenly love for jewelry and baubles! Your love of luxury comes from the knowledge of how good life can be. In truth, you're no extrovert, but you don't have to be. Others, awed by your energy and sensuality, find it hard to deny your wishes.

Now you notice another compelling presence in the room, beaming and drawing others too. It's probably a Leo Moon soul sister. Better keep those lioness claws in check. Competition between Moon Leos is not a pretty sight as you contend for center stage.

Pride is your biggest liability. If wounded, you will roar and complain until you are mollified. Because of the drama associated with your temper, others choose to be on your good side. They want to bask in your purrs, not incur your growls.

When you are hurt, you react like a wild animal without understanding why or how you came into such a state. This reactive lack of control can be your biggest problem. When you're injured, you seldom stop to consider what motivated the offending behavior. With reflection, you can keep the upper hand more often. Walking in another's footsteps takes constant effort. Fortunately, forgiveness is easy for you. You're generous and giving, both emotionally and financially.

As a Leo Moon woman, you take greater pride in your hair and looks than most. When the time comes, you're more likely than others to consider a face-lift. You love to adorn your body with beautiful clothes and jewelry and will spend money to look good. You have magnificent taste, usually more classic than trendsetting. This makes your showiness a bit less offensive. Your regal manner comes through no matter what.

In relationships, partners notice you love to be adored. Romance puts you in purr mode like no other sign. You radiate when you are in romantic bliss. For you, love is art. You adore the chase, the flirtation, and all the attention. You delight in the courtship ritual, the flowers, the dinners by candlelight. You reciprocate with enthusiasm and affection. You know how to keep love alive.

MOON IN LEO, SUN IN ARIES

You are full of get-up-and-go. Nothing will stop you once you decide you want that person, that experience, that object. Your raw energy makes you sexy. Your enthusiasm often creates good results, as long as you don't season it with too much impulsiveness.

Others see you as caring. Your willingness to pitch in and help wins admiration. You have no fear of getting your hands dirty and will do whatever it takes to finish a job. People appreciate your loyalty and endurance. When situations create demands, you meet them.

Even among Leo women, you are fiery and passionate. You'll tell others what you think and want without gilding the lily. For many men, you are too hot to handle. Taming your boldness will help you. Sometimes you crash into situations, forgetting the Leo finesse.

You are likely to develop an excellent relationship, especially if you choose a man with a fire Sun and/or Moon. You will live as two passionate, linked souls. It's crucial that you respect the man you choose. If you don't, you simply run over him like a Mack truck.

The smart beau will keep you on your Leo pedestal, enjoying you as a woman but also letting you know how important you are. In exchange, you harmonize with his fiery masculine side. You will rule the household while he conquers new horizons in the outside world.

With Aries SUN man: You dance a hot tango together and at the same time, share ideals. You'd like to heal the universe. Your life together is so simpatico, it seems as if you knew each other in a past life. To keep the relationship in peak form, you need to make a special time for the two of you.

With Taurus SUN man: He certainly will be a reliable provider and love the good life with you. You feel secure, but you could get bored. This man doesn't run on high octane like you do. He is an excellent lover and might be fun to romp with for a while. But you could find his practical interests too dreary.

With Gemini SUN man: He can charm your socks off, but is he all talk and no action? He could get bored when you want to do something noble for the world and he just wants to show off his wit. His body might be as dexterous as his mind. You might enjoy him as a charming fling. But as Mr. Forever? Never.

With Cancer SUN man: You will not like his strong ideas about running *your* household. He makes the perfect househusband or Mr. Mom, but is that what you want? You might find a permanent drizzle spoiling your parade here.

With Leo SUN man: The meeting of equals occurs here. This relationship can work if you remember to praise him. You like it, don't you? You could feel as if you were lovers in a past life, and maybe you were. Practice makes perfect.

With Virgo SUN man: You probably won't like his penchant for details. You could be very hard on him in your impatience to conquer new worlds. Though you both share a need to serve others, your styles are very different, and we know where roads paved with good intentions lead.

With Libra SUN man: You are opposites and attract each other magnetically. Libra basks in the comforts of life, which you relate to in your own way. You're naturally romantic. Your Leo universal commitment and fire might leave the more conventional Libra behind—or thrill him.

With Scorpio SUN man: This pairing is hot, hot, hot, but you want different things. Expect power plays and endless battles. The raw attraction is so overpowering, it isn't surprising you would give it a shot. But there is no peace here, only fire and sparks.

With Sagittarius SUN man: You love his need for adventure. An exciting love affair can deepen into genuine friendship. Expect an unconventional relationship with unusual satisfactions. You might want more stroking, but the action more than makes up for it.

With Capricorn SUN man: You might like his respect for authority and power. Beware. He is practical and materialistic. He could spoil your fun, though he knows how you like to be treated and is an excellent provider. Wake me up when it's over.

With Aquarius SUN man: The attraction stays vital for years, though you approach life differently. He's as quiet as you are explosive. Mutual respect and friendship are necessary. He cares about humanity and sees the forest for the trees.

With Pisces SUN man: You'll never lack for romance with your Pisces. You could bathe in his idealism. Yet putting his dreams into action could require your energy and practicality. This man could become dependent on you. You won't like that.

MOON IN LEO, SUN IN TAURUS

Among all the Leo Moon combinations, you are the one who most adores the good life. You want money and the luxury it buys. In return, you offer unusual stability, loyalty, and an appreciation of values. You're more traditional than most Leo Moons. You'll never forget your first love—whether or not you marry him.

You need romance, with all the trimmings. The ritual of courtship had better not end at the altar for you! Even in your old age you'll dine by candlelight. You could be very hard on a partner who doesn't pay heed.

Your earthy practicality carries you through rough times. You love to garden and grow beautiful flowers or wonderful herbs for your cooking, an important pastime. You are a true gourmet. Quality is your byword in food, love, or work. You give nothing less and expect it back.

As a lover, though demanding, you will give all. Making the right match is not the easiest because you can give off conflicting vibrations. You are likely to choose a practical, strong provider as your partner. He might not always be up to your stringent emotional demands, your need to be emulated and adored. After all, he is off working to make the money you so desire. Find balance here, and happiness will follow.

With Aries SUN man: Though this gentleman can light your fire, he might not provide the attention that keeps you glowing. He could also offend your sense of tradition. He is certainly his own man. You might find him inconsiderate or neglectful.

With Taurus SUN man: This man thoroughly understands you. You see eye-to-eye as you go about creating a quality life. He knows how to make you feel like a queen. But then you are one. Clashes can occur if either of you becomes stubborn.

With Gemini SUN man: A Gemini partner can charm you. You can talk to him about anything. Yet he probably isn't what you want in a man. He doesn't offer enough stability. Why ruin a wonderful friendship? Stop there.

With Cancer SUN man: There is a lot you like about this man and how he values tradition. He adds feeling and dimension to your life while you make him feel secure and valued by your glowing presence. A good match.

With Leo SUN man: There is a real kinship between you, as if you lived a past life together as husband and wife. Let's hope you didn't leave imbalances to correct this time around. He likes your style. You like his flair.

With Virgo SUN man: He loves your practical nature and you love his. However, your need to be center stage could be hard for him to understand and could cause friction. He is too sensible to fawn.

With Libra SUN man: You both appreciate beauty, and he finds you a beauty to behold. He might not have his feet enough on the ground to suit you. If you are willing to be his anchor, this could work.

With Scorpio SUN man: Opposites do attract here. However, you both want it your way and if your way isn't the same, sparks will fly. You'll hold out; he'll withdraw. Only your happy Leo Moon can ease this battle.

With Sagittarius SUN man: You are both interested in making and investing money. You share a passion about life, but some of the risks that Sag takes could send shivers up your back. Can you handle it?

With Capricorn SUN man: You both love prestige and money, the more the better. If you keep your common goal in mind, this pairing could be wonderfully enticing and steady. Your need to be worshiped could become a problem.

With Aquarius SUN man: You're the odd couple. Leo and Aquarius attract each other, but both are stubborn. You'll have a hard time cementing the relationship. Indeed, you might not even get to the first kiss! This is better as a friendship.

With Pisces SUN man: You enchant this gentleman, who needs your anchoring. In return for the stability, he will give you romance like you won't believe. A heavenly combination.

MOON IN LEO, SUN IN GEMINI

Lighthearted and witty, you possess magnetic charm. Your intellectual playfulness and verbal skills make you a fascinating conversationalist. Others seek you out to swap jokes, share, and brainstorm. You are a plethora of information and ideas.

The difference between you and other Gemini women is that you have Leo magnetism and energy to carry out the ideas that others just think about. You are a real doer. Attractive and dynamic, you can be a verbal snake charmer. People have a hard time resisting your requests.

What's wonderful is you walk your talk and you have the follow-through to fulfill your ambitions. Your sunny Leo Moon makes you a great optimist, ready to jump into a new experience. You remain young at heart, possessing positive, joyous feelings and a fast wit. While other Leo Moons could get stuck, you adjust with ease.

Your appeal to the opposite sex continues into your later years. With that youthfulness, you will always find a new suitor. Though you are intensely loving, you must work on fidelity—you are easily distracted if a situation isn't working. You could marry more than once.

With Aries SUN man: This combination radiates vitality. Aries adores your wit and resourcefulness, which feed his pioneering spirit. He appreciates your mind as well as your beautiful emotional nature. You are on your proper pedestal here.

With Taurus SUN man: This man could seem like a stick-in-the-mud, one you cannot budge. He is a nice guy, but probably can't feed your need for chitchat and fun. He is too earthy for your youthful style.

With Gemini SUN man: You have met your match here, a man who loves ideas as much as you. Mixing your senses of curiosity could lead to many an adventure. But does he have enough passion? You need to have your chimes rung.

With Cancer SUN man: Do both of you a favor and nix this one before it gets going. His heavy emotional neediness frosts you, and you drive him nuts with your penchant for flight and fun.

With Leo SUN man: This great pairing combines passion with true understanding. You naturally fulfill each other's needs. You take him on verbal adventures, playing out different scenarios that tweak his imagination and desire. He loves it!

With Virgo SUN man: You might like the mental tango here, though you will seldom agree about the important steps in a love relationship. Your passionate nature could trip him up.

With Libra SUN man: This man will delight in your wit and passion. Everything about you appeals to him. He sees you as the perfect woman. This is wonderful for your ego, and you can count on his willingness to court the queen well into old age.

With Scorpio SUN man: Steer clear, despite the intriguing attraction. This man could be too possessive and demanding. He needs to be with you to trust you, the beautiful butterfly of the zodiac. Who needs a guy with a net?

With Sagittarius SUN man: Your differences intrigue you, but unless you appreciate your variance in styles, trouble could brew. This type of attraction works best when both parties are mature. Once you find the magic, it will not disappear.

With Capricorn SUN man: You won't like him in the long run because he will dampen your spirit. Though his status and abilities are impressive, you will resent his need to comment on your "childishness." Nah-nah-nah, who needs you?

With Aquarius SUN man: This combo is wild. Aquarius brings out every ounce of jungle madness in the Lion. You admire his eccentricity and humor. You're crazy for each other.

With Pisces SUN man: Resist this one. His sweetness and caring might touch you, but in the long run he isn't the type of man you need. He's emotional and intuitive where you need an autonomous thinker.

MOON IN LEO, SUN IN CANCER

You are more sensitive, gentle, and concerned about your personal life than most Leo Moon women. You can be vulnerable, almost fragile. Yet you also possess unique strength. This mix has allure.

If your domestic life isn't up to snuff, you could feel off-center, even unfulfilled. You are the most likely of all Leo Moon women to have only one marriage. Your magnetism vitalizes your relationship and draws positives for your family or your favorite cause. Once you understand your powerful energy, you can bring great happiness to others and yourself.

You must live with moodiness, but this struggle helps you understand the changes people experience. You are an excellent nurturer, caretaker, or lover. You attract friends with ease. An intense dedication to others could lead you into community service. To feel complete, you must find an outlet for your caring nature.

The right man sees your inner beauty and helps stabilize your moodiness. He builds a castle upon stable foundations and makes you its queen. If he needs to entertain for business, all the better. He gets to show you off, and you appreciate the acknowledgment.

With Aries SUN man: You appreciate his willingness to take care of the family, including you. He will defend you all the way, even if you're wrong. But he needs to do more for the family than just defend it if this quirky combination is to work.

With Taurus SUN man: He is your cup of tea. He provides the financial and emotional security that you crave. But watch out if clashes degenerate into a war of wills. He won't give in; you'll lose.

With Gemini SUN man: You might enjoy him, but he cannot be the anchor you need. He appreciates your mind more than your wonderful emotional, sensual essence. You aren't interested in being valued like this. Don't settle.

With Cancer SUN man: Like spirits meet here. You have similar expectations of a deep, emotional life, though he is more reserved than you. He might seem understated and he could find you a bit flashy. Harmonize the differences and you've got a love for all seasons.

With Leo SUN man: This could be a heavenly combination if you just enjoy the ride and don't worry about who's in the driver's seat. There are overtones of a past-life marriage. Could be love at first sight!

With Virgo SUN man: You like the fact that he can run your house with efficiency. However, you might not appreciate his attention to minutiae, especially if it involves you or your housekeeping! In the long run, you'll tire of this wet mop.

With Libra SUN man: This isn't going to work because he is too flighty for you. You need someone who is grounded, not someone you need to grab as he whizzes by.

With Scorpio SUN man: There is no question who is going to rule the roost here—or is there? Yes, the crab's pincers could twitch when the scorpion becomes demanding and controlling. Deep passion helps iron out the kinks, or adds some.

With Sagittarius SUN man: You two have an odd energy. Though much about him turns you on, he might be too much of a risk-taker for you, the conservative security builder. For this to work, you must learn to risk—on him.

With Capricorn SUN man: There is a strong attraction. You love the master builder in this man, and he likes your need for a traditional home life. Your charisma only strengthens the bond.

With Aquarius SUN man: You're opposites, with the expected attraction. Yet this combo could be hard to hold together unless you can accept the Aquarian's flock of friends as your intimate family and mean it.

With Pisces SUN man: You love his spiritual, emotional quality. He responds to your need for security and is a nest-builder himself. He provides the endless romance you crave and adore. You've got a winner.

MOON IN LEO, SUN IN LEO

You are all Leo, a true representative of your sign. You are proud and expect to be treated regally. When not properly pampered, you're puzzled or offended.

You have that glowing Leo presence and creativity. Great energy fuels your imaginative ideas. You love to live and live to love.

Your sensuality and appeal are stronger than those of any other combination in the zodiac. As fiercely loyal as you are, you still tend to have flings and multiple marriages. You just love the opposite sex too much. It's difficult to see situations from any other point of view than yours, the queen's.

Having the Sun and Moon in the same sign brings many gifts along with the curse of not understanding other points of view. Your universe revolves around you. You can provoke jealousy of your many assets or a reaction of your self-involvement.

To develop success in relationships, you must learn to listen and to imagine what others go through. You aren't always right. Remember the cliché that there are three sides to every argument: yours, theirs, and the real story.

The more open you are to spiritual or emotional development, the happier your relationships will become. That is exactly what you want—a loving, powerful relationship.

With Aries SUN man: Though initially hot, this dance could become yesterday's mashed potatoes. He excites you, but this man simply does not fuss enough over you. That could frustrate your Leo need to be put on a pedestal.

With Taurus SUN man: You think you are right. He thinks he is. Power plays could ruin the attraction. You like the fact that he's a good earner, though. You love to spend. Is the price worth it?

With Gemini SUN man: His wit and intelligence draw you. He might not offer enough depth or emotionalism to keep your heart throbbing indefinitely. He makes a wonderful fling or friend.

With Cancer SUN man: You could find him a bit of a drag and at other times, a crybaby. His goals are simply different from yours. It's unlikely the twain will meet. If he gets hurt, he goes into his shell and ignores you. How dare he!

With Leo SUN man: As long as you agree, this combination is divine. You both like attention and are willing to share the limelight. Appearing as the radiant couple fulfills your fantasy of the happy-ever-after. He has the passion and love to meet you the whole way.

With Virgo SUN man: Unless this man is willing to shatter his patterns, this will not work. He might be attracted to your sunny ways. You might like or even admire him, but he is not the showy, adoring man you want. And you are not Pygmalion.

With Libra SUN man: This man can appreciate your finer attributes. He loves your style and the ritual of courtship. He brings you red roses, cards, and presents. Even better, he will accede to your demands.

With Scorpio SUN man: This could become a running war if it gets that far. You have colossal sexual passion, but everything else works against you. Leave, with a smile on your face.

With Sagittarius SUN man: He responds to a different drummer than you. He's involved with culture, legal matters, and the quality of civilization. Though he can love you to pieces, you will never be the center of his universe.

With Capricorn SUN man: This man can provide you with the baubles you require and enjoys you as a status symbol. You can have it your way unless you affect his financial or community standing. That's the deal.

With Aquarius SUN man: If you appreciate your differences, this can be an exciting match. You love love, and he loves his friends. As his significant sweetie, he will love you and be your best friend, but he might not feed your Leo ego.

With Pisces SUN man: He adores everything about you. He needs your strength and confidence. In return, he will indulge your every whim. He's likely to be a great lover.

MOON IN LEO, SUN IN VIRGO

Your sunny emotional nature is often shaded by a need to be realistic. The Leo Moon gives you a natural optimism, yet your Virgo Sun makes you somewhat tentative dealing with men and the outside world in general. You are nevertheless radiant and refined. You know what is appropriate.

Often you are asked to suggest gifts, offer ideas, and help with emotional problems. Others appreciate your discriminating palate. Sensitive and caring, you will sometimes take on pain rather than inflict it on another.

Your sensitivity makes you a polite, practical friend and partner. Beneath that veneer lurks the Leo need for passion. Though less so than for other Leo Moon women, you need your majestic presence to be acknowledged. You'll tolerate a slight or two, but it doesn't go unnoticed.

You want a man who adores you, yet can be the practical one in the partnership and run the household budget with finesse. You fuel the relationship with your care and love, qualities you also bestow on the outside world. You appreciate his taking care of business.

With Aries SUN man: You can admire the missionary in this gentleman, and sparks fly between you. If your Aries is detail-oriented, you can be one happy cat with him.

With Taurus SUN man: You like his practical money ways, yet he knows how to wine and dine you with great style. Romance flourishes naturally. There seems little to argue about.

With Gemini SUN man: His chatter might get to you. It feels as if he is all talk, no action. Being practical isn't part of his agenda. Worse yet, he doesn't have the passion you need. A no-no.

With Cancer SUN man: You have to do it all with this man. He needs you to run the household, stabilize him, and provide that Leo passion. If you are really into nurturing, this could work.

With Leo SUN man: You might feel a sense of instant recognition when you first meet this man. He can adore you the way you like. He appreciates your delicacy. You'll need to be the practical one here.

With Virgo SUN man: This tie resonates as if you had met before. You can trust this man to take care of the details while you go off and indulge your interests. You might like it.

With Libra SUN man: Though you could share romantic fantasies, don't push it. You might not like the way he makes his money and lives his life. You could become very critical of this sweet and gentle man.

With Scorpio SUN man: You are drawn by this man's power and resourcefulness. His depth intrigues you. The passion is very hot. So is the anger. You love him and you hate him.

With Sagittarius SUN man: Though you like this man's fiery willingness to go for it, you could find him irritating in the long run. He has little respect for detail and can be impractical. And you can be very critical. Nagdom awaits.

With Capricorn SUN man: He loves you and all you are about. He finds your realism refreshing and identifies with it. He builds empires, but provides security. You give him much to adore and show off.

With Aquarius SUN man: Steer away from this man, despite the attraction. In the long run, you will drive each other cuckoo. He is an adventurer and free spirit, uninterested in the realities or details of life.

With Pisces SUN man: This will only work if you are both mature and respect each other's differences. He finds you exotic. You adore his romantic qualities. Expect to do the budget. He is interested in the big picture. If you can put it together, this could last.

Moon in Leo, Sun in Libra

Along with your Leo sense of drama, you have artistic understanding and love beauty. It is often said that woman with Libra attributes are the most exquisite.

You will always want to be courted. Strong-willed despite that soft, charming exterior, you'll use your wiles to get what you want. You can be downright stubborn once you set sight on a goal. Until then, you're relatively open-minded.

Others understand your limits clearly and, within them, bask in your caring nature. Be sensitive to their insecurities. Sometimes you have difficulty identifying with them.

You do not feel complete without a relationship, commitment, and possibly marriage. Your Leo Moon penchant for romance and passion is filtered through a Libra Sun desire for commitment. You tend to fidelity, but if left alone or widowed, the need for partnership is so great, you'll probably find a new mate.

You are drawn to a conventional man, perhaps quite handsome, yet gentle. He values relationships. In fact, he might have a hard time revealing his feelings for fear of hurting yours. This could suit your Leo pride, as you don't like to be contradicted, but it is important to enable him to express his opinions—which, by the way, could change easily.

With Aries SUN man: There is so much heat in this combo, both of you could get singed. He might not have the finesse you like in a man, but you admire his values and energy. He could find you, sorry, a bit fluffy or vain. Still, the chemistry's there.

With Taurus SUN man: This combo is tough to call. As you are both Venus-ruled, you love the good life and enjoy courtship. However, you might not have the earthiness and endurance Taurus likes, and you could find him to be a stick-in-the-mud.

With Gemini SUN man: You could have an absolute hoot together. You love to share adventures and indulge each other's fantasies. Your fire takes this tie from mental to physical. A word of caution: fidelity. It isn't his strong suit, and that could provoke a reaction in you.

With Cancer SUN man: The traditional, marrying nature of the Cancer man appeals to you. However, his moodiness and emotional drama could be tough to take. If you hurt his feelings, he becomes the Crab and turns inward. Do you need this?

With Leo SUN man: This man appreciates your beauty and grace, and you find much to admire in him. These feelings can deepen into profound love that echoes through time. He puts you on that pedestal you love.

With Virgo SUN man: There's trouble here. You don't like his attention to details and business. He might seem like a nitpicker. He has trouble with your drama, intensity, and need for attention. Leave well enough alone.

With Libra SUN man: Wow. He delights in finding a soul mate who appreciates his finer sensibilities. Either of you could balk at taking the plunge if you overemphasize issues. Your passion could cause an unquenchable thirst in him—for more.

With Scorpio SUN man: You love the sensuality and his intense peering look, but he could disregard your need to be cherished. He might not provide the finery you want. He's probably too much a realist for you. Enjoy a hot time while it lasts.

With Sagittarius SUN man: This man has the right warmth. He's willing to take a risk, loves animals, and knows how to make the cat in you purr. He might not satisfy your need for courtship. More importantly, your values differ. For the short term, enjoy.

With Capricorn SUN man: Tension could run high. If your backgrounds are similar enough, this could work. He's very traditional and appreciates a beautiful bauble like you to show off. He'll wine and dine you because it is appropriate. He passionately shows you his adoration. But he could adore you as a symbol.

With Aquarius SUN man: This delightful man's ideas and eccentricity make you smile. You like his values and appreciate the way he honors friendship. His manner of courtship could be too offbeat. Forget your regal pedestal; he doesn't believe in such things.

With Pisces SUN man: There is a dangerous draw here. You might not be able to separate emotionally, even if you need to. His romantic ways delight you, but you need to anchor him, as he is often off on flights of fantasy. You two sure know how to party.

MOON IN LEO, SUN IN SCORPIO

You are full of conflict, intensity, and hot dynamic energy. You preen in the limelight and want to feel each moment. Though you can be constructive, negative happenings are better than none. Your looks spell drama, with a magnificent mane and penetrating eyes.

A strong libido can be your possession or your possessor. Your passion and power can be too hot and might even provoke you to opt for celibacy. Find a strong, creative outlet for these drives and you become mistress of your body and spirit.

Drawing the opposite sex is the least of your problems. You ooze sex appeal and know it. Men flock. With your need for passion and control, this could be the chart of Mata Hari or Cleopatra. It is the wise man who decides not to cross you. Yet you don't like a man without backbone.

You are drawn to deep, reserved men with insight and feeling, though it isn't always easy to read them. That's okay. Mystery intrigues you. Because you need a strong man, battles are inevitable. Your powerful personality and needs could lead to multiple marriages.

With Aries SUN man: This can be like lighting a torch. Both of you are ruled by Mars and don't mind an occasional skirmish if there is passionate making up afterward. You won't give in. Though fiery, he can let go and move on, a quality you admire.

With Taurus SUN man: Alas, you have met your match in stubbornness and withholding. A Taurus is very patient, but once he blows his fuse, beware. It could be worth adjusting your way of relating. You have a lot in common and adore the good life.

With Gemini SUN man: The sparks will fly. For the long run, though he's sexy and appealing, he doesn't have the endurance for you (in many ways). He probably won't have enough interest to last long term with someone as controlling as you!

With Cancer SUN man: You might need to tame your intensity with this man. Like you, he is emotional and loving, but when you raise your Scorpio stinger, he could retreat into his Crab shell. He adores you and has the depth to make the Leo in you purr.

With Leo SUN man: He absolutely loves your looks, style, and command. However, you could douse this man's fiery spirit if you smother the relationship with control. He could wander, possibly to never return. Meantime, passion fuels this pairing.

With Virgo SUN man: You will love seducing calm, cool, collected Virgo. You can't easily throw him for a loop, but you might find his lack of heroine worship a bit difficult to condone. After all, you are the queen.

With Libra SUN man: His sense of beauty and romanticism attract you, though he could have trouble with your intensity and strength. In the long run, he'll have trouble feeding that flame in your soul and he could run from your sizzling ways.

With Scorpio SUN man: Ooh-la-la! It's all or nothing here, but great times regardless. Your mutual stamina and understanding can get you through the battles. You understand how much fun making up is, and intuitively know your tie can outlast the strife.

With Sagittarius SUN man: You might think of this man as a fun tease and a great date. He is always up for adventure and will try it your way. Will you try it his? Probably not, so the best bet is friendship, even if it occasionally goes well beyond.

With Capricorn SUN man: This is a go. You can bring out the deep, undiscovered beast in a Capricorn man. He will always love you for introducing him to his torrid nature, and you will love being the means of discovery. Long term, he offers security and passion.

With Aquarius SUN man: You two could win the miserable couple of the year award should you attempt this match. You're both set in your ways. You might enjoy his kinkiness, but you cannot tolerate his detachment. Uh-uh. No way.

With Pisces SUN man: This man loves to love. He pleases you emotionally, but no way does he have your strength. If you're willing to be his pillar, he can bring you a long-lasting, peaceful, romantic relationship.

MOON IN LEO, SUN IN SAGITTARIUS

People appreciate your fire and enthusiasm. Men like your get-up-and-go. You are athletic and are willing to take wild leaps of faith. You get the job done. In fact, you're likely to breeze through it quickly. Wow, all this and you love animals too!

You don't hold back and expect the same of others. Sure, you need appreciation, but not perpetual adoration like many Leo Moons. You value the good life, but understand circumstances can interfere with romance. If a relationship gathers too much static, though, you'll move on to gain more time and attention. Flexible and understanding, you love a date to the ball game as much as to a good restaurant.

Unless heredity dealt you a tough hand, you probably are slender, long-limbed, and have beautiful hair. You don't play head games. You're direct and fiery in pursuit of the man you want, but if denied the object of your desire, you will just go on to better and different.

You tend to see greener grass on the other side of the fence and could have multiple marriages and many relationships. You want to experience life in its full complexity and love travel.

Men with similar fire and energy attract you, though Mr. Right could be a tad more judicious and logical than you. You need to share common interests or your relationship could suffer.

With Aries SUN man: Fire meets fire. This dynamic man is your match in every way. He likes your vitality and finds you a wonderful companion, friend, and lover. Because you enjoy each other so much, fighting is unlikely. Conflicts are quickly resolved.

With Taurus SUN man: You both value money and its rewards. But this man seems slow to you. While he drags his heels, you are off to the next challenge. The sensuality's nice, but timing is everything.

With Gemini SUN man: He is full of ideas, chatter, and fun; your enthusiastic responses make him happy. You have the energy to empower his ideas and inflame his passion. You might find his focus a bit scattered, given your appreciation of quality time.

With Cancer SUN man: You understand this man's traditional values, but you don't have the patience to deal with his hurt feelings when you act spontaneously. He takes things way too personally. You want to live, and he wants to feel.

With Leo SUN man: You adore each other. Be aware that, like you, he needs to be put up on a pedestal. If you can stand this, you could be great together. Paybacks are heaven. So is the passion and the sense that your love transcends time.

With Virgo SUN man: You might want to tell this man off. In fact, you're likely to. He doesn't see the big picture like you do. He gets caught up in details. Once you're out of bed, you two don't have the patience to tolerate each other.

With Libra SUN man: You find him charming, witty, and adorable, though you could go batty waiting for him to make decisions. He values your beauty. He will court and admire you—and might even join in your favorite sports. Have enough patience?

With Scorpio SUN man: This is a dangerous combination. Sexy Scorpio is possessive and could hold you down. You need freedom and space. He blows holes in your theories, and you don't feel valued.

With Sagittarius SUN man: Yes! This man meets many of your needs. You love to play together, and you have mutual interests. You respect each other's strengths and vitality and stoke each other's fire.

With Capricorn SUN man: This man is a solid provider, which appeals to you. So does the passion. Whether this works depends on how you adopt to his earthiness. He might not take to your adventures. You have to give each other space.

With Aquarius SUN man: His eccentricity and openness let him appreciate your freedom-loving ways. He likes a good adventure too. That makes you great friends, but there's also an intense attraction. You can't get enough of each other. And the magic lasts.

With Pisces SUN man: At first, you might enjoy his philosophical and romantic outlook. In the long run, you really don't like what he's all about or represents as a man. This is mixing oil with water. Wash this man right out of your hair!

MOON IN LEO, SUN IN CAPRICORN

What a powerhouse! You know what you want and are going to get it, emotionally, professionally, or socially. Your insatiable drive sustains a tremendous ambition. You will attain status or marry into it because you crave position and respectability. Money is the vehicle that gets you where you want to go.

You need to be noticed and admired, and you earn it with natural charm. Though lovely, you lack the spontaneity of many Moons in Leos. This can be a strength; your ability to reflect lets you weigh the likely consequences before acting. With age, you'll become more attractive—and more together. You are unlikely to fight if it can be avoided.

Though you like to be adored, you would rather it be shown through presents. To bejewel you is to love you. You link material gain and passion. You could judge a man by the quality of his gifts, material and physical.

You need a man who has a big savings account. You might be drawn to a politician or someone with a strong professional future. The right man adores you and wants to give you all you ask. You must rule the roost, though you create a comfortable nest. You make him the perfect wife and lover if he gives you what you want.

With Aries SUN man: His strong energy and commitment will draw your attention. You could decide to join forces. You feel light and alive in his presence. The love can grow deep, causing you to examine your values. Little things don't mean a lot to him.

With Taurus SUN man: There is something very comfortable about this man. He appreciates your need for security. Along with a strong sensuality, he offers romance and admires beauty. Should you cross him, watch out. He doesn't forgive easily.

With Gemini MAN: You will love his wit, charm, and intelligence. He could climb the corporate ladder. However, money and status don't ring his chimes. He loves ideas and experiences. He's more likely to write you poetry than give you jewels. He also could wander. He's a terrific mate—probably for somebody else.

With Cancer SUN man: Your strength inspires this man. He'll create the world you want. He will do everything in his power to make your life right. You have the attraction of opposites. It could be difficult to mesh at first. Once linked, it will be even harder to pry you apart.

With Leo SUN man: There is a great deal of passion and mutuality here. You both love money. He can probably afford you. He appreciates your practical side. He would prefer to live his life rather than worry about his investments. You can do that.

With Virgo SUN man: This man is practical and understands your financial needs. His cool ways could be hard on you, with all your passion. He is too practical to buy you the flashy baubles that make you feel loved. You need similar backgrounds and considerable give-and-take to make this match work.

With Libra SUN man: He loves beauty and enjoys your showy style and ability to save. You appreciate his good taste, gifts, and romantic ways. He might not have the depth, follow-through and passion you want. Be sure.

With Scorpio SUN man: This man is so intense and mentally provocative, he breaks down your barriers. More emotionally deep and brainy than materialistic, he can challenge your ideas like no other. The sex appeal is great. But can your ego take it?

With Sagittarius SUN man: This is the odd couple. He enjoys your brightness, showiness, and fervor. He offers security, though he cares more about prestige. On some level, you meet each other's needs and have fun frolicking.

With Capricorn SUN man: Talk about devoted! This man wants to build empires and share them with you. He has passion, adores and understands you, and fulfills many of your deepest desires. Your ability to draw others pleases him.

With Aquarius SUN man: This man doesn't see life the way you do and doesn't share your interests. He might be good for a quirky encounter or two, and could intrigue you in conversation. That could lead to friendship. Leave it at that unless you're into bickering.

With Pisces SUN man: He worships you and will do everything he can to provide what you want. You anchor him, and he feels secure with you. He'll let you run his finances and in exchange will romance you forever. You make a happy couple.

MOON IN LEO, SUN IN AQUARIUS

With your Sun and Moon in opposite signs, your often-conflicting vibes can drive others a little crazy, not to mention you. As you swing from one pole to the other, you might wonder if you will ever find stability.

You want passion, adoration, and traditional romance. You attract others. You care about humanity, see the big picture. You want a relationship in which love and friendship coexist. Above all, your partner must understand your need to be everyone's friend.

You often get tied up in causes, especially if they involve animal or human rights. These commitments let you escape from your emotional ups and downs. Sometimes you use excitement and perhaps uproar to create emotional distance. You can also get very stubborn if you don't have your way. You must resolve your conflicts if you want a good long-term relationship.

You seek a man who can be a friend above all. You'll like him even more if he's somewhat eccentric and marches to his own beat. Make sure that he appreciates the woman in you and can offer you the passion and excitement you crave. His understanding can make or break your relationship.

You could roam from one partner or another or decide to become celibate because the business of relating is so hard.

With Aries SUN man: He is full of get-up-and-go. You love to crusade together and have a strong friendship. His fieriness and strength give you a sense of balance, though he might not have time to fawn over you as much as you'd like.

With Taurus SUN man: This is a troublesome combination. The best you can hope for is friendship. You're both stubborn and could have titanic battles. In the long run, you won't like him because he is far too conservative.

With Gemini SUN man: What a hoot! You love his wit and sense of mischief. The two of you can go off playing forever. One of you needs to get practical, but it is unlikely unless necessity calls. Fun all the way.

With Cancer SUN man: His traditional values offend you. You'll probably feel as if he clings to you far too much. You might have difficulty sustaining a friendship, much less a commitment.

With Leo SUN man: The fires burns bright. He understands you and knows how to love you. He loves your sense of mischief. You can play your lives away. You both love others slightly too much. Watch out for jealousy.

With Virgo SUN man: You like his mind. He's more practical than most men. You also admire his need to serve others. In the long run, there's trouble. He doesn't have your sense of fun. Be friends.

With Libra SUN man: Your ups and downs could test this very patient, loving man. He loves a gentle, regal woman. That's you, if you choose to evolve. If anyone can tame your wildness, he can. This can be a lifetime love affair.

With Scorpio SUN man: Yikes! You are rigid, and so is he. There's an animal attraction, but that won't sustain you. He rains on your parade. In the long run, you'll nix him. So much the better for both of you.

With Sagittarius SUN man: His drama lights your fire. He provides friendship and understanding. He tends to be more conservative, and your values could clash. He's a realist and might not appreciate your imagination or moods. Do check him out, though.

With Capricorn SUN man: He's likely to annoy and irritate you. Even though you value money and its rewards, his selfish empire-building turns you off. You want someone who cares about people, not just himself. A doubtful duo.

With Aquarius SUN man: You both hear a different drummer. Let's hope they are in synch. Both of you have fixed agendas and you could clash if they differ. He loves your generosity and regal ways, and you share a sense of déjà vu.

With Pisces SUN man: You could find this man's emotionality a bit much, though you love his romantic style. Problems arrive if he isn't evolved and in touch with his spiritual essence. If he is, your romantic, healing bond can benefit others as well.

MOON IN LEO, SUN IN PISCES

Of the Leo Moons, you are the most romantic. In return for love you offer splendorous moments, undying loyalty, and care. You will be there not only for your lover, but for loved ones, friends, and everyone of importance to either of you. It takes little to move you to tears; others' feelings affect you nearly as much as your own.

You are able to project at will, taking on whatever image you desire. You can fulfill fantasies. You must keep a firm grip on reality, so great is your imagination. Your lucky partner will be forever fascinated by the scenarios you create.

You are a humanitarian, seductress, and actress. Others appreciate your sensitivity and your magical allure. If you don't pour your energies into home life, you could have an interesting career with an artistic or creative bent or perhaps as a healer.

As a lover you are supportive. You will be there, unless you feel scorned or unappreciated. You could suffer emotionally if drawn to someone who doesn't value you, and you might try to convince him how wonderful you are.

You are sensitive and feel a need to guard your emotions. The right man will honor your fragility and help you maximize your impressive assets. He needs to be as supportive and caring as you. If he has his own brand of magic, all the better.

With Aries SUN man: You love his sense of commitment as he gallops off on his charger. However, as much as you find him exciting and warm, he might not understand your sensitivity. Be careful before making a commitment.

With Taurus SUN man: You like his grounding and love of the good life. He will appreciate your need to be mother to all, yet help you keep perspective and not overdo. You delight in luxury and each other's sensuality. You're good for each other.

With Gemini SUN man: If you want him, there is no problem attracting this gentleman. In the long run, he is too flaky. He lacks the depth you crave. He might also get overwhelmed by your moodiness, which this relationship would only accentuate.

With Cancer SUN man: He appreciates your sensitivity, particularly to his feelings. He'll protect you and create the kind of home life that makes you feel safe and comfortable. You'll love his adoration. This is close to perfect.

With Leo SUN man: This man appreciates and adores you. That special magic you have for imagination adds luster to your relationship. He is touched by your caring ways and is proud of you. You can create Nirvana together, an eternal love.

With Virgo SUN man: The vitality of opposites attracting binds you. If you are mature and realize how much he offers, this can be an excellent relationship. You both have a great need to serve others. Your warm, sensual nature melts any barriers.

With Libra SUN man: Once the two of you connect, it might be hard for you to separate, even if the relationship doesn't work. He loves your finesse, glamour, and loving nature. Still, he might not be strong enough for you, though the caring is genuine.

With Scorpio SUN man: Believe it or not, this man is as emotional as you are. There could be a psychic connection as well. You have passion, though if you get stubborn and he wants his way, disagreements ensue. Somehow, you work it out.

With Sagittarius SUN man: You like his sense of adventure, but he might not have the necessary sensitivity. You find it hard to understand him. He admires your need to care for others, but doesn't appreciate your spirituality. You can do better.

With Capricorn SUN man: His concerns involve money and the here and now. Though you also enjoy the good life, you care more about the universe, love and the mystical. If you can both appreciate your differences, you will feel secure with him.

With Aquarius SUN man: You attract each other and could give this a noble try. In the long run, he just doesn't understand your deep feelings and emotionalism. You might always like and enjoy him, but you will feel incomplete. Punt.

With Pisces SUN man: He is a kindred spirit and will support your ideas and pursuits. You'll share feelings and flights of fantasy as few can. Your Leo fire will add spark and security to the mix. Don't let him become dependent. Help him to be his own man.

Moon in Virgo

*"I have always thought the actions of men the best inter-
preters of their thoughts"*
—JOHN LOCKE

You come home from a hard day of work. The phone is ringing off
the hook. You have messages. "Help, help, help! We need you!!"
Is this popularity?

You, of all Moon signs, can be counted on to pitch in and give your
most. Others know you as reliable and dedicated to your personal causes,
family, and friends. You are the ultimate soft touch. It's not that you
lose yourself in bursts of impulsive compassion. It's that you care on a
universal scale. You act on your thoughts and words.

Learning to say NO can be a hard lesson for Moon in Virgo. You
want to be helpful. You do what is needed with detached efficiency that
many another woman would envy. You fold, stack, and even organize
your laundry (or whatever is important to you) with the same focus
on detail.

No wonder so many nurses, editors, and accountants have your Moon
sign. You are great with the details. You rarely get overwhelmed, yet
you can overwhelm others with your precision. Your Virgo analytical
powers are a gift, not only to you but to those who are fortunate enough
to be close to you.

You strive for perfection. If you don't meet the grade, you can often
be self-critical. Your love and dedication are unsurpassed. You have a
constant need to take care of wounded souls and show them the right
road.

Right and wrong mean a lot to you. These concepts often motivate
you until you gain the recognition that all of us, including you, are
human. At this point, you are able to love more openly and with less

agenda than others. You will dedicate yourself selflessly. After all, isn't that loving?

You will attract suitors who want someone who is there for them and will give them the guidance they crave. You will be adored for your innocence, humility, and caring ways. Recognize how much you have to offer. Clearness, lovingness, and a cleanliness of spirit and body are your strengths.

Sometimes you may sacrifice your real desires in order to "look right" to the universe. When things go wrong in a relationship, you feel confused at best. At worst, you become highly critical of your partner. The problem is your standards are beyond reach for most people. You could go so far as to sacrifice your integrity and never be your true self in order to look good. A tendency to withhold what you know or feel for fear of judgment can overtake the fragile Virgo Moon woman.

You sure tend to want purity in this lifetime. You yearn for selfless love. Just learn to look at the big picture and not just at one detail in all your loving, emotional situations.

MOON IN VIRGO, SUN IN ARIES

You are a crusader, taking your need for service and putting it into action. Once you have adopted an idea or a pet cause, far be it from anyone to try to stop you. There is passion here. You are likely to express exactly what you feel, unlike other Virgo Moon combinations.

When you walk into a room, others sense your commitment and caring. Your nurturing ways attract others. You don't play games. You like people and are genuinely interested in their concerns.

The analytical Virgo and the passionate Aries empower you in seeking love; however, you could easily become obsessed by another. But for the most part, you suddenly tumble into love as the result of a sizzling friendship or work relationship. Working with a person is your ultimate courtship, especially if you like what he is all about.

Another Virgo Moon love scenario can occur if you try to heal someone and help him down the "right" path. Such situations can be enormously satisfying, breeding undying loyalty and care. However, the healed could become resentful, causing stress to develop even though you only meant well. If your security is based on another's dependence on you, this situation can be a double-edged sword.

You will be there for those you embrace, in spite of your other crusades. You will want the best for your significant sweetie, though you might have a somewhat detached way of showing it.

With Aries SUN man: When you meet this man, you could feel as if you have walked into one of your dreams. Problems could arrive after familiarity and passion become givens. Your perfectionist self could start nitpicking at this man who is all ideas and action and has little time for detail. Mute this criticism and you have a match made in heaven!

With Taurus SUN man: You could be a bit nervous as his slow, seething sensuality awakens a part of you that has been hidden. Your defenses could pop up, even though you love being loved like this. You might not approve of Taurus's love of the good life and his tendency to spend on pleasures. Nevertheless, there is a hot, sensual bond.

With Gemini SUN man: You like his mental acumen and brightness. Like you, he is efficient. But on another level, he always seems to be jumping from one idea to another, or one woman to another. He doesn't have endurance. Gemini is charming and interesting, but faithful? Maintain a friendship with this ultimate idea machine.

With Cancer SUN man: This is an emotional man. You might feel as if you could drown in his tears and woes. On the other hand, you could well decide to take him on as one of your causes, to heal. The Crab isn't likely to change in this lifetime. Eventually, you could become critical, driving him into his shell.

With Leo SUN man: This gentleman could knock your socks off with a smile. He is the lover of the zodiac and knows how to arouse tremendous passion. You enjoy his warm heart and giving ways. However, if this relationship is to last, you might need to turn your head the other way or learn to forgive his philandering. He simply is that way. Nothing personal.

With Virgo SUN man: This man innately understands you, and you understand him. He appreciates your innocence and concern with purity. Sometimes, as much as there is a deep and lasting bonding, you could yearn for a more passionate man. But what you have is close to perfect— and perfection is your ideal. Don't mess with success.

With Libra SUN man: This man is handsome, appealing, and courteous. You like his demeanor and attentive ways; your innocence and purity appeals to him. He cares about fairness and the common good, but in a different way than you. The magic could last here, but once you become familiar, your tendency to be critical and negative could get to him.

With Scorpio SUN man: This man can unearth you, and you might not be grounded for a long time. His intense, quiet ways fascinate you. This mystery man may appeal to your need for a committed, dominating man who, in his way, reciprocates your universal caring. You won't lose interest. This could be a lifetime sizzler.

With Sagittarius SUN man: This man is an excellent provider, but you must cope with his sometimes harebrained schemes. He isn't always practical, but he is unfailingly dynamic. He will not appreciate your demand for details, especially if you impose it on him. He will love you if you do what he doesn't do well, like run the budget and his life with your noteworthy efficiency. There is potential here.

With Capricorn SUN man: This man could provide the protection you need while you tend your favorite cause. He is likely to put you on a pedestal because you seem so totally balanced and perfect. There is always money here; this man is as practical as you. He doesn't have your concern for humanity. This could become a grating issue.

With Aquarius SUN man: He throws himself into some far-out crusades. This tendency could bother your practical Virgo side and have you wondering if you are wasting your time. He isn't of this world, face it. If you decide to help him through "his problems," count on having to run the household, budget, and most other practical details of everyday life. He won't mind, but can you respect him?

With Pisces SUN man: He needs healing and guidance, and there you are! He loves your nurturing and caring ways, though his emotions sometimes could make you very uncomfortable. He could have an addiction or two that causes problems. If healed, he will be indebted to you and you will be appreciated forever. However, he may be very me-oriented and needy.

Moon in Virgo, Sun in Taurus

You make a statement wherever you go: I have it together. And you do. You are organized, efficient and, above all, practical. You know how to mix the good times into your life and you know when to stop.

You have extraordinary abilities with money. You won't need a man to bring home the bacon. You won't be attracted to a man who is poverty-stricken unless you take in a starving artist ready to be discovered. If that happens, you will market him and make his fortune yours. Your have a strong esthetic sense and recognize talent.

There is a tremendous need for beauty in your environment. You run a household with precision but also with dignity. You love beauty. You surround yourself with plants and products of the earth.

As a lover, you have enormous patience and caring. You will stand by your man as he copes with setbacks. You are there for the long term. You will serve another selflessly, understanding and appreciating your partner's foibles.

Because of your extraordinary capacity for loving, you're likely to have a dynamic relationship. You will be equally as caring and loving with children and friends. You bring great humanity to your loving style.

You do tend to marry your first lover. You'll make him feel like the perfect man for you no matter what. This strength comes from your capacity to love endlessly, with depth and caring.

Unlike other Moon in Virgo women, you tend to not be as defensive or critical. You live your ideal of near perfection.

With Aries SUN man: This is a no-no. He is off conquering other worlds when you want him home enjoying the good things in life that the two of you have worked for. Your slow and easy pace could be somewhat irritating to him. He finds you too materialistic, and you find him lighter than Cocoa Puffs. Best left alone.

With Taurus SUN man: This could be a soul mate attraction. He is everything you want and admire in a man. He is even more sensual and grounded than you are. You could be the blushing bride forever with this man. Be careful that when you're feeling slightly vulnerable you don't attack him and push him away. He would rather hear the feelings.

With Gemini SUN man: You won't be able to keep up with him, and he won't slow down for you. You are about concrete results, and he is about ideas. The twain shall never meet, even if there is passion. You will end up being annoyed by him, and he will look at you as the supreme nag. If you try this relationship anyway, remember: I told you so.

With Cancer SUN man: His sentimentality could make your heart flutter. You really like this man. He says things that you can hardly believe, they are so emotional. He adores your practical and anchoring ways. The two of you relish the good life. He appreciates your ability to save money. He can be your greatest fan, and you are his world.

With Leo SUN man: You will always enjoy the finer things with him, and he will be more than ready to wine and dine you, expecting the evening to culminate in passion. The problem is that faithfulness is not part of his repertoire, and you demand it. When Virgo attacks this warm-hearted man, the romance fizzles. He must be adored if he is to stay with you.

With Virgo SUN man: You heat him up and introduce him to his true sensual self. You bring out the man in him. You both have the same fussiness about details, money, and precision. And there's the rub. If there is a flub-up, there could be recrimination and finger-pointing. Acknowledging your mutual power and fallibility is the key to success.

With Libra SUN man: This man loves your artistic nature and appreciates your need for beauty. He appreciates your ability to budget and be practical, something he can't do. He will always provide the roses and keep your heart fluttering. Just count on being the one to file the taxes!

With Scorpio SUN man: Before you know it, you could abandon your picky-detail-orientation in favor of the passion, intensity, and mystery. You could become overwhelmed by this very masculine partner who knows how to bring out your every feminine wile. You have quite different styles and need to appreciate that in each other. If you do, the bet here is forever.

With Sagittarius SUN man: His wildness with funds could have your hair standing straight up. You decide that he is dangerous and will jeopardize your need for security. Unlike you, he's not prone to work through details or appreciate the beauty in life. Though there could be an attraction, this relationship will take constant tuning to play well.

With Capricorn SUN man: For him, you are a beautiful bauble. He also likes your practical, yet loving nature. He will provide you with money, security, and prestige, enabling you to enjoy your love of service and luxury. All the while, an earthy sensuality keeps this relationship perking.

With Aquarius SUN man: Whatever attracted you to this man, it probably was illusion. This combo can only spell trouble. This man has none of the same values or priorities that you do. He doesn't have the intensity and depth you need. Practical? No. This relationship might work, but not in this lifetime.

With Pisces SUN man: You like the moody artist in this man, who is so romantic and almost formal about it, like in a Gothic novel. Your Virgo-ness cries to help him stabilize and not take on all the suffering of the universe. He needs your practicality and has myriad ways of thanking you. This could be long term if you are willing to be Mother Earth!

MOON IN VIRGO, SUN IN GEMINI

You live in the mental realm. You always have a thought to share, another point of view. Others are drawn to your brightness and wit. You exude life and spirit, yet in the midst of spouting great ideas, you remain practical.

You look for ways to help others. You want to serve humanity and save people from their darker sides. You care and have energy to show your caring. Others are drawn to your bright, clear eyes. You are constantly moving and use your hands to make points.

Emotionally, you are slightly prudish, a little shy and withdrawn. You feel vulnerable sharing your feelings. You need security and an earthy, stable atmosphere to flourish and express your loving nature.

You are drawn to a man who, like you, is animated and full of life. This trait does not often combine with the earthy practicality you need as well. You could easily have two major relationships in your life if you don't come to terms with this schism. The men you choose reflect your powerful duality. If you understand that your partner echoes your issues, then you could find a successful relationship.

In love, you are always exciting and dynamic. However, if disillusioned, your demeanor could take on a sarcastic, nitpicking quality. You could devour your loved one with criticism. You need first to tame your emotional currents and learn balance. Then you will enjoy the wonderful man you could choose.

With Aries SUN man: This man is likely to take your ideas and put them into action. You could be thrilled to see one of your theories made real by this fiery pioneer of the zodiac. He has the passion to sometimes quiet your mind. Ultimately you will want to run the budget and handle the details of life. He is too busy conquering the next frontier.

With Taurus SUN man: This combo, though very satisfying on a physical plane, may be hard on your mind. You could get bogged down with his dogmatic thoughts and decide he is really a self-indulgent bore. He might not understand your constant chatter and need to experience the world of ideas. He wants to live, and you want to read and think!

With Gemini SUN man: You like this man, and he likes you. The two of you could work together, cooking up brainy ideas or providing brilliant analyses. However, your earthy side might not match well with his wandering mind. You could need someone more reliable whom you can count on in the clinch. You'll be running the budget and taking care of the details.

With Cancer SUN man: You can count on it: Your logic doesn't work with this man. He couldn't care less about your ideas—he wants to know about your feelings. This man is vulnerable. He wants to know you are too. Both of you can create a wonderful home life, though you will be bored by his fountain of feelings and could need psychoanalysis to cope.

With Leo SUN man: You can be the fuel to light this man's fire. He loves the combination of your creative ideas and practical nature. Sometimes the terms you demand are bit too hard for this dauntless lover of the zodiac, but he will try. The problem is, if you push him too hard, he could turn to another woman.

With Virgo SUN man: This is the meeting of like souls. He is well grounded and knows how to take care of you so you can flourish. You feel secure, knowing he understands your need for self-sacrifice. However, your mental meandering could bore him at times, and you could become bored with his practical ideas. Can't he ever just flirt?

With Libra SUN man: You could be very hard on this man. He is frivolous, romantic, and caring but might not express it in the ways you want. He isn't dependable and can't make a decision. You become standoffish. However, you really like him and the diversity he offers you. You will have to nurture both him and yourself, but the fun could be well worth it.

With Scorpio SUN man: There's no lack of passion here as the Scorpion makes even the Virgin flame. You will want this man intensely. However, he is mysterious and sometimes withdraws. If this intrigues you, you'll do well. However, he cannot meander off into the world of ideas the way you do. You need to understand that.

With Sagittarius SUN man: This man is off charging with your last idea while you're generating the next one. He has the will and strength to make your dreams happen. Your styles are very different. If you can admire and learn from the differences, you will do well. You will have to find equilibrium in the constancy of change. Expect to handle the budget and practical details.

With Capricorn SUN man: He might be able to take care of you, but you will be oh, so bored. For this match to work, you need to enjoy the politics of Capricorn's power plays and enjoy discussing how to manipulate and win. He would find that, at times, you don't have the passion or the raw sensual needs that light his fire. Proceed with care.

With Aquarius SUN man: This man takes off like lightning with your ideas but suddenly they become his ideas. Fortunately, your ego can take it, but you might find that you want more than a humanitarian chasing after the latest cause. He will feel pulled down by your practical concerns. However, you love each other's mind.

With Pisces SUN man: You may be attracted to this man and want to help him direct his life in a meaningful way, but what is meaningful for you might not be for him. He needs a solid rock, not ideas. This moody man might knock your socks off at first, but after a while, you'll probably keep your socks, buckle your boots, and walk.

MOON IN VIRGO, SUN IN CANCER

You beautifully blend earth and water. You know when to be emotional and when to be practical. You're logical and dependable. You are the all-American girl who everyone loves.

Whenever there is a snafu, you pitch in. You value the traditional family. You want to take care of others. It is important for you to feel needed and cared about. You want to heal and you are willing to sacrifice for others.

Once you have chosen the man of your life, you are very likely to be happy and stay put. You need an emotionally caring soul like you, but perhaps someone slightly more emotional. It will help you feel more in control and secure. He will speak and share many of your feelings.

You touch the hearts of loved ones. You cook, and you nurture in any way possible. Those you love may sometimes complain of feeling suffocated, but they will be secure. Men who want commitment find you alluring, romantic, and ethereal. You have a watery, shimmering quality despite your practical nature. You seem to exude a sensual magic that knocks a guy's socks off. You epitomize femininity.

With Aries SUN man: This is a no-no for you. This man works long, hard hours and as a result, he might often come home late and seems to be a poor husband. Though caring and sometimes exciting, he doesn't offer you the grounded, day-to-day home life you crave. He needs adventure and conquest. You will rain on his parade.

With Taurus SUN man: You dig the Bull. He epitomizes the stability that allows you to be open about your needs. He provides the financial security to take care of your family's needs and then some. Above all, his sensuality and intensity will overwhelm your defenses. You two could be the love of each other's life.

With Gemini SUN man: The tension is high between you two. He unnerves you and worries you with his flightiness. You justifiably worry that he won't be there when you need him. He gives more of himself to work than you'd like. His fickle nature and lack of grounding will accentuate your discomfort. Please cancel.

With Cancer SUN man: Something about this man makes you want to take care of him and protect his sensitive, fragile nature. In return, he provides you with the security, love, and applause you need. Do own up to your bad moods. Curb the criticism and sarcasm and get to the heart of matters if you want to keep the flowing exchange.

With Leo SUN man: You could admire his passionate nature. He loves your radiant femininity. However, you could be unnerved by his wanderlust and the suspicion that there could be a mistress or two in the closet. You need more commitment and stability and you become cold, calculating, and critical. This could be a wonderful love affair but a difficult marriage.

With Virgo SUN man: He understands that you need security to flourish. He is attracted to your femininity and ethereal quality, though sometimes you find him cool or unemotional, which could make you feel insecure and caustic. He just doesn't relate to your emotional displays.

With Libra SUN man: This man loves romance and femininity. That is certainly your forte. However, he does not offer the stability or the emotional depth you seek. Face facts: That's how he is. Take it or leave it. He won't change you, and you won't change him. He could be a fun partner for a short ride, but then change trains.

With Scorpio SUN man: He'll appreciate your ability to use your fine mind when he is in a quandary and cannot see things clearly. Scorpio is masculine and macho, and you are feminine and ethereal. There is enough heat here to last a lifetime. You will feel safe to show him your vulnerabilities, and if you have a grumpy day or two, he won't care.

With Sagittarius SUN man: Don't even accept a dance with this man; he will tromp on your feet even if he doesn't mean to. For him, "the grass is always greener on the other side of the fence." You will cringe at his risk-taking and feel insecure. He doesn't seem to care about what is important to you.

With Capricorn SUN man: He offers you money, prestige, security, and the family values. He is tough, so when you feel somewhat cranky, it doesn't bother him, as long as it isn't a long-term habit. The two of you will have interesting discussions about investments, money, and long-term commitments.

With Aquarius SUN man: Ouch! Steer clear. He is more interested in his friends than his family. Unless you can make his friends part of your day-to-day family life, this isn't going to work. He will appreciate your focus on details, orderliness, and budget. However, he probably won't offer you the stability you crave and need.

With Pisces SUN man: This man is moody and emotional, and appreci-ates the caring, stability, and self-sacrifice you offer him. You will take delight in your importance to his well-being. Expect poetry, roses—a lifetime of courtship. He will not be able to say thank you in enough ways. This is bliss.

MOON IN VIRGO, SUN IN LEO

You are probably the most showy of the Moons in Virgo. Your natural finesse and delicacy mixed with that Leo presence make you a showstop-per. You draw men with ease and offer a lot more than most women. You are beautiful and dramatic, yet practical.

You value love, romance, and intense feelings, but you will never forget the budget, even though you enjoy beautiful baubles. You understand and care about others with intensity and are able to act with great sensitivity.

It is important for you to have a relationship, because you need someone to dote on and adore. You will not tolerate any affront to your pride and you expect as much back as you give. If disillusioned, you could become difficult, critical, and downright bitchy. No one wants to tangle with you when you're on the warpath!

You give mixed signals emotionally, and men sometimes have a hard time knowing which side of you to feed—the need for a big bank account or the love of frivolity and the moment. The right man will use his money to make you feel important.

Your biggest issue will be fidelity. You demand it. He could get discouraged if you don't match his passion.

With Aries SUN man: This man will put a smile on your face. He might or might not bring long-term happiness. You need a sense of humor, as courting isn't exactly his strong suit. He does include you in his fiery life. He admires your need for caring and service to others. Though he isn't Romeo, he adores you.

With Taurus SUN man: You like his dependability and superb money-making skills. He loves your luxurious, yet delicate style. However, he could be a bit too earthy and practical for you. He's worth it, though, as he sees to your comfort. You might not have every romantic fantasy fulfilled, but you won't have a reason to complain.

With Gemini SUN man: This man is full of ideas and perky flirtation. He makes you laugh and leaves you cheerful, but there isn't much in the relationship for you except those moments. Your security needs could be poorly taken care of. He has no time for your nitpicking and need for practicality.

With Cancer SUN man: This man, at first, will value you as a trinket, and a beautiful one at that. Your steamy emotional and dramatic ways will entice, but probably scare him. Once smitten, he will appreciate how you take care of him and love him. He would give the world, though he might not provide the romantic excitement you seek.

With Leo SUN man: And the party begins. You both love loving and the warmth of the moment. You could find yourself becoming judgmental when he doesn't meet your practical needs, or even worse, makes fun of your precision. You could also be hurt by his philandering, which could result from your criticism and sarcasm. Muzzle your mouth and this could work.

With Virgo SUN man: This man likes your femininity and wants you to take care of him. He gets critical at times and can dampen your more flamboyant personality. Uncharacteristically, you turn out to be the liberal in this combination, the one who takes risks. The question is: Is he ready for you?

With Libra SUN man: With your love of romance, you are vulnerable to this very affectionate and sweet man. He loves to be appreciated and cared about. He will understand that you are showing him caring by doing his laundry, though he appreciates more grandiose displays. Curb your sarcasm or you could damage this sweet creature.

With Scorpio SUN man: There is a tremendous passion in this relationship. Scorpio will storm your barriers. Though he isn't naturally a caretaker, you will feel cared for. He will seek your warmth. He won't have much energy or your need for planning and detail. Problems arise when you both want to have it your way and neither will give in.

With Sagittarius SUN man: You could like this man's risk-taking nature. He certainly knows how to have a good time. His need to wander insults your pride. You could also realize that he doesn't offer the security. He doesn't understand your need to serve others; he is into serving himself. Whether this relationship works depends on your self-sufficiency and depth of understanding.

With Capricorn SUN man: This man appreciates what a magnificent catch you are. You offer practicality and sensuality. You give devotion, yet have passion. You are feminine, but also wise in your choices. He also appreciates your focus on money and details. You will always knock his socks off. This is a go, the whole way.

With Aquarius SUN man: The two of you can stir up a party and have a ball. You take care of others. If this includes his friends, it will be a-okay. Meanwhile, you must handle the budget and other details. You could get tired of handling the lion's share at home and mommying his circle. If the party train stops, you could decide this man isn't worth the freight.

With Pisces SUN man: This man needs your nurturing ways to keep him. He also appreciates your ability to be practical when he isn't. You will be gratified by his romantic, loving ways. He knows you, appreciates you, and puts you on a pedestal. You will love it there and will only come down to do the budget. This relationship works.

MOON IN VIRGO, SUN IN VIRGO

You are the purest of the Moons in Virgo. You stand for all that is good about Virgo: the self-sacrifice, the concern for humanity, the healing. You can also manifest all that is difficult about Virgo: their driving need for perfection, self-criticism, and sarcasm brought on by disillusionment. With self-awareness, you can choose which attitude to assume.

You have a difficult time seeing yourself in relationship to your world. You tend to view events, people, and objects narrowly and need to learn to see the world through others' eyes.

You are dedicated, can be counted on in a pinch, and genuinely have an ability to detach from your feelings, if you so choose. You can maintain an element of distance that could discourage some suitors, yet to other men could be enticing. They want to heat you up and will go through whatever hurdles you present to accomplish that.

If your gene pool supports it, you are small and delicate. Your femininity comes out with ease. People are drawn to your soft, nurturing ways. You look good in white and often have a luminous quality. Yet you are likely to always dress practically.

You tend to fear outburst of emotions, and will run from them. A man who is tempted by you will learn to be easygoing, never volatile. Once you find your life-match, you will stay put. You learned at an early age the importance of family and togetherness.

With Aries SUN man: Ouch! This man has fire and get-up-and-go. He is prone to losing his temper and feeling his Wheaties. He is ruled by Mars, and he is all about passion, be it love, career, or family. The first time he loses his temper, you will be running for the hills. However, you make quite the team when working together. You'll have to work at it, though.

With Taurus SUN man: This man is earthy, patient, and understanding. He might treat you with great respect and dote on you when courting begins. He will be awed by your practical and efficient ways. You will enjoy his sensuality as he lures you off your pedestal and into a field of deep emotion. You sense you are safe with him, that it's okay to let down your guard. This blending could last.

With Gemini SUN man: You might never actually meet this man, as he is off tilting windmills or determining which way the air flows, talking about this idea or that idea. He is rarely in one spot very long. You share a love for talk, but the red flag is up here. He will never honor your security needs. He is from a different planet!

With Cancer SUN man: He is always emotional, though he may show the world a hard crust. You see through him. He will need you to keep his course steady in the real world and in his emotional realm. His loyalty is undying and will provide you with the love and family you yearn for.

With Leo SUN man: He loves your femininity and is drawn to your aloofness. Though charming, romantic, and passionate, his manner could put you off at the same time. Furthermore, he tends to stray, especially if he isn't greeted with adoration and admiration, which you're unlikely to give. He could cause you pain if you succumb to his purrs.

With Virgo SUN man: This is a case of two peas that need to be in the same pod. He offers comfort and seduction. As comfortable as he may seem, you could yearn for something new and different. Stay with it and you will develop a special kind of passion and caring. This is a go.

With Libra SUN man: This man is easygoing, charming, and affable. You like the way he dates and courts. Soon, though, you could begin to regard his values as superficial and wonder about his enjoyment of pretty things. He doesn't have enough meat-and-potato ethics. Why hurt this sweet man? Look for someone more your style.

With Scorpio SUN man: Buckle your seat belt. This man is intense and feeling to an extreme. He is curious about life and wonders about its mysteries, much as you do. His beliefs are evolving, though based on deep values. You admire his inquisitive mind and his strong sense of commitment. He will teach you about passion while overlooking a nit-picking comment or two.

With Sagittarius SUN man: This man is basically incompatible with you, though you will like his energy. You'll discover he's likely to pursue his interests with intensity, though not endurance. You could be a pretty little bauble to him, but don't count on him sticking around.

With Capricorn SUN man: You finally have found someone who appreciates your finer values and adores your feminine, receptive, practical ways. There is money, caring, and commitment here. You will love him for all that he gives you, and he will trust you completely with all that is important to him.

With Aquarius SUN man: You like this man's ideas and the way he appreciates his friends. Unfortunately, he doesn't understand your conservative, quiet ways. He thinks you are a prude. You could decide he is a lunatic as he takes sudden, dramatic stands. Seldom will you feel like joining his parades. The best way to deal with this one-man band is not to play.

With Pisces SUN man: You find yourself drawn to this man, yet wonder why. Don't try to change each other. He feels all and is highly empathetic; you refuse to feel and use your mind to detach, see, and discern. The combination could be potent if you understand each other. You achieve the balance of opposites, and the attraction.

MOON IN VIRGO, SUN IN LIBRA

You have an unusual magnetism and tend to draw men who are very different from you. However, you might differ from most Moons in Virgo in that you see purpose in frivolity and play. You are very attractive, and your femininity speaks through your work wardrobe.

You draw a man who reflects your lighter side, who isn't too intense about feelings yet enjoys courtship. His concern about what is fair and right will appeal to you. At times you could think he is frivolous in his zest for romance. His inability to make a decision could unnerve you.

Remember, he is your choice. He reflects what you are. If he irritates you, you could be angry at an aspect of your own nature.

Having a successful relationship requires your understanding conflicting drives in yourself. You must be careful not to project your issues on others. The man in your life simply fell in love with the woman you are. Now it is time to love the woman you are as well.

Partnership will always be a high priority for you. Once you are committed, and that may take you a while, you are in there for the long term.

With Aries SUN man: He has the ability to make decisions and take action while you are still debating the pros and cons. He cares about society and other people in a different way than you do. You admire him, and he admires your softness and nurturing ways. He supports you in your personal crusades. This is a fine match.

With Taurus SUN man: You share a concern with the quality of life. He saves his money to make your life more meaningful and enjoyable. He understands that if you aren't happy, you could go into your shell. Don't worry. He will lure you out. You could have a wonderful life with him.

With Gemini SUN man: You like his charm and his willingness to discuss anything at all. You find that he doesn't have time for your practical, efficient approach. It's fine with him if you want to serve the world and others. You will manage the budget in this relationship. With give-and-take, this combo can work.

With Cancer SUN man: This man is moody and wants to explore deep feelings, which can make you uncomfortable. Be aware that if you don't support his feelings, he will become the ultimate Crab, a real turnoff for you. Once the damage is done, you might never break through his shell again.

With Leo SUN man: You flip over this man's style of courtship. You might feel like you are in a dance that could last forever—and it could. He adores your feminine charm. He will give you the space to heal your universe and he will be proud of you. You will find that he always puts a smile on your face.

With Virgo SUN man: You could find this man too logical and cool. You understand this side of his nature, but you want amorous moments, romantic dinners, and a full courtship. He is too practical and doesn't take the time you need for the frivolous and beautiful. You will have to let go of some of those romantic fantasies. You might not be willing to pay the toll.

With Libra SUN man: Here is a man who delights your imagination and fits your fantasies. He is very romantic, and positively charming. You are instantly attracted and are sure that you have Mr. Right. When it comes to the practical details the job will fall on your shoulders. Is the romance worth it? Only you can decide.

With Scorpio SUN man: He knows how to set you hot in pursuit of him—odd, but true. There is something so mysterious about this man. He cares about what makes others ticks, so the two of you make quite a team. Eventually, you could be put off by his hedonistic ways when all you want is a dozen roses. He takes you down quirky paths.

With Sagittarius SUN man: This man is exciting and will take you on one adventure after another. You will wonder, though, whether all the cruising is worthy of you when there are few practical results. Though he appreciates your soft, gentle ways, he could have a bad case of wanderlust. Great flirtation, bad for the long term.

With Capricorn SUN man: He wants to talk about investments, not love. He might buy you a gift, but more likely a book than flowers. Though he can care about you very deeply, you could be put off by the lack of romance. If hooked for the long term, you can count on his providing you with security and wonderful trips. But for romance, this isn't the man.

With Aquarius SUN man: You could find this man adventuresome and enjoy his friendship. However, he really isn't your cup of tea. He can never give you the passion you need and desire. He is too concerned with causes and his friends. You could be great friends, but the love relationship will probably fizzle. He doesn't know how to tend to you.

With Pisces SUN man: For you, this man is the ultimate romantic. He can set your heart in a flurry, though you can't count on his long-term practicality. You care deeply about each other. Once hooked, you could have a difficult time separating. As long as you're content to be the household manager, he could continue to light up your life long term.

MOON IN VIRGO, SUN IN SCORPIO

Of all the Moon in Virgo women, you have the greatest need to penetrate the mysteries of life. You choose to do nothing halfway. You are extremely competitive and directed. You know what you want.

Intensity pervades your being. You probably have deep, penetrating eyes and a sense of direction that can put others ill at ease. You emanate understanding, sexuality, and commitment. You are not a woman to be toyed with.

The men you draw will pick up on your sensuality and high-voltage nature. You will have many choices. You could discard quite a few suitors until you find Mr. Right. He must be able to handle your hot nature, as well as your need for honesty and clarity.

When you have something to say, others hear it loud and clear. You are not diplomatic, but you sure are direct. Your mate needs to be tough enough to take your sarcasm and sometimes curt ways. You are worth it, and he will know it.

You are the force, the pillar in your relationship. You handle challenges easily. It is simple—your way or else.

With Aries SUN man: This man has strength and commitment, but might not be interested in your sometimes sardonic ways. You share a commitment to others, but he might not have the endurance to pursue you. You make it very hard, and he has too many other interests.

With Taurus SUN man: This man is not in a rush for anything. He likes your intensity and can handle your heat, even if it is directed toward him. He is a lover, not a fighter. All your logic will not make peace once the Bull turns because of too many snide comments. So don't take him for granted if you know what is good for you.

With Gemini SUN man: This man is interesting, but in no way does he have the staying power you need and demand. You may like to toy with his mind and play with his heart, but there is no bliss here. He will leave you just when you think everything is peachy keen.

With Cancer SUN man: You understand this man's intensity and caring; you have the same intense emotions, though you don't let them get out of control. You roll with the punches and have the strength to handle the tumult. This man needs your caring and efficiency. He will appreciate the form and shape you put into his life. You will be forever loyal.

With Leo SUN man: This man is romantic and provokes your sensual interest. Be careful not to crush his ego or he could leave you. If you try to overcome his will or have it your way too many times, he will go where the picking is more agreeable. Keep your critical ways to yourself if you want rapture with the Lion.

With Virgo SUN man: He is what you need and want emotionally. He will be good with details, providing the nest and security you demand. He can understand your sarcasm, if you understand his. Above all, he will remain permanently bonded when you expose him to the depth of his male passions and energy. Sexuality is the glue here.

With Libra SUN man: You could find this man charming. You might read more into his passion than is there. You will singe his soul and could be very hard on this gentle man. He will never forget you, but you must tame your wildness to make him comfortable. He does not give his trust easily. Be careful with criticism.

With Scorpio SUN man: He is the match of all matches. He meets your passion and is as curious as you. He understands you clearly. Be careful not to hammer at him. He will counter and can nail you with hurtful words. Respect is key to keeping this wonderful relationship level.

With Sagittarius SUN man: This match could be interesting for a brief time, but no way can this man hold your attention for long. He offers neither depth nor practicality. Also, he is a player, and with him, you will be too. You will get that bored. It's best to stop this relationship before it gets going.

With Capricorn SUN man: This man can meet your passion and commitment. He is tougher than you and can handle your sharp words. In fact, you could choose to be mum more often than not. Either that or you'll learn to be diplomatic. You don't have to change for him; he will appreciate you for who you are. He will also trust you implicitly.

With Aquarius SUN man: At best, this is a bad match that would be intelligent to forget, even in the short term. He could be critical of your painstaking precision; your emotions blow him out, and he finds your sharp words a tremendous turnoff. You might even have a hard time being friends, you are so different with so little in common.

With Pisces SUN man: The attraction here is strong, and you might find yourself in for the long haul. Be careful with your sharp insights and observations. Your Pisces can only take so much reality in his life or he will run away. Treat him with the gentleness he needs if you want a long-term relationship. He will adore you.

MOON IN VIRGO, SUN IN SAGITTARIUS

People can have a hard time reading you. There is a side of you that is very logical and dependable. You want to take care of others and be important to them. Your caring fosters security and stability. You want the same for yourself. In fact, the way you express your caring is the way you want to be cared for.

You are drawn to risk-taking men who live for adventure, not for you. You discover you like this excitement to a degree, but you want more out of your relationship. Somewhere between adventure and security, you need to find balance. This conflict in you seems to emerge in relationships. Unless you're very lucky, only when you resolve this conflict will you make successful relationship choices.

You draw the opposite sex with your flair and your adventurous, yet nurturing style. You are versatile and ready to try new things when the old ones don't work. You tend to be athletic and enjoy a good workout. Your love of sports earmarks you, as does your amorous agility.

With Aries SUN man: You could find each other together, sharing an escapade as the courtship begins. You find him exciting, and he likes your sense of adventure. He encourages you to be practical when taking risks, providing grounding you need. He appreciates your zest for thoroughness and details. Don't expect the same from him. Count on a lot of fun and cooperation.

With Taurus SUN man: You'll appreciate this man's sense of excellence and balance. Sometimes your rugged style of adventure hits a sour note with him. However, you do share a love of money. He will encourage you to be as practical and as thorough as possible. You will have many financial discussions. This can be a lifetime commitment.

With Gemini SUN man: This man entices you because he feeds you with ideas for new adventures. You may often laugh together; both of you see life with humor and detachment. You'd better count on being the practical one. Handle the budget and make sure the taxes are paid. He loves ideas and you, but he's not very grounded.

With Cancer SUN man: You could find this man a bit of a ninny. He whines a lot if he doesn't have it his way and he has overwhelming emotional moments. He is threatened by your sense of adventure. Curb the urge to take care of him.

With Leo SUN man: He may charm you enough to rein in your need for challenging experiences for a while. After all, he is quite the romantic prince. However, your thirst for details and practical concerns could bring him down. You could enjoy a passionate affair, but you will have a tough time making each other happy for the long haul.

With Virgo SUN man: This man allows you space to run household details and gives you the last word in practical matters. He might not understand why you take risks or seek challenges. He could become critical and put you down when you leave your practicality in the background. You could be upset that he isn't more like you. This could get worse as he gets older.

With Libra SUN man: This man is amused by your risk taking. You bring out something animalistic in him. He, the athlete or sports fan, loves to play with you. However, he won't understand why you sometimes get finicky about heartfelt issues. He will take your nitpicking personally, making this tie potentially shaky in the long run.

With Scorpio SUN man: Sometimes it seems as if he can do anything you can, better. He reads you well. You could be put out when playing or competing. He will win. He likes your precision and need for thoroughness. He helps you see your limits and allows you to understand yourself. This match is workable, but not easy.

With Sagittarius SUN man: The two of you share similar interests and a strong need to risk. You are likely to see the world, experiment, and enjoy capers together. What pleases him to no end is that he can count on your logic and ability to keep the details of projects together. You might not like being responsible for these matters, but no one is better at it than you. He adores you!

With Capricorn SUN man: You are creative with this man. He seems to open a spigot of energy and ideas for you. His values are similar to yours. You both want the material side of your universe to run smoothly. You can build together. However, you could become frustrated with his empire-building when you want to go skiing.

With Aquarius SUN man: This man offers friendship and will cheer you on as you attempt new challenges. He isn't threatened by your wanderlust or sense of adventure. He has similar needs. He expects you to understand his obsessions. He will count on you to run his budget and family with your Virgo precision. He admires that in you. This can work.

With Pisces SUN man: This man is moody and wants you close to him. You might not appreciate his artistic bent, especially when he wants to go to a concert and you want more earthy entertainment. Be careful not to put him down in your incisive way or he will not want to have anything to do with you. However, he does appreciate your caretaking ability.

MOON IN VIRGO, SUN IN CAPRICORN

You are meant for big things. You have ambition and a rainbow of qualities that will help you get there. You've got precision, detail-orientation, yet a sense of the big picture.

You might not draw men with the power of some Virgo moon women because you are rather particular in your tastes. You're less likely to accept flaws than others. You want a man who makes money, is firmly established, and skilled in his chosen field. You will need him to have foresight and the ability to plan for the future.

This is a big order, especially when you are younger. For this reason, it is likely you will meet your match later in life and marry when you are older. It is wise to be careful with attractions in your twenties. They might not last.

Once you find a partner, you will help your sweetie do whatever he needs to in order to be a success. You're likely to attain success as well. You are skilled in conversation and know how to handle touchy situations. You can be a diplomat or a stockbroker. You tell it as it is, in a manner others can hear.

You also are likely to be seen as better-looking as you get older. In fact, the quality of your life improves as you cross into your middle years.

With Aries SUN man: This man is ambitious and wants to conquer his universe. He will appreciate that when he brings the goods home, you know what to do with them. For this relationship to work, though, he needs to be a moneymaker. You will then love him forever.

With Taurus SUN man: This is a great match. He seeks a quality life and understands the need for money to make it happen. He doesn't want to see the savings account just accrue, however. He expects to enjoy the rewards of his labor, and yours. Count on special trips, beautiful jewelry, and a great deal of appreciation for your solid values.

With Gemini SUN man: You likes this man's dynamic ideas, but could be turned off by his constant need to talk. You might wish there were more action, not just brainy ideas. He has a tough time understanding your need for money and security. There could be a battle royal down the road, even if this gets rolling.

With Cancer SUN man: This is a very interesting combination. This man appreciates money and security, though he might not always be as skilled as you with practical matters. He is extremely emotional and appreciates your stability. You will love being put on a pedestal for all your wonderful traits. For the long term, this is a nifty partner.

With Leo SUN man: You and this man both like having money. He needs it for the good life, and you need it for security. The two of you could amass quite a fortune. However, you might be hurt by his roving eye, and he might not understand your open criticism and concern for detail. Proceed with caution.

With Virgo SUN man: This is a like spirit, but you demonstrate more vision and ability to see the big picture. To make this combo work, you need to compliment his skills. He will respond and love you forever for guiding him. Of the two of you, he could be the more critical. Get ready for a dose of your own medicine!

With Libra SUN man: You might find this man very appealing, but he isn't the empire builder you want. He also has problems making decisions, which at times could leave you frustrated. You get easily irritated by him. Once you start criticizing and he perceives himself as being attacked, you're headed for war, not peace. Forget this one.

With Scorpio SUN man: He is earthy and emotional. You give form to his strong drives and competitive needs. He has insight and penetrating points of view. These characteristics, mixed with your ambition, will make you a hard couple to beat. The two of you will take great delight in what you can do together. A definite go.

With Sagittarius SUN man: This man's hare-brained schemes for making money could make you shudder. You will not like his need to take risks and he will not identify or understand your need for the basics. You are too grounded; he is too flighty. That could leave you standing there watching someday as he flies away.

With Capricorn SUN man: He knows what he is doing in the business world and is practical. He too gets better with age, and the two of you are likely to romp hand in hand into your later years. You generate deep, intense passion as you create the balance of detail and challenge you need for a wonderful life. You both enjoy building and ruling your world together.

With Aquarius SUN man: Consider this man an alien creature and you won't be far off. You find that he isn't interested in establishing success, building a bank account, or making his life efficient and workable. He cares about the New Age, ideas, and his friends. Now, really. Do you want to discuss UFOs on your first date? I don't think so.

With Pisces SUN man: The Fish swims in two directions, and as emotional as this man is, he is also creative. He can amass huge sums of money, but for him it is a testimony to his art. You are perfect for him because you know how to handle what he creates and, in dry times, can help him find ways to tap his deep well of emotions and ideas. You are his anchor. He is your muse.

MOON IN VIRGO, SUN IN AQUARIUS

You are a beautiful but exotic bird. You walk your talk and have a very different way of thinking. You have unusual beliefs and have logical and seemingly grounded reasons for these ideas. Your nerves are rather highly strung.

You need a peaceful environment and get distraught when the fur flies. As a result, you could refuse to speak or say anything controversial. Or you might feel as if you must enforce politeness if you can't have peace. If you are in contact with your feelings, you are likely to shed many a tear if your home life isn't what you want.

Two marriages are more than likely for you. The man you choose when you are younger is often unsuitable as you get older. Also with age, your ideas become even more avant-garde.

You need financial security if you are to find contentment. You have the ability to save money if you choose. You are attracted to eccentric men who don't necessarily give you the security and bank account you'd like to have.

You could find yourself attacking your partner's habits. Do remember, you chose him, and he could reflect your offbeat nature. You also have a very calculating side. You might use sex to get what you want. You are not quite as innocent as the rest of the Moon in Virgo women, though you are capable of projecting a conventional image, ingenue that you are.

With Aries SUN man: This man is eccentric. He's prone to running off to pioneer his favorite cause. He will appreciate your following up details that he couldn't care less about. He'll thank you in his own style, making you feel truly appreciated. This is a go—the whole way. You have fun, sometimes unusual moments together, both being broad-minded.

With Taurus SUN man: You could find this man plain boring, though on some level he could soothe your soul and enrich your life. He doesn't understand your devotion to your friends. There might never be a meeting of minds here. This match is unlikely to last.

With Gemini SUN man: You find his duality exciting. You love his ideas, but he is far more conservative. You generate plenty of sexual energy, but you could be too emotionally demanding for him. You want proof of his caring. You need him to honor your sense of precision at home. He might indulge you, depending on his mood.

With Cancer SUN man: The constant emoting that you can expect with this man can clash with your passion for logic. You could feel threatened and suffocated by his outbursts. A side of you wants to take care of him and help him put order in his life, but in the long run, he is too much of a crybaby for you.

With Leo SUN man: This passionate extrovert could delight you. He adores humanity as much as you do. He is a lover first and you are a friend first, and this is where problems could begin. He lives and feels his sexuality. He could be offended by your lack of intensity and meandering. You will never feel secure with him, even with concerted manipulations.

With Virgo SUN man: This man nurtures your soul and wants to build a solid home life and family with you. He also wants financial security and likes you as a team playmate. He understands your need to sacrifice and take care of others. However, he will get lonely if you are off with your friends or causes too often. He needs a homebody.

With Libra SUN man: This man could be a bit fluffy for you. He will need you to run his life and take care of the details. He'll show his appreciation; he is a great lover. He's not heavy on passion, though he rewards your sense of adventure with surprising energy. You make an interesting couple.

With Scorpio SUN man: This combo spells trouble. Both of you can be very stubborn. If you decide it is your way or else, you could wait each other out until hell freezes over. He is as manipulative as you and often better at it. Don't plan to win. Also, your cerebral nature could frustrate him, and you might not relate to his passion.

With Sagittarius SUN man: This man's need for adventure intrigues you. You might just decide to follow along. You both value friendship and have pet causes. You could find him irritating in the long run, though, as he doesn't appreciate order the way you do. He finds you fussy; you think he's sloppy. Then the wars begin.

With Capricorn SUN man: You could find him too much of an anchor. He's somewhat critical of your need for adventure and the eccentric. You are bound for trouble here. He tends to be conservative, sensuous, and deep. You are more mental and liberal. It's unlikely you'll ever have a meeting of the minds.

With Aquarius SUN man: You have met your soul mate here. He is as eccentric as you and has similar values. He cares about his friends and will do almost anything to help them. As long as you don't ask him to join in, he will indulge your desire to better society and be proud of you. Your need to be Ms. Efficiency could unnerve him, especially if you demand the same of him.

With Pisces SUN man: Yes, he is weird and eccentric, but he will need you. His emotions are so effusive, you could feel as if you'll drown in them. You will feel a need to structure his life and limit his emotionality. That will cause him to resent you, and you could really put a crimp in his style. A definite no—though the attraction is there.

MOON IN VIRGO, SUN IN PISCES

Though Moon in Virgo women have a strong chance for marriage and fulfillment, you face the greatest challenges. The problem isn't your attractiveness. Your femininity pervades wherever you are, you ooze charisma, and men are drawn to you.

You are never quite sure how much to give or what to do. Your insecurity can affect your interactions. Do you follow your feelings or your thoughts? How do you attain what you want? You're likely to question yourself and feel uncertain in your actions.

You are an odd dichotomy. You have a practical efficiency that lets you think through problems. Yet you are emotional, creative, and somewhat out of control. Sometimes you can zero in on specifics while at other moments, you "feel" situations. You are strongly intuitive, yet your mind resists acting on your insights. Sometimes you feel at war with yourself.

The man you choose can reflect these internal struggles. You are attracted to an emotional, sensitive man. Such a man won't be as practical and anchored as you need. You won't have the security you need. Yet you chose him and need to look at what this choice reflects in you. Attacking his nature is really attacking that part of yourself. Once you make peace with yourself, you're far more likely to have a workable relationship.

You won't have trouble attracting men, and are likely to have at least two major relationships.

With Aries SUN man: You will not like this man. He is too practical for you and lacks creativity. Also he is fiery and confrontational, which hurts your fragile feelings. You want someone who is there for you and can handle your neediness. He can't, or won't.

With Taurus SUN man: This man is stable and helps ground you. He gives you permission to swing from one side of your nature to the other. He offers money and stability. He loves your creative, artistic ways. You bathe in his approval. He is enchanted by your romantic style. With him you could find a lifetime romance and partnership.

With Gemini SUN man: This man seems to bring out the worst in you. He questions your stability and gives you mixed signals. You are unnerved by his changing personality. He cannot feed your need for stability. You both have frequent trouble making decisions. What a mess! You are best off turning away from this attraction.

With Cancer SUN man: You are bound by strong emotions and feelings. You both love being close to water and share intimate moments there. You understand his need for gentleness, yet security. He understands your creativity, though he could be offended by your nitpicking. Tame that characteristic and you have a wonderful relationship.

With Leo SUN man: His romantic nature carries you away. Little did you think that love could be this wonderful. You fire his romantic nature with your beauty, elusiveness, and unpredictability. He can be stable as you swing from one pole to another. He likes your practical side. This can work.

With Virgo SUN man: This man could be confused dealing with you. He thinks you are in agreement, then receives an emotional outburst. He will want to help stabilize and nurture you. He will be practical, though sometimes critical. You could value his anchoring, though you might resent his lack of imagination. You need to resolve this conflict before committing to him.

With Libra SUN man: There is a hook here. Once you commit to a relationship, whether it works or not, you could have a difficult time wiggling away. You like his affectionate and romantic ways. He appreciates that he can count on you for details. However, he finds it difficult when you become overwrought, and you get frustrated by his indecision.

With Scorpio SUN man: This man can help you with your intense, sometimes overwhelming feelings. He has been there. He can relate to your dependability. When you become sharp and verbal, he understands. Better yet, when you are into an emotional frenzy, he can join in. This man has the passion to meet you at every juncture. A good bet.

With Sagittarius SUN man: This is a tension-laden relationship. His need to take off to explore new experiences could hurt and offend you. You don't understand or appreciate this trait. As you realize he simply doesn't offer you the security you want, you become negative, sharp, and caustic. He will be bored by your histrionics.

With Capricorn SUN man: This man offers stability and lets you experience the ups and downs of your natural personality. With and through him, you come to see your problems and conflicts. He might not provide the romantic energy that you want. This relationship can work if you value his gifts enough to get you past his limitations.

With Aquarius SUN man: This man is aloof and does not have patience for your swings from emotionality to a logical pursuit of order. He has neither trait, and you could feel as if you are floundering with this man. If you are tempted, don't succumb. There is little but unhappiness in this combination.

With Pisces SUN man: The two of you tease each other with romance, excitement, and joy. You will find a soul mate here whose artistic nature pleases you. You will, however, need to be the more rational one in the relationship. Take the lead with the budget and future planning. He will make it worthwhile for you.

Moon in Libra

"Charm is a way of getting the answer yes without having asked any clear questions."
ALBERT CAMUS

Without question, women with Moon in Libra are the zodiac's most enchanting. Their charm, even more than their beauty, can be irresistible. The combination is a wonderful gift.

You're innately able to relate skillfully as a diplomat or loving wife. Perhaps you learned these skills in another lifetime. This time around, you can use this talent to gain your desires. You expect, demand, and need peace in your immediate environment. Your skill at creating harmony is enhanced on some level by a fear of confrontation. If you hear yelling, you scamper off with your tail between your legs! Forced to deal with the situation, you do so with aplomb.

You are probably popular. You walk in, and the room lights up with beaming faces. Others know you to be kind, caring, and gentle. You are aware of what to say to bring a person out of the doldrums. Others feel appreciated by you, like royalty in your universe.

Because you fear hurting another's feelings, you're often indirect. If you have something negative to say, you dress it up in such pretty words, it could take a while for another to get your meaning. Once the lightbulb goes on, you'll be appreciated for your style.

You have the ability to see both sides of the coin, and will consider all points of view. This is a plus, but some potential partners might see you as wishy-washy. In truth, when you're not sure, you seldom fudge. You wait.

On the minus side, a Moon in Libra woman can become superficial, seeking out pleasure and the good things in life. At her worst, she can become a user, seeking fulfillment through others. This version of the

Libra Moon woman is needy and manipulates to control her partners. She's often afraid of revealing herself to others for fear of harsh judgments.

You are the queen of love. You might love passion, but without the frills you will not stick around. You want pink, romantic clouds in your life. Your lucky partner will feel as if he is the most special person in the world because of the way you treat him. You inspire deep loyalty and love.

A truly fortunate Moon in Libra will draw a partner who understands this aversion to confrontation. A healthy, fully accepted Moon in Libra is perhaps the happiest of all Moon signs. After all, Libra is the sign of marriage.

MOON IN LIBRA, SUN IN ARIES

You are a dichotomy. Your Moon sign is ruled by Venus, the goddess of love. Your Sun sign is ruled by Mars, the god of war. With this mix, you are likely to give off ambivalent vibes, to say the least! You often have trouble relating, as Venus and Mars present opposing energy, much like your Sun and Moon. You are a babe of the full moon, full of conflicts and oppositions.

Relating for you is a full-time and sometimes exhausting business. If you cannot resolve your issues, you might decide to remain single, or you could have multiple marriages. Yet within you there is a sadness, a craving that desperately needs filling. There is good reason to believe you will resolve these problems through introspection.

As Mars and Venus are the significators of your Moon and Sun, your sexiness is likely among the strongest of the Moons in Libra. You are the Cleopatra of the zodiac.

Count on one thing: There will be no shortage of suitors in your life. You will be the one going down the aisle at eighty with a twinkle in your eye. Your soon-to-be-husband will be skipping with mischief in his heart. You are supremely desirable, even if you find it tough to work through your issues. But why torture yourself and others? Deal with your conflicts. You possess the vaunted charms of the Libra Moons, spiced with unusually strong sexuality. You have a lot going for you.

With Aries SUN man: He is wonderful; he is awful. He is everything you want, but sometimes you hate him. What is going on here? Mr. Aries reflects the warlike part in you. He is tough enough to deal with you. He adores your femininity.

With Taurus SUN man: You might love Mr. Taurus, but something here bothers you subliminally. He, like you, is a lover and adores the quality life. He has similar sensuality. Taurus is strong. Once he makes his decisions (which are irrevocable), you could have fits if they don't suit you. The wars could be ferocious, yet there is something nice to explore here.

With Gemini SUN man: You have found the ultimate playmate. The two of you could talk forever as you debate ideas, discuss poetry, and evaluate art. He has the energy to run with some of your greatest schemes. He is Dr. Jekyll and Mr. Hyde. You could play many people with each other. Boredom will be an unknown.

With Cancer SUN man: When you meet this man, you would be wise to keep trucking along. He will provoke your warlike, bellicose side. Your poor Libra Moon nature will be crying inside. He is sentimental and clinging, not the action-oriented, dynamic idea man you covet. Forget this.

With Leo SUN man: When the going is good, it's terrific. You are one of the greatest romantics of the zodiac, and he is the greatest lover. The problem is that he is more committed to pleasure than to you. Eventually his philandering will get to you. This match makes a great affair but a potentially troublesome marriage unless both parties are committed to your inner repairs.

With Virgo SUN man: Uh-oh! The odds are that you are not attracted to this gentleman. All the better for both of you. He is picky, practical, and not what you want. What might draw you is his sense of commitment, but stay friends. You could successfully join forces for other things.

With Libra SUN man: You will melt in this man's arms and feel satisfied. The two of you are the ultimate romantics. This relationship could be rather syrupy to the rest of the world but to you two, perfect. Honor your individual issues, work them through, and you could have a lifetime romance here.

With Scorpio SUN man: Hot describes the attraction. He will buy you exotic oils and maybe a kinky toy. If you want to experience raw passion, you have it here with this man. You love his masculinity. It suits your femininity and vice versa. The shades will be pulled.

With Sagittarius SUN man: You like energy. The good news is you have enough to keep up with him. Your femininity is a raw turn-on for him, and his dynamism suits you fine. Your courtship might not be as classic as you'd like—something you will need to deal with—but the good times roll. This is an excellent combo.

With Capricorn SUN man: He is masculine, strong, and a leader. You like that. He might even court you stylishly, but ultimately his lack of frivolity will get to you. He is about making money. Everything serves a purpose. Why would he want to go dancing after you're hitched? He will never understand your long-term need for courtship.

With Aquarius SUN man: This match is a positive hoot for both of you, but you might not want to take it to the next level. This man's wild ideas will intrigue you, and his eccentricity might make you laugh. However, he simply doesn't know how to court you. Nothing personal, you realize. This is a great fling and friendship. No more, please.

With Pisces SUN man: This man is a romantic, and the draw is strong. Once zipped together, you might never be able to separate. Problems arrive when you realize he isn't the dynamic man you want. You attack, he gets hurt, you feel guilty. You apologize, kiss and make up, and then do it all over again.

MOON IN LIBRA, SUN IN TAURUS

If anyone understands the good life, it is you. You value beauty, peace, and serenity. Though you never look for conflict, you are capable of holding your own. In fact, you do not display the customary waffling of Moon in Libra. Once you make up your mind, the story is over and no one, absolutely no one, will change your mind.

Your commitment to a quality life must be shared by your partner. You expect it all—money, love, and poetry—in your day-to-day life. Because your commitment is so clear, it is more than likely you will make it a reality. You will probably marry once and achieve your goals, though a second marriage is not out of the question. You love your men with intensity and depth. Each one is the ultimate. And one ultimate could follow another. You are a true lover.

You exude a natural sensuality that men cannot miss. More than most Libra Moons, you might have a bit of a weight problem, especially in the hips and thighs. However, this adds to your sensual allure. There is something old-fashioned and charming in your Rubenesque figure.

With Aries SUN man: You might be put off by this man's bluntness and seeming lack of savoir faire, though there is a definite physical attraction. Should you choose to bond, he will challenge your desires, your belief system, and your very essence.

With Taurus SUN man: The problem with this vital and dynamic match is that if you both decide to have it your way, no one wins. You both value the same things in life. You make him happy, and he enthusiastically romances you. The sensuality of this combination could last a lifetime. You are a beautiful charm in his life.

With Gemini SUN man: There is a side of him that pleases you enormously. You can go to art openings, tell jokes, and flirt outrageously together. But when it comes to giving you the home life and the money you want, problems could arise. Mr. Gemini is very creative, and if he can make money, it could work.

With Cancer SUN man: This man values femininity, sensuality, and stability. He puts those qualities, and hence you, on a pedestal. However, you might be at a loss trying to deal with his tears, fragility, and victim mentality. You give Cancer a wonderful opportunity to grow and evolve. If he does, there will be many walks along the beach together.

With Leo SUN man: You love the vitality and masculinity that this man exudes. He is very romantic and caring. He's strong-willed like you and often feels he is right. But you know you are right, right? Because he loves good times like you love beauty, he might back off. Who wants a battle royale when you can have a good time? Be wise and give in if you like him.

With Virgo SUN man: This is a plus-and-minus situation. You like his practical, earthy nature, but you do not understand why he doesn't want to walk along the water and chat endlessly with you. He, on the other hand, finds you frivolous. Eventually, fights will break out. You might win, but you will never find what you want here.

With Libra SUN man: Yes, you love this man, and what is there not to love? He, like you, is the ultimate romantic. Note the instant recognition between you when you first meet. You intuitively know what to do for each other. Just hope he has the ability to make money, a very big plus for you. You need that bankroll. Nothing personal.

With Scorpio SUN man: The attraction is so primal, there might not be time to think about the plusses and minuses of this combo. You could disappear into intimacy, never to be seen again in this world. In the long run, this man is quiet and reserved, yet offers the stability you want. This is a true sizzler. You wish for nighttime, all the time.

With Sagittarius SUN man: He likes the good life, and if you can go along with some of his more bawdy interests, the sensuality and play could be long term. He's likely to be a moneymaker, though stability isn't his cup of tea. You need to be the keeper of the checkbook. He will take too many risks for your taste. A definite maybe!

With Capricorn SUN man: You build empires together and have few problems with the outside world. The intricacies of the relationship could be quite different. Though Capricorn will court you until the day you are married, he might go to another battlefield after you two are a *fait accompli*. You will be hard-pressed to find your needs met with this man.

With Aquarius SUN man: Though this man is amusing, he might be too much of a lightweight for you. He is fun, he makes merry, but no way does he have the sensuality to meet your libidinous nature. He doesn't know what romance is either. As for stability, you have to be an ostrich to think it is here.

With Pisces SUN man: Once the two of you tango, you could be in trouble, as this coupling has a long-term hook. You might find him emotional, and sometimes weak. You are the anchor here. He does provide oodles of romance. If anyone says good-bye, it will be you.

MOON IN LIBRA, SUN IN GEMINI

You walk into the room and exude excitement and desirability. Others are drawn to your sensuality, vivacious expressions, and animated gestures. There is something irresistible about you, both to women and to men. Women want you as a friend, as you certainly provide a good time. Men want you as their lover, as you implicitly promise lively sparks.

You demonstrate sensitivity in your thoughts and expressions. You are easily distracted and need a lot of activities to keep your mind stoked. Your energy is hard to match, and if there is a better way of doing something, you'll probably come up with it.

You have adaptability and are willing to go with the flow. Nothing seems to intimidate you in the world of ideas. You were given the gift of charm, which with your intellectualism, makes you a shining star.

If you are single, it is by choice, because you have yet to find anyone who could hold your interest long enough. You need a man who is bright, versatile, and a king in his own realm of work and ideas. You love romance and gentleness as much as you love thought. You want it all. You might marry several times, and somehow manage to look younger each time. You are the perpetual child.

With Aries SUN man: This blows hot energy into your life. Yes, he talks a good game; he wants to act on it too. There is a definite attraction there. You feed his fire. He might not be up to the kind of courtship you want, and you might not care as the steamy passions build. Check him out.

With Taurus SUN man: You both appreciate the finer sensibilities in life, but you might find him slow with the ideas. It is entirely possible you could tell a ha-ha and it could go right over him. You might find yourself bored. His earthiness buries you.

With Gemini SUN man: The peals of laughter could go on forever as you play out the many different personalities you both have. The problem is someone has to hush up once in a while in order to hear the other. Fortunately, your beauty and charm will occasionally stop him in his tracks. He will write you love poetry and give you roses. Life is a delight with this man.

With Cancer SUN man: Some combinations need to be forgotten about before they begin. Put this one in the discard pile. He is emotional and clinging, something that could send chills up your back. Say no before two nice people hurt each other.

With Leo SUN man: Conversation inevitably leads to flirtation; flirtation carries you to a love affair. You coquettishness will have Leo chasing you. He is charmed by your capricious ways, drawn by your desirability. There is romance to last a lifetime here. The laughter and flirtation won't stop.

With Virgo SUN man: You are unlikely to meet except at work, or perhaps the grocery store. I can see you two bumping into each other while shopping. He is lost in thought, calculating his bill while you blithely skip through the food aisles. Though there could be a collision, there isn't any glue here.

With Libra SUN man: Echoes of past lives float through your conversations and interactions. You wonder why he knows exactly what will make you happy, and he wonders how you can make him feel so at home. You have met your match. Make sure you have the same interests, and this relationship works.

With Scorpio SUN man: This man can singe your soul and mind. He manages to breeze through your chatter to the essence of what you're saying. He succumbs to your charm and magnetism. He will court you with ideas, dinners, and close-to-exhausting lovemaking. You might be very happy if you can handle a sarcastic comment or two.

With Sagittarius SUN man: You have met someone who does the opposite of you: acts without thinking. You think, but often don't act. If you can tolerate the differences and enjoy them, there is a lot of growth here for both of you. Life can be exciting and romantic with this adventuresome man. How you handle each other could make or break this relationship.

With Capricorn SUN man: His earthiness and materialism irritate you. He doesn't understand your love of flirtation, ideas, and talk. You don't like his need to gain—at everyone else's cost. After all, you care about your loved ones and intellectual commitments, not building empires. Once the initial flirtation fades, he becomes a deadly bore.

With Aquarius SUN man: He will play with ideas and introduce you to new, Bohemian outlooks. You actually find his eccentric gifts and courtship amusing. You will never feel threatened by him. He will enchant you, and you, him.

With Pisces SUN man: This is nothing less than a disaster. He is clinging and needy. You want to take off and see an avant-garde movie. He mopes that you left him. What you come home to might not be worth the hassle. If you like him, be good to him and leave him alone.

MOON IN LIBRA, SUN IN CANCER

You are emotional, sentimental, caring, and perhaps little too sensitive for your own good. The opposite sex is attracted to your allure and femininity. You do have a problem with moodiness. At times you even have trouble handling yourself!

You love family, romance, and all that is traditional and apple pie.

You want courtship, love, and marriage. You are very uncomfortable living with a man unmarried, though it is a possibility if you are gun-shy.

You have two sides: one enjoys the finer things of life and might be superficial, while the other is a perfect example of "still waters run deep." You need a man who stabilizes your emotional swings and sometimes makes decisions for you. You could waffle frequently, as you really don't want to hurt anyone or anything.

With your unusual warmth you have a real need for closeness and sensuality that may at times make others feel suffocated. You have a luminous quality and are beautiful wearing pearls and pinks. Your subtle looks lure and intrigue men. Your sensuality glows through your movements, eyes, and life-choices. A good meal to you is an epicurean treat. Lovemaking can be too. The hedonist in you will prevail.

With Aries SUN man: Ouch. He steps on your toes, emotionally and perhaps literally too. He might not even realize that he hurt you until he gets a very cold reception. Get used to his asking, "What did I do?" Yet there is an attraction. If you say yes, you'll both need to learn the art of compromise to make this work.

With Taurus SUN man: This man could be perfect for you. He is earthy and stabilizes your emotions. With him, you can reveal your true self. He also is a hedonist and gourmet. His values match yours, and you provide each other with a very special relationship. Green light.

With Gemini SUN man: His ideas and wit delight you. If he writes a short story or poem about you, you could be a goner—for a while. He doesn't understand your tears, wants to talk about your being upset when all you are looking for is a hug. This could be hard on both of you.

With Cancer SUN man: He is the man you have been dreaming about since you were a little girl! You will be romanced by the ocean, taken to many wonderful dinners, and protected by this sensitive soul of the zodiac. He expects the same depth and commitment back, though he loves your lightness. At times you might get uncomfortable with his emotional displays.

With Leo SUN man: This man is romantic and dynamic. You find him to be a lover who is hard to deny. Be careful. To hold on to him might be a whole different story. If you get clingy, he'll run. If you play hardball and are somewhat flirtatious with other men, he will chase you. The bottom line is you will need to work hard to keep him.

With Virgo SUN man: Though this man can be there for you and at times helps ground you, he doesn't understand your emotionality. He uses his mind to solve your tears. You will close down with him, even if you are a little interested. Forget romance. It won't happen. It simply isn't part of him.

With Libra SUN man: This is an interesting combo. He understands you. He lights up your heart and soul. You're the kind of couple who continues holding hands. You can't help but love him. He might feel uncomfortable with your emotionality. Nevertheless, count on his sensitivity. He won't ever want to see you cry. A close to perfect choice.

With Scorpio SUN man: This man is deep and feels with an intensity that could overwhelm you. His verbal attacks could be grueling and offend your sensitive side. You shut down and close off this relationship. That might be safer for you. Nevertheless, he is strong, a decision maker, and very attractive. This combo has a lot of pros and cons.

With Sagittarius SUN man: To this man, you are pretty, feminine, and alluring. However, if you want stability, a home life, and caring, continue looking. You like his vibrating excitement, but you will not be happy in the short or long term. Use his philosophy: The grass is greener on the other side of the fence. Move on.

With Capricorn SUN man: You are a good example of opposites attracting. You need money for security; he needs money for power. Yet you can count of him to provide for your needs. He will court you until he snags you, so be ready to hold out a bit. And should he upset you, the courtship restarts. He provides home, family, and occasional romancing. And there is always a hot attraction.

With Aquarius SUN man: You are delighted by his ideas and love of humanity, pets, and family. He is an oddball when it comes to romance, so don't expect anything traditional here and you won't be disappointed. He will not want your clinging and emotionality. So enjoy having him as a friend. This tie is a no-go for a long-term relationship.

With Pisces SUN man: You will absolutely adore this emotional man. You love that you both have deep needs. Pisces will always delight your heart with his emotional renderings. Make this work because you will never be able to leave each other. There is a karmic hook.

Moon in Libra, Sun in Leo

You are beautiful, charming, and dramatic. You are a magnet—irresistible to men. You have passion and romance, yet it takes a special man not to be intimidated by you. You are a Goddess of Love. You are feminine, sensual, and always warm.

If offended or wounded, you might have a difficult time forgiving the injuring party. You might never let a loved one know how much you hurt. It is this fear of hurt that could hamper you from finding true intimacy. For this reason, an enchanting and desirable as you are, there might not be depth in your relationships.

You tend to be preoccupied with all that is beautiful in life and, as a result, might be a runaway spender.

You make a man feel like a king; he will never forget the experience of being with you. However, if you should decide to let him be your significant sweetie, heaven forbid if he doesn't treat you like his queen. Your wanderlust comes into play.

You can be an extraordinary wife and partner, though you are demanding and will put your mate through his paces. You want constant romance, appreciation, and love. This could be hard on others, though you make it worth their time. If you get what you want, there is no more loyal and more passionate mate than you. It is your way or no one's.

With Aries SUN man: He has the fire to meet your passion, though he might not be interested in the delicacies you deem necessary. He has better things to do, like crusading to help humanity. He might consider you beautiful but demanding, a little vain and self-serving. You sizzle together, but don't make this a commitment—unless you can give up many of your musts.

With Taurus SUN man: Together, you see art shows and concerts, go to the finest restaurants, and inevitably have a good time. The attraction might be strong, but he has a slow and easy pace, and you are consumed by immediacy. If you can do it his way, this could be a lifetime courtship and bond. Mr. Taurus brings quality to your life.

With Gemini SUN man: He is a tease, and you love his humor. He is inventive, and your minds soar together. Adventure is the byword of this match. He will court you, but you will have to keep up with him. You are the gasoline, and he is the match. Stability derives from the longevity of the tie.

With Cancer SUN man: You will want to immediately turn the faucet off on this drippy man. He is emotional and can be clingy, something totally offensive to you. You will drown with him, and he will always be upset with you. Don't stop. Roll the dice and move on. You'll thank me.

With Leo SUN man: He likes to be treated like a king as much as you like to be a queen. Your dating will be a royal courtship if you both remember that the other is very proud. Both of you are generous, adore love, and are likely to create a very happy relationship. There could be an occasional meandering—but both of you understand these things.

With Virgo SUN man: This spells trouble, even if there is an attraction. He hurts you, you hurt him. He has a gift for precision and verbal sarcasm. He is practical and will tell you precisely how he feels about your frivolities. He wounds your pride, and you retaliate by running to another relationship. Do yourself a favor. Don't even try.

With Libra SUN man: His smile lights up your life, and to him, you are a magnet radiating warmth and beauty. It seems destined that you will court and fall in love. Liabilities? Not much. You are capable of making a decision; he wavers forever trying to come to a resolution. You will find his sweetness worth it. This is quite the love affair.

With Scorpio SUN man: He has a passionate nature that certainly might ring your chimes. Unless you can handle power plays, controlling behavior, and sarcasm, you will be singed or turned off. The sexual attraction is long term, but the problems intensify over the long run. Your pride will be stomped on, and you might find roving a major pastime, if not preoccupation.

With Sagittarius SUN man: Mr. Vitality and Energy does a fiery dance that never ends. You will not be bored with the zodiac's adventurer, but forget the type of romance you imagined. He is complex and complements your many-faceted beauty. You will travel with him and see much. Both of you need space, and if there is some vacillating or playing around, you're likely to pretend it never happened.

With Capricorn SUN man: This man has the bankroll to make you happy. He will wine and dine you to a tee. Once he has caught you, he is off to making more money (for him and you). Nevertheless, you are profoundly insulted by his lack of attention, and the fussing begins. He is too practical and earthy for your fiery, romantic nature. You will ultimately wander.

With Aquarius SUN man: "Hi," you say to this gentleman, who seems like everyone's friend. You are attracted, and so is he. You need to have a sense of humor when he brings you a cactus instead of a rose. If this is okay with you, the match could last. You will need to put up with his constant parade of friends.

With Pisces SUN man: Moonlight walks are frequent with this man. You will smile at his love letters and many offerings. With your passion, you offer him stability, yet you have the ability to understand his soft nature. Your strength becomes a must for him and he will want you forever. You are the stronger force here.

Moon in Libra, Sun in Virgo

You are probably very delicate emotionally and/or physically. To others, you seem like a China doll. You have the beauty and charm of the Libra Moon, yet the practicality bestowed by your Virgo Sun. In some ways, you have the whole package. You might have a hard time believing that you offer that much when you look at your love life. You might even decide you have bad luck with men. You do, but you don't. You might actually choose men who are emotionally unavailable, repeatedly, until you work this through. Remember, you are in control. You make the choices.

You want a man who is practical and can handle money. He needs to be efficient, allowing you to pursue your artistic interests. You also are very much tuned into what is spiritually beautiful and what is not. You are dedicated, love others, and have a need to show your sensitivity and caring. You make a loyal lover, friend, and supporter.

Excellence follows you into domestic life. You will manage the household and take care of all the details with precision. There will always be flowers and other fine details evident in your home. Others walk in and feel as if they can put up their feet and relax. You are there, ready to take care of them.

You wonder, with all that you have to offer, why relationships are so tough. Look to yourself and take responsibility, and you can change direction.

With Aries SUN man: You are very different people, yet you like his crusading ways and adventurous nature. He wants to exchange ideas and do for others, just like you. What is wonderful is that he expresses the same authenticity and dedication TO you. For him, you are a stable, yet beautiful woman. Together you establish a mutual admiration society.

With Taurus SUN man: This man understands both your love of beauty and your need for the practical. He echoes your requirements, but seems to unify them in an even better way. You will learn from him; he will love your willingness to defer. Here is a slow-building passion that could last a lifetime. The courtship never ends, yet this is a grounded, earthy relationship.

With Gemini SUN man: You love this man's dexterity and excitement. You might think you want to flirt with him for the rest of your life. Not so. Given time you will find him flighty. You will criticize him for his lack of grounding. As a result, he becomes cold and ignores you. Go for platonic friendship here.

With Cancer SUN man: There is an innate tension between you. His gooey devotion and emotionality might offend your finer sensibilities. You are practical and determined and do not understand his need for drama and scenes. You will criticize, and he will become the ultimate crab. It won't work. No way, no how.

With Leo SUN man: This man is a lover and a playboy. Though your Libra Moon wants to tame Leo, and he certainly finds you attractive, you might never be able to let down your guard and be yourself. If you do, he could wander. Please understand: This is a fun flirtation, but a tough commitment. You can do better.

With Virgo SUN man: You like this man's dependability, yet he is somewhat emotionally cold. If you want a successful relationship with this man, work through your issues. Otherwise the recriminations continue long term. The greatest passion you will have will be the battles. And forget courtship. He thinks it is frivolous.

With Libra SUN man: With this man you'll experience romance forever. The two of you are destined for emotional Nirvana. The rub is, if you want Libra to wear the pants and make decisions in the real world, forget it. You might even be the one proposing here. However, he will make it worth your while.

With Scorpio SUN man: This man is insightful and hot. He will bring you more than romance; he will introduce you to passion. At times you might find that he intimidates conservative you. If you get caustic and critical, he won't mind. Be prepared for someone who is more skilled than you with anger. This is one hot tamale.

With Sagittarius SUN man: You will not be able to tolerate his wanderlust, which makes you very uncomfortable. He is fun and full of adventure. You could make great friends, but lovers? No! You're destined to feel uncomfortable and uptight if you make it more. Be friends. He will adore you. He too senses this combo is off.

With Capricorn SUN man: He likes your energy, but even better, he can match your practicality. You will be comfortable with this security-minded man. He will court you and offer you a wonderful, solid life and commitment. On some level, you might get antsy as the relationship becomes old. This takes commitment on your part.

With Aquarius SUN man: You will laugh with this man and you will admire his dedication to his friends. If you hook up with him, you might find that you wish he'd treat you more like his friends. There might be a push-pull here that throws you off. Will he be able to feed your romantic nature and practical needs? Not in this lifetime. This couple is destined for misery.

With Pisces SUN man: You are attracted to the zodiac's ultimate romantic. Even if he isn't an artist, he has that temperament. He is needy too. Your desire to help comes into play right away. There is glue here. You love to be needed, and he needs you. The wonderful gift he brings is more romance than you ever dreamed of. You feel safe with him, even if you are the practical one.

MOON IN LIBRA, SUN IN LIBRA

You are the epitome of femininity and all that characterizes a Libra Moon. Your charm draws others, while your inner beauty radiates. You must share your inner self in order to experience the emotional completement of relationships.

Men fall madly in love with you. You might find your attractiveness difficult, as men only see your surface charm and seem to not want to get to know you more completely. This can be frustrating and hurtful. To counter this problem, run a tight courtship, giving both of you time to know each other.

You want to give all, yet there is still another side of you that can be superficial. To protect yourself, you might only let others know your beautiful surface. Unfortunately this defense will draw only shallow people.

Empathy and walking in another's shoes are odd concepts for you.

If someone gets mad at you, you might have a problem understanding why. You only see the world from your eyes.

You are drawn to men who reflect your inner energy. They could be romantic but also not strong at decision making. You might actually choose someone like you who hates confrontation. The problem with that is that the relationship might never touch your depths or open you up to the caring you can give. The two of you might wander away from each other even if you stay with the relationship. You are capable of a strong relationship, where you learn to deal with your feelings. Then you will have it all.

With Aries SUN man: You have just met the king of confrontation and you are attracted with a deadly passion. This could be a fabulous relationship, as he can teach you to talk about things that normally make you uncomfortable. But for this to work long term, you need to respect each other's differences. Consider this a blaze of passion.

With Taurus SUN man: This man is strong, yet understands your sensitivities. The good news is that he moves slowly, and you love the courtship. He offers it all: security, a beautiful life, and stability. One caution: You could become bored with him in the long run. He will not tolerate your playing around.

With Gemini SUN man: There is nothing here but fun and delightful moments. What is good for you here is his ability to discuss his feelings intellectually in a way that makes you feel comfortable. This is a lively, yet nonthreatening relationship. Together you will sound like a pair of magpies and you will be free as birds.

With Cancer SUN man: Discomfort is high with this man. He and you have different styles and never will the twain meet. He is emotional and needy, and you will feel like you just met your albatross. You have. Say "no thank you" and when he asks you on a date. He might be attracted to you, but it won't work.

With Leo SUN man: There might be no time for you to evaluate whether this is good or bad for you. His fiery zeal will overwhelm you and unglue you, but you love it. Neither of you will have time to wander on the other. Though Leo is generous and caring, he does have a temper. You must learn to deal with confrontation with this man. Do it. It is worth it.

With Virgo SUN man: OOPS. You just ran into a problem. Not that this man isn't nice, but you are nearly the antithesis of each other. Unless there is some planetary glue that is unique to this man, it isn't going to happen, nor should it. His practical and critical nature is quite offensive to you.

With Libra SUN man: Woman, meet man. Same meets same. The attraction is dynamite and dreamy. There will always be an element of superficiality, as neither of you wants to deal with anything "heavy." As a couple, you will choose beauty over utility. Why pay bills when you can go to Mexico with the same money?

With Scorpio SUN man: You are attracted to this very masculine man as he zeros in on your extraordinary femininity. He is deep and mysterious. He could intrigue you, yet he might want more feelings and depth from you. You will learn about deep emotions and confrontation should you choose to hang out. The decision is yours.

With Sagittarius SUN man: Look at the long term and what this man offers—adventure, travel, and constant activity. This actually might be very enticing, though he could love his racehorse more than you once you become a *fait accompli.* You might not like the relationship once the initial bloom fades. If you can't accept his many hobbies and passions, give up now.

With Capricorn SUN man: Take the lead and say no. He is about power and money. You are about that which is artistic, beautiful, and feminine. You will never be happy with him, and he finds you superficial. He does recognize a beautiful woman like you. So it is up to you to say no.

With Aquarius SUN man: This is a wild tour of an eccentric, perhaps insane world for you. As conservative as you are, he is liberal. Never dream of having normal times here. Though this is a romp and a half, it will frustrate as a long-term commitment. You might want an everlasting friendship with who knows what else tossed in. He is a delight late at night.

With Pisces SUN man: There is a deep tie that might be hard to dissolve once the relationship takes off. You love his dynamite imagination. Every day is full of romance. Though instability isn't a problem for you, his neediness and emotions are. You simply cannot understand them. Eventually, he'll feel that you don't care, and the romance stops.

MOON IN LIBRA, SUN IN SCORPIO

On the outside, you are a very passionate, sexy, bright woman. You know what to say to get the reaction you want and you exude security and confidence.

On the inside, there might be a war raging. You are intense and perceptive, and want to experience life in depth, yet you are very uncomfortable with this need. You don't like to have your emotional boat rocked. You could get scared of feelings when you think you are losing control. This inner war can take quite a toll on your life.

You might always be a bit at odds with your more superficial tendencies and demand more of yourself. You are promised lifetime growth should you choose that course. Otherwise, after bouncing from one relationship to another, you will go for the superficiality of the dating game. You might be too frightened to face your emotional demons.

You need a man with deep emotions and commitment. Once hooked, it could be rather intense because of your ever-changing complex emotional development. It is quite possible you might need two marriages because of how you metamorphose. Not that one man is better than the other, but rather they represent that period of your growth. Your relationships will be direct reflections of the emotional steps you will take.

With Aries SUN man: Once you two tango, you are unlikely to forget this man. He is hot, enthusiastic, and meets many of your requirements. You might never separate after your first date, except for his periodic crusades. The passion will more than make up for any lack of romantic frills. Lucky you. Lucky him.

With Taurus SUN man: This is such a dynamic attraction, you are a goner after the first date. He is earthy, stable, and strong and he will help you voice your feelings. Your biggest problem could be formalizing the tie or getting it off the ground, but once you do, neither will back away. There is a lot to be learned from each other. A forever combination.

With Gemini SUN man: You like his charm and easy ways. You wish you had his social ease. However, he makes a better friend than lover because he does not offer the grounding you want. He lives for ideas and might not have time for such details as security and stability. This could make you uneasy, and before you know it, nasty verbal sparring begins. Uh-oh.

With Cancer SUN man: He evokes a deep emotional response from you, though on some level there is irritation. He doesn't understand your need for freedom and could become clingy or needy. You have a decision to make. He will offer you security and a wonderful home life. Is the price of freedom worth it? Toasty fun behind closed doors makes it an even tougher choice.

With Leo SUN man: This man is the personification of the fun and happiness you love. You have good times together and could date, love, and romance for the rest of your lives. However, he is strong-willed, and when you decide you are right, there is no changing your mind. Potentially you could have the War of the Roses. Think about it. You might want to pretend to be wrong sometimes.

With Virgo SUN man: Virgo is practical and earthy. He also has a sharp tongue, something that you have been accused of having, so he won't hold a grudge if you have a bout. He offers stability, but your need for romance and frivolous fun cries out. The intimate connection might not be enough to make up for the difference.

With Libra SUN man: You share an innate understanding. He meets your need for a wonderful, peaceful life. Don't attack him because of his lack of decisiveness or practicality. Remember, he represents an aspect of your nature, and bashing him is like bashing yourself. You need to come to terms with your conflicts if this relationship is to work.

With Scorpio SUN man: Talk about being too hot to handle! The physical attraction is so potent, you might not be able to say no to this man. It is meld over matter here. He could be the strong man of your dreams, though don't be surprised if he puts down your need for frills. This is a relationship that can last. Others will marvel at your passion for each other years later.

With Sagittarius SUN man: He likes to play, and so do you. He is up for adventure, and that resonates with your love of danger and the mysterious. In the long run, he doesn't have the intensity you crave. You will hurt him. Be kind and don't play with his soul, mind, or body. You like being honorable. Do the right thing.

With Capricorn SUN man: This man is appetizing and passionate. You seem to be a match for him, on the baseball field, behind closed doors, anywhere. You entertain his clients and delight him in many ways. He won't mind paying for your trivialities, but he might not be able to frolic the way you'd like. Nevertheless, this tie is most workable.

With Aquarius SUN man: You think he is funny, and he makes a great friend. You might even have romantic fantasies about him. He means it when he says enough, and no amount of manipulation will change his mind. There could be a major clash even before this relationship gets off the ground.

With Pisces SUN man: You love his imagination as he takes you on one mental adventure after another. Romancing seems natural to him, and you respond big time. His artistic nature appeals to you, and you can put some order in his life. He will always need you, and you will love helping him. It stabilizes you. You can find long-term love with this man.

MOON IN LIBRA, SUN IN SAGITTARIUS

You have unusual vitality and energy. You are an excellent athlete, yet you love doing girl things. You can't deny your femininity. Others admire your desirability and grace. You will always express your feelings, but in ways that others can hear. You are sensitive, yet direct. Want more compliments? You don't hold grudges and are loving, caring, and full of answers. You won't make problems where there are none. You're sensible, level, and intelligent.

Because of your naturally athletic disposition and the magnetic Libra Moon, men seem to fall all over you, so much so that it might be difficult to avoid multiple relationships. It is just that you are so exciting and you get so enthusiastic about the opposite sex. You love men. You love them as friends as well as lovers. They feel your approval and want more.

The kind of man who will make you happy will be dynamic, energetic, and willing to risk. You like the mystery in his adventuresome nature. Together, you will explore the world. You will want it all and you will choose a man who can offer it.

You will not settle down before you are ready. You want to experience all you can. And you will.

With Aries SUN man: He is fiery and full of magnetism. You enjoy yourself to the max with him. The attraction is binding and will not die very easily. Though you will have your angry moments, affection will ease you through them. This is a long-term match, especially if you are both willing to share some of the other's interests. An excellent choice.

With Taurus SUN man: This man could be too slow for you, as you are off like a flash of lightning. If you do stick with him awhile, you'll discover someone who is appreciative and will offer you security and a launching pad to the world. You might want to check him out.

With Gemini SUN man: With your busy schedules, you could have a hard time getting together. You love his ideas and imagination. He will love his ability to take his ideas and make them real. Between you exists a natural sense of mischief and adventure. You might never want kids, as you enjoy being children yourselves, romping together!

With Cancer SUN man: You will find that he just doesn't get it, nor do you. He wants to set up house and make it happen. When you say no, he will back off, lick his wounds, and emotionally shut down. You will have problems nearly from the get-go.

With Leo SUN man: You might even give up tennis for his passionate games. You will be taken by surprise and swept off your feet. In return, your vitality and energy will always have him wondering what you are up to. You will certainly keep his life exciting. This is a mutually happy couple.

With Virgo SUN man: You will not like his criticism. Your experimental and open nature will threaten him. He will think of you as frivolous, accuse you of taking unnecessary risks. Even if there is an attraction, this could be a disaster. If so, it is more likely you will play awhile and leave him. He gets hurt. Not you.

With Libra SUN man: You have made a good choice if you are eyeing this gentleman. In a past life, you might have been the man and he the woman. Consider this: Some of the problems you have as a couple might relate to your deep pasts. For the here and now you get to perfect what is naturally good to begin with. You both are huge flirts, and this adds to the steamy attraction. Hop on this one.

With Scorpio SUN man: You are out of your league here. He is deep and dark. He will always be suspicious of you as you bat your eyelids at the male gender. If he thinks he has reason to be jealous, the paybacks and recriminations could be downright painful. He will hurt deeply. And you can't be who you really are with him. This is out.

With Sagittarius SUN man: You two might be so busy wandering and exploring the world together, you could get lost or worst yet, lose each other. However, there's a likelihood of true love and a bonding of like souls. If he ever asks, don't fool around and play coy, say yes. You will always turn each other on mentally, physically, and spiritually.

With Capricorn SUN man: To make this work will take true talent. You like his ability to accrue money, establish a power base, and be a go-getter. He is conservative and can seem like a stick-in-the-mud. All your seduction cannot get him out of his mold. However, there is much comfort for you with this man, providing he can give you space.

With Aquarius SUN man: Peals of laughter mark this relationship. You make great friends and adore each other. You might find his courtship a bit offbeat. He could give you dandelions instead of roses, but you will forgive him, as the good times are thrilling. You will never stop laughing and loving together.

With Pisces SUN man: There is a high attraction, but also a deep tension here. Though you love his style, you cannot endure his clingy ways and dependence on you. You will feel as if you could drown with him when you really want someone you can soar with. This isn't a good choice and worse, could be one that is close to impossible to disengage from.

MOON IN LIBRA, SUN IN CAPRICORN

You are an ever-moving bundle of energy. Others find this vitality very attractive, though few can keep up with you. You are always ready for the next adventure, phone call, or invitation.

You are extremely feminine, but your interest in succeeding in life also dominates. For some of you this might portend a strong career. For the majority, it means a dynamic mate, with all the accruements of the good life and marriage. You will want a solid bank account, quality home life, and accomplished children.

You are sensuous and alluring, yet your feet are firmly planted. You tend to make excellent choices for yourself and never lose sight of your priorities and needs. Because you take such good care of yourself, you have a great deal to give.

You will want to be romanced with style and splendor. You expect physical, concrete testimony of his caring and you will settle for nothing less. You will control the courtship, mainly by your unspoken demands, which he will meet or you'll let him fall by the wayside. After all, you know what you want.

You are capable of that discipline and want to maintain one lifetime marriage. There could, however, be an affair or two to take the edge off your occasional boredom. But leave your marriage? No way.

With Aries SUN man: He is full of energy, vivacity, and spirit. He will go for whatever he wants, and that includes you. He knows perfection when he sees it—you! Feel complimented, but if you think this will be an easy match, you are wrong. He has a temper. There will be a lot of yelling, but a lot of kissing and making up.

With Taurus SUN man: This is the kind of match that makes fifty-year marriages. He is stable and a good earner. He appreciates your artistic nature and your great femininity. He will forever put you on a pedestal. The sensuality is intense and consuming. You will travel, see the world together, and love forever. Neither of you will forget that the marriage comes first.

With Gemini SUN man: You will immediately like this dynamic, interesting man. You will want to talk, exchange ideas, and flirt, flirt, flirt! This can work IF he's a good moneymaker. You won't be happy if he is a starving writer. His sometimes flighty ways could be slightly unnerving, but he will adore you. The constant twists are exciting.

With Cancer SUN man: He needs your stability and sense of direction. Together you build quite a handsome bank account and estate. He worships your womanliness. You will have many romantic strolls together. There are opportunities for both of you to grow here, for him attaining stability, and for you, learning to let go and be emotional.

With Leo SUN man: The passion between you is like an explosion when you touch. Intuitively, you know how to entice him into a permanent bond. He won't have much time to wander. He will be too busy making money and making sure you beam. He could find you demanding, but the plusses way outweigh the negatives.

With Virgo SUN man: There is stability here, but if you are looking for excitement, you might be barking up the wrong tree. His strong suit isn't courting. The odd thing is that you will date and you might marry. But you will never known the intense love and romance you are capable of. All is quiet, and way too boring.

With Libra SUN man: Most definitely this could be the love affair of your lifetime. There is magic here. The problems occur when you look for the details that make your life work. He doesn't have a practical bone in him. You will have to wear the pants in this household and not let him realize it if you want a lifetime romance.

With Scorpio SUN man: He brings out the animal in you and could easily become an addiction. However, at times your superficiality gets to him. He doesn't understand all the fluff you need to make you happy; he could also question your thirst for substantial sums of money. Consider giving up some of these tendencies for this relationship. You will be a couple who always wants to disappear together.

With Sagittarius SUN man: You might find this man a challenge and somewhat engaging. But he might not make enough money to keep you happy. Also, he is so into risk-taking that you could get chills up your back. Your financial security is at risk here. So is your emotional security. He careens from one woman to another. Need to know any more?

With Capricorn SUN man: In many ways, this is your ideal man. He can make money and take care of your costly whims. He gives the structure and form you crave. However, the sweet, cooing words could die off once he takes you as a given. You might wander on him. The intimate scenes are great with Mr. Capricorn, so you will always come home.

With Aquarius SUN man: This is a fun time. However, toss stability and long-term prospects to the wind. He is always out with his friends. He might not realize what he has done. If you tell him, he will tell you to become more independent. This man might be an excellent friend, but nothing more. Be his pal, and he will be there forever.

With Pisces SUN man: You are anchored; he is a loose cannon. He can't offer you stability, but he does have money, as he is very creative, possibly artistic. He will need you to manage the money he makes. You will love the enchanting romantic web he weaves. He will forever adore you and put you on a pedestal—if you take care of him. Do you want to?

MOON IN LIBRA, SUN IN AQUARIUS

You are light, airy, and fun. Others describe as a people-person. You might even find it difficult to be alone, though you have an independent streak.

Your superb relating style nurtured by your love of people makes you ever popular. You could, if you wish, have a long list of lovers. That's a strong possibility, as you love romance so much. Once the wooing ends, you get disillusioned. You will always be friends with your exes, but you want more than just friendship.

You are beautiful and exotic-looking. You are like a magnet to the opposite sex. They can't get enough of you or close enough to you.

Though you love a classic courtship, you like an original twist to your love beat. There is uniqueness in your lovemaking style. This too binds you and your sweetie.

You are capable of an excellent relationship. However, you might opt for as many as four major relationships during your life. You do, after all, like variety and change. At the same time, you offer to your friends and loved ones friendship and tender devotion.

With Aries SUN man: With this man, you are like the match that lights the TNT. You can work through problems if there is mutual respect. He finds you very womanly, and you like his fiery ways. He frequently crusades, giving you plenty of time to socialize and hang out with your friends. When he comes home, both of you are happy to see each other.

With Taurus SUN man: He might be a bit too conservative and slow for you. What's nice is that he appreciates your sense of delicacy and refinement. Both of you greatly enjoy gourmet experiences, the arts, and intellectual discussions. However, for the long term, you will get bored. Also, he can be as stubborn as you.

With Gemini SUN man: You are as delighted by this man as he is with you. Your courtship will be a whirlwind of fun, laughter, and exciting new vistas. It is okay with him that you want it your way. He really doesn't care, as long as you give him freedom. He will appreciate your soft, romantic ways and will court you for the rest of your life.

With Cancer SUN man: You poor dear. If you decide to be more than friends, you might need a permanent investment in Kleenex. He cries and whines, and you might dissolve in tears having to deal with this weeping willow. It might even be hard to have a friendship with Cancer after he turns into a Crab because you hurt his feelings.

With Leo SUN man: He is a lover and knows how to make you tingle down to your toes with desire for him. He has as much to learn about friendship from you as you will learn about loving from him. As long as both of you respect your intellectual differences and aren't into being right, this could be a lifetime go. Both of you like the opposite sex a little too much to maintain strict monogamy. But who is telling?

With Virgo SUN man: Clearly this is a match to steer far away from. You are likely to make each other unhappy. There seems to be little joy to be found here. He experiences you as wifty—off in your dreams and superficial. You know he is a nag—critical and oh, so boring. Get into dump mode fast here.

With Libra SUN man: You absolutely adore him to pieces. He knows how to speak to you. He is sensitive. And you're the complete woman he wants. You seem to intuitively know the right moves to please each other. You will forgive and actually cherish his eccentricities, such as struggling to make up his mind or having a hard time committing. You understand; you have similar issues.

With Scorpio SUN man: This man is intense and intriguing. You might even call him weird. Still, you like him and, given time and chemistry, you could passionately love him. However, he might find you a bit too detached once the courtship is over. The physical magnetism is undeniable here. P.S. He will win all the fights, so don't even try.

With Sagittarius SUN man: In this man, you've found a lifetime friend and adventurer. He will take risks and enjoy life, much as you do. You will like his sudden interludes of romance, and you'll enjoy his pioneering as a change of pace. He thinks the grass is greener on the other side of the fence until he meets you. Count on adventure, fun, and love.

With Capricorn SUN man: You might be attracted to his energy, but that is where it begins and ends. He will find you superficial, eccentric, and weird. You will think he is stodgy beyond belief. Why bother?

With Aquarius SUN man: It's important that you like each other's friends, and that they get along with each other, because both of you are devoted to friendships. You'll want to stage parties for your entire circle. He will love your delicate ways and your beauty. He'll also appreciate your tactfulness when he acts like a raging bull. Together, you have a unique way of looking at life.

With Pisces SUN man: You might be attracted. Unfortunately he is weird enough to attract your attention and become your boyfriend. He might drown you in his neediness and emotions. This is very hard on your need for space and freedom, yet you might feel too guilt-ridden to dump him. Welcome to chains and shackles.

MOON IN LIBRA, SUN IN PISCES

You cry at the movies, you cry when a friend tells you a sad story. You feel everything. You care a lot about the well-being of others. There is not a more sentimental person in the world than you. You are fragile, yet you are gentle with those in your immediate circle. Men often sense you as needy and could back away from you, perceiving you as a clinging vine.

Yet you are a very attractive and talented woman who offers much. You have an ethereal, magical quality with your exceptional femininity.

You want, you crave romance, yet you might settle for less. You are responsive to a man's neediness and dependency and have the capacity to get tied up in difficult relationships. You need to be clear about what YOU want from a relationship. Though you desire a sensitive man, you will want someone who is strong and can take the lead. You want a relationship with moments of enchantment. Somehow, you feel as if all your relationships are destined. And in some sense, you are right.

You will grow and change considerably during your lifetime. You might marry twice if your first spouse does not grow with you. This is quite possible because you tend to do too much for your partner, so that he comes to think you will always be there. Not so. You will jolt him with your sudden willingness to throw in the towel. The problem is you might have been saying you weren't happy but your actions undermined your words. Curb this tendency to be savior to so many if you want stronger relationships with those closest to you.

With Aries SUN man: He will appreciate your support, but he won't let you smother him. He will be off saving others. You can join him in his crusades and, when he comes home, relish the flames that you ignite. You are just plain good together. He will keep your spirits up, and you won't mope much with the Ram.

With Taurus SUN man: This man loves and understands your fragility. He appreciates your beauty and love of the good life. He provides security and stability, but he won't need you. You will need him. With him, you will be able to become the full, dynamic woman you have always wanted to be. There will be security, sensuality, and love in this match. This is a lifetime opportunity.

With Gemini SUN man: Craziness happens between you. You love his vitality, wit, and charm. You will have an idea of how he "should" be. Forget it. He is his own man, and you won't change him. Don't try being Miss Clingy either or he will race off in a cloud of dust. He won't understand your gothic feelings. This match will be touchy at best.

With Cancer SUN man: You could write the book on codependency here, but it's a happy story. If you get together, you're destined for a strong connection. You will love the way he can cry with you. There is also a strong sensual connection. He might not understand your sudden moments of detachment. Treat this man with love and you might live forever in your romantic castle on the water.

With Leo SUN man: The Lion's ability to court you and take your imagination through many delightful meanderings will make you want to be his. He loves grand passion, and you certainly can provide it. Be smart. Turn the other way should he wander a little. Not many women provide beauty, sensitivity, sensuality, and passion.

With Virgo SUN man: You attract as opposites. He is practical; you are in another world. He is logical, whereas you are a bundle of emotions. Where is the tie? You both love to serve others. If you can respect each other's style, this could be a go. Yet there is always a side of you that feels a bit incomplete. No candlelight dinners here unless he is saving on electricity!

With Libra SUN man: You will adore this man, and what is there to not adore? He meets your emotional needs. You both value romance, but you take him into mystical, sensual realms that he never knew existed. He won't ever leave you; he loves you to pieces. The problem is, neither of you is practical. You will nurture him and encourage him to take charge. He might or might not.

With Scorpio SUN man: He feels as deeply as you, though he might not show it the way you do. You know how the other feels, and indeed, there is a psychic tie. He is strong and will stabilize you. However, when you detach, he might feel a little put out. Jealousy could very well be the outcome, but that can be romantic too. After all, you are really cared about.

With Sagittarius SUN man: Steer clear of Mr. Risk-taker. He might make a wonderfully romantic figure to chase, but this match will not work. He will never be there for you and you will frequently be left hurting. Be smart and keep this man as your friend. You can have great talks together.

With Capricorn SUN man: This man spells stability and security. The initial courtship will delight you, but once this relationship is established, you might be dismayed. You might throw dramatic scenes. He will be confused, and neither of you will be happy. He will never understand what he sees as your perpetual state of PMS.

With Aquarius SUN man: Say no to this man for the long run, though there is an attraction. You will find fun in intimate moments. He's a huge flirt and a good friend. But the minute you become a weeping willow, he will split. Those kind of feelings scare the living daylights out of him.

With Pisces SUN man: He understands you, loves you, and wants only for you to be yourself with him. Cry, and he will cry along. He has your same sense of romance and drama. You appreciate his sensitive, creative nature. He loves your femininity and ethereal quality. Together you will experience all that is sensual, artistic, and romantic.

Moon in Scorpio

"Power is the ultimate aphrodisiac."
HENRY KISSINGER

You are shrouded by mystery. Because of your intense eyes and quality of remoteness, others are drawn to you, yet intimidated. You walk, talk, and act with sensuality, magic, and deep knowledge. You personify sexual enchantment and desirability.

You have tremendous strength and resilience. You're capable of attaining deep psychological levels, and can process your issues and clear their effect from your life. You are likely to reinvent yourself. However, until then, you can be a real tiger for others to deal with.

You demand complete and total loyalty. If you don't have that, you feel insecure, crushed, and betrayed. The real issue is you need to have total control in order to feel in control of your life. With this need, you unleash many unpleasant consequences on your loved ones if they don't follow YOUR guidelines. No one who tangles with you will ever forget your displeasure. Few will go into combat with you. They would prefer to give in.

But ultimately, what kind of relationship can you have if you do not allow your partners to display their colors? You see that your relationship won't have the depth you want if you limit your partner's expression. Your demands can lead to unhappiness and failure.

This pattern will repeat until you decide to work on your enormous need for control. You will experience fear, vulnerability. But feelings that others will never know should you decide to change. This isn't easy work, but it is great work.

You are likely to experience quite a few relationships as you work through your issues. You might be fortunate and find someone with the strength and dynamic power to understand you on the first shot. If so, your marriage will last.

Once someone falls in love with you, your magnetism might make it difficult to leave you. Men want you, often with little regard to the emotional cost. You are a powerful woman.

Once committed, you will work on your relationship, twist it, pull it apart, do whatever you need to make it work. However, if you're still in the early evolution of your Scorpio Moon personality, you could be very tough to deal with. The punishments you deal out can be hard to take. You might not see it, but those on the receiving end sure do. You are capable of creating one of those passionate, gothic novel love stories if all goes well.

You are the combination of extremes. It is all or nothing. This separates you from all the other Moon signs. No one can love more deeply and compassionately than you. However, no one can turn on or dislike someone with the same intensity either. Remember: The highest form of control is no control at all.

Moon in Scorpio, Sun in Aries

You have a fiery quality in addition to your strong Moon in Scorpio. You have incredible get-up-and-go, sprinkled with enthusiasm. Once focused, nothing will stop you. Your insistence and dynamic power can sometimes overwhelm the mere mortals who surround you. They will pull back and make way for you in nearly any realm of life.

You are more likely to lasso the man you want than any other Moon sign combination. Remember, you nearly always get what you want. The problem comes after the challenge is over. You might not want the man you so much coveted. What is interesting about your chase is that it is subtle enough that the man in question might think he did the chasing!

You are a formidable partner as well as enemy. You are an asset to anyone's team, if they give you the control you desire. If hard-pressed or pushed, you can demonstrate a powerful temper. You need a strong mate who can take your inevitable flare-ups.

You are among the most sexual of Scorpio Moon women, and for that reason want a committed relationship. You also are loyal and devoted once you trust your partner. You might feel jealous at times, but as you grow, this becomes less of an issue. Though you want to marry only once, the strength of your partner will determine whether your first marriage works.

With Aries SUN man: He is the match that lights you. He will forgive you when you approach a problem in a convoluted way. He doesn't have time to get that oblique. He loves you the way you are. Never forget, though, that he has a temper too. If you push too hard, you will get rammed.

With Taurus SUN man: He holds a monopoly on obstinacy. Nothing will turn him around once he makes a decision. You, yes you, will have to give in. There is an amazing sensual blending here of a nature that only Taurus can expose you to. If you can handle his laid-back nature and learn to say you're sorry, this could work. And be most steamy!

With Gemini SUN man: Here's a guy with great personality and sparkling wit. But he's not for you. Yes, there is a dynamic attraction, and you love hanging out with him. Both of you look for reasons as to why the universe does what it does. Though you have a mind-meld here, he lacks the physical passion to match you on other levels.

With Cancer SUN man: Like you, he can learn to form his emotions and use them to empower himself. He finds you like the Rock of Gibraltar. He cannot take your stinging comments and might eventually curl up in a ball, never to be vulnerable to you again. You must be very well behaved if you want this relationship to be happy ever after. He is the only one allowed to have a stinger.

With Leo SUN man: It isn't an easy match, yet it's one that has enough sexual glue to last. He will rage and roar at your insults. He might get so angry, he could want to play with other sweeter, young things. However, he will never experience the heat and intensity you offer. "Make love, not war" needs to be the household slogan. There is nothing halfway here.

With Virgo SUN man: This man is deliberate and practical, which you can appreciate. He has a sharp tongue, and when he decides to attack you, you know you have been chastised. Your animal ways heat him up to an intensity he is likely to never forget. You might not have the energetic, dynamic man you seek. Can you give that up?

With Libra SUN man: You might find there is a deep attraction between you, but pulling it together might take more than Houdini. He will run on the first attack and vanish. He hates confrontation; you are confrontational. Be careful, though. He could vanish at any given moment. And it could be forever.

With Scorpio SUN man: Though you like to be in control, you will lose it here. Partially because the passion is so fierce, you will be helpless and vulnerable. You both need to be committed to growth and to getting past your vindictive tendencies. This relationship could be whatever both of you want it to be—World War III or the love of your life.

With Sagittarius SUN man: This man amazes you with his great energy, but you might be hard-pressed to find the intensity here that you so deeply desire. Though you really like him, he might ultimately prove to be too wifty. He isn't into your type of games. He doesn't have time, even with all that you offer.

With Capricorn SUN man: This man can match your passion. Eventually, he will get fed up with Scorpio negative traits. He can't be controlled. It might not be worth the effort anyway. He is interested but ultimately it is your call. See: You are in control after all!

With Aquarius SUN man: You like his independence and unconventional ways. He is his own person. As easygoing as he is, he can be as obstinate as you. Your passion intrigues him and adds another dimension to his creative lovemaking. You like this man, but ultimately decide he is a cold fish. Again, another one that is your call.

With Pisces SUN man: This man is needy, though possibly very active, creative, and dynamic. He will buckle under your Scorpio ways and lovestyle. Count on being dominant. If you hurt him with your stinging comments, he might actually like it. On some level, he expects abuse and pain in loving. The problem is how neurotic this could get—for both of you.

MOON IN SCORPIO, SUN IN TAURUS

You certainly are a complex creature, as you have complex feelings and seem to be overly concerned with being right and in control. Yes, you are extremely alluring and charming, yet one immediately gets a strong sense that you are no lightweight. You also give off conflicting impressions, reflecting your inner conflicts. You want security above all.

You're a black belt in the art of manipulation. You might actually believe manipulation is how to make a relationship work. Unless you outgrow this tendency, you might find yourself going through men like panty hose.

When a man who is strong, yet gentle, crosses your path, you might stop. You need someone like this. He must also have financial promise if you are going to spend your life with him. You will expect a full courtship and love ritual. This process will make you feel more secure; you need the slow pace, but will keep every small gift as symbols of his caring.

Many of you will marry once, most likely your first love. You have tremendous passion. If you allow yourself to be free and not defensive, you and your partner will get to know the hot lady who lives inside of you. Taming the wildness inside of you is a full-time occupation. But what a glorious, full person you can become.

With Aries SUN man: When he meets you, this man might take off running as fast as he can. You are attractive to him, but he senses the human powerhouse he just ran into. He wants to be the dominant person in his relationship. He knows it wouldn't be him here. Don't pine away for this man. He made the right decision for both of you.

With Taurus SUN man: He will give you the slow, easy courtship you need. There will be sensuality, security, and understanding with this man. He knows how to get close, and that might lead you to lower your defenses. It is scary having someone know you so well. Be careful how hard you push him away in your defensive moments. You could lose this very special man.

With Gemini SUN man: This man isn't your cup of tea, though he is interesting. How can someone be so light, witty, and whimsical? You might admire these qualities and wish you were like him, but he can't offer you what you want. He is attracted to you. This could be a fun romp, but nothing else. He won't stick around.

With Cancer SUN man: This man wants material security as much as you do, and he's likely to provide it. He is very emotional, and by contrast you seem like the Rock of Gibraltar. If you nip at him too much, he will develop a hard, crablike shell. He might stay with you, but the emotional intimacy will be lost. The odd thing is both of you could be comfortable without the intense sharing.

With Leo SUN man: Talk about passion, heat, and uncontrollable emotions! He senses the animal in you and, as the King of Love, he will chase you until you become his. You will be dewy-eyed; the problems begin when you become difficult. He is into romance, not power plays. However, he won't give in either. He will just go off and play with someone else, leaving you hurt and betrayed. Do you want this?

With Virgo SUN man: You can count on his serenity, logic, and helpfulness to stabilize you and encourage you to live life to the fullest. However, fullest to him is half a cup to you. He will never have the emotional heat you have, though he will enjoy your blazing sexuality. Both of you could be happy. He just won't understand the depth of your feelings.

With Libra SUN man: You have found the zodiac's weakling, in your terms. He can't make a decision. He will cower at your mood swings and head for the hills. He is so charming, you might want to take a spin with him. Remember, this is a truly gentle soul. Do be nice.

With Scorpio SUN man: He is powerful and dynamic, so sexy and hot, your fires will be continually stoked. You will know what it is like to be consumed, and he will love every moment of it. Remember, he is as jealous as you are, so be very careful with him. You don't want the battle to even begin. This is love on all levels. And a scorcher too.

With Sagittarius SUN man: You find that this man is hard to keep up with. He loves money, but he will risk and gamble. Heaven forbid! You cannot do this. If you ever catch up with him, have a fling, but forget the long term. No, no, no!

With Capricorn SUN man: There's security aplenty with this man. He has money, power, and seemingly control over his environment. He is very sexy, and with him, you display the power of your sexuality. You will feel so comfortable with him, you can even share your fears and worries. He will respond in a big way. You can find stability and happiness here.

With Aquarius SUN man: To you, he is the madman of the zodiac. You love his quirky sexuality; you like his eccentricities. With him you will find insecurity, unpredictability, and other women at every twist and turn. But they are friends! You can't tolerate this in any way, shape, or form. You'd become a nervous wreck.

With Pisces SUN man: You reach out for this emotional man, as you identify with him. You will be feeling and caring with him. However, you could get distraught, as he provides instability. You could love each other, yet at some point you will attack him. He will get very upset. You need to resolve some of your neediness to have a happy relationship here.

MOON IN SCORPIO, SUN IN GEMINI

This is an exquisite combination. You have the depth of a Scorpio Moon. You are capable of great transformation. You are able to verbalize the emotional highs and lows of this powerful Moon. Because of your willingness to talk, you will be able to negotiate many of your issues, such as jealousy and a total need for control. However, you could talk another to death as you work through the issue of the moment.

You are bright, flirtatious, and sensual. Others are attracted. They cannot deny your charisma. It is important for you to pick and choose from among your many would-be suitors. After all, you have it all, and your charm brings others in for a closer look.

You could enjoy multiple relationships, as you feel safe that way and are lured by your need for constant variety. If you are to settle down, you need to find someone with the versatility and desirability that you have.

You need a man who appreciates variety and excitement, just like you. Your experimenting and being open is key to your relationship. You're unlikely to lose a man, as he will be too attracted to leave. You are not only bright, but also one hot mama. You will make a sensual wife and a wonderful partner who will never, ever be boring.

With Aries SUN man: You could easily flip over him, and he over you. He loves your ideas and might be off making them realities before you can count to ten. He makes you feel valued and cared about. He has heat and natural magnetism that can match your eternal flame. The two of you could easily have it all. Say yes to the first date.

With Taurus SUN man: He can talk ideas, but is interested in the arts and money. He has a deep, easy sensuality that will draw you to him. This can be an excellent match if you can get past the fact that he isn't as mental as you. He is even; you are intense. You do a nice balancing act together. Your dance is long term, with a chemistry that keeps on cooking.

With Gemini SUN man: Here you have the ultimate playmate. Ideas flash, and you seem to have your own language together. He's a bit of a flirt and a playboy, but your sexuality could anchor him. It doesn't get much better, and he knows it. This is a lifetime adventure. The two of you make your own amusement park.

With Cancer SUN man: This man is moody and loves your emotionality. However, your ideas and fine mental acumen have no place in his world. You will get angry and give a Scorpion punch that will leave him curled up. Ultimately, this cannot work because you will not like each other forever. However, for a little snuggling, it's okay.

With Leo SUN man: He is romantic and sensual. Your ideas and flirtation reel him in faster than he would like. He is quite the playboy, but don't worry. Your sizzling love nature will have him coming back, again and again and again. Plus, he will love your mind and want to share his world with you. This could be a perfect match if you know when NOT to get stubborn.

With Virgo SUN man: He likes your sensuality and is drawn to you. However, you won't like his pickiness and critical ways. He doesn't understand your need to think, experiment, and discuss. For you it is exciting and revealing. For him, it is needless chatter. You will end up verbally battering each other in the long run.

With Libra SUN man: This man has the charm and wit to meet your constantly inquiring mind. The flirtation between you could be naughty and exquisite. At a restaurant others might eavesdrop on your seductive exchange. Your passion makes him smolder. This man who has trouble committing will have no problem with you. You just need to learn to talk about your jealousy rather than act on it.

With Scorpio SUN man: He is as hot as you and loves your love-dance. You two act like you are wild animals in the jungle. However, when you talk, he might not get it. If he does respond, you could find your controlling games transform to a wonderful loving negotiation. You will love the way he touches your soul. You could have it all.

With Sagittarius SUN man: You and he have a strong attraction. He has the courage to act on your ideas. This is quite flattering to you. He does risk, and somehow this could threaten your need for material security. That's where the problem lies. There is no lack of passion and adoration between you. If you can handle the lack of security, this could work.

With Capricorn SUN man: This man is intensely drawn to you, is willing to court you, love you, and give you half of his empire. His mind, however, might be off working on moneymaking schemes rather than enjoying your ideas, discourse, and witty exchanges. If you have friends who can satisfy this strong need in you, you could be happy. But with this man, you won't have it all.

With Aquarius SUN man: His far-out, inventive mind intrigues and draws you. You will have a picnic no matter what you do together. You will love how he mixes his mind with his passion. This might work, as long as you can be secure. He loves his friends almost more than you. It might be best to keep this as a naughty friendship.

With Pisces SUN man: You cannot deal with this poor man's inability to process. You can identify with his propensity to be a victim, as that is one of your specialties. But you know there is more to life than being down-and-out. He can't do what you can; he doesn't have the same ability to transform. Ultimately you will attack him and crucify him. Pass on this one.

MOON IN SCORPIO, SUN IN CANCER

You are emotional, sensitive, and intuitive. You sometimes know what is coming before it does. This ability enhances your capacity to understand and relate.

You have a natural way of connecting and understanding. Others are drawn to your wisdom. However, you have traveled a difficult route to come to terms with your sensitivity. You have faced deep emotions and perhaps have sunk low, enabling you to soar later. You understand life's ups and downs. You reach out and are there for others as they slide into their emotional valleys.

You're likely to have ethereal looks, with big, deep eyes. You aren't afraid of eye contact. Others feel as if you see through them.

More than most Moons in Scorpio, you realize that you have no control over others. Ironically, because of your ability to connect, you have more influence than you realize.

Men who are drawn to you often have courage and the ability to appreciate your gifts and stability. Sure, you can bite, but you are too empathetic to inflict hurt thoughtlessly. Still, you aren't a toy to be played with.

If you are hurt, you're likely to close down for a while. Your trust is a very powerful gift. Should you choose to withdraw it, your loved ones will feel the loss keenly. You don't need to revert to vengeance and power plays. You have enough power within to control yourself and your choices. You are greatly gifted. Your presence is welcomed—or sorely missed.

With Aries SUN man: Though an attraction exists between you, this man is fiery and, with you, could create little but steam. You might be disappointed that he doesn't want to spend hours at home with the family. He is a crusader, a pioneer, and unless his pet cause is his familial rights (which you could identify with), your interests probably won't mesh.

With Taurus SUN man: Where you are emotionally deep, he is grounded and profound. Dates are romantic, intense, and have a slow, steady pace. You can trust this man. He will delight in your special recipes and love of home. You feed each other sexually, emotionally, and spiritually. Count on a lifetime of romance.

With Gemini SUN man: You could find yourself in serious emotional pain if you even try here. There might not even be enough draw for a friendship, yet there can be a sexual attraction. You sense his erotic dexterity, and he understands your steamy sensuality. Still, stay away.

With Cancer SUN man: Both of you are emotional and tend to withdraw when hurt. Your mutual love of water can have you holding hands, walking along a romantic shore—or, playing on water beds. Like water, moonlight soothes your souls. You intuitively know how to love each other. This bonding can be your dream come true.

With Leo SUN man: The attraction is intense and hot, yet difficult for both of you to manage. At some point you could start putting each other down. Your aloofness and hypnotic qualities draw him. You will douse his enthusiasm and call him superficial when he hurts your feelings. And problems just continue to mount.

With Virgo SUN man: He is cool, practical, and detached. He will have a tough time understanding you deeply; you won't be able to comprehend him either. These differences could affect your lovemaking. He is detail-oriented; you are passionate. You could learn to coexist well. But is this what you want?

With Libra SUN man: Other than sexuality, there is little happening here. In fact, you could irritate each other and start bickering with your first encounter. He will run from your deep feelings, and you will consider his avoidance of confrontation and lack of intensity wimpy. No way, José!

With Scorpio SUN man: This is heavenly. He can be as intuitive and mesmerizing as you. You are like two streams flowing into one river together. The sensuality is out of this world, and your understanding is natural. Loving each other just is. Listen to each other's bugaboos and you won't get into trouble. This is as good as it gets.

With Sagittarius SUN man: Steer clear here, though you are attracted to his moneymaking skills. Everything else screams for you to stay miles away. He is a wanderer, a risker. You will be shrieking or sobbing before you know it. And where is he? Gone.

With Capricorn SUN man: He offers you stability, grounding, and security. He will love your ethereal quality and adore you as a bedmate. You might find him comforting in some ways, though he will never understand your depth and emotionality. This relationship requires mutual respect. The attraction is long term, a love that lasts.

With Aquarius SUN man: Though you have a mutual interest in the occult and spirituality, that is where it begins and ends. He is flighty and involved in ideas. You have great difficulty relating to him and vice versa. Why bother?

With Pisces SUN man: This man needs you and will do whatever is necessary to maintain the kind of relationship that will keep you happy and close. You will be the dominant one, almost certainly. There is an intuitive sensual understanding between you. He is uncanny. He knows how to have you vibrating with his sensual magic. In other realms, you wear the pants.

MOON IN SCORPIO, SUN IN LEO

Others feel your presence when you walk into a room. You radiate excitement, vitality, and depth. Your presence is an invitation to live life with joy and commitment.

People have trouble saying no to you, which can be more of a problem than it might seem. Yet later, they might resent what they agreed to or did to court your favor. What did you do? In fact, you will respect people more if they do not compromise their integrity.

You are showy, beautiful, and deep. But wow, are you stubborn. You offer a lot, but you're determined to have things run as you think they should. You have a tendency to wear the pants in any relationship; you're that strong and dominant, yet still very feminine.

You choose strong men. Weak ones don't interest you. You enjoy a strong man's submission and his appreciation as well. It's not that every day goes by smoothly. You like the ups and downs of conflicting egos. It only adds to the passion.

You would like one marriage, but are likely to have more. The problem is your strength. Unless you find a man equal to you, relationships break down.

Meeting your emotional needs proves to be a challenge in your life. Sometimes you feel lonely. The irony of your powerful charisma is that it brings people to you, but also prevents you from forming open, sharing friendships. There always seems to be another agenda.

With Aries SUN man: You are two torches ablaze, with their fires merging. This man is as into living as you and very much committed to you. You will share grand passion with him and learn many different ways of relating. It is fine with him if you command the emotional ship; he has too much on his plate anyway. You will never burn each other out.

With Taurus SUN man: He is sedate, while you are explosive. He is artistic, while you are charismatic. You appreciate the differences, as does he. He will help you build long-term security. The courtship goes way past normal wooing. It adds to the steaminess you share and will continue through the years. This man's an excellent bet, though your battles could be tough. He is as stubborn as you.

With Gemini SUN man: You are drawn to his childlike joy, his grownup mind, and his teenage desire to experiment sexually. The good news is you can have it your way. He adds another dimension to your life, like a breath of fresh air. Odds are good for a long-term, magical exchange and commitment.

With Cancer SUN man: He will give in to you. He'll provide a home for you equal to your magnificence. He will understand your strength, adore your depth, and be an enthusiastic lover. So what is wrong? You are likely to get bored. Inevitably, you will find yourself with a major case of wanderlust. If you decide the grass is greener elsewhere, bye-bye.

With Leo SUN man: He is everything you ever wanted in a man, though he needs to be appreciated and adored for his Lion ways. You will have a big problem if the magic ever wears off. The romps are endless, and the quality of life magnificent. You find he is a like spirit. He used to be a player until he met you. He knows what he has.

With Virgo SUN man: Though you could *like* Mr. Virgo, there is nothing much more here than a romp in the hay. A friendship is even difficult because he will always want more, and it just ain't there, no matter how hard you try. Scratch him off your list.

With Libra SUN man: In this man you've chosen the gentle and the pretty. It is a good thing that you wear the pants, because he cannot make a decision. He is the king of waffling. He will court you and absolutely adore your femininity, depth, and strength. He might feel put out when you tell him off and vanish, but not for long. Your charisma saves the day.

With Scorpio SUN man: Neither villains nor life's outrageous twists can interfere with the torrid state of this affair. He might growl, but he can't say no to you. You are the honey he craves in his life. You both want control. Why not divide up your domain so both of you can control? You will love each other forever. Whether you can live together forever depends on your communication.

With Sagittarius SUN man: This man is always off tilting at windmills but will fall flat on his face when he sees you. He will want you, and you definitely will have a good time. You'll be two frisky colts together. However, when you get serious and deep, he gets scared and takes off. If you can handle his trepidation, you could have a fiery match here.

With Capricorn SUN man: He has the stability women long for. He offers you his allegiance and will share his empire. You will have the money to play with and a man who honors your depth. But a playmate, no. He is all about work, and you are about living life to the fullest. This is a conflict of interests. You won't change him either.

With Aquarius SUN man: He is about friendship and camaraderie; you are about living and loving. Yet the twain do meet here. You find him a huge flirt who is erotically adventuresome. However, he can't relate to your emotionality and ponds of feelings. It isn't there for him. Understand that before you enter into this match.

With Pisces SUN man: Mr. Emotional reads your true depth quite clearly. He will cling to you for security. This might be okay for you, as he is quite the romantic and will make every moment an adventure. You will help him mobilize his unusual talents and make money with them. This is an arty, love affair that could last the whole way.

MOON IN SCORPIO, SUN IN VIRGO

You are grounded, practical, and think before you act. You mean well and want the best for everyone. Because you tame the torrential emotions of the Scorpio Moon with the reflective, thoughtful Virgo qualities, you are easy to get along with compared to your sister Scorpio Moons.

However, you are demanding. You know what you want and will not settle for less. You are practical and make grounded choices emotionally and professionally. Your high-quality choices reflect your efficient, caring nature.

You are a very attractive woman and, genes willing, diminutive in some ways. You move quietly and gently. You have a profound sense of what is right and wrong, which you carry into your relationships. At some point, you fought a battle between your lustful nature and your high morality. You put form and shape to your emotions.

You want a man who can be practical and take care of your worlds together. You have enough feelings for both of you, so if he is a bit detached, that's okay. You would rather have a good provider, a kind husband, and a nurturing father. You appreciate his attention to details and management of the finances.

Courtship doesn't need to be as sultry as for other Scorpio Moons. You find happiness if he pitches in and makes your life easier. You might appreciate roses, but you are just as happy if he fixes your plumbing. The right man will comfort you when you are overwhelmed by feelings and help you sift through them.

With Aries SUN man: Though he is oh, so desirable and hot, he doesn't fulfill your needs. He has lots of spark and is not one to be contained. In the long run, you will attack him for not being more practical, and he won't understand at all. He's been the same person from day one.

With Taurus SUN man: You are definitely attracted, and he is waiting and willing. He likes your grounding, but is also attracted to your passion. He will court you carefully, drawing out the animal in you. He offers much and helps you connect with the emotional volcano that seethes within. You feel safe, comfortable, and well loved.

With Gemini SUN man: He can play head games beyond your imagination. He is a tease and full of ideas. You sense his sensuality and want to romp with him. However, the problem is that practicality is not in his vocabulary. You will discard him once you discover that you can't mold him. Keep Mr. Gemini as a friend.

With Cancer SUN man: He is loving and understands your depth. He appreciates and values your prim side. Together you build a wonderful life with many emotional high points. He will lean on your judgment and practicality and can provide the security you need. Remember, he doesn't respond to sharp words. Gentleness and logic are the way to his soul.

With Leo SUN man: He is dashing and wonderfully romantic. You might be attracted and even have a taste or two, but in the long run, this is a huge nix. He won't be the logical, dependable man you want. He is a wildfire, full of life. You will get tired of his need for adoration, and he will start playing where he is worshiped. For happiness, look elsewhere.

With Virgo SUN man: You like this man. If you think YOU are practical, check this guy out. The only problem could be if you define order differently, as both of you demand it. He has the logic and clarity you seek. You will arouse passion in him. He will never want to leave you. You might snap at each other on occasion, but you both understand that kind of communication.

With Libra SUN man: You will be very hard on this impractical man. He is sweet and loving, but flunks as far as being your type. You will criticize and nitpick, but you can never change him. You will be dissatisfied, and he will be hurt. Leave this one alone for both your sakes.

With Scorpio SUN man: It almost seems he was married to you in a past life. He loves your ways and your ability to be a practical, passionate partner. He likes your sometimes prudish behavior, especially since he knows the seething passion that lies beneath the surface. You will win your fights because you are more logical. He will admire you even if he loses!

With Sagittarius SUN man: You find this man thrilling, but more in the context of a horror movie. There is nothing wrong with him, there is nothing wrong with you, but you are very different people. He is off yonder, full of adventure. You want what is practical and works. No risks for you. And that means no to this match.

With Capricorn SUN man: He is as practical and earthy as you, only he seems to have bigger plans. You can go along, except when his moneymaking ideas scare you. You need to trust his business acumen. He really gets into your steamy emotions and intensity. He finds you close to perfect; he can be your ideal partner. He will help you grow throughout your life.

With Aquarius SUN man: Oops! Turn the other way and walk. He might be caring about others, but that is where the similarity ends. He is eccentric and somewhat unpredictable. He has none of the same desires as you, and practical? Could you define that?

With Pisces SUN man: Here is the ultimate challenge and reward. You are nearly opposites, though you have a common intensity of feelings. You might be able to discipline your emotions, while for him, they slosh in every direction. He needs your sensibility and support to unleash his true creative power. You will be the practical one here, but he will say thank you in so many ways!

MOON IN SCORPIO, SUN IN LIBRA

You personify passion and romance. You radiate femininity no matter what you do. You have a strong, emotional temperament and know what you want, though you sometimes shy away from asking for that. You have power and strength that deceives others. You project as light, accessible, and desirable.

Men respond to your qualities and want to get to know you, though they have no idea what a tiger they've found. You might never display your intense Scorpio characteristics until you are deeply connected.

You can be very rigid about what you want. This is a reaction to your sometimes having difficulty making a decision. Once you land, you stay put. To get you to change your mind is a tough challenge.

Partnership is very important to you, and often you speak in terms of "we" when there is none. Everyone is your pal. Sometimes you have a problem discerning acquaintances from friends. Part of this problem comes from your driving need for partnership. Also you are sometimes satisfied with the superficial and don't look deeper.

You want a man who appreciates the lighter side of life and who can relate to the artist and romantic in you. Fairness is an important characteristic as well. He needs to remember you will always want roses and romance. As you emotionally develop, your profound Scorpio Moon becomes more dominant. Then you find yourself dissatisfied with "his" superficial ways. Why isn't there more feeling and emotion? He reflects a side of your nature, and you chose him. Accept him, and you will accept yourself.

With Aries SUN man: The attraction is very strong; he is passionate and direct, and wants you. You light his fire and feed it. Once he discovers how steamy you really are beneath that exterior, he is addicted. You like his fairness, directness, and concern for others. If you can forgive his crusades and absences, this love affair can last forever.

With Taurus SUN man: This man is an artist on some level. You will share luxurious meals and enchanting dates. You'll love his quiet, earthy approach. You tumble in love steadily and perhaps permanently. Your depth is like glue to this deeply practical man. Together, you build the sensuality. You have found your Rock of Gibraltar.

With Gemini SUN man: He will have you laughing from the get-go, and you might chortle together for a long time. He is intellectual in his courtship. He writes poems and love letters, and tweaks your imagination. Your heat might surprise him, but he can get into it. You love his inventive lovemaking. And so this could go for a lifetime.

With Cancer SUN man: He offers the traditional symbols you desire: home, family, romance. Yet he gets gooey. You draw understanding from your deeply emotional side, but you might not like the way he emotes in nearly all situations. You could find yourself criticizing him and then him turning into his nickname: the Crab.

With Leo SUN man: He can knock your socks off. The traditional attraction between Leo and Scorpio comes into play, and the passion is intense. He is romantic; you are hot. He will not wander on you because he will be too busy taking care of you. It is as important to him as to you. However, when you fight, both of you are too stubborn to give in. Now somebody has to, to make this work. Is he worth it? I think so.

With Virgo SUN man: You will be unhappy as this man criticizes your need to buy flowers (can't plants do?) and your love of the frivolous. He doesn't like paying for expensive dinners when you can cook such meals, unsurpassed in his opinion by any restaurant. And a lot cheaper. Even if there is some sexual energy, discard this relationship or forget the things you want.

With Libra SUN man: You love his delightful charm and wit. He knows how to court you perfectly, and of course, you will tumble into his arms, madly in love. However, you will be the stronger one here, needing to make the decisions. This could make you uncomfortable as the months become years. After all, who takes care of whom here?

With Scorpio SUN man: The chemistry overwhelms you both. The sparks fly, and you might not care that you never made it out the door on your first date. Eventually you might ask for more ritual. He will give you ritual all right, so much so that you won't even dream of looking elsewhere. A matching of passion and depth here.

With Sagittarius SUN man: He is full of adventure, but perhaps is a little too unconventional in his choices for you. Do you really want to go to a baseball game on your first date? He will give you a kitten instead of flowers. Your intense femininity stokes his interest so much that he might give up his wanderlust. Expect fun and adventure.

With Capricorn SUN man: Yes he knows how to court and he can make strong decisions for both of you. This might or might not be okay with you, depending on your need for control. You will always have money and security, though eventually he will forget the flowers and other symbols of romance. He will often say yes to anything. That's your ace.

With Aquarius SUN man: His eccentricities will make you laugh, and the two of you will be great buddies. Now if you get serious, there is something lacking here for the long term. He has neither the depth nor the intensity to sustain you. And courtship is downright weird with him. Stay friends.

With Pisces SUN man: This man draws you like honey does a bear. You will adore his artistry in all realms, and he is a kindred soul emotionally. However, he is needy and you might find yourself always trying to keep him whole. Once you bond, separating is close to impossible. The two of you are hooked.

MOON IN SCORPIO, SUN IN SCORPIO

You sizzle. Within you lie smoldering passions and intense feelings. Sometimes they overwhelm you, and you become reactive. Because you're so sensitive, you could judge that someone is hurting you, when no hurt is intended. You have been known to be vindictive and difficult. Yet the men cannot stay away from you.

Your biggest asset is your depth and innate wisdom. You are a powerful lover and demand total loyalty and control. You could want to experiment and know several different kinds of people and relationships during your lifetime.

You tend to be one-sided. You sometimes cannot understand others, or, more likely, you attach your reasons to their behavior, often missing the mark. You must learn to ask, which could be hard for you as you fear making yourself vulnerable. Actually, others will see it as a mark of an inquiring, open person.

You will grow enormously through such study of human behavior and become rich in your knowledge of others. You will also learn to use your need for control for self-discipline. For you, the meaning of "the highest control is no control" is baffling, but can become a profound revelation.

You will want a man like you: strong, reserved, and willing to penetrate the recesses of the mind. He might be a bit quiet and withdrawn, but you will be able to sense where he's at. There might be a near-telepathic connection. He needs to read through your sometimes defensive but strong reactions. The more evolved and loving he is, the more you will grow.

With Aries SUN man: This man is expressive, strong, and confrontational. You might be desperately attracted, as he will be to you, but don't think this match is easy. He will not tolerate your games and designs. You will never understand each other, unless you are willing to communicate continually, and you realize he is a different person than you.

With Taurus SUN man: He is slow and easy. He understands you, and there is a strong sexual bonding. He tends to be quiet and sometimes withdrawn, like you. You might need to spell out your thinking, because sometimes he is bullheaded. You cannot find a more gentle, tender, yet strong man. An excellent long-term choice.

With Gemini SUN man: He is the opposite of you. He's full of talk and is happy performing a monologue. He might even start answering himself and pretending he is you. The humor could be endless, and you could gain insight about other people's thoughts and feelings from him. He won't stick around if you attack him, as he is charming and can have many women. There is sexual glue here.

With Cancer SUN man: He expects to be understood and indulged, as you do. Though eventually you can come to an understanding, there might be some hard moments. If you criticize, he will become cold and remote. You love his warmth, feelings, and passion, so honor his needs. You could nest a long time with this man. You seem to read each other cold.

With Leo SUN man: This man is dynamic, strong, and a terrific lover. He will zero in on you and want to explore the dark recesses of your mind, body, and soul. The passion is as good as it gets. However, he won't tolerate vindictiveness or jealousy. He'd rather go off to where the picking is better, despite the great passion. Careful. He could break your heart.

With Virgo SUN man: This man is one cool cucumber. What you go through is unfathomable to him. He provides stability, practicality, and strong judgments. If you are naughty, sarcastic, and vindictive, he knows the words to chastise you. You have tremendous sexual power over this man, and can use it to gain what you want. If you want control, you can have it here.

With Libra SUN man: He is flighty; you are deep. He'd rather not feel; you can't help but feel. He can't make a decision; you are strong-willed. Your emotionality could get to him and he could feel as if he is drowning with you. You might feel like you have a long-term flake on your hands. Maybe, maybe not. Oops! I sound like him.

With Scorpio SUN man: It might be interesting to see your male counterpart. You are probably stronger than he is and will win the battles. In between the holdouts and power plays, there is wild passion. Eventually you will iron out your conflicts, though you will keep each other under lock and key. You both are so possessive!

With Sagittarius SUN man: He is a foreigner to you and best left that way. He might toy with you, but once your anger boils up, he will decide he doesn't want that kind of relationship. He is about living and enjoying. He doesn't understand control struggles. And he doesn't want to either.

With Capricorn SUN man: Your tough stands will roll over this man like water. You will have to learn to relate differently if you want to communicate. It is worth it because this man is just as sensual as you are. You can have many wonderful times together if you just let go and lighten up. In exchange, he will provide money, stability, and great lovemaking. Say yes.

With Aquarius SUN man: He wonders if you're an alien enchantress. He has never seen such sexiness, but he doesn't understand your lack of verbalizing and chatter. He might or might not pick up on your depth, but he is everyone's friend, and that can irritate you. You want your partner to be yours.

With Pisces SUN man: Pisces often plays the martyr, and that can even be a bit of a turn-on for them. So it is okay with them if once in a while you get difficult; it only charges up their love energy. There is an intuitive level to your intimate encounters that you cannot have with any other man. You can trust him with your feelings. He will understand.

MOON IN SCORPIO, SUN IN SAGITTARIUS

You are a combination of steamy feelings and hot action. Whether these characteristics blend or become part of an internal juggling act is your call. Sometimes you feel betrayed by your impulsive actions; other times it seems as if your powerful feelings undo you. You are your own harshest critic.

You are an active person; you are deep. It has been said there is nothing sexier than energy, which you have in abundance. Yet you have the deep mysterious ways of a Scorpio Moon. Often you might say little and let your body language speak.

Men find you extremely desirable, even if you're withdrawn or unavailable. You adore playing, getting into a hard game of a racquetball or going to a fun spectator sport. Your dexterity is much admired.

You do have deep feelings. Learn to own your feelings and discuss them, and you will be well on the path to a quality relationship. As for passion, you'll always have that!

You want an active playmate for a suitor, lover, and husband. You prefer someone who isn't afraid of you or life, who is willing to take a risk. The two of you will be busier than most couples would dream of. You will want to go everywhere and do everything. Then there will be your private times, which are much the same. It's important that you don't sacrifice one side of yourself for another. Your attractiveness will bring you many choices, so be very picky.

With Aries SUN man: The two of you explode in passion. He will tolerate your overwhelming feelings and try to help you with them. He won't make judgments either, but you might when he is running around on his latest campaign. You might feel as if he is running away from you. He isn't. Understand this and you can be very happy with another fiery spirit like yours.

With Taurus SUN man: He provides words for your melody. There is a pull between you that is undeniable. The attraction can carry you through a lifetime. He will understand your inner self perhaps better than you. He is a moneymaker and will provide the best of life. He will love your physical nature, and you will love his endurance. The two of you make fine music together.

With Gemini SUN man: This could be a torrid love affair, but it could easily encounter trouble. You'll adore his mind and his physical dexterity. But eventually, you'll lose respect for him, judging that he's all words and no action. You want someone who lives his words. Long after the relationship has ended, you could enjoy a toasty reunion.

With Cancer SUN man: He is emotional and evokes strong feelings in you. You need to be gentle with this man, because if hurt, he could close you out. He loves his home and isn't an adventurer either. However, he is physically active, and that you like. If you are wise, the differences between you can be a great strength rather than a problem.

With Leo SUN man: He is a romantic and whisks you off your feet. You will intrigue him with your energy, deep sensuality, and mysterious nature. You are the handful that he has been looking for. But are you sure you want him? He is very self-indulgent, but always a good time. Both of you are so stubborn. Your battles could be titanic, and the making up sublime.

With Virgo SUN man: This man is a cold fish in your book. He's detached, careful, and practical; you are fiery and impulsive. Your differences are so great, they probably can never be resolved. You might not even be attracted. Just as well.

With Libra SUN man: He is the air that feeds your flame. The passion between you will constantly regenerate. Be careful with your anger, though. You could blow him out and have him running. But with the kind of attachment that exists between you, he will return. He isn't the decision-maker, you are. So decide what you want here.

With Scorpio SUN man: You melt together into a sea of oblivion. There is little to think about or consider. It just is. You feel perfect for each other. He has physical stamina, and you are a fiery live wire. Though there will be power struggles, as you both are always right, but you discover it's worth it when you kiss and make up. This is a lifetime sizzler.

With Sagittarius SUN man: You like everything about this man. He is passionate, lively, and adventuresome. The two of you could frolic from one escapade to another and never be bored. He will not identify with your feelings, but they won't bother him. On the other hand, you might be too busy to drift into overwhelmingly emotional scenarios. This match could be long term.

With Capricorn SUN man: There is a deep sensuality that he rouses in you. Expect many sizzling times together. If you can adapt to his passion for money, you'll have a good thing going. He will provide for your whims (especially if they are investments) and he'll stabilize your heavy undercurrents. Both of you will want a total commitment here, and it can last.

With Aquarius SUN man: This man can appreciate your fun-loving nature. You actually give him insight into his far-out ways. You understand his deep interest in aliens and the avant-garde. After all, you like the occult. This can be a fun affair. However, problems develop if you expect him to identify with your feelings. He is oh, so detached.

With Pisces SUN man: You are emotionally drawn to this mound of emotions and feelings. You keep trying to cheer him up by offering him tickets to the football game. He doesn't get it; you don't get it. Just forget it! Eventually you will be on the opposite sides of the fence.

MOON IN SCORPIO, SUN IN CAPRICORN

You are a wonderful blend of boundless emotions and are grounded practically. You know what you want and you won't be sidetracked. Men find you a formidable partner who expects to be treated equally. You will want to partake in your partner's life and help create the quality of life you expect.

You have a mystical quality that draws others and allows you to understand their thoughts and feelings, perhaps before they do. You want to help others realize what is possible. Resourcefulness marks your relationships, life, and career. You always have an answer.

You will get better with age. Your desirability will increase as you greet maturity. You offer wisdom, a smoldering sensuality, and a high level of intensity. Men who are drawn to you want a woman who is strong, stable, and sexy. You offer even more. Physically, you are earthy and alluring. Men know you have substance emotionally and physically. You are there; you are real. Even your walk intimates sensuality.

You will choose a man who is grounded and makes sound choices. He needs to be a provider with a good sense of finances. He needs to reflect a wisdom similar to yours, though you will be the more emotional onc. You'll want him to understand and appreciate boundless feelings. You want to touch his heart and not frighten him.

With Aries SUN man: This man has passion and determination. He loves your heat, but might have a problem with your seriousness. Though he likes power and money as you do, there is more to life than that. He needs someone who can frolic and experience life in his style. This match is good for a fling, but destined for hassles.

With Taurus SUN man: Don't count on separating once you merge. You will always want each other. Better yet, you see eye-to-eye about life, money, and priorities. He will indulge a little too much, in your opinion. But you can deal with that and maybe even learn to like it! You grow old happily together.

With Gemini SUN man: Odds are, you will be attracted. There is a learning experience here for both of you, but the chances of longevity are slim. He doesn't understand your emotions or your practicality. He is about ideas and wit with a splash of drama. Don't bark up this tree.

With Cancer SUN man: Provided that you respect each other's differences, there will be much love and spiritual bonding. He needs your logic and practical touch; you like his drive for security and his emotional panorama. You make music together. And your private time has an emotional tenor that is unique, even to you. This is a yes.

With Leo SUN man: You like the way this man handles his money, but at times you judge him frivolous and superficial. He makes you laugh and has the ability to get you going full throttle. Curb the sarcastic remarks and criticism or else he could run into another's arms. He doesn't have the same type of commitment you have. It is playtime!

With Virgo SUN man: He is earthy, logical, and cold. Though you can turn up the heat, you might not be happy here. Life could be boring with this man, even if he can provide you with the financial and domestic life you demand. It will be an easy life with him, but you will want more passion than he's capable of providing. Is he worth the sacrifice?

With Libra SUN man: He is nearly the opposite of you and what you seek, if that is possible. He is romantic, light, and certainly not practical. You will inadvertently irritate him with your sarcasm, need for power, and demanding ways. He cannot and will not be what you want, ever. Why not leave well enough alone?

With Scorpio SUN man: You might stop in your tracks when you meet this man. He reads you loud and clear. He enjoys pleasuring you and thus himself. Emotions, intimacy, and mystery bind you for life. Can he be practical and make money? That will depend on other factors in his chart, but do check him out. You probably can't resist him anyhow.

With Sagittarius SUN man: You'll cause this man a lot of pain sooner or later. Your emotions will burn him out, and he will need to move on to preserve himself. You could attack him because he isn't the practical, earthy man you want. Why bother?

With Capricorn SUN man: Here is a man who ultimately is your ideal. He has great moneymaking potential. He's interested in stability and building strong foundations. Above all, he delights in your sensual magnetism and desirability. You are the heat that melts his barriers. You open him up to new worlds. He will be saying thank you forever. And in a way you like.

With Aquarius SUN man: This man could force you to redefine your concept of impractical. He is kooky, in your book. Your best bet is a friendship. He will want an occasional romp and might please you momentarily. He's interesting, but that is about all.

With Pisces SUN man: You identify with this creative, emotional man, though he's sometimes a marshmallow. He just wants to love and enjoy life. You can touch his feelings and help him structure his world on a more logical basis. You understand both sides of the coin. To turn him on, just massage his feet. He will say yes, yes, yes.

MOON IN SCORPIO, SUN IN AQUARIUS

You are sexy, intense, and emotional. You want to experience yourself to the fullest, yet your emotional storms could overwhelm you. You can be quite defensive and have trouble opening up to others.

You are fun, lively, and uniquely exotic. You're a good friend, yet your body language seems to promise men so much more. While capable of falling madly in love, you're so tender inside, you fear rejection or hurt. Yet you yearn for one committed relationship in which you can be free to be yourself. If you find such a partner, you won't ever leave. What is also great about you is that life will never be boring for the lucky man you choose.

You seek friendship first in a relationship. With it, you feel you can trust a potential suitor. You might test this friendship many times before you reveal your true loving nature. You can love as few can, with a special heat. Mr. Right be a freethinker, open to your ideas. You will walk a Bohemian path together.

You're likely to choose someone far more detached than you, which sometimes can be a problem. You could also try to trigger his emotions. What would be better is to honor and express your own high level of feelings. If he can't deal with that side of you, you really don't want him.

You promise excitement, intrigue, and mysterious adventures. You need to feel in control to unlock your natural sensuality. You must learn that no one can control you except you yourself. Then you will be master of your own ship and less frightened of emotional wounding.

With Aries SUN man: He is fire and passion mixed with fun and commitment. He appreciates your friendship, but you might throw him into a tizzy with your defensive emotional dance. He won't get it and, if he has an inkling, he might not want to get it! There's laughter aplenty, and he responds to your directness. This relationship can go either way.

With Taurus SUN man: You might feel there is an invisible rubber band holding you to him. The draw is mutual, and you could be wobbling to each other's beat for a lifetime. He doesn't delight in friendship the way you do. He wants to meet the deep, mysterious woman in you. He will pull and work to help you reveal this side. This requires commitment from you in the fullest sense.

With Gemini SUN man: This appeals to you. Naturally naughty, you both will enjoy special times together, especially in unusual settings. Remain playful, and love will last here. Gemini will be intrigued by your intensity, but if your behavior gets too twisted, he will bail out big time. You need to resolve some of the emotional spins you take yourself and others through if you want this to work.

With Cancer SUN man: He senses your Scorpio potency and wants to know you in the complete context of the word. Problems occur if you detach too much. He feels hurt and withdraws. Problems could multiply when you are discussing his behavior if you indulge in your naturally witty sarcasm. He curls up into a hard shell, never to be exposed again. I don't know about this match. It's passionate, but potentially devastating to both of you.

With Leo SUN man: Both are stubborn and right all the time. But what melts the resistance is the sizzling intimacy. You won't get rid of each other, so you might as well work it out. Leo has a loving heat that warms you down to your tiptoes. He also appreciates your sense of camaraderie. You are so passionate, he won't be inclined to wander.

With Virgo SUN man: He loves the way you warm up his life. You are hot, even if sometimes remote. The good news is that he can be as sarcastic as you and it is okay with him if occasionally you go off into an emotional frenzy. This match can work as long as you see his coolness as a plus. Together you will want to heal your universe and well could.

With Libra SUN man: You might offer friendship but secretly desire him as a lover. He is a good mix, and your passionate Scorpio womanly ways will keep him forever interested. Because you will put up with his waffling and indecision, he will put up with your sarcasm and emotionality. Fair is fair. This could be a long-term dance with quite a few different steps.

With Scorpio SUN man: The game begins as he works to bring forth your hidden passion. He is similar to you, sarcasm and all. You'd better agree on most things, because you're both always right. Your disagreements could degenerate into battles. Only you'll know if the passion is worth it.

With Sagittarius SUN man: He makes you laugh. You find his adventures, risks, and spirit delightful and exciting. Here is one of your lifetime playmates and friends. If you can keep the relationship on this level, it could be long term. However, your deeply feeling side could seem unfulfilled. Then trouble begins. He will run when you attack.

With Capricorn SUN man: He is drawn to your Scorpio charisma. He appreciates your emotionality, but he could find your detached friendliness too sappy. It will take black magic to make him interested in your spiritual and occult concerns. If you don't talk, and just romp, this match could work, but it probably won't last.

With Aquarius SUN man: You find a man who is as eccentric as you on some level. He adores his friends, can be detached, and yet resonates to your Scorpio passions. Know you are desirable and trust your bonding. Things could get weirder and weirder, thus more exciting with the two of you. Don't tell. Your friends won't understand.

With Pisces SUN man: There is a sense of a spiritual and emotional bonding here. He will handle your sarcasm and intensity. He doesn't mind a little pain here or there. It tells him how alive he is and how deeply he can feel. But if you detach, he will hate it. On the other hand, you might need to detach, because you feel you could drown in these emotional waters.

MOON IN SCORPIO, SUN IN PISCES

You were born emotional and will die emotional. Though the saying is "still waters run deep," you are a case of rushing white water with tumultuous depths. You like yourself and the way you live your life once you learn to navigate the churning waters of your soul.

You have a great deal of intuitive, psychic knowledge that enhances your day-to-day life. You follow this inner knowledge and let it guide your life.

Your looks have an ethereal, soft quality. You seem to flow from room to room rather than walk. Your eyes speak of the qualities within. You don't need to worry about sex appeal. You draw the men, but few have the courage to test your waters. They fear drowning.

You give all with total commitment. Often, you see people as what they could be, rather than what they are. The issue for you is when to stop healing and helping, which you do so well.

You want a partner who also is feeling and intuitive. You are drawn to someone artistic and creative who has a need to also express his high libidinal energies. He could also be a doctor or healer. On the other hand, you could be drawn to a man who needs you to heal and mend him. Be forewarned here. It would hurt you a lot to end this tie, but it might be necessary.

You are likely to have two major relationships. Both will be deep and meaningful.

With Aries SUN man: There is fire here and much steam. The steam is mainly physical. Without it, this combo falls flat. He is a great guy, but not for you. He might know better than even to try here. Some people are best left unknown.

With Taurus SUN man: He will love your emotionality and sensitivity, but he looks at life differently. If there is mutual respect, you can grow through each other. He will indulge you. You might like it enough to stay put for a lifetime. He promises you a wonderful life.

With Gemini SUN man: There are some things that never should happen this lifetime. This match is one of them. If you have already gotten started with a Gemini, you know that this can't work. You have nothing to bond except an occasionally hot workout. He doesn't like emotions.

With Cancer SUN man: This man could ring your chimes. You've met a soul mate, someone who plumbs the abyss of the soul like you. You understand each other and neither of you are thrown off by emotional storms. He wants a home and a family, and you can be his anchor forever. You have an uncanny sense of what each other needs. This tie can endure.

With Leo SUN man: The sexual energy between the Scorpion and the Lion are renowned, but the power plays are too. Leo adores the romantic qualities of Pisces and can really feed that side of you. In some ways, you love his passion and dreamy nature. But he's unlikely to ever understand your deep side. If you can life with that, then give it a go.

With Virgo SUN man: He can't conceive of the emotional regions you frequent. Yet there is a high attraction. You like his logical mind; he appreciates your imagination. Though you will get along, you might feel empty because you cannot share your totality with him.

With Libra SUN man: The connection here seems destined, karmic. It could be hard to separate once you bond. However, you will have a hard time finding happiness together. He is flighty, though well intentioned. You feel his sweetness and might want to cuddle some, but long term? Not in this lifetime.

With Scorpio SUN man: You don't know what hit you and neither does he. He is your ultimate match, with the passion to meet you around every curve and twist. You both are possessive steamily sensual, and can't have enough of each other. Because you want each other so much, you might find it difficult to let anyone else into your lives.

With Sagittarius SUN man: Keep going and don't stop. He will not be able to deal with your emotionality. He is into doing and acting. Now when it comes to action with you, he loves your intimate moments, but that is where the compatibility ends, if there is any. You might not even like him as a lover. Skip away, happy and free.

With Capricorn SUN man: You totally turn him on. He can offer you stability and love. His dynamic power attracts you, and you experience a different way of looking at life through his eyes. Your sensitive outlook helps him gain perspective as well. He can share everything with you, without fear of your judgment. You have an uncanny way of reaching his soul. You make a great team.

With Aquarius SUN man: He is as detached as you can be emotional. There is no glue, though he certainly is intrigued by your obvious sensuality and womanliness. Let the intrigue and barrier hold firm. It belongs there.

With Pisces SUN man: He needs you to keep himself together, and he will appreciate your strength and devotion. He will give back in many ways. There is an extraordinary bonding here. Your smoldering sensuality has a remarkable, psychic dimension of space and time. You both have it, making your love life unbeatable. Go for it.

Moon in Sagittarius

"Tomorrow is our permanent address."
E.E. CUMMINGS

You don't walk, you bound into rooms, the epitome of exuberance and energy. Others admire the way you're always full of spirit, yet a great source of wisdom. Nothing could possibly be wrong as you smile and greet life with enthusiasm, waiting for its next offering. Others wonder how you could be so lucky when they aren't.

Moon in Sagittarius women have an innate sense of superiority based on their knowledge and moral understanding. Others sense it, and bow to it. You have a need to show how great and wonderful life can be, if others would just follow your sense of cosmic order or system.

You believe wholeheartedly that life will get better. The result is your miniholocausts *do* turn out better for you than for most signs, because you have the ability to turn your thoughts into reality.

The problem with this type of thinking is that often you don't deal with the reality of situations. You avoid today's issue while waiting for a better tomorrow. Or you could delude yourself into thinking things are wonderful and will only get better.

With love, this optimism can play out in two different ways. You can go from man to man, always convinced that there is yet someone better around the corner. And who knows, you may just be right! Or you can choose to stay with one man forever, ignoring problems and thinking that clearly, you have the best of all men. It is wonderful to consider this the best of all relationships, the best of all worlds, but sometimes being an ostrich can cause you problems. One day, you discover your relationship isn't so great. Your partner might leave you, or you may realize there is no longer any personal interaction.

You do need to remain sensitive to your loved ones and listen to them. Honor feelings, and you can have a dynamic interaction. Also please understand you might not have all the answers, though the philosophical being in you says yes, yes, you do!

You are a very attractive woman who can enjoy sports with ease, more so than most women. You are not only a participant, but also a spectator. Because of your willingness to not get stuck in sexual role models, your appeal is strong to men who want companions as much as lovers. You are both lover and friend.

The man you choose will have to be open to your insights and wisdom. You don't want to fight, you want to be right. He needs to share your interests and hobbies. He will need to have fire and get-up-and-go. You also want companionship from him and the willingness to bounce from one idea to another.

You can be passionate and fiery, making the best out of each moment, vigorously living life. With this orientation, there is a tendency to overindulge and go to extremes in some areas of your life. Remember, of all Moon signs, you love living most, and you can take that to the edge.

MOON IN SAGITTARIUS, SUN IN ARIES

No one can ever complain about your lack of energy. You are all fire and enthusiasm. You tend to be impulsive and run off with wild ideas and schemes. Sometimes they turn out well. Other times, to the world, they might not, but you will find something positive out of the worst possible experience! Your imagination, combined with your combustible nature, makes you dynamic, full of energy, and fun.

You are interested in action, accomplishment, and acting on your ideas. You will hop over walls, rather than run into them. You do not know the word impossible. Everything is possible. You live that philosophy; you are that philosophy. Others, meanwhile, are flabbergasted at the speed with which you whiz by them mentally, emotionally, and physically. There is no stopping you.

Raw charisma seeps out of you at every twist and turn. No surprise to anyone, you have a gang of admirers running fast to keep up with you! It is important to stop, think, and decide what kind of man and relationship you desire.

You will need a man with as much energy as you (if that is possible), whose zest for life equals yours. You need a man who, though an intellect, will not have your need to avoid the facts. A little reality, as much as you don't like it, might be very good. Your partner must believe in equal rights because in many areas of your life together, you will want to wear the pants! He needs to be secure to take your wanderings and sometimes competitive nature.

With Aries SUN man: You are welcome to lecture about your systems of reality and life. He might roll his eyes occasionally because he is into action, not talk. He has the virility to complement your zest for living. The two of you smolder together and explode in flames. This can be forever. He tolerates your eccentricities as you do his.

With Taurus SUN man: You hit a brick wall with this man. There is no bypassing this. He is slow and steady; you are full of tumultuous action. This match is a big NO. He can be sultry, and you like that, but he will never be able to match you, and probably won't like you or love you. Besides, he likes the traditional roles—he Tarzan, you Jane.

With Gemini SUN man: He blows hot air on your blazing personality and sensuality. You experience a bonding that few could even dream of. He loves ideas, but he would rather play with them than live them. He doesn't mind sitting home while you take off like a cannonball. He adores your ardor, in all respects. You appreciate that he is president of your fan club.

With Cancer SUN man: Some combinations are destined to failure. This one is, no matter what the plusses are. He may seem spirited, but ultimately he is a wet rag. You hate having water thrown on you. Need I say more? NO!

With Leo SUN man: He loves the chase, and you will love the pounce. This is a wonderfully romantic couple, though you need to let him know how very special he is. He is a player, but you will look the other way, knowing that this is clearly the best of all possible worlds. He will thank you for your generosity in many ways.

With Virgo SUN man: Who wants to be criticized? Not you. Promise: This man will criticize. You are both perfectionists, but in very different ways, and you will continually grate on each other. Unless one of you likes being made into hash, forget it.

With Libra SUN man: He is laid back, something that is foreign to you. He won't commit. However, the passion will never ebb. The love-making and romance make you feel extremely feminine and valued. Yet he loves it when you're enjoying baseball with him. If you are willing to talk about feelings, the relationship can work, with oodles and oodles of love.

With Scorpio SUN man: Both of you are physically passionate, throwing caution to the wind and just letting it happen. Apart from your intimate moments, he could be too reserved for you. This man is very jealous and possessive. He won't like it when you play football with the guys. Trouble brews easily and can ignite quickly into major conflict. Proceed with caution.

With Sagittarius SUN man: Together you go off on your personal tour of a fantasy life, sharing adventures and bounding over obstacles. Problems could develop with the practical matters. Who will diaper the baby or pay the bills? Why bother with these trivialities when you can be off loving and living? Somehow you will make it, though the IRS could be hot on your heels.

With Capricorn SUN man: He is about structure and reality. Though you could have a discussion about the way life ''should'' be, your outlooks are different and have little in common. He loves your combustible sexuality, but he can't identify with your wanderlust and need to experience life. No thank you. Maybe in another incarnation.

With Aquarius SUN man: Discuss philosophy with him, he loves it. Take a risk, he will be behind you, observing and cheering you on. He is airy and detached, yet with you, he sizzles. You can count on his perceptions to help you work through impasses, big and small. You are like salt and pepper together, adding what the other lacks, adding that extra spice to life.

With Pisces SUN man: You are truly foreign elements together. You don't speak the same language and have no understanding of what the other is about. He is nearly the opposite of what you want. He revels in the ups and downs of the moment. You don't understand his moping. You ask, why bother? Don't ask me!

MOON IN SAGITTARIUS, SUN IN TAURUS

You are certainly an unusual combination, with foresight and vision. Unlike your sister Sagittarius Moons, you're always practical in your suggestions and ideas. Because you have the experience of success, you are strong about what you think is right.

You manifest a sense of intellectual superiority and could unwittingly put down others. By letting others know where they are "faulty" in their thinking, you feel as if you're doing them a favor.

The man you choose needs to match your zest, yet have the ability to be earthy and practical. Mr. Right must have the strength and savoir faire to handle you. You will seek a companion with common artistic and intellectual interests. Above all, this man must have moneymaking skills that meet your criteria.

You expect to be fifty-fifty in nearly every area except courtship. You will demand the flowers, dinners, and gestures or you could become quite difficult and tell him off. With you, if you sublimate your feelings, they will come out in physical excess. Express your depth, emotions, and above all, spirit.

Men find you earthy, grounded, and sensual. You want to look good and do what you need to feel good. You may have to fight the battle of the bulge with your Sun-Moon combination.

With Aries SUN man: He is a freethinker and acts on his moral code. He will tell you when you are wrong. Yet you admire his energy and integrity. Much depends on whether you have common interests and if he can provide the sense of security you desire. The passion is there to support this tie.

With Taurus SUN man: Recognize you are both stubborn, want it your way, and your way is right. Depending on your defenses, you could either confront or run away. Running away might work because he will lure and court you back into his pasture. Being with you ignites his passion and leads to adventure. You will always be secure with this man.

With Gemini SUN man: He is in his head; you are in your body. You want action; he wants to think. Yet his love of ideas, culture, and exchange of wit very much appeal to you. The emotional and sensual dance could last. However, pulling your differences together into a sane, healthy relationship is another issue. Unless he is properly bankrolled, he might not give you enough security.

With Cancer SUN man: He is quite traditional and wants you to be Mommy, woman, and lover. Though you understand this, shackling you with housework and husband-care could be a bit much, even for stable you. He will make it worth it to you, catering to your whims financially, emotionally, and sexually. It might be worth considering.

With Leo SUN man: He discovers what an earthy animal he has in you. If he doesn't watch it, you could take off. You keep him on his tiptoes, and he loves your independence. Count on money and romance here, though you need to defer to him. Remember: he is King of the Beasts. Take a risk with him, and you will know grand passion.

With Virgo SUN man: He understands your need for the practical and chimes in with you. You will take the lead here and might need to thaw his cold exterior! Together you will feel like the earth moved beneath you. However, he won't like your independent streak. In life he is the accountant and you are the economic engine.

With Libra SUN man: Your courtship could make a romantic novel— he with his arduous, yet tender ways, you slowly, reluctantly giving him what he covets. You could be doing the same dance as an old married couple. The embers will stay forever hot. Liabilities? You have to be the practical one. That's all.

With Scorpio SUN man: He senses your seething sensuality. He likes your values and determination. Your experimental nature could challenge, yet scare him. There is action here, but it could be difficult to pull together—though fun to try. If you can take his hard, incisive comments, the fires are worth it.

With Sagittarius SUN man: He is like an Olympic runner as he speeds by you. It is your decision if you want to join the chase. You can count on his independence and willingness to risk. You have a telepathic bond and can live in harmony. Let go of your demand for security and you will have the match of a lifetime.

With Capricorn SUN man: Do stop and meet this gentleman. He is grounded, a sensual treat. He is into power, something that intrigues you. The two of you will love scheming together and could turn pie-in-the-sky dreams into reality. The problem is that he won't take kindly to your wandering too far from the fold. How far is too far? That is for you to find out.

With Aquarius SUN man: He is a great friend and romp for you. The sexual tie could scald, but he is not an earthy, practical man. He lives in another world. In fact, in your book he might be ET. This doesn't mean you can't be friends. However, long-term commitment is doubtful.

With Pisces SUN man: You will enjoy the rapture of the first kiss and the intensity of your dynamic bonding. You will be his Earth and anchor; you will find in him your muse. However, he will cling when you are looking for a new adventure. If it is the racetrack or the baseball field, fine. He will want to join you everywhere. He is like glue.

MOON IN SAGITTARIUS, SUN IN GEMINI

You are a complex and captivating woman. You want it all. You should be able to realize your desires, but you give off ambivalent energy, especially in relating. You are desirable and attractive; men want you. However, they aren't sure what you want, and for that matter, neither are you.

You want someone who will pioneer new universes with you. You need a steady diet of risking. You are sure of yourself. You take action on your ideas.

Yet you choose a man who loves ideas, especially yours. When it comes to passion, he is an intellect first, not an intense fighter, lover, or risk-taker.

If you want someone to worship and appreciate you, he might not need to have all the same virtues. You are not sure of your boundaries.

Often, you but don't get the meaning of experiences. Sometimes you swing so completely into the risk, you miss the point. On the other hand, you can overthink and overtalk. Your passion can scare you. You need a partner who can give you insight during your meanderings. You seek; however, you must also learn to find. Balancing this polarity will help you heal and make you complete.

With Aries SUN man: He meets your energy with his . . . no matter what your field of play. The romp of two intense spirits joins in sexual dance. With him, you feel a unity that you have with few men. You see him anchor your mind and body. He balances them and with excellence. Go for this. It could be a lifetime commitment.

With Taurus SUN man: This man has a type of grounding, sensuality, and understanding that is foreign to you. You want a man full of ideas, fun, and vivacity. He is slow and steady. He provides security. You don't care. You are off on an adventure, risking, leaving him behind. Toss away this stick-in-the-mud.

With Gemini SUN man: He will put you on a pedestal and he will think your crusades are marvelous. He might discuss the pros and cons, but he admires your action and willingness to risk. Though he is charming and attractive, he will not be the active member of this partnership. With your physical dexterity and energy, you will take his naughty ideas and play them out. Please keep the shades pulled.

With Cancer SUN man: Everything is wrong here. He wants a homebody; you want to wander. You want to intellectually discuss feelings; he wants to feel them. You talk out; he acts out. Both of you are destined to be uncomfortable with each other. He douses your fire with water. There is a lot of anger and steam with this combo.

With Leo SUN man: No one has time to question this combination. He will always be running after you, courting you, and wondering what you are up to. In quiet moments, your wit and intelligence will delight him. He makes a wonderful lover and husband. If one of you strays, the other will look the other way. You are both clear that you have a good thing going.

With Virgo SUN man: You are very intelligent and directed. You know when to call a halt to the impossible. This match is beyond impossible. It's ridiculous. He is picky and looks at the little picture. You are enthusiastic and look at the big picture. He snuffs your fire, and you make him seethe like a volcano. NO.

With Libra SUN man: He is a romantic and cares about the relationship, though he might be commitment-phobic. He needs his space, which you give with pleasure. You have so much to do, so many tales to spin. He will delight you with his tender offerings. You like his fair mind and legal interest. He wants what is right for all. You might never get married, but you could love forever.

With Scorpio SUN man: He smolders; he is an intellectual. In some way he might be very appealing to you. Problems occur when you take off and he doesn't like it. He will feel he owns you, that you are his. You aren't into being possessed. You are into living. Only if you two can juggle the meeting of two powers can this work.

With Sagittarius SUN man: You are two like spirits that tear off into the world to experience life to the ultimate. You will risk and gamble, even with your relationship. You are adrenaline junkies, but you will criticize his lack of reason. Excuse me, whose lack of reason? You are two peas in a pod. He is your soul mate.

With Capricorn SUN man: You like his mental acumen and interest in ideas, money, and power. You are interested in living, and he certainly can provide the dough to finance your romps. He is a workaholic, so it is wonderful that you have these projects. As for intimacy, remember he is into power and will use his manly powers to make you happy.

With Aquarius SUN man: His adventures are different from yours. He will consider taking a rocket ship to the moon; you will be happy at the racetrack. You will be the conservative of the combo, hard as it is to believe! As delightful and sizzling as he is, you could discard him as a kook. If you don't, a marriage of your two spirits and bodies will provide companionship and laughter forever.

With Pisces SUN man: The tension is so thick between you, you can cut it. He might be a charming romantic, but there is an emotional drip that is constant. You don't want to be clung to, do you? Then move on.

MOON IN SAGITTARIUS, SUN IN CANCER

You are vibrant, active, and emotional. You have fire and energy to meet life's demands. You negotiate life's bounces with ease, always feeling you can succeed. It is very hard to get you down, but if you do fall apart, you are emotional, clinging, and needy.

You have many moods, which you will learn to use to guide your adventures and decisions. You are highly intuitive. The key is to learn balance and to understand the strength of your two sides. You cannot fire off and avoid feeling.

You are loving and would heal the world. But you will always opt for your immediate family. You will philosophize about the world and what to do to improve conditions. You could also adopt foster children. You will make an excellent mother and caretaker. You act on your concerns and causes.

You'll attract men. The fact that you enjoy your body and movement adds to your allure. Along with your nurturing, caring quality, what is there not to like? You are either full-chested or full-faced, with an ethereal quality. You're there, then you're gone. You exude sexual magic and have a touch of the coquette. You love flirting and the game of woman meets man. You are sure the world revolves around relationships, love, risking, and family values. And in your world, you are certainly right.

With Aries SUN man: This is putting a match to dynamite. Which way the explosion blows is anyone's guess. He is a pioneer and backs your world-healing crusades. Together you can move mountains. However, he might not understand your emotionality and sentimentality, though he won't put you down for your feelings. This could be the torrid affair of lovers meeting in the Peace Corps!

With Taurus SUN man: He provides and appreciates a quality personal life. He likes your values. He wants a family and home with you, but you MUST take time off from your crusading to go to the theater to make him happy. You love to eat together. Yes, this can work.

With Gemini SUN man: He feels inspired when he watches the way you live your life, not that he will change his style. He can speak about world change; you can act on it. The attraction is magnetic, but difficult to consummate. He is detached and intellectual. Emotional you could be left yelling and screaming with this cool cucumber.

With Cancer SUN man: You are emotional triggers for each other. You cry, care, and love in harmony. This quality adds to the thunder of your romance. You are both lightning-struck. As long as your crusades involve his interests, both of you will be happy. His values are similar to yours; his passion is equal. This could be one happy household with many romantic moments.

With Leo SUN man: This man is a real lion in the world of romance and good living. You like his fire and can easily be seduced into his lair. However, when sanity dawns, you might not approve of his hedonistic ways. He is about living, and you are about changing the world. Better not risk in this playpen.

With Virgo SUN man: You like his practical solutions to your emotional crises. You nurture him, and he feels safe. You could be stunned by his intensity once he unleashes his quiet masculinity. He wants to serve, as you want to heal. However, you need to have similar ethics and commitments. If so, this man offers a life of stability.

With Libra SUN man: He is a charming man, fun to flirt with but a bad idea for a long-term commitment. He will not understand, and actually will shy away from, your emotional side. To please him, you would have to subdue part of yourself. He cares about what is fair, but is in no way interested in your causes. Best left as friends, or this could be painful.

With Scorpio SUN man: He meets you with intensity and could bowl you over. You are gentle, and he can be very sharp-tongued. Your feelings could get hurt, and you could run away—or curl into a ball. Neither are great outcomes for the long term. Stay clear unless he is an unusually tame Scorp.

With Sagittarius SUN man: Finally you have met someone with electricity and energy; you could venture out into the world together. You both love discussing religion and life until you're blue in the face. The sensuality is great. He might never be as emotional as you. If that isn't okay, proceed with caution. Otherwise, this is a party the whole way.

With Capricorn SUN man: He is very attractive to you. He offers stability, security, and a wonderful home. He will also be very proud of your dedication and desire to take care of others. He might shake his head at your need to risk or take flying leaps of faith. There is always a strong attraction between you. Always.

With Aquarius SUN man: You are a friend and lover to this zodiac beatnik. You love talking to him. He too is a cause person and wants to save the universe. There is a friendship here, though he will never have your sensitive, feeling nature. As lovers, you soar into other realms, though if you hook up for life, don't expect him to change. It is as it is.

With Pisces SUN man: Together you cry, feel, and campaign. He will do everything you want to add quality to your lives. However, he might get upset at your sense of independence. He is into constant companionship and cuddling. Can you handle that over the long haul? Guess it depends on how good he is!

MOON IN SAGITTARIUS, SUN IN LEO

No one can accuse you of dragging your feet. You might suddenly turn in an opposite direction, as you are impulsive, but slow? Sorry, not in this lifetime.

You can be a delight to the right man. You will chase, pounce, and attack. He just needs to tell you the whole way how very wonderful you are. Your need for adulation can get a bit heavy for a partner. You are good, you know it, and you want to know HE knows it.

Love and romance are very important to you. You need them as part of your daily fare, just as you need challenge. You don't feel complete without some passion and a budding romance in your life. You love so much that you might have a whole string of men—two husbands mini-mum. Of course, you can choose otherwise.

You offer passion and warmth to your partner. In return, you expect loyalty, romance, and a life play partner.

Travel, exploring your passions, and learning more about the world can be lifetime preoccupations. You will want to share your experiences. You find life much better with a friend, lover, and companion. You do tend to push others away because you are stubborn and must have it your way. Though you are generous, expansive, and forgiving when crossed, you are quite a handful.

With Aries SUN man: You have met another spark plug. However, his ego isn't as vested as yours in admiration, which is a good thing. You blaze together to become a wildfire. Your mutual passion will never be controlled, but is to be experienced. He doesn't care. He will adore you as you are. The feeling is mutual!

With Taurus SUN man: Both of you are bullish, and that is the biggest obstacle. Plus, he is too busy sniffing the flowers to go into full gallop and stay up with you. He loves beauty and living, but, unlike you, at a slower, easier pace. Together the animal in you comes out. For the long run, you need to let go of your need to always be right if this is to work.

With Gemini SUN man: Ah, to be adored like this is many a woman's dream. He will love your spirit. He is airy and feeds your fire. He experiences life on the fullest terms, as you do, though you need to indulge his heady discussions. Freedom is a byword for both of you. Passion is a given. Lucky you. Lucky him.

With Cancer SUN man: Stop now. Don't go down this path. This can be a huge mistake for both of you. Yes, he will worship and adore you. However, he needs a partner there to constantly support him emotionally. Is that you? No. He will not appreciate your independence. He will withdraw from you and possibly head to another woman.

With Leo SUN man: You are both flashes of energy, love, and fire. If your spirits are to blend, the admiration must be mutual. Constant strok-ing needs to be a daily habit. Just as the fires blaze, the disagreements could nearly burn you out. Somehow you must work your differences through to be content, or one of you will start playing in a different yard.

With Virgo SUN man: He sill simply irritate you. You will not appreciate his snide remarks, especially if they are directed toward you. He is practical. You are idealistic. Please say no.

With Libra SUN man: You will be lured by his quiet, boyish ways and charm. He is ambivalent, which makes the chase all the more enticing. He excites you with romantic innuendos, and your imagination goes wild. He will love you because you make up for what he lacks. The catch is as good as the chase.

With Scorpio SUN man: You could be attracted to the sheer animal in this man. His sensual looks and mysterious ways lure you. However, you will never be what he wants and vice versa. He doesn't do admiration. Forget this for the long term, though as far as a playmate, mmm!

With Sagittarius SUN man: He is off running as fast as you. You might have trouble keeping up with him, but once he notices you, he will stop dead in his tracks. He senses your generosity and great femininity. There are rarely arguments here, as he is so much like you. This heavenly match is not boring. It is all fire and heat. Go with it.

With Capricorn SUN man: He is a powerhouse, sensual and accomplished. You know there will be money. He adores your femininity, though he will be shocked if you pursue him. Don't worry. Lay back. The magic is mutual. It is good to have role reversal once in a while.

With Aquarius SUN man: He likes your hot nature, and you like the way he cares about his friends. Mutual respect is a must here, as you have very different styles. There is a lot to be learned from each other. He won't mind it when you decide to take off. You share passion, love, and friendship. You make a couple that is invited everywhere because of the joy you radiate.

With Pisces SUN man: He radiates mystery, romance, and feelings. However, he wants you with him, not off on some adventure. Are you ready for glue? If you can tolerate having him along on all your quests, so be it. You both have a tendency to excess, and neither of you wants to put the brakes on. Expect lots of loving times.

Moon in Sagittarius, Sun in Virgo

You care a lot about your immediate world and surroundings. You want to pitch in and help wherever you can. However, this desire comes with terms. You must do things your way or else you could become uncomfortable. You have a need for control and precision that prevents you from risking.

You have much energy, passion, and stamina once you decide to commit. What you project has very little to do with the real woman inside. Sorting out your ambivalent vibes is key to your success in relationships.

You want a man who is earthy, practical, and grounded. Though you are drawn to such a man, there is a side of you that puts him down for not being a go-getter, more passionate and dynamic. Remember, you chose him, and he represents a side of you. No one can be more critical than you. To succeed in relationships, you need to resolve this schism. A wild woman coexists in you with a conservative lady. You come to terms with this inner splintering through reflection and self-understanding. Above all, do not attack yourself, a tendency you have.

When relationships fail, you often throw yourself into your work or a project. You might find it safer and easier to give in this manner. Or you could wander from relationship to relationship, knowing something is off.

With Aries SUN man: He has none of your pickiness, but cares about others and willingly puts himself on the line. Let your passions meet and you are unlikely to separate. He won't care if you have an occasional snap attack, if you can deal with his temper. It serves you to be lovers and not warriors. It's more fun that way.

With Taurus SUN man: This man meets your expectations. He's earthy and lives life to the max. He is artistic or has a creativity that you might not appreciate sometimes. Besides his smoldering sensuality, his ability is to make money. You like both a lot. You will travel the world together, enjoying the best of love and life.

With Gemini SUN man: No question, you're attracted. There is a lot going on between you. You love his mind, vision, and laissez-faire attitude. However, if you start to pick at him, he will move on. There is no reason for this sexy man to put up with that. Just as well, as he doesn't have a practical bone in him.

With Cancer SUN man: He is emotional, loving, and tender. He appreciates your ability to make sense of what confuses him, yet he will hate your running critique. He will put up a hard exterior that you won't be able to break through. He also doesn't appreciate your need to take off and wander. Better not.

With Leo SUN man: The world is intense with this fiery romantic. You will be charmed out of your finickiness, and he will kindle your fires. Fuss all you want, he will set you ablaze with passion. If you want to be the practical one in the relationship, fine, just appreciate all he offers or he could wander off.

With Virgo SUN man: He is all you want—detailed and direct. He will offer security, earthiness, and practicality. He will have a fit when you attack him for not being flamboyant like you. Remember, please, you chose this man. Because of him, you can indulge your animated, energetic Moon. Can work, if YOU behave yourself.

With Libra SUN man: This is a gentle man with none of the practical abilities and earthiness you desire. He is full of fun and romance, which lures even the wildest of women. Loving this man is a pleasure, but living with him is a whole other issue. Don't count on this forever.

With Scorpio SUN man: His steamy nature might have you cowering. You won't want to cross him; he is more sarcastic than you. If you can tolerate his demands, you might be okay. You both love to excess, so the nighttime is your meat and potatoes. You are open, and he is secretive, which could make you uncomfortable. There are pros and cons.

With Sagittarius SUN man: You need to run the budget here. You might not want to as your flamboyant, sensual spirits meet. There could be a lot of risking, wildness, and soaring, passionate moments. The problem is the morning after, when you see the damages left by the uncontrollable firestorm you two create. If you can play both roles, all the more power to you and this relationship.

With Capricorn SUN man: He is an earthy, practical man who appreciates your abilities to manage the household and take care of others. He wants to create. He would love you to be his companion, handling the details. He will never be flamboyant, but he will be powerful. You make a happy bird and bee together.

With Aquarius SUN man: He is a friendly type who likes your sense of adventure and playfulness. He too can be detached, calm, and collected, but you will need to handle the finances. He has other, more far-out interests. You both like to take care of others. If you choose each other as your projects, it could be a very nice match.

With Pisces SUN man: There is a definite attraction and there is a definite problem. He is emotional and needy; you are practical and independent. You can offer each other a lot if you can rise above criticism. However, it may be hard for him to transcend his clinginess. This will never be an easy match. You can have it if you want to put in the work.

MOON IN SAGITTARIUS, SUN IN LIBRA

You are one of the feline tigers, yet few can identify you immediately. They are taken by your soft radiance and easy smile. You cover your volatile, energetic nature with fluff and femininity, often smiling, knowing the right thing to say. You tend to be very diplomatic, never wanting to hurt anyone's feelings. For that reason, you can sometimes fudge the truth. This can be a problem with some men, as they may never feel secure with you.

There are other reasons to feel insecure. You are a supreme lover of men and enjoy your entourage. You like everything about maleness. As feminine as you are, you are very comfortable with male activities. You like baseball and football. Why not? There are many more of the opposite sex around.

You pose quite the challenge to a man. He will have his hands full holding on to you. In fact, you can't be held. You stick around because you so choose. You tend to play around, and though this may be work for a while, at some point you might make a conscious decision to settle down.

You are likely to have more than one marriage because of your natural love of the opposite sex, though you could have one very special man who knows how to light your fire forever.

With Aries SUN man: He is ruled by Mars, the planet of masculinity. The chemistry will never wear away, though you will need to adjust to his challenging ways and hot temper. He doesn't appreciate games. But then with this man, kissing and making up is worth it. This match will work better if you share a cause or hobby.

With Taurus SUN man: He is sensual, arty, and has practicality, something you sorely lack. He will demand monogamy, so you might want to meet him after you sow your wild oats. You will always be surrounded by love, beauty, and quality. Travel, fine restaurants, and touring the arts keep you both content, acute, and ever desirable. A good last stop.

With Gemini SUN man: He is out there making the most of the adventure of life. He will want a playmate, someone with similar energy, who wants to experience life, talk concepts, and debate the pros and cons. You are as romantic as he is. You will love the little touches he adds to your life. You are both flirts, so a little naughtiness won't bother either of you.

With Cancer SUN man: Though this man, like most, is attracted to the ephemeral, feline image you project, he won't be able to put up with your nonsense and shenanigans. He needs stability and a mommy. You are a lot of things, but not that.

With Leo SUN man: You have found your male match. He can outflirt you, outlove you, and outcharm you. And you love it. Both of you are fiery and great lovers. You both tend to stray, so you will be too busy to keep track of the other—which might be perfect. This is a coupling akin to a fairy-tale love story. Is there a choice?

With Virgo SUN man: Fortunately, nothing may ever happen here, as his practical, earthy nature is a total turnoff to you. He will criticize you; you'll be bored. Just forget it.

With Libra SUN man: You find him delightful and fun, day and night. You do a bewitching dance around each other, and both of you could fall permanently in love. Your fiery, risky nature makes him want you more. He can handle your wildness. You might bring out a side of him that he never knew existed. He will love it. An excellent combination.

With Scorpio SUN man: He has penetrating eyes that look right through you. He might like your femininity, but he wonders about your ability to stay put with him. He could toy with you and you with him. The odds of this being long term are practically zip. The passion is nice, but not worth the aggravation in the long run.

With Sagittarius SUN man: He dances to your tune and wants you on the baseball field with him, taking the next flight to Portugal, or just living your life beside him. He likes your soft, romantic femininity. He knows there is more. You will need to work on this to keep it together, but the commitment is worthwhile. You're good for each other.

With Capricorn SUN man: He can just plain aggravate you as he tries to make you settle down and be anchored. For what, you ask. You want your freedom. No way are you going to be tied down! He is a nice man; at least give him that!

With Aquarius SUN man: He adores your spirit and your womanliness. He will allow you to fly and be free, picking and choosing when to join you. You will give great parties together. You add the softness and atmosphere, while he provides excitement. You two make the social scene worth it. Your private life works similarly. Use your imagination.

With Pisces SUN man: There is an inevitable draw here. You love his romantic nature so much that he nearly puts you into a trance. Unfortunately, that state cannot continue forever, as he NEEDS you, and you get the creepy-crawlies without space. Nevertheless, separating is close to impossible. You like the mystic moments.

MOON IN SAGITTARIUS, SUN IN SCORPIO

You are passionately fiery and independent, but anyone meeting you knows there is something dark and mysterious within. You will learn to deal with your hidden fires, obsessions, and extreme nature. Your fiery moon only adds an element of the extreme, so even you want to go "whoa" and stop this ride. Your libido is high and needs an outlet. Your creativity could overwhelm you, yet could produce greatness.

Others sense your magic and depth and are intrigued. Yet few can handle your profound nature and heated passion. You want a man who has similar depth, who seeks reasons and ponders the universe. Unfortunately, there is a tendency to choose men who are also remote and perhaps emotionally unavailable.

For you to learn to trust anyone, much less a member of the opposite sex, takes a lot of work. There is a side of you that loves to have a companion, very close and snugly. You could project as a libertine or free spirit as a defensive maneuver. It is a lot easier than being hurt. Or is it? You tend to deny yourself the powerful, dynamic bonding you want and can have. As a result, you'll feel slightly empty.

Once committed, you are a loving companion. You are loyal, caring, and lusty. You can make any man happy. The issue is whether he can make you happy.

With Aries SUN man: Give this man a shot. You will think you have seen the fires of Vesuvius, and so will he. This man is always off on an adventure, so you might not fear his closeness too much. In some ways, he meets your need for a remote man. You can be comfortable here, yet be steamy and fiery all in one.

With Taurus SUN man: Opposites attract here with a magnetic force that will make it hard to pry you apart. He is even and steady, providing you with a sense of safety as you reveal your vulnerabilities. He can handle all your facets and finds you a diamond in the rough. He will help you polish your rougher edges. He will praise, marry, and love you.

With Gemini SUN man: He laughs, he plays, and he charms. You enter a whirlwind love affair in which you are as free as birds. This can work if your intensely possessive nature never comes into play. He is in some sense unavailable, and that meets a need for you. Don't criticize him after he is caught. You wanted this.

With Cancer SUN man: This deeply emotional man evokes a harmonic note in you. The two of you could have a smoldering love relationship. You will want your privacy as a couple because there is so much going on. He will like your passion, especially when it is directed at making a home and family. Once hooked, you seem destined to stay together.

With Leo SUN man: He is the zodiac's lover. Don't think you will go unnoticed. You spell mystery, enchantment, and sexuality. He will chase you and want to drag you into his lair. Eventually the sparks will ignite. You could feel as if there is a lot going on here. The battles are rough, but the passion makes you feel alive.

With Virgo SUN man: He is quiet and practical, and you can feel secure with him. But somehow he is cold and remote. You can share physical heat, but he will never identify with your hot ways and deep feelings. He is a cool bird, while you are a sizzling tiger. Never the twain shall met.

With Libra SUN man: He's like a wind fanning your sparks. You will become one flame together, but it is unlikely that he can identify with your deeply feeling nature. Try though he may, he can't bridge that gap. You could find him distant. It isn't his intention. It is his nature. You could wander, as you want so much more.

With Scorpio SUN man: You find a man who has knowledge of your sensual depth and intensity. He also has a similar need for reasons and understanding. There is nothing else but the two of you and the moment. He likes your physical prowess and limber body. You will play more than tennis together for a long time, maybe forever.

With Sagittarius SUN man: He adores you and reads you cold. He could ask you out to play racquetball, but much more will happen. And you both know it from the get-go. You both like exploring, even more so together. Compulsive, overindulging in all realms mark you as a couple. And you like it that way.

With Capricorn SUN man: He reaches out and touches the deep, unexplored areas of your soul. He can deal with your intensity. He loves it. You find him steadfast and strong. This match can work, but you need to tame your wanderlust and experimental nature. He is so hot that you may never want to leave.

With Aquarius SUN man: Experimental and eccentric describe this man to a tee. You will love playing with him and like his originality in all realms. Do not expect to have a meeting of the souls here. He might be open to it, but he doesn't have the deep, needy nature you do. Play with him, love him, but don't look for anything but lightness here.

With Pisces SUN man: Passion meets passion, depth meets depth. You both indulge in emoting to no end, experiencing all and loving totally. You are safe with this man, as he is more vulnerable than you, if that is possible You are the problem, not he. Every so often you need to take off and be a free spirit. He will pout, but your embraces make up for it nicely.

Moon in Sagittarius, Sun in Sagittarius

You are a perpetual optimist, and with this mind-set comes a fiery nature, high energy, and a natural sensuality. You love to move. The feeling of air rushing through your hair is an aphrodisiac. What others consider a physical effort can be the joy of feeling your muscles working. You are a true sensualist, loving the current of life running through your body.

You do not fear risk and you could send chills up some backs as you gamble and plunge ahead in life. You want to experience it all, FEEL it.

Men discover early on that you are vital, alive, and a challenge. You will be drawn to a fiery type, not a weeping willow. You want strength and energy.

No one ever questions how wild or loving you can be as a partner. You will be adventuresome, open to forgiving and to going to the next step. Your main requirement is that your freedom needs to honored. That's hard for some to imagine—freedom with commitment—but those are your terms, or there will be no life-dance with you!

Problems occur because you cannot understand or identify with others. It is difficult for you to fathom why everyone doesn't want to live their lives with passion and drive. When others have problems because you are so one-sided, you can't find alternatives. As a result, you could have quite a few relationships until you find one that works.

With Aries SUN man: His fire is directed toward causes, yours is into living to the fullest. However, you can easily jump onto his bandwagon, and he yours. Risking and adventure are the norm. When he starts his fiery crusade to win your heart, soul, mind, and body, you will nudge him on to the next step. Naughty you. A fine melding of souls.

With Taurus SUN man: You both are committed to the business of living. You do this with very different styles. He is into the quality, good life. You are into quality living. Both of you live to the extreme and overindulge. He is grounded and bonds, but this can work. If he trusts you, he will give you all the freedom you want. Your intimate times will have you soaring.

With Gemini SUN man: You are opposites in life and living. You are forever taking off, whereas his mind is perpetually wandering. If you respect your different styles, you could be a very happy couple. He ignites you, feeding your flames with ideas, flirtation, and a naughtiness unknown to him. You will have all the freedom you want, but he will demand the same.

With Cancer SUN man: This man wasn't designed for you and he will constantly be weeping as you take off on your next whirl. You like his ability to feel and love, but you will hate having Mr. Albatross around your neck!

With Leo SUN man: This man is enough to stop you dead in your tracks. His romantic ways and obvious sensuality draw you. You might not want to stray far with him, but if you do, he will run after you. He loves your physical vitality. You will teach him about living, and he will teach you about loving. A perfect match!

With Virgo SUN man: No, no, no! He is picky and not into living as much as structuring his materialistic world. He will think the way you risk is horrible, and he will nitpick and criticize. Meanwhile, you will never stick around for this one, never.

With Libra SUN man: He is charming, adorable, and romantic. He's active and loves to move around like you. The romance and consequent heated moments could be exquisite, but he is not a risk-taker. You could send scary chills up his spine. He can give you space, but he won't commit to a lasting relationship unless you make him feel very secure.

With Scorpio SUN man: You could find the experience, the big picture with this man very painful. He is possessive, grasping, and doesn't know what freedom means. However, the merging of two different types of passions could have your pots boiling. This is a real scorcher, bound to singe your heart.

With Sagittarius SUN man: You and he are soul mates and understand each other clearly. Unless you have similar interests, you could wander into different playgrounds and forget each other—at least for a while. This can work, but you need to be the judge. You'll probably go for it, as you are such a risk-taker!

With Capricorn SUN man: He is nearly the opposite of you. He wants form and structure. You want movement and energy. You are fiery; he is earthy. He takes risks only when they are well researched—nothing impulsive for him. You could feel like you are in quicksand with him, losing your vitality. Walk around this one.

With Aquarius SUN man: This guy is a giggle and more. He loves risks, though his are even more bizarre than yours. He loves exploring and definitely hears a different drummer. This man makes you look conservative! You add spark to his life, though he could snub your conservative ways. Make peace, don't judge, and you'll have a friend forever. If you want more, it is there. He can be wild.

With Pisces SUN man: You don't like the feeling of drowning, do you? Then head the other direction. He is artistic, creative, and so emotional. He needs someone there who can stabilize him and love him. He will not be able to handle your adventures. Do not go here.

MOON IN SAGITTARIUS, SUN IN CAPRICORN

You want a solid life, money, and stability. You want a relationship that lasts forever. However, your freedom-loving soul keeps coming out and sabotaging your choices. It takes a special man to understand and help you through these swings. You will find him once you become more conscious of your inner conflicts.

You yearn for stability, emotional security, and control in your life. For that reason, you project a stoic, conservative front. You are likely to choose a man who offers this kind of stability, the life you thought you had dreamed of. The problem is that true stability for you comes from understanding your enormous energy and ability to experience.

As a wife, you can be a splendid companion, very sensitive, sensual, and desirable. There will never be a dull moment as you flip from one side of your nature to the other. You come through for your partner in a big way. Nothing you do is halfway.

Some find your multifaceted personality confusing. You draw men who match one side of your nature or the other. You could, if not at peace with yourself, attack your partner periodically. Actually, you are projecting, showing your lack of self-acceptance. As a result, if you marry young or have not yet evolved, you could have two marriages.

With Aries SUN man: He invites your wild side to come out and play. You could see him as a risk but in reality, he will be a joy, as he allows you to be whole. You discover that he can provide the kind of security that allows you to be comfortable. If you choose this path, the fires are eternal.

With Taurus SUN man: It makes no difference what face you choose to show him: He likes it. He appreciates and fulfills your need for stability and earthiness. Yet when the woman with blazing spirit and passion appears on the scene, he says "yes." He will open you up to the wonders of life from his arms to the other side of the world. Say "yes" back!

With Gemini SUN man: He challenges you on many levels. He wanders mentally and is consumed by a passion for ideas. Your response is to express your passion for action. If these passions combine, call out the National Guard! Despite the potential heat, he might not be able to offer you a practical life.

With Cancer SUN man: Nobody said that this wasn't an interesting match, but then no one said it was an easy one either. You have very different styles. You want him to be powerful and in control. He wants security as much as you, but he is emotional and clinging. Your need for action could be stymied with this man. Recriminations back and forth could ensue.

With Leo SUN man: He is passionate, romantic, and a showstopper. Because he loves the quality life so much, he tends to make money. You like this characteristic in him because you feel security comes through the bankroll. Emotionally, he knows how to make you twang. He is likely to understand both sides of your nature.

With Virgo SUN man: You want a practical and earthy man, but your need for heat, vitality, and energy could be left short. This man is very restrained. You will never be able to unlock your total womanliness with him. If that is okay with you, then go for it with your eyes open.

With Libra SUN man: If you are looking for stability and wealth in this lifetime, keep on truckin'. As delightful as he is, this man cannot make a decision. He will pull on your heartstrings. If you can let out your free-spirited nature, you might be able to enjoy a long-term connection.

With Scorpio SUN man: The aura of mystery and sensuality flows from him, and you can't help it, you want him. On some level you like his commanding, possessive temperament and feel safe with his strength. When you introduce him to the spirited lady within you, he will be even more drawn to you. He will be demanding. Count on it.

With Sagittarius SUN man: Once bonded, you have a union of souls and may never part. The good news is that you might not need to, as you live together harmoniously. He helps you contact your emotional depth. He encourages you to be yourself. How secure you will feel depends on the quality of your relationship and your ability to release certain prejudices.

With Capricorn SUN man: He is everything you thought you wanted and more. He provides you with a stable income and can be quite grounded. You will always resent that you cannot be free-spirited and adventuresome. He looks at you dumbfounded, not sure how to handle you if you become a wild woman. Remember, he is into control, and that means controlling you too.

With Aquarius SUN man: You find the ultimate friend and playmate in this man. He is always ready for the next adventure. You might have such a good time together that you take the next step. You like the physical tie, but you are likely to berate him for not providing the security you want. You have a choice here.

With Pisces SUN man: There is something very appealing about this man. You figure with your sense of direction, you can CHANGE him into a powerhouse. But you really can't change anyone but yourself. So if this match depends on his metamorphosis, go another direction.

MOON IN SAGITTARIUS, SUN IN AQUARIUS

You are a pleasure-seeker by nature. You pioneer freedom, independence, and adventure. You project trendiness, combined with an exotic touch. You are bundle of fire and air and somewhat explosive should you set your eye on a goal. Nothing will stop you.

You are attractive to men because you are so intuitive and vivacious. Your vibrant love of life comes through no matter what you do. Men can only imagine what it might be like to be with such a bundle of grace, vitality, and energy. You will need a playmate and partner who meets your energy, and who may also have a touch of the unusual.

You are probably slender, athletic, and ready to pop up at the racquet-ball club or take off on a motorcycle. You could be just as comfortable at an art show or opera. Your mind is equal to your physical vitality. You don't need to be. You care about experiences.

You are likely to marry more than once, especially if you marry at an early age. You will want a man who is his own thinker, whom others might classify as eccentric. You will respect his integrity and strength of character. He won't need to have a huge bank account, but must have commitment and show dedication. You aren't picky about romantic styles, though your way of courtship could have your friends shaking their heads.

With Aries SUN man: You have found an adventurer here, a man who could suddenly go on safari if it suited him. You are turned on by this way-out behavior and want to be friends and more. You will choose each other not only for love, but also because you like each other. With this kind of bonding, how can you go wrong?

With Taurus SUN man: Nice guy, perhaps for another lifetime. He is conservative and doesn't walk anywhere near a wild path. He won't know what to make of you, so untraditional, not that he won't be attracted. Be friends.

With Gemini SUN man: He is unusual, though he is an idea man all the way. He will like your quickness in responding to him. You'll act on his ideas, which will flatter him. You get him off his intellectual duff to come play with you. You can't help yourselves. Plan on a good time with this man for the long haul.

With Cancer SUN man: Though this man makes a fabulous husband and partner, he isn't for you. He wants a traditional life, and when you do your thing, he could fall off his chair. He knows better, you know better. Trouble could still happen!

With Leo SUN man: With this man there is passion and love that you might not find with many others. You are opposites, but there is so much physical glue and romance that you will be smitten. He likes a chase, and you will give him one. You'll be happy no matter what you're up to together. Ah, love at first sight.

With Virgo SUN man: His logical ways could make you think he is a Vulcan. You like weirdness and you might have an eccentric here. There will be tension because he is not used to nor does he want such a vibrant, independent woman. The bonding is touching, but needs to be worked with. You must understand each other for this match to stay together.

With Libra SUN man: You will want to get to know this gentleman better. It doesn't make any difference that he can't make a decision and is allergic to commitment. You will entice him with your freedom and independence. He finds you very attractive, exciting, and dynamic. This can be a great love affair.

With Scorpio SUN man: This is a tense connection at best. As free-spirited as you are, he is possessive. You both tend to think that you are right, that your way is the only way. And that means the highway. Don't play.

With Sagittarius SUN man: You move in harmony. You work as one. You think alike and feel alike. Your blending is exciting, with many unexpected twists. If he is a little strange, you love him all the more. You will not be bored, nor will he with this excellent match. And as time passes, it only becomes more fun.

With Capricorn SUN man: You find this man the ultimate stick-in-the-mud. And we would prefer to not mention what he thinks of you. You both are well advised to not even consider each other.

With Aquarius SUN man: To some, the two of you seem Looney Tunes. They may be jealous because it is so obvious how much fun you're having. You don't seem like a normal couple with normal problems. What bothers others doesn't faze the two of you. Life has many exotic twists for you if you stick together.

With Pisces SUN man: Tensions are very high between you. You are simply two very different people. Nothing is wrong, but it doesn't feel right. You can play together, but it won't go anywhere. Just don't be hard on each other.

MOON IN SAGITTARIUS, SUN IN PISCES

You are a feeling, loving woman who will go to great lengths to help others. You have the energy to realize your goals. Sometimes you will question your own strength and can get weepy. Being able to feel as intensely is a plus, not a negative. It is simply you, going to excess as you are wont to do.

You are very attractive with a somewhat ethereal, feminine look. You have lots of vitality and raw energy. Men are attracted to this blend of the feminine and masculine, and find you quite exotic. You could marry more than once and have your share of relationships in exploring the blending of your dual nature.

Part of the reason you could have several relationships is that you give off ambivalent vibes. Sometimes you seem independent and other times fragile and ultrasensitive. You might not realize how confusing you can be to men. You might not be sure which voice to respond to, and your spontaneity makes choosing difficult.

You want a partner who is strong and creative, and understands your moodiness. Passion must be as important to him as it is you. Yet you will demand space to do your own things. You will always be intense, whether for some nurturing, loving activity or in taking an adventurous risk. You are artistic, talented, and devoted. You will experience many facets of life because of your capacity to feel and pick up on others. Mr. Right will give you space to play out your many sides.

With Aries SUN man: Both of you feel a burning attraction. He brings out the raw, passionate woman in you. However, when you become emotional, feeling, and empathic, he won't know quite what to do or say. If you expect him to partake in these emotional tempests, you are barking up the wrong tree. But he has a lot to offer.

With Taurus SUN man: This man understands you on many levels. He is feeling, yet grounded. He can talk about emotions, understand them, and help you work through your feelings. He will adore your risk-taking nature and invite you to adventure with him. This is a deeply sensual bonding. With him, you will feel unified.

With Gemini SUN man: The tension is inordinately high here. It is as if he is on the opposite end of a rubber band you are holding. Though there seems to be movement toward each other, ultimately the tie could snap. He lives in a world of thought and has no patience for emotional displays. You will think he's a cold fish. Think before you take this leap.

With Cancer SUN man: You have met a man who understands your sensitivities and has his own. Together you create an unusually sensual tie, as you are intuitive about each other. You walk into magical realms simply by touching and sharing. The added passion of your fiery moon won't bother him one iota.

With Leo SUN man: He is one passionate, hot tamale and you love it. You stoke his romantic passion with your intensely independent manner. He is enthralled by your multifaceted personality. To make this relationship bloom, you must praise him for his chivalrous ways. He loves it and gives you many opportunities to repeat the compliment.

With Virgo SUN man: The draw is there, though the compatibility might not be. His picky comments do nothing but irritate you, encouraging you to run away. You are loving, emotional, and sensitive. He is always rational, earthy, and oh, so reasonable. He's attracted to your intensity, but this isn't a go. You feel as if you just took a shower with him. A cold shower.

With Libra SUN man: His imaginative courtship and gentle smile lures you. You have found a fellow romantic who appreciates the artistic and creative. Your passion only fans his desire more. You will be okay with his inability to make up his mind. It really isn't important to you. You know you were meant to be together. Don't figure on ever separating.

With Scorpio SUN man: He is even hotter and more feeling than you. His mysterious ways add to his allure, but you read right through them. Don't let him know; he will be upset if he thinks you figured him out! Sometimes he's a bit jealous—after all, you are more independent than he. He's worth playing coy. Everything you share is excessive, especially the loving.

With Sagittarius SUN man: You and this man are on a perpetual merry-go-round. Like you, he loves to play or take off on the next adventure. You will feel joined at the hip. Hope he will have something in his astrological makeup that will help him understand the poetic, sensitive woman in you. Otherwise, as happy as you could be, there might be a sense of something lacking.

With Capricorn SUN man: In many ways this man offers form, stability, and financial well being. You can be emotional with him and he will tune in. He is turned on by your zest and vitality. Careful, though. If you become too big for your britches and insist on doing your own thing, he could go where the pickings are more to his liking.

With Aquarius SUN man: You can be great friends and go on explorations together. You will love having him at your party, but that is where it all ends. He doesn't understand emotionality, nor does he want to. This is a wild friendship with a little loving tossed in. It would be a mistake to make any more of it.

With Pisces SUN man: This is the emotional, gentle man you want. You will take his interests as yours. He could sometimes be annoyed by your energy and drive. He is just envious. In many ways, you will feel as if you are living out a fairy tale together, there is so much imaginative interplay between you.

Moon in Capricorn

"Don't threaten me with love, Baby. Let's just go walking in the rain."

BILLIE HOLIDAY

When you were very young, you learned to be adult in behavior. You never got to romp and play as a kid; now, your inner child may never come to surface. In fact, you might not even recognize the child within you, as you were taught to repress your feelings at an early age.

Image is a high priority for you. It is important that others respect you and see you as in control of your life. Somehow, if you don't have others' homage, you feel as if having nothing. Respect is important, but you will come to learn that it's even more important to respect yourself, including your feelings and emotions. Expect this to be one of your lifetime lessons. Until you connect with your self-esteem, you could often become the person you think others will respect, sacrificing yourself.

You project with a sense of direction, confidence, and control. However, you seem like a fortress emotionally. A man who is attracted to you will need to penetrate your defenses. You want a knight in shining armor whom you can be proud of. But he also needs to catapult your walls.

The lifetime issue for you emotionally is: Do you want a relationship that looks good but might have little emotional content? Or you do you want to risk, be vulnerable, and have an emotional blending as well as a dynamic relationship? The former seems easier, but could leave you empty. The latter will be harder work, but worthwhile.

Though desirable, you might choose to marry late in life, after you work through many of your issues. That is not to say that you won't have your fill of relationships. Each bonding will help you step up the ladder of vulnerability, if that is what you choose. You are very serious-minded about everything, including relationships and transformation.

You possess a high energy level, a need for movement that makes you interesting to the opposite sex. Though you could dress your body in business garb or drab clothes, your movements reveal a very sensual, vital woman. You will be more comfortable with your sensuality as you get older. You are a woman who ripens with age.

You fill the role of wife to the max, and others wonder how you manage to do it so well. You are concerned with image, remember? You do nothing halfway. Whatever is expected of you as a partner will be done with excellence.

MOON IN CAPRICORN, SUN IN ARIES

You are a bundle of energy and activity. You're sure of what you want and where you are heading. You have no intention of letting anyone stop you. You have an innate restlessness that is hard to control. You can't stay still for all the tea in China.

Because of your high vitality, you draw others with ease. Men feel your sexiness, whether or not you hide it. You are likely to be bold, direct, and animated. Though there is a side of you that is coy, you are quite direct about your sexuality and desires. You draw a man who is responsive to these needs. You could very well have relationships for sex, as much as for companionship. You are quite capable of sorting the two.

In that sense, men understand you loud and clear, as they often make similar distinctions. However, with all of this, you will seek a man who is committed to his ideals and has a sense of energy, directness, and willingness to do what is necessary to get what he wants. You want someone with drive, energy, and determination. You might be willing to fudge a little on traditional structure in this relationship, though in the long run, you will create a very dynamic life and family structure with your partner.

Though you aren't one for intimate cooing and sharing, the passions you share with Mr. Right will open you up to more vulnerability than you expected. The word ardent will describe your work, your life, and your relationship.

With Aries SUN man: He is your picture-perfect man, at least the one you want in your heart and dreams. He is a crusader, energetic, and passionate. In some way, his heat touches your soul and you feel merged, even before it happens! This can work long term. Because you are so much alike, much goes unsaid, but is understood.

With Taurus SUN man: He brings you a unique emotional softness and security. He plays your heartstrings like a musician, and you feel safe enough to lower some of your barriers. What is great here is the depth, feeling, and growth. He will provide the security and baubles that you need. This could be a go, with a sensuality that Cupid would admire.

With Gemini SUN man: He is full of whoopee and fun. He is always flitting from one idea to another. He tends to give up, and you will batter him for that! However, there is a sensual heat between you that keeps bringing you together. He is good for the moment, bad for commitment! Play him accordingly.

With Cancer SUN man: He too desires respectability. He shares your need for motion. However, he is not the fiery man you want. He is security-oriented and wants a family, but may embarrass you when he starts to cry. You will have to deal with your feelings here!

With Leo SUN man: You are about commitment; he is about love. There is fire here and the need for respect on both your parts. Your souls will dissolve into one. His commitment is to the good life, which he will provide. And you will know grand passion. He could be more than you can handle.

With Virgo SUN man: You find here a man who has precision and can make you feel secure. But dynamic? Action-oriented? I don't think so, unless other astrological influences come into play. You can be happy, but you will yearn for passion. With this man, passion could be a foreign word.

With Libra SUN man: He never stays still and loves to move. However, he isn't fiery or directed the way you'd like. Unlike you, he seems to be incapable of a decision. However, he is a charmer and a romantic. There is an eternal push and pull between you. You're well advised to let him be. In the long run, you will feel as if you compromised in choosing him.

With Scorpio SUN man: You will find he has a sturdy sense of commitment and an animal majesty that brings out the Ram in you. You must respect him or he won't put up with you. You can build a strong commitment together, but it must be based on mutual respect, a meeting of two equal powers. Neither of you can control the other.

With Sagittarius SUN man: He is a bundle of fire, energy, and then zoom, he is gone. You like the energy, but the flakiness is another issue. You want someone solid and committed to your type of values. Though you certainly will enjoy passionate moments with him, you could find yourself ultimately dissatisfied with this man.

With Capricorn SUN man: He reads you cold, and you read him. Your goals in life are similar, and you create a mutual empire together that others cannot help but admire. The intimacy is odd, in that it works on an unspoken level. Sometimes you wish he could have more passion and fire. Wishing is okay, but in reality, he is a wonderful choice.

With Aquarius SUN Man: Yes, he is fun and you might very well be friends. You like his universal caring and causes. However, you are too conservative for him, and you do not appreciate his wildness, except perhaps when the shades are pulled. Some things are best left undone. This relationship is one of them.

With Pisces SUN man: He is emotional, creative, and feeling. For him, structure stabilizes his feelings; for you, it protects your feelings. Eventually, however, you could turn on him, as he is not the fiery, determined gentleman you want as a mate. Still, there is a lot to be learned here. And you offer each other much.

MOON IN CAPRICORN, SUN IN TAURUS

You are clear about what you want, and you know how to make it happen. You will follow the logical, utilitarian route. Your stamina will bring you success. However, you demand and expect control.

Your sensuality speaks through your clothes and your choices, no matter how prim you are. It is possible that you perpetually wage the battle of the bulge. Your keen sense of balance and color comes out in your appearance, drawing others.

Because of the soft sensuality that frames you, others might mistake you for an easy mark. Wrong. You are grounded, earthy, and not to be toyed with. In a nice and firm manner you let another know your boundaries.

You will have many suitors, and if ever alone you won't for long. You're likely to marry your first love. Mr. Right must have the moneymaking capacity to provide a quality life. You will be drawn to luxury and want it as testimony of his caring. He needs to provide you and the family with a big house and many vacations.

Your partner needs to have strong feelings, a sense of balance, and a love of the arts. He will be able to express his depth and caring. Indulgence could be a theme for both of you, as you want only the best together. With him, you will feel safe to express your vulnerabilities. There will be a tie of trust.

With Aries SUN man: He is a bundle of energy, off on a crusade to make life more enjoyable for the people he cares about. He might not have the quiet stability you seek from your mate. There is high energy between you, though ultimately, you might want to bypass him. You want someone earthier, and maybe a little less impulsive.

With Taurus SUN man: He is stubborn and, like you, when he digs his heels in, it is his way or no way. Fortunately, before you get to loggerheads, there is a lot of give-and-take. Conflict probably will not be necessary, as you are so much alike once you get down to the bottom line. The sensuality hums between you.

With Gemini SUN man: There is no question that you are attracted to this man. There are sparks between you, but they can become the sparks of dissension rather than passion. You find him flaky. He finds you sensual, but difficult and too grounded for his taste.

With Cancer SUN man: Together, you build strong foundations. He loves romantic walks on the beach and knows how to make you leave your earthy grounding for the fever of love. This is a long-term match with a great deal of feeling. Enjoy candlelight dinners and strolls hand in hand. You make history together.

With Leo SUN man: You have just met the epitome of romance, and you like his courtship. He senses your sensuality, which could disorient him for a long time. Financial gain is a strong likelihood here, and with it comes a very good life. You'll need to look the other way, however, because he is a bit of a player.

With Virgo SUN man: He is practical, but not dynamic. You understand his picky detail-orientation, but you want more than that out of life. You can cohabit together easily, but life could become dull. He might not understand your need for luxury, intensity, and power. You could be too much for him to handle, but he will adore you. You are the dynamo here.

With Libra SUN man: You tune into his finer sensibilities and artistic nature. He picks up on your sensuality and hardy earthiness. He loses himself to your passions and love of indulgence. You treat him to a universe of depth he might have never experienced. You must wear the pants here and make the decisions.

With Scorpio SUN man: You are on a seesaw together. When one goes up, the other goes down, yet you have common issues. You simply play them out differently. You must respect your different styles to make this work. The seething emotional and sensual draw will force you to work issues through. He presents you with intrigue, mystery, and magic. You steam together.

With Sagittarius SUN man: He is fiery and independent, with a roving eye. You will not tolerate this on any level. He does have some interesting wisdom to share with you. Show him you are wise too: Keep this relationship on an intellectual level.

With Capricorn SUN man: He is into control, money, and power. You like your rhythm together. You see eye-to-eye about life. He intuitively knows you and is charmed by your vulnerability and artistic manner. You know there will always be stability here. You talk the same language—in the day and at play. This is a winning couple.

With Aquarius SUN man: He is lively, different, and a bit weird. He will be your friend, and you can be his. But forget anything else.

With Pisces SUN man: He is artistic, sensitive, and loving. He cannot thank you enough for the understanding and stability you provide in his life. You adore romance, and he offers that even into old age. You work well together, melding into a harmonious, loving couple. You will be his fortress, and he will be your Romeo.

MOON IN CAPRICORN, SUN IN GEMINI

Control is a major issue in all realms of your life. You will undermine anything that feels out of control and blow it up. You also do this emotionally. It could take many years for you to recognize the value of vulnerability. One of your lessons is letting go of the need to control others, and learning to control yourself.

You are probably quite attractive, slender, and tall. Your high energy and physique draw others. You have big eyes, agility, and grace. You don't dress for attention, but rather for function, though you always look good. After all, you want to be admired and respected, and your physical presentation is part of your image.

Once you learn to quiet the constant verbal chatter in your mind, you will be able to get in touch with the intense feelings that rage within. Your feelings run you, but you might not be conscious of them. Once you come to terms with your intensity, you can become a wonderfully loving partner. You are always loyal, faithful, and honest.

You will expect a mate who can debate with you, share ideas, and enjoy the use of intellect as much as you. It is okay if he isn't very intense about feelings. If he has humor and you can laugh over the rough moments, all the better!

You could go through several relationships before you find the right person. This is the result of your transformation in adulthood and your need for diversity, change, and excitement.

With Aries SUN man: He is a man of passionate currents. He has blazing, strong emotions, yet an extremely keen intellect. You like his energy and mind, but you will not be able to suppress his feelings. Your defenses could become impenetrable as a result. Unless you can open to him, let go.

With Taurus SUN man: He is like a lullaby at night for you. He could be very bright and concerned with intellectual matters. However, forget the heavy-duty repartee. That isn't his style. In fact, some of your ha-has go over his head. You could feel very comfortable here, yet attack him for not being the word whiz you are.

With Gemini SUN man: You dance a jig when you meet this man, you are so happy. You are able to experience the exchange of mind and body here. This match could be very nice, but be careful. His love of excitement could have him playing in other yards too! Can you accept this?

With Cancer SUN man: You have meet your antithesis. He is emotional, acknowledging his helplessness. He is changeable but, unlike you, he is moody, not intellectually fickle. You ultimately want the same things: home, family, and security. However, you could get bored by his drippiness, and he will be insecure because he really can't reach you emotionally.

With Leo SUN man: Meet the lover of the zodiac! He charms, has a way with words and with women. You're likely to tumble hook, line, and sinker. He will like your playfulness, but you need to demonstrate some of that deep passion to hold him. This may be a very scary proposition, but one you will take on anyway if this relationship is to work.

With Virgo SUN man: He is mental like you, but not in the style you like. He focuses on practical matters, not fun and frolic. Repartee, exchanges of wit, and great humor aren't his style. You would be safe here—and very bored.

With Libra SUN man: He is delightful, light, and witty. This could be Nirvana superficially, but he will not offer you security. You will ache for structure and stability. Still, he is very appealing.

With Scorpio SUN man: This man is intense and brilliant. He can match you on every level and twist words. Be careful, sarcasm is one of his specialties. You will fall in love with his mind and quite possibly his body. He loves your wit and senses your earthy stability. There is an element of spontaneous combustion here, and it could happen over and over.

With Sagittarius SUN man: He is as much a man of action as you are a woman of ideas. You add sparks to his life and you are complimented by his adoration. This man travels and has wanderlust. Though there is a long-term attraction, there is a long-term problem too. He won't provide security. This is like jumping into a wildfire.

With Capricorn SUN man: Your Moon and his Sun kiss. He understands you as you do him. Neither of you will push the other beyond your limits. This mutuality is pivotal to the relationship's success. Your laughter and lightness amuse him, though occasionally he will want to muzzle you! Nothing personal, you realize.

With Aquarius SUN man: You feel you've tumbled into the perfect playmate, as you giggle and roll with laughter. There is an innate sense of naughtiness here with lots of good times, mischief, and flirtation. However, unless he has something anchored in his chart, you might never feel secure.

With Pisces SUN man: You know how it feels when you hear fingernails against a blackboard? This man is like that sound to you and always will be. If you get past the first reaction, you could find a sense of stability in the constant emoting. Yech! This isn't for you at all!

MOON IN CAPRICORN, SUN IN CANCER

You are a charming combination of mixed messages and vibrations. But within these seemingly opposite voices, there are some key themes. You want security, at any cost. Family is important to you. You don't like feeling out of control, though you are often vulnerable and helpless. You have the ability to build defenses that could take an A-bomb to bring down.

However, meeting you for the first time, no one would pick up such vital information, as you are charming, ethereal, and seemingly soft and sweet. Your magnetism draws, yet there is a very firm, directed woman beneath this surface.

You question yourself constantly about boundaries. How much is too much or not enough? This back and forth marks your thinking. You wonder whether to do what you feel rather than doing what you think. Such confusion!

Landing the right man is an unlikely first-round accomplishment. You will want a man who is emotional, caring, and somewhat possessive. His possessiveness will make you feel secure and help you express your emotions. You want a romantic courtship, trips by waters, meals at wonderful restaurants.

You offer stability yet excitement because of your diversity and full moon moodiness. You will be a beautiful hostess, wife, and mother. You will nurture and love those in your care. You feel safe because they need you. Protecting yourself and yet loving seems to be what you are about.

With Aries SUN man: He will trigger you in nearly every possible way. The good news is you could lose a lot of weight running away from him. If you like confrontation and brash emotions, you've got it here. Keep running. You need the exercise!

With Taurus SUN man: There is good and there is great. This is nothing less than great. He offers stability, romance, earthy sensuality, and one experience after another. He strokes your heart, and you find you are loved beyond what you thought possible. You will be great together, no matter what you do. Don't say no!

With Gemini SUN man: Much goes on behind the scenes here, and it's not good stuff. He is the inverse of what you seek, though he can pursue you romantically. He is intellectual; you want feelings, security, and structure. Don't bark up this tree.

With Cancer SUN man: He offers you love, security, and feeling. You will call the shots as he does his love dance. Cupid's arrow strikes both of you. You have a good thing going, spiced with a continuous feverish attraction.

With Leo SUN man: He is romantic and emotional about love. He will be an excellent provider, no question about it, and a wonderful lover too. The real issue is whether you can feel secure with him. If not, steer clear or else you will become the Princess of Negativity.

With Virgo SUN man: Not a detail goes past this man unnoticed. He is practical and a nurturer. However, if you expect him to understand your emotional nature, forget it. Nevertheless, together you can build a very happy life. The romance could be warmer, but the peace of mind is wonderful.

With Libra SUN man: He is romantic and gentle. That is where the plusses end for this couple. You won't be happy, as he won't be able to identify with your emotional ups and downs. And structure? It won't happen. Move on.

With Scorpio SUN man: You will feel as if you are on a tropical island with him. Your interactions are steamy and emotional. There is nothing to regret here except that you might not be able to cool off, even after years. This man is strong and determined, and will love you forever. This is a passionate love match, a dream come true.

With Sagittarius SUN man: You need to relax when you meet this man, because he isn't what you want. Just mellow, chill out, and enjoy him as a friend. That is the best possible outcome for this combo.

With Capricorn SUN man: You hum the same tune as this man. You will live like king and queen together. You both have your share of defenses, but you speak the same language. Your rainbow of feelings adds great tone to the relationship, pushing and extending the sensual spectrum wider and wider.

With Aquarius SUN man: He is a good friend, a bit exotic and not for you. Your goals don't dance together, and there really isn't a match. So much for that.

With Pisces SUN man: You cry, he joins in. You might need to buy stock in Kleenex if you decide to be a couple. There is an emotional tenderness and empathy that few will ever experience. Your more practical side saves the day. At least someone will remember to pay the bills here! This is the nest of true love.

Moon in Capricorn, Sun in Leo

You are strength, magnetism, and presence all wrapped up into one. Getting what you want is a prime directive for you and you don't understand anything less. You are able to make a big difference in any realm once you decide your intentions. You draw the opposite sex with ease, but you put suitors through quite a set of challenges. What better way to find out all about them?

You seek out a dramatic, charismatic man. He needs to provide you with security and be able to wine and dine you in the best of style. Romance is important to you. You judge it as testimony of caring. For that reason, it is important that the courtship never end.

You and your partner will be a very romantic couple with all the accruements that go with relationships. You both will want only the best.

You are very proud and a little remote. Those who understand you realize this is part of your defense mechanism. You can't always be open. You will be forgiven for this trait because you are a generous lover. You give 100 percent.

If someone hurts you, you will find it difficult to be open again to that person. One of your biggest needs is to learn to forgive yourself as well as others. If wounded, you could turn to collecting material possessions rather than allowing love in your life. In that case, you will never feel as if you have enough.

With Aries SUN man: The embers here explode when you meet each other. Your flamboyant and passionate style turns this man on. He likes that you are sensible, anchored, and directed. You will enjoy his fiery nature, though at times you will need to curb your need for control. Another case of spontaneous combustion!

With Taurus SUN man: He is romantic and anchored. Count on being appreciated. You will be romanced as if there is no tomorrow. You can have it all here. However, if you should get into a power struggle, there will be no winner. Learn to not always be the ruling monarch and you can have a loving, secure relationship with all the accruements you have dreamed about.

With Gemini SUN man: He responds to your coquetry with wit, eagerness, and flirtation. You like his spirit, full of humor and happiness. Though the loving is fun A-okay, you will learn that he can not provide the security and stability you seek. He is always off tilting at windmills. Here today, gone tomorrow.

With Cancer SUN man: There is a definite attraction here that could last. You are very different people with different styles, but you share a deep concern about security. Your sunny temperament intrigues this man. He is quite the romantic, and you will love his intense courtship. You build empires in the clouds together.

With Leo SUN man: Here two powers face each other. You can either work together or against each other. There is great natural magnetism, and your ground rules are the same. You both need praise and worship. If you aren't capable of this mutuality, this match falls flat. If you can, WOW!

With Virgo SUN man: You will be offended by his quiet style, though you'll appreciate the fact that he can handle a budget and make good choices. However, you will never have the dynamic man you seek. Your energies are off. If you are willing to settle, then this is a good compromise.

With Libra SUN man: He has a way with the women, and even you can tumble into his collection of the smitten. Be realistic about him. As much as he is a romantic dream, he is a practical nightmare. He is not strong with reality or making good decisions. If you are willing to wear the pants, this is great!

With Scorpio SUN man: Fires rarely rage so out of control as they do here. The passion bug bites both of you as you learn how to meld your love and life. He might love and adore you, but he will never worship a heroine. You might not care either, as he offers so much else you are seeking. This is a go.

With Sagittarius SUN man: You like his fiery style. He has a sense of wanderlust and magic that intrigues you. You might even decide to play with him for a while, but for the long run, he is a bad bet. His risk-taking will make you very nervous.

With Capricorn SUN man: You two are like bread and butter together, and probably anything after this man will seem like margarine. You understand each other clearly and know how to touch each other emotionally, mentally, and physically. Living together is a snap; you know you were meant to be together. He will love your flashiness and finds you beautiful. The admiration is mutual.

With Aquarius SUN man: Some people just make you want to giggle. He is one of them. There is a tremendous appeal and attraction between you. You view life in terms of people, popularity, and socializing. His style is detached and platonic; yours is rich and loving. However, the two of you play and party well together. He is a fun romp, though making you secure isn't his primary interest. This match is great for the short term.

With Pisces SUN man: The dance he weaves around you is exciting, dramatic, and loving. The romantic butterflies soar forever for you. His emotional level will make you feel secure, even if his bankroll doesn't. He needs you to ground him and help him create the success both of you want. There is a positive give-and-take here.

MOON IN CAPRICORN, SUN IN VIRGO

You are clear and directed. You may project much less dynamically than the true person within. You often wonder at others who are more impulsive and wild than you. You see no reason to cause yourself trouble.

There is a strong likelihood that you are petite, if your gene pool supports it. Yet you have a big way of letting others know exactly what is on your mind. You are commanding and direct. Because you are so together, you make good choices. You offer a lot in a relationship: commitment, stability, and nurturing. Others can count on you. You draw members of the opposite sex, who value these qualities and want a wonderful wife, companion, and partner.

Often people do not sense the dynamic businesswoman and powerhouse within you. You are ambitious and will look for someone who offers status and security. You might have a strong career. Though you believe in traditional marriage, you are a modern woman.

The man you choose will be practical and financially secure and have dynamic potential. For you to want him, your ethics and morals need to match. You will demand this assurance before you reveal your womanly self. You are capable of tremendous caring and vulnerability once you open up. Therefore, you make your choices with scrupulous care. You don't want to be burned. Once more, you seize control of your life and make your choices accordingly.

With Aries SUN man: You have met a passionate pistol, someone who goes after what he wants. You won't have much control here, so do think before you leap. He can light your fire and offer security, but calm, I don't think so! You might criticize him for his flamboyant style and cause problems when there are none.

With Taurus SUN man: He lures you with wonderfully seductive, romantic dates. He slowly nurtures the flames of love between you. He brushes you with tender moments, touches you with his soft ways, and seduces you. You will never know passion as you do with him. The good news is that he is a hot choice in all areas.

With Gemini SUN man: There are some partners one knows intuitively not to tango with. This is one. His flightiness annoys you; he might even suggest (heaven forbid) that you are boring. Tensions run high, yet there could be a physical attraction. Still, stay away.

With Cancer SUN man: You can't stop yourself, and why should you? This man is emotional, loving, and caring. He will provide security. You will always feel safe to express your feelings with him. He understands vulnerability. You will love the way he gives all, even his checkbook. He knows he can trust you with everything. There is a deep foundation of trust here.

With Leo SUN man: He is a runner and a player, the last thing you want. If you are lucky, he won't notice you, or you him. Steer clear. He is trouble. He might be a financial powerhouse, but move on.

With Virgo SUN man: You like him; you two are very similar. You will be the more ambitious one, and you could give him a helpful push or two. Still, you feel good with what he offers you. He is a little cool and detached in romance, but you love feeling your womanly power with him. You like what you can do to him!

With Libra SUN man: This man is about love and romance. However, he doesn't really have a practical bone in him. Though you could fall in love with him, you could attack him for not being what you want. He likes your strength and practicality and will want you. But in the long run, you become cold and attacking. This isn't good for either of you.

With Scorpio SUN man: This man is a tidal wave of passion. He's mysterious and deep, and understands you with ease. He appreciates the simplicity with which you organize your life. His intensity of feeling gives you permission to lose control sometimes. You are both powerful. Together you create a special life. Go for it.

With Sagittarius SUN man: He is a risk-taker, something you can't tolerate, and don't want to. Laugh, enjoy superficialities, and don't bother to let this go any deeper.

With Capricorn SUN man: Like meets like. You both are very clear about your future and what you want. It is more likely that these objectives are the same, promising a real match. Your precision and ability to organize and handle details please him. He trusts you, likes you, and will make you tingle to your tiptoes. There is no question here. Yes!

With Aquarius SUN man: He is strange, cool, and detached. Precision is not his strong suit, nor is practicality. You know what you want, and it isn't him. Friendship is a possibility.

With Pisces SUN man: He serves others, cares about them, and expresses his healing qualities. In that way you are the same, though he could be more altruistic (and less practical). You will fall in love with this caring, romantic spirit. For both of your sakes, you will have to keep your hands on the checkbook. He is worth it. You will know depth and feeling here.

MOON IN CAPRICORN, SUN IN LIBRA

You give off mixed signals. You want security, control, and money and aren't likely to settle for anything less. You could also hide from your feelings and refuse to let down your guard.

Yet you project differently. You are very soft, delicate, and attractive. You seem to be somewhat indecisive, soft and willowy. However, that exterior has very little to do with what is inside, though men are likely to be attracted to what they first see.

Romance and courtship delight you to the point that you might judge a man on his courtship and not on his essence. You could fall madly in love, only to later find that your love choice doesn't offer the security and structure you want. For that reason, you might become contrary or feel disappointed by "love."

With your confusing projection, you are likely to draw someone who only sees your surface and might not read your depth. Recognize that you want more, and perhaps need to reveal more of yourself, even if you aren't comfortable being vulnerable and open.

You will want a man who takes care of the total you, though your heart will be drawn to a romantic man with a rose in his hand and a sweet compliment on his lips. For that reason, you could have more than one marriage until you find the right man. That's a man who will nurture your vulnerable, emotional side as well as court the delightful woman.

With Aries SUN man: Yin has met yang, male meets female. He is drawn to your feminine side. However, your need for power could throw him off. He is his own man. To make this relationship work, respect each other's styles and don't get into power struggles. On the physical plane, there is much going on here to encourage that extra effort.

With Taurus SUN man: He understands your complexity, appreciates your femininity, and loves your power. He will wine and dine you to the hilt as you tumble head over heels in love. You two are like the salt of the earth. You belong together. The longer you know each other, the clearer it becomes. Count on his gentle, loving strength to guide and cherish you well.

With Gemini SUN man: He presents a dashing figure, and you tumble. You need to love the moment to be with this man, and not look to the long term. He doesn't offer security, as he is changeable—some people might say flighty. The romantic twists are feverish. You will find it hard to say no.

With Cancer SUN man: He is more emotional than you. At times you could become embarrassed by his exposed feelings. You'll have romantic moments aplenty. Learn not to judge each other if this relationship is to work. There is great potential for growth here. He will need your control and penchant for structure to build the security you both desire.

With Leo SUN man: You are vitally drawn, like two beasts in the wild. He loves to chase, and you adore being caught. Together you can create an empire. Money is important to him, and power is key to you. You will love going out together and demonstrating the quality life you lead as a couple. You are proud to be the other half.

With Virgo SUN man: You will suffer if you expect to change him into the Romeo of your fantasies. Try not to project if you are attracted. Look at him as his own man. You will find that he is earthy and practical, and can offer the anchoring you crave. If you can appreciate this and not spurn his love-style, this is a go.

With Libra SUN man: There is a side of him that is every bit as romantic as you. The quiet, soft moments could send you both into Nirvana. However, you will land with a big clang. Your earthy side suddenly says: Who is this man who can't make a decision or organize his life?

With Scorpio SUN man: This man has intensity and masculinity. He is a force beyond your control. You find this extremely enticing and can't stay away. if you can replace candlelight dinners with torrid tangos, you are A-okay. He is a mystery and a power. You are stepping onto cloud nine.

With Sagittarius SUN man: He is a lively man, but it will take all your femininity and soft ways to draw him in. It isn't that you are unattractive; it is simply that he is always on to the next adventure. He is a risk-taker; you won't like that. Weigh this carefully before leaping.

With Capricorn SUN man: Your sense of bonding speaks for itself. You have little choice because you could be committed before you blink. At a later date, you might fuss because there isn't romance on a par with your dreams, but wait, you are happy on a profound level. Don't mess with a good thing.

With Aquarius SUN man: You are intrigued, but the courtship is atypical to say the least. You might laugh at this Bohemian figure. You will like him more if you keep him as a friend. Even if he wanted to, he couldn't anchor you. Plus, he is a bit of a playboy!

With Pisces SUN man: Your romantic styles are different, yet you revel in each other's love tempo. He will amaze you with his capacity for emotional catharsis, which sometimes overwhelms you. By being there for him, you stabilize him. It will be you who creates the structure of the relationship and your life together.

Moon in Capricorn, Sun in Scorpio

Many describe you as mysterious and distant, but you are really a case of still waters running deep. You have a lot to share, though you are picky about whom you choose to reveal yourself to. This quality of discrimination weaves through your life.

You exude sexuality when you walk into a room. Some would describe you as sultry. You move with self-assurance. Others want to know more. You have strong, deep eyes and don't shy away from eye contact. This gives others a sense you know all and fear little.

You are strong at recognizing your limits. It is important for you to know someone and size him up before deciding to be close. Though you are capable of grand passion, you will hold back until you feel secure. You have the good fortune of knowing what you want, which allows you strong self-control and direction.

Don't let anyone kid you: You chose the man in your life, though you might permit him to think that he zeroed in on you. Actually not only did you pick him, you also control the relationship by your reactions. You simply want to establish that the gentleman cares sufficiently for you to reveal your magnificent colors. There is a voluptuous quality to your body. You love feeling, touching, eating—all that is sensual. At times, you will need to ask yourself what is more important: the relationship or having control If you opt for love, you will have a wonderful tie.

With Aries SUN man: You're hot, he's hot. If your torrid passion doesn't burn each other out, you'll find that to feel comfortable, you must hold the reins. This man is a wild stallion, not easily handled. He isn't into control, but he can't be controlled either. Frankly, my dear, as much as you love him, he could drive you nuts.

With Taurus SUN man: Opposites make for heated moments. He's one of the few lovers who can deal with your heated, tumultuous displays. He understands what you want and will help you create it. He is docile (so it seems) until he has had enough. Then you are the red flag, and he is the charging bull. You must learn your limits if you want him!

With Gemini SUN man: You know what you want, and though this gentleman is charming, bright, and lively, he ain't it! He isn't easily controlled, as he is off here, there, and everywhere. He might run even faster if he senses your dynamic power and magnetism. Despite the attraction, even if you catch up with him, you will find he is too much of a lightweight for you.

With Cancer SUN man: He is as emotional as you, though he senses your need for control, which fortunately isn't one of his issues. However, your needs for security match. This relationship can last. The touching is uncanny, building to towering passion. You opt for growth, emotionality, and true love with Mr. Cancer.

With Leo SUN man: There is something wild and uncontrollable about this combination. Though this match can last long term, the wars are incredible. You are both fixed and rigid, though he is such a lover, he may have you backing down before you know it. He will provide for you as his queen, but remember, he is king!

With Virgo SUN man: He is earthy and sensual, and warms up to you with ease. His heat builds slowly, but with you he becomes a steamroller. You can count on his devotion, and he will treat your love like a cherished plant, knowing to tend it, water it, and nourish it. You can count on him providing whatever you want. This tie is stable. Play it long term.

With Libra SUN man: There is something innately contrary about this combination. You are both active, dynamic people. He wants exchanges on a light, easy, flirtatious level, whereas you are powerfully sensual, much like a river running into the ocean. Your mix isn't there in courtship, marriage, or life. No.

With Scorpio SUN man: Union is inevitable, deep, and profound. There is communication by touch, and nothing will be denied. However, he needs control as much as you. You need to trust each other and nurture your love to keep this relationship together. If there is commitment and devotion, you could have it all.

With Sagittarius SUN man: His passion is like a blaze of fire that rushes by you. It's there, and then it is gone. You are stable and present. This combination might work for a very short while, but any more than that, no, unless he is made of some unusual astrological fabric. He risks with money, feelings, and life; you build with money, feelings, and life. Forget it!

With Capricorn SUN man: This is a rendezvous with destiny. You are meant to be together and sense a hidden agenda. There is an otherworldly knowledge of each other and your needs. Together, you are powers and will build a sturdy, loving relationship. You'll have it all—security, intensity, and someone who intuitively understands you. There is faith and trust between you.

With Aquarius SUN man: There are some things that are just plain funny. This match is one of them. Whatever is happening between you, it is an odd combination. He is eccentric, a freedom-loving soul. You will never control him, and he might take off for Never-Never Land once he senses your heated passions and controlling nature.

With Pisces SUN man: He is sweet, water looking for form and passion. You are it! You both flow into each other with unusual mutuality and understanding. Your touching and loving replenish each other. Your stability will add to his security. He will want to give all. You only need to pave the way.

MOON IN CAPRICORN, SUN IN SAGITTARIUS

You are strong. You want solid foundations to protect yourself from worldly shocks and upsets. You have a sense of design, how "things" should be, and you will strive mightily to make it so. You will risk, after you weigh the ramifications.

You will have excellent earning capacity and will seek financial security above all in your relationships. You will be moody at times, but knowing there is money in your savings account for a rainy day will always cheer you up.

You tend to choose men who are emotionally unavailable for relationships or who can't give you what you want. This stems from a feeling that you don't deserve any better. Working on your self-esteem is important for you to create the quality relationship you deserve. You will be drawn to a daredevil type man who embodies on some level your inner spirit. He will tend to be wild in one area or another.

Though you might hide your sensuality, it comes through loud and clear to a sensitive man. He sees you as a rose yet to bud. You relate to men well once you relax. You are probably athletic, love sports, and participate in many male activities. You make a great companion and understand the opposite sex. That is probably why you could have a vulnerability to naughty boys. You basically like them.

You make a tough partner in that as much as you like your naughty men, you demand a lot. You want stability, security, and a traditional setup. However, it may be tough to get that kind of life from your mischievous choices. Remember, you have chosen them, and the responsibility lies with you.

With Aries SUN man: He appeals to the wild, fascinating animal side of you. You feel as if there is a merger of souls here, though you could be shy and reticent about how he arouses you. The problem here is that as strong as the attraction is, at some point, you decide to be sane, or shall we say more proper?

With Taurus SUN man: You like his stability and earthy ways. He will give you all that is proper and right. You like the image, the love, and the sweet nurturing that come with this man. He also tunes into the cavernous sensuality that lies below your surface. Here there is a merger of body and mind.

With Gemini SUN man: Your attraction is magical and strong enough that you will be compelled to work through any problems between you. You need to understand that this man is light and airy and won't threaten you. However, unless he has an unusually strong moneymaking profession, he might not keep you secure. But you will stick with him. Love him for what he is!

With Cancer SUN man: Opposites attract here, and you have much to learn from this man. He will help you feel at peace with the raging currents within you. You like his preoccupation with money and security, something you have in common. On the outside, you are very different, but there is a lot of mutuality. He loves your mix of earth and sparks.

With Leo SUN man: Mr. Romantic pops into your life, and you will not say no to him. You will want him to know the vibrant physical lady in you. He provides the type of lifestyle you want. You will play ball with him and feel amazingly complete. This is a home run.

With Virgo SUN man: He offers you all that you want and all that you have been seeking in the concrete world. However, in the realm of passion, you could be sorely lacking. You could think this is it, and then later, start spitting accusations because there isn't enough warmth. And that will cool things off even more.

With Libra SUN man: He will coax out that part of you that you choose to keep hidden. You will be very comfortable with him. As much as you adore him, you might put him down for not being more of a businessman. You need to revolve this conflict within you if this match is to work.

With Scorpio SUN man: There is an odd sense of possession here. He might have to ''own'' you and ''control'' you. Conversations flow with ease, and you have similar needs, though what makes one of you secure might not do it for the other. This relationship is about growth and his need to tame your independent, fiery spirit. Do you want that?

With Sagittarius SUN man: Naughty spirits merge here, and trouble happens. Do remember it takes two to tango and you are one of them!

You will want to play forever, but there is a side of you that is too logical for such shenanigans. This can work if you give up being judgmental.

With Capricorn SUN man: This is a meeting of minds and souls. He knows what to do to make you happy on one level. However, you might be tough on him because he is all business and no play. In many ways, he is perfect for you. He will force you inadvertently to work through some of your fear issues.

With Aquarius SUN man: He is a little more mischievous than you, and you read him cold. There is a wonderful friendship here; you can decide to let it develop into more. However, if you are looking for stability, you are barking up the wrong tree. There is a sensual element that makes you want to possess him. Therefore, you might try this anyway.

With Pisces SUN man: Though you connect emotionally with this man, he will irritate you and leave you climbing the walls. He is very much a clinging vine, one that you can't easily get away from. This really puts a damper on you. You would be wise not to play.

Moon in Capricorn, Sun in Capricorn

Far be it for anyone to question your motives and desires. You could even get huffy! Your sensuality and magnetism make it tough for anyone to stay angry at you very long. There is an innate implication of talent, strength, and inborn ability to survive.

One of your greatest strengths, and at the same time one of your greatest weaknesses, is your self-assuredness. Your way is the right way, the only way. This attitude gives you the courage to fight battles and the determination to win. But sometimes in relationships, you cannot understand the other side or opinion. It is hard for you to accept that both of you might be right, or that perhaps there is another side to the story.

Because of your air of self-assurance, men are drawn to you. They will pursue you, giving you many choices. As determined as you are about everything, you will want to have a good marriage as well. However, because of your lack of perception, you might find yourself with more than one trip down the aisle.

Mr. Right needs to be established and conservative, a force to be dealt with. You expect to be proud of him and want him to be proud of you. How you appear as a couple is important to you. You don't want the world to see a problem or a disagreement. Because of your strong boundaries, it is likely that you will need someone who doesn't dig too deeply into your psyche. You aren't big on being vulnerable.

With Aries SUN man: His energy will draw you; his volatility will repel you. This choice is not to be touched if possible. You are both very strong, and never will there be a meeting of the minds. At best, you tolerate each other.

With Taurus SUN man: To the world this looks like apple pie and vanilla ice cream. And indeed, it is a loving, peaceful relationship where the love is replenished, guided, and planned for. Because the trust is so high, passions could permanently bind you both. Though you are different, there is mutual respect. He will teach you about the good life and quality loving.

With Gemini SUN man: There isn't much common ground. You live in the physical plane; he lives in the world of the mind. You find him fluffy. No matter how debonair a figure this man presents, leave him alone!

With Cancer SUN man: You are a boulder of strength to him, made of fine marble. You are very different people, though you want the same things in life. He does not withhold feelings unless hurt; you rarely share your feelings. Once trust and respect are established, you can grow throughout life in this relationship. And toasty? Whew!

With Leo SUN man: He is fire and passion. In his charming, debonair way, he breaks past your barriers and has you acting out and loving it (for the most part)! You will not have control here, nor will he. You sizzle and burn together. To the world, you are a glamorous couple. He will provide and love you. The real issue is whether you can take being this exposed.

With Virgo SUN man: He is quiet and dependable, and likes you. You are the power. You will unearth him. He sees you as a passionate creature, one whom he will love and adore forever. You are safe here and know it. Together you could build a life, marriage, and all you have ever wanted. I can't promise excitement, however.

With Libra SUN man: He's nice, you're nice, and it isn't meant to be. You are direct and know precisely what you want. He is loving, yet his feelings are fleeting. This man is a wonderful boy toy for you, but as long-term material, no way, unless you like a lightweight relationship.

With Scorpio SUN man: This man is reserved, intense, and deep. You will want to know him. This relationship is actually his call. If he appreciates security and power, he will win a marathon race for you. If that isn't his fancy, he will smile, and that is where it ends. Don't even attempt to control him, manipulate him, or play hardball.

With Sagittarius SUN man: This represents only problems for both of you. It is unlikely you will want him, but if you do, his risky love of women and the good life will fry you. Why bother?

With Capricorn SUN man: You are like twins, with the same needs and desires. Naturally, there is mutuality here. The real issue is whether you are ready for a mutual admiration society. Ultimately it could get a bit dull unless he has something very different in his chart than you do in yours.

With Aquarius SUN man: He is dangerous for you, though you are drawn to his smiling, wicked ways. You cannot believe someone could ever walk such a different course. Do get to know him, but you will never understand him. You won't want him as your significant other either. You might be lifetime friends with many a giggle.

With Pisces SUN man: You will fall in love with his romantic ways, and the fact that he adores you won't hurt. He will tease and tempt you into all sorts of indulgences. Together you offer each other many different experiences, and safety as well. You will be his piece of land in raging waters, and he will be the spark of your life.

MOON IN CAPRICORN, SUN IN AQUARIUS

You are an interesting twist of bold liberalism and conservative neediness. Your choices are not only an adventure in the voting booth, but in life. Of course you seem logical to yourself. To other, especially men, you are intriguing and fascinating. However, actually relating to this mixed bag is a challenging task. It takes openness, want, and humor.

You present a Bohemian, offbeat front. You seem very intellectual, though impulsiveness breaks up the veneer. You might have difficulty contacting your own emotional depths. At some point in your life you learned to build walls around your feelings as someone trespassed on your emotions.

In relationships, your attractiveness is not an issue. The problem is your choices. In fact, because of this, you could have two marriages, especially if you marry early. You might choose an offbeat partner, someone who, like you, marches to his own drummer. You want spirit, force of will, and independence. It is okay with you if he is not a feeler as much as a thinker. You will feel safe with him. In the long run, however, you might experience an emotional void, especially if you get more in contact with your feelings. You're never boring and you're open to new ideas. However, making emotional changes is hard for you. You need someone who is patient and loving.

With Aries SUN man: Excellent communications earmark this relationship. He has a lot to say, and you want to hear it. Friendship and good communications create chemistry. At some point, however, if he doesn't have a conservative streak in him, you could go on the attack. Phooey! Just enjoy Mr. Aries. He is A-okay.

With Taurus SUN man: He appeals to your emotional needs and is very secure in dealing with your whimsical, contradictory nature. Together, you can build a wonderful life, as long as you don't expect him to be as eccentric as you. He is a born conservative, artist, and bon vivant!

With Gemini SUN man: The fireworks between you and this man resemble the Fourth of July. There are sparks of passion and of anger. He is hot and full of play, mischief, and seduction. You have a ball with him. However, your more practical side could lead you to anger that he doesn't offer you more. After all, he is sooo good.

With Cancer SUN man: The attraction is always present, yet pulling it together could be an act for Houdini. His concerns are similar to yours. He worries about money and security. He spews emotions and doesn't understand your need for independence. You are like rubber bands; this relationship is always a stretch.

With Leo SUN man: Both of you are social animals, though you have very different styles. You are detached, yet very caring; he is loving and romantic. You build a strong tie on the common ground of mutual concern. He finds you very passionate; you have nothing to complain about either. This is a match all the way.

With Virgo SUN man: Both of you have an altruistic streak. You want to help your friends and others. He wants to help all of humanity. Your practical nature appeals to him. You will be a sunburst in his life, warming him with true heat and passion. He will thank you forever for that gift.

With Libra SUN man: He is ethereal and loving, and has quite a way with women. He is a diplomat, whereas you tell it like it is. Nevertheless, the room temperature goes up when you're together. Please don't condemn him for not being as practical as you. It is your specialty, not his. Naughtiness and flirtation reign here.

With Scorpio SUN man: Two powers meet here. You are both eccentric and march to different drummers. However, his depth and magnetism have you clamoring to know him better. You can't push here. It is his way or no one's. Together you make a volcano seem cool. Expect long-term intensity that keeps building and building. You have it all here.

With Sagittarius SUN man: You have a natural friend here who is as adventuresome as you. You are likely to run away together, thinking it is forever. It could be, depending on how you handle the lack of security. He could make a lot of money, but he could also lose it. He is an innate risk-taker. Still, you find him a delight!

With Capricorn SUN man: You have a date here with destiny. You feel as if you have known this man forever. You know how to please each other in all areas of your lives. The comfort and loving will make it nearly impossible to say no, nor would you want to. He isn't your wild man, and you don't care!! He will demand a commitment.

With Aquarius SUN man: Ooh-la-la! The two of you will certainly take off on a mad romp, but you are both fairly rigid. It is your way or no one's. Though there can be intrigue, naughtiness, and wildness, this relationship, given time, will fall flat, with both of you going your own way.

With Pisces SUN man: Your airy side could respond to the amusement and sensuality this man provides. He goes from one extreme to another. You might not like his neediness, though, when it emerges. On some level, you find it threatening. Be careful about letting this tie develop too far.

MOON IN CAPRICORN, SUN IN PISCES

Emotionally, you are strong and know exactly what you desire. However, your presentation is emotional, and others might not realize what a pillar of strength you really are. You're in command of your ship, and know exactly what you want and where you are going.

You have a soft, ethereal quality that again belies the inner strength that marks you. You will get even better with age, manifesting a womanliness that many would aspire to. Men are clearly attracted. Your sumptuousness implies a real love of life and its experiences. You move with ease and are comfortable with your body.

You have a strong ethical system despite your sensuous, fun exterior. You guard your feelings because you know your vulnerabilities. Yet when the time comes to get to know you, you will reveal yourself appropriately. Because of the way you handle your feelings, you will be very successful in your life. You have an innate wisdom that emerged at an early age.

You want an emotional, creative, feeling man. You are willing to sort through one relationship after another until you find Mr. Right. You will not lack for suitors and relationships in the process. In fact, it is unlikely that you will be alone unless you make that choice. You will be content in your later life.

With Aries SUN man: You are sensitive, feeling, and nurturing. This man is full of get-up-and-go as he races along. He is passionate, but perhaps not as emotional or sensitive as you would like. You are better off letting go.

With Taurus SUN man: He meets your qualifications to a tee. He is indulgent, loves the good life, and yet comes from solid foundations, like you. Together, you will experience Nirvana. This is easily a lifetime match. There are strong positive money indicators as well. You will release your emotional, sensual self to very firm, capable hands.

With Gemini SUN man: Turn away from this man. He isn't what you want on any level. He could be interesting for a conversation or two, but that is about it.

With Cancer SUN man: He has an innate sense of touch and timing. Before you know it, you melt in his hands. You can look forward to a lifetime of sensual treats, though you will provide the stability. He can make money, but you need to handle finances for the household. The tenderness between you is very special to this combination.

With Leo SUN man: This is a dangerous, karmic tie. Once hooked, you could have a difficult time letting go. He is fiery and adoring. You like these qualities, though he could lack the gentle knowledge to deal with a woman as sensitive as you. He will provide security and good times. Sometimes, though, your feelings could be hurt.

With Virgo SUN man: You find this man one cool cucumber. He finds you a paradox: sometimes so grounded, yet other times extremely emotional and out of control. He will criticize you because he doesn't get it. And he is unlikely to. What you can hope for, at best, is acceptance.

With Libra SUN man: Once linked here, you might not be able to say good-bye. This is a case of a thousand breakups, yet you could still be together! You are emotional and deep; he is romantic and light. You want much more, and he doesn't know how to provide it. Yet you find him lovable and adore him for who he is. In a way, this is true loving, yet it is unsatisfactory on some level.

With Scorpio SUN man: He is mysterious, sensual, and alluring. You can scarcely say no, and the question is, why should you? Romance arrives in depth and full form. You feel cared about and adored. He is enchanted by your sensitivity, and your soul sings to him. Everything is positive here, for both of you. Make this so.

With Sagittarius SUN man: The tension is rather high between you. He doesn't want the same things as you and is unlikely to change. The connection is dubious if anything.

With Capricorn SUN man: You are two powers that meet. You have more dimension and inner strength than he knows. Your emotional receptivity adds an awareness that will always surprise him. However, you might get bored. Compared to your majesty, he falls a bit flat.

With Aquarius SUN man: No, no, no! He doesn't understand emotional depth; he is not interested in security, as you understand it. Swap a joke or two and move on. Please.

With Pisces SUN man: This man is lyrical, enchanting, and emotional. You feel together you can hit all the notes, and you do. He plays your tune well, knows how to touch you, move you, and fulfill your dreams. He needs your sensibility to manage his money and create stability. You share emotions, tenderness, and a love few could hope for.

Moon in Aquarius

"Two roads diverged in a wood, and I—I took the one less traveled by, And that has made all the difference."
ROBERT FROST

To some, you might seem remote and inaccessible. When you hear this, you shake your head, not understanding. After all, you are friendly, care about humanity and, above all, are everyone's friend, even protector to some. You have a natural disposition to consider the common good and to sell short your emotional needs. And that is what others pick up—your fear of close emotional attachment. It is quite clear you can function with or without a relationship.

You have coped in diverse ways. Freedom and space are your mantra, as you are easily threatened by those pulling in too close. You can be quite rebellious and obstinate, sabotaging your close relationships. Moons in Aquarius are known for great emotional dramas (to distance others) and multiple relationships (protection from that special one!).

One of the side effects of not knowing your real emotional core is that you become vulnerable or dependent on a loved one to build security, compliment you, and love you. You could be devastated by a clear, insightful comment. Rather than expose yourself to his pain, you choose to distance, and you are the queen of cooking up defense mechanisms to create this space. You could choose a very difficult man to justify this distance, rage, and uproar.

You are unique in your magnetism and appeal. Generally, great charisma comes with this Moon position. You pride yourself on being different, perhaps avant-garde. There is no question you have an enchanting, bewitching appeal. You are exciting and electric.

You make a responsive, caring partner once you decide you have met a man who gives you the distance you need. Trust and friendship are key factors. If this man understands your friendship and your fear of intimacy, you could be comfortable. You are fun, full of excitement, and always concerned about some form of equal rights.

You will fight ferociously for what you feel is right. You don't back down. You will do the same for your chosen mate and what he believes in. You must respect his mind and beliefs to bond with him, and for that reason, his causes will become your causes. You'll be his friend, ally, and partner.

You can be a creative, exciting, exotic lover. You feel like a kid in a sandbox in intimate situations, adding a zestful enthusiasm. Men sense your enthusiasm and they want to know you better. There will never be a shortage of lovers.

MOON IN AQUARIUS, SUN IN ARIES

You are full of energy, passion, and raw magnetism. The distinctive, electric quality of Aquarius mixed with passionate Aries traits cooks up a batch of get-up-and-go. You evoke strong responses. People either love your or hate you, with few in between.

You are definitely committed to your cause, a crusader by nature.

You are headstrong. It would take a collision with a freight train to stop you once you make up your mind! You have a similar passion in love, once you decide you like a certain man. You will always have applicants for Mr. Right. Men sense your vital, simmering passion that lies right beneath the surface. However, you will make the choice, and you'll be an active force in the relationship, if not the pursuer.

Mr. Right needs to be a self-starter, as you are not about to mommy him. He needs to be whole, his own person. You desire a meeting of two strong, independent forces. You will appreciate it if he has an element of impulsiveness or carefree behavior. The more eccentric he is, the more likely you are to be struck by Cupid's arrow.

You are capable of a very special relationship that can endure. The issue is whether you'll hold out for the right man rather than settle. You won't have a space issue with your partner, as there will be so much camaraderie, you will feel comfortable.

With Aries SUN man: He is a man of spirit, zeal, and fire. His initial intensity could frighten you, but you'll like and admire his loyalty. This match can work especially well if you have a common cause and some of his hot energy is funneled there. You two can make an important difference together. You will come to rely on his heated responses.

With Taurus SUN man: He is easygoing and hides his intensity. But you quickly recognize he is not the right man. He's conservative, and his greatest commitment is to the good life and building his own version of Fort Knox. You can't respect his values and you won't like him.

With Gemini SUN man: You are definitely intrigued by this charming mind-juggler. He plays with ideas, trying many different approaches. He will flirt, make you laugh, and help you see the total picture. He loves play in all forms. Though you are attracted, you could nix him, as you judge him to be superficial and lacking commitment.

With Cancer SUN man: He is the exact opposite of what you want. He is clingy and emotional, traits that give you the creepy-crawlies! However, if you decide to put him on your list of causes, you will try to foster his independence. Try as you might, ultimately this is a no-go.

With Leo SUN man: His biggest crusade will be getting you to respond to him. He is a lover and idealistic. He adores people and is very social. He will like your passion for life, as long as it includes him. To make this relationship work, the friendship must be tight. You could take life-long delight in each other, as long as you don't expect him to be like you.

With Virgo SUN man: He too is into "service," and you could be very comfortable with him. You won't find passion here, but you will like his dedication. You will never be threatened by this man and you will feel a quiet, dedicated loving. You could opt for this relationship.

With Libra SUN man: An explosive attraction lets him break down your natural resistance. You are forced to deal with the emotional discomfort. He could get involved in one of your causes, but expect him to be more interested in a loving, congenial relationship. You will admire his values, particularly that fairness is so important to him. Passions will always be bubbling to the surface.

With Scorpio SUN man: He is intense and committed, but he seeks answers and might not be a crusader at all. Nevertheless, you appreciate his intellectual outlook. Past that, he will be history. You won't tolerate his manipulations as he attempts to get you under his control. NEVER!

With Sagittarius SUN man: He is a risker, fiery, and always ready to experiment—especially if the experiment involves you!! He has some pet causes; whether you accept them as worthy is another issue. You delight in his humor, laughter, and toasty passion. Count on feverish moments mixed with tons of space. You'll like it.

With Capricorn SUN man: It is doubtful you will like, much less respect, the empire-builder of the zodiac. He is into money and power. It is more likely that you will be involved in a campaign that might offend him. You'll probably be on opposite sides of the fence.

With Aquarius SUN man: Criticizing him is criticizing yourself, you are so much alike. Your choices might be very different, but you are both humanitarians, with similar natures, detachment, and commitment. Your hot passion could keep him permanently aflame, burning for you more and more. This relationship is a kiss with destiny.

With Pisces SUN man: He is emotional, yet very caring about others. His universal caring appeals to you, but his neediness has you heading for the hills as fast as you can run. You might want to consider a friendship here.

MOON IN AQUARIUS, SUN IN TAURUS

You are an enigma to those around you. You seem to be anchored and directed, and know what you want. You value the good life and stability. You demand a quality relationship. You can be very stubborn, wanting what you want and not always seeing matters from another's perspective. This sense of determination makes you a difficult person to tangle with. You usually win.

You are curvaceous and alluring. You give off magnetic, earthy vibes. Stability is key to you. You don't like abrupt change. You want home, family, and a quality life. It is quite likely that you will marry or hook up with your first love. You need a certain level of consistency and stability in your life, especially your love life.

You tend to sabotage yourself in relationships. You might not recognize that deep within you there is a fear of intimacy. Your rigid rules and ways can turn off even the most attentive lovers. You need to recognize your fear and process it if you are ever to have the quality relationship and life to which you aspire.

You are a wonderful partner. You will be your mate's friend and understand him, yet you will be his Aphrodite as well, loving him and appreciating him for all he offers. You are very special. Know it and expect just that in return. Once you have let go of your rigid, distancing ways, you will love the comforts of intimacy and a close relationship.

With Aries SUN man: His enthusiasm is a turn-on to you. However, if he gets too exotic with his crusades, you might not want to let this relationship develop too far. You want a family man, someone there for you. You could turn on this man and become testy. He really isn't your picture of what a man should be.

With Taurus SUN man: He knows how to lure you, offering a magical courtship. A man who values friendship, he will give you the space to face your demons. He sees you as a total woman he deeply cares for, not a possession. By wanting the best for you, he fosters the friendship you value. You enjoy his style when he decides to seduce you. There is much desire and loving here.

With Gemini SUN man: He is funny, witty, and charming. You can talk about anything with him. This man connects with your independent streak. He too needs space. Both of you fear closeness, but he even more than you. He could use a bit more stability, yet there is a wonderful love affair and friendship here. Just don't read anything more into it.

With Cancer SUN man: He is emotional and needs a woman who can identify with his feelings. You can offer him friendship and structure, but feel his feelings? I think not. Yet because he worships the ground you walk on, you might give this match a whirl. Ultimately, though he offers you all, you could feel penned in.

With Leo SUN man: This can be a mad love affair that can continue lifelong. With the twinkle in his eye, he helps you see yourself more clearly. Fevers rage. The chemistry is undeniable. You have very different styles, but he likes what you are about. Together, you build a secure, comfortable life, always loving and prizing each other. Yet there is space. Love soars here.

With Virgo SUN man: He is precise, earthy, and detailed. He knows what is important to him. Into service and dedication, he appeals to you with his quiet ways. You feel stability here. He won't mind giving you space, but it is you who must heat up the temperature. Be forewarned.

With Libra SUN man: This man is gentle and romantic, which appeals to you. Like you, he prefers beauty and softness, but no way does he have your backbone and strength. In the long run, this difference could be a plus if you like giving the commands.

With Scorpio SUN man: The chemistry here is magical; you are both attracted. As strong as you can be, he is as tough. Be lovers, but stay that way. You'll admire each other, but he will not tolerate your putting your friends in front of him. Be warned, you will lose all battles here. It is his way, or not at all. Are you ready to submit? Or at least pretend?

With Sagittarius SUN man: He has fire and energy. There is something so personable about him that you want to come out and play. The problem is that you must look the other way, because monogamy isn't his strong suit. You want more security, even if the embers of desire burn.

With Capricorn SUN man: He will pursue you intensely, because he is used to having what he wants. You have a decision to make here. He will want commitment. Though he won't challenge your need for freedom, don't count on him understanding you. You make quite a handsome couple.

With Aquarius SUN man: He introduces you to a part of yourself that you might not yet know. You become alive with passion, joy, and commitment. You read each other and can live happily together. The only problem is that he could be too eccentric for your taste, except maybe in private moments. You might not have a choice, as the romance and attraction are overwhelming.

With Pisces SUN man: He is gentle, caring, and emotional. You stabilize him and help him put form to his creativity. You might create an interesting relationship here if you can tolerate his neediness. If you have come to terms with your need for space and fear of closeness, this could work. The soft and gentle moments could be worth it.

MOON IN AQUARIUS, SUN IN GEMINI

Your unique style is light, airy, and dreamy. You breeze by others with an aura of destiny, always on the move. Your humor, laughter, and joy come through. You even laugh when there are problems, talking and seeking solutions and probably enjoying the uproar. Others admire your stamina, your easiness, and your ability to absorb.

You probably are quite slender, move with ease, and have strong eyes or features. Your wit, exotic ways, and liberal attitude draw members of the opposite sex. It is easy to have a good time with you. No one would dream of having a celebration without you. You are everyone's friend.

Truth be known, you fear intimacy and often make choices that allow the space you need. You could choose a difficult partner whose behavior justifies your tantrums and emotional upheaval. These are your forms of distancing.

You need a partner with the wit, vigor, and brightness that you exude. He doesn't need to be as eccentric as you. A more traditional man is okay. You will want to talk and share; he needs to be verbal and intellectual. You will expect the same level of friendship that you give, and indeed, you deserve it as well.

The right man needs to understand you clearly and love you for the freedom-loving, happy person you are.

With Aries SUN man: You become his kindling as his desire bursts into flame. He loves your airy, light ways and finds your repartee fun. He is a man of action. He adds fire to his commitments. This is a great combination. He will keep you glowing, and you stoke his fires. There is a profound friendship as well as love present.

With Taurus SUN man: He has charm and a desire to know you. There are good times and perhaps some passion, but you will not appreciate his groundedness. You want to be a free spirit. You could hurt him with your recriminations. It just won't work.

With Gemini SUN man: With a cup of coffee in your hands, you two easily tease, twist with words, and flirt with fantasies. You love imagination, ideas, and loving. You will create your own worlds. Both of you are dexterous and wild together, flashing your sensuality and offerings. Expect a lifetime of love and enjoyment, a merger of like spirits.

With Cancer SUN man: You are a romantic, as he is, but his need for a traditional structure could make you uncomfortable. You like Thanksgiving dinner, but you aren't up for the drippy scenes and the emotional responses. You want less control and more freedom. Keep on romping, please.

With Leo SUN man: The passion you discover with him makes you want to be his friend, lover, and companion. You both love people and ideas, though your styles are different. He delights in your liberal views, but watch it, because if not sufficiently anchored, he could go off and play. Keep the pace active and lively for him, and this can work.

With Virgo SUN man: He is practical and verbal, but he wants to see material results. You aren't interested in those details, though you could feel comfortable with his detachment. However, haggling is probably inevitable, and you could flee the scene. This isn't for you. He doesn't appreciate you.

With Libra SUN man: Here's another kindred spirit who loves repartee and flirtation. Love grows, though you could be the one who must make the demands. Never fear, he can't say no. There's lifetime love and fun here. Others don't understand the giggling that endures even into old age.

With Scorpio SUN man: No one can deny the raw magnetism. He wants to know what makes you tick, wants to know you inside and out. Problems occur when he tries to control you. Remember, you tend to pick difficult men so you can create distance. You are as responsible for this can of worms as he is. Careful.

With Sagittarius SUN man: The two of you are like a comet, streaking in the sky. He gives your ideas form and loves who you are. He needs space as much as you do, so the two of you can easily coexist. You both need to understand that your differences are okay. He acts; you think. Together, you make a powerful duo.

With Capricorn SUN man: He is hard on your freedom-loving nature, though he is profoundly attracted, as you are. The two of you can tango together, but you will inevitably step on each other's feet. Sexual glue is fine, but you can't seem to resolve the other issues. You simply are too different.

With Aquarius SUN man: This smacks of the kiss of destiny. He is distant and remote, like you, though you might not be as conscious of it as he. He resonates with that primitive inner core in you that needs to emerge. If you understand yourself, this combo can happy for the long term.

With Pisces SUN man: You will not want to deal with this emotional sponge. He will make you want to cry about his problems, but you will feel so hemmed in! Say no or you could emotionally batter each other. Here are two nice people who don't belong together.

MOON IN AQUARIUS, SUN IN CANCER

You are very sensitive, loving, and caring. Your trademark is that you're there for friends and loved ones. You possess an unusual loyalty that makes friends as important to you as your family. You stay in touch, reach out for others, and share experiences. You seek understanding and value feedback.

You are extremely sensual and alluring, drawing others to you. The sense that you care pervades. You have an excellent sense of humor, even about yourself. Because you are so sharing, others believe they can share their secrets and fears. You are the keeper of many secrets.

The right man needs to be sensitive and concerned with others. You will expect him to be a nurturer or a caretaker. You'll want to rely on his inner wisdom and caring. He doesn't have to look at life in the liberal way you do, but you won't tolerate his putting down some of your way-out interests. For a relationship to work to its fullest level, he must have at least some interest in your hobbies.

You will want to marry once, but because of your unusual independent streak and complexities, there may be two marriages. When you are younger, you might defensively avoid some of your deeper feelings. You will handle them, for you must, as a relationship is very important to you.

With Aries SUN man: There is an innate tension between you. A friendship most definitely exists here. However, if you act on the physical attraction, havoc could result. He is fiery and explosive, something you don't want to deal with. You are walking into a minefield if you let this relationship develop.

With Taurus SUN man: You have found a real homebody. Despite his stability, he is willing to take a spin in some of the more exotic mental territories you travel. However, you could decide he is too stuck and too staid for you. Take another look and don't act from a fixed position. Besides soaring sensuality, he has much to offer. Give it a shot.

With Gemini SUN man: You like his vigorous spirit and mental energy. You might not be sure of what you want here, because he has difficulty anchoring in any other world but that of the mind. Nevertheless, you intrigue him as he does you. There is a sensual magnetism that makes you both wild. This is quite the merry-go-round.

With Cancer SUN man: He is sensual and has a magical sense of worlds beyond the material realm. A spiritual tie draws you both deeper. Together you plunder the hidden regions of your souls and hearts. At times, your intellect blocks the emotional onslaught. You need this in order to not feel suffocated. Your Cancer man will understand.

With Leo SUN man: There is mischief afoot here. He is debonair and daring. He's quite the romantic figure. You both are social beasts and cannot play enough. Count on stroking his ego; he demands that. Don't even dream that he will be a quiet homebody; he wants love and liveliness forever.

With Virgo SUN man: He is quiet and dedicated. You can identify with his need for intellect over feelings. However, you will always know something is lacking here. The emotionality and sensitivity you crave are not possible with this man, though you could share a calm life. Is that what you want?

With Libra SUN man: He is a delight and a charmer. You sense his sensitivity. However, compared to the depth you are capable of, he could seem superficial. The physical attraction is strong, and you might still decide to go for a romp. Don't expect much more, and you don't go wrong.

With Scorpio SUN man: You have run into a soul who will travel the recesses of his mind and fearlessly faces his inner demons. There is a tie here that is uncanny and sensual. Together you flood your worlds with deep emotionality. Like you, he is interested in the hows and whys of the universe. Don't shy away from this pillar of strength.

With Sagittarius SUN man: He is your friend and has enough steam and energy to carry both of you to new places. However, he is a wanderer, and you crave someone to anchor and settle down with. It isn't him. He certainly is a good time, though, and your eccentricity charges his fantasies.

With Capricorn SUN man: You find a sturdy attraction here, which will force you to work through any issues you might have. He might not probe the secrets of the universe; he is too busy making money and establishing the security you crave. You will be comfortable. Just don't demand that he be like you. Your shared passion cinches it.

With Aquarius SUN man: Your souls chime together. You intuitively know what each other wants. You will opt for a Bohemian life together, greeting the untraditional with glee. You could sometimes jolt this man with your profound sensitivities. You share a wonderful love and life.

With Pisces SUN man: He reaches the deepest corners of your soul. You find him creative, interesting, and incredibly sensual and romantic.

Whether the relationship's worth it depends on how much he is willing to give back. Sometimes you will be uncomfortable with his neediness. You must decide what is okay here, and whether he matches up.

MOON IN AQUARIUS, SUN IN LEO

You are a force, with energy so strong that others sense your presence when you walk into a room. People turn around for no reason as you walk through a door. You have chemistry, warmth, and a strong smile. You probably have big eyes, a full mane of hair, and a wonderful way with others.

You have a tendency to mix love and friendship. Some men think that they are courting you when you think they offer friendship. Or vice versa. Confusion marks your relationships. You might respond explosively.

The right man needs to be able to handle this volatile behavior and help you define your needs. At the same time, you will expect a full courtship with dynamic scenarios. Yet you offer friendship more than passionate affection. This can be very complicated to someone trying to court you. You need to feel safe by maintaining a friendly detachment, but you expect men to put themselves on the line, professing undying love. You will want your man to be very showy and somewhat of a catch. You don't mind other women flirting with him; that only makes you feel more desirable because he is yours.

Because of your inner schism, it is quite possible you will have two marriages. You will grow from relationship to relationship. What you choose at an early age could be much different from what you want when you become older and wiser.

With Aries SUN man: He could zip by you, but don't think he doesn't notice you. He likes your energy, picks up on your sensuality, and senses your conflicts. You are "interesting," in his book. You find that he has commitment, loyalty, and so much raw magnetism, you can scarcely breathe.

With Taurus SUN man: He is seductive and easygoing, and has his feet firmly planted on the ground. He might be desperately attracted to you, but in the long run, you will find him a stick-in-the-mud, or maybe a pet rock. Let him be.

With Gemini SUN man: This man is charming and witty. He makes you laugh and adores you. Your magic does not go unnoticed, and you experience strong currents of emotions with him. He can play friends, be very naughty, and still be a wonderfully romantic lover. This man needs variety, which is a natural for you.

With Cancer SUN man: He is romantic and enticing, yet you could unintentionally drive him away. He must have more solidity than you can provide. You might have a good time with him, but he won't benefit. Be nice, leave him alone.

With Leo SUN man: He knows exactly what to do to make you his, so he thinks. But you are quirky, remember? Just when he thinks you are his, you do the unexpected. You will constantly keep him interested by your unpredictability, and there is strong romance here. The attraction is high, but only works if you can respect your differences.

With Virgo SUN man: He is quiet, deliberate, and can't deal with your full moon spirit. As an on going commentary, he will criticize your inability to let go. There is a strong possibility of common interests, but that is where the compatibility stops.

With Libra SUN man: He is easy and charming, and will knock you off your feet. He's intrigued by your emotional flips. You excite him, both as a friend and a lover. He accepts you, with all your facets. To him, you are perfect as you are. You love being cared about and accepted. Love grows and is well tended here.

With Scorpio SUN man: He challenges you, playing havoc with your ideas and beliefs. You are extremely reactive to him, trying all your wiles to get what you want. Enjoy the passion here. However, for this match to succeed in the long run, you'll need a lot more than that. Be realistic about your interests and priorities.

With Sagittarius SUN man: He is a traveler, a wanderer, so you will never feel crushed by his attention. The bond of friendship is strong, and the moments merry. He cannot resist the magic that whirls around you. The sum total of this tie is excellent and good for the long term. The embers could burn forever.

With Capricorn SUN man: He is practical and earthy. You might like the lifestyle he can provide. He understands your heat and magnetism. You will have space, as he is probably a workaholic, allowing you to go off, flirt, and be the world's friend. This can actually work!

With Aquarius SUN man: You click. It is as if you have known each other for a lifetime. This connection delights you; you seem to be able to live in harmony. He might lack some of the passion you dream of, but you get along. You bewitch his heart and body. He will want you and you alone.

With Pisces SUN man: He has a way with words and an imagination that creates one romantic fantasy after another. You adore his drama and romance. However, when you need space from this tropical tie, he gets upset. He wants you all the time. And what is this friendship business? He wants a lover. You might eventually feel out of sorts and unappreciated.

MOON IN AQUARIUS, SUN IN VIRGO

You are extremely logical and direct. Others find you an endless resource for solutions, details, and ideas.

You draw a man who likes coolness and aloofness. However, just when a man thinks he understands you, you do something quirky that throws him off. Of course this keeps the intrigue alive. Part of your surprising behavior comes from suppressing your feelings. This gives you a tendency to act out. You often don't really know the basis of your actions.

Your relationships are an interesting brew. You want to be nurturing and caring, though somehow your nitpicking, precise, cool nature comes through. In relationships, this behavior could be maddening. You often don't understand why partners scream and yell. They want more "feeling" from you. You feel secure that you're cared for, but stunned by such displays.

You would like your man to be calm, cool, and intellectual. It would be better for you if he didn't fly off the handle, because in a comfortable situation you're more likely to get in touch with your feelings. If your partner gets snappy and critical, you will understand. You don't want a display of romance, love, and smoldering passion as much as you want someone loyal on whom you can count.

In relationships, you will be loyal, ethical, and devoted. Yet, you always will feel a mild discomfort with emotions and love relationships.

With Aries SUN man: He is full of heat, sparks, and passion. This could be very hard on cool, cucumber you. However, you like this man and what he is about. In the long run, unfortunately, you will attack him for not being more logical. He is no Vulcan!

With Taurus SUN man: He is earthy and grounded. Though he can be logical, he is very sensuous and romantic. You might be comfortable with his advances, but to your surprise, there is much passion here. You might want more of a friendship with this man, and need one to be at ease with his love nature.

With Gemini SUN man: You have met a similar spirit; this man dwells in the mind and might be uncomfortable with huge displays of emotions. Practical, he isn't. He's a Don Quixote of ideas, not realities. You might have a ball playing with him, as there is only fun, nothing heavy. In the long run, you will be on his case for not being more reasonable.

With Cancer SUN man: You have met the Prince of Feelings, and he will let you know it. Though you like his dedication and ethics, you will not be comfortable with his drippy displays. If you are found, it will be running for the hills.

With Leo SUN man: He is the lover of the zodiac and cares about people in much more passionate ways than you. He is like kindling wood to you, and you might want to give this a shot. It could work, but know in advance he will never accept your criticism. Love him as he is or forget it. Respect each other's styles and you could be headed for the alter.

With Virgo SUN man: He is precise, detailed, and exact. You feel very comfortable relating to him. You know he won't provoke any difficult passionate displays. With time, you might long for a little more camaraderie and warmth. But that has more to do with your issues than who he is. Don't expect him to change!

With Libra SUN man: He is polite and quite appealing. Your heart will throb when you meet this romantic. Because he is so easygoing, you might not be threatened and will love his friendship and dedication. He is exactly who he projects to be. Don't think of changing him. A promise: You will have to be the practical one here.

With Scorpio SUN man: He is like a steaming underground hot spring. He is hot, demanding, and penetrating. You will like his mind, but could be threatened by his scalding sensual pursuit. You could emphasize friendship, but actually you are distancing. He is a very scary person to you. You'll find plenty of feelings with this man—probably more than you want.

With Sagittarius SUN man: He is off exploring. You like him and could join him on an adventure or two. But pull back and look at him. He is a risk-taker and could be very wild. This isn't what you need, though you might very much want him. Don't complain with whatever choice you make.

With Capricorn SUN man: This man is dependable and logical, and will provide for you as if you are his queen. You will always be happy with him if you can handle his need to "own" you. He won't understand your romps with friends, but then he is too busy working to put a halt to this. Sensuality bonds you forever.

With Aquarius SUN man: He is your soul mate and understands exactly what you need. He will never threaten you emotionally. Your detachment might be important should he wander a little. You understand his way-out interests and passions; you have your set of them too. He might be practical, if it so suits him. Be smart. Count on being the one who does the taxes here. This is a go.

With Pisces SUN man: Both of you care about service and dedication, though he is passionate about these issues. He can be downright melodramatic about nearly everything. The magic between you forces a confrontation of two different styles. It will take a lot to work this out. You both must really want it.

MOON IN AQUARIUS, SUN IN LIBRA

Say hello to a born flirt. Yes, that is you! You are extremely attractive, feminine, and easygoing. You are definitely a people-person. You cannot imagine being without a partner. You think in terms of "we," and you simply enjoy life more as part of a couple.

You are sought after and might have a whole string of lovers and admirers. You may have dated at an unusually early age. It is likely that you will marry young.

With your wandering eye, you could have a difficult time staying in one relationship. It isn't that your man will leave, but rather that you cannot commit. After all, what is more exciting in life than men?

For a woman who loves men so much, what makes a man Mr. Right? You expect romance, champagne, roses, and all that goes with a traditional courtship, one of the best parts of a relationship, according to you. The right man needs to be fair of face and mind. You want someone you can be proud of, as all man, as you are all woman. Because you sometimes want to do odd things, you will want an understanding man who won't judge you.

You will always need a lot of activity, going out even after committing with a band on your finger. If your man doesn't do this, he will quickly become Mr. Wrong. And though you can be lovely, if angered, you could be critical and difficult.

With Aries SUN man: Now this is a blast. He charges you up, and you fan his flames. You are vibrant, dynamic people. He thinks in terms of "I," and you think in terms of "we," yet the strength of your passion motivates you to work it out. Work on the friendship as well.

With Taurus SUN man: This is a very romantic man, and you sure like his style. You are both ruled by Venus, so there is great mutuality and sensuality. Your flirting is okay as long as it is only with him. Should you spend too much time with your male buddies, he will see red! Think before committing.

With Gemini SUN man: You instinctively feel complete with this man as he pens romantic love letters to you. You will always enjoy his mind. Your passions and love needs are very similar. He will adore your quirkiness. He is okay with your flirting and your friends because he is very much the same way. Listen to his ideas and he will be yours forever.

With Cancer SUN man: This man could have you mooning after him for a very long time. He is sweet, emotional, and takes you on wonderful adventures. But there is an "oh, no!" He will cling and be dependent, particularly when you get quirky or cavort with friends. He might turn on you and decide to channel his emotions through someone else.

With Leo SUN man: He is your knight in shining armor. You both care about people, though you have different styles. He wants to love them all, and you want to like them all. Yet this match can work out if you learn from each other. This relationship takes commitment, but can work.

With Virgo SUN man: Well, he's a nice thought. Don't let him become more. He is picky and practical; something feels bizarre to you. And where is the romance? He wonders why you need it. Leave this alone.

With Libra SUN man: You've found your ideal. You see eye-to-eye. He appreciates your unpredictability, and if you want an adventure or two with friends, it won't bother him, but be careful. Remember, like you, he is a "we" person, and if you aren't there, someone else could be.

With Scorpio SUN man: You might like to stick your toe in, but be careful: Don't go much farther. He is a whirlpool of sensuality and emotion that you might drown in. He can become sarcastic, deciding you are superficial, yet you still are intrigued by his uniqueness and his masculinity. These are shark-infested waters for you.

With Sagittarius SUN man: Your first date could be to water-test his hand-built toy submarine; this kind of fun isn't exactly romantic, but it could be interesting. You will have to make a decision here, as there is an extraordinary friendship. He can make you happy in many ways if you are willing to compromise about the romantic moments.

With Capricorn SUN man: He is a moneymaker, and you will be secure here. There might be a side of you that feels he isn't fair, and you don't like his power obsession. If you can get this man to transfer his focus to romancing you, then consider him. Otherwise, forget him.

With Aquarius SUN man: You are meeting destiny and karma here. You won't be able to stay away once the bewitching passion begins. You love well together, communicate superbly, and adore being together. He brings out your stranger side, but then who cares? You won't even worry about the romance, so strong is the bond.

With Pisces SUN man: There is a hook here, and it is hard to determine who is the fish and who is the bait. Once snared, you can't pull away from each other. Delightful, sentimental, romantic moments are his specialty. Expect some clinging, but he could be worth it.

MOON IN AQUARIUS, SUN IN SCORPIO

You are exotic. You have strong, penetrating eyes that reveal the magic in your soul. You don't have time for the superficial. You seek depth, meaning, and the unexpected. Your charisma stops men in their tracks. Few can handle your power and enchanting manner.

You want a strong man, with depth and intensity, someone who can think. You don't have time for men who run away from your feline power. You are a lioness who scratches way beyond the surface.

Your man must be direct and honest with you. You can be liberal about certain matters, but when it comes to your passions, you won't be played with. No one will forget your vengeance.

Your biggest issue is rigidity. Being demanding and dominant can be difficult in relationships. With this trademark, relationships easily degenerate into battles. There is a conflict within you. You want unspoken loyalty, yet need space. It is hard for men to give you space with the seductiveness you exude. Sometimes you will cause a fight in order to gain distance. Wouldn't it be better to openly honor your need for space?

Once you decide to commit, you are in there for the long haul. It is hard for you to admit failure. You will stick to it, to the very end. Because you are so strong, you are likely to choose a similar personality, increasing the chance that you will have multiple relationships, and quite possibility, marriages.

With Aries SUN man: He is hot stuff, but in a much different way than you. This could be a go as long as you muzzle your need to be critical. He appreciates your intensity, ethics, and flare. Bring your exotic touch to the bedroom, and with his vitality, neither of you may be seen again.

With Taurus SUN man: He is earthy, sensual, and provides a delightful courtship. The fires could burn, but you must respect each other's styles. Both of you are very fixed in your opinions. Negotiation will have to become an art form for both of you two!

With Gemini SUN man: He is a hoot and a great time. Contact between you can be fiery. Mirth and sensuality blend here, and you could be very content. You appreciate his intellectualism. At times he can be scattered. Don't criticize him. That is part of the package.

With Cancer SUN man: You find this man emotional and sensitive. However, he is most needy. You will feel like the Crab put his pincers in you sometimes when relating to him. Your free spirit may cry. As appealing as he is, be careful!

With Leo SUN man: With the appeal that exists, it could be very tough to say "no." You both love people, though you have different ways of expressing it. If you simply enjoy each other, and don't criticize, then this can work. You will feel like you are in the Sahara Desert. It is hot, very hot.

With Virgo SUN man: When he runs into you, he will redefine his understanding of different and intense. There is an attraction because of similar values, and a need to serve others. You might never fully understand each other, but you sure could like each other. Your bonfire charges him!

With Libra SUN man: He is affectionate and easy. You might love playing with him, and he never minds a game or two. However, if you decide to challenge him and attack, he will leave. Remember, he is very desirable to many and knows he doesn't need problems.

With Scorpio SUN man: He is intense and deep like you. You two can love and battle together, yet still be happy. Your need to sometimes flake out and this could irk him, but in the long run, he will take it as a challenge. There is more than fun and games here; there are sizzling times. You can do this!

With Sagittarius SUN man: He is a wonderful friend and a delightful adventurer. Off you go romping. However, take note: He isn't serious, deep, or intense, qualities you seek in Mr. Right. Do take responsibility instead of using nasty criticism when you discover he isn't perfect.

With Capricorn SUN man: Your depth appeals to this man in a profound, soulful way. However, he might not be your cup of tea, as he is very materialistic, something you don't respect. You want more than "things" out of life. Don't go here.

With Aquarius SUN man: The two of you could give it a spin and end up going around the world together. Reality is of very little concern to either of you. You two could seek adventure forever. You simply love being together. This is an unconventional but wonderful match.

With Pisces SUN man: This man is a creative, romantic joy. He understands your love of the exotic. You like his emotionalism, but he has a hard time giving you freedom, something you need as much as air and water. Though there is love, there are profound differences.

MOON IN AQUARIUS, SUN IN SAGITTARIUS

Your independence marks you as a survivor who can take care of yourself. You are a thinker and like making your own decisions. When you choose a partner, it is because you value the camaraderie and friendship a relationship presents. You are likely to have your share of suitors and could have as many as four major relationships. Really!

You are athletic, bright, and easygoing. Your dynamic energy attracts men, often because they like buddying with you. You can be found playing softball or taking a risk with your career. You like action, not talk.

Emotionally, you need independence and space. You want to love and care for a significant other, yet because of your individuality you are afraid of not being appreciated, and perhaps feeling overwhelmed. Worry less and go with the flow. Choose someone who has similar independence and interests.

Men love your ability to risk. You will look for a man with strong energy like yours, someone who shares your interests. All the better if he needs to explore and experience life. So do you.

You are quite attractive. If there are slender people in your family, you're likely to be among them. The right man must believe the sexes are equal. No kowtowing for you! He needs to value your friendship, want your enthusiasm, and be okay if you beat him in his favorite sport.

With Aries SUN man: He is passionate and adoring. He's always off on a crusade—or at least a dry run. Fine with you; you will either join in or go off on your own adventure. There is a constant hot desert wind blowing on your relationship. There is enough in common that this could be the real deal.

With Taurus SUN man: You might like a date or two with this man. You appreciate his moneymaking skills, but the real issue boils down to whether he can give you the space you need and not feel jeopardized. He might want something more connected, in his terms.

With Gemini SUN man: Life just became a dynamite adventure. He sparks your interest with ideas, fantasies, and the unbelievable. You act on them. He is flattered. The tie between you is incendiary. You can have the ball of your life with this man, and he with you. Others will envy the hoot you have together.

With Cancer SUN man: You might want to cross him from your list of potential suitors. There is nothing wrong with him, but then in your book, there will be nothing right with him. He feels. You do. Don't.

With Leo SUN man: Snap, crackle, and pop! And don't forget the sizzle! He will be so busy running after you that he will forget all his potential mates, wanting only you to play with. You share unusual understanding, depth, and loving. This looks like the romance of a lifetime. You pitch, he will catch.

With Virgo SUN man: You have different agendas. The clash isn't that obvious until you need to parachute jump, and then you could tangle.

He'll yell about expenses, the stupidity of the act. The best way to avoid this calamity is not to jump.

With Libra SUN man: He is a gentle man, yet he is drawn to your unconventionality and high energy. He will love getting on the baseball field with you. Plan on making time for romantic dances. He needs them. This could be dreamy for you and fun for him. Making it long term will take commitment on both of your parts. You are both players!

With Scorpio SUN man: Dear me. He likes your vitality, but you are better off as buddies. He is possessive, falls into control games, and can be contrary. You will look at him, toss him to the side, and go on. Don't forget to say no, thank you.

With Sagittarius SUN man: Both of you are always off trying something new. Though there is good glue and magic, both of your wanderings could take away from the enchantment of this tie. In fact, you could become memories without even realizing that you have separated.

With Capricorn SUN man: He will not tolerate you and probably isn't attracted. He doesn't like your independence, forward-looking nature, and lack of tolerance for building HIS empire. No go.

With Aquarius SUN man: He tweaks your imagination with his mischievous smile and seemingly knowing ways. There is an element of ESP between the two of you. Love abounds here. You make an excellent couple, enjoying fun, understanding, and friendship. And both of you are oh, so naughty together.

With Pisces SUN man: He will have a problem with you. You are not likely to stick around to hear him chant his love poetry under your balcony. You will be somewhere else as he pines away. You aren't comfortable with emotional closeness and needs. He will be miserable as you take off with the guys to play!

Moon in Aquarius, Sun in Capricorn

You project as distant, aloof, and independent, but beneath it all, you need a lot of security. You tend to be very hard on yourself and on men. Somehow you need to come to terms with your conflicting needs. Part of you screams for freedom and yet you demand security.

You could feel very insecure dealing with men. You might not know how to share your feelings with men and could be somewhat frightened of them. Instead of working through this issue, you could very well find yourself attracted to a sequence of emotionally unavailable men, perhaps subconsciously.

You need to learn that you made these choices. Then you will be able to change them and find someone who will give you greater satisfaction. He could be quiet, wise. It is likely he will offer unusual material security. Because he is probably a workaholic, you won't feel smothered by him and will be comfortable.

If you are unable to see into your inner workings, then two marriages are likely. You will keep trying, as you do value the institution of marriage.

You will attract a man who wants a woman with her feet firmly planted on the ground, with perhaps an exotic touch or two! You are so versatile, it will be hard for a man to become bored with you.

With Aries SUN man: He is fiery, demonstrative, and very appealing. He probably will be secure financially. There is a great friendship possible between you. You might find him a bit too controversial at times. This tie is dependent on how much you want him.

With Taurus SUN man: His easy style prevents you from panicking, yet allows you to change and grow. You become more mellow dealing with him, though there could be some battle of the wills here. You are both stubborn. Though this match might not last long term, it could open your horizons and become an important relationship for you. He is well intentioned and, luckily for you, he is hot stuff too.

With Gemini SUN man: He tweaks your imagination, and the two of you are like rippling waves teasing and playing. There is a strong physical attraction here, one hard to deny. He will have a jovial manner that makes you ready and willing, but he might not offer you the financial security you crave.

With Cancer SUN man: There is magic between you. You are a cool cucumber compared to his hot emotionalism. Around him, you feel safe because you know what is going on. The attraction is deep, and you both want to establish security. But you must be able to tolerate his clingy moments. The fun romps seem to encourage working this relationship through.

With Leo SUN man: The two of you adore each other and can't say no to the magic of opposites. Heated moments and raw passion bring you irrevocably together. You will play together and throw parties for your big entourage of friends. He is likely to have the money to keep you secure. Expect a lifetime of sparks.

With Virgo SUN man: Your needs are akin to his. You find even with the comfort and security he offers, you could be bored. You might wander. How are you going to feel about that? Be sure you can commit to this man before you let this go too far.

With Libra SUN man: He ropes you in with his charming and desirable ways. Before you know it, you are head over heels in love. Understand that he will never be stable and often can't seem to make a decision. You could find yourself pulling your hair out!

With Scorpio SUN man: You can find deep and profound passion with this man. He understands you perhaps better than you do. He wants to nurture you and love you, but you will have to make choices that please him. You need to think carefully here, even if he is a torch for you.

With Sagittarius SUN man: He is mischievous, fun, and full of life. He is into enjoying life and might not be able to nurture your confidence. You can share a great friendship, a mutuality, and even a burning desire. You eventually could be threatened by his wanderlust, but until then it is a ball!

With Capricorn SUN man: He could very well stir your fancy, as he is everything you want. He is stable and secure, fitting your ideal to a tee. This can be a heavenly treat as long as he likes your exotic twists. You are a bolt of lightning in his life. He is the anchor you crave.

With Aquarius SUN man: This is a happy merger of two spirited people who like each other. He intuitively knows how to light your fire, and you are his soul mate. However, you need to work through your emotional issues because this match isn't staid and secure. But it could be exquisite and joyful.

With Pisces SUN man: He hits poignant notes in you—and you want to stabilize him. Your ability to understand and empathize with him opens deep caring. You will both need to work on emotional stability. He will have a problem with your need to be free. This is an odd tie, perhaps too difficult to be completely workable.

MOON IN AQUARIUS, SUN IN AQUARIUS

You are the center of your universe and you see life in terms of YOU. It isn't that you don't care about others, but rather you tend to be one-sided. With both your Sun and Moon in the same sign, you don't get other points of view.

With this position comes many blessings, including great creativity and an allure that speaks for itself. Though you can be quirky, men are drawn to you. There is a sense that you know something they don't. They want to explore your magic and mystery.

The issue is: What do you want? You could easily have four relationships or marriages. It might save some heartbreak if you stop and think about your ideal man. It is likely you will opt for a very unusual man. You like eccentric, even weird men. You want to learn about different walks of life and are drawn to spicy, unique personalities.

You could opt more for companionship and friendship and be very happy. You aren't always comfortable with closeness and neediness.

As a woman and partner, you guarantee adventure and excitement. You could suddenly hop the next plane to India. The right man needs not only to appreciate your adventures but will also want to jump in. You could uproot at the drop of a hat. You are rigid in your commitment to uproar, the unexpected, and change.

With Aries SUN man: This man likes your unique qualities and dynamite energy. He's neither conventional nor unconventional. Your spirit will appeal to him and force him to stop. You blow hot air on his torrid temperament—a toasty recipe. Neither of you will ever know boredom together.

With Taurus SUN man: Ms. Unconventional, please meet Mr. Conventional. You are a bird in flight, and he stays planted. Need I say any more? Opt for friendship.

With Gemini SUN man: He will pose many fantasies and ideas for you to act on. He loves your spirit that can take off at any given moment. He's an armchair traveler, but he will decide to get limber and join you. You are off to Never-Never Land together. Others will only hear your peals of laughter.

With Cancer SUN man: He needs roots, home, and security. You need none of the above. You might want to stop and chat awhile, to see what the other side of life is like. But past that, forget it.

With Leo SUN man: He leaves a litter of lovers and passions behind him once he meets you. Your unique spirit, detachment, and magnetism draws him in, as he rarely is drawn. There is a magnetic draw between you that makes separating close to impossible. Make it your pleasure to deal with him.

With Virgo SUN man: He is detached, but not experimental. You will be bored after the first hello. He offers little of what you need, except perhaps a motive to go to India.

With Libra SUN man: You like his refreshing, easy ways, and it is okay with you if he cannot make up his mind. That will permit an adventure or two on the side. He is romantic and warm whenever you are with each other. Your unique spirit takes him on a fantasy spin that may never end. You appreciate his loving style.

With Scorpio SUN man: He is intrigued, and so are you. There is so much mystery you offer each other that you might decide to romp together for a while. If you do, it could be one of those wondrous lifetime moments. You'll never forget this liaison, though it could merely be a passage for you.

With Sagittarius SUN man: He loves it! He loves you! He has had dreams of a woman like you who could be more adventuresome than he. He will skip from one greener pasture to the next, all over the world, for you. When you rest, his heat will recharge you. This is a passionate love affair that will last.

With Capricorn SUN man: He is practical and earthy. He was good at building blocks as a kid and now he is still building, but on a grander scale. As a child you were the type who kicked his blocks over and made a mess. Nothing much has changed. This match could be highly frustrating, for both of you.

With Aquarius SUN man: I don't know if you can have more freedom than with this man. He is unusual, eccentric, and a true wanderer. You will leap on his ship. How long you stay together depends on both your commitment and his. Few will know joy mixed with liberation like this.

With Pisces SUN man: He is sentimental and loves the world. He certainly sees you as a bright and shiny bauble. He wants a shot, but that is where it should end. You will remember this encounter. It has such sweet overtones.

MOON IN AQUARIUS, SUN IN PISCES

There are wild mood swings here, not only for you but for anyone involved with you. You don't intend it that way, but that's you. Men adore your ethereal smile and dreamy eyes.

When people get to know you, they are often surprised. You can be so cool and rational in relationships that others are jolted. You need to be cool and in control to remain comfortable. You also have a strong sense of intuition and sense what is going on with others.

Your dedication is deep and loving. To be your loving self translates as expressing the depth of your commitment to humanity.

Because of this quality, men throw themselves at you; they want to be your patient so you can help them. If they understand and accept your nurturing with that touch of detachment, you can be their partner and love. You need to verbalize who you are so that others can get a clearer picture of the whole you.

As a partner you are devoted to making your partner's life work. However, if you don't feel appreciated, it could be splitsville. You need someone very special who accepts you and loves you as you are. Often you attract a partner who wants to change you. That won't happen. You will be drawn to an emotional and feeling man, one who can express what you don't or can't. You prize this quality.

With Aries SUN man: This man is a pistol, full of energy. He will love your independence, caring, and nurturing. He finds you a fellow soul mate in that you care about others nearly as much as he does. You two could save the world and at the same time light up each other's lives.

With Taurus SUN man: You mix, play, and party to your heart's desire with this man. He sees you as sweet, loving, and dreamy. However, he could get irritated when you get an idea stuck in your mind. You could decide even if the good times are great, the bad ones aren't worth it.

With Gemini SUN man: Together there is a sense of adventure and caring. You share common ideas and want to be partners in play. He isn't emotional, yet he is changeable. Though there is much delight in adventuring with him, he might irritate you. He isn't your vision of what a man needs to be.

With Cancer SUN man: He is a lovable, caring man who simply needs you. You will love taking care of and stabilizing him. You like his sensitivity and feel alive with him. You have an uncanny sense of what makes him tick. You teach him to feel empowered. In exchange, he worships the ground you walk on. You won't be sorry!

With Leo SUN man: You can't help it: You want him, and he knocks your socks off. You will weave magic together. You both love the human race. You will throw great parties and strive to heal on a universal level, as well as those close to you. Together, you light each other's worlds.

With Virgo SUN man: You like the fact that he also wants to take care of others and cares about the world. However, he is logical and practical when you want him to be emotional. You need to realize he might be more effective than you on the same mission. He will never cramp your space, and together you make quite the team.

With Libra SUN man: This is a forever connection. You both need space, yet demand romance. You may be stormier than he is used to, but he will love you anyway. He is sweet and gentle, just what you want. The electricity is high voltage. You won't burn each other out, only recharge together.

With Scorpio SUN man: He is intensely interested in you. He's perceptive and subtle, and reads you loud and clear. His sexiness could light your burner, but you might be uncomfortable with his intensity, comments, and need for closeness. The one who gets hurt here is you. Be very careful. You are walking on eggshells.

With Sagittarius SUN man: When he is off hooting it up, you could find his presence sorely missed. You want him to be with you but not challenge your space. There is friendship and delight here, but long-term possibilities other than friendship are problematic. He is a wanderer. Remember that.

With Capricorn SUN man: This man is there for you, and is ever so practical. You will always have security with him. He might conduct quite the courtship, and he won't care if you take an independent twist or two. You can live together agreeably, but you won't have a partner in causes.

With Aquarius SUN man: Once more you meet a person who has similar space needs and relishes your independence and free spirit. The two of you act on naughty ideas, delighting each other with your sensual imagination. The play is endless. You learn to understand him and love him. He has a unique sweetness that warms your heart.

With Pisces SUN man: The two of you do quite a dance together. Outwardly, you're a dreamy couple with much touching and sharing. Privately, you help him through crises, and the bonding is very tight. Do plan an occasional vacation away, just to maintain that free spirit of yours.

Moon in Pisces

"Your heart often knows things before your mind does."
POLLY ADLER

A Pisces Moon feels deeply. You frequently feel like a bundle of sentiments, not knowing exactly where to direct them or what to do with them.

In some way you are a conduit through which emotions, yours and others, flow. One of your most important lessons is learning to identify YOUR feelings. Clearing feelings, or learning how to manage them, is instrumental to your well-being.

Moon in Pisces allows a great deal of depth, emotionalism, inspiration, and possibly self-indulgence. The wisdom of a Pisces Moon woman is expressed in the level of understanding she has achieved. Pisces knows no boundaries, and the emotions here seem to beg for definition and answers.

An unevolved Moon in Pisces woman tends to seek in others their ideals of perfection, and as a result experiences much disappointment. You lose yourself in your ivory tower, seeking life as it "should" be, being unrealistic about life and people. When others let you down, you seek a higher plane, pulling yourself up or putting the other down, making them wrong. The results are confusion, misunderstandings, and unsuccessful relationships.

An evolved Moon in Pisces woman learns to forgive her own imperfections and those of others. Then real communication can begin, and positive interactions and bonding are more likely. When you are able to clearly hear what others want, you seek to help them create that ideal. It is on this level that you can come to know the unconditional love you seek.

It is likely that you are very attractive and sensitive. You feel another's pain and want to share it and help. You have a tendency to be negative or a complainer, so with all the beauty in the world, it is hard for many to want to become close to you. Heal yourself and you will heal your world. That is the path to the relationship you desire.

Often Moon in Pisces women have several marriages until they evolve. They could suffer from overindulgence, lack of dietary care, and discipline in general. There could be bouts of crying, self-pity, and sympathy-seeking. This is not the true you. It is simply a rung in the ladder to finding yourself.

When you do heal, you will successfully seek relationships based on empathetic bonding. You can then share your dreams and open to the inspiration of your loved ones. No one can have as sensitive and nurturing a relationship as you. Once you get there, you will treasure your tie, loving your partner as your muse, love, and inspiration.

MOON IN PISCES, SUN IN ARIES

Men are attracted to you and want to know you. This could pose quite a challenge, as you might not know yourself. At an early age, you learned to hide your feelings and emotions because they weren't appreciated or perhaps were misunderstood. You might have spent time hiding away, daydreaming about what life could be or imagining your knight in shining armor. At heart you are a true romantic. The right man will tap into this childlike romanticism.

You can delight a man. You have a penchant for love. You tend to put your man on a pedestal. You will appreciate each card from him, each date. You'll save matchbooks from restaurants, dry flowers he has given you.

When this romantic tale is unwinding, you are at your best. The problem with putting your man on a pedestal is that, inevitably, he will fall off. And you will be disillusioned. But who put him there?

Though you will date often and learn through these experiences, it is likely you will have one marriage. Your ties are intense, and you might be uncomfortable with your feelings at times. You will either relieve them through your crusade of the moment, or learn to process them. Your partner might also help you work these intense passions through.

With Aries SUN man: You are a pistol, and he is your bullet. Together you will crusade to change the world. You make a powerful couple with passion and commitment. He loves your softness and sentimentality.

There is a very romantic-feeling quality to your love. Both of you feel adored and understood.

With Taurus SUN man: Your sentimentality and sweet ways melt him. He makes you feel steady and secure, as you never have before. You'll fall hook, line, and sinker. However, your fiery independence can sometimes throw him off. You might eventually notice that though he provides you with a magnificent sanctuary, he doesn't grow.

With Gemini SUN man: He adds sparkle to your life, but the bubble will burst if you get overly sentimental and clingy. He will split. He likes lots of action on the home front, something that might make you feel off-kilter. Yet he offers great courtship, writing poetry and adding ideas to your newest cause. This is an open question of emotional chemistry.

With Cancer SUN man: You will share tears, making each other's woes your own. You'll sensitively touch each other, knowing how to make each other feel better. There is a sensual quality here that is a showstopper. However, unless he understands you as the pioneer who loves society, there could be some crabby moments!

With Leo SUN man: He is the man you might have dreamed of as a child. He is charming, funny, and powerful. There is no question you will succumb to his masculinity and become his. You stir each other's fantasies. This combination can easily endure. Say yes, though you might have already!

With Virgo SUN man: He is dedicated, dependable, and finds your interest in service and others delightful. You have very different solutions and responses to problems, and there is much to be learned from each other. However, somehow your sweet sentimentality could get lost. Make a careful call here.

With Libra SUN man: You will stop in your tracks, even if you are very busy when this man goes by. He is a diamond, a treasure trove in your opinion. Your styles are very different, yet you are like a hook and eye together once latched. He could be the love of your life. Let the dream begin.

With Scorpio SUN man: He is a whirlpool of emotions and feelings, like you. Once you touch, you reach a whole new level of communication. You have an uncanny sense of touch that soothes your souls. You will pioneer waters that few will ever swim. Lucky you.

With Sagittarius SUN man: You might be drawn to his energy and even go to a baseball game together, but let it end there. You are a woman who needs monogamy. Your self-destructive sides comes out when you find out his path is strewn with lady loves.

With Capricorn SUN man: This man is your protector in this world, shielding you from ugliness and offering you his caring. You will have a beautiful home and sanctuary. He will understand your feelings, though he can't identify with them. Sooner or later, you might grumble because he is a bit too mercenary for your style.

With Aquarius SUN man: He is intuitive and direct about liking you. There is constant eruption and change with him. He will join you in your crusades and offer you a wonderful friendship, but that is where it ends—or should.

With Pisces SUN man: He plucks your heartstrings, and the magic begins. He is your knight in shining armor. You turn your home into your own fairy tale castle and are happy together. He adores your fiery energy when it comes to helping those in trouble, including him. This is a home run.

MOON IN PISCES, SUN IN TAURUS

Of all Pisces Moon women, you seem to be best able to stabilize yourself and use your emotions to empower you. You come out a winner time after time because you understand your feelings and can mobilize them to get what you want. You willingly take off your rose-colored glasses and work with reality.

Others love your easy, understanding nature. It makes them comfortable. You understand their pains and desires. With your extraordinary empathy, mixed with a practical nature, you help others find solutions. Others learn to depend upon, love, and trust you.

You will know a rare form of loving, and once you decide on a partner, you are likely to be a wonderful wife. You will create a sturdy family relationship in a home where others are welcomed. You will be surrounded by devoted family and friends.

You are extremely sensuous, and attract men with ease. There might be some degree of fullness in your body structure, but that only adds to your appeal. You have the ability to evoke strong self-discipline to counter overindulgence and not follow the bad dietary habits associated with your Pisces Moon.

The same inclination toward overindulgence makes for good times. Friends want to be with you, and you are frequently invited to parties. When single, your dance card is often filled. Because you are so sought after, you need to know what you want from a relationship.

With Aries SUN man: Expect fire and confrontation. Though you like his leadership and energy, you don't dig his temper, which inevitably comes out. It is simply part of him. Don't try to work this out. This is a case of different personalities that do not mesh. Remember, there are many fish in the sea.

With Taurus SUN man: Expect a romantic courtship with all the touching little thoughts and meaningful gifts. You find this man easygoing and wonderful. Once in a while you will butt heads, as you both can be set in your ways. But you won't care. He is worth it.

With Gemini SUN man: Some things are meant not to happen. This relationship is one of them. Grounding is unlikely with him. He could also irritate the daylights out of you. You will put him down and he will be off in a cloud of dust.

With Cancer SUN man: You experience the world together, connecting on deep emotional and sensual levels. You share intuitive knowledge and a treasure of feelings. Water soothes both of your souls. You add structure to his world. However, be careful. His fragility is at least as great as yours. Don't make him withdraw.

With Leo SUN man: He is passionate and romantic. You can't deny the attraction, and why would you? You both are romantic and passionate. Problems occur when you both decide you are right and won't give way. Your commitment needs to include a willingness to compromise.

With Virgo SUN man: You will be drawn to each other. He is patient and stable, a careful builder. You share and value practicality. On another plane, you share a raw passion that will thrill you both. There is much respect and loving here.

With Libra SUN man: This is an interesting match, one that isn't easy to make work. Yet the tie between you is a strong one and hard to break.

He provides magic and enchantment, something you cannot resist. You will never understand each other, yet you will always love each other.

With Scorpio SUN man: He is the sorcerer king of sensuality, and knows how to enchant you forever. You both are determined to have what you want. You seem to weave an emotional web around his stubborn ways, and he happily falls deep into it. Both of you will have eyes only for each other. Say hello to love and passion.

With Sagittarius SUN man: Fidelity isn't his strong suit, and you might be very depressed at what goes on. You could become the self-pitying, forlorn version of Moon in Pisces with him. Don't do this to yourself, please.

With Capricorn SUN man: Together you build a secure, luxurious life. You see eye-to-eye on nearly everything. Your smoldering sensuality cinches it between you and adds to your commitment. He will always appreciate your sensitivity and understanding.

With Aquarius SUN man: You really do not have much in common. He doesn't want to settle down, isn't patient with your practical comments, and is uncomfortable with your highly tuned sensitivity.

With Pisces SUN man: He adores you and your loving ways. The mutuality between you is unique. You sense and feel each other. The uncanny sensuality sends you both over the rainbow. Warning: With him, count on being the practical one.

MOON IN PISCES, SUN IN GEMINI

You have the unique gift of being able to express your feelings in a way that others understand. You also can help others discover their feelings. You are a treasure trove of guidance and information, once you have resolved your own struggles.

You are a tender, attractive woman with a great deal of humor and wit. You seek grounding and want a partner who offers it. As with other Pisces Moons, you are highly desirable. You're quite possibly slender, with sensual, magnetic ways. Your personality helps people feel at peace with you. You need to make good choices and not get sucked in by another's sad story. It is one thing to be empathetic, another to buy in.

Because you are an easy touch, it is likely that you could have more than one marriage. You find commitment difficult, as you discover that when the going gets tough, you long to escape. Escapes can take many forms, but probably will be in the realm of overindulgence. You are also susceptible to side love affairs, which will not help your marriage.

Try not to commit until you are ready, as much as you want security. Real security can only come from within. When you understand that, you will become a more viable partner and friend. You will offer excitement, fun, and sensitivity to the lucky man you chose.

With Aries SUN man: His fiery ways delight your mind and imagination. One feeds off the other. However, he might not be able to understand your emotionality. You will have to work very hard to "communicate" what you are feeling. It might be worth it, because the stimulation is strong on many levels.

With Taurus SUN man: You feel emotionally stable with this man. He's romantic, but not adventuresome, and eventually you could find him boring. He also will not tolerate your playing and flirting with other men. This might feel good, but committing to it long term is another story.

With Gemini SUN man: You sound like two parrots chirping and squawking together. You talk, you talk, you talk. The problem is, will the talking ever end and the playing begin? This man has a sense of mischief that delights your heart and body. You will romp together happily, but he isn't always comfortable with your high emotional notes. But then neither are you! This can work.

With Cancer SUN man: He amplifies your emotional tones. You feel and love each other. You share an uncanny sense of touch, a knowing what to do when the other is down. Talk all you want, but this man is into feeling, being, and sharing with you. You might find yourself hooked, and you could stay that way.

With Leo SUN man: You love his alluring style, and your romantic dance enthralls him. Your wit and charm will keep him in heavy pursuit. You are both players, but because you feel what is good for the goose is great for the gander, you're likely to stay put. This is a lifetime relationship, a happily ever after.

With Virgo SUN man: This man is attractive to you because he is so rational and intellectual. Yet he has none of the swinging vitality that emanates from you. He simply doesn't know what to do with it. The passion here can be intense, but don't be fooled and make more of this relationship than is there.

With Libra SUN man: His courtship style delights your sense of romance. You are charmed by his wit and gentleness; he is thrilled with your intellect. There is much loving, enchantment, and laughter. Once connected, you will have a difficult time leaving each other. So much the better!

With Scorpio SUN man: Your loving ways and emotional sensitivities draw him. He is deeply passionate and emotional. He feels with you he will find solace, and he will. Your wit and airy ways provoke his sexual imagination. He is like a wildfire with you. Let it burn!

With Sagittarius SUN man: Trouble alert! You are desperately attracted. However, he cannot foster the climate you need to feel emotionally safe. He will never understand your poetry and style. You could feel as if struck by lightning here, but beware the monsoon of tears that follows.

With Capricorn SUN man: The beast in him responds to you. He finds you provocative, someone he must have and love. You will hesitate, sensing his will and power. You know the chemistry is there. He will want you as his hostess, wife, and friend. He will love your mind and body. He will try to understand your strong empathy, but might never really understand it.

With Aquarius SUN man: You act like two naughty kids playing doctor. The fun goes on, though he cannot satisfy your deep emotional needs. But who knows, you might have so much fun that you won't care! This is truly playtime.

With Pisces SUN man: The merger of two like spirits ends your search for solace. Your empathy needs no words, just touching. In many ways this is true love. Who wouldn't feel secure with what you two have?

MOON IN PISCES, SUN IN CANCER

You are emotional and sensitive, and have deep wisdom. You are not comfortable around light, flaky people. Your pastimes reflect your feeling nature. You need time outdoors to center.

You shine. You might be drawn to pearls and opals that reflect your multifaceted personality. Depending on your mood and the moment, you reveal different sides of yourself. Men find you fascinating, a glowing, ever-changing gem. You are so utterly feminine, you will draw many men, though they might not suit you.

You offer sensitivity, security, and loyalty. You love the quality life and help create good times for loved ones and friends. You seek financial security. You want one marriage and will work hard to maintain it. You can be easily disillusioned because of your fragile vulnerability. If that should happen, you could become negative, difficult, and contrary. Once in that cycle, you might find it hard to break.

Whatever mode you are in, it is hard for you to pull out and stop. You are an all-or-nothing woman. Nothing is done halfway.

You seek a partner with similar spirit, a man who can relate to you on an emotional, soulful level. He needs to be able to provide material as well as emotional security.

With Aries SUN man: He is a dart, and you are like water. He might strike you, but he will sink in your tidal pools. You can admire him and like him, but let it go at that. His fire and energy are not compatible with your soulful ways. He cares, but in a fiery, universal manner.

With Taurus SUN man: This man is the salt of the earth. He gives form to feelings and emotions. With him you find form in the currents of feeling that run through you. He will teach you not to give in to each whim and opt for the whole. This is a wonderful life-choice.

With Gemini SUN man: When you meet this man, you might feel you have encountered a different species. He is of the mind and has no concept of the emotional depths within you. Even his definition of a good time is much different from yours. Consider doing lunch, then going your different ways.

With Cancer SUN man: Your head might spin when you sense his feelings as well as yours. There is a fusion here, as both of you are deeply empathetic and easily merge into one. The sensuality here leaves you feeling exposed but loved. Expect a lifetime of love and feeling.

With Leo SUN man: He is romantic and dashing. You will inadvertently drown him with your emotional excesses and feelings. He likes action. You like feeling. You play a whole different game.

With Virgo SUN man: This man is stable, persistent, and detached. You might hit him like a hurricane with your emotional blast. He can help you see more logical ways to do things, if you are receptive. You will initiate him to grand passion. He will love you forever for that!

With Libra SUN man: You make magic together, and he knows how to charm you to your very tiptoes. He is light and airy and will never know how deeply you feel. There is a basic incompatibility that makes this relationship a dud. However, he is cute, don't you think?

With Scorpio SUN man: He is a riptide in your waters. He is as sensual as sensual can get. Love builds steadily with a great deal of intuition and inner knowledge. You spend hours dreaming and staring into each other's eyes. You say much, but in a language others cannot understand. You are in the hot tub of life and loving here.

With Sagittarius SUN man: He is fire and action. It is possible that unless he has strong water elements in his chart, he will never notice you. That's okay; you would feel worse if you had a relationship with him!

With Capricorn SUN man: Opposites attract here, and though he knows nothing of your emotional currents, he senses your passion and heat. Love is well taken care of. He allows you security and the freedom to be. In return, you fulfill his whims and desires.

With Aquarius SUN man: Again, it is unlikely that you will have eyes for each other, unless there is a unique quality in his chart. He will never be able to understand you and wants to be free. He will find you drippy. Sorry.

With Pisces SUN man: Emotions meet, and you have a bonding that is out of this world. The pleasures are undeniable, sometimes quite out of control. You tend to play together as if there is no tomorrow. You will live and love without limits with this man. You won't be able to say no.

MOON IN PISCES, SUN IN LEO

Romance and loving are a must for your daily living. You are a strong presence. Eyes turn toward you as you charm others. Underneath your magnificent exterior lies a very emotional woman. You have a penchant for drama, but this quality can push others away. As beautiful as you are, you might often find yourself isolated.

When you're together, your natural style is steamy and intense; few can resist or want to. You are capable of great passion. You can melt defenses, creating deep loving. You can be trusted with love. You have a very strong picture of what love looks like. You might think a loved one should share every wound, so you can heal them. You need to let others be whole, independent, and come to you on their own terms.

You offer a nurturing, caring relationship. You might think you want quiet and calm, but deep down, you crave action and drama. And if you don't have them, you become bored.

You unconsciously seek a man who is dramatic, active, and amorous. Generosity and security are big plusses. The problem is that you always want your love relationship to be running full throttle, not giving it times off to recharge. For this reason, you might go through a sequence of relationships trying to find the right man. You need to understand yourself first to fulfill your potential. Then you will be secure and not need the love switch flipped constantly on high.

With Aries SUN man: He is committed, unpretentious, and fiery. You can expect a dashing, whirlwind courtship, but he will never understand your deeply emotional side. Plug that emotional energy into healing the world with him and you could sizzle away together.

With Taurus SUN man: He conducts a slow and easy courtship while you chomp at the bit. You play femme fatale as you attempt to quicken the pace. The problem is already apparent in this tie. You want it your way and will manipulate in any direction to make it so. He is the way he is. The frustration is high.

With Gemini SUN man: He is exciting, dashing, and daring. You think you want to make him yours. Think again. After the initial spark, he is overwhelmed by your emotionality. Light and airy is how he likes it. Take a peek in the mirror. That isn't you! The sparks of passion might change all too soon to anger. Play this as a fling.

With Cancer SUN man: You are kindred spirits. It is questionable here who is healing whom. Empathetic bonding adds to the sensual tie. You'll take turns being dramatic. That's okay. The negative? He might not be that dashing knight you so dreamed of. If you can let go of your pictures, you can have a loving lifetime tie with this man.

With Leo SUN man: Finally, your knight in shining armor has arrived. He will love your romantic, endearing side. He adores the dramatic scenarios the two of you create. Your imagination knows no limits, and he will often tap you as a resource. This is the kind of loving novels are written about.

With Virgo SUN man: Opposites attract, and there is a sense you belong to each other. Yet as strong as the embers glow here, there is a problem keeping them burning. Eventually you will cause him a lot of pain, making demands that he can't fulfill. Yet if you accept him for who he is, the relationship could be okay, though not great.

With Libra SUN man: He will tease and coerce you to come closer to him, and you will. You might sense something is off. You will be so locked in by the time you identify it that it could be inconsequential. After all, you want to heal others. Now you can help him get more in touch with his core.

With Scorpio SUN man: Passions boil up, searing both of you, again and again. He is a controller. You might have a hard time with that, as you are very strong and have a clear picture of how things should be. As suitable as this match is, both of you will need to learn to negotiate and compromise.

With Sagittarius SUN man: You will fall in love with him and want him to settle down, something that isn't likely to happen. He has wander- lust. You will feel what is good for the goose is great for the gander. There will be many dramas here, which on some level you like. But, sadly, little happiness. You will be saying "if only."

With Capricorn SUN man: Your essence appeals to him, and he finds you very different. He loves grand displays, which you are so capable of. The passion between you seems to solidify what his money can't. As a couple, you will specialize in grand entries. You both love power and the limelight. Go for this if you like his style.

With Aquarius SUN man: He is detached and values friendship where you are about passion and loving. There is an attraction that can't be denied, but this combo can only work with great mutual respect and caring. Your tumultuous emotions will make him pity himself for having to put up with this Brouhaha. Think twice.

With Pisces SUN man: A kiss and you know this is it. There is a glue that goes from the emotional to the physical to the mental. You live well together; you love well together. There are many romantic twists and turns here. You'll have enough variety to keep you busy for a lifetime.

MOON IN PISCES, SUN IN VIRGO

Women born under a full moon have an unusual allure and appeal. You have this magic. You swing back and forth, much like the Moon changes shape—moody, beautiful, and dynamic. You draw men with ease. Relating to them is a whole different story.

You have a strong need to be of service to others and are highly compassionate. You will take care of others in some form, perhaps through your work. You are a "soft touch." Once someone discovers that about you, your weak spot is exposed. It is important to learn to say no when you are uncomfortable with a request.

You want a strong man who is dedicated like you. It is okay with you if he isn't passionate or emotional. You want dedication more than words, sensitivity more than emotions, and always kindness.

You offer compassion, dedication, and loyalty. You will do whatever is necessary to make a partner happy, even playing the role of his fantasy woman. However, if you become disillusioned, you could wander and perhaps have an affair. You crave an emotionally fulfilling relationship and will always work for that. When something isn't working, you need to let go of it. Insecurity doesn't become you. Stand up for your integrity and be who you are.

With Aries SUN man: He is passionate and directed. You might not want him, as interesting as he is. You are best off starting to get to know him and aiming toward a friendship. Then make a decision.

With Taurus SUN man: There could be a veritable meltdown when the two of you meet. This is a slow-building relationship, well tended by him. What you don't understand about relating, he will teach you. It is his pleasure. This is a good long-term match.

With Gemini SUN man: If you run into him, do a U-turn and head the other way. He is nothing but trouble for you and vice versa. This can't possibly work. He isn't the committing type and hates emotional displays. You aren't meant for each other.

With Cancer SUN man: He is emotional like you and connects on a soulful level. You feel as if you are meant to dance together. You will have to be the rational one when things get crazy. Sensual sparks bond you even more tightly. There is a sense of connection without words. You and he know you belong together.

With Leo SUN man: Romeo just went by and he is enough to trigger the wildest, most torrid fantasy. There is likely to be an instant connection, but be smart and let it go. In the long run, his passions melt your barriers and you will be very vulnerable. Should he decide to go philandering, which is his nature, you will be left standing in a puddle of tears.

With Virgo SUN man: He is there for you, much devoted. You connect on an intellect level. He represents your cool side, and his logic is dependable. You will bring out fiery passion in him when you show him your multifaceted personality. Your touch will enthrall him and bind him to you. Count on his emotional display in private moments.

With Libra SUN man: This man means well and likes you. He senses your deep emotionality and is intrigued. He isn't right for you, though once the romance begins, it might be hard to pull away. You are deep; he is somewhat superficial. This adds up to a rough ride through the tunnel of love.

With Scorpio SUN man: You can really be yourself with this man. Surges of feelings wipe him out and overwhelm him, like you. Because he seems to embody both your detachment and emotionality, you feel a real connection. Love grows by leaps and bounds in his hands.

With Sagittarius SUN man: This man is about fire and adventure. And though he is certainly hot stuff, he is not the right stuff. Don't take it personally; he belongs to no one. You have met a true free spirit.

With Capricorn SUN man: You have encountered a man who builds and creates from his thoughts. He will appreciate your logical ideas and questions. He will adore it when you act out your fantasies with him. You play well together. You will find him the Rock of Gibraltar— and quite possibly the love of your life. This is a merger of different powers.

With Aquarius SUN man: He is cool, detached, and clever too. All this appeals to you. However, when he gets the idea that deep waters run under your surface, he might vanish. He will be your friend, but nothing more.

With Pisces SUN man: He wears his feelings on his shirtsleeve, letting you know just how much you are cared for. You automatically feel safe.

You love each other with a natural tenderness and delight. You are a couple that keeps vanishing to your private world. Others are envious.

MOON IN PISCES, SUN IN LIBRA

You are delightful, feminine, and romantic. You have the charm and ease that many wish for. Others notice your softness. You would do nothing to hurt another and you will do all you can to make others' lives work.

Attractiveness is your middle name, and combined with your lovely ways and personality, you are irresistible. Then add your deep femininity. Few can say no to you.

You are extremely versatile and offer a man many things. You will always be his feminine partner. He'll wear the pants. You love being the other half. You can be a superb wife, healer, and lover. You can be indecisive, and, therefore, a man who is clear and directed can be a gift.

It takes quite a courtship, which is very important to you, to lure you into a relationship. In fact, you might judge the quality of what a man offers by the tempo of his love-dance. Inside, you know these values are superficial, but you can't help your light, flaky side.

You will expect the courtship to last forever, and you will do your best to make sure of that. If your mate becomes bored with the love-dance, you will do your best to revive it. If you don't succeed, you might wander. This is why you so much need a sense for commitment.

With Aries SUN man: He is as masculine as you are feminine. You are receptive, and he is directed. There is much more than raw magnetism here. There isn't time for thought here, as passion rules. He has enough zest to keep you busy for a long time.

With Taurus SUN man: He is sensual candy that you want to take your time enjoying. You both love romance, pleasure, and quality. Though there is a tendency to go way overboard together, and you need days to recuperate, the love builds. You find him an anchor, and he thinks you are his womanly treat of a lifetime.

With Gemini SUN man: He is great for a fling, but a no-go for the long term. He lures, cajoles, and tempts you with his intelligence, sentimental offerings, and sexual energy. The problem is that he doesn't want an anchor, and eventually you would become that to him. Great fun is promised here, but not permanence. Now you know.

With Cancer SUN man: He is intense and wants you. Count on romantic walks, trips to the water, dinner at the best restaurants. The courtship will get an "A" in your book. You have the potential for a deep, loving relationship with one of the most romantic ties possible. He loves your affable ways.

With Leo SUN man: You will never, ever be able to complain about the lack of loving here. This man is romantic and is enthralled by your imagination and amorous desires. You will keep this zodiac flirt put because of your charm, femininity, and depth. He loves it, and he loves you. This can last forever.

With Virgo SUN man: Though you are attracted, he is rather detached, if levelheaded. He will love your flirting and all that follows it. You will always need to warm him up. Do you want this? You can count on one thing. He will want you. A toss-up.

With Libra SUN man: He is as tender as you are. You both love to tease and let it all hang out. You drive each other into sweet torment. He might be a flirt, he might have a hard time committing, but he isn't leaving you. You can bet on him.

With Scorpio SUN man: You have met someone who pushes all your buttons. Your head will spin with this master lover and seducer. He knows where and how to touch. You will meld with this man.

With Sagittarius SUN man: He might be tempted by you, the princess of femininity, and you love his energy and ability to risk. This can be a royal romp, but you will find that when you try to set up a nest together, the wars begin. You want him to play, and he is always off with the guys—enough! Remember: This is play. No more.

With Capricorn SUN man: He wants to talk business when you wink at him. But don't think he doesn't notice you. However, as much as you can forgive him for his work orientation, he will always annoy you. You might do better if you continue looking. Just keep thinking how much he annoys you.

With Aquarius SUN man: My, he can flirt even more than you, but his thoughts are more wicked! The wooing is wild and out of control. However, this is another tie you might want to keep as a naughty friendship. He needs freedom. You need love and romance. You will not be able to bring these different interests together for any length of time.

With Pisces SUN man: In your hearts you want the same thing and you are both deeply connected. It is obvious. When you meet, you will look into his eyes and feel that you have known him forever. The intensity will send flares over your household for the rest of your life. This link can lead to marriage.

MOON IN PISCES, SUN IN SCORPIO

You might suddenly become quiet and turn inward. Others wonder why the sudden silence. Actually you are picking up on feelings: others' and yours. You might be aware of how strong your psychic abilities are. This skill is at the base of your choices.

Others sense your yearning sensuality. Your eyes are puddles of promise and knowledge. You have an aura of mystery, excitement, and enchantment. Men want to know you better, but they might be insecure about how to proceed. You are bewitching. You seem to have magic up your sleeve.

Others also feel your warmth. They want to know your depth. You have the illusive quality of water, filling the available vessel. You make others feel whole, loved, and complete. You have an intuitive, uncanny sense of touch.

You are obviously a very special partner and mate, one who will give all, who does not hold back. You expect total loyalty and, if you find your partner has strayed, you could feel deeply hurt. You want to trust those around you, but you could become skeptical after several emotional jolts.

You seek a man who is reserved and penetrating, and wants to experience the deep, feeling levels you seem to promise. He might be possessive, but you have a similar need. You want and demand a quality relationship, a man to share life's pleasures with.

With Aries SUN man: He is who he is—a fiery hotshot. But he might not be what you need to charge your battery. He means well and cares. Together you and he make steam, and eventually both of you could get scalded. Move along.

With Taurus SUN man: You are a magnet to him, throwing him into whirlpools of feelings and caring. He will give form to your emotions, and you will introduce him to his depths. This is a long-term, stable combination. You will be seduced by his touch and his grounded courtship. Yes, you are safe.

With Gemini SUN man: There might be flickers and a spark or two. However, he dwells in his mind and isn't ready to deal with your puddles of feelings. Though he finds you sexy, he will run. You are doing nothing wrong. This just isn't meant to be.

With Cancer SUN man: With him, you feel complete. Together, you seem to do the right thing, make the right choices. This combination is as exciting as Niagara Falls, and that is where it is heading. The honeymoon here could be forever. You move as a unit.

With Leo SUN man Few can say no to the King of Lovers, you included. He is steamy, loving, and romantic. Count on torrents of passion. However, this storm is likely to turn into a hurricane. Consider this a lethal attraction. Be prepared, as you are both stubborn. You are very different, and might never see eye-to-eye.

With Virgo SUN man: You would like to be rational, but your passions and feelings consume you like tidal waves. He knows intuitively how to anchor you, though you might feel a yearning wanderlust. It feels as if something is lacking. It is. He doesn't have your emotional currents, and can't swim with them.

With Libra SUN man: As charming as he is, this man is not your style of lover. Where you live through your emotions, he sees through impressions that he tests and evaluates. Again, a case of very different, nice people who don't belong together.

With Scorpio SUN man: You have met Nirvana with this man. He offers your ideal of loving. He will brush your soul, and there will be fiery, angry moments as you establish what you need. There is resolution here—then great satisfaction. Go for it.

With Sagittarius SUN man: He is fiery and wild. You might notice him, but you're unlikely to pay much heed. He needs his space and loves women in general. He doesn't know how to stroke your soul and mind. Body, maybe. Still, move on.

With Capricorn SUN man: Count on stability and earthiness here. He is intensely hot and powerful, though he is unlikely to even be capable of imagining your emotional plunges and highs. You have compatibility, but not kinship. If you can be happy without a soul mate union, this could work.

With Aquarius SUN man: If he is turning right, you go left. His unpredictability could have you on a shrink's sofa for a very long time. His quirks are like a Richter scale 7 earthquake for you. No.

With Pisces SUN man: There is an unusual bond here. Both of you are sensitive, artistic, and telepathic. You are on the same wavelength. You seem to naturally wrap your lives and souls around each other. You live and love well together. You can stop looking now.

MOON IN PISCES, SUN IN SAGITTARIUS

If you ever go to a dating service, your portfolio will reflect your natural dichotomy: wants freedom; needs deep emotional attachments. Sound familiar? This is a hard combination to satisfy because it depends on which need is stronger, and how connected you are to your feelings.

You are athletic, spirited, and deeply sensitive. Though you can project as sound and strong, inside there is a fragile, caring person. Be aware of your deep needs and that sometimes you try to escape them by defensive maneuvering. It is possible you will choose men who are unavailable but, when they are around, are extremely deep and emotional. You could feel needy and helpless and respond by whining and playing victim. That could push away those who might want to be close to you.

You want a partner who doesn't threaten your need for space, yet who is there for you. You want him to have sparkle and pizzazz. He knows when to risk and when to be close. He must understand you and read you clearly, be okay with your mood swings and, indeed, love you with them.

You will accept his business trips, nights out with the guys, and sporting events.

You might have two marriages as you look for the perfect fit. It could take up to four. But never fear, there's a great relationship out there for you.

With Aries SUN man: You just stuck your finger in an electrical socket. The two of you develop your own magnetic force field. There is a lot of passionate play here, but he might not be on your emotional wavelength. Think before acting on fantasy. You aren't changing him; you can only change yourself.

With Taurus SUN man: There is synchronization here. This man is even-tempered, though strong. He will take risks and do his ''thing,'' yet he will be dedicated to you. Together, there will be lots of indulgence, many late nights, romantic moments, and laughter galore.

With Gemini SUN man: If you want more conflict, another side, a different point of view, celebrate. You have found it with this man. He is full of ideas and easily gives you space. However, he can't meet your intimacy needs. He is a good time, though.

With Cancer SUN man: Consider how much snuggling you can take and how many breaths of fresh air you'll need to grab. Once you calculate, make your choice. Though you will have a clinging vine, he knows how to make you tremble for his touch. An interesting call.

With Leo SUN man: Temperatures soar when you meet this gentleman. You can count on him firing up your passions and dreams. He is okay with emotionalism. It is another testimony to your caring. Declare your independence, and he smiles, understands, and becomes more seductive! An excellent match here.

With Virgo SUN man: Though there's strong attraction, you're an odd couple. He is picky, detailed, and detached. You are passionate, independent, and a risk-taker. You're hard to imagine together, but it does happen. As loudly as the drum beats between you, as much you are out of synch.

With Libra SUN man: This might not work, but once you find each other and tug at each other's heartstrings, there could be no way out. There is superglue between you. He is a romantic like you and can work with your independence. Your emotional scenes can get a bit heavy for him. Yet there is much joy.

With Scorpio SUN man: High-voltage emotions surge through the two of you. You naturally belong together. He is sometimes silent and withdrawn. You understand, and it gives you space. Use the moments well. There is an intensity here that few can experience.

With Sagittarius SUN man: He has your freedom-loving nature. He's debonair and exciting. However, you will have to come to terms with your emotional neediness. He won't know what to do with it. Relating to him provides an excellent opportunity to balance your polarities. Go for it.

With Capricorn SUN man: He is the salt of the earth and can tolerate demonstrative, wild scenes, yet help you stabilize. Your risk-taking could send chills up his back, which is where the problems begin. Even if he is a workaholic, he won't take kindly to your leaving for China for a month. Think carefully. This man is powerful and strong. But he wants you around.

With Aquarius SUN man: You seem to be two naughty kids into mischief. There is a deep friendship here, yet he will never be your emotional anchor. As much fun as he is, you are selling out part of yourself with him. However, you could still laugh and play forever together.

With Pisces SUN man: You have an indescribable soul connection. You are natural lovers. Your souls, bodies, and minds bond. You will need to cope with your occasional thirst for independence. But you can do it! And with him, you will want to.

MOON IN PISCES, SUN IN CAPRICORN

You are emotional and can throw quite a tantrum. But you're also capable of being practical, someone who doesn't miss a trick. This combination can play out in many different ways. You're likely to know how to have your practicality serve your emotional sensuality, and vice versa.

People may see you as highly organized, but know you're capable of going ballistic. Your ability to use your different facets makes you one successful woman. Men find you fascinating. You can be a tower of strength, yet be a soft, emotionally vulnerable woman. You are an enigma to them. Consequently, you have many choices. Of course, you will not be attracted to every man, but your compassion will help you find something attractive and likable in each person.

You probably have a strongly defined image of what you want in a relationship. You seek a powerful man, one who is in control and can provide you the emotional and material shelter you want. You can be free with your feelings and flourish with Mr. Right.

Your partner could be older, or seem more mature than his age. Because you will probably marry once, it's possible you will marry at an older age. You are capable of and expect a life commitment.

With Aries SUN man: Though he is an excellent provider, he might not be your cup of tea. He is action-oriented and seldom stays put. You like a man you can find. That might not be possible here.

With Taurus SUN man: He fits. You fit. A perfect match. Not only is he stable and on his way to affluence, he is sensual, loving, and indulgent. You can merge your facets with his and have one shiny gem of a relationship. You are a great couple on many levels, inspiring others with the strength of your commitment.

With Gemini SUN man: He is charming and witty. Invite him to one of your parties, not into your heart. He won't be the stable man you want and he will abhor your emotional drama.

With Cancer SUN man: Your temperature rises when he enters the room. You feel his poetry, know he wants the same security as you, that he is very sensual. There are some relationships that make it through every bump because of the sheer power of chemistry. Bingo!

With Leo SUN man: This zodiac Romeo has interesting ties with you. Once you are in his arms, both of you might never want to let go. The rebellion could be wild as you buck the inevitable. This is an exciting ride, with love, passion, and lots of sparks. Oh yes, he will offer you security.

With Virgo SUN man: He is a wizard of efficiency and will be there for you. He might not always be able to deal with your emotional ups and downs, and could become critical. Either you are both respectful of the differences, or this is a time bomb.

With Libra SUN man: Yes, you could really dig him and he, you. You can intertwine forever, but recognize one thing: He isn't practical, and won't be. You will have to do the budget, if you can pry yourself away from him long enough.

With Scorpio SUN man: He is dark, mysterious, and very sexy. Your heart thumps when this soul enters the scene. He is electric to you; beyond the initial shock is only high-voltage pleasure. He offers stability, resonates with you emotionally, and likes your every facet. What is there to say no to? This is heavy-duty.

With Sagittarius SUN man: Being with this man is a fun idea, but it's practically inconceivable that much will happen for the long haul. You and he have very little in common unless there are some unusual factors in his chart.

With Capricorn SUN man: There is naughtiness afoot here. You two are both stable powers, capable of establishing your own secure empires.

Because there is so much happening in your separate endeavors, you can afford to be frivolous together. This is the kind of mischief that leads to a lifetime relationship.

With Aquarius SUN man: Please don't. He is airy and eccentric. You are conservative and emotional. Don't even think about it.

With Pisces SUN man: You feel as if you've always known each other, and the news is that you probably will know each other from here on in. This is a hard-core connection with love, tenderness, sensual electricity, and fathomless understanding. You will need a break once in a while, perhaps to balance your joint checkbook!

MOON IN PISCES, SUN IN AQUARIUS

You use your emotions as a guide. Your intuitive, psychic abilities let you read people, gain a sense of direction, and often help you make money. You see people clearly and accurately. Sometimes you know them better than they know themselves.

You have a unique ability to pull away and see the big picture in an unemotional context. Blessed with a superior ability to process along with your homing instinct, you are very easygoing and successful.

You offer warmth, understanding, and nurturing. There is comfort with the person you choose to share your special sensitivity with. You will feel his pain and make it yours. Yet because of your remarkable ability to detach, you are able to come up with dynamic solutions and ideas. You are a very special friend with undying loyalty.

You have a unique look, perhaps bordering on the ethereal, and your looks are changeable. You love watery blues and greens with a touch of purple or violet. You melt into your environs and seem to pick up the looks of those around you, or somehow project the surrounding atmosphere.

You seek a man who will be your friend, understand you, and forgive anything. It is okay if he's somewhat distant or detached, because for you that provides a certain ease. But he must understand your emotionality. He needs to follow his own drummer and see you as the unique, special person you are.

With Aries SUN man: You like his fire and read him cold. He knows how to pull you in and be very close to you. But your styles are very different, and you are likely to scald each other. Your mixed messages will confuse him, sometimes feeding his fire, other times throwing water on him.

With Taurus SUN man: Did you know you were stubborn? Well, you get to see just how stubborn and fixed you are with this man. You must learn to flex if you want happiness here. He is grounded and understands you.

With Gemini SUN man: His mind is forever active with ideas, and you will jolt him when you decide to run with his more eccentric suggestions. Not only does he not relate to your emotionality, he could flee from it. Be careful here. Yet there is an attraction.

With Cancer SUN man: Both of you love the good life filled with pleasure, wonderful food, and delightful moments. You have great sensual chemistry. However, when you detach, he might get insecure. You need to tell him what goes on within you. He will understand.

With Leo SUN man: The chemistry between the two of you will always be volatile and hot. When you become logical and quick, he is thrilled. You both love people and can entertain from now to forever. This is a joyous sharing of passion and deep friendship. Why resist?

With Virgo SUN man: Both of you are able to detach. Yet you both care deeply about others and each other. Count on providing the spark for passion, not that he will turn away from it. Let this happen. Don't be surprised if you also work together as a team.

With Libra SUN man: You might be here today but gone tomorrow. However, so could he. You both love your space. This is an incredible hookup. He delights in your mischief, perspective, and fun. His gentle and loving ways melt your heart. You are his; he is yours. The depth of the loving, merged with your mutual sense of humor, make this a great go.

With Scorpio SUN man: He is an abyss of emotions and understands when your reservoir of feelings spills over. Problems could come if he gets possessive and jealous. Remember, you are the world's friend, and he wants you where he can find you, close to him. Something will have to give: you, he, or the relationship.

With Sagittarius SUN man: You blow hot air on his sparks, igniting him. Not only is there passion here, but also trouble. When you get emotional, he feels as if you've doused him with cold water. You will rain on his parade, so he will take his parade elsewhere. Watch it here.

With Capricorn SUN man: Count on his conservatism. He will judge your eccentric ideas as off the wall. He is an emotional anchor for you and will take care of you. However, the constant smashing of your ideas and vitality will wear you down. This is at best problematic.

With Aquarius SUN man: One idea only gets more wicked than the last. You feed each other's naughtiness and fantasies. You can play, talk, and wander together. He will have to be a special type of Aquarian to handle your feelings when they overflow. You'll know if he is right for you.

With Pisces SUN man: You give your friendship, yet he draws out your raw passions. You are emotional twins; he is as feeling and tender as you. Love is in good hands here. You share an intuitive sense of touching, loving, and nurturing. To the outside world, there might be too much drama. These scenes are your meat and potatoes. Feast with him.

Moon in Pisces, Sun in Pisces

Your message comes across loud and clear as you speak your mind intuitively and emotionally. Your actions directly reflect your true nature. You're able to maintain a sense of stability even if you find yourself swinging from one emotional pole to the other. That is your consistency; perpetual change and emoting.

You have been bestowed with charisma and raw magnetism aplenty. Your suitors pursue ardently. Your desirability allows you to be picky. Your biggest problem is your strong empathy and need to care for others, which makes you a soft touch. You are a sucker (excuse me) for a hard luck story.

Titanic loves mark your life. Music touches your soul, water recharges your body, and loving energizes your heart.

You can have trouble seeing the big picture or seeing a situation in which you are involved from a perspective other than your own. In relationships you could find it difficult to resolve problems. You feel you must give in totally or have it your way. You are okay with pain and discomfort. In fact, a twang or two seems to be part of loving in your book.

You will seek a man who has the same sense of loving and emotional qualities as you, a man who rolls with change. However, you could also

choose a man who is deeply needy. You might be okay with this because
you love to nurture and heal.

With Aries SUN man: He is hot-headed and emotional in your book.
You're probably right, given that you absorb others' energy easily. The
two of you are not destined for a relationship. In fact, it might even be
a challenge to have a friendship!

With Taurus SUN man: He is receptive and gives form to your feeling
as they spill over him. He is sweet and gentle, yet firm. You will always
feel secure in his arms and can let your feelings envelop him. His
grounded sensuality has you dancing from one star to the next. Love is
secure and stable with this man.

With Gemini SUN man: Your instincts are usually right on. When you
feel like running the other way after you meet this gentleman, do it!
There is nothing wrong with him. In fact, he is affable, bright, and
charming. But the two of you are a problem together. Follow your intuition and bail.

With Cancer SUN man: His loving is as deep as yours. Together it is
as if two bodies of water have joined. Sometimes it is hard to tell which
are your feelings or his. You achieve a sense of oneness here. You like
the same things: walks by the sea, wonderfully sensual meals, and fun
indulgences. There are few problems here, so don't make any!

With Leo SUN man: He is passionate and romantic. You might fall
into his arms and love could grow. The long haul is a different story.
He is independent and does his thing; he will love you, but be careful
with your clinginess. Let your feelings flow in positive ways and he will
hang out with you for a while, and maybe even longer.

With Virgo SUN man: He is your zodiac and personality opposite. As
intimate and empathic as you are, he is detached and cool. Yet there is
a searing attraction between you that is hard to control. The common
ground is that you both care greatly about others and want to nurture
and serve. Just remember, your styles are like day and night!

With Libra SUN man: This can be an enchanting interlude, and please
note "interlude." You can let it go on much longer because the romantic
moments are tender and full of novel promise. Ultimately, you are too
emotional for him and he is too flighty for you. Have fun and keep
a perspective.

With Scorpio SUN man: Here heat and passion meet romance and emotion. This can't miss. This man might be quiet or distant at times, but you don't have a problem because there is telepathy between you. Much is unspoken, but with the physical and soulful bonding you have, it is irrelevant. You touch true love here.

With Sagittarius SUN man: This really isn't meant to be. He will upset you with his devoted intensity, which might last a few moments, days, or maybe weeks, before he fires up his engines and takes off. You will be left a miserable, drippy mess. Don't do this to yourself.

With Capricorn SUN man: He is earthy and stable, and offers security and solace. The heated moments could cinch it as you sense this recipe will cook for a long time. Your femininity and ethereal qualities charm him while you respond to his stoic ethics and caring. Both of you can be happy here.

With Aquarius SUN man: Let him run by you. You could find his ideas interesting and weird, but that is where it ends. He is another one who you might not be able to tame, because he values independence more than intimacy. Friendship might work.

With Pisces SUN man: The fish rules here, and this could be mighty interesting. You are obviously very similar, see eye-to-eye, and have like needs. Emotions blend. You live and love with ease together. The biggest hassle could be who gets the foot massage tonight. Probably both of you will, as indulgence and touching is natural to you both.

CHARTS

The following moon sign charts give the exact day—and time of day—on which the moon changes signs and moves into the sign shown in the left column.

To read charts, first locate your date of birth in the center column. If you find your birth date, check the time in the right column. The times are Eastern Standard, and are shown in military time, meaning 1:00 is 1:00 A.M. and 13:00 is 1 P.M. If you were born in Central Standard time, add one hour to the time shown. If you were born in Pacific Standard Time, add three hours.

If the time to the right of your birth date equals or is *earlier than* the time of day you were born, your moon sign is in the left column. If the time in the right column is *later than* your birth time, go to the line *before* your date. Your moon sign is in the left column.

If you don't find your exact birth date, use the first date given that is *before* your date. Your moon sign is in the left column.

For example, if you were born Feb. 24, 1936 at 9:10 A.M. Eastern Standard Time, your moon is in Aries. If you were born Feb. 24, 1936 at 7:32 A.M. EST, your moon is in Pisces. If you were born Feb. 25, 1936 at any time of day, your moon is in Aries. If you were born Feb. 26, 1936 at 7 A.M. Pacific Standard Time, your moon is in Taurus, but if you were born that day at 7 A.M. Eastern Standard Time, your moon is in Aries.

If you don't know the exact time of your birth, and you were born on a day the Moon changed signs, you might want to read the chapters for the moon sign shown for your birth date and the moon sign on the line *before* that date. See which description fits you best. If your birth date isn't shown, always use the line with the next date *before* your birth date to find your moon sign.

So curl up with paper and pencil and look up your moon sign. Then read the corresponding chapter. When you've finished reading about yourself, don't forget to look up your favorite people as well. You will learn to understand them in greater depth once their moon traits are revealed.

These charts cover the dates of 1930 to 2005. If you were born on a date not mentioned here, you may contact ASTROLABE at (508) 896-5081. Astrolabe can calculate your exact natal planetary positions, including the Moon, for $5.00. You may also contact Jacqueline Bigar's business line at (609) 354-0803.

Aqu	01/01/1930	13:28	Gem	04/30/1930	05:25	Lib	08/25/1930	21:58
Pis	01/04/1930	02:03	Can	05/02/1930	08:53	Sco	08/28/1930	00:11
Ari	01/06/1930	13:26	Leo	05/04/1930	11:31	Sag	08/30/1930	06:04
Tau	01/08/1930	21:57	Vir	05/06/1930	14:10	Cap	09/01/1930	15:35
Gem	01/11/1930	02:33	Lib	05/08/1930	17:29	Aqu	09/04/1930	03:27
Can	01/13/1930	03:33	Sco	05/10/1930	22:06	Pis	09/06/1930	16:06
Leo	01/15/1930	02:36	Sag	05/13/1930	04:38	Ari	09/09/1930	04:20
Vir	01/17/1930	01:57	Cap	05/15/1930	13:39	Tau	09/11/1930	15:17
Lib	01/19/1930	03:44	Aqu	05/18/1930	01:03	Gem	09/13/1930	23:59
Sco	01/21/1930	09:25	Pis	05/20/1930	13:33	Can	09/16/1930	05:41
Sag	01/23/1930	18:56	Ari	05/23/1930	00:53	Leo	09/18/1930	08:17
Cap	01/26/1930	06:52	Tau	05/25/1930	09:13	Vir	09/20/1930	08:44
Aqu	01/28/1930	19:34	Gem	05/27/1930	14:05	Lib	09/22/1930	08:43
Pis	01/31/1930	07:58	Can	05/29/1930	16:24	Sco	09/24/1930	10:07
Ari	02/02/1930	19:22	Leo	05/31/1930	17:44	Sag	09/26/1930	14:35
Tau	02/05/1930	04:47	Vir	06/02/1930	19:36	Cap	09/28/1930	22:49
Gem	02/07/1930	11:06	Lib	06/04/1930	23:04	Aqu	10/01/1930	10:09
Can	02/09/1930	13:53	Sco	06/07/1930	04:30	Pis	10/03/1930	22:47
Leo	02/11/1930	13:59	Sag	06/09/1930	11:56	Ari	10/06/1930	10:51
Vir	02/13/1930	13:14	Cap	06/11/1930	21:20	Tau	10/08/1930	21:13
Lib	02/15/1930	13:51	Aqu	06/14/1930	08:38	Gem	10/11/1930	05:28
Sco	02/17/1930	17:44	Pis	06/16/1930	21:11	Can	10/13/1930	11:28
Sag	02/20/1930	01:49	Ari	06/19/1930	09:13	Leo	10/15/1930	15:18
Cap	02/22/1930	13:12	Tau	06/21/1930	18:34	Vir	10/17/1930	17:25
Aqu	02/25/1930	01:56	Gem	06/23/1930	23:58	Lib	10/19/1930	18:42
Pis	02/27/1930	14:12	Can	06/26/1930	01:56	Sco	10/21/1930	20:32
Ari	03/02/1930	01:07	Leo	06/28/1930	02:05	Sag	10/24/1930	00:24
Tau	03/04/1930	10:17	Vir	06/30/1930	02:28	Cap	10/26/1930	07:27
Gem	03/06/1930	17:15	Lib	07/02/1930	04:46	Aqu	10/28/1930	17:53
Can	03/08/1930	21:33	Sco	07/04/1930	09:56	Pis	10/31/1930	06:22
Leo	03/10/1930	23:24	Sag	07/06/1930	17:48	Ari	11/02/1930	18:33
Vir	03/12/1930	23:53	Cap	07/09/1930	03:49	Tau	11/05/1930	04:36
Lib	03/15/1930	00:43	Aqu	07/11/1930	15:22	Gem	11/07/1930	11:57
Sco	03/17/1930	03:46	Pis	07/14/1930	03:56	Can	11/09/1930	17:04
Sag	03/19/1930	10:24	Ari	07/16/1930	16:25	Leo	11/11/1930	20:44
Cap	03/21/1930	20:40	Tau	07/19/1930	02:52	Vir	11/13/1930	23:41
Aqu	03/24/1930	09:04	Gem	07/21/1930	09:37	Lib	11/16/1930	02:26
Pis	03/26/1930	21:22	Can	07/23/1930	12:20	Sco	11/18/1930	05:36
Ari	03/29/1930	07:58	Leo	07/25/1930	12:18	Sag	11/20/1930	10:00
Tau	03/31/1930	16:22	Vir	07/27/1930	11:34	Cap	11/22/1930	16:42
Gem	04/02/1930	22:41	Lib	07/29/1930	12:18	Aqu	11/25/1930	02:23
Can	04/05/1930	03:10	Sco	07/31/1930	16:05	Pis	11/27/1930	14:32
Leo	04/07/1930	06:08	Sag	08/02/1930	23:24	Ari	11/30/1930	03:05
Vir	04/09/1930	08:10	Cap	08/05/1930	09:34	Tau	12/02/1930	13:30
Lib	04/11/1930	10:17	Aqu	08/07/1930	21:26	Gem	12/04/1930	20:30
Sco	04/13/1930	13:45	Pis	08/10/1930	10:02	Can	12/07/1930	00:30
Sag	04/15/1930	19:49	Ari	08/12/1930	22:31	Leo	12/09/1930	02:52
Cap	04/18/1930	05:06	Tau	08/15/1930	09:36	Vir	12/11/1930	05:03
Aqu	04/20/1930	16:58	Gem	08/17/1930	17:45	Lib	12/13/1930	08:04
Pis	04/23/1930	05:22	Can	08/19/1930	22:00	Sco	12/15/1930	12:19
Ari	04/25/1930	16:08	Leo	08/21/1930	22:56	Sag	12/17/1930	17:54
Tau	04/28/1930	00:06	Vir	08/23/1930	22:13	Cap	12/20/1930	01:11

Aqu	12/22/1930	10:43	Gem	04/20/1931	11:54	Lib	08/16/1931	07:44
Pis	12/24/1930	22:35	Can	04/22/1931	19:41	Sco	08/18/1931	09:10
Ari	12/27/1930	11:28	Leo	04/25/1931	01:02	Sag	08/20/1931	12:47
Tau	12/29/1930	22:50	Vir	04/27/1931	04:08	Cap	08/22/1931	18:58
Gem	01/01/1931	06:33	Lib	04/29/1931	05:34	Aqu	08/25/1931	03:38
Can	01/03/1931	10:19	Sco	05/01/1931	06:25	Pis	08/27/1931	14:27
Leo	01/05/1931	11:31	Sag	05/03/1931	08:14	Ari	08/30/1931	02:56
Vir	01/07/1931	12:06	Cap	05/05/1931	12:36	Tau	09/01/1931	15:58
Lib	01/09/1931	13:48	Aqu	05/07/1931	20:36	Gem	09/04/1931	03:42
Sco	01/11/1931	17:40	Pis	05/10/1931	08:01	Can	09/06/1931	12:13
Sag	01/13/1931	23:50	Ari	05/12/1931	20:55	Leo	09/08/1931	16:46
Cap	01/16/1931	08:01	Tau	05/15/1931	08:53	Vir	09/10/1931	18:03
Aqu	01/18/1931	18:03	Gem	05/17/1931	18:26	Lib	09/12/1931	17:42
Pis	01/21/1931	05:54	Can	05/20/1931	01:24	Sco	09/14/1931	17:40
Ari	01/23/1931	18:54	Leo	05/22/1931	06:26	Sag	09/16/1931	19:39
Tau	01/26/1931	07:09	Vir	05/24/1931	10:06	Cap	09/19/1931	00:48
Gem	01/28/1931	16:17	Lib	05/26/1931	12:50	Aqu	09/21/1931	09:18
Can	01/30/1931	21:07	Sco	05/28/1931	15:07	Pis	09/23/1931	20:28
Leo	02/01/1931	22:23	Sag	05/30/1931	17:47	Ari	09/26/1931	09:09
Vir	02/03/1931	21:56	Cap	06/01/1931	22:07	Tau	09/28/1931	22:06
Lib	02/05/1931	21:55	Aqu	06/04/1931	05:22	Gem	10/01/1931	10:02
Sco	02/08/1931	00:05	Pis	06/06/1931	16:00	Can	10/03/1931	19:36
Sag	02/10/1931	05:21	Ari	06/09/1931	04:43	Leo	10/06/1931	01:47
Cap	02/12/1931	13:39	Tau	06/11/1931	16:53	Vir	10/08/1931	04:33
Aqu	02/15/1931	00:14	Gem	06/14/1931	02:20	Lib	10/10/1931	04:49
Pis	02/17/1931	12:23	Can	06/16/1931	08:37	Sco	10/12/1931	04:17
Ari	02/20/1931	01:20	Leo	06/18/1931	12:35	Sag	10/14/1931	04:51
Tau	02/22/1931	13:52	Vir	06/20/1931	15:32	Cap	10/16/1931	08:18
Gem	02/25/1931	00:11	Lib	06/22/1931	18:22	Aqu	10/18/1931	15:39
Can	02/27/1931	06:46	Sco	06/24/1931	21:34	Pis	10/21/1931	02:32
Leo	03/01/1931	09:23	Sag	06/27/1931	01:26	Ari	10/23/1931	15:20
Vir	03/03/1931	09:20	Cap	06/29/1931	06:34	Tau	10/26/1931	04:11
Lib	03/05/1931	08:32	Aqu	07/01/1931	13:56	Gem	10/28/1931	15:47
Sco	03/07/1931	09:03	Pis	07/04/1931	00:09	Can	10/31/1931	01:25
Sag	03/09/1931	12:31	Ari	07/06/1931	12:39	Leo	11/02/1931	08:38
Cap	03/11/1931	19:39	Tau	07/09/1931	01:12	Vir	11/04/1931	13:06
Aqu	03/14/1931	06:03	Gem	07/11/1931	11:12	Lib	11/06/1931	15:02
Pis	03/16/1931	18:26	Can	07/13/1931	17:29	Sco	11/08/1931	15:20
Ari	03/19/1931	07:23	Leo	07/15/1931	20:40	Sag	11/10/1931	15:39
Tau	03/21/1931	19:43	Vir	07/17/1931	22:21	Cap	11/12/1931	17:51
Gem	03/24/1931	06:18	Lib	07/20/1931	00:06	Aqu	11/14/1931	23:41
Can	03/26/1931	14:02	Sco	07/22/1931	02:56	Pis	11/17/1931	09:32
Leo	03/28/1931	18:28	Sag	07/24/1931	07:18	Ari	11/19/1931	22:08
Vir	03/30/1931	19:56	Cap	07/26/1931	13:22	Tau	11/22/1931	10:59
Lib	04/01/1931	19:48	Aqu	07/28/1931	21:24	Gem	11/24/1931	22:10
Sco	04/03/1931	19:50	Pis	07/31/1931	07:45	Can	11/27/1931	07:08
Sag	04/05/1931	21:52	Ari	08/02/1931	20:09	Leo	11/29/1931	14:05
Cap	04/08/1931	03:21	Tau	08/05/1931	09:04	Vir	12/01/1931	19:15
Aqu	04/10/1931	12:40	Gem	08/07/1931	20:00	Lib	12/03/1931	22:43
Pis	04/13/1931	00:48	Can	08/10/1931	03:09	Sco	12/06/1931	00:42
Ari	04/15/1931	13:47	Leo	08/12/1931	06:30	Sag	12/08/1931	02:04
Tau	04/18/1931	01:49	Vir	08/14/1931	07:24	Cap	12/10/1931	04:18

Aqu	12/12/1931	09:10	Gem	04/09/1932	13:26	Lib	08/05/1932	19:55
Pis	12/14/1931	17:50	Can	04/12/1932	00:45	Sco	08/07/1932	22:49
Ari	12/17/1931	05:49	Leo	04/14/1932	09:20	Sag	08/10/1932	01:32
Tau	12/19/1931	18:45	Vir	04/16/1932	14:20	Cap	08/12/1932	04:38
Gem	12/22/1931	05:59	Lib	04/18/1932	15:59	Aqu	08/14/1932	08:54
Can	12/24/1931	14:20	Sco	04/20/1932	15:33	Pis	08/16/1932	15:14
Leo	12/26/1931	20:15	Sag	04/22/1932	14:57	Ari	08/19/1932	00:19
Vir	12/29/1931	00:40	Cap	04/24/1932	16:15	Tau	08/21/1932	11:56
Lib	12/31/1931	04:17	Aqu	04/26/1932	21:05	Gem	08/24/1932	00:33
Sco	01/02/1932	07:23	Pis	04/29/1932	05:55	Can	08/26/1932	11:49
Sag	01/04/1932	10:15	Ari	05/01/1932	17:46	Leo	08/28/1932	20:02
Cap	01/06/1932	13:37	Tau	05/04/1932	06:45	Vir	08/31/1932	00:57
Aqu	01/08/1932	18:43	Gem	05/06/1932	19:19	Lib	09/02/1932	03:31
Pis	01/11/1932	02:50	Can	05/09/1932	06:34	Sco	09/04/1932	05:06
Ari	01/13/1932	14:07	Leo	05/11/1932	15:45	Sag	09/06/1932	06:59
Tau	01/16/1932	03:02	Vir	05/13/1932	22:11	Cap	09/08/1932	10:12
Gem	01/18/1932	14:46	Lib	05/16/1932	01:31	Aqu	09/10/1932	15:16
Can	01/20/1932	23:21	Sco	05/18/1932	02:13	Pis	09/12/1932	22:31
Leo	01/23/1932	04:39	Sag	05/20/1932	01:47	Ari	09/15/1932	08:01
Vir	01/25/1932	07:46	Cap	05/22/1932	02:13	Tau	09/17/1932	19:33
Lib	01/27/1932	10:07	Aqu	05/24/1932	05:30	Gem	09/20/1932	08:13
Sco	01/29/1932	12:43	Pis	05/26/1932	12:58	Can	09/22/1932	20:12
Sag	01/31/1932	16:06	Ari	05/29/1932	00:09	Leo	09/25/1932	05:31
Cap	02/02/1932	20:39	Tau	05/31/1932	13:04	Vir	09/27/1932	11:05
Aqu	02/05/1932	02:48	Gem	06/03/1932	01:31	Lib	09/29/1932	13:21
Pis	02/07/1932	11:15	Can	06/05/1932	12:20	Sco	10/01/1932	13:43
Ari	02/09/1932	22:17	Leo	06/07/1932	21:14	Sag	10/03/1932	14:03
Tau	02/12/1932	11:04	Vir	06/10/1932	04:05	Cap	10/05/1932	16:00
Gem	02/14/1932	23:26	Lib	06/12/1932	08:40	Aqu	10/07/1932	20:44
Can	02/17/1932	09:01	Sco	06/14/1932	10:59	Pis	10/10/1932	04:26
Leo	02/19/1932	14:47	Sag	06/16/1932	11:45	Ari	10/12/1932	14:35
Vir	02/21/1932	17:24	Cap	06/18/1932	12:31	Tau	10/15/1932	02:24
Lib	02/23/1932	18:21	Aqu	06/20/1932	15:12	Gem	10/17/1932	15:02
Sco	02/25/1932	19:20	Pis	06/22/1932	21:26	Can	10/20/1932	03:25
Sag	02/27/1932	21:39	Ari	06/25/1932	07:34	Leo	10/22/1932	13:56
Cap	03/01/1932	02:07	Tau	06/27/1932	20:07	Vir	10/24/1932	21:01
Aqu	03/03/1932	09:00	Gem	06/30/1932	08:34	Lib	10/27/1932	00:14
Pis	03/05/1932	18:15	Can	07/02/1932	19:06	Sco	10/29/1932	00:29
Ari	03/08/1932	05:35	Leo	07/05/1932	03:18	Sag	10/30/1932	23:40
Tau	03/10/1932	18:19	Vir	07/07/1932	09:32	Cap	11/01/1932	23:55
Gem	03/13/1932	07:02	Lib	07/09/1932	14:12	Aqu	11/04/1932	03:06
Can	03/15/1932	17:45	Sco	07/11/1932	17:27	Pis	11/06/1932	10:07
Leo	03/18/1932	00:54	Sag	07/13/1932	19:37	Ari	11/08/1932	20:24
Vir	03/20/1932	04:17	Cap	07/15/1932	21:36	Tau	11/11/1932	08:33
Lib	03/22/1932	04:56	Aqu	07/18/1932	00:45	Gem	11/13/1932	21:13
Sco	03/24/1932	04:34	Pis	07/20/1932	06:34	Can	11/16/1932	09:31
Sag	03/26/1932	05:06	Ari	07/22/1932	15:52	Leo	11/18/1932	20:34
Cap	03/28/1932	08:08	Tau	07/25/1932	03:54	Vir	11/21/1932	05:07
Aqu	03/30/1932	14:31	Gem	07/27/1932	16:26	Lib	11/23/1932	10:06
Pis	04/02/1932	00:05	Can	07/30/1932	03:06	Sco	11/25/1932	11:36
Ari	04/04/1932	11:53	Leo	08/01/1932	10:55	Sag	11/27/1932	10:58
Tau	04/07/1932	00:43	Vir	08/03/1932	16:14	Cap	11/29/1932	10:17

Aqu	12/01/1932	11:47	Gem	03/30/1933	10:13	Lib	07/27/1933	06:44
Pis	12/03/1932	17:08	Can	04/01/1933	22:49	Sco	07/29/1933	12:20
Ari	12/06/1932	02:35	Leo	04/04/1933	10:15	Sag	07/31/1933	15:26
Tau	12/08/1932	14:41	Vir	04/06/1933	18:32	Cap	08/02/1933	16:40
Gem	12/11/1932	03:25	Lib	04/08/1933	22:59	Aqu	08/04/1933	17:22
Can	12/13/1932	15:27	Sco	04/11/1933	00:31	Pis	08/06/1933	19:11
Leo	12/16/1932	02:12	Sag	04/13/1933	00:52	Ari	08/08/1933	23:42
Vir	12/18/1932	11:08	Cap	04/15/1933	01:54	Tau	08/11/1933	07:45
Lib	12/20/1932	17:31	Aqu	04/17/1933	05:02	Gem	08/13/1933	18:57
Sco	12/22/1932	20:51	Pis	04/19/1933	10:54	Can	08/16/1933	07:32
Sag	12/24/1932	21:41	Ari	04/21/1933	19:14	Leo	08/18/1933	19:22
Cap	12/26/1932	21:31	Tau	04/24/1933	05:31	Vir	08/21/1933	05:07
Aqu	12/28/1932	22:24	Gem	04/26/1933	17:18	Lib	08/23/1933	12:28
Pis	12/31/1932	02:17	Can	04/29/1933	05:58	Sco	08/25/1933	17:44
Ari	01/02/1933	10:14	Leo	05/01/1933	18:06	Sag	08/27/1933	21:20
Tau	01/04/1933	21:36	Vir	05/04/1933	03:39	Cap	08/29/1933	23:51
Gem	01/07/1933	10:19	Lib	05/06/1933	09:16	Aqu	09/01/1933	02:00
Can	01/09/1933	22:15	Sco	05/08/1933	11:05	Pis	09/03/1933	04:44
Leo	01/12/1933	08:26	Sag	05/10/1933	10:42	Ari	09/05/1933	09:15
Vir	01/14/1933	16:41	Cap	05/12/1933	10:15	Tau	09/07/1933	16:35
Lib	01/16/1933	23:02	Aqu	05/14/1933	11:47	Gem	09/10/1933	03:01
Sco	01/19/1933	03:23	Pis	05/16/1933	16:34	Can	09/12/1933	15:25
Sag	01/21/1933	05:54	Ari	05/19/1933	00:46	Leo	09/15/1933	03:30
Cap	01/23/1933	07:17	Tau	05/21/1933	11:26	Vir	09/17/1933	13:12
Aqu	01/25/1933	08:57	Gem	05/23/1933	23:31	Lib	09/19/1933	19:50
Pis	01/27/1933	12:32	Can	05/26/1933	12:11	Sco	09/21/1933	23:59
Ari	01/29/1933	19:21	Leo	05/29/1933	00:32	Sag	09/24/1933	02:48
Tau	02/01/1933	05:40	Vir	05/31/1933	11:04	Cap	09/26/1933	05:23
Gem	02/03/1933	18:04	Lib	06/02/1933	18:14	Aqu	09/28/1933	08:27
Can	02/06/1933	06:13	Sco	06/04/1933	21:23	Pis	09/30/1933	12:27
Leo	02/08/1933	16:15	Sag	06/06/1933	21:31	Ari	10/02/1933	17:51
Vir	02/10/1933	23:42	Cap	06/08/1933	20:33	Tau	10/05/1933	01:18
Lib	02/13/1933	04:58	Aqu	06/10/1933	20:42	Gem	10/07/1933	11:18
Sco	02/15/1933	08:46	Pis	06/12/1933	23:51	Can	10/09/1933	23:29
Sag	02/17/1933	11:42	Ari	06/15/1933	06:51	Leo	10/12/1933	12:01
Cap	02/19/1933	14:22	Tau	06/17/1933	17:12	Vir	10/14/1933	22:23
Aqu	02/21/1933	17:28	Gem	06/20/1933	05:25	Lib	10/17/1933	05:07
Pis	02/23/1933	21:56	Can	06/22/1933	18:06	Sco	10/19/1933	08:26
Ari	02/26/1933	04:42	Leo	06/25/1933	06:17	Sag	10/21/1933	09:54
Tau	02/28/1933	14:20	Vir	06/27/1933	17:01	Cap	10/23/1933	11:13
Gem	03/03/1933	02:17	Lib	06/30/1933	01:09	Aqu	10/25/1933	13:49
Can	03/05/1933	14:42	Sco	07/02/1933	05:56	Pis	10/27/1933	18:17
Leo	03/08/1933	01:16	Sag	07/04/1933	07:31	Ari	10/30/1933	00:41
Vir	03/10/1933	08:41	Cap	07/06/1933	07:15	Tau	11/01/1933	08:53
Lib	03/12/1933	13:02	Aqu	07/08/1933	07:05	Gem	11/03/1933	19:02
Sco	03/14/1933	15:27	Pis	07/10/1933	09:02	Can	11/06/1933	07:05
Sag	03/16/1933	17:18	Ari	07/12/1933	14:32	Leo	11/08/1933	19:57
Cap	03/18/1933	19:47	Tau	07/14/1933	23:49	Vir	11/11/1933	07:23
Aqu	03/20/1933	23:39	Gem	07/17/1933	11:44	Lib	11/13/1933	15:11
Pis	03/23/1933	05:15	Can	07/20/1933	00:24	Sco	11/15/1933	18:51
Ari	03/25/1933	12:50	Leo	07/22/1933	12:18	Sag	11/17/1933	19:34
Tau	03/27/1933	22:32	Vir	07/24/1933	22:35	Cap	11/19/1933	19:24

Aqu	11/21/1933	20:21	Gem	03/20/1934	05:51	Lib	07/17/1934	11:46
Pis	11/23/1933	23:50	Can	03/22/1934	17:13	Sco	07/19/1934	20:30
Ari	11/26/1933	06:12	Leo	03/25/1934	06:03	Sag	07/22/1934	01:26
Tau	11/28/1933	15:03	Vir	03/27/1934	17:44	Cap	07/24/1934	03:02
Gem	12/01/1933	01:45	Lib	03/30/1934	02:35	Aqu	07/26/1934	02:43
Can	12/03/1933	13:53	Sco	04/01/1934	08:34	Pis	07/28/1934	02:21
Leo	12/06/1933	02:48	Sag	04/03/1934	12:36	Ari	07/30/1934	03:46
Vir	12/08/1933	14:59	Cap	04/05/1934	15:45	Tau	08/01/1934	08:26
Lib	12/11/1933	00:17	Aqu	04/07/1934	18:42	Gem	08/03/1934	16:49
Sco	12/13/1933	05:26	Pis	04/09/1934	21:52	Can	08/06/1934	04:13
Sag	12/15/1933	06:48	Ari	04/12/1934	01:40	Leo	08/08/1934	17:08
Cap	12/17/1933	06:08	Tau	04/14/1934	06:56	Vir	08/11/1934	05:59
Aqu	12/19/1933	05:37	Gem	04/16/1934	14:42	Lib	08/13/1934	17:33
Pis	12/21/1933	07:15	Can	04/19/1934	01:27	Sco	08/16/1934	02:50
Ari	12/23/1933	12:16	Leo	04/21/1934	14:10	Sag	08/18/1934	09:10
Tau	12/25/1933	20:43	Vir	04/24/1934	02:19	Cap	08/20/1934	12:26
Gem	12/28/1933	07:43	Lib	04/26/1934	11:31	Aqu	08/22/1934	13:17
Can	12/30/1933	20:06	Sco	04/28/1934	17:06	Pis	08/24/1934	13:08
Leo	01/02/1934	08:56	Sag	04/30/1934	20:01	Ari	08/26/1934	13:44
Vir	01/04/1934	21:08	Cap	05/02/1934	21:53	Tau	08/28/1934	16:55
Lib	01/07/1934	07:20	Aqu	05/05/1934	00:06	Gem	08/30/1934	23:56
Sco	01/09/1934	14:09	Pis	05/07/1934	03:26	Can	09/02/1934	10:41
Sag	01/11/1934	17:17	Ari	05/09/1934	08:09	Leo	09/04/1934	23:32
Cap	01/13/1934	17:36	Tau	05/11/1934	14:24	Vir	09/07/1934	12:16
Aqu	01/15/1934	16:56	Gem	05/13/1934	22:38	Lib	09/09/1934	23:22
Pis	01/17/1934	17:17	Can	05/16/1934	09:17	Sco	09/12/1934	08:19
Ari	01/19/1934	20:28	Leo	05/18/1934	21:55	Sag	09/14/1934	15:03
Tau	01/22/1934	03:27	Vir	05/21/1934	10:34	Cap	09/16/1934	19:35
Gem	01/24/1934	13:54	Lib	05/23/1934	20:42	Aqu	09/18/1934	22:06
Can	01/27/1934	02:24	Sco	05/26/1934	02:50	Pis	09/20/1934	23:13
Leo	01/29/1934	15:11	Sag	05/28/1934	05:28	Ari	09/23/1934	00:13
Vir	02/01/1934	03:00	Cap	05/30/1934	06:12	Tau	09/25/1934	02:47
Lib	02/03/1934	12:58	Aqu	06/01/1934	06:55	Gem	09/27/1934	08:34
Sco	02/05/1934	20:30	Pis	06/03/1934	09:07	Can	09/29/1934	18:14
Sag	02/08/1934	01:13	Ari	06/05/1934	13:32	Leo	10/02/1934	06:44
Cap	02/10/1934	03:22	Tau	06/07/1934	20:17	Vir	10/04/1934	19:30
Aqu	02/12/1934	03:57	Gem	06/10/1934	05:13	Lib	10/07/1934	06:20
Pis	02/14/1934	04:27	Can	06/12/1934	16:14	Sco	10/09/1934	14:31
Ari	02/16/1934	06:39	Leo	06/15/1934	04:52	Sag	10/11/1934	20:31
Tau	02/18/1934	12:04	Vir	06/17/1934	17:51	Cap	10/14/1934	01:03
Gem	02/20/1934	21:17	Lib	06/20/1934	04:58	Aqu	10/16/1934	04:32
Can	02/23/1934	09:22	Sco	06/22/1934	12:23	Pis	10/18/1934	07:09
Leo	02/25/1934	22:13	Sag	06/24/1934	15:48	Ari	10/20/1934	09:28
Vir	02/28/1934	09:45	Cap	06/26/1934	16:24	Tau	10/22/1934	12:35
Lib	03/02/1934	19:01	Aqu	06/28/1934	16:02	Gem	10/24/1934	17:57
Sco	03/05/1934	01:58	Pis	06/30/1934	16:38	Can	10/27/1934	02:47
Sag	03/07/1934	06:58	Ari	07/02/1934	19:39	Leo	10/29/1934	14:42
Cap	03/09/1934	10:21	Tau	07/05/1934	01:48	Vir	11/01/1934	03:35
Aqu	03/11/1934	12:35	Gem	07/07/1934	10:56	Lib	11/03/1934	14:40
Pis	03/13/1934	14:25	Can	07/09/1934	22:21	Sco	11/05/1934	22:31
Ari	03/15/1934	17:00	Leo	07/12/1934	11:07	Sag	11/08/1934	03:32
Tau	03/17/1934	21:47	Vir	07/15/1934	00:06	Cap	11/10/1934	06:56

Aqu	11/12/1934	09:52	Gem	03/10/1935	05:11	Lib	07/07/1935	09:52
Pis	11/14/1934	12:56	Can	03/12/1935	13:53	Sco	07/09/1935	21:14
Ari	11/16/1934	16:26	Leo	03/15/1935	01:48	Sag	07/12/1935	05:27
Tau	11/18/1934	20:47	Vir	03/17/1935	14:51	Cap	07/14/1935	10:02
Gem	11/21/1934	02:48	Lib	03/20/1935	03:07	Aqu	07/16/1935	11:53
Can	11/23/1934	11:26	Sco	03/22/1935	13:44	Pis	07/18/1935	12:31
Leo	11/25/1934	22:54	Sag	03/24/1935	22:23	Ari	07/20/1935	13:33
Vir	11/28/1934	11:51	Cap	03/27/1935	04:48	Tau	07/22/1935	16:21
Lib	11/30/1934	23:38	Aqu	03/29/1935	08:41	Gem	07/24/1935	21:42
Sco	12/03/1934	08:05	Pis	03/31/1935	10:14	Can	07/27/1935	05:43
Sag	12/05/1934	12:51	Ari	04/02/1935	10:31	Leo	07/29/1935	16:04
Cap	12/07/1934	15:08	Tau	04/04/1935	11:19	Vir	08/01/1935	04:07
Aqu	12/09/1934	16:33	Gem	04/06/1935	14:36	Lib	08/03/1935	16:55
Pis	12/11/1934	18:31	Can	04/08/1935	21:50	Sco	08/06/1935	04:57
Ari	12/13/1934	21:52	Leo	04/11/1935	08:52	Sag	08/08/1935	14:24
Tau	12/16/1934	02:57	Vir	04/13/1935	21:46	Cap	08/10/1935	20:09
Gem	12/18/1934	09:59	Lib	04/16/1935	10:00	Aqu	08/12/1935	22:21
Can	12/20/1934	19:11	Sco	04/18/1935	20:09	Pis	08/14/1935	22:19
Leo	12/23/1934	06:37	Sag	04/21/1935	04:06	Ari	08/16/1935	21:56
Vir	12/25/1934	19:32	Cap	04/23/1935	10:13	Tau	08/18/1935	23:09
Lib	12/28/1934	07:59	Aqu	04/25/1935	14:43	Gem	08/21/1935	03:26
Sco	12/30/1934	17:41	Pis	04/27/1935	17:40	Can	08/23/1935	11:18
Sag	01/01/1935	23:25	Ari	04/29/1935	19:26	Leo	08/25/1935	22:01
Cap	01/04/1935	01:43	Tau	05/01/1935	21:10	Vir	08/28/1935	10:21
Aqu	01/06/1935	02:04	Gem	05/04/1935	00:27	Lib	08/30/1935	23:08
Pis	01/08/1935	02:18	Can	05/06/1935	06:50	Sco	09/02/1935	11:21
Ari	01/10/1935	04:03	Leo	05/08/1935	16:55	Sag	09/04/1935	21:47
Tau	01/12/1935	08:25	Vir	05/11/1935	05:26	Cap	09/07/1935	05:07
Gem	01/14/1935	15:43	Lib	05/13/1935	17:48	Aqu	09/09/1935	08:43
Can	01/17/1935	01:38	Sco	05/16/1935	03:53	Pis	09/11/1935	09:14
Leo	01/19/1935	13:27	Sag	05/18/1935	11:12	Ari	09/13/1935	08:21
Vir	01/22/1935	02:19	Cap	05/20/1935	16:20	Tau	09/15/1935	08:11
Lib	01/24/1935	14:59	Aqu	05/22/1935	20:08	Gem	09/17/1935	10:49
Sco	01/27/1935	01:45	Pis	05/24/1935	23:13	Can	09/19/1935	17:27
Sag	01/29/1935	09:09	Ari	05/27/1935	01:59	Leo	09/22/1935	03:50
Cap	01/31/1935	12:46	Tau	05/29/1935	04:59	Vir	09/24/1935	16:19
Aqu	02/02/1935	13:25	Gem	05/31/1935	09:11	Lib	09/27/1935	05:05
Pis	02/04/1935	12:47	Can	06/02/1935	15:44	Sco	09/29/1935	17:06
Ari	02/06/1935	12:50	Leo	06/05/1935	01:20	Sag	10/02/1935	03:40
Tau	02/08/1935	15:23	Vir	06/07/1935	13:26	Cap	10/04/1935	12:01
Gem	02/10/1935	21:36	Lib	06/10/1935	01:59	Aqu	10/06/1935	17:20
Can	02/13/1935	07:24	Sco	06/12/1935	12:34	Pis	10/08/1935	19:26
Leo	02/15/1935	19:35	Sag	06/14/1935	19:56	Ari	10/10/1935	19:20
Vir	02/18/1935	08:33	Cap	06/17/1935	00:20	Tau	10/12/1935	18:53
Lib	02/20/1935	21:02	Aqu	06/19/1935	02:55	Gem	10/14/1935	20:18
Sco	02/23/1935	08:04	Pis	06/21/1935	04:56	Can	10/17/1935	01:22
Sag	02/25/1935	16:39	Ari	06/23/1935	07:21	Leo	10/19/1935	10:36
Cap	02/27/1935	22:03	Tau	06/25/1935	10:54	Vir	10/21/1935	22:44
Aqu	03/02/1935	00:15	Gem	06/27/1935	16:06	Lib	10/24/1935	11:31
Pis	03/04/1935	00:13	Can	06/29/1935	23:27	Sco	10/26/1935	23:14
Ari	03/05/1935	23:41	Leo	07/02/1935	09:13	Sag	10/29/1935	09:17
Tau	03/08/1935	00:44	Vir	07/04/1935	21:09	Cap	10/31/1935	17:31

Aqu	11/02/1935	23:37	Gem	02/28/1936	11:31	Lib	06/26/1936	04:23
Pis	11/05/1935	03:19	Can	03/01/1936	17:26	Sco	06/28/1936	16:53
Ari	11/07/1935	04:54	Leo	03/04/1936	02:21	Sag	07/01/1936	04:27
Tau	11/09/1935	05:29	Vir	03/06/1936	13:18	Cap	07/03/1936	13:33
Gem	11/11/1935	06:52	Lib	03/09/1936	01:26	Aqu	07/05/1936	19:56
Can	11/13/1935	10:58	Sco	03/11/1936	14:03	Pis	07/08/1936	00:09
Leo	11/15/1935	18:51	Sag	03/14/1936	02:05	Ari	07/10/1936	03:10
Vir	11/18/1935	06:10	Cap	03/16/1936	11:50	Tau	07/12/1936	05:46
Lib	11/20/1935	18:52	Aqu	03/18/1936	17:52	Gem	07/14/1936	08:39
Sco	11/23/1935	06:36	Pis	03/20/1936	19:58	Can	07/16/1936	12:28
Sag	11/25/1935	16:08	Ari	03/22/1936	19:31	Leo	07/18/1936	17:58
Cap	11/27/1935	23:27	Tau	03/24/1936	18:37	Vir	07/21/1936	01:54
Aqu	11/30/1935	05:00	Gem	03/26/1936	19:32	Lib	07/23/1936	12:31
Pis	12/02/1935	09:02	Can	03/28/1936	23:53	Sco	07/26/1936	00:54
Ari	12/04/1935	11:52	Leo	03/31/1936	08:04	Sag	07/28/1936	12:55
Tau	12/06/1935	14:03	Vir	04/02/1936	19:07	Cap	07/30/1936	22:23
Gem	12/08/1935	16:37	Lib	04/05/1936	07:31	Aqu	08/02/1936	04:25
Can	12/10/1935	20:54	Sco	04/07/1936	20:05	Pis	08/04/1936	07:35
Leo	12/13/1935	04:07	Sag	04/10/1936	08:02	Ari	08/06/1936	09:21
Vir	12/15/1935	14:33	Cap	04/12/1936	18:22	Tau	08/08/1936	11:12
Lib	12/18/1935	02:58	Aqu	04/15/1936	01:48	Gem	08/10/1936	14:12
Sco	12/20/1935	15:02	Pis	04/17/1936	05:37	Can	08/12/1936	18:52
Sag	12/23/1935	00:43	Ari	04/19/1936	06:20	Leo	08/15/1936	01:20
Cap	12/25/1935	07:27	Tau	04/21/1936	05:37	Vir	08/17/1936	09:45
Aqu	12/27/1935	11:45	Gem	04/23/1936	05:37	Lib	08/19/1936	20:17
Pis	12/29/1935	14:42	Can	04/25/1936	08:23	Sco	08/22/1936	08:36
Ari	12/31/1935	17:15	Leo	04/27/1936	15:04	Sag	08/24/1936	21:09
Tau	01/02/1936	20:11	Vir	04/30/1936	01:22	Cap	08/27/1936	07:34
Gem	01/05/1936	00:04	Lib	05/02/1936	13:43	Aqu	08/29/1936	14:11
Can	01/07/1936	05:29	Sco	05/05/1936	02:16	Pis	08/31/1936	17:05
Leo	01/09/1936	13:03	Sag	05/07/1936	13:54	Ari	09/02/1936	17:43
Vir	01/11/1936	23:06	Cap	05/09/1936	23:56	Tau	09/04/1936	18:04
Lib	01/14/1936	11:11	Aqu	05/12/1936	07:47	Gem	09/06/1936	19:55
Sco	01/16/1936	23:38	Pis	05/14/1936	12:51	Can	09/09/1936	00:17
Sag	01/19/1936	10:10	Ari	05/16/1936	15:13	Leo	09/11/1936	07:13
Cap	01/21/1936	17:18	Tau	05/18/1936	15:47	Vir	09/13/1936	16:20
Aqu	01/23/1936	21:01	Gem	05/20/1936	16:12	Lib	09/16/1936	03:13
Pis	01/25/1936	22:34	Can	05/22/1936	18:19	Sco	09/18/1936	15:32
Ari	01/27/1936	23:36	Leo	05/24/1936	23:43	Sag	09/21/1936	04:24
Tau	01/30/1936	01:38	Vir	05/27/1936	08:48	Cap	09/23/1936	15:52
Gem	02/01/1936	05:39	Lib	05/29/1936	20:38	Aqu	09/25/1936	23:51
Can	02/03/1936	11:59	Sco	06/01/1936	09:11	Pis	09/28/1936	03:38
Leo	02/05/1936	20:26	Sag	06/03/1936	20:36	Ari	09/30/1936	04:09
Vir	02/08/1936	06:48	Cap	06/06/1936	06:03	Tau	10/02/1936	03:26
Lib	02/10/1936	18:46	Aqu	06/08/1936	13:16	Gem	10/04/1936	03:37
Sco	02/13/1936	07:24	Pis	06/10/1936	18:27	Can	10/06/1936	06:29
Sag	02/15/1936	18:56	Ari	06/12/1936	21:46	Leo	10/08/1936	12:46
Cap	02/18/1936	03:20	Tau	06/14/1936	23:48	Vir	10/10/1936	22:02
Aqu	02/20/1936	07:46	Gem	06/17/1936	01:30	Lib	10/13/1936	09:19
Pis	02/22/1936	08:55	Can	06/19/1936	04:09	Sco	10/15/1936	21:47
Ari	02/24/1936	08:35	Leo	06/21/1936	09:07	Sag	10/18/1936	10:37
Tau	02/26/1936	08:51	Vir	06/23/1936	17:15	Cap	10/20/1936	22:36

Aqu	10/23/1936	07:59	Gem	02/18/1937	00:22	Lib	06/16/1937	01:09
Pis	10/25/1936	13:26	Can	02/20/1937	04:04	Sco	06/18/1937	12:31
Ari	10/27/1936	15:09	Leo	02/22/1937	08:51	Sag	06/21/1937	01:25
Tau	10/29/1936	14:34	Vir	02/24/1937	15:05	Cap	06/23/1937	13:57
Gem	10/31/1936	13:50	Lib	02/26/1937	23:27	Aqu	06/26/1937	00:53
Can	11/02/1936	15:01	Sco	03/01/1937	10:23	Pis	06/28/1937	09:36
Leo	11/04/1936	19:37	Sag	03/03/1937	23:08	Ari	06/30/1937	15:50
Vir	11/07/1936	04:00	Cap	03/06/1937	11:22	Tau	07/02/1937	19:34
Lib	11/09/1936	15:15	Aqu	03/08/1937	20:34	Gem	07/04/1937	21:15
Sco	11/12/1936	03:52	Pis	03/11/1937	01:49	Can	07/06/1937	21:53
Sag	11/14/1936	16:33	Ari	03/13/1937	03:59	Leo	07/08/1937	23:00
Cap	11/17/1936	04:20	Tau	03/15/1937	04:54	Vir	07/11/1937	02:16
Aqu	11/19/1936	14:10	Gem	03/17/1937	06:19	Lib	07/13/1937	09:05
Pis	11/21/1936	21:03	Can	03/19/1937	09:26	Sco	07/15/1937	19:36
Ari	11/24/1936	00:35	Leo	03/21/1937	14:36	Sag	07/18/1937	08:20
Tau	11/26/1936	01:28	Vir	03/23/1937	21:44	Cap	07/20/1937	20:50
Gem	11/28/1936	01:12	Lib	03/26/1937	06:47	Aqu	07/23/1937	07:19
Can	11/30/1936	01:41	Sco	03/28/1937	17:51	Pis	07/25/1937	15:20
Leo	12/02/1936	04:44	Sag	03/31/1937	06:32	Ari	07/27/1937	21:15
Vir	12/04/1936	11:32	Cap	04/02/1937	19:16	Tau	07/30/1937	01:31
Lib	12/06/1936	21:56	Aqu	04/05/1937	05:38	Gem	08/01/1937	04:29
Sco	12/09/1936	10:28	Pis	04/07/1937	11:58	Can	08/03/1937	06:34
Sag	12/11/1936	23:07	Ari	04/09/1937	14:27	Leo	08/05/1937	08:36
Cap	12/14/1936	10:25	Tau	04/11/1937	14:39	Vir	08/07/1937	11:55
Aqu	12/16/1936	19:42	Gem	04/13/1937	14:35	Lib	08/09/1937	17:58
Pis	12/19/1936	02:43	Can	04/15/1937	16:03	Sco	08/12/1937	03:37
Ari	12/21/1936	07:26	Leo	04/17/1937	20:12	Sag	08/14/1937	15:59
Tau	12/23/1936	10:05	Vir	04/20/1937	03:16	Cap	08/17/1937	04:37
Gem	12/25/1936	11:24	Lib	04/22/1937	12:51	Aqu	08/19/1937	15:04
Can	12/27/1936	12:37	Sco	04/25/1937	00:21	Pis	08/21/1937	22:27
Leo	12/29/1936	15:14	Sag	04/27/1937	13:05	Ari	08/24/1937	03:23
Vir	12/31/1936	20:46	Cap	04/30/1937	01:56	Tau	08/26/1937	06:56
Lib	01/03/1937	05:55	Aqu	05/02/1937	13:07	Gem	08/28/1937	10:01
Sco	01/05/1937	17:58	Pis	05/04/1937	20:56	Can	08/30/1937	13:03
Sag	01/08/1937	06:43	Ari	05/07/1937	00:46	Leo	09/01/1937	16:21
Cap	01/10/1937	17:53	Tau	05/09/1937	01:31	Vir	09/03/1937	20:35
Aqu	01/13/1937	02:24	Gem	05/11/1937	00:56	Lib	09/06/1937	02:49
Pis	01/15/1937	08:28	Can	05/13/1937	01:01	Sco	09/08/1937	12:00
Ari	01/17/1937	12:48	Leo	05/15/1937	03:28	Sag	09/10/1937	23:59
Tau	01/19/1937	16:07	Vir	05/17/1937	09:19	Cap	09/13/1937	12:51
Gem	01/21/1937	18:53	Lib	05/19/1937	18:35	Aqu	09/15/1937	23:50
Can	01/23/1937	21:38	Sco	05/22/1937	06:18	Pis	09/18/1937	07:19
Leo	01/26/1937	01:08	Sag	05/24/1937	19:10	Ari	09/20/1937	11:30
Vir	01/28/1937	06:30	Cap	05/27/1937	07:53	Tau	09/22/1937	13:49
Lib	01/30/1937	14:50	Aqu	05/29/1937	19:12	Gem	09/24/1937	15:46
Sco	02/02/1937	02:11	Pis	06/01/1937	03:57	Can	09/26/1937	18:24
Sag	02/04/1937	14:59	Ari	06/03/1937	09:21	Leo	09/28/1937	22:14
Cap	02/07/1937	02:33	Tau	06/05/1937	11:35	Vir	10/01/1937	03:29
Aqu	02/09/1937	10:59	Gem	06/07/1937	11:45	Lib	10/03/1937	10:32
Pis	02/11/1937	16:09	Can	06/09/1937	11:32	Sco	10/05/1937	19:55
Ari	02/13/1937	19:12	Leo	06/11/1937	12:45	Sag	10/08/1937	07:44
Tau	02/15/1937	21:35	Vir	06/13/1937	17:01	Cap	10/10/1937	20:46

Aqu	10/13/1937	08:36		Gem	02/08/1938	15:07		Lib	06/06/1938	04:36
Pis	10/15/1937	17:03		Can	02/10/1938	17:25		Sco	06/08/1938	13:02
Ari	10/17/1937	21:31		Leo	02/12/1938	18:33		Sag	06/10/1938	23:57
Tau	10/19/1937	23:09		Vir	02/14/1938	19:57		Cap	06/13/1938	12:21
Gem	10/21/1937	23:40		Lib	02/16/1938	23:29		Aqu	06/16/1938	01:07
Can	10/24/1937	00:47		Sco	02/19/1938	06:37		Pis	06/18/1938	13:02
Leo	10/26/1937	03:43		Sag	02/21/1938	17:34		Ari	06/20/1938	22:38
Vir	10/28/1937	09:02		Cap	02/24/1938	06:28		Tau	06/23/1938	04:49
Lib	10/30/1937	16:47		Aqu	02/26/1938	18:36		Gem	06/25/1938	07:24
Sco	11/02/1937	02:49		Pis	03/01/1938	04:13		Can	06/27/1938	07:27
Sag	11/04/1937	14:46		Ari	03/03/1938	11:16		Leo	06/29/1938	06:45
Cap	11/07/1937	03:50		Tau	03/05/1938	16:29		Vir	07/01/1938	07:24
Aqu	11/09/1937	16:18		Gem	03/07/1938	20:33		Lib	07/03/1938	11:10
Pis	11/12/1937	02:06		Can	03/09/1938	23:45		Sco	07/05/1938	18:49
Ari	11/14/1937	07:59		Leo	03/12/1938	02:23		Sag	07/08/1938	05:45
Tau	11/16/1937	10:11		Vir	03/14/1938	05:06		Cap	07/10/1938	18:22
Gem	11/18/1937	10:10		Lib	03/16/1938	09:09		Aqu	07/13/1938	07:05
Can	11/20/1937	09:48		Sco	03/18/1938	15:54		Pis	07/15/1938	18:55
Leo	11/22/1937	10:56		Sag	03/21/1938	02:02		Ari	07/18/1938	05:02
Vir	11/24/1937	14:56		Cap	03/23/1938	14:32		Tau	07/20/1938	12:30
Lib	11/26/1937	22:22		Aqu	03/26/1938	02:55		Gem	07/22/1938	16:42
Sco	11/29/1937	08:47		Pis	03/28/1938	12:50		Can	07/24/1938	17:54
Sag	12/01/1937	21:05		Ari	03/30/1938	19:33		Leo	07/26/1938	17:25
Cap	12/04/1937	10:07		Tau	04/01/1938	23:42		Vir	07/28/1938	17:17
Aqu	12/06/1937	22:39		Gem	04/04/1938	02:33		Lib	07/30/1938	19:35
Pis	12/09/1937	09:20		Can	04/06/1938	05:07		Sco	08/02/1938	01:51
Ari	12/11/1937	16:54		Leo	04/08/1938	08:04		Sag	08/04/1938	12:02
Tau	12/13/1937	20:49		Vir	04/10/1938	11:51		Cap	08/07/1938	00:33
Gem	12/15/1937	21:42		Lib	04/12/1938	17:02		Aqu	08/09/1938	13:14
Can	12/17/1937	21:03		Sco	04/15/1938	00:22		Pis	08/12/1938	00:44
Leo	12/19/1937	20:49		Sag	04/17/1938	10:20		Ari	08/14/1938	10:34
Vir	12/21/1937	22:58		Cap	04/19/1938	22:31		Tau	08/16/1938	18:25
Lib	12/24/1937	04:53		Aqu	04/22/1938	11:10		Gem	08/18/1938	23:50
Sco	12/26/1937	14:45		Pis	04/24/1938	21:52		Can	08/21/1938	02:39
Sag	12/29/1937	03:12		Ari	04/27/1938	05:08		Leo	08/23/1938	03:26
Cap	12/31/1937	16:17		Tau	04/29/1938	09:01		Vir	08/25/1938	03:43
Aqu	01/03/1938	04:31		Gem	05/01/1938	10:44		Lib	08/27/1938	05:26
Pis	01/05/1938	15:06		Can	05/03/1938	11:51		Sco	08/29/1938	10:27
Ari	01/07/1938	23:28		Leo	05/05/1938	13:42		Sag	08/31/1938	19:28
Tau	01/10/1938	05:05		Vir	05/07/1938	17:17		Cap	09/03/1938	07:30
Gem	01/12/1938	07:49		Lib	05/09/1938	23:06		Aqu	09/05/1938	20:10
Can	01/14/1938	08:21		Sco	05/12/1938	07:16		Pis	09/08/1938	07:28
Leo	01/16/1938	08:09		Sag	05/14/1938	17:40		Ari	09/10/1938	16:40
Vir	01/18/1938	09:13		Cap	05/17/1938	05:51		Tau	09/12/1938	23:53
Lib	01/20/1938	13:28		Aqu	05/19/1938	18:37		Gem	09/15/1938	05:23
Sco	01/22/1938	21:56		Pis	05/22/1938	06:08		Can	09/17/1938	09:09
Sag	01/25/1938	09:52		Ari	05/24/1938	14:34		Leo	09/19/1938	11:25
Cap	01/27/1938	22:58		Tau	05/26/1938	19:16		Vir	09/21/1938	13:01
Aqu	01/30/1938	10:59		Gem	05/28/1938	20:51		Lib	09/23/1938	15:19
Pis	02/01/1938	20:58		Can	05/30/1938	20:52		Sco	09/25/1938	19:57
Ari	02/04/1938	04:54		Leo	06/01/1938	21:09		Sag	09/28/1938	04:03
Tau	02/06/1938	10:58		Vir	06/03/1938	23:22		Cap	09/30/1938	15:20

Aqu	10/03/1938	03:57	Gem	01/30/1939	01:49	Lib	05/27/1939	15:06
Pis	10/05/1938	15:26	Can	02/01/1939	04:21	Sco	05/29/1939	19:47
Ari	10/08/1938	00:21	Leo	02/03/1939	04:05	Sag	06/01/1939	02:15
Tau	10/10/1938	06:42	Vir	02/05/1939	03:02	Cap	06/03/1939	10:50
Gem	10/12/1938	11:09	Lib	02/07/1939	03:30	Aqu	06/05/1939	21:40
Can	10/14/1938	14:30	Sco	02/09/1939	07:22	Pis	06/08/1939	10:04
Leo	10/16/1938	17:19	Sag	02/11/1939	15:25	Ari	06/10/1939	22:09
Vir	10/18/1938	20:09	Cap	02/14/1939	02:42	Tau	06/13/1939	07:41
Lib	10/20/1938	23:43	Aqu	02/16/1939	15:22	Gem	06/15/1939	13:30
Sco	10/23/1938	05:00	Pis	02/19/1939	03:51	Can	06/17/1939	16:05
Sag	10/25/1938	12:55	Ari	02/21/1939	15:23	Leo	06/19/1939	16:57
Cap	10/27/1938	23:39	Tau	02/24/1939	01:18	Vir	06/21/1939	17:56
Aqu	10/30/1938	12:08	Gem	02/26/1939	08:46	Lib	06/23/1939	20:31
Pis	11/02/1938	00:08	Can	02/28/1939	13:05	Sco	06/26/1939	01:25
Ari	11/04/1938	09:34	Leo	03/02/1939	14:29	Sag	06/28/1939	08:39
Tau	11/06/1938	15:40	Vir	03/04/1939	14:16	Cap	06/30/1939	17:53
Gem	11/08/1938	19:03	Lib	03/06/1939	14:26	Aqu	07/03/1939	04:54
Can	11/10/1938	20:59	Sco	03/08/1939	17:00	Pis	07/05/1939	17:17
Leo	11/12/1938	22:50	Sag	03/10/1939	23:24	Ari	07/08/1939	05:49
Vir	11/15/1938	01:38	Cap	03/13/1939	09:36	Tau	07/10/1939	16:26
Lib	11/17/1938	06:03	Aqu	03/15/1939	22:01	Gem	07/12/1939	23:18
Sco	11/19/1938	12:26	Pis	03/18/1939	10:31	Can	07/15/1939	02:14
Sag	11/21/1938	20:57	Ari	03/20/1939	21:40	Leo	07/17/1939	02:30
Cap	11/24/1938	07:38	Tau	03/23/1939	06:58	Vir	07/19/1939	02:08
Aqu	11/26/1938	19:58	Gem	03/25/1939	14:14	Lib	07/21/1939	03:10
Pis	11/29/1938	08:29	Can	03/27/1939	19:18	Sco	07/23/1939	07:04
Ari	12/01/1938	19:02	Leo	03/29/1939	22:14	Sag	07/25/1939	14:10
Tau	12/04/1938	01:59	Vir	03/31/1939	23:38	Cap	07/27/1939	23:51
Gem	12/06/1938	05:18	Lib	04/03/1939	00:49	Aqu	07/30/1939	11:15
Can	12/08/1938	06:07	Sco	04/05/1939	03:22	Pis	08/01/1939	23:41
Leo	12/10/1938	06:17	Sag	04/07/1939	08:48	Ari	08/04/1939	12:21
Vir	12/12/1938	07:38	Cap	04/09/1939	17:46	Tau	08/06/1939	23:46
Lib	12/14/1938	11:28	Aqu	04/12/1939	05:33	Gem	08/09/1939	08:05
Sco	12/16/1938	18:13	Pis	04/14/1939	18:04	Can	08/11/1939	12:19
Sag	12/19/1938	03:31	Ari	04/17/1939	05:12	Leo	08/13/1939	13:08
Cap	12/21/1938	14:39	Tau	04/19/1939	13:55	Vir	08/15/1939	12:19
Aqu	12/24/1938	02:59	Gem	04/21/1939	20:15	Lib	08/17/1939	12:04
Pis	12/26/1938	15:40	Can	04/24/1939	00:42	Sco	08/19/1939	14:21
Ari	12/29/1938	03:13	Leo	04/26/1939	03:54	Sag	08/21/1939	20:14
Tau	12/31/1938	11:46	Vir	04/28/1939	06:26	Cap	08/24/1939	05:33
Gem	01/02/1939	16:19	Lib	04/30/1939	09:02	Aqu	08/26/1939	17:09
Can	01/04/1939	17:20	Sco	05/02/1939	12:36	Pis	08/29/1939	05:42
Leo	01/06/1939	16:32	Sag	05/04/1939	18:10	Ari	08/31/1939	18:14
Vir	01/08/1939	16:08	Cap	05/07/1939	02:34	Tau	09/03/1939	05:47
Lib	01/10/1939	18:10	Aqu	05/09/1939	13:41	Gem	09/05/1939	15:00
Sco	01/12/1939	23:55	Pis	05/12/1939	02:08	Can	09/07/1939	20:50
Sag	01/15/1939	09:10	Ari	05/14/1939	13:39	Leo	09/09/1939	23:10
Cap	01/17/1939	20:44	Tau	05/16/1939	22:26	Vir	09/11/1939	23:08
Aqu	01/20/1939	09:15	Gem	05/19/1939	04:06	Lib	09/13/1939	22:39
Pis	01/22/1939	21:51	Can	05/21/1939	07:22	Sco	09/15/1939	23:44
Ari	01/25/1939	09:41	Leo	05/23/1939	09:33	Sag	09/18/1939	04:02
Tau	01/27/1939	19:28	Vir	05/25/1939	11:51	Cap	09/20/1939	12:12

Aqu	09/22/1939	23:24	Gem	01/20/1940	05:31	Lib	05/17/1940	04:40
Pis	09/25/1939	11:59	Can	01/22/1940	10:33	Sco	05/19/1940	06:11
Ari	09/28/1939	00:21	Leo	01/24/1940	12:09	Sag	05/21/1940	08:00
Tau	09/30/1939	11:28	Vir	01/26/1940	12:12	Cap	05/23/1940	11:35
Gem	10/02/1939	20:37	Lib	01/28/1940	12:43	Aqu	05/25/1940	18:18
Can	10/05/1939	03:15	Sco	01/30/1940	15:18	Pis	05/28/1940	04:39
Leo	10/07/1939	07:09	Sag	02/01/1940	20:36	Ari	05/30/1940	17:18
Vir	10/09/1939	08:45	Cap	02/04/1940	04:27	Tau	06/02/1940	05:43
Lib	10/11/1939	09:15	Aqu	02/06/1940	14:21	Gem	06/04/1940	15:48
Sco	10/13/1939	10:19	Pis	02/09/1940	01:58	Can	06/06/1940	23:01
Sag	10/15/1939	13:37	Ari	02/11/1940	14:49	Leo	06/09/1940	04:00
Cap	10/17/1939	20:22	Tau	02/14/1940	03:35	Vir	06/11/1940	07:40
Aqu	10/20/1939	06:39	Gem	02/16/1940	14:08	Lib	06/13/1940	10:43
Pis	10/22/1939	19:05	Can	02/18/1940	20:45	Sco	06/15/1940	13:31
Ari	10/25/1939	07:27	Leo	02/20/1940	23:17	Sag	06/17/1940	16:34
Tau	10/27/1939	18:09	Vir	02/22/1940	23:11	Cap	06/19/1940	20:44
Gem	10/30/1939	02:30	Lib	02/24/1940	22:29	Aqu	06/22/1940	03:15
Can	11/01/1939	08:40	Sco	02/26/1940	23:14	Pis	06/24/1940	12:56
Leo	11/03/1939	13:00	Sag	02/29/1940	02:55	Ari	06/27/1940	01:13
Vir	11/05/1939	15:56	Cap	03/02/1940	10:03	Tau	06/29/1940	13:51
Lib	11/07/1939	18:03	Aqu	03/04/1940	20:07	Gem	07/02/1940	00:14
Sco	11/09/1939	20:14	Pis	03/07/1940	08:07	Can	07/04/1940	07:10
Sag	11/11/1939	23:42	Ari	03/09/1940	21:00	Leo	07/06/1940	11:11
Cap	11/14/1939	05:42	Tau	03/12/1940	09:43	Vir	07/08/1940	13:44
Aqu	11/16/1939	15:00	Gem	03/14/1940	20:51	Lib	07/10/1940	16:06
Pis	11/19/1939	03:00	Can	03/17/1940	04:56	Sco	07/12/1940	19:07
Ari	11/21/1939	15:35	Leo	03/19/1940	09:13	Sag	07/14/1940	23:05
Tau	11/24/1939	02:21	Vir	03/21/1940	10:19	Cap	07/17/1940	04:17
Gem	11/26/1939	10:08	Lib	03/23/1940	09:47	Aqu	07/19/1940	11:22
Can	11/28/1939	15:10	Sco	03/25/1940	09:34	Pis	07/21/1940	20:58
Leo	11/30/1939	18:34	Sag	03/27/1940	11:32	Ari	07/24/1940	09:01
Vir	12/02/1939	21:23	Cap	03/29/1940	17:00	Tau	07/26/1940	21:55
Lib	12/05/1939	00:22	Aqu	04/01/1940	02:14	Gem	07/29/1940	09:03
Sco	12/07/1939	03:57	Pis	04/03/1940	14:11	Can	07/31/1940	16:31
Sag	12/09/1939	08:32	Ari	04/06/1940	03:09	Leo	08/02/1940	20:19
Cap	12/11/1939	14:51	Tau	04/08/1940	15:38	Vir	08/04/1940	21:50
Aqu	12/13/1939	23:43	Gem	04/11/1940	02:31	Lib	08/06/1940	22:49
Pis	12/16/1939	11:14	Can	04/13/1940	11:02	Sco	08/09/1940	00:46
Ari	12/19/1939	00:02	Leo	04/15/1940	16:43	Sag	08/11/1940	04:29
Tau	12/21/1939	11:30	Vir	04/17/1940	19:34	Cap	08/13/1940	10:15
Gem	12/23/1939	19:36	Lib	04/19/1940	20:22	Aqu	08/15/1940	18:07
Can	12/26/1939	00:02	Sco	04/21/1940	20:33	Pis	08/18/1940	04:10
Leo	12/28/1939	02:04	Sag	04/23/1940	21:49	Ari	08/20/1940	16:14
Vir	12/30/1939	03:29	Cap	04/26/1940	01:50	Tau	08/23/1940	05:16
Lib	01/01/1940	05:43	Aqu	04/28/1940	09:39	Gem	08/25/1940	17:12
Sco	01/03/1940	09:36	Pis	04/30/1940	20:56	Can	08/28/1940	01:52
Sag	01/05/1940	15:12	Ari	05/03/1940	09:51	Leo	08/30/1940	06:31
Cap	01/07/1940	22:30	Tau	05/05/1940	22:11	Vir	09/01/1940	07:56
Aqu	01/10/1940	07:42	Gem	05/08/1940	08:33	Lib	09/03/1940	07:54
Pis	01/12/1940	19:03	Can	05/10/1940	16:33	Sco	09/05/1940	08:16
Ari	01/15/1940	07:55	Leo	05/12/1940	22:21	Sag	09/07/1940	10:37
Tau	01/17/1940	20:15	Vir	05/15/1940	02:16	Cap	09/09/1940	15:46

Aqu	09/11/1940	23:52	Gem	01/09/1941	03:26	Lib	05/07/1941	16:10
Pis	09/14/1940	10:25	Can	01/11/1941	12:32	Sco	05/09/1941	16:33
Ari	09/16/1940	22:43	Leo	01/13/1941	18:38	Sag	05/11/1941	15:49
Tau	09/19/1940	11:45	Vir	01/15/1941	22:45	Cap	05/13/1941	16:04
Gem	09/22/1940	00:04	Lib	01/18/1941	01:59	Aqu	05/15/1941	19:15
Can	09/24/1940	09:56	Sco	01/20/1941	05:03	Pis	05/18/1941	02:34
Leo	09/26/1940	16:08	Sag	01/22/1941	08:16	Ari	05/20/1941	13:34
Vir	09/28/1940	18:41	Cap	01/24/1941	12:01	Tau	05/23/1941	02:26
Lib	09/30/1940	18:46	Aqu	01/26/1941	17:05	Gem	05/25/1941	15:09
Sco	10/02/1940	18:12	Pis	01/29/1941	00:35	Can	05/28/1941	02:35
Sag	10/04/1940	18:54	Ari	01/31/1941	11:02	Leo	05/30/1941	12:14
Cap	10/06/1940	22:29	Tau	02/02/1941	23:40	Vir	06/01/1941	19:37
Aqu	10/09/1940	05:44	Gem	02/05/1941	12:08	Lib	06/04/1941	00:15
Pis	10/11/1940	16:17	Can	02/07/1941	21:56	Sco	06/06/1941	02:12
Ari	10/14/1940	04:50	Leo	02/10/1941	04:06	Sag	06/08/1941	02:23
Tau	10/16/1940	17:49	Vir	02/12/1941	07:20	Cap	06/10/1941	02:32
Gem	10/19/1940	05:59	Lib	02/14/1941	09:07	Aqu	06/12/1941	04:41
Can	10/21/1940	16:17	Sco	02/16/1941	10:52	Pis	06/14/1941	10:34
Leo	10/23/1940	23:49	Sag	02/18/1941	13:37	Ari	06/16/1941	20:30
Vir	10/26/1940	04:09	Cap	02/20/1941	17:53	Tau	06/19/1941	09:02
Lib	10/28/1940	05:36	Aqu	02/23/1941	00:02	Gem	06/21/1941	21:43
Sco	10/30/1940	05:24	Pis	02/25/1941	08:18	Can	06/24/1941	08:50
Sag	11/01/1940	05:20	Ari	02/27/1941	18:54	Leo	06/26/1941	17:54
Cap	11/03/1940	07:22	Tau	03/02/1941	07:23	Vir	06/29/1941	01:02
Aqu	11/05/1940	13:04	Gem	03/04/1941	20:11	Lib	07/01/1941	06:16
Pis	11/07/1940	22:46	Can	03/07/1941	07:03	Sco	07/03/1941	09:33
Ari	11/10/1940	11:13	Leo	03/09/1941	14:17	Sag	07/05/1941	11:12
Tau	11/13/1940	00:12	Vir	03/11/1941	17:51	Cap	07/07/1941	12:21
Gem	11/15/1940	11:59	Lib	03/13/1941	18:51	Aqu	07/09/1941	14:36
Can	11/17/1940	21:51	Sco	03/15/1941	19:02	Pis	07/11/1941	19:42
Leo	11/20/1940	05:38	Sag	03/17/1941	20:08	Ari	07/14/1941	04:34
Vir	11/22/1940	11:09	Cap	03/19/1941	23:26	Tau	07/16/1941	16:29
Lib	11/24/1940	14:23	Aqu	03/22/1941	05:34	Gem	07/19/1941	05:09
Sco	11/26/1940	15:44	Pis	03/24/1941	14:30	Can	07/21/1941	16:14
Sag	11/28/1940	16:18	Ari	03/27/1941	01:39	Leo	07/24/1941	00:47
Cap	11/30/1940	17:50	Tau	03/29/1941	14:13	Vir	07/26/1941	07:03
Aqu	12/02/1940	22:13	Gem	04/01/1941	03:05	Lib	07/28/1941	11:40
Pis	12/05/1940	06:35	Can	04/03/1941	14:42	Sco	07/30/1941	15:08
Ari	12/07/1940	18:26	Leo	04/05/1941	23:24	Sag	08/01/1941	17:49
Tau	12/10/1940	07:26	Vir	04/08/1941	04:20	Cap	08/03/1941	20:17
Gem	12/12/1940	19:07	Lib	04/10/1941	05:54	Aqu	08/05/1941	23:32
Can	12/15/1940	04:19	Sco	04/12/1941	05:31	Pis	08/08/1941	04:51
Leo	12/17/1940	11:15	Sag	04/14/1941	05:07	Ari	08/10/1941	13:13
Vir	12/19/1940	16:34	Cap	04/16/1941	06:38	Tau	08/13/1941	00:32
Lib	12/21/1940	20:36	Aqu	04/18/1941	11:32	Gem	08/15/1941	13:09
Sco	12/23/1940	23:29	Pis	04/20/1941	20:07	Can	08/18/1941	00:36
Sag	12/26/1940	01:36	Ari	04/23/1941	07:34	Leo	08/20/1941	09:14
Cap	12/28/1940	03:58	Tau	04/25/1941	20:22	Vir	08/22/1941	14:52
Aqu	12/30/1940	08:09	Gem	04/28/1941	09:10	Lib	08/24/1941	18:21
Pis	01/01/1941	15:35	Can	04/30/1941	20:55	Sco	08/26/1941	20:48
Ari	01/04/1941	02:34	Leo	05/03/1941	06:33	Sag	08/28/1941	23:13
Tau	01/06/1941	15:28	Vir	05/05/1941	13:04	Cap	08/31/1941	02:18

Aqu	09/02/1941	06:38	Gem	12/29/1941	23:26	Lib	04/27/1942	22:48
Pis	09/04/1941	12:52	Can	01/01/1942	11:40	Sco	04/30/1942	00:57
Ari	09/06/1941	21:29	Leo	01/03/1942	22:31	Sag	05/02/1942	01:02
Tau	09/09/1941	08:32	Vir	01/06/1942	07:41	Cap	05/04/1942	01:05
Gem	09/11/1941	21:05	Lib	01/08/1942	14:47	Aqu	05/06/1942	02:56
Can	09/14/1941	09:08	Sco	01/10/1942	19:23	Pis	05/08/1942	07:43
Leo	09/16/1941	18:35	Sag	01/12/1942	21:30	Ari	05/10/1942	15:31
Vir	09/19/1941	00:27	Cap	01/14/1942	22:06	Tau	05/13/1942	01:36
Lib	09/21/1941	03:16	Aqu	01/16/1942	22:53	Gem	05/15/1942	13:14
Sco	09/23/1941	04:23	Pis	01/19/1942	01:44	Can	05/18/1942	01:48
Sag	09/25/1941	05:24	Ari	01/21/1942	08:08	Leo	05/20/1942	14:20
Cap	09/27/1941	07:44	Tau	01/23/1942	18:18	Vir	05/23/1942	01:05
Aqu	09/29/1941	12:17	Gem	01/26/1942	06:43	Lib	05/25/1942	08:20
Pis	10/01/1941	19:18	Can	01/28/1942	19:02	Sco	05/27/1942	11:30
Ari	10/04/1941	04:37	Leo	01/31/1942	05:36	Sag	05/29/1942	11:37
Tau	10/06/1941	15:51	Vir	02/02/1942	13:56	Cap	05/31/1942	10:43
Gem	10/09/1941	04:22	Lib	02/04/1942	20:17	Aqu	06/02/1942	11:00
Can	10/11/1941	16:52	Sco	02/07/1942	00:55	Pis	06/04/1942	14:14
Leo	10/14/1941	03:28	Sag	02/09/1942	04:06	Ari	06/06/1942	21:11
Vir	10/16/1941	10:34	Cap	02/11/1942	06:18	Tau	06/09/1942	07:15
Lib	10/18/1941	13:52	Aqu	02/13/1942	08:27	Gem	06/11/1942	19:11
Sco	10/20/1941	14:24	Pis	02/15/1942	11:51	Can	06/14/1942	07:49
Sag	10/22/1941	14:00	Ari	02/17/1942	17:46	Leo	06/16/1942	20:18
Cap	10/24/1941	14:40	Tau	02/20/1942	02:57	Vir	06/19/1942	07:32
Aqu	10/26/1941	18:02	Gem	02/22/1942	14:47	Lib	06/21/1942	16:03
Pis	10/29/1941	00:51	Can	02/25/1942	03:14	Sco	06/23/1942	20:49
Ari	10/31/1941	10:38	Leo	02/27/1942	14:04	Sag	06/25/1942	22:07
Tau	11/02/1941	22:18	Vir	03/01/1942	22:04	Cap	06/27/1942	21:29
Gem	11/05/1941	10:51	Lib	03/04/1942	03:22	Aqu	06/29/1942	21:01
Can	11/07/1941	23:25	Sco	03/06/1942	06:49	Pis	07/01/1942	22:47
Leo	11/10/1941	10:47	Sag	03/08/1942	09:27	Ari	07/04/1942	04:10
Vir	11/12/1941	19:28	Cap	03/10/1942	12:08	Tau	07/06/1942	13:22
Lib	11/15/1941	00:20	Aqu	03/12/1942	15:30	Gem	07/09/1942	01:10
Sco	11/17/1941	01:38	Pis	03/14/1942	20:08	Can	07/11/1942	13:50
Sag	11/19/1941	00:53	Ari	03/17/1942	02:41	Leo	07/14/1942	02:07
Cap	11/21/1941	00:12	Tau	03/19/1942	11:39	Vir	07/16/1942	13:07
Aqu	11/23/1941	01:47	Gem	03/21/1942	23:00	Lib	07/18/1942	22:00
Pis	11/25/1941	07:09	Can	03/24/1942	11:32	Sco	07/21/1942	04:01
Ari	11/27/1941	16:26	Leo	03/26/1942	23:02	Sag	07/23/1942	06:57
Tau	11/30/1941	04:18	Vir	03/29/1942	07:35	Cap	07/25/1942	07:37
Gem	12/02/1941	16:59	Lib	03/31/1942	12:35	Aqu	07/27/1942	07:36
Can	12/05/1941	05:21	Sco	04/02/1942	14:53	Pis	07/29/1942	08:49
Leo	12/07/1941	16:42	Sag	04/04/1942	16:04	Ari	07/31/1942	12:56
Vir	12/10/1941	02:11	Cap	04/06/1942	17:41	Tau	08/02/1942	20:47
Lib	12/12/1941	08:44	Aqu	04/08/1942	20:56	Gem	08/05/1942	07:54
Sco	12/14/1941	11:50	Pis	04/11/1942	02:19	Can	08/07/1942	20:29
Sag	12/16/1941	12:09	Ari	04/13/1942	09:49	Leo	08/10/1942	08:38
Cap	12/18/1941	11:26	Tau	04/15/1942	19:17	Vir	08/12/1942	19:08
Aqu	12/20/1941	11:54	Gem	04/18/1942	06:36	Lib	08/15/1942	03:30
Pis	12/22/1941	15:33	Can	04/20/1942	19:09	Sco	08/17/1942	09:36
Ari	12/24/1941	23:24	Leo	04/23/1942	07:20	Sag	08/19/1942	13:33
Tau	12/27/1941	10:43	Vir	04/25/1942	17:01	Cap	08/21/1942	15:45

Aqu	08/23/1942	17:06	Gem	12/19/1942	21:45	Lib	04/18/1943	00:39
Pis	08/25/1942	18:54	Can	12/22/1942	09:45	Sco	04/20/1943	07:02
Ari	08/27/1942	22:39	Leo	12/24/1942	22:34	Sag	04/22/1943	10:55
Tau	08/30/1942	05:28	Vir	12/27/1942	11:09	Cap	04/24/1943	13:39
Gem	09/01/1942	15:40	Lib	12/29/1942	21:43	Aqu	04/26/1943	16:20
Can	09/04/1942	03:59	Sco	01/01/1943	04:38	Pis	04/28/1943	19:35
Leo	09/06/1942	16:14	Sag	01/03/1943	07:32	Ari	04/30/1943	23:39
Vir	09/09/1942	02:29	Cap	01/05/1943	07:34	Tau	05/03/1943	04:56
Lib	09/11/1942	10:03	Aqu	01/07/1943	06:41	Gem	05/05/1943	12:16
Sco	09/13/1942	15:17	Pis	01/09/1943	07:02	Can	05/07/1943	22:16
Sag	09/15/1942	18:57	Ari	01/11/1943	10:21	Leo	05/10/1943	10:38
Cap	09/17/1942	21:47	Tau	01/13/1943	17:21	Vir	05/12/1943	23:20
Aqu	09/20/1942	00:26	Gem	01/16/1943	03:38	Lib	05/15/1943	09:42
Pis	09/22/1942	03:33	Can	01/18/1943	15:53	Sco	05/17/1943	16:18
Ari	09/24/1942	07:57	Leo	01/21/1943	04:43	Sag	05/19/1943	19:32
Tau	09/26/1942	14:34	Vir	01/23/1943	17:02	Cap	05/21/1943	20:59
Gem	09/29/1942	00:05	Lib	01/26/1943	03:46	Aqu	05/23/1943	22:23
Can	10/01/1942	12:02	Sco	01/28/1943	11:49	Pis	05/26/1943	00:57
Leo	10/04/1942	00:34	Sag	01/30/1943	16:33	Ari	05/28/1943	05:15
Vir	10/06/1942	11:11	Cap	02/01/1943	18:14	Tau	05/30/1943	11:24
Lib	10/08/1942	18:31	Aqu	02/03/1943	18:09	Gem	06/01/1943	19:29
Sco	10/10/1942	22:45	Pis	02/05/1943	18:07	Can	06/04/1943	05:44
Sag	10/13/1942	01:09	Ari	02/07/1943	20:00	Leo	06/06/1943	18:02
Cap	10/15/1942	03:13	Tau	02/10/1943	01:17	Vir	06/09/1943	07:02
Aqu	10/17/1942	06:00	Gem	02/12/1943	10:25	Lib	06/11/1943	18:21
Pis	10/19/1942	10:05	Can	02/14/1943	22:24	Sco	06/14/1943	01:57
Ari	10/21/1942	15:36	Leo	02/17/1943	11:17	Sag	06/16/1943	05:35
Tau	10/23/1942	22:52	Vir	02/19/1943	23:19	Cap	06/18/1943	06:29
Gem	10/26/1942	08:18	Lib	02/22/1943	09:28	Aqu	06/20/1943	06:33
Can	10/28/1942	19:59	Sco	02/24/1943	17:24	Pis	06/22/1943	07:36
Leo	10/31/1942	08:47	Sag	02/26/1943	22:57	Ari	06/24/1943	10:53
Vir	11/02/1942	20:17	Cap	03/01/1943	02:17	Tau	06/26/1943	16:51
Lib	11/05/1942	04:20	Aqu	03/03/1943	03:55	Gem	06/29/1943	01:26
Sco	11/07/1942	08:25	Pis	03/05/1943	04:54	Can	07/01/1943	12:13
Sag	11/09/1942	09:46	Ari	03/07/1943	06:41	Leo	07/04/1943	00:38
Cap	11/11/1942	10:17	Tau	03/09/1943	10:54	Vir	07/06/1943	13:44
Aqu	11/13/1942	11:48	Gem	03/11/1943	18:38	Lib	07/09/1943	01:42
Pis	11/15/1942	15:27	Can	03/14/1943	05:50	Sco	07/11/1943	10:38
Ari	11/17/1942	21:30	Leo	03/16/1943	18:40	Sag	07/13/1943	15:35
Tau	11/20/1942	05:37	Vir	03/19/1943	06:42	Cap	07/15/1943	17:06
Gem	11/22/1942	15:34	Lib	03/21/1943	16:20	Aqu	07/17/1943	16:45
Can	11/25/1942	03:16	Sco	03/23/1943	23:21	Pis	07/19/1943	16:30
Leo	11/27/1942	16:08	Sag	03/26/1943	04:22	Ari	07/21/1943	18:07
Vir	11/30/1942	04:28	Cap	03/28/1943	08:04	Tau	07/23/1943	22:53
Lib	12/02/1942	13:53	Aqu	03/30/1943	10:56	Gem	07/26/1943	07:03
Sco	12/04/1942	19:05	Pis	04/01/1943	13:26	Can	07/28/1943	18:03
Sag	12/06/1942	20:32	Ari	04/03/1943	16:17	Leo	07/31/1943	06:42
Cap	12/08/1942	20:06	Tau	04/05/1943	20:37	Vir	08/02/1943	19:44
Aqu	12/10/1942	19:56	Gem	04/08/1943	03:41	Lib	08/05/1943	07:50
Pis	12/12/1942	21:56	Can	04/10/1943	14:03	Sco	08/07/1943	17:39
Ari	12/15/1942	03:04	Leo	04/13/1943	02:39	Sag	08/10/1943	00:06
Tau	12/17/1942	11:16	Vir	04/15/1943	14:57	Cap	08/12/1943	03:07

Aqu	08/14/1943	03:35	Gem	12/10/1943	00:32	Lib	04/06/1944	23:20
Pis	08/16/1943	03:06	Can	12/12/1943	08:46	Sco	04/09/1944	10:10
Ari	08/18/1943	03:32	Leo	12/14/1943	19:36	Sag	04/11/1944	19:01
Tau	08/20/1943	06:39	Vir	12/17/1943	08:21	Cap	04/14/1944	01:54
Gem	08/22/1943	13:34	Lib	12/19/1943	20:54	Aqu	04/16/1944	06:45
Can	08/25/1943	00:07	Sco	12/22/1943	06:45	Pis	04/18/1944	09:27
Leo	08/27/1943	12:48	Sag	12/24/1943	12:42	Ari	04/20/1944	10:35
Vir	08/30/1943	01:46	Cap	12/26/1943	15:22	Tau	04/22/1944	11:28
Lib	09/01/1943	13:32	Aqu	12/28/1943	16:20	Gem	04/24/1944	13:59
Sco	09/03/1943	23:18	Pis	12/30/1943	17:16	Can	04/26/1944	19:48
Sag	09/06/1943	06:37	Ari	01/01/1944	19:33	Leo	04/29/1944	05:35
Cap	09/08/1943	11:11	Tau	01/03/1944	23:58	Vir	05/01/1944	18:03
Aqu	09/10/1943	13:16	Gem	01/06/1944	06:43	Lib	05/04/1944	06:38
Pis	09/12/1943	13:45	Can	01/08/1944	15:47	Sco	05/06/1944	17:17
Ari	09/14/1943	14:08	Leo	01/11/1944	02:57	Sag	05/09/1944	01:25
Tau	09/16/1943	16:14	Vir	01/13/1944	15:37	Cap	05/11/1944	07:32
Gem	09/18/1943	21:42	Lib	01/16/1944	04:28	Aqu	05/13/1944	12:09
Can	09/21/1943	07:10	Sco	01/18/1944	15:26	Pis	05/15/1944	15:34
Leo	09/23/1943	19:33	Sag	01/20/1944	22:51	Ari	05/17/1944	18:02
Vir	09/26/1943	08:29	Cap	01/23/1944	02:25	Tau	05/19/1944	20:15
Lib	09/28/1943	19:55	Aqu	01/25/1944	03:08	Gem	05/21/1944	23:26
Sco	10/01/1943	05:03	Pis	01/27/1944	02:47	Can	05/24/1944	05:03
Sag	10/03/1943	12:01	Ari	01/29/1944	03:14	Leo	05/26/1944	14:04
Cap	10/05/1943	17:10	Tau	01/31/1944	06:06	Vir	05/29/1944	01:58
Aqu	10/07/1943	20:38	Gem	02/02/1944	12:17	Lib	05/31/1944	14:36
Pis	10/09/1943	22:43	Can	02/04/1944	21:39	Sco	06/03/1944	01:30
Ari	10/12/1943	00:11	Leo	02/07/1944	09:19	Sag	06/05/1944	09:26
Tau	10/14/1943	02:26	Vir	02/09/1944	22:07	Cap	06/07/1944	14:40
Gem	10/16/1943	07:06	Lib	02/12/1944	10:53	Aqu	06/09/1944	18:11
Can	10/18/1943	15:27	Sco	02/14/1944	22:22	Pis	06/11/1944	20:57
Leo	10/21/1943	03:11	Sag	02/17/1944	07:13	Ari	06/13/1944	23:40
Vir	10/23/1943	16:08	Cap	02/19/1944	12:31	Tau	06/16/1944	02:51
Lib	10/26/1943	03:36	Aqu	02/21/1944	14:25	Gem	06/18/1944	07:10
Sco	10/28/1943	12:12	Pis	02/23/1944	14:08	Can	06/20/1944	13:28
Sag	10/30/1943	18:13	Ari	02/25/1944	13:31	Leo	06/22/1944	22:25
Cap	11/01/1943	22:35	Tau	02/27/1944	14:36	Vir	06/25/1944	09:57
Aqu	11/04/1943	02:08	Gem	02/29/1944	19:05	Lib	06/27/1944	22:39
Pis	11/06/1943	05:15	Can	03/03/1944	03:38	Sco	06/30/1944	10:09
Ari	11/08/1943	08:10	Leo	03/05/1944	15:19	Sag	07/02/1944	18:37
Tau	11/10/1943	11:32	Vir	03/08/1944	04:17	Cap	07/04/1944	23:40
Gem	11/12/1943	16:31	Lib	03/10/1944	16:54	Aqu	07/07/1944	02:13
Can	11/15/1943	00:22	Sco	03/13/1944	04:11	Pis	07/09/1944	03:38
Leo	11/17/1943	11:27	Sag	03/15/1944	13:29	Ari	07/11/1944	05:18
Vir	11/20/1943	00:20	Cap	03/17/1944	20:12	Tau	07/13/1944	08:16
Lib	11/22/1943	12:17	Aqu	03/19/1944	23:53	Gem	07/15/1944	13:11
Sco	11/24/1943	21:07	Pis	03/22/1944	00:57	Can	07/17/1944	20:21
Sag	11/27/1943	02:33	Ari	03/24/1944	00:41	Leo	07/20/1944	05:50
Cap	11/29/1943	05:42	Tau	03/26/1944	01:01	Vir	07/22/1944	17:24
Aqu	12/01/1943	08:00	Gem	03/28/1944	03:58	Lib	07/25/1944	06:07
Pis	12/03/1943	10:35	Can	03/30/1944	10:59	Sco	07/27/1944	18:15
Ari	12/05/1943	13:59	Leo	04/01/1944	21:54	Sag	07/30/1944	03:48
Tau	12/07/1943	18:29	Vir	04/04/1944	10:48	Cap	08/01/1944	09:40

Aqu	08/03/1944	12:09	Gem	11/29/1944	06:54	Lib	03/27/1945	21:14
Pis	08/05/1944	12:34	Can	12/01/1944	10:17	Sco	03/30/1945	09:49
Ari	08/07/1944	12:43	Leo	12/03/1944	16:52	Sag	04/01/1945	22:06
Tau	08/09/1944	14:19	Vir	12/06/1944	03:03	Cap	04/04/1945	08:50
Gem	08/11/1944	18:37	Lib	12/08/1944	15:27	Aqu	04/06/1945	16:27
Can	08/14/1944	02:03	Sco	12/11/1944	03:41	Pis	04/08/1945	20:09
Leo	08/16/1944	12:08	Sag	12/13/1944	13:48	Ari	04/10/1945	20:36
Vir	08/19/1944	00:00	Cap	12/15/1944	21:20	Tau	04/12/1945	19:39
Lib	08/21/1944	12:44	Aqu	12/18/1944	02:43	Gem	04/14/1945	19:31
Sco	08/24/1944	01:12	Pis	12/20/1944	06:38	Can	04/16/1945	22:14
Sag	08/26/1944	11:50	Ari	12/22/1944	09:41	Leo	04/19/1945	04:51
Cap	08/28/1944	19:11	Tau	12/24/1944	12:23	Vir	04/21/1945	15:02
Aqu	08/30/1944	22:42	Gem	12/26/1944	15:25	Lib	04/24/1945	03:14
Pis	09/01/1944	23:13	Can	12/28/1944	19:43	Sco	04/26/1945	15:51
Ari	09/03/1944	22:27	Leo	12/31/1944	02:19	Sag	04/29/1945	03:55
Tau	09/05/1944	22:29	Vir	01/02/1945	11:49	Cap	05/01/1945	14:38
Gem	09/08/1944	01:14	Lib	01/04/1945	23:43	Aqu	05/03/1945	23:03
Can	09/10/1944	07:46	Sco	01/07/1945	12:12	Pis	05/06/1945	04:20
Leo	09/12/1944	17:49	Sag	01/09/1945	22:53	Ari	05/08/1945	06:24
Vir	09/15/1944	05:59	Cap	01/12/1945	06:27	Tau	05/10/1945	06:23
Lib	09/17/1944	18:47	Aqu	01/14/1945	10:55	Gem	05/12/1945	06:11
Sco	09/20/1944	07:10	Pis	01/16/1945	13:26	Can	05/14/1945	07:51
Sag	09/22/1944	18:15	Ari	01/18/1945	15:20	Leo	05/16/1945	12:57
Cap	09/25/1944	02:53	Tau	01/20/1945	17:47	Vir	05/18/1945	21:56
Aqu	09/27/1944	08:08	Gem	01/22/1945	21:34	Lib	05/21/1945	09:42
Pis	09/29/1944	09:56	Can	01/25/1945	03:04	Sco	05/23/1945	22:19
Ari	10/01/1944	09:29	Leo	01/27/1945	10:32	Sag	05/26/1945	10:10
Tau	10/03/1944	08:45	Vir	01/29/1945	20:08	Cap	05/28/1945	20:23
Gem	10/05/1944	10:00	Lib	02/01/1945	07:45	Aqu	05/31/1945	04:34
Can	10/07/1944	14:56	Sco	02/03/1945	20:21	Pis	06/02/1945	10:23
Leo	10/10/1944	00:03	Sag	02/06/1945	07:56	Ari	06/04/1945	13:49
Vir	10/12/1944	12:04	Cap	02/08/1945	16:28	Tau	06/06/1945	15:22
Lib	10/15/1944	00:54	Aqu	02/10/1945	21:10	Gem	06/08/1945	16:14
Sco	10/17/1944	13:02	Pis	02/12/1945	22:51	Can	06/10/1945	18:01
Sag	10/19/1944	23:48	Ari	02/14/1945	23:12	Leo	06/12/1945	22:20
Cap	10/22/1944	08:47	Tau	02/17/1945	00:05	Vir	06/15/1945	06:06
Aqu	10/24/1944	15:17	Gem	02/19/1945	03:01	Lib	06/17/1945	17:05
Pis	10/26/1944	18:52	Can	02/21/1945	08:42	Sco	06/20/1945	05:35
Ari	10/28/1944	19:52	Leo	02/23/1945	16:58	Sag	06/22/1945	17:26
Tau	10/30/1944	19:44	Vir	02/26/1945	03:13	Cap	06/25/1945	03:13
Gem	11/01/1944	20:28	Lib	02/28/1945	14:56	Aqu	06/27/1945	10:35
Can	11/04/1944	00:05	Sco	03/03/1945	03:32	Pis	06/29/1945	15:50
Leo	11/06/1944	07:44	Sag	03/05/1945	15:43	Ari	07/01/1945	19:28
Vir	11/08/1944	18:58	Cap	03/08/1945	01:35	Tau	07/03/1945	22:03
Lib	11/11/1944	07:43	Aqu	03/10/1945	07:38	Gem	07/06/1945	00:19
Sco	11/13/1944	19:46	Pis	03/12/1945	09:48	Can	07/08/1945	03:10
Sag	11/16/1944	06:01	Ari	03/14/1945	09:31	Leo	07/10/1945	07:43
Cap	11/18/1944	14:18	Tau	03/16/1945	08:54	Vir	07/12/1945	14:58
Aqu	11/20/1944	20:46	Gem	03/18/1945	10:05	Lib	07/15/1945	01:12
Pis	11/23/1944	01:17	Can	03/20/1945	14:31	Sco	07/17/1945	13:28
Ari	11/25/1944	03:55	Leo	03/22/1945	22:31	Sag	07/20/1945	01:34
Tau	11/27/1944	05:21	Vir	03/25/1945	09:10	Cap	07/22/1945	11:27

Aqu	07/24/1945	18:15	Gem	11/19/1945	15:02	Lib	03/17/1946	20:40
Pis	07/26/1945	22:25	Can	11/21/1945	15:13	Sco	03/20/1946	07:04
Ari	07/29/1945	01:06	Leo	11/23/1945	18:11	Sag	03/22/1946	19:29
Tau	07/31/1945	03:28	Vir	11/26/1945	00:59	Cap	03/25/1946	08:16
Gem	08/02/1945	06:22	Lib	11/28/1945	11:18	Aqu	03/27/1946	18:49
Can	08/04/1945	10:22	Sco	11/30/1945	23:42	Pis	03/30/1946	01:24
Leo	08/06/1945	15:52	Sag	12/03/1945	12:28	Ari	04/01/1946	04:15
Vir	08/08/1945	23:24	Cap	12/06/1945	00:22	Tau	04/03/1946	04:55
Lib	08/11/1945	09:21	Aqu	12/08/1945	10:32	Gem	04/05/1946	05:24
Sco	08/13/1945	21:24	Pis	12/10/1945	18:19	Can	04/07/1946	07:20
Sag	08/16/1945	09:54	Ari	12/12/1945	23:13	Leo	04/09/1946	11:37
Cap	08/18/1945	20:29	Tau	12/15/1945	01:28	Vir	04/11/1946	18:19
Aqu	08/21/1945	03:30	Gem	12/17/1945	02:01	Lib	04/14/1946	03:13
Pis	08/23/1945	07:04	Can	12/19/1945	02:27	Sco	04/16/1946	14:03
Ari	08/25/1945	08:29	Leo	12/21/1945	04:30	Sag	04/19/1946	02:29
Tau	08/27/1945	09:33	Vir	12/23/1945	09:44	Cap	04/21/1946	15:27
Gem	08/29/1945	11:46	Lib	12/25/1945	18:44	Aqu	04/24/1946	02:54
Can	08/31/1945	15:59	Sco	12/28/1945	06:42	Pis	04/26/1946	10:52
Leo	09/02/1945	22:19	Sag	12/30/1945	19:31	Ari	04/28/1946	14:44
Vir	09/05/1945	06:35	Cap	01/02/1946	07:10	Tau	04/30/1946	15:29
Lib	09/07/1945	16:48	Aqu	01/04/1946	16:36	Gem	05/02/1946	15:03
Sco	09/10/1945	04:47	Pis	01/06/1946	23:45	Can	05/04/1946	15:22
Sag	09/12/1945	17:36	Ari	01/09/1946	04:54	Leo	05/06/1946	18:03
Cap	09/15/1945	05:10	Tau	01/11/1946	08:24	Vir	05/08/1946	23:57
Aqu	09/17/1945	13:17	Gem	01/13/1946	10:41	Lib	05/11/1946	08:53
Pis	09/19/1945	17:17	Can	01/15/1946	12:32	Sco	05/13/1946	20:08
Ari	09/21/1945	18:10	Leo	01/17/1946	15:03	Sag	05/16/1946	08:45
Tau	09/23/1945	17:52	Vir	01/19/1946	19:40	Cap	05/18/1946	21:40
Gem	09/25/1945	18:31	Lib	01/22/1946	03:31	Aqu	05/21/1946	09:29
Can	09/27/1945	21:38	Sco	01/24/1946	14:39	Pis	05/23/1946	18:37
Leo	09/30/1945	03:46	Sag	01/27/1946	03:26	Ari	05/26/1946	00:02
Vir	10/02/1945	12:33	Cap	01/29/1946	15:16	Tau	05/28/1946	02:02
Lib	10/04/1945	23:16	Aqu	02/01/1946	00:22	Gem	05/30/1946	01:53
Sco	10/07/1945	11:23	Pis	02/03/1946	06:31	Can	06/01/1946	01:28
Sag	10/10/1945	00:16	Ari	02/05/1946	10:37	Leo	06/03/1946	02:39
Cap	10/12/1945	12:31	Tau	02/07/1946	13:46	Vir	06/05/1946	06:56
Aqu	10/14/1945	22:04	Gem	02/09/1946	16:44	Lib	06/07/1946	14:57
Pis	10/17/1945	03:32	Can	02/11/1946	19:58	Sco	06/10/1946	02:04
Ari	10/19/1945	05:08	Leo	02/13/1946	23:50	Sag	06/12/1946	14:49
Tau	10/21/1945	04:29	Vir	02/16/1946	05:02	Cap	06/15/1946	03:38
Gem	10/23/1945	03:49	Lib	02/18/1946	12:36	Aqu	06/17/1946	15:14
Can	10/25/1945	05:10	Sco	02/20/1946	23:04	Pis	06/20/1946	00:41
Leo	10/27/1945	09:55	Sag	02/23/1946	11:40	Ari	06/22/1946	07:18
Vir	10/29/1945	18:11	Cap	02/26/1946	00:00	Tau	06/24/1946	10:54
Lib	11/01/1945	05:07	Aqu	02/28/1946	09:32	Gem	06/26/1946	12:06
Sco	11/03/1945	17:28	Pis	03/02/1946	15:23	Can	06/28/1946	12:10
Sag	11/06/1945	06:17	Ari	03/04/1946	18:22	Leo	06/30/1946	12:47
Cap	11/08/1945	18:34	Tau	03/06/1946	20:07	Vir	07/02/1946	15:45
Aqu	11/11/1945	04:57	Gem	03/08/1946	22:11	Lib	07/04/1946	22:21
Pis	11/13/1945	12:02	Can	03/11/1946	01:28	Sco	07/07/1946	08:41
Ari	11/15/1945	15:22	Leo	03/13/1946	06:13	Sag	07/09/1946	21:19
Tau	11/17/1945	15:46	Vir	03/15/1946	12:32	Cap	07/12/1946	10:04

Aqu	07/14/1946	21:15	Gem	11/10/1946	00:06	Lib	03/07/1947	22:51
Pis	07/17/1946	06:14	Can	11/12/1946	00:15	Sco	03/10/1947	04:50
Ari	07/19/1946	12:57	Leo	11/14/1946	01:53	Sag	03/12/1947	14:34
Tau	07/21/1946	17:34	Vir	11/16/1946	06:04	Cap	03/15/1947	02:59
Gem	07/23/1946	20:17	Lib	11/18/1946	13:12	Aqu	03/17/1947	15:34
Can	07/25/1946	21:43	Sco	11/20/1946	22:57	Pis	03/20/1947	01:55
Leo	07/27/1946	22:57	Sag	11/23/1946	10:43	Ari	03/22/1947	09:21
Vir	07/30/1946	01:32	Cap	11/25/1946	23:38	Tau	03/24/1947	14:27
Lib	08/01/1946	07:04	Aqu	11/28/1946	12:28	Gem	03/26/1947	18:15
Sco	08/03/1946	16:22	Pis	11/30/1946	23:27	Can	03/28/1947	21:25
Sag	08/06/1946	04:35	Ari	12/03/1946	07:04	Leo	03/31/1947	00:21
Cap	08/08/1946	17:22	Tau	12/05/1946	10:46	Vir	04/02/1947	03:30
Aqu	08/11/1946	04:22	Gem	12/07/1946	11:28	Lib	04/04/1947	07:39
Pis	08/13/1946	12:39	Can	12/09/1946	10:49	Sco	04/06/1947	13:56
Ari	08/15/1946	18:36	Leo	12/11/1946	10:46	Sag	04/08/1947	23:12
Tau	08/17/1946	22:58	Vir	12/13/1946	13:09	Cap	04/11/1947	11:08
Gem	08/20/1946	02:21	Lib	12/15/1946	19:07	Aqu	04/13/1947	23:50
Can	08/22/1946	05:05	Sco	12/18/1946	04:42	Pis	04/16/1947	10:45
Leo	08/24/1946	07:37	Sag	12/20/1946	16:48	Ari	04/18/1947	18:24
Vir	08/26/1946	10:54	Cap	12/23/1946	05:49	Tau	04/20/1947	22:54
Lib	08/28/1946	16:15	Aqu	12/25/1946	18:28	Gem	04/23/1947	01:26
Sco	08/31/1946	00:49	Pis	12/28/1946	05:42	Can	04/25/1947	03:21
Sag	09/02/1946	12:30	Ari	12/30/1946	14:29	Leo	04/27/1947	05:43
Cap	09/05/1946	01:22	Tau	01/01/1947	20:04	Vir	04/29/1947	09:14
Aqu	09/07/1946	12:39	Gem	01/03/1947	22:24	Lib	05/01/1947	14:23
Pis	09/09/1946	20:44	Can	01/05/1947	22:26	Sco	05/03/1947	21:35
Ari	09/12/1946	01:47	Leo	01/07/1947	21:53	Sag	05/06/1947	07:08
Tau	09/14/1946	05:02	Vir	01/09/1947	22:45	Cap	05/08/1947	18:54
Gem	09/16/1946	07:44	Lib	01/12/1947	02:54	Aqu	05/11/1947	07:40
Can	09/18/1946	10:41	Sco	01/14/1947	11:16	Pis	05/13/1947	19:19
Leo	09/20/1946	14:12	Sag	01/16/1947	23:03	Ari	05/16/1947	03:54
Vir	09/22/1946	18:37	Cap	01/19/1947	12:09	Tau	05/18/1947	08:50
Lib	09/25/1946	00:40	Aqu	01/22/1947	00:36	Gem	05/20/1947	10:50
Sco	09/27/1946	09:12	Pis	01/24/1947	11:21	Can	05/22/1947	11:26
Sag	09/29/1946	20:32	Ari	01/26/1947	20:09	Leo	05/24/1947	12:18
Cap	10/02/1946	09:28	Tau	01/29/1947	02:44	Vir	05/26/1947	14:49
Aqu	10/04/1946	21:25	Gem	01/31/1947	06:51	Lib	05/28/1947	19:53
Pis	10/07/1946	06:08	Can	02/02/1947	08:37	Sco	05/31/1947	03:42
Ari	10/09/1946	11:03	Leo	02/04/1947	09:00	Sag	06/02/1947	13:53
Tau	10/11/1946	13:19	Vir	02/06/1947	09:42	Cap	06/05/1947	01:51
Gem	10/13/1946	14:36	Lib	02/08/1947	12:40	Aqu	06/07/1947	14:37
Can	10/15/1946	16:22	Sco	02/10/1947	19:28	Pis	06/10/1947	02:45
Leo	10/17/1946	19:34	Sag	02/13/1947	06:15	Ari	06/12/1947	12:31
Vir	10/20/1946	00:35	Cap	02/15/1947	19:11	Tau	06/14/1947	18:44
Lib	10/22/1946	07:32	Aqu	02/18/1947	07:37	Gem	06/16/1947	21:20
Sco	10/24/1946	16:40	Pis	02/20/1947	17:56	Can	06/18/1947	21:31
Sag	10/27/1946	04:02	Ari	02/23/1947	01:56	Leo	06/20/1947	21:06
Cap	10/29/1946	16:58	Tau	02/25/1947	08:06	Vir	06/22/1947	22:01
Aqu	11/01/1946	05:35	Gem	02/27/1947	12:45	Lib	06/25/1947	01:51
Pis	11/03/1946	15:30	Can	03/01/1947	15:57	Sco	06/27/1947	09:16
Ari	11/05/1946	21:26	Leo	03/03/1947	17:59	Sag	06/29/1947	19:45
Tau	11/07/1946	23:47	Vir	03/05/1947	19:46	Cap	07/02/1947	08:02

Aqu	07/04/1947	20:48	Gem	10/31/1947	09:34	Lib	02/26/1948	04:05
Pis	07/07/1947	09:02	Can	11/02/1947	12:31	Sco	02/28/1948	06:23
Ari	07/09/1947	19:33	Leo	11/04/1947	15:03	Sag	03/01/1948	12:42
Tau	07/12/1947	03:10	Vir	11/06/1947	17:54	Cap	03/03/1948	22:50
Gem	07/14/1947	07:15	Lib	11/08/1947	21:42	Aqu	03/06/1948	11:13
Can	07/16/1947	08:13	Sco	11/11/1947	03:02	Pis	03/08/1948	23:52
Leo	07/18/1947	07:33	Sag	11/13/1947	10:33	Ari	03/11/1948	11:32
Vir	07/20/1947	07:18	Cap	11/15/1947	20:37	Tau	03/13/1948	21:39
Lib	07/22/1947	09:33	Aqu	11/18/1947	08:44	Gem	03/16/1948	05:44
Sco	07/24/1947	15:41	Pis	11/20/1947	21:15	Can	03/18/1948	11:12
Sag	07/27/1947	01:40	Ari	11/23/1947	07:52	Leo	03/20/1948	13:56
Cap	07/29/1947	14:01	Tau	11/25/1947	15:04	Vir	03/22/1948	14:41
Aqu	08/01/1947	02:49	Gem	11/27/1947	18:54	Lib	03/24/1948	15:01
Pis	08/03/1947	14:48	Can	11/29/1947	20:30	Sco	03/26/1948	16:49
Ari	08/06/1947	01:18	Leo	12/01/1947	21:30	Sag	03/28/1948	21:47
Tau	08/08/1947	09:41	Vir	12/03/1947	23:23	Cap	03/31/1948	06:33
Gem	08/10/1947	15:16	Lib	12/06/1947	03:13	Aqu	04/02/1948	18:18
Can	08/12/1947	17:49	Sco	12/08/1947	09:24	Pis	04/05/1948	06:55
Leo	08/14/1947	18:05	Sag	12/10/1947	17:48	Ari	04/07/1948	18:27
Vir	08/16/1947	17:48	Cap	12/13/1947	04:13	Tau	04/10/1948	03:57
Lib	08/18/1947	19:03	Aqu	12/15/1947	16:15	Gem	04/12/1948	11:18
Sco	08/20/1947	23:45	Pis	12/18/1947	04:58	Can	04/14/1948	16:40
Sag	08/23/1947	08:34	Ari	12/20/1947	16:35	Leo	04/16/1948	20:15
Cap	08/25/1947	20:30	Tau	12/23/1947	01:09	Vir	04/18/1948	22:29
Aqu	08/28/1947	09:17	Gem	12/25/1947	05:46	Lib	04/21/1948	00:16
Pis	08/30/1947	21:02	Can	12/27/1947	07:02	Sco	04/23/1948	02:49
Ari	09/02/1947	07:01	Leo	12/29/1947	06:41	Sag	04/25/1948	07:31
Tau	09/04/1947	15:09	Vir	12/31/1947	06:46	Cap	04/27/1948	15:21
Gem	09/06/1947	21:17	Lib	01/02/1948	09:10	Aqu	04/30/1948	02:15
Can	09/09/1947	01:10	Sco	01/04/1948	14:51	Pis	05/02/1948	14:43
Leo	09/11/1947	03:02	Sag	01/06/1948	23:40	Ari	05/05/1948	02:26
Vir	09/13/1947	03:50	Cap	01/09/1948	10:40	Tau	05/07/1948	11:46
Lib	09/15/1947	05:15	Aqu	01/11/1948	22:53	Gem	05/09/1948	18:19
Sco	09/17/1947	09:11	Pis	01/14/1948	11:34	Can	05/11/1948	22:37
Sag	09/19/1947	16:49	Ari	01/16/1948	23:42	Leo	05/14/1948	01:38
Cap	09/22/1947	03:57	Tau	01/19/1948	09:40	Vir	05/16/1948	04:13
Aqu	09/24/1947	16:36	Gem	01/21/1948	16:00	Lib	05/18/1948	07:06
Pis	09/27/1947	04:23	Can	01/23/1948	18:22	Sco	05/20/1948	10:55
Ari	09/29/1947	13:57	Leo	01/25/1948	17:59	Sag	05/22/1948	16:21
Tau	10/01/1947	21:14	Vir	01/27/1948	16:55	Cap	05/25/1948	00:08
Gem	10/04/1947	02:42	Lib	01/29/1948	17:28	Aqu	05/27/1948	10:30
Can	10/06/1947	06:46	Sco	01/31/1948	21:28	Pis	05/29/1948	22:45
Leo	10/08/1947	09:40	Sag	02/03/1948	05:25	Ari	06/01/1948	10:53
Vir	10/10/1947	11:56	Cap	02/05/1948	16:29	Tau	06/03/1948	20:41
Lib	10/12/1947	14:31	Aqu	02/08/1948	04:58	Gem	06/06/1948	03:04
Sco	10/14/1947	18:45	Pis	02/10/1948	17:36	Can	06/08/1948	06:27
Sag	10/17/1947	01:53	Ari	02/13/1948	05:36	Leo	06/10/1948	08:10
Cap	10/19/1947	12:14	Tau	02/15/1948	16:07	Vir	06/12/1948	09:48
Aqu	10/22/1947	00:38	Gem	02/17/1948	23:54	Lib	06/14/1948	12:33
Pis	10/24/1947	12:44	Can	02/20/1948	04:07	Sco	06/16/1948	17:02
Ari	10/26/1947	22:29	Leo	02/22/1948	05:05	Sag	06/18/1948	23:28
Tau	10/29/1947	05:15	Vir	02/24/1948	04:21	Cap	06/21/1948	07:50

Aqu	06/23/1948	18:14	Gem	10/20/1948	17:13	Lib	02/15/1949	12:43
Pis	06/26/1948	06:22	Can	10/23/1948	00:20	Sco	02/17/1949	13:53
Ari	06/28/1948	18:55	Leo	10/25/1948	05:09	Sag	02/19/1949	17:49
Tau	07/01/1948	05:39	Vir	10/27/1948	07:52	Cap	02/22/1949	00:50
Gem	07/03/1948	12:45	Lib	10/29/1948	09:15	Aqu	02/24/1949	10:26
Can	07/05/1948	16:05	Sco	10/31/1948	10:31	Pis	02/26/1949	21:53
Leo	07/07/1948	16:52	Sag	11/02/1948	13:11	Ari	03/01/1949	10:35
Vir	07/09/1948	17:03	Cap	11/04/1948	18:39	Tau	03/03/1949	23:31
Lib	07/11/1948	18:30	Aqu	11/07/1948	03:41	Gem	03/06/1949	11:03
Sco	07/13/1948	22:28	Pis	11/09/1948	15:33	Can	03/08/1949	19:20
Sag	07/16/1948	05:10	Ari	11/12/1948	04:11	Leo	03/10/1949	23:31
Cap	07/18/1948	14:13	Tau	11/14/1948	15:23	Vir	03/13/1949	00:22
Aqu	07/21/1948	01:02	Gem	11/17/1948	00:00	Lib	03/14/1949	23:39
Pis	07/23/1948	13:12	Can	11/19/1948	06:10	Sco	03/16/1949	23:25
Ari	07/26/1948	01:56	Leo	11/21/1948	10:31	Sag	03/19/1949	01:31
Tau	07/28/1948	13:32	Vir	11/23/1948	13:47	Cap	03/21/1949	07:04
Gem	07/30/1948	21:59	Lib	11/25/1948	16:32	Aqu	03/23/1949	16:10
Can	08/02/1948	02:18	Sco	11/27/1948	19:18	Pis	03/26/1949	03:49
Leo	08/04/1948	03:12	Sag	11/29/1948	22:52	Ari	03/28/1949	16:40
Vir	08/06/1948	02:32	Cap	12/02/1948	04:16	Tau	03/31/1949	05:28
Lib	08/08/1948	02:29	Aqu	12/04/1948	12:32	Gem	04/02/1949	17:01
Sco	08/10/1948	04:56	Pis	12/06/1948	23:45	Can	04/05/1949	02:08
Sag	08/12/1948	10:49	Ari	12/09/1948	12:29	Leo	04/07/1949	07:58
Cap	08/14/1948	19:51	Tau	12/12/1948	00:07	Vir	04/09/1949	10:30
Aqu	08/17/1948	07:02	Gem	12/14/1948	08:42	Lib	04/11/1949	10:46
Pis	08/19/1948	19:22	Can	12/16/1948	13:59	Sco	04/13/1949	10:27
Ari	08/22/1948	08:04	Leo	12/18/1948	17:02	Sag	04/15/1949	11:24
Tau	08/24/1948	20:02	Vir	12/20/1948	19:18	Cap	04/17/1949	15:16
Gem	08/27/1948	05:39	Lib	12/22/1948	21:59	Aqu	04/19/1949	22:59
Can	08/29/1948	11:31	Sco	12/25/1948	01:38	Pis	04/22/1949	10:07
Leo	08/31/1948	13:39	Sag	12/27/1948	06:28	Ari	04/24/1949	23:00
Vir	09/02/1948	13:19	Cap	12/29/1948	12:46	Tau	04/27/1949	11:39
Lib	09/04/1948	12:35	Aqu	12/31/1948	21:07	Gem	04/29/1949	22:46
Sco	09/06/1948	13:34	Pis	01/03/1949	07:58	Can	05/02/1949	07:42
Sag	09/08/1948	17:51	Ari	01/05/1949	20:40	Leo	05/04/1949	14:10
Cap	09/11/1948	01:57	Tau	01/08/1949	09:01	Vir	05/06/1949	18:10
Aqu	09/13/1948	12:58	Gem	01/10/1949	18:30	Lib	05/08/1949	20:06
Pis	09/16/1948	01:26	Can	01/12/1949	23:54	Sco	05/10/1949	20:53
Ari	09/18/1948	14:01	Leo	01/15/1949	02:06	Sag	05/12/1949	21:57
Tau	09/21/1948	01:44	Vir	01/17/1949	02:51	Cap	05/15/1949	00:57
Gem	09/23/1948	11:38	Lib	01/19/1949	04:02	Aqu	05/17/1949	07:18
Can	09/25/1948	18:45	Sco	01/21/1949	06:59	Pis	05/19/1949	17:25
Leo	09/27/1948	22:33	Sag	01/23/1949	12:09	Ari	05/22/1949	06:01
Vir	09/29/1948	23:39	Cap	01/25/1949	19:21	Tau	05/24/1949	18:41
Lib	10/01/1948	23:29	Aqu	01/28/1949	04:26	Gem	05/27/1949	05:26
Sco	10/03/1948	23:58	Pis	01/30/1949	15:26	Can	05/29/1949	13:37
Sag	10/06/1948	02:55	Ari	02/02/1949	04:03	Leo	05/31/1949	19:35
Cap	10/08/1948	09:31	Tau	02/04/1949	16:56	Vir	06/02/1949	23:52
Aqu	10/10/1948	19:42	Gem	02/07/1949	03:39	Lib	06/05/1949	02:56
Pis	10/13/1948	08:02	Can	02/09/1949	10:20	Sco	06/07/1949	05:12
Ari	10/15/1948	20:35	Leo	02/11/1949	12:58	Sag	06/09/1949	07:23
Tau	10/18/1948	07:53	Vir	02/13/1949	13:04	Cap	06/11/1949	10:40

Aqu	06/13/1949	16:26	Gem	10/10/1949	20:01	Lib	02/06/1950	00:18
Pis	06/16/1949	01:38	Can	10/13/1949	06:50	Sco	02/08/1950	02:50
Ari	06/18/1949	13:44	Leo	10/15/1949	14:33	Sag	02/10/1950	05:50
Tau	06/21/1949	02:29	Vir	10/17/1949	18:41	Cap	02/12/1950	09:44
Gem	06/23/1949	13:18	Lib	10/19/1949	19:47	Aqu	02/14/1950	14:57
Can	06/25/1949	21:00	Sco	10/21/1949	19:18	Pis	02/16/1950	22:11
Leo	06/28/1949	01:59	Sag	10/23/1949	19:07	Ari	02/19/1950	08:00
Vir	06/30/1949	05:26	Cap	10/25/1949	21:11	Tau	02/21/1950	20:11
Lib	07/02/1949	08:21	Aqu	10/28/1949	02:51	Gem	02/24/1950	09:02
Sco	07/04/1949	11:21	Pis	10/30/1949	12:22	Can	02/26/1950	20:02
Sag	07/06/1949	14:45	Ari	11/02/1949	00:34	Leo	03/01/1950	03:29
Cap	07/08/1949	19:02	Tau	11/04/1949	13:36	Vir	03/03/1950	07:23
Aqu	07/11/1949	01:09	Gem	11/07/1949	01:54	Lib	03/05/1950	08:59
Pis	07/13/1949	10:01	Can	11/09/1949	12:34	Sco	03/07/1950	09:55
Ari	07/15/1949	21:42	Leo	11/11/1949	20:59	Sag	03/09/1950	11:38
Tau	07/18/1949	10:35	Vir	11/14/1949	02:41	Cap	03/11/1950	15:07
Gem	07/20/1949	21:55	Lib	11/16/1949	05:35	Aqu	03/13/1950	20:52
Can	07/23/1949	05:51	Sco	11/18/1949	06:18	Pis	03/16/1950	04:59
Leo	07/25/1949	10:17	Sag	11/20/1949	06:15	Ari	03/18/1950	15:21
Vir	07/27/1949	12:35	Cap	11/22/1949	07:19	Tau	03/21/1950	03:32
Lib	07/29/1949	14:19	Aqu	11/24/1949	11:25	Gem	03/23/1950	16:27
Sco	07/31/1949	16:43	Pis	11/26/1949	19:35	Can	03/26/1950	04:16
Sag	08/02/1949	20:25	Ari	11/29/1949	07:17	Leo	03/28/1950	13:02
Cap	08/05/1949	01:36	Tau	12/01/1949	20:21	Vir	03/30/1950	18:00
Aqu	08/07/1949	08:34	Gem	12/04/1949	08:27	Lib	04/01/1950	19:39
Pis	08/09/1949	17:45	Can	12/06/1949	18:30	Sco	04/03/1950	19:35
Ari	08/12/1949	05:19	Leo	12/09/1949	02:26	Sag	04/05/1950	19:37
Tau	08/14/1949	18:17	Vir	12/11/1949	08:30	Cap	04/07/1950	21:30
Gem	08/17/1949	06:22	Lib	12/13/1949	12:44	Aqu	04/10/1950	02:25
Can	08/19/1949	15:13	Sco	12/15/1949	15:12	Pis	04/12/1950	10:38
Leo	08/21/1949	20:06	Sag	12/17/1949	16:31	Ari	04/14/1950	21:31
Vir	08/23/1949	21:54	Cap	12/19/1949	17:59	Tau	04/17/1950	09:59
Lib	08/25/1949	22:23	Aqu	12/21/1949	21:25	Gem	04/19/1950	22:53
Sco	08/27/1949	23:19	Pis	12/24/1949	04:20	Can	04/22/1950	11:00
Sag	08/30/1949	02:01	Ari	12/26/1949	15:04	Leo	04/24/1950	20:56
Cap	09/01/1949	07:04	Tau	12/29/1949	03:57	Vir	04/27/1950	03:28
Aqu	09/03/1949	14:37	Gem	12/31/1949	16:12	Lib	04/29/1950	06:24
Pis	09/06/1949	00:26	Can	01/03/1950	01:55	Sco	05/01/1950	06:36
Ari	09/08/1949	12:13	Leo	01/05/1950	08:57	Sag	05/03/1950	05:50
Tau	09/11/1949	01:11	Vir	01/07/1950	14:05	Cap	05/05/1950	06:07
Gem	09/13/1949	13:45	Lib	01/09/1950	18:08	Aqu	05/07/1950	09:23
Can	09/15/1949	23:50	Sco	01/11/1950	21:27	Pis	05/09/1950	16:34
Leo	09/18/1949	06:04	Sag	01/14/1950	00:15	Ari	05/12/1950	03:18
Vir	09/20/1949	08:32	Cap	01/16/1950	03:06	Tau	05/14/1950	15:58
Lib	09/22/1949	08:41	Aqu	01/18/1950	07:07	Gem	05/17/1950	04:52
Sco	09/24/1949	08:20	Pis	01/20/1950	13:42	Can	05/19/1950	16:50
Sag	09/26/1949	09:21	Ari	01/22/1950	23:38	Leo	05/22/1950	03:05
Cap	09/28/1949	13:07	Tau	01/25/1950	12:07	Vir	05/24/1950	10:49
Aqu	09/30/1949	20:13	Gem	01/28/1950	00:42	Lib	05/26/1950	15:25
Pis	10/03/1949	06:19	Can	01/30/1950	10:48	Sco	05/28/1950	17:00
Ari	10/05/1949	18:27	Leo	02/01/1950	17:33	Sag	05/30/1950	16:43
Tau	10/08/1949	07:26	Vir	02/03/1950	21:35	Cap	06/01/1950	16:26

Aqu	06/03/1950	18:17	Gem	09/30/1950	17:26	Lib	01/27/1951	11:45
Pis	06/05/1950	23:58	Can	10/03/1950	05:59	Sco	01/29/1951	17:03
Ari	06/08/1950	09:44	Leo	10/05/1950	16:39	Sag	01/31/1951	20:15
Tau	06/10/1950	22:12	Vir	10/07/1950	23:52	Cap	02/02/1951	21:52
Gem	06/13/1950	11:04	Lib	10/10/1950	03:27	Aqu	02/04/1951	23:04
Can	06/15/1950	22:44	Sco	10/12/1950	04:30	Pis	02/07/1951	01:29
Leo	06/18/1950	08:36	Sag	10/14/1950	04:44	Ari	02/09/1951	06:43
Vir	06/20/1950	16:30	Cap	10/16/1950	05:54	Tau	02/11/1951	15:33
Lib	06/22/1950	22:08	Aqu	10/18/1950	09:27	Gem	02/14/1951	03:18
Sco	06/25/1950	01:17	Pis	10/20/1950	15:53	Can	02/16/1951	15:51
Sag	06/27/1950	02:25	Ari	10/23/1950	00:59	Leo	02/19/1951	03:00
Cap	06/29/1950	02:48	Tau	10/25/1950	12:03	Vir	02/21/1951	11:41
Aqu	07/01/1950	04:19	Gem	10/28/1950	00:22	Lib	02/23/1951	18:00
Pis	07/03/1950	08:52	Can	10/30/1950	13:02	Sco	02/25/1951	22:30
Ari	07/05/1950	17:24	Leo	11/02/1950	00:37	Sag	02/28/1951	01:49
Tau	07/08/1950	05:13	Vir	11/04/1950	09:19	Cap	03/02/1951	04:29
Gem	07/10/1950	18:01	Lib	11/06/1950	14:08	Aqu	03/04/1951	07:10
Can	07/13/1950	05:33	Sco	11/08/1950	15:27	Pis	03/06/1951	10:46
Leo	07/15/1950	14:51	Sag	11/10/1950	14:51	Ari	03/08/1951	16:16
Vir	07/17/1950	22:04	Cap	11/12/1950	14:26	Tau	03/11/1951	00:33
Lib	07/20/1950	03:33	Aqu	11/14/1950	16:14	Gem	03/13/1951	11:36
Sco	07/22/1950	07:26	Pis	11/16/1950	21:39	Can	03/16/1951	00:05
Sag	07/24/1950	09:54	Ari	11/19/1950	06:39	Leo	03/18/1951	11:43
Cap	07/26/1950	11:39	Tau	11/21/1950	18:07	Vir	03/20/1951	20:38
Aqu	07/28/1950	13:56	Gem	11/24/1950	06:38	Lib	03/23/1951	02:20
Pis	07/30/1950	18:18	Can	11/26/1950	19:12	Sco	03/25/1951	05:35
Ari	08/02/1950	02:03	Leo	11/29/1950	07:01	Sag	03/27/1951	07:40
Tau	08/04/1950	13:05	Vir	12/01/1950	16:53	Cap	03/29/1951	09:51
Gem	08/07/1950	01:43	Lib	12/03/1950	23:27	Aqu	03/31/1951	13:02
Can	08/09/1950	13:26	Sco	12/06/1950	02:18	Pis	04/02/1951	17:44
Leo	08/11/1950	22:35	Sag	12/08/1950	02:16	Ari	04/05/1951	00:16
Vir	08/14/1950	05:02	Cap	12/10/1950	01:16	Tau	04/07/1951	08:52
Lib	08/16/1950	09:30	Aqu	12/12/1950	01:35	Gem	04/09/1951	19:40
Sco	08/18/1950	12:48	Pis	12/14/1950	05:10	Can	04/12/1951	08:04
Sag	08/20/1950	15:35	Ari	12/16/1950	12:59	Leo	04/14/1951	20:17
Cap	08/22/1950	18:23	Tau	12/19/1950	00:09	Vir	04/17/1951	06:06
Aqu	08/24/1950	21:53	Gem	12/21/1950	12:49	Lib	04/19/1951	12:12
Pis	08/27/1950	03:02	Can	12/24/1950	01:17	Sco	04/21/1951	14:54
Ari	08/29/1950	10:45	Leo	12/26/1950	12:44	Sag	04/23/1951	15:39
Tau	08/31/1950	21:19	Vir	12/28/1950	22:40	Cap	04/25/1951	16:19
Gem	09/03/1950	09:45	Lib	12/31/1950	06:19	Aqu	04/27/1951	18:32
Can	09/05/1950	21:53	Sco	01/02/1951	10:56	Pis	04/29/1951	23:14
Leo	09/08/1950	07:33	Sag	01/04/1951	12:37	Ari	05/02/1951	06:26
Vir	09/10/1950	13:53	Cap	01/06/1951	12:31	Tau	05/04/1951	15:46
Lib	09/12/1950	17:27	Aqu	01/08/1951	12:36	Gem	05/07/1951	02:51
Sco	09/14/1950	19:26	Pis	01/10/1951	14:56	Can	05/09/1951	15:13
Sag	09/16/1950	21:12	Ari	01/12/1951	21:06	Leo	05/12/1951	03:49
Cap	09/18/1950	23:49	Tau	01/15/1951	07:10	Vir	05/14/1951	14:42
Aqu	09/21/1950	04:00	Gem	01/17/1951	19:35	Lib	05/16/1951	22:03
Pis	09/23/1950	10:09	Can	01/20/1951	08:05	Sco	05/19/1951	01:21
Ari	09/25/1950	18:31	Leo	01/22/1951	19:11	Sag	05/21/1951	01:43
Tau	09/28/1950	05:08	Vir	01/25/1951	04:25	Cap	05/23/1951	01:07

Aqu	05/25/1951	01:42	Gem	09/20/1951	12:47	Lib	01/17/1952	18:19
Pis	05/27/1951	05:05	Can	09/23/1951	00:34	Sco	01/20/1952	02:43
Ari	05/29/1951	11:54	Leo	09/25/1951	13:07	Sag	01/22/1952	07:21
Tau	05/31/1951	21:33	Vir	09/28/1951	00:04	Cap	01/24/1952	08:38
Gem	06/03/1951	09:02	Lib	09/30/1951	08:07	Aqu	01/26/1952	08:06
Can	06/05/1951	21:31	Sco	10/02/1951	13:22	Pis	01/28/1952	07:45
Leo	06/08/1951	10:11	Sag	10/04/1951	16:48	Ari	01/30/1952	09:33
Vir	06/10/1951	21:45	Cap	10/06/1951	19:30	Tau	02/01/1952	14:51
Lib	06/13/1951	06:30	Aqu	10/08/1951	22:19	Gem	02/03/1952	23:55
Sco	06/15/1951	11:15	Pis	10/11/1951	01:46	Can	02/06/1952	11:44
Sag	06/17/1951	12:25	Ari	10/13/1951	06:19	Leo	02/09/1952	00:36
Cap	06/19/1951	11:37	Tau	10/15/1951	12:37	Vir	02/11/1952	13:01
Aqu	06/21/1951	11:04	Gem	10/17/1951	21:22	Lib	02/13/1952	23:59
Pis	06/23/1951	12:50	Can	10/20/1951	08:42	Sco	02/16/1952	08:44
Ari	06/25/1951	18:13	Leo	10/22/1951	21:24	Sag	02/18/1952	14:41
Tau	06/28/1951	03:17	Vir	10/25/1951	09:00	Cap	02/20/1952	17:49
Gem	06/30/1951	14:51	Lib	10/27/1951	17:24	Aqu	02/22/1952	18:48
Can	07/03/1951	03:27	Sco	10/29/1951	22:08	Pis	02/24/1952	19:01
Leo	07/05/1951	16:00	Sag	11/01/1951	00:19	Ari	02/26/1952	20:12
Vir	07/08/1951	03:35	Cap	11/03/1951	01:40	Tau	02/29/1952	00:03
Lib	07/10/1951	13:03	Aqu	11/05/1951	03:43	Gem	03/02/1952	07:36
Sco	07/12/1951	19:18	Pis	11/07/1951	07:23	Can	03/04/1952	18:40
Sag	07/14/1951	22:01	Ari	11/09/1951	12:53	Leo	03/07/1952	07:30
Cap	07/16/1951	22:13	Tau	11/11/1951	20:07	Vir	03/09/1952	19:51
Aqu	07/18/1951	21:41	Gem	11/14/1951	05:15	Lib	03/12/1952	06:16
Pis	07/20/1951	22:29	Can	11/16/1951	16:27	Sco	03/14/1952	14:19
Ari	07/23/1951	02:22	Leo	11/19/1951	05:12	Sag	03/16/1952	20:14
Tau	07/25/1951	10:07	Vir	11/21/1951	17:35	Cap	03/19/1952	00:18
Gem	07/27/1951	21:07	Lib	11/24/1951	03:07	Aqu	03/21/1952	02:54
Can	07/30/1951	09:42	Sco	11/26/1951	08:30	Pis	03/23/1952	04:39
Leo	08/01/1951	22:07	Sag	11/28/1951	10:19	Ari	03/25/1952	06:34
Vir	08/04/1951	09:17	Cap	11/30/1951	10:22	Tau	03/27/1952	10:06
Lib	08/06/1951	18:34	Aqu	12/02/1951	10:45	Gem	03/29/1952	16:36
Sco	08/09/1951	01:22	Pis	12/04/1951	13:08	Can	04/01/1952	02:39
Sag	08/11/1951	05:30	Ari	12/06/1951	18:18	Leo	04/03/1952	15:09
Cap	08/13/1951	07:18	Tau	12/09/1951	02:04	Vir	04/06/1952	03:39
Aqu	08/15/1951	07:53	Gem	12/11/1951	11:54	Lib	04/08/1952	13:54
Pis	08/17/1951	08:53	Can	12/13/1951	23:22	Sco	04/10/1952	21:12
Ari	08/19/1951	11:59	Leo	12/16/1951	12:04	Sag	04/13/1952	02:07
Tau	08/21/1951	18:26	Vir	12/19/1951	00:51	Cap	04/15/1952	05:41
Gem	08/24/1951	04:27	Lib	12/21/1951	11:39	Aqu	04/17/1952	08:43
Can	08/26/1951	16:44	Sco	12/23/1951	18:38	Pis	04/19/1952	11:40
Leo	08/29/1951	05:09	Sag	12/25/1951	21:25	Ari	04/21/1952	14:56
Vir	08/31/1951	15:59	Cap	12/27/1951	21:23	Tau	04/23/1952	19:15
Lib	09/03/1951	00:31	Aqu	12/29/1951	20:36	Gem	04/26/1952	01:41
Sco	09/05/1951	06:48	Pis	12/31/1951	21:11	Can	04/28/1952	11:06
Sag	09/07/1951	11:10	Ari	01/03/1952	00:43	Leo	04/30/1952	23:12
Cap	09/09/1951	14:05	Tau	01/05/1952	07:43	Vir	05/03/1952	11:56
Aqu	09/11/1951	16:11	Gem	01/07/1952	17:42	Lib	05/05/1952	22:37
Pis	09/13/1951	18:21	Can	01/10/1952	05:34	Sco	05/08/1952	05:48
Ari	09/15/1951	21:48	Leo	01/12/1952	18:19	Sag	05/10/1952	09:49
Tau	09/18/1951	03:42	Vir	01/15/1952	07:00	Cap	05/12/1952	12:08

Aqu	05/14/1952	14:14	Gem	09/09/1952	11:07	Lib	01/06/1953	17:36
Pis	05/16/1952	17:05	Can	09/11/1952	20:24	Sco	01/09/1953	04:43
Ari	05/18/1952	21:07	Leo	09/14/1952	08:38	Sag	01/11/1953	12:12
Tau	05/21/1952	02:29	Vir	09/16/1952	21:41	Cap	01/13/1953	15:54
Gem	05/23/1952	09:37	Lib	09/19/1952	09:41	Aqu	01/15/1953	16:57
Can	05/25/1952	19:06	Sco	09/21/1952	19:43	Pis	01/17/1953	17:07
Leo	05/28/1952	06:59	Sag	09/24/1952	03:32	Ari	01/19/1953	18:08
Vir	05/30/1952	19:57	Cap	09/26/1952	09:05	Tau	01/21/1953	21:21
Lib	06/02/1952	07:25	Aqu	09/28/1952	12:23	Gem	01/24/1953	03:21
Sco	06/04/1952	15:18	Pis	09/30/1952	13:52	Can	01/26/1953	12:07
Sag	06/06/1952	19:20	Ari	10/02/1952	14:34	Leo	01/28/1953	23:06
Cap	06/08/1952	20:46	Tau	10/04/1952	16:06	Vir	01/31/1953	11:35
Aqu	06/10/1952	21:27	Gem	10/06/1952	20:15	Lib	02/03/1953	00:31
Pis	06/12/1952	23:01	Can	10/09/1952	04:16	Sco	02/05/1953	12:20
Ari	06/15/1952	02:29	Leo	10/11/1952	15:50	Sag	02/07/1953	21:19
Tau	06/17/1952	08:11	Vir	10/14/1952	04:50	Cap	02/10/1953	02:31
Gem	06/19/1952	16:03	Lib	10/16/1952	16:44	Aqu	02/12/1953	04:16
Can	06/22/1952	02:04	Sco	10/19/1952	02:09	Pis	02/14/1953	03:58
Leo	06/24/1952	14:02	Sag	10/21/1952	09:11	Ari	02/16/1953	03:31
Vir	06/27/1952	03:06	Cap	10/23/1952	14:28	Tau	02/18/1953	04:51
Lib	06/29/1952	15:17	Aqu	10/25/1952	18:28	Gem	02/20/1953	09:28
Sco	07/02/1952	00:24	Pis	10/27/1952	21:22	Can	02/22/1953	17:48
Sag	07/04/1952	05:26	Ari	10/29/1952	23:34	Leo	02/25/1953	05:05
Cap	07/06/1952	07:02	Tau	11/01/1952	01:59	Vir	02/27/1953	17:51
Aqu	07/08/1952	06:54	Gem	11/03/1952	06:02	Lib	03/02/1953	06:41
Pis	07/10/1952	06:59	Can	11/05/1952	13:13	Sco	03/04/1953	18:31
Ari	07/12/1952	08:57	Leo	11/07/1952	23:57	Sag	03/07/1953	04:19
Tau	07/14/1952	13:46	Vir	11/10/1952	12:46	Cap	03/09/1953	11:09
Gem	07/16/1952	21:38	Lib	11/13/1952	00:56	Aqu	03/11/1953	14:36
Can	07/19/1952	08:05	Sco	11/15/1952	10:17	Pis	03/13/1953	15:16
Leo	07/21/1952	20:20	Sag	11/17/1952	16:32	Ari	03/15/1953	14:39
Vir	07/24/1952	09:24	Cap	11/19/1952	20:40	Tau	03/17/1953	14:45
Lib	07/26/1952	21:53	Aqu	11/21/1952	23:51	Gem	03/19/1953	17:35
Sco	07/29/1952	08:03	Pis	11/24/1952	02:55	Can	03/22/1953	00:30
Sag	07/31/1952	14:36	Ari	11/26/1952	06:09	Leo	03/24/1953	11:15
Cap	08/02/1952	17:27	Tau	11/28/1952	09:54	Vir	03/27/1953	00:04
Aqu	08/04/1952	17:41	Gem	11/30/1952	14:53	Lib	03/29/1953	12:51
Pis	08/06/1952	17:05	Can	12/02/1952	22:09	Sco	04/01/1953	00:19
Ari	08/08/1952	17:33	Leo	12/05/1952	08:23	Sag	04/03/1953	09:58
Tau	08/10/1952	20:46	Vir	12/07/1952	20:57	Cap	04/05/1953	17:29
Gem	08/13/1952	03:37	Lib	12/10/1952	09:34	Aqu	04/07/1953	22:26
Can	08/15/1952	13:53	Sco	12/12/1952	19:38	Pis	04/10/1953	00:48
Leo	08/18/1952	02:19	Sag	12/15/1952	01:58	Ari	04/12/1953	01:19
Vir	08/20/1952	15:22	Cap	12/17/1952	05:17	Tau	04/14/1953	01:32
Lib	08/23/1952	03:41	Aqu	12/19/1952	07:02	Gem	04/16/1953	03:28
Sco	08/25/1952	14:09	Pis	12/21/1952	08:46	Can	04/18/1953	08:54
Sag	08/27/1952	21:52	Ari	12/23/1952	11:30	Leo	04/20/1953	18:27
Cap	08/30/1952	02:22	Tau	12/25/1952	15:46	Vir	04/23/1953	06:53
Aqu	09/01/1952	04:02	Gem	12/27/1952	21:48	Lib	04/25/1953	19:40
Pis	09/03/1952	04:00	Can	12/30/1952	05:53	Sco	04/28/1953	06:51
Ari	09/05/1952	03:57	Leo	01/01/1953	16:17	Sag	04/30/1953	15:52
Tau	09/07/1952	05:48	Vir	01/04/1953	04:41	Cap	05/02/1953	22:54

Aqu	05/05/1953	04:12	Gem	08/30/1953	16:07	Lib	12/27/1953	12:11
Pis	05/07/1953	07:46	Can	09/01/1953	22:31	Sco	12/30/1953	00:42
Ari	05/09/1953	09:49	Leo	09/04/1953	08:05	Sag	01/01/1954	11:38
Tau	05/11/1953	11:12	Vir	09/06/1953	19:47	Cap	01/03/1954	19:45
Gem	05/13/1953	13:28	Lib	09/09/1953	08:27	Aqu	01/06/1954	01:08
Can	05/15/1953	18:16	Sco	09/11/1953	21:05	Pis	01/08/1954	04:43
Leo	05/18/1953	02:48	Sag	09/14/1953	08:31	Ari	01/10/1954	07:27
Vir	05/20/1953	14:31	Cap	09/16/1953	17:20	Tau	01/12/1954	10:10
Lib	05/23/1953	03:16	Aqu	09/18/1953	22:28	Gem	01/14/1954	13:30
Sco	05/25/1953	14:31	Pis	09/21/1953	00:05	Can	01/16/1954	18:01
Sag	05/27/1953	23:07	Ari	09/22/1953	23:30	Leo	01/19/1954	00:25
Cap	05/30/1953	05:17	Tau	09/24/1953	22:46	Vir	01/21/1954	09:14
Aqu	06/01/1953	09:45	Gem	09/27/1953	00:02	Lib	01/23/1954	20:30
Pis	06/03/1953	13:12	Can	09/29/1953	04:57	Sco	01/26/1954	09:03
Ari	06/05/1953	16:01	Leo	10/01/1953	13:54	Sag	01/28/1954	20:42
Tau	06/07/1953	18:41	Vir	10/04/1953	01:41	Cap	01/31/1954	05:26
Gem	06/09/1953	22:03	Lib	10/06/1953	14:28	Aqu	02/02/1954	10:37
Can	06/12/1953	03:18	Sco	10/09/1953	02:56	Pis	02/04/1954	13:03
Leo	06/14/1953	11:28	Sag	10/11/1953	14:19	Ari	02/06/1954	14:14
Vir	06/16/1953	22:37	Cap	10/13/1953	23:50	Tau	02/08/1954	15:47
Lib	06/19/1953	11:16	Aqu	10/16/1953	06:34	Gem	02/10/1954	18:54
Sco	06/21/1953	22:57	Pis	10/18/1953	09:54	Can	02/13/1954	00:11
Sag	06/24/1953	07:47	Ari	10/20/1953	10:26	Leo	02/15/1954	07:36
Cap	06/26/1953	13:28	Tau	10/22/1953	09:47	Vir	02/17/1954	17:00
Aqu	06/28/1953	16:51	Gem	10/24/1953	10:05	Lib	02/20/1954	04:14
Pis	06/30/1953	19:08	Can	10/26/1953	13:25	Sco	02/22/1954	16:43
Ari	07/02/1953	21:24	Leo	10/28/1953	20:56	Sag	02/25/1954	05:00
Tau	07/05/1953	00:24	Vir	10/31/1953	08:04	Cap	02/27/1954	14:57
Gem	07/07/1953	04:42	Lib	11/02/1953	20:51	Aqu	03/01/1954	21:06
Can	07/09/1953	10:55	Sco	11/05/1953	09:11	Pis	03/03/1954	23:31
Leo	07/11/1953	19:28	Sag	11/07/1953	20:06	Ari	03/05/1954	23:40
Vir	07/14/1953	06:28	Cap	11/10/1953	05:18	Tau	03/07/1954	23:33
Lib	07/16/1953	19:04	Aqu	11/12/1953	12:30	Gem	03/10/1954	01:07
Sco	07/19/1953	07:17	Pis	11/14/1953	17:17	Can	03/12/1954	05:38
Sag	07/21/1953	16:59	Ari	11/16/1953	19:35	Leo	03/14/1954	13:18
Cap	07/23/1953	23:05	Tau	11/18/1953	20:15	Vir	03/16/1954	23:22
Aqu	07/26/1953	02:02	Gem	11/20/1953	20:55	Lib	03/19/1954	10:58
Pis	07/28/1953	03:07	Can	11/22/1953	23:33	Sco	03/21/1954	23:26
Ari	07/30/1953	03:56	Leo	11/25/1953	05:40	Sag	03/24/1954	11:56
Tau	08/01/1953	05:57	Vir	11/27/1953	15:41	Cap	03/26/1954	22:54
Gem	08/03/1953	10:11	Lib	11/30/1953	04:06	Aqu	03/29/1954	06:37
Can	08/05/1953	17:00	Sco	12/02/1953	16:30	Pis	03/31/1954	10:15
Leo	08/08/1953	02:16	Sag	12/05/1953	03:08	Ari	04/02/1954	10:39
Vir	08/10/1953	13:34	Cap	12/07/1953	11:32	Tau	04/04/1954	09:43
Lib	08/13/1953	02:08	Aqu	12/09/1953	17:59	Gem	04/06/1954	09:41
Sco	08/15/1953	14:43	Pis	12/11/1953	22:46	Can	04/08/1954	12:30
Sag	08/18/1953	01:29	Ari	12/14/1953	02:06	Leo	04/10/1954	19:06
Cap	08/20/1953	08:52	Tau	12/16/1953	04:22	Vir	04/13/1954	05:03
Aqu	08/22/1953	12:27	Gem	12/18/1953	06:27	Lib	04/15/1954	16:58
Pis	08/24/1953	13:11	Can	12/20/1953	09:41	Sco	04/18/1954	05:32
Ari	08/26/1953	12:46	Leo	12/22/1953	15:23	Sag	04/20/1954	17:55
Tau	08/28/1953	13:11	Vir	12/25/1953	00:25	Cap	04/23/1954	05:11

Aqu	04/25/1954	14:01	Gem	08/21/1954	03:56	Lib	12/17/1954	07:52
Pis	04/27/1954	19:21	Can	08/23/1954	07:50	Sco	12/19/1954	19:43
Ari	04/29/1954	21:08	Leo	08/25/1954	13:23	Sag	12/22/1954	08:35
Tau	05/01/1954	20:42	Vir	08/27/1954	20:44	Cap	12/24/1954	20:40
Gem	05/03/1954	20:07	Lib	08/30/1954	06:12	Aqu	12/27/1954	07:00
Can	05/05/1954	21:31	Sco	09/01/1954	17:49	Pis	12/29/1954	15:09
Leo	05/08/1954	02:30	Sag	09/04/1954	06:32	Ari	12/31/1954	20:55
Vir	05/10/1954	11:23	Cap	09/06/1954	18:10	Tau	01/03/1955	00:23
Lib	05/12/1954	23:04	Aqu	09/09/1954	02:30	Gem	01/05/1955	02:04
Sco	05/15/1954	11:42	Pis	09/11/1954	06:54	Can	01/07/1955	03:00
Sag	05/17/1954	23:53	Ari	09/13/1954	08:22	Leo	01/09/1955	04:41
Cap	05/20/1954	10:48	Tau	09/15/1954	08:44	Vir	01/11/1955	08:43
Aqu	05/22/1954	19:48	Gem	09/17/1954	09:55	Lib	01/13/1955	16:15
Pis	05/25/1954	02:07	Can	09/19/1954	13:14	Sco	01/16/1955	03:15
Ari	05/27/1954	05:32	Leo	09/21/1954	19:04	Sag	01/18/1955	16:01
Tau	05/29/1954	06:33	Vir	09/24/1954	03:11	Cap	01/21/1955	04:09
Gem	05/31/1954	06:41	Lib	09/26/1954	13:11	Aqu	01/23/1955	13:58
Can	06/02/1954	07:46	Sco	09/29/1954	00:52	Pis	01/25/1955	21:10
Leo	06/04/1954	11:36	Sag	10/01/1954	13:41	Ari	01/28/1955	02:19
Vir	06/06/1954	19:06	Cap	10/04/1954	02:03	Tau	01/30/1954	06:06
Lib	06/09/1954	05:59	Aqu	10/06/1954	11:44	Gem	02/01/1955	09:02
Sco	06/11/1954	18:30	Pis	10/08/1954	17:16	Can	02/03/1955	11:36
Sag	06/14/1954	06:37	Ari	10/10/1954	18:58	Leo	02/05/1955	14:29
Cap	06/16/1954	17:05	Tau	10/12/1954	18:32	Vir	02/07/1955	18:43
Aqu	06/19/1954	01:25	Gem	10/14/1954	18:10	Lib	02/10/1955	01:34
Pis	06/21/1954	07:36	Can	10/16/1954	19:50	Sco	02/12/1955	11:39
Ari	06/23/1954	11:43	Leo	10/19/1954	00:42	Sag	02/15/1955	00:07
Tau	06/25/1954	14:09	Vir	10/21/1954	08:45	Cap	02/17/1955	12:34
Gem	06/27/1954	15:42	Lib	10/23/1954	19:12	Aqu	02/19/1955	22:32
Can	06/29/1954	17:35	Sco	10/26/1954	07:11	Pis	02/22/1955	05:09
Leo	07/01/1954	21:17	Sag	10/28/1954	19:58	Ari	02/24/1955	09:06
Vir	07/04/1954	03:57	Cap	10/31/1954	08:35	Tau	02/26/1955	11:46
Lib	07/06/1954	13:54	Aqu	11/02/1954	19:21	Gem	02/28/1955	14:24
Sco	07/09/1954	02:04	Pis	11/05/1954	02:33	Can	03/02/1955	17:40
Sag	07/11/1954	14:18	Ari	11/07/1954	05:42	Leo	03/04/1955	21:49
Cap	07/14/1954	00:39	Tau	11/09/1954	05:48	Vir	03/07/1955	03:09
Aqu	07/16/1954	08:19	Gem	11/11/1954	04:51	Lib	03/09/1955	10:21
Pis	07/18/1954	13:32	Can	11/13/1954	04:59	Sco	03/11/1955	20:05
Ari	07/20/1954	17:07	Leo	11/15/1954	08:03	Sag	03/14/1955	08:13
Tau	07/22/1954	19:52	Vir	11/17/1954	14:53	Cap	03/16/1955	21:01
Gem	07/24/1954	22:30	Lib	11/20/1954	01:03	Aqu	03/19/1955	07:46
Can	07/27/1954	01:41	Sco	11/22/1954	13:13	Pis	03/21/1955	14:44
Leo	07/29/1954	06:10	Sag	11/25/1954	02:01	Ari	03/23/1955	18:09
Vir	07/31/1954	12:51	Cap	11/27/1954	14:23	Tau	03/25/1955	19:31
Lib	08/02/1954	22:15	Aqu	11/30/1954	01:18	Gem	03/27/1955	20:42
Sco	08/05/1954	10:03	Pis	12/02/1954	09:37	Can	03/29/1955	23:06
Sag	08/07/1954	22:32	Ari	12/04/1954	14:34	Leo	04/01/1955	03:21
Cap	08/10/1954	09:19	Tau	12/06/1954	16:22	Vir	04/03/1955	09:31
Aqu	08/12/1954	16:54	Gem	12/08/1954	16:16	Lib	04/05/1955	17:34
Pis	08/14/1954	21:16	Can	12/10/1954	16:06	Sco	04/08/1955	03:38
Ari	08/16/1954	23:37	Leo	12/12/1954	17:48	Sag	04/10/1955	15:42
Tau	08/19/1954	01:26	Vir	12/14/1954	22:55	Cap	04/13/1955	04:40

Aqu	04/15/1955	16:19	Gem	08/11/1955	18:33	Lib	12/07/1955	09:49
Pis	04/18/1955	00:27	Can	08/13/1955	20:50	Sco	12/09/1955	19:00
Ari	04/20/1955	04:29	Leo	08/15/1955	22:34	Sag	12/12/1955	06:34
Tau	04/22/1955	05:29	Vir	08/18/1955	00:58	Cap	12/14/1955	19:23
Gem	04/24/1955	05:24	Lib	08/20/1955	05:34	Aqu	12/17/1955	08:19
Can	04/26/1955	06:09	Sco	08/22/1955	13:38	Pis	12/19/1955	20:01
Leo	04/28/1955	09:09	Sag	08/25/1955	01:04	Ari	12/22/1955	05:05
Vir	04/30/1955	14:58	Cap	08/27/1955	13:56	Tau	12/24/1955	10:32
Lib	05/02/1955	23:26	Aqu	08/30/1955	01:34	Gem	12/26/1955	12:32
Sco	05/05/1955	10:04	Pis	09/01/1955	10:22	Can	12/28/1955	12:17
Sag	05/07/1955	22:19	Ari	09/03/1955	16:23	Leo	12/30/1955	11:37
Cap	05/10/1955	11:18	Tau	09/05/1955	20:36	Vir	01/01/1956	12:32
Aqu	05/12/1955	23:28	Gem	09/07/1955	23:58	Lib	01/03/1956	16:44
Pis	05/15/1955	08:52	Can	09/10/1955	03:01	Sco	01/06/1956	01:01
Ari	05/17/1955	14:19	Leo	09/12/1955	06:02	Sag	01/08/1956	12:33
Tau	05/19/1955	16:11	Vir	09/14/1955	09:33	Cap	01/11/1956	01:34
Gem	05/21/1955	15:56	Lib	09/16/1955	14:36	Aqu	01/13/1956	14:19
Can	05/23/1955	15:33	Sco	09/18/1955	22:20	Pis	01/16/1956	01:47
Leo	05/25/1955	16:53	Sag	09/21/1955	09:12	Ari	01/18/1956	11:16
Vir	05/27/1955	21:17	Cap	09/23/1955	22:01	Tau	01/20/1956	18:11
Lib	05/30/1955	05:08	Aqu	09/26/1955	10:06	Gem	01/22/1956	22:05
Sco	06/01/1955	15:54	Pis	09/28/1955	19:12	Can	01/24/1956	23:19
Sag	06/04/1955	04:24	Ari	10/01/1955	00:45	Leo	01/26/1956	23:06
Cap	06/06/1955	17:21	Tau	10/03/1955	03:51	Vir	01/28/1956	23:18
Aqu	06/09/1955	05:30	Gem	10/05/1955	05:59	Lib	01/31/1956	01:57
Pis	06/11/1955	15:31	Can	10/07/1955	08:23	Sco	02/02/1956	08:34
Ari	06/13/1955	22:23	Leo	10/09/1955	11:42	Sag	02/04/1956	19:13
Tau	06/16/1955	01:49	Vir	10/11/1955	16:11	Cap	02/07/1956	08:08
Gem	06/18/1955	02:36	Lib	10/13/1955	22:14	Aqu	02/09/1956	20:52
Can	06/20/1955	02:15	Sco	10/16/1955	06:23	Pis	02/12/1956	07:52
Leo	06/22/1955	02:37	Sag	10/18/1955	17:08	Ari	02/14/1956	16:48
Vir	06/24/1955	05:26	Cap	10/21/1955	05:51	Tau	02/16/1956	23:48
Lib	06/26/1955	11:56	Aqu	10/23/1955	18:32	Gem	02/19/1956	04:50
Sco	06/28/1955	22:05	Pis	10/26/1955	04:37	Can	02/21/1956	07:49
Sag	07/01/1955	10:34	Ari	10/28/1955	10:45	Leo	02/23/1956	09:10
Cap	07/03/1955	23:29	Tau	10/30/1955	13:29	Vir	02/25/1956	10:05
Aqu	07/06/1955	11:17	Gem	11/01/1955	14:23	Lib	02/27/1956	12:22
Pis	07/08/1955	21:08	Can	11/03/1955	15:11	Sco	02/29/1956	17:45
Ari	07/11/1955	04:33	Leo	11/05/1955	17:20	Sag	03/03/1956	03:10
Tau	07/13/1955	09:19	Vir	11/07/1955	21:37	Cap	03/05/1956	15:33
Gem	07/15/1955	11:42	Lib	11/10/1955	04:15	Aqu	03/08/1956	04:19
Can	07/17/1955	12:30	Sco	11/12/1955	13:13	Pis	03/10/1956	15:11
Leo	07/19/1955	13:04	Sag	11/15/1955	00:17	Ari	03/12/1956	23:25
Vir	07/21/1955	15:07	Cap	11/17/1955	12:59	Tau	03/15/1956	05:32
Lib	07/23/1955	20:17	Aqu	11/20/1955	01:58	Gem	03/17/1956	10:11
Sco	07/26/1955	05:19	Pis	11/22/1955	13:09	Can	03/19/1956	13:47
Sag	07/28/1955	17:24	Ari	11/24/1955	20:46	Leo	03/21/1956	16:31
Cap	07/31/1955	06:19	Tau	11/27/1955	00:26	Vir	03/23/1956	18:53
Aqu	08/02/1955	17:52	Gem	11/29/1955	01:11	Lib	03/25/1956	22:01
Pis	08/05/1955	03:03	Can	12/01/1955	00:47	Sco	03/28/1956	03:19
Ari	08/07/1955	09:59	Leo	12/03/1955	01:08	Sag	03/30/1956	11:57
Tau	08/09/1955	15:02	Vir	12/05/1955	03:50	Cap	04/01/1956	23:38

Aqu	04/04/1956	12:24		Gem	08/01/1956	06:16		Lib	11/26/1956	19:11
Pis	04/06/1956	23:36		Can	08/03/1956	08:31		Sco	11/29/1956	00:35
Ari	04/09/1956	07:46		Leo	08/05/1956	08:26		Sag	12/01/1956	07:59
Tau	04/11/1956	13:02		Vir	08/07/1956	07:50		Cap	12/03/1956	17:36
Gem	04/13/1956	16:30		Lib	08/09/1956	08:51		Aqu	12/06/1956	05:16
Can	04/15/1956	19:15		Sco	08/11/1956	13:22		Pis	12/08/1956	17:57
Leo	04/17/1956	22:00		Sag	08/13/1956	22:01		Ari	12/11/1956	05:37
Vir	04/20/1956	01:17		Cap	08/16/1956	09:48		Tau	12/13/1956	14:14
Lib	04/22/1956	05:36		Aqu	08/18/1956	22:37		Gem	12/15/1956	19:06
Sco	04/24/1956	11:45		Pis	08/21/1956	10:47		Can	12/17/1956	20:51
Sag	04/26/1956	20:26		Ari	08/23/1956	21:29		Leo	12/19/1956	21:11
Cap	04/29/1956	07:44		Tau	08/26/1956	06:23		Vir	12/21/1956	21:56
Aqu	05/01/1956	20:27		Gem	08/28/1956	12:58		Lib	12/24/1956	00:40
Pis	05/04/1956	08:15		Can	08/30/1956	16:51		Sco	12/26/1956	06:09
Ari	05/06/1956	17:05		Leo	09/01/1956	18:14		Sag	12/28/1956	14:20
Tau	05/08/1956	22:23		Vir	09/03/1956	18:20		Cap	12/31/1956	00:37
Gem	05/11/1956	01:00		Lib	09/05/1956	19:04		Aqu	01/02/1957	12:25
Can	05/13/1956	02:21		Sco	09/07/1956	22:28		Pis	01/05/1957	01:04
Leo	05/15/1956	03:52		Sag	09/10/1956	05:46		Ari	01/07/1957	13:22
Vir	05/17/1956	06:40		Cap	09/12/1956	16:46		Tau	01/09/1957	23:25
Lib	05/19/1956	11:26		Aqu	09/15/1956	05:28		Gem	01/12/1957	05:44
Sco	05/21/1956	18:27		Pis	09/17/1956	17:33		Can	01/14/1957	08:05
Sag	05/24/1956	03:47		Ari	09/20/1956	03:47		Leo	01/16/1957	07:50
Cap	05/26/1956	15:11		Tau	09/22/1956	12:00		Vir	01/18/1957	07:04
Aqu	05/29/1956	03:52		Gem	09/24/1956	18:25		Lib	01/20/1957	07:56
Pis	05/31/1956	16:09		Can	09/26/1956	22:59		Sco	01/22/1957	12:04
Ari	06/03/1956	02:03		Leo	09/29/1956	01:48		Sag	01/24/1957	19:52
Tau	06/05/1956	08:21		Vir	10/01/1956	03:24		Cap	01/27/1957	06:32
Gem	06/07/1956	11:08		Lib	10/03/1956	05:01		Aqu	01/29/1957	18:42
Can	06/09/1956	11:42		Sco	10/05/1956	08:19		Pis	02/01/1957	07:20
Leo	06/11/1956	11:45		Sag	10/07/1956	14:47		Ari	02/03/1957	19:42
Vir	06/13/1956	13:04		Cap	10/10/1956	00:49		Tau	02/06/1957	06:37
Lib	06/15/1956	16:59		Aqu	10/12/1956	13:09		Gem	02/08/1957	14:33
Sco	06/18/1956	00:04		Pis	10/15/1956	01:24		Can	02/10/1957	18:38
Sag	06/20/1956	09:56		Ari	10/17/1956	11:34		Leo	02/12/1957	19:18
Cap	06/22/1956	21:43		Tau	10/19/1956	19:07		Vir	02/14/1957	18:16
Aqu	06/25/1956	10:25		Gem	10/22/1956	00:28		Lib	02/16/1957	17:49
Pis	06/27/1956	22:54		Can	10/24/1956	04:23		Sco	02/18/1957	20:07
Ari	06/30/1956	09:42		Leo	10/26/1956	07:27		Sag	02/21/1957	02:24
Tau	07/02/1956	17:25		Vir	10/28/1956	10:09		Cap	02/23/1957	12:27
Gem	07/04/1956	21:25		Lib	10/30/1956	13:10		Aqu	02/26/1957	00:43
Can	07/06/1956	22:19		Sco	11/01/1956	17:24		Pis	02/28/1957	13:25
Leo	07/08/1956	21:42		Sag	11/03/1956	23:57		Ari	03/03/1957	01:30
Vir	07/10/1956	21:35		Cap	11/06/1956	09:25		Tau	03/05/1957	12:20
Lib	07/12/1956	23:55		Aqu	11/08/1956	21:19		Gem	03/07/1957	21:02
Sco	07/15/1956	05:56		Pis	11/11/1956	09:50		Can	03/10/1957	02:44
Sag	07/17/1956	15:38		Ari	11/13/1956	20:35		Leo	03/12/1957	05:11
Cap	07/20/1956	03:41		Tau	11/16/1956	04:12		Vir	03/14/1957	05:19
Aqu	07/22/1956	16:28		Gem	11/18/1956	08:44		Lib	03/16/1957	04:59
Pis	07/25/1956	04:50		Can	11/20/1956	11:17		Sco	03/18/1957	06:14
Ari	07/27/1956	15:53		Leo	11/22/1956	13:10		Sag	03/20/1957	10:55
Tau	07/30/1956	00:39		Vir	11/24/1956	15:32		Cap	03/22/1957	19:34

Aqu	03/25/1957	07:17	Gem	07/22/1957	11:32	Lib	11/17/1957	08:25
Pis	03/27/1957	19:59	Can	07/24/1957	16:04	Sco	11/19/1957	10:17
Ari	03/30/1957	07:54	Leo	07/26/1957	17:16	Sag	11/21/1957	12:52
Tau	04/01/1957	18:11	Vir	07/28/1957	16:59	Cap	11/23/1957	17:29
Gem	04/04/1957	02:29	Lib	07/30/1957	17:20	Aqu	11/26/1957	01:17
Can	04/06/1957	08:37	Sco	08/01/1957	20:01	Pis	11/28/1957	12:16
Leo	04/08/1957	12:23	Sag	08/04/1957	01:48	Ari	12/01/1957	00:56
Vir	04/10/1957	14:12	Cap	08/06/1957	10:24	Tau	12/03/1957	12:47
Lib	04/12/1957	15:08	Aqu	08/08/1957	21:02	Gem	12/05/1957	21:59
Sco	04/14/1957	16:45	Pis	08/11/1957	09:02	Can	12/08/1957	04:15
Sag	04/16/1957	20:44	Ari	08/13/1957	21:46	Leo	12/10/1957	08:23
Cap	04/19/1957	04:08	Tau	08/16/1957	10:00	Vir	12/12/1957	11:28
Aqu	04/21/1957	14:54	Gem	08/18/1957	19:50	Lib	12/14/1957	14:22
Pis	04/24/1957	03:23	Can	08/21/1957	01:47	Sco	12/16/1957	17:35
Ari	04/26/1957	15:21	Leo	08/23/1957	03:50	Sag	12/18/1957	21:31
Tau	04/29/1957	01:17	Vir	08/25/1957	03:25	Cap	12/21/1957	02:47
Gem	05/01/1957	08:46	Lib	08/27/1957	02:42	Aqu	12/23/1957	10:19
Can	05/03/1957	14:07	Sco	08/29/1957	03:46	Pis	12/25/1957	20:41
Leo	05/05/1957	17:53	Sag	08/31/1957	08:08	Ari	12/28/1957	09:12
Vir	05/07/1957	20:36	Cap	09/02/1957	16:06	Tau	12/30/1957	21:36
Lib	05/09/1957	22:57	Aqu	09/05/1957	02:50	Gem	01/02/1958	07:21
Sco	05/12/1957	01:49	Pis	09/07/1957	15:04	Can	01/04/1958	13:20
Sag	05/14/1957	06:13	Ari	09/10/1957	03:44	Leo	01/06/1958	16:21
Cap	05/16/1957	13:14	Tau	09/12/1957	15:57	Vir	01/08/1958	17:59
Aqu	05/18/1957	23:12	Gem	09/15/1957	02:25	Lib	01/10/1958	19:52
Pis	05/21/1957	11:20	Can	09/17/1957	09:48	Sco	01/12/1958	23:02
Ari	05/23/1957	23:33	Leo	09/19/1957	13:29	Sag	01/15/1958	03:49
Tau	05/26/1957	09:42	Vir	09/21/1957	14:10	Cap	01/17/1958	10:13
Gem	05/28/1957	16:46	Lib	09/23/1957	13:33	Aqu	01/19/1958	18:22
Can	05/30/1957	21:05	Sco	09/25/1957	13:41	Pis	01/22/1958	04:42
Leo	06/01/1957	23:45	Sag	09/27/1957	16:27	Ari	01/24/1958	17:03
Vir	06/04/1957	01:59	Cap	09/29/1957	23:00	Tau	01/27/1958	05:56
Lib	06/06/1957	04:45	Aqu	10/02/1957	09:04	Gem	01/29/1958	16:47
Sco	06/08/1957	08:41	Pis	10/04/1957	21:17	Can	01/31/1958	23:39
Sag	06/10/1957	14:10	Ari	10/07/1957	09:56	Leo	02/03/1958	02:36
Cap	06/12/1957	21:37	Tau	10/09/1957	21:47	Vir	02/05/1958	03:10
Aqu	06/15/1957	07:23	Gem	10/12/1957	08:00	Lib	02/07/1958	03:23
Pis	06/17/1957	19:15	Can	10/14/1957	15:53	Sco	02/09/1958	05:03
Ari	06/20/1957	07:45	Leo	10/16/1957	20:58	Sag	02/11/1958	09:12
Tau	06/22/1957	18:38	Vir	10/18/1957	23:22	Cap	02/13/1958	15:55
Gem	06/25/1957	02:05	Lib	10/21/1957	00:03	Aqu	02/16/1958	00:51
Can	06/27/1957	06:00	Sco	10/23/1957	00:31	Pis	02/18/1958	11:39
Leo	06/29/1957	07:31	Sag	10/25/1957	02:34	Ari	02/21/1958	00:02
Vir	07/01/1957	08:23	Cap	10/27/1957	07:41	Tau	02/23/1958	13:04
Lib	07/03/1957	10:16	Aqu	10/29/1957	16:32	Gem	02/26/1958	00:51
Sco	07/05/1957	14:10	Pis	11/01/1957	04:18	Can	02/28/1958	09:15
Sag	07/07/1957	20:20	Ari	11/03/1957	16:59	Leo	03/02/1958	13:25
Cap	07/10/1957	04:35	Tau	11/06/1957	04:37	Vir	03/04/1958	14:14
Aqu	07/12/1957	14:43	Gem	11/08/1957	14:08	Lib	03/06/1958	13:35
Pis	07/15/1957	02:32	Can	11/10/1957	21:23	Sco	03/08/1958	13:35
Ari	07/17/1957	15:14	Leo	11/13/1957	02:35	Sag	03/10/1958	15:57
Tau	07/20/1957	02:57	Vir	11/15/1957	06:07	Cap	03/12/1958	21:37

Aqu	03/15/1958	06:28	Gem	07/12/1958	10:45	Lib	11/07/1958	20:15
Pis	03/17/1958	17:41	Can	07/14/1958	19:15	Sco	11/09/1958	20:29
Ari	03/20/1958	06:16	Leo	07/17/1958	00:30	Sag	11/11/1958	20:03
Tau	03/22/1958	19:15	Vir	07/19/1958	03:41	Cap	11/13/1958	20:55
Gem	03/25/1958	07:19	Lib	07/21/1958	06:11	Aqu	11/16/1958	00:54
Can	03/27/1958	16:52	Sco	07/23/1958	08:57	Pis	11/18/1958	08:57
Leo	03/29/1958	22:44	Sag	07/25/1958	12:25	Ari	11/20/1958	20:28
Vir	04/01/1958	00:59	Cap	07/27/1958	16:53	Tau	11/23/1958	09:30
Lib	04/03/1958	00:53	Aqu	07/29/1958	22:53	Gem	11/25/1958	22:00
Sco	04/05/1958	00:17	Pis	08/01/1958	07:12	Can	11/28/1958	08:50
Sag	04/07/1958	01:08	Ari	08/03/1958	18:14	Leo	11/30/1958	17:40
Cap	04/09/1958	05:01	Tau	08/06/1958	07:04	Vir	12/03/1958	00:17
Aqu	04/11/1958	12:42	Gem	08/08/1958	19:16	Lib	12/05/1958	04:30
Pis	04/13/1958	23:39	Can	08/11/1958	04:24	Sco	12/07/1958	06:28
Ari	04/16/1958	12:22	Leo	08/13/1958	09:42	Sag	12/09/1958	07:01
Tau	04/19/1958	01:15	Vir	08/15/1958	12:06	Cap	12/11/1958	07:46
Gem	04/21/1958	13:02	Lib	08/17/1958	13:17	Aqu	12/13/1958	10:39
Can	04/23/1958	22:45	Sco	08/19/1958	14:50	Pis	12/15/1958	17:12
Leo	04/26/1958	05:43	Sag	08/21/1958	17:48	Ari	12/18/1958	03:45
Vir	04/28/1958	09:39	Cap	08/23/1958	22:39	Tau	12/20/1958	16:37
Lib	04/30/1958	11:05	Aqu	08/26/1958	05:27	Gem	12/23/1958	05:08
Sco	05/02/1958	11:14	Pis	08/28/1958	14:25	Can	12/25/1958	15:32
Sag	05/04/1958	11:44	Ari	08/31/1958	01:35	Leo	12/27/1958	23:32
Cap	05/06/1958	14:21	Tau	09/02/1958	14:23	Vir	12/30/1958	05:40
Aqu	05/08/1958	20:30	Gem	09/05/1958	03:06	Lib	01/01/1959	10:20
Pis	05/11/1958	06:27	Can	09/07/1958	13:20	Sco	01/03/1959	13:41
Ari	05/13/1958	18:57	Leo	09/09/1958	19:40	Sag	01/05/1959	15:55
Tau	05/16/1958	07:49	Vir	09/11/1958	22:18	Cap	01/07/1959	17:50
Gem	05/18/1958	19:13	Lib	09/13/1958	22:44	Aqu	01/09/1959	20:52
Can	05/21/1958	04:22	Sco	09/15/1958	22:49	Pis	01/12/1959	02:40
Leo	05/23/1958	11:13	Sag	09/18/1958	00:17	Ari	01/14/1959	12:10
Vir	05/25/1958	15:59	Cap	09/20/1958	04:13	Tau	01/17/1959	00:32
Lib	05/27/1958	18:55	Aqu	09/22/1958	11:04	Gem	01/19/1959	13:15
Sco	05/29/1958	20:33	Pis	09/24/1958	20:33	Can	01/21/1959	23:45
Sag	05/31/1958	21:53	Ari	09/27/1958	08:07	Leo	01/24/1959	07:13
Cap	06/03/1958	00:23	Tau	09/29/1958	20:58	Vir	01/26/1959	12:12
Aqu	06/05/1958	05:33	Gem	10/02/1958	09:49	Lib	01/28/1959	15:54
Pis	06/07/1958	14:24	Can	10/04/1958	20:59	Sco	01/30/1959	19:05
Ari	06/10/1958	02:20	Leo	10/07/1958	04:50	Sag	02/01/1959	22:10
Tau	06/12/1958	15:12	Vir	10/09/1958	08:48	Cap	02/04/1959	01:29
Gem	06/15/1958	02:30	Lib	10/11/1958	09:43	Aqu	02/06/1959	05:40
Can	06/17/1958	11:02	Sco	10/13/1958	09:11	Pis	02/08/1959	11:51
Leo	06/19/1958	17:03	Sag	10/15/1958	09:09	Ari	02/10/1959	20:55
Vir	06/21/1958	21:21	Cap	10/17/1958	11:24	Tau	02/13/1959	08:47
Lib	06/24/1958	00:42	Aqu	10/19/1958	17:04	Gem	02/15/1959	21:39
Sco	06/26/1958	03:30	Pis	10/22/1958	02:20	Can	02/18/1959	08:49
Sag	06/28/1958	06:11	Ari	10/24/1958	14:10	Leo	02/20/1959	16:37
Cap	06/30/1958	09:32	Tau	10/27/1958	03:07	Vir	02/22/1959	21:05
Aqu	07/02/1958	14:45	Gem	10/29/1958	15:49	Lib	02/24/1959	23:28
Pis	07/04/1958	22:57	Can	11/01/1958	03:08	Sco	02/27/1959	01:14
Ari	07/07/1958	10:18	Leo	11/03/1958	12:01	Sag	03/01/1959	03:33
Tau	07/09/1958	23:08	Vir	11/05/1958	17:45	Cap	03/03/1959	07:05

Aqu	03/05/1959	12:16	Gem	07/02/1959	07:05	Lib	10/29/1959	03:40
Pis	03/07/1959	19:25	Can	07/04/1959	19:03	Sco	10/31/1959	05:13
Ari	03/10/1959	04:53	Leo	07/07/1959	05:07	Sag	11/02/1959	05:01
Tau	03/12/1959	16:36	Vir	07/09/1959	13:14	Cap	11/04/1959	05:05
Gem	03/15/1959	05:30	Lib	07/11/1959	19:26	Aqu	11/06/1959	07:14
Can	03/17/1959	17:27	Sco	07/13/1959	23:32	Pis	11/08/1959	12:36
Leo	03/20/1959	02:21	Sag	07/16/1959	01:41	Ari	11/10/1959	21:10
Vir	03/22/1959	07:27	Cap	07/18/1959	02:41	Tau	11/13/1959	08:04
Lib	03/24/1959	09:26	Aqu	07/20/1959	04:05	Gem	11/15/1959	20:16
Sco	03/26/1959	09:53	Pis	07/22/1959	07:41	Can	11/18/1959	08:56
Sag	03/28/1959	10:32	Ari	07/24/1959	14:54	Leo	11/20/1959	21:03
Cap	03/30/1959	12:49	Tau	07/27/1959	01:43	Vir	11/23/1959	07:07
Aqu	04/01/1959	17:41	Gem	07/29/1959	14:23	Lib	11/25/1959	13:39
Pis	04/04/1959	01:23	Can	08/01/1959	02:23	Sco	11/27/1959	16:20
Ari	04/06/1959	11:33	Leo	08/03/1959	12:08	Sag	11/29/1959	16:11
Tau	04/08/1959	23:31	Vir	08/05/1959	19:29	Cap	12/01/1959	15:11
Gem	04/11/1959	12:24	Lib	08/08/1959	00:55	Aqu	12/03/1959	15:35
Can	04/14/1959	00:46	Sco	08/10/1959	04:59	Pis	12/05/1959	19:16
Leo	04/16/1959	10:53	Sag	08/12/1959	07:58	Ari	12/08/1959	03:00
Vir	04/18/1959	17:27	Cap	08/14/1959	10:18	Tau	12/10/1959	13:56
Lib	04/20/1959	20:18	Aqu	08/16/1959	12:54	Gem	12/13/1959	02:23
Sco	04/22/1959	20:33	Pis	08/18/1959	16:59	Can	12/15/1959	15:00
Sag	04/24/1959	19:59	Ari	08/20/1959	23:52	Leo	12/18/1959	02:57
Cap	04/26/1959	20:33	Tau	08/23/1959	09:58	Vir	12/20/1959	13:28
Aqu	04/28/1959	23:56	Gem	08/25/1959	22:18	Lib	12/22/1959	21:27
Pis	05/01/1959	06:58	Can	08/28/1959	10:32	Sco	12/25/1959	01:59
Ari	05/03/1959	17:18	Leo	08/30/1959	20:32	Sag	12/27/1959	03:14
Tau	05/06/1959	05:38	Vir	09/02/1959	03:30	Cap	12/29/1959	02:37
Gem	05/08/1959	18:34	Lib	09/04/1959	07:56	Aqu	12/31/1959	02:15
Can	05/11/1959	06:56	Sco	09/06/1959	10:52	Pis	01/02/1960	04:19
Leo	05/13/1959	17:40	Sag	09/08/1959	13:20	Ari	01/04/1960	10:22
Vir	05/16/1959	01:36	Cap	09/10/1959	16:04	Tau	01/06/1960	20:22
Lib	05/18/1959	06:06	Aqu	09/12/1959	19:43	Gem	01/09/1960	08:44
Sco	05/20/1959	07:23	Pis	09/15/1959	00:54	Can	01/11/1960	21:22
Sag	05/22/1959	06:50	Ari	09/17/1959	08:16	Leo	01/14/1960	08:58
Cap	05/24/1959	06:23	Tau	09/19/1959	18:12	Vir	01/16/1960	19:03
Aqu	05/26/1959	08:10	Gem	09/22/1959	06:15	Lib	01/19/1960	03:13
Pis	05/28/1959	13:43	Can	09/24/1959	18:49	Sco	01/21/1960	08:58
Ari	05/30/1959	23:19	Leo	09/27/1959	05:36	Sag	01/23/1960	12:01
Tau	06/02/1959	11:37	Vir	09/29/1959	13:02	Cap	01/25/1960	12:58
Gem	06/05/1959	00:35	Lib	10/01/1959	17:07	Aqu	01/27/1960	13:19
Can	06/07/1959	12:43	Sco	10/03/1959	18:53	Pis	01/29/1960	14:57
Leo	06/09/1959	23:18	Sag	10/05/1959	19:54	Ari	01/31/1960	19:39
Vir	06/12/1959	07:49	Cap	10/07/1959	21:39	Tau	02/03/1960	04:16
Lib	06/14/1959	13:40	Aqu	10/10/1959	01:13	Gem	02/05/1960	15:58
Sco	06/16/1959	16:37	Pis	10/12/1959	07:06	Can	02/08/1960	04:36
Sag	06/18/1959	17:14	Ari	10/14/1959	15:20	Leo	02/10/1960	16:07
Cap	06/20/1959	17:01	Tau	10/17/1959	01:40	Vir	02/13/1960	01:34
Aqu	06/22/1959	18:00	Gem	10/19/1959	13:40	Lib	02/15/1960	08:54
Pis	06/24/1959	22:10	Can	10/22/1959	02:22	Sco	02/17/1960	14:23
Ari	06/27/1959	06:27	Leo	10/24/1959	14:02	Sag	02/19/1960	18:11
Tau	06/29/1959	18:10	Vir	10/26/1959	22:47	Cap	02/21/1960	20:38

Aqu	02/23/1960	22:32	Gem	06/21/1960	04:45	Lib	10/18/1960	06:31
Pis	02/26/1960	01:04	Can	06/23/1960	17:09	Sco	10/20/1960	12:04
Ari	02/28/1960	05:37	Leo	06/26/1960	05:51	Sag	10/22/1960	15:15
Tau	03/01/1960	13:19	Vir	06/28/1960	17:52	Cap	10/24/1960	17:27
Gem	03/04/1960	00:07	Lib	07/01/1960	03:45	Aqu	10/26/1960	19:57
Can	03/06/1960	12:36	Sco	07/03/1960	10:07	Pis	10/28/1960	23:26
Leo	03/09/1960	00:23	Sag	07/05/1960	12:40	Ari	10/31/1960	04:11
Vir	03/11/1960	09:46	Cap	07/07/1960	12:33	Tau	11/02/1960	10:27
Lib	03/13/1960	16:18	Aqu	07/09/1960	11:43	Gem	11/04/1960	18:44
Sco	03/15/1960	20:36	Pis	07/11/1960	12:20	Can	11/07/1960	05:25
Sag	03/17/1960	23:37	Ari	07/13/1960	16:07	Leo	11/09/1960	17:59
Cap	03/20/1960	02:14	Tau	07/15/1960	23:49	Vir	11/12/1960	06:23
Aqu	03/22/1960	05:09	Gem	07/18/1960	10:40	Lib	11/14/1960	16:06
Pis	03/24/1960	09:02	Can	07/20/1960	23:08	Sco	11/16/1960	21:51
Ari	03/26/1960	14:30	Leo	07/23/1960	11:45	Sag	11/19/1960	00:15
Tau	03/28/1960	22:13	Vir	07/25/1960	23:30	Cap	11/21/1960	01:01
Gem	03/31/1960	08:31	Lib	07/28/1960	09:32	Aqu	11/23/1960	02:04
Can	04/02/1960	20:45	Sco	07/30/1960	16:54	Pis	11/25/1960	04:49
Leo	04/05/1960	09:00	Sag	08/01/1960	21:03	Ari	11/27/1960	09:51
Vir	04/07/1960	19:01	Cap	08/03/1960	22:24	Tau	11/29/1960	16:59
Lib	04/10/1960	01:34	Aqu	08/05/1960	22:20	Gem	12/02/1960	02:00
Sco	04/12/1960	05:00	Pis	08/07/1960	22:42	Can	12/04/1960	12:52
Sag	04/14/1960	06:37	Ari	08/10/1960	01:22	Leo	12/07/1960	01:20
Cap	04/16/1960	08:01	Tau	08/12/1960	07:36	Vir	12/09/1960	14:12
Aqu	04/18/1960	10:32	Gem	08/14/1960	17:29	Lib	12/12/1960	01:08
Pis	04/20/1960	14:55	Can	08/17/1960	05:42	Sco	12/14/1960	08:11
Ari	04/22/1960	21:23	Leo	08/19/1960	18:17	Sag	12/16/1960	11:05
Tau	04/25/1960	05:50	Vir	08/22/1960	05:41	Cap	12/18/1960	11:15
Gem	04/27/1960	16:16	Lib	08/24/1960	15:08	Aqu	12/20/1960	10:49
Can	04/30/1960	04:22	Sco	08/26/1960	22:22	Pis	12/22/1960	11:48
Leo	05/02/1960	16:58	Sag	08/29/1960	03:18	Ari	12/24/1960	15:34
Vir	05/05/1960	03:57	Cap	08/31/1960	06:08	Tau	12/26/1960	22:30
Lib	05/07/1960	11:28	Aqu	09/02/1960	07:34	Gem	12/29/1960	08:01
Sco	05/09/1960	15:05	Pis	09/04/1960	08:51	Can	12/31/1960	19:21
Sag	05/11/1960	15:54	Ari	09/06/1960	11:26	Leo	01/03/1961	07:53
Cap	05/13/1960	15:50	Tau	09/08/1960	16:44	Vir	01/05/1961	20:47
Aqu	05/15/1960	16:51	Gem	09/11/1960	01:31	Lib	01/08/1961	08:30
Pis	05/17/1960	20:24	Can	09/13/1960	13:10	Sco	01/10/1961	17:08
Ari	05/20/1960	02:55	Leo	09/16/1960	01:45	Sag	01/12/1961	21:38
Tau	05/22/1960	12:00	Vir	09/18/1960	13:06	Cap	01/14/1961	22:39
Gem	05/24/1960	22:54	Lib	09/20/1960	21:57	Aqu	01/16/1961	21:55
Can	05/27/1960	11:06	Sco	09/23/1960	04:17	Pis	01/18/1961	21:32
Leo	05/29/1960	23:49	Sag	09/25/1960	08:41	Ari	01/20/1961	23:27
Vir	06/01/1960	11:36	Cap	09/27/1960	11:53	Tau	01/23/1961	04:51
Lib	06/03/1960	20:29	Aqu	09/29/1960	14:32	Gem	01/25/1961	13:50
Sco	06/06/1960	01:18	Pis	10/01/1960	17:14	Can	01/28/1961	01:21
Sag	06/08/1960	02:29	Ari	10/03/1960	20:46	Leo	01/30/1961	14:04
Cap	06/10/1960	01:47	Tau	10/06/1960	02:09	Vir	02/02/1961	02:47
Aqu	06/12/1960	01:23	Gem	10/08/1960	10:17	Lib	02/04/1961	14:26
Pis	06/14/1960	03:18	Can	10/10/1960	21:18	Sco	02/06/1961	23:49
Ari	06/16/1960	08:43	Leo	10/13/1960	09:54	Sag	02/09/1961	06:00
Tau	06/18/1960	17:33	Vir	10/15/1960	21:38	Cap	02/11/1961	08:49

Aqu	02/13/1961	09:13	Gem	06/11/1961	06:39	Lib	10/08/1961	06:03
Pis	02/15/1961	08:52	Can	06/13/1961	15:49	Sco	10/10/1961	16:18
Ari	02/17/1961	09:41	Leo	06/16/1961	03:15	Sag	10/13/1961	00:19
Tau	02/19/1961	13:22	Vir	06/18/1961	16:11	Cap	10/15/1961	06:23
Gem	02/21/1961	20:51	Lib	06/21/1961	04:31	Aqu	10/17/1961	10:35
Can	02/24/1961	07:48	Sco	06/23/1961	13:49	Pis	10/19/1961	13:09
Leo	02/26/1961	20:34	Sag	06/25/1961	19:04	Ari	10/21/1961	14:35
Vir	03/01/1961	09:11	Cap	06/27/1961	20:59	Tau	10/23/1961	16:06
Lib	03/03/1961	20:20	Aqu	06/29/1961	21:17	Gem	10/25/1961	19:24
Sco	03/06/1961	05:23	Pis	07/01/1961	21:52	Can	10/28/1961	02:03
Sag	03/08/1961	12:02	Ari	07/04/1961	00:12	Leo	10/30/1961	12:29
Cap	03/10/1961	16:18	Tau	07/06/1961	05:01	Vir	11/02/1961	01:16
Aqu	03/12/1961	18:28	Gem	07/08/1961	12:27	Lib	11/04/1961	13:41
Pis	03/14/1961	19:25	Can	07/10/1961	22:13	Sco	11/06/1961	23:38
Ari	03/16/1961	20:32	Leo	07/13/1961	09:56	Sag	11/09/1961	06:50
Tau	03/18/1961	23:26	Vir	07/15/1961	22:54	Cap	11/11/1961	11:58
Gem	03/21/1961	05:31	Lib	07/18/1961	11:37	Aqu	11/13/1961	15:58
Can	03/23/1961	15:22	Sco	07/20/1961	22:03	Pis	11/15/1961	19:17
Leo	03/26/1961	03:48	Sag	07/23/1961	04:41	Ari	11/17/1961	22:09
Vir	03/28/1961	16:28	Cap	07/25/1961	07:27	Tau	11/20/1961	01:03
Lib	03/31/1961	03:20	Aqu	07/27/1961	07:41	Gem	11/22/1961	04:58
Sco	04/02/1961	11:35	Pis	07/29/1961	07:12	Can	11/24/1961	11:20
Sag	04/04/1961	17:33	Ari	07/31/1961	07:56	Leo	11/26/1961	21:01
Cap	04/06/1961	21:51	Tau	08/02/1961	11:19	Vir	11/29/1961	09:24
Aqu	04/09/1961	01:02	Gem	08/04/1961	18:03	Lib	12/01/1961	22:06
Pis	04/11/1961	03:31	Can	08/07/1961	03:56	Sco	12/04/1961	08:28
Ari	04/13/1961	05:55	Leo	08/09/1961	15:59	Sag	12/06/1961	15:23
Tau	04/15/1961	09:16	Vir	08/12/1961	04:59	Cap	12/08/1961	19:29
Gem	04/17/1961	14:55	Lib	08/14/1961	17:43	Aqu	12/10/1961	22:10
Can	04/19/1961	23:50	Sco	08/17/1961	04:43	Pis	12/13/1961	00:41
Leo	04/22/1961	11:42	Sag	08/19/1961	12:42	Ari	12/15/1961	03:43
Vir	04/25/1961	00:30	Cap	08/21/1961	17:06	Tau	12/17/1961	07:38
Lib	04/27/1961	11:32	Aqu	08/23/1961	18:24	Gem	12/19/1961	12:47
Sco	04/29/1961	19:26	Pis	08/25/1961	18:02	Can	12/21/1961	19:49
Sag	05/02/1961	00:23	Ari	08/27/1961	17:48	Leo	12/24/1961	05:25
Cap	05/04/1961	03:39	Tau	08/29/1961	19:36	Vir	12/26/1961	17:29
Aqu	05/06/1961	06:23	Gem	09/01/1961	00:53	Lib	12/29/1961	06:25
Pis	05/08/1961	09:22	Can	09/03/1961	10:00	Sco	12/31/1961	17:41
Ari	05/10/1961	12:55	Leo	09/05/1961	22:00	Sag	01/03/1962	01:21
Tau	05/12/1961	17:24	Vir	09/08/1961	11:04	Cap	01/05/1962	05:23
Gem	05/14/1961	23:34	Lib	09/10/1961	23:32	Aqu	01/07/1962	06:59
Can	05/17/1961	08:16	Sco	09/13/1961	10:21	Pis	01/09/1962	07:53
Leo	05/19/1961	19:44	Sag	09/15/1961	18:53	Ari	01/11/1962	09:34
Vir	05/22/1961	08:37	Cap	09/18/1961	00:40	Tau	01/13/1962	13:01
Lib	05/24/1961	20:16	Aqu	09/20/1961	03:42	Gem	01/15/1962	18:41
Sco	05/27/1961	04:33	Pis	09/22/1961	04:35	Can	01/18/1962	02:39
Sag	05/29/1961	09:09	Ari	09/24/1961	04:39	Leo	01/20/1962	12:49
Cap	05/31/1961	11:19	Tau	09/26/1961	05:41	Vir	01/23/1962	00:53
Aqu	06/02/1961	12:44	Gem	09/28/1961	09:32	Lib	01/25/1962	13:51
Pis	06/04/1961	14:50	Can	09/30/1961	17:18	Sco	01/28/1962	01:52
Ari	06/06/1961	18:23	Leo	10/03/1961	04:43	Sag	01/30/1962	10:57
Tau	06/08/1961	23:37	Vir	10/05/1961	17:45	Cap	02/01/1962	16:08

Aqu	02/03/1962	17:56	Gem	06/01/1962	12:40	Lib	09/28/1962	04:07
Pis	02/05/1962	17:52	Can	06/03/1962	16:56	Sco	09/30/1962	16:48
Ari	02/07/1962	17:50	Leo	06/06/1962	00:23	Sag	10/03/1962	04:38
Tau	02/09/1962	19:34	Vir	06/08/1962	11:12	Cap	10/05/1962	14:33
Gem	02/12/1962	00:18	Lib	06/10/1962	23:50	Aqu	10/07/1962	21:19
Can	02/14/1962	08:19	Sco	06/13/1962	11:43	Pis	10/10/1962	00:26
Leo	02/16/1962	19:03	Sag	06/15/1962	21:02	Ari	10/12/1962	00:39
Vir	02/19/1962	07:26	Cap	06/18/1962	03:28	Tau	10/13/1962	23:43
Lib	02/21/1962	20:21	Aqu	06/20/1962	07:48	Gem	10/15/1962	23:51
Sco	02/24/1962	08:35	Pis	06/22/1962	10:58	Can	10/18/1962	03:05
Sag	02/26/1962	18:45	Ari	06/24/1962	13:42	Leo	10/20/1962	10:30
Cap	03/01/1962	01:36	Tau	06/26/1962	16:34	Vir	10/22/1962	21:30
Aqu	03/03/1962	04:51	Gem	06/28/1962	20:09	Lib	10/25/1962	10:12
Pis	03/05/1962	05:15	Can	07/01/1962	01:18	Sco	10/27/1962	22:47
Ari	03/07/1962	04:31	Leo	07/03/1962	08:55	Sag	10/30/1962	10:18
Tau	03/09/1962	04:40	Vir	07/05/1962	19:21	Cap	11/01/1962	20:16
Gem	03/11/1962	07:35	Lib	07/08/1962	07:47	Aqu	11/04/1962	04:01
Can	03/13/1962	14:26	Sco	07/10/1962	20:04	Pis	11/06/1962	08:50
Leo	03/16/1962	00:56	Sag	07/13/1962	06:00	Ari	11/08/1962	10:44
Vir	03/18/1962	13:32	Cap	07/15/1962	12:30	Tau	11/10/1962	10:44
Lib	03/21/1962	02:27	Aqu	07/17/1962	16:06	Gem	11/12/1962	10:43
Sco	03/23/1962	14:27	Pis	07/19/1962	17:59	Can	11/14/1962	12:49
Sag	03/26/1962	00:47	Ari	07/21/1962	19:33	Leo	11/16/1962	18:39
Cap	03/28/1962	08:44	Tau	07/23/1962	21:56	Vir	11/19/1962	04:33
Aqu	03/30/1962	13:41	Gem	07/26/1962	01:56	Lib	11/21/1962	16:57
Pis	04/01/1962	15:41	Can	07/28/1962	08:00	Sco	11/24/1962	05:32
Ari	04/03/1962	15:40	Leo	07/30/1962	16:20	Sag	11/26/1962	16:42
Tau	04/05/1962	15:25	Vir	08/02/1962	02:57	Cap	11/29/1962	01:59
Gem	04/07/1962	16:59	Lib	08/04/1962	15:17	Aqu	12/01/1962	09:24
Can	04/09/1962	22:13	Sco	08/07/1962	03:55	Pis	12/03/1962	14:52
Leo	04/12/1962	07:36	Sag	08/09/1962	14:46	Ari	12/05/1962	18:16
Vir	04/14/1962	19:56	Cap	08/11/1962	22:15	Tau	12/07/1962	19:58
Lib	04/17/1962	08:52	Aqu	08/14/1962	02:05	Gem	12/09/1962	21:07
Sco	04/19/1962	20:35	Pis	08/16/1962	03:15	Can	12/11/1962	23:21
Sag	04/22/1962	06:26	Ari	08/18/1962	03:25	Leo	12/14/1962	04:20
Cap	04/24/1962	14:18	Tau	08/20/1962	04:19	Vir	12/16/1962	12:59
Aqu	04/26/1962	20:06	Gem	08/22/1962	07:27	Lib	12/19/1962	00:40
Pis	04/28/1962	23:38	Can	08/24/1962	13:34	Sco	12/21/1962	13:16
Ari	05/01/1962	01:11	Leo	08/26/1962	22:29	Sag	12/24/1962	00:31
Tau	05/03/1962	01:48	Vir	08/29/1962	09:35	Cap	12/26/1962	09:17
Gem	05/05/1962	03:16	Lib	08/31/1962	22:00	Aqu	12/28/1962	15:41
Can	05/07/1962	07:28	Sco	09/03/1962	10:45	Pis	12/30/1962	20:19
Leo	05/09/1962	15:35	Sag	09/05/1962	22:24	Ari	01/01/1963	23:46
Vir	05/12/1962	03:10	Cap	09/08/1962	07:18	Tau	01/04/1963	02:32
Lib	05/14/1962	16:01	Aqu	09/10/1962	12:24	Gem	01/06/1963	05:13
Sco	05/17/1962	03:41	Pis	09/12/1962	14:00	Can	01/08/1963	08:41
Sag	05/19/1962	13:01	Ari	09/14/1962	13:32	Leo	01/10/1963	14:01
Cap	05/21/1962	20:07	Tau	09/16/1962	13:01	Vir	01/12/1963	22:07
Aqu	05/24/1962	01:29	Gem	09/18/1962	14:29	Lib	01/15/1963	09:04
Pis	05/26/1962	05:29	Can	09/20/1962	19:25	Sco	01/17/1963	21:34
Ari	05/28/1962	08:14	Leo	09/23/1962	04:06	Sag	01/20/1963	09:19
Tau	05/30/1962	10:16	Vir	09/25/1962	15:30	Cap	01/22/1963	18:22

Aqu	01/25/1963	00:12	Gem	05/22/1963	20:53	Lib	09/18/1963	02:59
Pis	01/27/1963	03:34	Can	05/24/1963	21:29	Sco	09/20/1963	14:10
Ari	01/29/1963	05:43	Leo	05/27/1963	00:59	Sag	09/23/1963	02:49
Tau	01/31/1963	07:54	Vir	05/29/1963	08:21	Cap	09/25/1963	15:14
Gem	02/02/1963	11:03	Lib	05/31/1963	19:08	Aqu	09/28/1963	01:01
Can	02/04/1963	15:40	Sco	06/03/1963	07:37	Pis	09/30/1963	06:45
Leo	02/06/1963	22:05	Sag	06/05/1963	19:59	Ari	10/02/1963	08:46
Vir	02/09/1963	06:35	Cap	06/08/1963	07:05	Tau	10/04/1963	08:49
Lib	02/11/1963	17:17	Aqu	06/10/1963	16:21	Gem	10/06/1963	08:58
Sco	02/14/1963	05:38	Pis	06/12/1963	23:19	Can	10/08/1963	11:01
Sag	02/16/1963	17:56	Ari	06/15/1963	03:45	Leo	10/10/1963	15:54
Cap	02/19/1963	03:58	Tau	06/17/1963	05:53	Vir	10/12/1963	23:34
Aqu	02/21/1963	10:21	Gem	06/19/1963	06:43	Lib	10/15/1963	09:23
Pis	02/23/1963	13:15	Can	06/21/1963	07:46	Sco	10/17/1963	20:52
Ari	02/25/1963	14:04	Leo	06/23/1963	10:44	Sag	10/20/1963	09:31
Tau	02/27/1963	14:38	Vir	06/25/1963	16:56	Cap	10/22/1963	22:19
Gem	03/01/1963	16:38	Lib	06/28/1963	02:40	Aqu	10/25/1963	09:18
Can	03/03/1963	21:07	Sco	06/30/1963	14:47	Pis	10/27/1963	16:34
Leo	03/06/1963	04:14	Sag	07/03/1963	03:10	Ari	10/29/1963	19:38
Vir	03/08/1963	13:33	Cap	07/05/1963	14:01	Tau	10/31/1963	19:41
Lib	03/11/1963	00:34	Aqu	07/07/1963	22:34	Gem	11/02/1963	18:47
Sco	03/13/1963	12:51	Pis	07/10/1963	04:52	Can	11/04/1963	19:07
Sag	03/16/1963	01:25	Ari	07/12/1963	09:15	Leo	11/06/1963	22:24
Cap	03/18/1963	12:32	Tau	07/14/1963	12:14	Vir	11/09/1963	05:13
Aqu	03/20/1963	20:19	Gem	07/16/1963	14:26	Lib	11/11/1963	15:07
Pis	03/23/1963	00:02	Can	07/18/1963	16:44	Sco	11/14/1963	02:56
Ari	03/25/1963	00:36	Leo	07/20/1963	20:14	Sag	11/16/1963	15:38
Tau	03/26/1963	23:56	Vir	07/23/1963	02:06	Cap	11/19/1963	04:21
Gem	03/29/1963	00:13	Lib	07/25/1963	11:02	Aqu	11/21/1963	15:50
Can	03/31/1963	03:14	Sco	07/27/1963	22:38	Pis	11/24/1963	00:30
Leo	04/02/1963	09:45	Sag	07/30/1963	11:07	Ari	11/26/1963	05:24
Vir	04/04/1963	19:19	Cap	08/01/1963	22:10	Tau	11/28/1963	06:48
Lib	04/07/1963	06:49	Aqu	08/04/1963	06:24	Gem	11/30/1963	06:14
Sco	04/09/1963	19:13	Pis	08/06/1963	11:44	Can	12/02/1963	05:44
Sag	04/12/1963	07:47	Ari	08/08/1963	15:05	Leo	12/04/1963	07:19
Cap	04/14/1963	19:25	Tau	08/10/1963	17:36	Vir	12/06/1963	12:27
Aqu	04/17/1963	04:32	Gem	08/12/1963	20:15	Lib	12/08/1963	21:21
Pis	04/19/1963	09:51	Can	08/14/1963	23:39	Sco	12/11/1963	09:03
Ari	04/21/1963	11:28	Leo	08/17/1963	04:16	Sag	12/13/1963	21:52
Tau	04/23/1963	10:50	Vir	08/19/1963	10:40	Cap	12/16/1963	10:20
Gem	04/25/1963	10:06	Lib	08/21/1963	19:25	Aqu	12/18/1963	21:27
Can	04/27/1963	11:27	Sco	08/24/1963	06:38	Pis	12/21/1963	06:27
Leo	04/29/1963	16:25	Sag	08/26/1963	19:14	Ari	12/23/1963	12:39
Vir	05/02/1963	01:13	Cap	08/29/1963	06:56	Tau	12/25/1963	15:56
Lib	05/04/1963	12:41	Aqu	08/31/1963	15:35	Gem	12/27/1963	16:57
Sco	05/07/1963	01:15	Pis	09/02/1963	20:35	Can	12/29/1963	17:06
Sag	05/09/1963	13:41	Ari	09/04/1963	22:50	Leo	12/31/1963	18:08
Cap	05/12/1963	01:12	Tau	09/07/1963	00:01	Vir	01/02/1964	21:48
Aqu	05/14/1963	10:49	Gem	09/09/1963	01:45	Lib	01/05/1964	05:09
Pis	05/16/1963	17:31	Can	09/11/1963	05:07	Sco	01/07/1964	16:03
Ari	05/18/1963	20:46	Leo	09/13/1963	10:29	Sag	01/10/1964	04:48
Tau	05/20/1963	21:20	Vir	09/15/1963	17:46	Cap	01/12/1964	17:13

Aqu	01/15/1964	03:46	Gem	05/12/1964	06:00	Lib	09/07/1964	04:19
Pis	01/17/1964	12:02	Can	05/14/1964	05:52	Sco	09/09/1964	11:20
Ari	01/19/1964	18:09	Leo	05/16/1964	07:31	Sag	09/11/1964	21:47
Tau	01/21/1964	22:22	Vir	05/18/1964	12:02	Cap	09/14/1964	10:29
Gem	01/24/1964	01:03	Lib	05/20/1964	19:40	Aqu	09/16/1964	22:45
Can	01/26/1964	02:50	Sco	05/23/1964	05:57	Pis	09/19/1964	08:20
Leo	01/28/1964	04:44	Sag	05/25/1964	18:02	Ari	09/21/1964	14:42
Vir	01/30/1964	08:08	Cap	05/28/1964	06:59	Tau	09/23/1964	18:45
Lib	02/01/1964	14:25	Aqu	05/30/1964	19:31	Gem	09/25/1964	21:45
Sco	02/04/1964	00:12	Pis	06/02/1964	06:00	Can	09/28/1964	00:39
Sag	02/06/1964	12:34	Ari	06/04/1964	13:00	Leo	09/30/1964	03:52
Cap	02/09/1964	01:09	Tau	06/06/1964	16:18	Vir	10/02/1964	07:41
Aqu	02/11/1964	11:37	Gem	06/08/1964	16:49	Lib	10/04/1964	12:44
Pis	02/13/1964	19:08	Can	06/10/1964	16:16	Sco	10/06/1964	19:56
Ari	02/16/1964	00:08	Leo	06/12/1964	16:34	Sag	10/09/1964	06:01
Tau	02/18/1964	03:44	Vir	06/14/1964	19:27	Cap	10/11/1964	18:31
Gem	02/20/1964	06:47	Lib	06/17/1964	01:54	Aqu	10/14/1964	07:14
Can	02/22/1964	09:48	Sco	06/19/1964	11:49	Pis	10/16/1964	17:31
Leo	02/24/1964	13:10	Sag	06/22/1964	00:02	Ari	10/19/1964	00:02
Vir	02/26/1964	17:29	Cap	06/24/1964	13:00	Tau	10/21/1964	03:23
Lib	02/28/1964	23:46	Aqu	06/27/1964	01:20	Gem	10/23/1964	05:02
Sco	03/02/1964	08:54	Pis	06/29/1964	11:54	Can	10/25/1964	06:36
Sag	03/04/1964	20:46	Ari	07/01/1964	19:51	Leo	10/27/1964	09:13
Cap	03/07/1964	09:34	Tau	07/04/1964	00:40	Vir	10/29/1964	13:25
Aqu	03/09/1964	20:34	Gem	07/06/1964	02:41	Lib	10/31/1964	19:23
Pis	03/12/1964	04:03	Can	07/08/1964	02:56	Sco	11/03/1964	03:24
Ari	03/14/1964	08:14	Leo	07/10/1964	03:00	Sag	11/05/1964	13:43
Tau	03/16/1964	10:29	Vir	07/12/1964	04:43	Cap	11/08/1964	02:05
Gem	03/18/1964	12:25	Lib	07/14/1964	09:41	Aqu	11/10/1964	15:07
Can	03/20/1964	15:11	Sco	07/16/1964	18:31	Pis	11/13/1964	02:26
Leo	03/22/1964	19:14	Sag	07/19/1964	06:27	Ari	11/15/1964	10:08
Vir	03/25/1964	00:41	Cap	07/21/1964	19:26	Tau	11/17/1964	13:55
Lib	03/27/1964	07:47	Aqu	07/24/1964	07:29	Gem	11/19/1964	14:57
Sco	03/29/1964	17:03	Pis	07/26/1964	17:34	Can	11/21/1964	15:03
Sag	04/01/1964	04:40	Ari	07/29/1964	01:23	Leo	11/23/1964	15:58
Cap	04/03/1964	17:35	Tau	07/31/1964	06:59	Vir	11/25/1964	19:02
Aqu	04/06/1964	05:23	Gem	08/02/1964	10:26	Lib	11/28/1964	00:54
Pis	04/08/1964	13:44	Can	08/04/1964	12:12	Sco	11/30/1964	09:30
Ari	04/10/1964	18:07	Leo	08/06/1964	13:10	Sag	12/02/1964	20:23
Tau	04/12/1964	19:36	Vir	08/08/1964	14:50	Cap	12/05/1964	08:52
Gem	04/14/1964	20:05	Lib	08/10/1964	18:51	Aqu	12/07/1964	21:56
Can	04/16/1964	21:23	Sco	08/13/1964	02:31	Pis	12/10/1964	09:58
Leo	04/19/1964	00:40	Sag	08/15/1964	13:44	Ari	12/12/1964	19:11
Vir	04/21/1964	06:16	Cap	08/18/1964	02:37	Tau	12/15/1964	00:30
Lib	04/23/1964	14:07	Aqu	08/20/1964	14:37	Gem	12/17/1964	02:19
Sco	04/26/1964	00:00	Pis	08/23/1964	00:11	Can	12/19/1964	02:01
Sag	04/28/1964	11:45	Ari	08/25/1964	07:14	Leo	12/21/1964	01:30
Cap	05/01/1964	00:41	Tau	08/27/1964	12:22	Vir	12/23/1964	02:42
Aqu	05/03/1964	13:04	Gem	08/29/1964	16:15	Lib	12/25/1964	07:04
Pis	05/05/1964	22:41	Can	08/31/1964	19:12	Sco	12/27/1964	15:11
Ari	05/08/1964	04:14	Leo	09/02/1964	21:35	Sag	12/30/1964	02:20
Tau	05/10/1964	06:08	Vir	09/05/1964	00:12	Cap	01/01/1965	15:06

Aqu	01/04/1965	04:03	Gem	05/02/1965	15:25	Lib	08/28/1965	08:52
Pis	01/06/1965	16:05	Can	05/04/1965	17:38	Sco	08/30/1965	11:54
Ari	01/09/1965	02:06	Leo	05/06/1965	19:49	Sag	09/01/1965	18:59
Tau	01/11/1965	09:08	Vir	05/08/1965	22:47	Cap	09/04/1965	05:50
Gem	01/13/1965	12:46	Lib	05/11/1965	03:04	Aqu	09/06/1965	18:32
Can	01/15/1965	13:33	Sco	05/13/1965	09:09	Pis	09/09/1965	06:55
Leo	01/17/1965	12:57	Sag	05/15/1965	17:31	Ari	09/11/1965	17:49
Vir	01/19/1965	12:55	Cap	05/18/1965	04:19	Tau	09/14/1965	02:55
Lib	01/21/1965	15:28	Aqu	05/20/1965	16:49	Gem	09/16/1965	10:04
Sco	01/23/1965	22:01	Pis	05/23/1965	05:13	Can	09/18/1965	14:59
Sag	01/26/1965	08:32	Ari	05/25/1965	15:17	Leo	09/20/1965	17:34
Cap	01/28/1965	21:20	Tau	05/27/1965	21:46	Vir	09/22/1965	18:29
Aqu	01/31/1965	10:16	Gem	05/30/1965	00:57	Lib	09/24/1965	19:15
Pis	02/02/1965	21:54	Can	06/01/1965	02:04	Sco	09/26/1965	21:47
Ari	02/05/1965	07:42	Leo	06/03/1965	02:46	Sag	09/29/1965	03:42
Tau	02/07/1965	15:22	Vir	06/05/1965	04:32	Cap	10/01/1965	13:29
Gem	02/09/1965	20:34	Lib	06/07/1965	08:29	Aqu	10/04/1965	01:47
Can	02/11/1965	23:12	Sco	06/09/1965	15:03	Pis	10/06/1965	14:12
Leo	02/13/1965	23:53	Sag	06/12/1965	00:09	Ari	10/09/1965	00:52
Vir	02/16/1965	00:05	Cap	06/14/1965	11:20	Tau	10/11/1965	09:15
Lib	02/18/1965	01:45	Aqu	06/16/1965	23:50	Gem	10/13/1965	15:38
Sco	02/20/1965	06:45	Pis	06/19/1965	12:27	Can	10/15/1965	20:25
Sag	02/22/1965	15:57	Ari	06/21/1965	23:27	Leo	10/17/1965	23:50
Cap	02/25/1965	04:16	Tau	06/24/1965	07:15	Vir	10/20/1965	02:12
Aqu	02/27/1965	17:13	Gem	06/26/1965	11:16	Lib	10/22/1965	04:20
Pis	03/02/1965	04:37	Can	06/28/1965	12:18	Sco	10/24/1965	07:31
Ari	03/04/1965	13:43	Leo	06/30/1965	11:58	Sag	10/26/1965	13:09
Tau	03/06/1965	20:48	Vir	07/02/1965	12:11	Cap	10/28/1965	22:05
Gem	03/09/1965	02:12	Lib	07/04/1965	14:43	Aqu	10/31/1965	09:49
Can	03/11/1965	06:02	Sco	07/06/1965	20:38	Pis	11/02/1965	22:21
Leo	03/13/1965	08:22	Sag	07/09/1965	05:52	Ari	11/05/1965	09:20
Vir	03/15/1965	09:55	Cap	07/11/1965	17:28	Tau	11/07/1965	17:28
Lib	03/17/1965	12:04	Aqu	07/14/1965	06:07	Gem	11/09/1965	22:53
Sco	03/19/1965	16:32	Pis	07/16/1965	18:44	Can	11/12/1965	02:28
Sag	03/22/1965	00:37	Ari	07/19/1965	06:12	Leo	11/14/1965	05:13
Cap	03/24/1965	12:06	Tau	07/21/1965	15:12	Vir	11/16/1965	07:54
Aqu	03/27/1965	00:57	Gem	07/23/1965	20:46	Lib	11/18/1965	11:09
Pis	03/29/1965	12:30	Can	07/25/1965	22:51	Sco	11/20/1965	15:36
Ari	03/31/1965	21:17	Leo	07/27/1965	22:36	Sag	11/22/1965	21:56
Tau	04/03/1965	03:27	Vir	07/29/1965	21:54	Cap	11/25/1965	06:45
Gem	04/05/1965	07:53	Lib	07/31/1965	22:54	Aqu	11/27/1965	18:02
Can	04/07/1965	11:23	Sco	08/03/1965	03:20	Pis	11/30/1965	06:39
Leo	04/09/1965	14:22	Sag	08/05/1965	11:49	Ari	12/02/1965	18:21
Vir	04/11/1965	17:13	Cap	08/07/1965	23:22	Tau	12/05/1965	03:09
Lib	04/13/1965	20:38	Aqu	08/10/1965	12:08	Gem	12/07/1965	08:26
Sco	04/16/1965	01:42	Pis	08/13/1965	00:36	Can	12/09/1965	10:55
Sag	04/18/1965	09:31	Ari	08/15/1965	11:55	Leo	12/11/1965	12:07
Cap	04/20/1965	20:23	Tau	08/17/1965	21:26	Vir	12/13/1965	13:35
Aqu	04/23/1965	09:03	Gem	08/20/1965	04:19	Lib	12/15/1965	16:33
Pis	04/25/1965	21:00	Can	08/22/1965	08:03	Sco	12/17/1965	21:40
Ari	04/28/1965	06:11	Leo	08/24/1965	09:00	Sag	12/20/1965	05:00
Tau	04/30/1965	12:02	Vir	08/26/1965	08:35	Cap	12/22/1965	14:26

Aqu	12/25/1965	01:43	Gem	04/22/1966	23:25	Lib	08/18/1966	17:04
Pis	12/27/1965	14:16	Can	04/25/1966	05:47	Sco	08/20/1966	18:23
Ari	12/30/1965	02:38	Leo	04/27/1966	10:08	Sag	08/22/1966	22:51
Tau	01/01/1966	12:44	Vir	04/29/1966	12:48	Cap	08/25/1966	06:36
Gem	01/03/1966	19:05	Lib	05/01/1966	14:30	Aqu	08/27/1966	16:55
Can	01/05/1966	21:38	Sco	05/03/1966	16:23	Pis	08/30/1966	04:47
Leo	01/07/1966	21:49	Sag	05/05/1966	19:52	Ari	09/01/1966	17:26
Vir	01/09/1966	21:34	Cap	05/08/1966	02:12	Tau	09/04/1966	05:58
Lib	01/11/1966	22:53	Aqu	05/10/1966	11:51	Gem	09/06/1966	16:51
Sco	01/14/1966	03:08	Pis	05/12/1966	23:54	Can	09/09/1966	00:24
Sag	01/16/1966	10:39	Ari	05/15/1966	12:13	Leo	09/11/1966	03:59
Cap	01/18/1966	20:44	Tau	05/17/1966	22:47	Vir	09/13/1966	04:24
Aqu	01/21/1966	08:25	Gem	05/20/1966	06:39	Lib	09/15/1966	03:32
Pis	01/23/1966	20:57	Can	05/22/1966	11:58	Sco	09/17/1966	03:33
Ari	01/26/1966	09:31	Leo	05/24/1966	15:36	Sag	09/19/1966	06:20
Tau	01/28/1966	20:41	Vir	05/26/1966	18:21	Cap	09/21/1966	12:53
Gem	01/31/1966	04:42	Lib	05/28/1966	20:59	Aqu	09/23/1966	22:48
Can	02/02/1966	08:39	Sco	05/31/1966	00:11	Pis	09/26/1966	10:48
Leo	02/04/1966	09:12	Sag	06/02/1966	04:38	Ari	09/28/1966	23:28
Vir	02/06/1966	08:10	Cap	06/04/1966	11:10	Tau	10/01/1966	11:45
Lib	02/08/1966	07:50	Aqu	06/06/1966	20:20	Gem	10/03/1966	22:42
Sco	02/10/1966	10:15	Pis	06/09/1966	07:56	Can	10/06/1966	07:11
Sag	02/12/1966	16:33	Ari	06/11/1966	20:25	Leo	10/08/1966	12:22
Cap	02/15/1966	02:25	Tau	06/14/1966	07:28	Vir	10/10/1966	14:25
Aqu	02/17/1966	14:25	Gem	06/16/1966	15:24	Lib	10/12/1966	14:28
Pis	02/20/1966	03:04	Can	06/18/1966	20:03	Sco	10/14/1966	14:21
Ari	02/22/1966	15:29	Leo	06/20/1966	22:28	Sag	10/16/1966	15:59
Tau	02/25/1966	02:51	Vir	06/23/1966	00:07	Cap	10/18/1966	20:56
Gem	02/27/1966	12:00	Lib	06/25/1966	02:22	Aqu	10/21/1966	05:40
Can	03/01/1966	17:47	Sco	06/27/1966	06:03	Pis	10/23/1966	17:19
Leo	03/03/1966	19:55	Sag	06/29/1966	11:31	Ari	10/26/1966	06:02
Vir	03/05/1966	19:35	Cap	07/01/1966	18:50	Tau	10/28/1966	18:04
Lib	03/07/1966	18:48	Aqu	07/04/1966	04:14	Gem	10/31/1966	04:27
Sco	03/09/1966	19:47	Pis	07/06/1966	15:39	Can	11/02/1966	12:41
Sag	03/12/1966	00:19	Ari	07/09/1966	04:15	Leo	11/04/1966	18:35
Cap	03/14/1966	08:55	Tau	07/11/1966	16:02	Vir	11/06/1966	22:08
Aqu	03/16/1966	20:34	Gem	07/14/1966	00:49	Lib	11/08/1966	23:53
Pis	03/19/1966	09:17	Can	07/16/1966	05:43	Sco	11/11/1966	00:53
Ari	03/21/1966	21:32	Leo	07/18/1966	07:26	Sag	11/13/1966	02:36
Tau	03/24/1966	08:30	Vir	07/20/1966	07:46	Cap	11/15/1966	06:36
Gem	03/26/1966	17:40	Lib	07/22/1966	08:38	Aqu	11/17/1966	14:03
Can	03/29/1966	00:21	Sco	07/24/1966	11:32	Pis	11/20/1966	00:52
Leo	03/31/1966	04:10	Sag	07/26/1966	17:04	Ari	11/22/1966	13:30
Vir	04/02/1966	05:30	Cap	07/29/1966	01:04	Tau	11/25/1966	01:35
Lib	04/04/1966	05:39	Aqu	07/31/1966	11:01	Gem	11/27/1966	11:29
Sco	04/06/1966	06:29	Pis	08/02/1966	22:35	Can	11/29/1966	18:48
Sag	04/08/1966	09:54	Ari	08/05/1966	11:14	Leo	12/02/1966	00:00
Cap	04/10/1966	17:01	Tau	08/07/1966	23:36	Vir	12/04/1966	03:47
Aqu	04/13/1966	03:41	Gem	08/10/1966	09:36	Lib	12/06/1966	06:42
Pis	04/15/1966	16:12	Can	08/12/1966	15:39	Sco	12/08/1966	09:17
Ari	04/18/1966	04:26	Leo	08/14/1966	17:49	Sag	12/10/1966	12:13
Tau	04/20/1966	14:59	Vir	08/16/1966	17:34	Cap	12/12/1966	16:30

Aqu	12/14/1966	23:19	Gem	04/13/1967	03:13	Lib	08/09/1967	04:33
Pis	12/17/1966	09:17	Can	04/15/1967	13:35	Sco	08/11/1967	06:43
Ari	12/19/1966	21:38	Leo	04/17/1967	20:52	Sag	08/13/1967	09:52
Tau	12/22/1966	10:06	Vir	04/20/1967	00:40	Cap	08/15/1967	14:18
Gem	12/24/1966	20:12	Lib	04/22/1967	01:40	Aqu	08/17/1967	20:16
Can	12/27/1966	02:56	Sco	04/24/1967	01:18	Pis	08/20/1967	04:18
Leo	12/29/1966	06:56	Sag	04/26/1967	01:27	Ari	08/22/1967	14:47
Vir	12/31/1966	09:32	Cap	04/28/1967	03:54	Tau	08/25/1967	03:20
Lib	01/02/1967	12:03	Aqu	04/30/1967	09:58	Gem	08/27/1967	16:07
Sco	01/04/1967	15:15	Pis	05/02/1967	19:47	Can	08/30/1967	02:33
Sag	01/06/1967	19:27	Ari	05/05/1967	08:09	Leo	09/01/1967	09:06
Cap	01/09/1967	00:53	Tau	05/07/1967	21:08	Vir	09/03/1967	12:05
Aqu	01/11/1967	08:05	Gem	05/10/1967	09:07	Lib	09/05/1967	13:02
Pis	01/13/1967	17:44	Can	05/12/1967	19:09	Sco	09/07/1967	13:43
Ari	01/16/1967	05:47	Leo	05/15/1967	02:47	Sag	09/09/1967	15:39
Tau	01/18/1967	18:38	Vir	05/17/1967	07:50	Cap	09/11/1967	19:42
Gem	01/21/1967	05:37	Lib	05/19/1967	10:29	Aqu	09/14/1967	02:08
Can	01/23/1967	12:49	Sco	05/21/1967	11:29	Pis	09/16/1967	10:53
Leo	01/25/1967	16:19	Sag	05/23/1967	12:05	Ari	09/18/1967	21:46
Vir	01/27/1967	17:35	Cap	05/25/1967	13:58	Tau	09/21/1967	10:20
Lib	01/29/1967	18:32	Aqu	05/27/1967	18:43	Gem	09/23/1967	23:20
Sco	01/31/1967	20:43	Pis	05/30/1967	03:18	Can	09/26/1967	10:43
Sag	02/03/1967	00:55	Ari	06/01/1967	15:06	Leo	09/28/1967	18:40
Cap	02/05/1967	07:09	Tau	06/04/1967	04:03	Vir	09/30/1967	22:36
Aqu	02/07/1967	15:16	Gem	06/06/1967	15:51	Lib	10/02/1967	23:33
Pis	02/10/1967	01:19	Can	06/09/1967	01:16	Sco	10/04/1967	23:13
Ari	02/12/1967	13:16	Leo	06/11/1967	08:18	Sag	10/06/1967	23:32
Tau	02/15/1967	02:17	Vir	06/13/1967	13:22	Cap	10/09/1967	02:04
Gem	02/17/1967	14:14	Lib	06/15/1967	16:57	Aqu	10/11/1967	07:45
Can	02/19/1967	22:45	Sco	06/17/1967	19:24	Pis	10/13/1967	16:37
Leo	02/22/1967	03:02	Sag	06/19/1967	21:19	Ari	10/16/1967	03:57
Vir	02/24/1967	04:03	Cap	06/21/1967	23:46	Tau	10/18/1967	16:40
Lib	02/26/1967	03:44	Aqu	06/24/1967	04:10	Gem	10/21/1967	05:37
Sco	02/28/1967	04:09	Pis	06/26/1967	11:50	Can	10/23/1967	17:26
Sag	03/02/1967	06:52	Ari	06/28/1967	22:52	Leo	10/26/1967	02:38
Cap	03/04/1967	12:35	Tau	07/01/1967	11:42	Vir	10/28/1967	08:17
Aqu	03/06/1967	21:03	Gem	07/03/1967	23:37	Lib	10/30/1967	10:29
Pis	03/09/1967	07:40	Can	07/06/1967	08:46	Sco	11/01/1967	10:25
Ari	03/11/1967	19:52	Leo	07/08/1967	14:57	Sag	11/03/1967	09:51
Tau	03/14/1967	08:53	Vir	07/10/1967	19:06	Cap	11/05/1967	10:44
Gem	03/16/1967	21:17	Lib	07/12/1967	22:19	Aqu	11/07/1967	14:46
Can	03/19/1967	07:08	Sco	07/15/1967	01:17	Pis	11/09/1967	22:43
Leo	03/21/1967	13:01	Sag	07/17/1967	04:21	Ari	11/12/1967	09:58
Vir	03/23/1967	15:06	Cap	07/19/1967	07:59	Tau	11/14/1967	22:51
Lib	03/25/1967	14:49	Aqu	07/21/1967	12:59	Gem	11/17/1967	11:39
Sco	03/27/1967	14:10	Pis	07/23/1967	20:28	Can	11/19/1967	23:11
Sag	03/29/1967	15:08	Ari	07/26/1967	06:59	Leo	11/22/1967	08:46
Cap	03/31/1967	19:10	Tau	07/28/1967	19:40	Vir	11/24/1967	15:44
Aqu	04/02/1967	02:49	Gem	07/31/1967	07:59	Lib	11/26/1967	19:47
Pis	04/05/1967	13:28	Can	08/02/1967	17:31	Sco	11/28/1967	21:12
Ari	04/08/1967	01:56	Leo	08/04/1967	23:24	Sag	11/30/1967	21:09
Tau	04/10/1967	14:55	Vir	08/07/1967	02:35	Cap	12/02/1967	21:25

Aqu	12/04/1967	23:57	Gem	04/02/1968	01:39	Lib	07/29/1968	16:31
Pis	12/07/1967	06:19	Can	04/04/1968	14:11	Sco	07/31/1968	21:10
Ari	12/09/1967	16:43	Leo	04/07/1968	00:26	Sag	08/03/1968	00:09
Tau	12/12/1967	05:31	Vir	04/09/1968	07:03	Cap	08/05/1968	01:57
Gem	12/14/1967	18:17	Lib	04/11/1968	09:59	Aqu	08/07/1968	03:37
Can	12/17/1967	05:22	Sco	04/13/1968	10:31	Pis	08/09/1968	06:45
Leo	12/19/1967	14:20	Sag	04/15/1968	10:23	Ari	08/11/1968	12:54
Vir	12/21/1967	21:20	Cap	04/17/1968	11:23	Tau	08/13/1968	22:36
Lib	12/24/1967	02:25	Aqu	04/19/1968	14:57	Gem	08/16/1968	10:50
Sco	12/26/1967	05:35	Pis	04/21/1968	21:46	Can	08/18/1968	23:14
Sag	12/28/1967	07:08	Ari	04/24/1968	07:32	Leo	08/21/1968	09:38
Cap	12/30/1967	08:11	Tau	04/26/1968	19:21	Vir	08/23/1968	17:20
Aqu	01/01/1968	10:24	Gem	04/29/1968	08:10	Lib	08/25/1968	22:43
Pis	01/03/1968	15:36	Can	05/01/1968	20:49	Sco	08/28/1968	02:37
Ari	01/06/1968	00:46	Leo	05/04/1968	07:52	Sag	08/30/1968	05:40
Tau	01/08/1968	13:02	Vir	05/06/1968	15:56	Cap	09/01/1968	08:21
Gem	01/11/1968	01:53	Lib	05/08/1968	20:19	Aqu	09/03/1968	11:19
Can	01/13/1968	12:52	Sco	05/10/1968	21:28	Pis	09/05/1968	15:27
Leo	01/15/1968	21:08	Sag	05/12/1968	20:53	Ari	09/07/1968	21:49
Vir	01/18/1968	03:10	Cap	05/14/1968	20:31	Tau	09/10/1968	07:06
Lib	01/20/1968	07:46	Aqu	05/16/1968	22:23	Gem	09/12/1968	18:54
Sco	01/22/1968	11:27	Pis	05/19/1968	03:53	Can	09/15/1968	07:28
Sag	01/24/1968	14:23	Ari	05/21/1968	13:14	Leo	09/17/1968	18:25
Cap	01/26/1968	16:56	Tau	05/24/1968	01:15	Vir	09/20/1968	02:14
Aqu	01/28/1968	20:06	Gem	05/26/1968	14:11	Lib	09/22/1968	06:59
Pis	01/31/1968	01:16	Can	05/29/1968	02:42	Sco	09/24/1968	09:38
Ari	02/02/1968	09:40	Leo	05/31/1968	13:52	Sag	09/26/1968	11:30
Tau	02/04/1968	21:15	Vir	06/02/1968	22:50	Cap	09/28/1968	13:44
Gem	02/07/1968	10:08	Lib	06/05/1968	04:48	Aqu	09/30/1968	17:10
Can	02/09/1968	21:33	Sco	06/07/1968	07:29	Pis	10/02/1968	22:21
Leo	02/12/1968	05:49	Sag	06/09/1968	07:41	Ari	10/05/1968	05:35
Vir	02/14/1968	11:01	Cap	06/11/1968	07:05	Tau	10/07/1968	15:07
Lib	02/16/1968	14:20	Aqu	06/13/1968	07:46	Gem	10/10/1968	02:43
Sco	02/18/1968	16:59	Pis	06/15/1968	11:43	Can	10/12/1968	15:23
Sag	02/20/1968	19:47	Ari	06/17/1968	19:50	Leo	10/15/1968	03:07
Cap	02/22/1968	23:11	Tau	06/20/1968	07:24	Vir	10/17/1968	11:56
Aqu	02/25/1968	03:36	Gem	06/22/1968	20:21	Lib	10/19/1968	17:04
Pis	02/27/1968	09:42	Can	06/25/1968	08:42	Sco	10/21/1968	19:05
Ari	02/29/1968	18:14	Leo	06/27/1968	19:30	Sag	10/23/1968	19:32
Tau	03/03/1968	05:27	Vir	06/30/1968	04:25	Cap	10/25/1968	20:13
Gem	03/05/1968	18:16	Lib	07/02/1968	11:08	Aqu	10/27/1968	22:43
Can	03/08/1968	06:20	Sco	07/04/1968	15:19	Pis	10/30/1968	03:54
Leo	03/10/1968	15:25	Sag	07/06/1968	17:04	Ari	11/01/1968	11:51
Vir	03/12/1968	20:50	Cap	07/08/1968	17:23	Tau	11/03/1968	22:01
Lib	03/14/1968	23:21	Aqu	07/10/1968	18:03	Gem	11/06/1968	09:47
Sco	03/17/1968	00:32	Pis	07/12/1968	21:03	Can	11/08/1968	22:26
Sag	03/19/1968	01:53	Ari	07/15/1968	03:52	Leo	11/11/1968	10:43
Cap	03/21/1968	04:34	Tau	07/17/1968	14:30	Vir	11/13/1968	20:53
Aqu	03/23/1968	09:16	Gem	07/20/1968	03:12	Lib	11/16/1968	03:25
Pis	03/25/1968	16:15	Can	07/22/1968	15:30	Sco	11/18/1968	06:05
Ari	03/28/1968	01:32	Leo	07/25/1968	01:54	Sag	11/20/1968	06:03
Tau	03/30/1968	12:54	Vir	07/27/1968	10:09	Cap	11/22/1968	05:19

Aqu	11/24/1968	06:01	Gem	03/22/1969	21:12	Lib	07/20/1969	00:18
Pis	11/26/1968	09:53	Can	03/25/1969	09:18	Sco	07/22/1969	08:03
Ari	11/28/1968	17:25	Leo	03/27/1969	21:36	Sag	07/24/1969	12:09
Tau	12/01/1968	03:57	Vir	03/30/1969	07:52	Cap	07/26/1969	13:08
Gem	12/03/1968	16:05	Lib	04/01/1969	15:02	Aqu	07/28/1969	12:34
Can	12/06/1968	04:43	Sco	04/03/1969	19:21	Pis	07/30/1969	12:31
Leo	12/08/1968	17:02	Sag	04/05/1969	21:56	Ari	08/01/1969	14:55
Vir	12/11/1968	03:58	Cap	04/08/1969	00:04	Tau	08/03/1969	21:02
Lib	12/13/1968	12:06	Aqu	04/10/1969	02:46	Gem	08/06/1969	06:49
Sco	12/15/1968	16:30	Pis	04/12/1969	06:41	Can	08/08/1969	18:57
Sag	12/17/1968	17:27	Ari	04/14/1969	12:13	Leo	08/11/1969	07:38
Cap	12/19/1968	16:32	Tau	04/16/1969	19:43	Vir	08/13/1969	19:32
Aqu	12/21/1968	16:00	Gem	04/19/1969	05:28	Lib	08/16/1969	05:50
Pis	12/23/1968	18:00	Can	04/21/1969	17:16	Sco	08/18/1969	13:52
Ari	12/26/1968	00:03	Leo	04/24/1969	05:50	Sag	08/20/1969	19:11
Tau	12/28/1968	09:57	Vir	04/26/1969	16:56	Cap	08/22/1969	21:47
Gem	12/30/1968	22:10	Lib	04/29/1969	00:42	Aqu	08/24/1969	22:35
Can	01/02/1969	10:52	Sco	05/01/1969	04:49	Pis	08/26/1969	23:04
Leo	01/04/1969	22:54	Sag	05/03/1969	06:18	Ari	08/29/1969	00:58
Vir	01/07/1969	09:41	Cap	05/05/1969	06:56	Tau	08/31/1969	05:50
Lib	01/09/1969	18:32	Aqu	05/07/1969	08:28	Gem	09/02/1969	14:24
Sco	01/12/1969	00:30	Pis	05/09/1969	12:04	Can	09/05/1969	01:57
Sag	01/14/1969	03:17	Ari	05/11/1969	18:08	Leo	09/07/1969	14:35
Cap	01/16/1969	03:38	Tau	05/14/1969	02:28	Vir	09/10/1969	02:19
Aqu	01/18/1969	03:16	Gem	05/16/1969	12:41	Lib	09/12/1969	12:00
Pis	01/20/1969	04:21	Can	05/19/1969	00:30	Sco	09/14/1969	19:24
Ari	01/22/1969	08:44	Leo	05/21/1969	13:11	Sag	09/17/1969	00:41
Tau	01/24/1969	17:12	Vir	05/24/1969	01:05	Cap	09/19/1969	04:13
Gem	01/27/1969	04:53	Lib	05/26/1969	10:05	Aqu	09/21/1969	06:30
Can	01/29/1969	17:36	Sco	05/28/1969	15:03	Pis	09/23/1969	08:22
Leo	02/01/1969	05:28	Sag	05/30/1969	16:29	Ari	09/25/1969	10:56
Vir	02/03/1969	15:40	Cap	06/01/1969	16:06	Tau	09/27/1969	15:29
Lib	02/05/1969	23:59	Aqu	06/03/1969	16:04	Gem	09/29/1969	23:06
Sco	02/08/1969	06:17	Pis	06/05/1969	18:13	Can	10/02/1969	09:52
Sag	02/10/1969	10:22	Ari	06/07/1969	23:37	Leo	10/04/1969	22:24
Cap	02/12/1969	12:27	Tau	06/10/1969	08:06	Vir	10/07/1969	10:20
Aqu	02/14/1969	13:30	Gem	06/12/1969	18:48	Lib	10/09/1969	19:47
Pis	02/16/1969	15:03	Can	06/15/1969	06:52	Sco	10/12/1969	02:17
Ari	02/18/1969	18:48	Leo	06/17/1969	19:34	Sag	10/14/1969	06:32
Tau	02/21/1969	02:02	Vir	06/20/1969	07:53	Cap	10/16/1969	09:35
Gem	02/23/1969	12:41	Lib	06/22/1969	18:03	Aqu	10/18/1969	12:21
Can	02/26/1969	01:10	Sco	06/25/1969	00:29	Pis	10/20/1969	15:25
Leo	02/28/1969	13:10	Sag	06/27/1969	02:58	Ari	10/22/1969	19:17
Vir	03/02/1969	23:05	Cap	06/29/1969	02:43	Tau	10/25/1969	00:33
Lib	03/05/1969	06:33	Aqu	07/01/1969	01:49	Gem	10/27/1969	08:00
Sco	03/07/1969	11:55	Pis	07/03/1969	02:27	Can	10/29/1969	18:12
Sag	03/09/1969	15:47	Ari	07/05/1969	06:16	Leo	11/01/1969	06:34
Cap	03/11/1969	18:39	Tau	07/07/1969	13:53	Vir	11/03/1969	18:59
Aqu	03/13/1969	21:09	Gem	07/10/1969	00:31	Lib	11/06/1969	04:58
Pis	03/16/1969	00:04	Can	07/12/1969	12:47	Sco	11/08/1969	11:16
Ari	03/18/1969	04:27	Leo	07/15/1969	01:28	Sag	11/10/1969	14:29
Tau	03/20/1969	11:21	Vir	07/17/1969	13:41	Cap	11/12/1969	16:08

Aqu	11/14/1969	17:52	Gem	03/12/1970	18:36	Lib	07/10/1970	01:02
Pis	11/16/1969	20:52	Can	03/15/1970	04:18	Sco	07/12/1970	11:39
Ari	11/19/1969	01:32	Leo	03/17/1970	16:39	Sag	07/14/1970	18:25
Tau	11/21/1969	07:52	Vir	03/20/1970	05:29	Cap	07/16/1970	21:18
Gem	11/23/1969	15:59	Lib	03/22/1970	16:56	Aqu	07/18/1970	21:44
Can	11/26/1969	02:10	Sco	03/25/1970	02:09	Pis	07/20/1970	21:37
Leo	11/28/1969	14:22	Sag	03/27/1970	09:05	Ari	07/22/1970	22:43
Vir	12/01/1969	03:13	Cap	03/29/1970	13:59	Tau	07/25/1970	02:19
Lib	12/03/1969	14:15	Aqu	03/31/1970	17:08	Gem	07/27/1970	08:53
Sco	12/05/1969	21:28	Pis	04/02/1970	19:00	Can	07/29/1970	18:14
Sag	12/08/1969	00:41	Ari	04/04/1970	20:32	Leo	08/01/1970	05:44
Cap	12/10/1969	01:19	Tau	04/06/1970	23:03	Vir	08/03/1970	18:34
Aqu	12/12/1969	01:27	Gem	04/09/1970	04:02	Lib	08/06/1970	07:32
Pis	12/14/1969	02:56	Can	04/11/1970	12:34	Sco	08/08/1970	18:56
Ari	12/16/1969	06:56	Leo	04/14/1970	00:16	Sag	08/11/1970	03:06
Tau	12/18/1969	13:35	Vir	04/16/1970	13:06	Cap	08/13/1970	07:24
Gem	12/20/1969	22:28	Lib	04/19/1970	00:33	Aqu	08/15/1970	08:30
Can	12/23/1969	09:08	Sco	04/21/1970	09:14	Pis	08/17/1970	08:01
Leo	12/25/1969	21:21	Sag	04/23/1970	15:14	Ari	08/19/1970	07:50
Vir	12/28/1969	10:19	Cap	04/25/1970	19:26	Tau	08/21/1970	09:47
Lib	12/30/1969	22:16	Aqu	04/27/1970	22:42	Gem	08/23/1970	15:04
Sco	01/02/1970	07:02	Pis	04/30/1970	01:37	Can	08/25/1970	23:59
Sag	01/04/1970	11:31	Ari	05/02/1970	04:32	Leo	08/28/1970	11:38
Cap	01/06/1970	12:28	Tau	05/04/1970	08:05	Vir	08/31/1970	00:36
Aqu	01/08/1970	11:47	Gem	05/06/1970	13:18	Lib	09/02/1970	13:25
Pis	01/10/1970	11:37	Can	05/08/1970	21:17	Sco	09/05/1970	00:53
Ari	01/12/1970	13:49	Leo	05/11/1970	08:22	Sag	09/07/1970	09:57
Tau	01/14/1970	19:20	Vir	05/13/1970	21:10	Cap	09/09/1970	15:50
Gem	01/17/1970	04:07	Lib	05/16/1970	09:01	Aqu	09/11/1970	18:33
Can	01/19/1970	15:13	Sco	05/18/1970	17:49	Pis	09/13/1970	18:56
Leo	01/22/1970	03:40	Sag	05/20/1970	23:10	Ari	09/15/1970	18:35
Vir	01/24/1970	16:32	Cap	05/23/1970	02:12	Tau	09/17/1970	19:21
Lib	01/27/1970	04:42	Aqu	05/25/1970	04:25	Gem	09/19/1970	23:03
Sco	01/29/1970	14:33	Pis	05/27/1970	06:58	Can	09/22/1970	06:41
Sag	01/31/1970	20:48	Ari	05/29/1970	10:27	Leo	09/24/1970	17:54
Cap	02/02/1970	23:20	Tau	05/31/1970	15:03	Vir	09/27/1970	06:53
Aqu	02/04/1970	23:18	Gem	06/02/1970	21:10	Lib	09/29/1970	19:33
Pis	02/06/1970	22:37	Can	06/05/1970	05:25	Sco	10/02/1970	06:35
Ari	02/08/1970	23:18	Leo	06/07/1970	16:17	Sag	10/04/1970	15:30
Tau	02/11/1970	03:00	Vir	06/10/1970	05:02	Cap	10/06/1970	22:09
Gem	02/13/1970	10:29	Lib	06/12/1970	17:27	Aqu	10/09/1970	02:25
Can	02/15/1970	21:17	Sco	06/15/1970	03:00	Pis	10/11/1970	04:29
Leo	02/18/1970	09:53	Sag	06/17/1970	08:38	Ari	10/13/1970	05:12
Vir	02/20/1970	22:41	Cap	06/19/1970	11:04	Tau	10/15/1970	05:59
Lib	02/23/1970	10:29	Aqu	06/21/1970	12:00	Gem	10/17/1970	08:44
Sco	02/25/1970	20:22	Pis	06/23/1970	13:12	Can	10/19/1970	14:59
Sag	02/28/1970	03:37	Ari	06/25/1970	15:52	Leo	10/22/1970	01:13
Cap	03/02/1970	07:53	Tau	06/27/1970	20:35	Vir	10/24/1970	13:57
Aqu	03/04/1970	09:33	Gem	06/30/1970	03:24	Lib	10/27/1970	02:36
Pis	03/06/1970	09:48	Can	07/02/1970	12:21	Sco	10/29/1970	13:14
Ari	03/08/1970	10:17	Leo	07/04/1970	23:26	Sag	10/31/1970	21:23
Tau	03/10/1970	12:44	Vir	07/07/1970	12:11	Cap	11/03/1970	03:32

Aqu	11/05/1970	08:10	Gem	03/02/1971	22:02	Lib	06/29/1971	20:22
Pis	11/07/1970	11:32	Can	03/05/1971	04:48	Sco	07/02/1971	08:45
Ari	11/09/1970	13:51	Leo	03/07/1971	14:56	Sag	07/04/1971	18:58
Tau	11/11/1970	15:50	Vir	03/10/1971	03:10	Cap	07/07/1971	02:02
Gem	11/13/1970	18:48	Lib	03/12/1971	16:05	Aqu	07/09/1971	06:26
Can	11/16/1970	00:24	Sco	03/15/1971	04:31	Pis	07/11/1971	09:14
Leo	11/18/1970	09:36	Sag	03/17/1971	15:22	Ari	07/13/1971	11:32
Vir	11/20/1970	21:50	Cap	03/19/1971	23:36	Tau	07/15/1971	14:11
Lib	11/23/1970	10:38	Aqu	03/22/1971	04:28	Gem	07/17/1971	17:47
Sco	11/25/1970	21:23	Pis	03/24/1971	06:07	Can	07/19/1971	22:57
Sag	11/28/1970	05:01	Ari	03/26/1971	05:45	Leo	07/22/1971	06:16
Cap	11/30/1970	10:05	Tau	03/28/1971	05:15	Vir	07/24/1971	16:10
Aqu	12/02/1970	13:44	Gem	03/30/1971	06:44	Lib	07/27/1971	04:12
Pis	12/04/1970	16:55	Can	04/01/1971	11:52	Sco	07/29/1971	16:50
Ari	12/06/1970	20:03	Leo	04/03/1971	21:06	Sag	08/01/1971	03:49
Tau	12/08/1970	23:24	Vir	04/06/1971	09:16	Cap	08/03/1971	11:30
Gem	12/11/1970	03:33	Lib	04/08/1971	22:16	Aqu	08/05/1971	15:46
Can	12/13/1970	09:33	Sco	04/11/1971	10:27	Pis	08/07/1971	17:34
Leo	12/15/1970	18:21	Sag	04/13/1971	21:02	Ari	08/09/1971	18:27
Vir	12/18/1970	06:04	Cap	04/16/1971	05:38	Tau	08/11/1971	19:56
Lib	12/20/1970	19:01	Aqu	04/18/1971	11:44	Gem	08/13/1971	23:11
Sco	12/23/1970	06:26	Pis	04/20/1971	15:07	Can	08/16/1971	04:50
Sag	12/25/1970	14:26	Ari	04/22/1971	16:08	Leo	08/18/1971	12:58
Cap	12/27/1970	19:01	Tau	04/24/1971	16:06	Vir	08/20/1971	23:19
Aqu	12/29/1970	21:23	Gem	04/26/1971	16:59	Lib	08/23/1971	11:23
Pis	12/31/1970	23:08	Can	04/28/1971	20:44	Sco	08/26/1971	00:08
Ari	01/03/1971	01:27	Leo	05/01/1971	04:35	Sag	08/28/1971	11:56
Tau	01/05/1971	05:00	Vir	05/03/1971	16:03	Cap	08/30/1971	20:53
Gem	01/07/1971	10:09	Lib	05/06/1971	04:59	Aqu	09/02/1971	02:02
Can	01/09/1971	17:09	Sco	05/08/1971	17:03	Pis	09/04/1971	03:50
Leo	01/12/1971	02:24	Sag	05/11/1971	03:07	Ari	09/06/1971	03:43
Vir	01/14/1971	13:58	Cap	05/13/1971	11:08	Tau	09/08/1971	03:38
Lib	01/17/1971	02:53	Aqu	05/15/1971	17:19	Gem	09/10/1971	05:25
Sco	01/19/1971	15:03	Pis	05/17/1971	21:38	Can	09/12/1971	10:22
Sag	01/22/1971	00:14	Ari	05/20/1971	00:10	Leo	09/14/1971	18:38
Cap	01/24/1971	05:32	Tau	05/22/1971	01:31	Vir	09/17/1971	05:29
Aqu	01/26/1971	07:35	Gem	05/24/1971	03:01	Lib	09/19/1971	17:47
Pis	01/28/1971	08:01	Can	05/26/1971	06:26	Sco	09/22/1971	06:33
Ari	01/30/1971	08:36	Leo	05/28/1971	13:17	Sag	09/24/1971	18:43
Tau	02/01/1971	10:49	Vir	05/30/1971	23:48	Cap	09/27/1971	04:52
Gem	02/03/1971	15:35	Lib	06/02/1971	12:26	Aqu	09/29/1971	11:37
Can	02/05/1971	23:07	Sco	06/05/1971	00:35	Pis	10/01/1971	14:35
Leo	02/08/1971	09:06	Sag	06/07/1971	10:27	Ari	10/03/1971	14:40
Vir	02/10/1971	20:58	Cap	06/09/1971	17:45	Tau	10/05/1971	13:42
Lib	02/13/1971	09:50	Aqu	06/11/1971	23:02	Gem	10/07/1971	13:54
Sco	02/15/1971	22:21	Pis	06/14/1971	03:01	Can	10/09/1971	17:11
Sag	02/18/1971	08:44	Ari	06/16/1971	06:06	Leo	10/12/1971	00:32
Cap	02/20/1971	15:36	Tau	06/18/1971	08:39	Vir	10/14/1971	11:17
Aqu	02/22/1971	18:42	Gem	06/20/1971	11:24	Lib	10/16/1971	23:47
Pis	02/24/1971	19:05	Can	06/22/1971	15:30	Sco	10/19/1971	12:30
Ari	02/26/1971	18:29	Leo	06/24/1971	22:13	Sag	10/22/1971	00:31
Tau	02/28/1971	18:54	Vir	06/27/1971	08:06	Cap	10/24/1971	11:04

Aqu	10/26/1971	19:10	Gem	02/21/1972	08:36	Lib	06/18/1972	15:39
Pis	10/28/1971	23:55	Can	02/23/1972	12:53	Sco	06/21/1972	03:43
Ari	10/31/1971	01:25	Leo	02/25/1972	19:15	Sag	06/23/1972	16:14
Tau	11/02/1971	00:55	Vir	02/28/1972	03:39	Cap	06/26/1972	03:36
Gem	11/04/1971	00:28	Lib	03/01/1972	14:00	Aqu	06/28/1972	13:02
Can	11/06/1971	02:16	Sco	03/04/1972	02:00	Pis	06/30/1972	20:18
Leo	11/08/1971	07:57	Sag	03/06/1972	14:36	Ari	07/03/1972	01:21
Vir	11/10/1971	17:44	Cap	03/09/1972	01:48	Tau	07/05/1972	04:24
Lib	11/13/1971	06:05	Aqu	03/11/1972	09:41	Gem	07/07/1972	06:05
Sco	11/15/1971	18:49	Pis	03/13/1972	13:38	Can	07/09/1972	07:29
Sag	11/18/1971	06:29	Ari	03/15/1972	14:36	Leo	07/11/1972	10:06
Cap	11/20/1971	16:36	Tau	03/17/1972	14:28	Vir	07/13/1972	15:17
Aqu	11/23/1971	00:51	Gem	03/19/1972	15:13	Lib	07/15/1972	23:50
Pis	11/25/1971	06:47	Can	03/21/1972	18:26	Sco	07/18/1972	11:15
Ari	11/27/1971	10:02	Leo	03/24/1972	00:47	Sag	07/20/1972	23:46
Tau	11/29/1971	11:08	Vir	03/26/1972	09:48	Cap	07/23/1972	11:09
Gem	12/01/1971	11:26	Lib	03/28/1972	20:42	Aqu	07/25/1972	20:06
Can	12/03/1971	12:52	Sco	03/31/1972	08:48	Pis	07/28/1972	02:28
Leo	12/05/1971	17:17	Sag	04/02/1972	21:27	Ari	07/30/1972	06:50
Vir	12/08/1971	01:41	Cap	04/05/1972	09:20	Tau	08/01/1972	09:57
Lib	12/10/1971	13:19	Aqu	04/07/1972	18:37	Gem	08/03/1972	12:33
Sco	12/13/1971	02:01	Pis	04/09/1972	23:56	Can	08/05/1972	15:18
Sag	12/15/1971	13:36	Ari	04/12/1972	01:31	Leo	08/07/1972	18:56
Cap	12/17/1971	23:06	Tau	04/14/1972	00:54	Vir	08/10/1972	00:24
Aqu	12/20/1971	06:32	Gem	04/16/1972	00:17	Lib	08/12/1972	08:28
Pis	12/22/1971	12:09	Can	04/18/1972	01:47	Sco	08/14/1972	19:20
Ari	12/24/1971	16:09	Leo	04/20/1972	06:47	Sag	08/17/1972	07:49
Tau	12/26/1971	18:45	Vir	04/22/1972	15:25	Cap	08/19/1972	19:37
Gem	12/28/1971	20:38	Lib	04/25/1972	02:35	Aqu	08/22/1972	04:42
Can	12/30/1971	23:02	Sco	04/27/1972	14:56	Pis	08/24/1972	10:27
Leo	01/02/1972	03:22	Sag	04/30/1972	03:30	Ari	08/26/1972	13:40
Vir	01/04/1972	10:51	Cap	05/02/1972	15:28	Tau	08/28/1972	15:43
Lib	01/06/1972	21:33	Aqu	05/05/1972	01:34	Gem	08/30/1972	17:56
Sco	01/09/1972	10:03	Pis	05/07/1972	08:27	Can	09/01/1972	21:12
Sag	01/11/1972	21:56	Ari	05/09/1972	11:33	Leo	09/04/1972	01:54
Cap	01/14/1972	07:25	Tau	05/11/1972	11:47	Vir	09/06/1972	08:15
Aqu	01/16/1972	14:03	Gem	05/13/1972	10:57	Lib	09/08/1972	16:37
Pis	01/18/1972	18:28	Can	05/15/1972	11:17	Sco	09/11/1972	03:16
Ari	01/20/1972	21:35	Leo	05/17/1972	14:39	Sag	09/13/1972	15:42
Tau	01/23/1972	00:17	Vir	05/19/1972	21:57	Cap	09/16/1972	04:07
Gem	01/25/1972	03:14	Lib	05/22/1972	08:36	Aqu	09/18/1972	14:03
Can	01/27/1972	07:02	Sco	05/24/1972	21:01	Pis	09/20/1972	20:08
Leo	01/29/1972	12:22	Sag	05/27/1972	09:33	Ari	09/22/1972	22:43
Vir	01/31/1972	19:56	Cap	05/29/1972	21:12	Tau	09/24/1972	23:27
Lib	02/03/1972	06:06	Aqu	06/01/1972	07:15	Gem	09/27/1972	00:15
Sco	02/05/1972	18:18	Pis	06/03/1972	14:51	Can	09/29/1972	02:39
Sag	02/08/1972	06:38	Ari	06/05/1972	19:27	Leo	10/01/1972	07:25
Cap	02/10/1972	16:49	Tau	06/07/1972	21:14	Vir	10/03/1972	14:31
Aqu	02/12/1972	23:35	Gem	06/09/1972	21:24	Lib	10/05/1972	23:35
Pis	02/15/1972	03:10	Can	06/11/1972	21:45	Sco	10/08/1972	10:27
Ari	02/17/1972	04:50	Leo	06/14/1972	00:11	Sag	10/10/1972	22:52
Tau	02/19/1972	06:11	Vir	06/16/1972	06:03	Cap	10/13/1972	11:43

Aqu	10/15/1972	22:50	Gem	02/10/1973	23:09	Lib	06/08/1973	16:16
Pis	10/18/1972	06:12	Can	02/13/1973	01:44	Sco	06/11/1973	01:52
Ari	10/20/1972	09:21	Leo	02/15/1973	04:12	Sag	06/13/1973	13:43
Tau	10/22/1972	09:37	Vir	02/17/1973	07:31	Cap	06/16/1973	02:37
Gem	10/24/1972	09:03	Lib	02/19/1973	12:59	Aqu	06/18/1973	15:18
Can	10/26/1972	09:45	Sco	02/21/1973	21:36	Pis	06/21/1973	02:28
Leo	10/28/1972	13:15	Sag	02/24/1973	09:15	Ari	06/23/1973	10:47
Vir	10/30/1972	20:00	Cap	02/26/1973	22:03	Tau	06/25/1973	15:36
Lib	11/02/1972	05:27	Aqu	03/01/1973	09:21	Gem	06/27/1973	17:17
Sco	11/04/1972	16:46	Pis	03/03/1973	17:31	Can	06/29/1973	17:08
Sag	11/07/1972	05:16	Ari	03/05/1973	22:36	Leo	07/01/1973	16:56
Cap	11/09/1972	18:11	Tau	03/08/1973	01:50	Vir	07/03/1973	18:31
Aqu	11/12/1972	06:02	Gem	03/10/1973	04:31	Lib	07/05/1973	23:25
Pis	11/14/1972	14:55	Can	03/12/1973	07:29	Sco	07/08/1973	08:06
Ari	11/16/1972	19:43	Leo	03/14/1973	11:08	Sag	07/10/1973	19:48
Tau	11/18/1972	20:52	Vir	03/16/1973	15:42	Cap	07/13/1973	08:45
Gem	11/20/1972	20:05	Lib	03/18/1973	21:49	Aqu	07/15/1973	21:14
Can	11/22/1972	19:31	Sco	03/21/1973	06:15	Pis	07/18/1973	08:07
Leo	11/24/1972	21:12	Sag	03/23/1973	17:26	Ari	07/20/1973	16:43
Vir	11/27/1972	02:25	Cap	03/26/1973	06:16	Tau	07/22/1973	22:40
Lib	11/29/1972	11:16	Aqu	03/28/1973	18:12	Gem	07/25/1973	01:57
Sco	12/01/1972	22:43	Pis	03/31/1973	02:54	Can	07/27/1973	03:10
Sag	12/04/1972	11:22	Ari	04/02/1973	07:47	Leo	07/29/1973	03:29
Cap	12/07/1972	00:06	Tau	04/04/1973	09:58	Vir	07/31/1973	04:35
Aqu	12/09/1972	11:53	Gem	04/06/1973	11:12	Lib	08/02/1973	08:13
Pis	12/11/1972	21:31	Can	04/08/1973	13:05	Sco	08/04/1973	15:36
Ari	12/14/1972	03:58	Leo	04/10/1973	16:31	Sag	08/07/1973	02:37
Tau	12/16/1972	06:58	Vir	04/12/1973	21:47	Cap	08/09/1973	15:30
Gem	12/18/1972	07:24	Lib	04/15/1973	04:50	Aqu	08/12/1973	03:52
Can	12/20/1972	06:57	Sco	04/17/1973	13:52	Pis	08/14/1973	14:13
Leo	12/22/1972	07:34	Sag	04/20/1973	01:02	Ari	08/16/1973	22:15
Vir	12/24/1972	11:04	Cap	04/22/1973	13:49	Tau	08/19/1973	04:13
Lib	12/26/1972	18:22	Aqu	04/25/1973	02:20	Gem	08/21/1973	08:26
Sco	12/29/1972	05:10	Pis	04/27/1973	12:08	Can	08/23/1973	11:07
Sag	12/31/1972	17:51	Ari	04/29/1973	17:53	Leo	08/25/1973	12:49
Cap	01/03/1973	06:30	Tau	05/01/1973	20:01	Vir	08/27/1973	14:34
Aqu	01/05/1973	17:47	Gem	05/03/1973	20:16	Lib	08/29/1973	17:52
Pis	01/08/1973	03:02	Can	05/05/1973	20:35	Sco	09/01/1973	00:19
Ari	01/10/1973	09:57	Leo	05/07/1973	22:37	Sag	09/03/1973	10:25
Tau	01/12/1973	14:24	Vir	05/10/1973	03:13	Cap	09/05/1973	23:01
Gem	01/14/1973	16:40	Lib	05/12/1973	10:31	Aqu	09/08/1973	11:30
Can	01/16/1973	17:38	Sco	05/14/1973	20:09	Pis	09/10/1973	21:39
Leo	01/18/1973	18:40	Sag	05/17/1973	07:42	Ari	09/13/1973	04:55
Vir	01/20/1973	21:24	Cap	05/19/1973	20:30	Tau	09/15/1973	09:58
Lib	01/23/1973	03:17	Aqu	05/22/1973	09:17	Gem	09/17/1973	13:47
Sco	01/25/1973	12:53	Pis	05/24/1973	20:04	Can	09/19/1973	17:01
Sag	01/28/1973	01:10	Ari	05/27/1973	03:13	Leo	09/21/1973	19:56
Cap	01/30/1973	13:53	Tau	05/29/1973	06:27	Vir	09/23/1973	22:59
Aqu	02/02/1973	00:54	Gem	05/31/1973	06:52	Lib	09/26/1973	03:01
Pis	02/04/1973	09:21	Can	06/02/1973	06:21	Sco	09/28/1973	09:19
Ari	02/06/1973	15:28	Leo	06/04/1973	06:49	Sag	09/30/1973	18:48
Tau	02/08/1973	19:53	Vir	06/06/1973	09:52	Cap	10/03/1973	07:02

Aqu	10/05/1973	19:48	Gem	02/01/1974	11:52	Lib	05/30/1974	00:17
Pis	10/08/1973	06:23	Can	02/03/1974	14:05	Sco	06/01/1974	06:10
Ari	10/10/1973	13:28	Leo	02/05/1974	14:11	Sag	06/03/1974	14:22
Tau	10/12/1973	17:36	Vir	02/07/1974	13:52	Cap	06/06/1974	00:49
Gem	10/14/1973	20:08	Lib	02/09/1974	15:11	Aqu	06/08/1974	13:02
Can	10/16/1973	22:29	Sco	02/11/1974	19:59	Pis	06/11/1974	01:43
Leo	10/19/1973	01:25	Sag	02/14/1974	05:01	Ari	06/13/1974	12:51
Vir	10/21/1973	05:19	Cap	02/16/1974	17:16	Tau	06/15/1974	20:45
Lib	10/23/1973	10:29	Aqu	02/19/1974	06:21	Gem	06/18/1974	00:58
Sco	10/25/1973	17:28	Pis	02/21/1974	18:15	Can	06/20/1974	02:21
Sag	10/28/1973	02:58	Ari	02/24/1974	04:12	Leo	06/22/1974	02:30
Cap	10/30/1973	14:57	Tau	02/26/1974	12:11	Vir	06/24/1974	03:12
Aqu	11/02/1973	03:58	Gem	02/28/1974	18:10	Lib	06/26/1974	05:57
Pis	11/04/1973	15:25	Can	03/02/1974	21:59	Sco	06/28/1974	11:41
Ari	11/06/1973	23:18	Leo	03/04/1974	23:48	Sag	06/30/1974	20:21
Tau	11/09/1973	03:25	Vir	03/07/1974	00:33	Cap	07/03/1974	07:19
Gem	11/11/1973	04:59	Lib	03/09/1974	01:53	Aqu	07/05/1974	19:41
Can	11/13/1973	05:46	Sco	03/11/1974	05:40	Pis	07/08/1974	08:25
Leo	11/15/1973	07:20	Sag	03/13/1974	13:21	Ari	07/10/1974	20:10
Vir	11/17/1973	10:42	Cap	03/16/1974	00:42	Tau	07/13/1974	05:21
Lib	11/19/1973	16:16	Aqu	03/18/1974	13:38	Gem	07/15/1974	10:52
Sco	11/22/1973	00:07	Pis	03/21/1974	01:33	Can	07/17/1974	12:55
Sag	11/24/1973	10:11	Ari	03/23/1974	11:02	Leo	07/19/1974	12:43
Cap	11/26/1973	22:13	Tau	03/25/1974	18:09	Vir	07/21/1974	12:10
Aqu	11/29/1973	11:17	Gem	03/27/1974	23:32	Lib	07/23/1974	13:20
Pis	12/01/1973	23:31	Can	03/30/1974	03:39	Sco	07/25/1974	17:45
Ari	12/04/1973	08:49	Leo	04/01/1974	06:40	Sag	07/28/1974	02:00
Tau	12/06/1973	14:07	Vir	04/03/1974	08:56	Cap	07/30/1974	13:11
Gem	12/08/1973	15:57	Lib	04/05/1974	11:23	Aqu	08/02/1974	01:46
Can	12/10/1973	15:52	Sco	04/07/1974	15:26	Pis	08/04/1974	14:26
Leo	12/12/1973	15:45	Sag	04/09/1974	22:28	Ari	08/07/1974	02:14
Vir	12/14/1973	17:21	Cap	04/12/1974	08:57	Tau	08/09/1974	12:12
Lib	12/16/1973	21:54	Aqu	04/14/1974	21:34	Gem	08/11/1974	19:14
Sco	12/19/1973	05:44	Pis	04/17/1974	09:43	Can	08/13/1974	22:47
Sag	12/21/1973	16:20	Ari	04/19/1974	19:19	Leo	08/15/1974	23:25
Cap	12/24/1973	04:41	Tau	04/22/1974	01:53	Vir	08/17/1974	22:43
Aqu	12/26/1973	17:43	Gem	04/24/1974	06:11	Lib	08/19/1974	22:46
Pis	12/29/1973	06:10	Can	04/26/1974	09:17	Sco	08/22/1974	01:38
Ari	12/31/1973	16:33	Leo	04/28/1974	12:03	Sag	08/24/1974	08:35
Tau	01/02/1974	23:36	Vir	04/30/1974	15:00	Cap	08/26/1974	19:15
Gem	01/05/1974	02:59	Lib	05/02/1974	18:39	Aqu	08/29/1974	07:52
Can	01/07/1974	03:28	Sco	05/04/1974	23:44	Pis	08/31/1974	20:29
Leo	01/09/1974	02:42	Sag	05/07/1974	07:05	Ari	09/03/1974	07:57
Vir	01/11/1974	02:42	Cap	05/09/1974	17:15	Tau	09/05/1974	17:50
Lib	01/13/1974	05:21	Aqu	05/12/1974	05:34	Gem	09/08/1974	01:35
Sco	01/15/1974	11:55	Pis	05/14/1974	18:03	Can	09/10/1974	06:39
Sag	01/17/1974	22:13	Ari	05/17/1974	04:19	Leo	09/12/1974	08:53
Cap	01/20/1974	10:48	Tau	05/19/1974	11:09	Vir	09/14/1974	09:12
Aqu	01/22/1974	23:50	Gem	05/21/1974	14:53	Lib	09/16/1974	09:17
Pis	01/25/1974	12:00	Can	05/23/1974	16:45	Sco	09/18/1974	11:15
Ari	01/27/1974	22:31	Leo	05/25/1974	18:12	Sag	09/20/1974	16:47
Tau	01/30/1974	06:41	Vir	05/27/1974	20:26	Cap	09/23/1974	02:22

Aqu	09/25/1974	14:38	Gem	01/22/1975	18:23	Lib	05/20/1975	13:05
Pis	09/28/1974	03:14	Can	01/24/1975	22:19	Sco	05/22/1975	15:26
Ari	09/30/1974	14:25	Leo	01/26/1975	22:59	Sag	05/24/1975	18:51
Tau	10/02/1974	23:38	Vir	01/28/1975	22:14	Cap	05/27/1975	00:31
Gem	10/05/1974	07:00	Lib	01/30/1975	22:14	Aqu	05/29/1975	09:10
Can	10/07/1974	12:29	Sco	02/02/1975	00:54	Pis	05/31/1975	20:32
Leo	10/09/1974	16:02	Sag	02/04/1975	07:11	Ari	06/03/1975	09:01
Vir	10/11/1974	17:56	Cap	02/06/1975	16:42	Tau	06/05/1975	20:18
Lib	10/13/1974	19:11	Aqu	02/09/1975	04:17	Gem	06/08/1975	04:49
Sco	10/15/1974	21:24	Pis	02/11/1975	16:45	Can	06/10/1975	10:21
Sag	10/18/1974	02:15	Ari	02/14/1975	05:22	Leo	06/12/1975	13:44
Cap	10/20/1974	10:45	Tau	02/16/1975	17:09	Vir	06/14/1975	16:10
Aqu	10/22/1974	22:20	Gem	02/19/1975	02:34	Lib	06/16/1975	18:41
Pis	10/25/1974	10:56	Can	02/21/1975	08:18	Sco	06/18/1975	21:59
Ari	10/27/1974	22:12	Leo	02/23/1975	10:12	Sag	06/21/1975	02:35
Tau	10/30/1974	06:59	Vir	02/25/1975	09:36	Cap	06/23/1975	08:56
Gem	11/01/1974	13:22	Lib	02/27/1975	08:39	Aqu	06/25/1975	17:33
Can	11/03/1974	18:01	Sco	03/01/1975	09:35	Pis	06/28/1975	04:33
Leo	11/05/1974	21:30	Sag	03/03/1975	14:07	Ari	06/30/1975	17:02
Vir	11/08/1974	00:18	Cap	03/05/1975	22:41	Tau	07/03/1975	04:54
Lib	11/10/1974	02:59	Aqu	03/08/1975	10:10	Gem	07/05/1975	13:57
Sco	11/12/1974	06:23	Pis	03/10/1975	22:49	Can	07/07/1975	19:22
Sag	11/14/1974	11:40	Ari	03/13/1975	11:18	Leo	07/09/1975	21:49
Cap	11/16/1974	19:42	Tau	03/15/1975	22:52	Vir	07/11/1975	22:55
Aqu	11/19/1974	06:39	Gem	03/18/1975	08:42	Lib	07/14/1975	00:22
Pis	11/21/1974	19:11	Can	03/20/1975	15:48	Sco	07/16/1975	03:23
Ari	11/24/1974	06:59	Leo	03/22/1975	19:30	Sag	07/18/1975	08:32
Tau	11/26/1974	16:04	Vir	03/24/1975	20:20	Cap	07/20/1975	15:46
Gem	11/28/1974	21:57	Lib	03/26/1975	19:51	Aqu	07/23/1975	00:56
Can	12/01/1974	01:21	Sco	03/28/1975	20:08	Pis	07/25/1975	11:59
Leo	12/03/1974	03:31	Sag	03/30/1975	23:11	Ari	07/28/1975	00:27
Vir	12/05/1974	05:40	Cap	04/02/1975	06:08	Tau	07/30/1975	12:53
Lib	12/07/1974	08:43	Aqu	04/04/1975	16:45	Gem	08/01/1975	23:01
Sco	12/09/1974	13:14	Pis	04/07/1975	05:17	Can	08/04/1975	05:16
Sag	12/11/1974	19:35	Ari	04/09/1975	17:44	Leo	08/06/1975	07:43
Cap	12/14/1974	04:04	Tau	04/12/1975	04:53	Vir	08/08/1975	07:53
Aqu	12/16/1974	14:48	Gem	04/14/1975	14:14	Lib	08/10/1975	07:51
Pis	12/19/1974	03:12	Can	04/16/1975	21:26	Sco	08/12/1975	09:30
Ari	12/21/1974	15:35	Leo	04/19/1975	02:13	Sag	08/14/1975	14:00
Tau	12/24/1974	01:44	Vir	04/21/1975	04:42	Cap	08/16/1975	21:25
Gem	12/26/1974	08:15	Lib	04/23/1975	05:41	Aqu	08/19/1975	07:09
Can	12/28/1974	11:15	Sco	04/25/1975	06:39	Pis	08/21/1975	18:32
Leo	12/30/1974	12:05	Sag	04/27/1975	09:21	Ari	08/24/1975	07:02
Vir	01/01/1975	12:33	Cap	04/29/1975	15:09	Tau	08/26/1975	19:44
Lib	01/03/1975	14:22	Aqu	05/02/1975	00:34	Gem	08/29/1975	06:53
Sco	01/05/1975	18:39	Pis	05/04/1975	12:34	Can	08/31/1975	14:33
Sag	01/08/1975	01:40	Ari	05/07/1975	01:02	Leo	09/02/1975	18:08
Cap	01/10/1975	10:59	Tau	05/09/1975	12:02	Vir	09/04/1975	18:29
Aqu	01/12/1975	22:03	Gem	05/11/1975	20:44	Lib	09/06/1975	17:38
Pis	01/15/1975	10:23	Can	05/14/1975	03:07	Sco	09/08/1975	17:45
Ari	01/17/1975	23:03	Leo	05/16/1975	07:38	Sag	09/10/1975	20:41
Tau	01/20/1975	10:20	Vir	05/18/1975	10:45	Cap	09/13/1975	03:12

Aqu	09/15/1975	12:51	Gem	01/12/1976	18:19	Lib	05/10/1976	01:38
Pis	09/18/1975	00:32	Can	01/15/1976	01:59	Sco	05/12/1976	02:02
Ari	09/20/1975	13:07	Leo	01/17/1976	06:15	Sag	05/14/1976	02:04
Tau	09/23/1975	01:43	Vir	01/19/1976	08:25	Cap	05/16/1976	03:32
Gem	09/25/1975	13:12	Lib	01/21/1976	10:11	Aqu	05/18/1976	08:03
Can	09/27/1975	22:05	Sco	01/23/1976	12:48	Pis	05/20/1976	16:27
Leo	09/30/1975	03:19	Sag	01/25/1976	16:51	Ari	05/23/1976	04:07
Vir	10/02/1975	05:03	Cap	01/27/1976	22:24	Tau	05/25/1976	17:07
Lib	10/04/1975	04:38	Aqu	01/30/1976	05:34	Gem	05/28/1976	05:22
Sco	10/06/1975	04:09	Pis	02/01/1976	14:47	Can	05/30/1976	15:38
Sag	10/08/1975	05:35	Ari	02/04/1976	02:17	Leo	06/01/1976	23:36
Cap	10/10/1975	10:30	Tau	02/06/1976	15:13	Vir	06/04/1976	05:20
Aqu	10/12/1975	19:10	Gem	02/09/1976	03:15	Lib	06/06/1976	08:59
Pis	10/15/1975	06:40	Can	02/11/1976	11:57	Sco	06/08/1976	10:57
Ari	10/17/1975	19:20	Leo	02/13/1976	16:32	Sag	06/10/1976	12:06
Tau	10/20/1975	07:43	Vir	02/15/1976	17:59	Cap	06/12/1976	13:46
Gem	10/22/1975	18:51	Lib	02/17/1976	18:14	Aqu	06/14/1976	17:31
Can	10/25/1975	03:56	Sco	02/19/1976	19:14	Pis	06/17/1976	00:44
Leo	10/27/1975	10:18	Sag	02/21/1976	22:19	Ari	06/19/1976	11:32
Vir	10/29/1975	13:45	Cap	02/24/1976	03:54	Tau	06/22/1976	00:21
Lib	10/31/1975	14:54	Aqu	02/26/1976	11:49	Gem	06/24/1976	12:36
Sco	11/02/1975	15:07	Pis	02/28/1976	21:42	Can	06/26/1976	22:28
Sag	11/04/1975	16:10	Ari	03/02/1976	09:22	Leo	06/29/1976	05:39
Cap	11/06/1975	19:46	Tau	03/04/1976	22:18	Vir	07/01/1976	10:45
Aqu	11/09/1975	03:00	Gem	03/07/1976	10:55	Lib	07/03/1976	14:34
Pis	11/11/1975	13:42	Can	03/09/1976	20:57	Sco	07/05/1976	17:33
Ari	11/14/1975	02:17	Leo	03/12/1976	02:54	Sag	07/07/1976	20:05
Tau	11/16/1975	14:37	Vir	03/14/1976	04:58	Cap	07/09/1976	22:50
Gem	11/19/1975	01:13	Lib	03/16/1976	04:44	Aqu	07/12/1976	02:54
Can	11/21/1975	09:35	Sco	03/18/1976	04:18	Pis	07/14/1976	09:37
Leo	11/23/1975	15:47	Sag	03/20/1976	05:34	Ari	07/16/1976	19:40
Vir	11/25/1975	20:04	Cap	03/22/1976	09:49	Tau	07/19/1976	08:11
Lib	11/27/1975	22:47	Aqu	03/24/1976	17:19	Gem	07/21/1976	20:40
Sco	11/30/1975	00:36	Pis	03/27/1976	03:34	Can	07/24/1976	06:39
Sag	12/02/1975	02:33	Ari	03/29/1976	15:37	Leo	07/26/1976	13:17
Cap	12/04/1975	05:58	Tau	04/01/1976	04:33	Vir	07/28/1976	17:23
Aqu	12/06/1975	12:13	Gem	04/03/1976	17:15	Lib	07/30/1976	20:13
Pis	12/08/1975	21:52	Can	04/06/1976	04:05	Sco	08/01/1976	22:55
Ari	12/11/1975	10:06	Leo	04/08/1976	11:35	Sag	08/04/1976	02:03
Tau	12/13/1975	22:38	Vir	04/10/1976	15:15	Cap	08/06/1976	05:54
Gem	12/16/1975	09:11	Lib	04/12/1976	15:53	Aqu	08/08/1976	10:58
Can	12/18/1975	16:48	Sco	04/14/1976	15:14	Pis	08/10/1976	18:00
Leo	12/20/1975	21:53	Sag	04/16/1976	15:15	Ari	08/13/1976	03:49
Vir	12/23/1975	01:27	Cap	04/18/1976	17:43	Tau	08/15/1976	16:05
Lib	12/25/1975	04:27	Aqu	04/20/1976	23:48	Gem	08/18/1976	04:54
Sco	12/27/1975	07:28	Pis	04/23/1976	09:28	Can	08/20/1976	15:33
Sag	12/29/1975	10:53	Ari	04/25/1976	21:37	Leo	08/22/1976	22:29
Cap	12/31/1975	15:17	Tau	04/28/1976	10:37	Vir	08/25/1976	02:03
Aqu	01/02/1976	21:33	Gem	04/30/1976	23:04	Lib	08/27/1976	03:41
Pis	01/05/1976	06:35	Can	05/03/1976	09:52	Sco	08/29/1976	05:05
Ari	01/07/1976	18:21	Leo	05/05/1976	18:09	Sag	08/31/1976	07:28
Tau	01/10/1976	07:09	Vir	05/07/1976	23:20	Cap	09/02/1976	11:29

Aqu	09/04/1976	17:20	Gem	01/01/1977	14:42	Lib	04/30/1977	10:11
Pis	09/07/1976	01:12	Can	01/04/1977	02:11	Sco	05/02/1977	11:22
Ari	09/09/1976	11:19	Leo	01/06/1977	11:20	Sag	05/04/1977	10:59
Tau	09/11/1976	23:30	Vir	01/08/1977	18:23	Cap	05/06/1977	10:55
Gem	09/14/1976	12:32	Lib	01/10/1977	23:47	Aqu	05/08/1977	13:01
Can	09/17/1976	00:05	Sco	01/13/1977	03:44	Pis	05/10/1977	18:29
Leo	09/19/1976	08:09	Sag	01/15/1977	06:18	Ari	05/13/1977	03:30
Vir	09/21/1976	12:14	Cap	01/17/1977	08:02	Tau	05/15/1977	15:04
Lib	09/23/1976	13:27	Aqu	01/19/1977	10:13	Gem	05/18/1977	03:50
Sco	09/25/1976	13:33	Pis	01/21/1977	14:31	Can	05/20/1977	16:35
Sag	09/27/1976	14:22	Ari	01/23/1977	22:20	Leo	05/23/1977	04:13
Cap	09/29/1976	17:13	Tau	01/26/1977	09:41	Vir	05/25/1977	13:29
Aqu	10/01/1976	22:50	Gem	01/28/1977	22:36	Lib	05/27/1977	19:27
Pis	10/04/1976	07:10	Can	01/31/1977	10:19	Sco	05/29/1977	21:55
Ari	10/06/1976	17:49	Leo	02/02/1977	19:11	Sag	05/31/1977	21:53
Tau	10/09/1976	06:11	Vir	02/05/1977	01:16	Cap	06/02/1977	21:07
Gem	10/11/1976	19:14	Lib	02/07/1977	05:36	Aqu	06/04/1977	21:44
Can	10/14/1976	07:23	Sco	02/09/1977	09:04	Pis	06/07/1977	01:36
Leo	10/16/1976	16:49	Sag	02/11/1977	12:11	Ari	06/09/1977	09:35
Vir	10/18/1976	22:23	Cap	02/13/1977	15:14	Tau	06/11/1977	20:57
Lib	10/21/1976	00:25	Aqu	02/15/1977	18:45	Gem	06/14/1977	09:49
Sco	10/23/1976	00:16	Pis	02/17/1977	23:46	Can	06/16/1977	22:28
Sag	10/24/1976	23:49	Ari	02/20/1977	07:23	Leo	06/19/1977	09:53
Cap	10/27/1976	00:56	Tau	02/22/1977	18:06	Vir	06/21/1977	19:28
Aqu	10/29/1976	05:05	Gem	02/25/1977	06:50	Lib	06/24/1977	02:34
Pis	10/31/1976	12:54	Can	02/27/1977	19:02	Sco	06/26/1977	06:41
Ari	11/02/1976	23:46	Leo	03/02/1977	04:24	Sag	06/28/1977	08:01
Tau	11/05/1976	12:23	Vir	03/04/1977	10:18	Cap	06/30/1977	07:48
Gem	11/08/1976	01:20	Lib	03/06/1977	13:34	Aqu	07/02/1977	07:56
Can	11/10/1976	13:27	Sco	03/08/1977	15:36	Pis	07/04/1977	10:32
Leo	11/12/1976	23:35	Sag	03/10/1977	17:41	Ari	07/06/1977	17:03
Vir	11/15/1976	06:46	Cap	03/12/1977	20:40	Tau	07/09/1977	03:33
Lib	11/17/1976	10:33	Aqu	03/15/1977	01:00	Gem	07/11/1977	16:15
Sco	11/19/1976	11:31	Pis	03/17/1977	07:05	Can	07/14/1977	04:49
Sag	11/21/1976	11:03	Ari	03/19/1977	15:23	Leo	07/16/1977	15:51
Cap	11/23/1976	11:04	Tau	03/22/1977	02:06	Vir	07/19/1977	00:58
Aqu	11/25/1976	13:31	Gem	03/24/1977	14:39	Lib	07/21/1977	08:09
Pis	11/27/1976	19:48	Can	03/27/1977	03:16	Sco	07/23/1977	13:12
Ari	11/30/1976	06:01	Leo	03/29/1977	13:39	Sag	07/25/1977	16:04
Tau	12/02/1976	18:41	Vir	03/31/1977	20:24	Cap	07/27/1977	17:14
Gem	12/05/1976	07:38	Lib	04/02/1977	23:38	Aqu	07/29/1977	18:04
Can	12/07/1976	19:20	Sco	04/05/1977	00:39	Pis	07/31/1977	20:24
Leo	12/10/1976	05:12	Sag	04/07/1977	01:09	Ari	08/03/1977	01:55
Vir	12/12/1976	12:54	Cap	04/09/1977	02:41	Tau	08/05/1977	11:18
Lib	12/14/1976	18:13	Aqu	04/11/1977	06:24	Gem	08/07/1977	23:29
Sco	12/16/1976	21:01	Pis	04/13/1977	12:50	Can	08/10/1977	12:03
Sag	12/18/1976	21:53	Ari	04/15/1977	21:52	Leo	08/12/1977	22:56
Cap	12/20/1976	22:12	Tau	04/18/1977	09:02	Vir	08/15/1977	07:25
Aqu	12/22/1976	23:49	Gem	04/20/1977	21:37	Lib	08/17/1977	13:48
Pis	12/25/1976	04:36	Can	04/23/1977	10:24	Sco	08/19/1977	18:35
Ari	12/27/1976	13:32	Leo	04/25/1977	21:42	Sag	08/21/1977	22:02
Tau	12/30/1976	01:43	Vir	04/28/1977	05:51	Cap	08/24/1977	00:30

Aqu	08/26/1977	02:41	Gem	12/22/1977	11:51	Lib	04/20/1978	13:51
Pis	08/28/1977	05:46	Can	12/25/1977	00:29	Sco	04/22/1978	18:38
Ari	08/30/1977	11:12	Leo	12/27/1977	12:51	Sag	04/24/1978	20:59
Tau	09/01/1977	19:52	Vir	12/30/1977	00:13	Cap	04/26/1978	22:27
Gem	09/04/1977	07:27	Lib	01/01/1978	09:30	Aqu	04/29/1978	00:28
Can	09/06/1977	20:02	Sco	01/03/1978	15:34	Pis	05/01/1978	04:00
Leo	09/09/1977	07:13	Sag	01/05/1978	18:03	Ari	05/03/1978	09:27
Vir	09/11/1977	15:33	Cap	01/07/1978	17:54	Tau	05/05/1978	16:52
Lib	09/13/1977	21:06	Aqu	01/09/1978	17:05	Gem	05/08/1978	02:18
Sco	09/16/1977	00:44	Pis	01/11/1978	17:50	Can	05/10/1978	13:41
Sag	09/18/1977	03:28	Ari	01/13/1978	22:06	Leo	05/13/1978	02:16
Cap	09/20/1977	06:04	Tau	01/16/1978	06:30	Vir	05/15/1978	14:14
Aqu	09/22/1977	09:12	Gem	01/18/1978	18:06	Lib	05/17/1978	23:22
Pis	09/24/1977	13:30	Can	01/21/1978	06:50	Sco	05/20/1978	04:38
Ari	09/26/1977	19:40	Leo	01/23/1978	19:02	Sag	05/22/1978	06:30
Tau	09/29/1977	04:21	Vir	01/26/1978	05:56	Cap	05/24/1978	06:41
Gem	10/01/1977	15:33	Lib	01/28/1978	15:07	Aqu	05/26/1978	07:10
Can	10/04/1977	04:08	Sco	01/30/1978	22:02	Pis	05/28/1978	09:37
Leo	10/06/1977	15:57	Sag	02/02/1978	02:12	Ari	05/30/1978	14:52
Vir	10/09/1977	00:57	Cap	02/04/1978	03:49	Tau	06/01/1978	22:50
Lib	10/11/1977	06:29	Aqu	02/06/1978	04:04	Gem	06/04/1978	08:53
Sco	10/13/1977	09:10	Pis	02/08/1978	04:47	Can	06/06/1978	20:30
Sag	10/15/1977	10:27	Ari	02/10/1978	07:57	Leo	06/09/1978	09:07
Cap	10/17/1977	11:51	Tau	02/12/1978	14:51	Vir	06/11/1978	21:34
Aqu	10/19/1977	14:36	Gem	02/15/1978	01:24	Lib	06/14/1978	07:54
Pis	10/21/1977	19:26	Can	02/17/1978	13:55	Sco	06/16/1978	14:27
Ari	10/24/1977	02:34	Leo	02/20/1978	02:09	Sag	06/18/1978	17:00
Tau	10/26/1977	11:53	Vir	02/22/1978	12:38	Cap	06/20/1978	16:51
Gem	10/28/1977	23:08	Lib	02/24/1978	21:02	Aqu	06/22/1978	16:07
Can	10/31/1977	11:39	Sco	02/27/1978	03:27	Pis	06/24/1978	16:57
Leo	11/03/1977	00:02	Sag	03/01/1978	08:01	Ari	06/26/1978	20:53
Vir	11/05/1977	10:15	Cap	03/03/1978	10:57	Tau	06/29/1978	04:21
Lib	11/07/1977	16:50	Aqu	03/05/1978	12:50	Gem	07/01/1978	14:37
Sco	11/09/1977	19:41	Pis	03/07/1978	14:46	Can	07/04/1978	02:33
Sag	11/11/1977	20:03	Ari	03/09/1978	18:08	Leo	07/06/1978	15:12
Cap	11/13/1977	19:50	Tau	03/12/1978	00:19	Vir	07/09/1978	03:44
Aqu	11/15/1977	21:00	Gem	03/14/1978	09:48	Lib	07/11/1978	14:47
Pis	11/18/1977	00:59	Can	03/16/1978	21:49	Sco	07/13/1978	22:45
Ari	11/20/1977	08:13	Leo	03/19/1978	10:11	Sag	07/16/1978	02:48
Tau	11/22/1977	18:09	Vir	03/21/1978	20:48	Cap	07/18/1978	03:32
Gem	11/25/1977	05:48	Lib	03/24/1978	04:41	Aqu	07/20/1978	02:41
Can	11/27/1977	18:20	Sco	03/26/1978	10:00	Pis	07/22/1978	02:26
Leo	11/30/1977	06:52	Sag	03/28/1978	13:36	Ari	07/24/1978	04:46
Vir	12/02/1977	18:05	Cap	03/30/1978	16:23	Tau	07/26/1978	10:51
Lib	12/05/1977	02:16	Aqu	04/01/1978	19:04	Gem	07/28/1978	20:30
Sco	12/07/1977	06:32	Pis	04/03/1978	22:20	Can	07/31/1978	08:28
Sag	12/09/1977	07:21	Ari	04/06/1978	02:51	Leo	08/02/1978	21:10
Cap	12/11/1977	06:26	Tau	04/08/1978	09:22	Vir	08/05/1978	09:28
Aqu	12/13/1977	05:59	Gem	04/10/1978	18:27	Lib	08/07/1978	20:29
Pis	12/15/1977	08:09	Can	04/13/1978	05:58	Sco	08/10/1978	05:10
Ari	12/17/1977	14:12	Leo	04/15/1978	18:30	Sag	08/12/1978	10:41
Tau	12/19/1977	23:54	Vir	04/18/1978	05:43	Cap	08/14/1978	13:01

Aqu	08/16/1978	13:14	Gem	12/12/1978	12:54	Lib	04/10/1979	13:43
Pis	08/18/1978	13:05	Can	12/14/1978	22:50	Sco	04/12/1979	23:14
Ari	08/20/1978	14:30	Leo	12/17/1978	10:37	Sag	04/15/1979	06:17
Tau	08/22/1978	19:06	Vir	12/19/1978	23:33	Cap	04/17/1979	11:21
Gem	08/25/1978	03:31	Lib	12/22/1978	11:38	Aqu	04/19/1979	15:01
Can	08/27/1978	14:59	Sco	12/24/1978	20:30	Pis	04/21/1979	17:40
Leo	08/30/1978	03:39	Sag	12/27/1978	01:05	Ari	04/23/1979	19:51
Vir	09/01/1978	15:46	Cap	12/29/1978	02:14	Tau	04/25/1979	22:27
Lib	09/04/1978	02:15	Aqu	12/31/1978	01:53	Gem	04/28/1979	02:49
Sco	09/06/1978	10:37	Pis	01/02/1979	02:08	Can	04/30/1979	10:12
Sag	09/08/1978	16:38	Ari	01/04/1979	04:41	Leo	05/02/1979	20:56
Cap	09/10/1978	20:19	Tau	01/06/1979	10:18	Vir	05/05/1979	09:40
Aqu	09/12/1978	22:08	Gem	01/08/1979	18:42	Lib	05/07/1979	21:46
Pis	09/14/1978	23:09	Can	01/11/1979	05:14	Sco	05/10/1979	07:09
Ari	09/17/1978	00:50	Leo	01/13/1979	17:16	Sag	05/12/1979	13:23
Tau	09/19/1978	04:43	Vir	01/16/1979	06:09	Cap	05/14/1979	17:25
Gem	09/21/1978	11:57	Lib	01/18/1979	18:40	Aqu	05/16/1979	20:25
Can	09/23/1978	22:31	Sco	01/21/1979	04:50	Pis	05/18/1979	23:18
Leo	09/26/1978	11:01	Sag	01/23/1979	11:06	Ari	05/21/1979	02:30
Vir	09/28/1978	23:10	Cap	01/25/1979	13:26	Tau	05/23/1979	06:20
Lib	10/01/1978	09:15	Aqu	01/27/1979	13:11	Gem	05/25/1979	11:28
Sco	10/03/1978	16:47	Pis	01/29/1979	12:25	Can	05/27/1979	18:50
Sag	10/05/1978	22:05	Ari	01/31/1979	13:12	Leo	05/30/1979	05:07
Cap	10/08/1978	01:51	Tau	02/02/1979	17:03	Vir	06/01/1979	17:40
Aqu	10/10/1978	04:42	Gem	02/05/1979	00:33	Lib	06/04/1979	06:11
Pis	10/12/1978	07:12	Can	02/07/1979	11:05	Sco	06/06/1979	16:03
Ari	10/14/1978	10:06	Leo	02/09/1979	23:25	Sag	06/08/1979	22:13
Tau	10/16/1978	14:22	Vir	02/12/1979	12:17	Cap	06/11/1979	01:22
Gem	10/18/1978	21:05	Lib	02/15/1979	00:36	Aqu	06/13/1979	03:05
Can	10/21/1978	06:52	Sco	02/17/1979	11:10	Pis	06/15/1979	04:55
Leo	10/23/1978	19:03	Sag	02/19/1979	18:50	Ari	06/17/1979	07:52
Vir	10/26/1978	07:31	Cap	02/21/1979	22:59	Tau	06/19/1979	12:18
Lib	10/28/1978	17:50	Aqu	02/24/1979	00:11	Gem	06/21/1979	18:22
Sco	10/31/1978	00:51	Pis	02/25/1979	23:52	Can	06/24/1979	02:24
Sag	11/02/1978	05:02	Ari	02/27/1979	23:54	Leo	06/26/1979	12:47
Cap	11/04/1978	07:40	Tau	03/02/1979	02:10	Vir	06/29/1979	01:13
Aqu	11/06/1978	10:03	Gem	03/04/1979	07:58	Lib	07/01/1979	14:07
Pis	11/08/1978	13:06	Can	03/06/1979	17:33	Sco	07/04/1979	00:55
Ari	11/10/1978	17:11	Leo	03/09/1979	05:47	Sag	07/06/1979	07:54
Tau	11/12/1978	22:35	Vir	03/11/1979	18:42	Cap	07/08/1979	11:06
Gem	11/15/1978	05:44	Lib	03/14/1979	06:41	Aqu	07/10/1979	11:58
Can	11/17/1978	15:16	Sco	03/16/1979	16:48	Pis	07/12/1979	12:23
Leo	11/20/1978	03:08	Sag	03/19/1979	00:36	Ari	07/14/1979	13:57
Vir	11/22/1978	15:56	Cap	03/21/1979	05:56	Tau	07/16/1979	17:42
Lib	11/25/1978	03:05	Aqu	03/23/1979	08:51	Gem	07/19/1979	00:00
Sco	11/27/1978	10:36	Pis	03/25/1979	10:04	Can	07/21/1979	08:40
Sag	11/29/1978	14:22	Ari	03/27/1979	10:47	Leo	07/23/1979	19:29
Cap	12/01/1978	15:43	Tau	03/29/1979	12:37	Vir	07/26/1979	08:01
Aqu	12/03/1978	16:35	Gem	03/31/1979	17:08	Lib	07/28/1979	21:05
Pis	12/05/1978	18:36	Can	04/03/1979	01:24	Sco	07/31/1979	08:45
Ari	12/07/1978	22:40	Leo	04/05/1979	12:57	Sag	08/02/1979	17:04
Tau	12/10/1978	04:50	Vir	04/08/1979	01:51	Cap	08/04/1979	21:21

Aqu	08/06/1979	22:27	Gem	12/02/1979	18:01	Lib	03/30/1980	11:48
Pis	08/08/1979	22:05	Can	12/04/1979	23:02	Sco	04/02/1980	00:20
Ari	08/10/1979	22:10	Leo	12/07/1979	07:08	Sag	04/04/1980	11:33
Tau	08/13/1979	00:22	Vir	12/09/1979	18:32	Cap	04/06/1980	20:41
Gem	08/15/1979	05:41	Lib	12/12/1979	07:28	Aqu	04/09/1980	02:58
Can	08/17/1979	14:17	Sco	12/14/1979	19:07	Pis	04/11/1980	06:06
Leo	08/20/1979	01:28	Sag	12/17/1979	03:35	Ari	04/13/1980	06:39
Vir	08/22/1979	14:11	Cap	12/19/1979	08:53	Tau	04/15/1980	06:10
Lib	08/25/1979	03:13	Aqu	12/21/1979	12:11	Gem	04/17/1980	06:41
Sco	08/27/1979	15:11	Pis	12/23/1979	14:49	Can	04/19/1980	10:12
Sag	08/30/1979	00:37	Ari	12/25/1979	17:39	Leo	04/21/1980	17:51
Cap	09/01/1979	06:33	Tau	12/27/1979	21:07	Vir	04/24/1980	05:11
Aqu	09/03/1979	08:58	Gem	12/30/1979	01:32	Lib	04/26/1980	18:09
Pis	09/05/1979	09:02	Can	01/01/1980	07:29	Sco	04/29/1980	06:34
Ari	09/07/1979	08:29	Leo	01/03/1980	15:47	Sag	05/01/1980	17:21
Tau	09/09/1979	09:13	Vir	01/06/1980	02:48	Cap	05/04/1980	02:13
Gem	09/11/1979	12:55	Lib	01/08/1980	15:37	Aqu	05/06/1980	09:02
Can	09/13/1979	20:27	Sco	01/11/1980	03:54	Pis	05/08/1980	13:32
Leo	09/16/1979	07:25	Sag	01/13/1980	13:15	Ari	05/10/1980	15:43
Vir	09/18/1979	20:15	Cap	01/15/1980	18:50	Tau	05/12/1980	16:23
Lib	09/21/1979	09:10	Aqu	01/17/1980	21:24	Gem	05/14/1980	17:07
Sco	09/23/1979	20:53	Pis	01/19/1980	22:32	Can	05/16/1980	19:52
Sag	09/26/1979	06:35	Ari	01/21/1980	23:51	Leo	05/19/1980	02:15
Cap	09/28/1979	13:38	Tau	01/24/1980	02:31	Vir	05/21/1980	12:32
Aqu	09/30/1979	17:48	Gem	01/26/1980	07:10	Lib	05/24/1980	01:10
Pis	10/02/1979	19:22	Can	01/28/1980	14:02	Sco	05/26/1980	13:35
Ari	10/04/1979	19:27	Leo	01/30/1980	23:08	Sag	05/29/1980	00:03
Tau	10/06/1979	19:44	Vir	02/02/1980	10:21	Cap	05/31/1980	08:13
Gem	10/08/1979	22:08	Lib	02/04/1980	23:04	Aqu	06/02/1980	14:28
Can	10/11/1979	04:09	Sco	02/07/1980	11:45	Pis	06/04/1980	19:09
Leo	10/13/1979	14:12	Sag	02/09/1980	22:17	Ari	06/06/1980	22:22
Vir	10/16/1979	02:51	Cap	02/12/1980	05:11	Tau	06/09/1980	00:29
Lib	10/18/1979	15:43	Aqu	02/14/1980	08:18	Gem	06/11/1980	02:22
Sco	10/21/1979	03:01	Pis	02/16/1980	08:53	Can	06/13/1980	05:29
Sag	10/23/1979	12:08	Ari	02/18/1980	08:42	Leo	06/15/1980	11:22
Cap	10/25/1979	19:10	Tau	02/20/1980	09:35	Vir	06/17/1980	20:47
Aqu	10/28/1979	00:15	Gem	02/22/1980	12:59	Lib	06/20/1980	08:54
Pis	10/30/1979	03:28	Can	02/24/1980	19:34	Sco	06/22/1980	21:25
Ari	11/01/1979	05:08	Leo	02/27/1980	05:10	Sag	06/25/1980	08:00
Tau	11/03/1979	06:15	Vir	02/29/1980	16:53	Cap	06/27/1980	15:45
Gem	11/05/1979	08:25	Lib	03/03/1980	05:39	Aqu	06/29/1980	21:02
Can	11/07/1979	13:24	Sco	03/05/1980	18:22	Pis	07/02/1980	00:47
Leo	11/09/1979	22:15	Sag	03/08/1980	05:37	Ari	07/04/1980	03:45
Vir	11/12/1979	10:20	Cap	03/10/1980	14:00	Tau	07/06/1980	06:29
Lib	11/14/1979	23:15	Aqu	03/12/1980	18:44	Gem	07/08/1980	09:33
Sco	11/17/1979	10:28	Pis	03/14/1980	20:09	Can	07/10/1980	13:44
Sag	11/19/1979	18:55	Ari	03/16/1980	19:40	Leo	07/12/1980	20:02
Cap	11/22/1979	01:00	Tau	03/18/1980	19:13	Vir	07/15/1980	05:11
Aqu	11/24/1979	05:36	Gem	03/20/1980	20:48	Lib	07/17/1980	16:54
Pis	11/26/1979	09:16	Can	03/23/1980	01:56	Sco	07/20/1980	05:33
Ari	11/28/1979	12:16	Leo	03/25/1980	10:59	Sag	07/22/1980	16:41
Tau	11/30/1979	14:54	Vir	03/27/1980	22:51	Cap	07/25/1980	00:43

Aqu	07/27/1980	05:34	Gem	11/22/1980	01:27	Lib	03/20/1981	10:30
Pis	07/29/1980	08:10	Can	11/24/1980	02:19	Sco	03/22/1981	22:13
Ari	07/31/1980	09:53	Leo	11/26/1980	06:22	Sag	03/25/1981	10:50
Tau	08/02/1980	11:55	Vir	11/28/1980	14:37	Cap	03/27/1981	22:50
Gem	08/04/1980	15:09	Lib	12/01/1980	02:13	Aqu	03/30/1981	08:14
Can	08/06/1980	20:12	Sco	12/03/1980	14:59	Pis	04/01/1981	13:39
Leo	08/09/1980	03:23	Sag	12/06/1980	02:56	Ari	04/03/1981	15:24
Vir	08/11/1980	12:54	Cap	12/08/1980	13:10	Tau	04/05/1981	15:03
Lib	08/14/1980	00:32	Aqu	12/10/1980	21:34	Gem	04/07/1981	14:47
Sco	08/16/1980	13:14	Pis	12/13/1980	04:02	Can	04/09/1981	16:33
Sag	08/19/1980	01:06	Ari	12/15/1980	08:20	Leo	04/11/1981	21:37
Cap	08/21/1980	10:09	Tau	12/17/1980	10:35	Vir	04/14/1981	05:55
Aqu	08/23/1980	15:31	Gem	12/19/1980	11:39	Lib	04/16/1981	16:37
Pis	08/25/1980	17:42	Can	12/21/1980	13:03	Sco	04/19/1981	04:38
Ari	08/27/1980	18:10	Leo	12/23/1980	16:33	Sag	04/21/1981	17:14
Tau	08/29/1980	18:40	Vir	12/25/1980	23:33	Cap	04/24/1981	05:30
Gem	08/31/1980	20:50	Lib	12/28/1980	10:04	Aqu	04/26/1981	15:55
Can	09/03/1980	01:40	Sco	12/30/1980	22:35	Pis	04/28/1981	22:54
Leo	09/05/1980	09:22	Sag	01/02/1981	10:40	Ari	05/01/1981	01:55
Vir	09/07/1980	19:30	Cap	01/04/1981	20:40	Tau	05/03/1981	01:58
Lib	09/10/1980	07:22	Aqu	01/07/1981	04:11	Gem	05/05/1981	01:01
Sco	09/12/1980	20:05	Pis	01/09/1981	09:41	Can	05/07/1981	01:18
Sag	09/15/1980	08:26	Ari	01/11/1981	13:42	Leo	05/09/1981	04:40
Cap	09/17/1980	18:44	Tau	01/13/1981	16:44	Vir	05/11/1981	11:55
Aqu	09/20/1980	01:28	Gem	01/15/1981	19:16	Lib	05/13/1981	22:24
Pis	09/22/1980	04:26	Can	01/17/1981	22:07	Sco	05/16/1981	10:37
Ari	09/24/1980	04:36	Leo	01/20/1981	02:21	Sag	05/18/1981	23:13
Tau	09/26/1980	03:53	Vir	01/22/1981	09:02	Cap	05/21/1981	11:19
Gem	09/28/1980	04:21	Lib	01/24/1981	18:44	Aqu	05/23/1981	21:59
Can	09/30/1980	07:46	Sco	01/27/1981	06:48	Pis	05/26/1981	06:04
Leo	10/02/1980	14:57	Sag	01/29/1981	19:10	Ari	05/28/1981	10:42
Vir	10/05/1980	01:19	Cap	02/01/1981	05:36	Tau	05/30/1981	12:09
Lib	10/07/1980	13:30	Aqu	02/03/1981	12:53	Gem	06/01/1981	11:48
Sco	10/10/1980	02:14	Pis	02/05/1981	17:20	Can	06/03/1981	11:39
Sag	10/12/1980	14:36	Ari	02/07/1981	20:00	Leo	06/05/1981	13:43
Cap	10/15/1980	01:35	Tau	02/09/1981	22:10	Vir	06/07/1981	19:25
Aqu	10/17/1980	09:51	Gem	02/12/1981	00:51	Lib	06/10/1981	04:54
Pis	10/19/1980	14:29	Can	02/14/1981	04:42	Sco	06/12/1981	16:53
Ari	10/21/1980	15:41	Leo	02/16/1981	10:10	Sag	06/15/1981	05:30
Tau	10/23/1980	14:55	Vir	02/18/1981	17:33	Cap	06/17/1981	17:20
Gem	10/25/1980	14:17	Lib	02/21/1981	03:12	Aqu	06/20/1981	03:35
Can	10/27/1980	16:00	Sco	02/23/1981	14:54	Pis	06/22/1981	11:42
Leo	10/29/1980	21:39	Sag	02/26/1981	03:28	Ari	06/24/1981	17:17
Vir	11/01/1980	07:18	Cap	02/28/1981	14:44	Tau	06/26/1981	20:15
Lib	11/03/1980	19:30	Aqu	03/02/1981	22:48	Gem	06/28/1981	21:20
Sco	11/06/1980	08:18	Pis	03/05/1981	03:10	Can	06/30/1981	21:57
Sag	11/08/1980	20:24	Ari	03/07/1981	04:47	Leo	07/02/1981	23:47
Cap	11/11/1980	07:14	Tau	03/09/1981	05:22	Vir	07/05/1981	04:26
Aqu	11/13/1980	16:09	Gem	03/11/1981	06:41	Lib	07/07/1981	12:42
Pis	11/15/1980	22:19	Can	03/13/1981	10:06	Sco	07/10/1981	00:01
Ari	11/18/1980	01:20	Leo	03/15/1981	16:02	Sag	07/12/1981	12:34
Tau	11/20/1980	01:49	Vir	03/18/1981	00:19	Cap	07/15/1981	00:18

Aqu	07/17/1981	10:00	Gem	11/12/1981	09:59	Lib	03/10/1982	11:34
Pis	07/19/1981	17:25	Can	11/14/1981	09:37	Sco	03/12/1982	19:16
Ari	07/21/1981	22:42	Leo	11/16/1981	11:33	Sag	03/15/1982	06:02
Tau	07/24/1981	02:17	Vir	11/18/1981	16:52	Cap	03/17/1982	18:46
Gem	07/26/1981	04:41	Lib	11/21/1981	01:33	Aqu	03/20/1982	06:52
Can	07/28/1981	06:40	Sco	11/23/1981	12:36	Pis	03/22/1982	16:00
Leo	07/30/1981	09:20	Sag	11/26/1981	00:59	Ari	03/24/1982	21:35
Vir	08/01/1981	13:55	Cap	11/28/1981	13:51	Tau	03/27/1982	00:38
Lib	08/03/1981	21:24	Aqu	12/01/1981	02:07	Gem	03/29/1982	02:43
Sco	08/06/1981	07:58	Pis	12/03/1981	12:14	Can	03/31/1982	05:08
Sag	08/08/1981	20:21	Ari	12/05/1981	18:47	Leo	04/02/1982	08:36
Cap	08/11/1981	08:19	Tau	12/07/1981	21:29	Vir	04/04/1982	13:18
Aqu	08/13/1981	17:55	Gem	12/09/1981	21:29	Lib	04/06/1982	19:26
Pis	08/16/1981	00:33	Can	12/11/1981	20:40	Sco	04/09/1982	03:32
Ari	08/18/1981	04:48	Leo	12/13/1981	21:08	Sag	04/11/1982	14:06
Tau	08/20/1981	07:43	Vir	12/16/1981	00:38	Cap	04/14/1982	02:40
Gem	08/22/1981	10:17	Lib	12/18/1981	07:58	Aqu	04/16/1982	15:16
Can	08/24/1981	13:16	Sco	12/20/1981	18:38	Pis	04/19/1982	01:17
Leo	08/26/1981	17:09	Sag	12/23/1981	07:10	Ari	04/21/1982	07:21
Vir	08/28/1981	22:31	Cap	12/25/1981	19:58	Tau	04/23/1982	09:57
Lib	08/31/1981	06:02	Aqu	12/28/1981	07:52	Gem	04/25/1982	10:47
Sco	09/02/1981	16:10	Pis	12/30/1981	18:00	Can	04/27/1982	11:43
Sag	09/05/1981	04:23	Ari	01/02/1982	01:31	Leo	04/29/1982	14:09
Cap	09/07/1981	16:47	Tau	01/04/1982	06:01	Vir	05/01/1982	18:44
Aqu	09/10/1981	02:57	Gem	01/06/1982	07:47	Lib	05/04/1982	01:32
Pis	09/12/1981	09:32	Can	01/08/1982	08:00	Sco	05/06/1982	10:24
Ari	09/14/1981	12:54	Leo	01/10/1982	08:20	Sag	05/08/1982	21:16
Tau	09/16/1981	14:29	Vir	01/12/1982	10:37	Cap	05/11/1982	09:49
Gem	09/18/1981	15:58	Lib	01/14/1982	16:16	Aqu	05/13/1982	22:43
Can	09/20/1981	18:39	Sco	01/17/1982	01:46	Pis	05/16/1982	09:44
Leo	09/22/1981	23:08	Sag	01/19/1982	13:59	Ari	05/18/1982	17:03
Vir	09/25/1981	05:28	Cap	01/22/1982	02:49	Tau	05/20/1982	20:20
Lib	09/27/1981	13:40	Aqu	01/24/1982	14:23	Gem	05/22/1982	20:53
Sco	09/29/1981	23:52	Pis	01/26/1982	23:48	Can	05/24/1982	20:38
Sag	10/02/1981	11:59	Ari	01/29/1982	06:57	Leo	05/26/1982	21:27
Cap	10/05/1981	00:47	Tau	01/31/1982	12:02	Vir	05/29/1982	00:43
Aqu	10/07/1981	11:59	Gem	02/02/1982	15:19	Lib	05/31/1982	07:02
Pis	10/09/1981	19:31	Can	02/04/1982	17:17	Sco	06/02/1982	16:11
Ari	10/11/1981	22:59	Leo	02/06/1982	18:49	Sag	06/05/1982	03:31
Tau	10/13/1981	23:42	Vir	02/08/1982	21:15	Cap	06/07/1982	16:11
Gem	10/15/1981	23:41	Lib	02/11/1982	02:02	Aqu	06/10/1982	05:07
Can	10/18/1981	00:52	Sco	02/13/1982	10:16	Pis	06/12/1982	16:42
Leo	10/20/1981	04:34	Sag	02/15/1982	21:44	Ari	06/15/1982	01:18
Vir	10/22/1981	11:05	Cap	02/18/1982	10:35	Tau	06/17/1982	06:06
Lib	10/24/1981	19:56	Aqu	02/20/1982	22:13	Gem	06/19/1982	07:33
Sco	10/27/1981	06:37	Pis	02/23/1982	07:08	Can	06/21/1982	07:12
Sag	10/29/1981	18:47	Ari	02/25/1982	13:15	Leo	06/23/1982	06:56
Cap	11/01/1981	07:45	Tau	02/27/1982	17:31	Vir	06/25/1982	08:36
Aqu	11/03/1981	19:49	Gem	03/01/1982	20:49	Lib	06/27/1982	13:30
Pis	11/06/1981	04:50	Can	03/03/1982	23:47	Sco	06/29/1982	22:01
Ari	11/08/1981	09:36	Leo	03/06/1982	02:50	Sag	07/02/1982	09:25
Tau	11/10/1981	10:43	Vir	03/08/1982	06:26	Cap	07/04/1982	22:14

Aqu	07/07/1982	11:01	Gem	11/02/1982	19:21	Lib	02/28/1983	15:30
Pis	07/09/1982	22:33	Can	11/04/1982	20:58	Sco	03/02/1983	18:50
Ari	07/12/1982	07:47	Leo	11/06/1982	23:10	Sag	03/05/1983	02:15
Tau	07/14/1982	13:58	Vir	11/09/1982	02:39	Cap	03/07/1983	13:29
Gem	07/16/1982	17:02	Lib	11/11/1982	07:45	Aqu	03/10/1983	02:29
Can	07/18/1982	17:45	Sco	11/13/1982	14:42	Pis	03/12/1983	14:46
Leo	07/20/1982	17:34	Sag	11/15/1982	23:51	Ari	03/15/1983	00:58
Vir	07/22/1982	18:19	Cap	11/18/1982	11:21	Tau	03/17/1983	09:03
Lib	07/24/1982	21:45	Aqu	11/21/1982	00:19	Gem	03/19/1983	15:18
Sco	07/27/1982	04:57	Pis	11/23/1982	12:41	Can	03/21/1983	19:51
Sag	07/29/1982	15:47	Ari	11/25/1982	22:05	Leo	03/23/1983	22:42
Cap	08/01/1982	04:35	Tau	11/28/1982	03:30	Vir	03/26/1983	00:17
Aqu	08/03/1982	17:16	Gem	11/30/1982	05:35	Lib	03/28/1983	01:48
Pis	08/06/1982	04:22	Can	12/02/1982	05:57	Sco	03/30/1983	04:56
Ari	08/08/1982	13:19	Leo	12/04/1982	06:25	Sag	04/01/1983	11:20
Tau	08/10/1982	19:59	Vir	12/06/1982	08:32	Cap	04/03/1983	21:29
Gem	08/13/1982	00:20	Lib	12/08/1982	13:11	Aqu	04/06/1983	10:05
Can	08/15/1982	02:39	Sco	12/10/1982	20:34	Pis	04/08/1983	22:29
Leo	08/17/1982	03:39	Sag	12/13/1982	06:26	Ari	04/11/1983	08:35
Vir	08/19/1982	04:39	Cap	12/15/1982	18:14	Tau	04/13/1983	15:57
Lib	08/21/1982	07:21	Aqu	12/18/1982	07:11	Gem	04/15/1983	21:13
Sco	08/23/1982	13:21	Pis	12/20/1982	19:54	Can	04/18/1983	01:13
Sag	08/25/1982	23:11	Ari	12/23/1982	06:33	Leo	04/20/1983	04:25
Cap	08/28/1982	11:41	Tau	12/25/1982	13:34	Vir	04/22/1983	07:11
Aqu	08/31/1982	00:22	Gem	12/27/1982	16:47	Lib	04/24/1983	10:03
Pis	09/02/1982	11:09	Can	12/29/1982	17:11	Sco	04/26/1983	14:04
Ari	09/04/1982	19:22	Leo	12/31/1982	16:32	Sag	04/28/1983	20:28
Tau	09/07/1982	01:25	Vir	01/02/1983	16:49	Cap	05/01/1983	06:00
Gem	09/09/1982	05:56	Lib	01/04/1983	19:44	Aqu	05/03/1983	18:08
Can	09/11/1982	09:17	Sco	01/07/1983	02:16	Pis	05/06/1983	06:42
Leo	09/13/1982	11:45	Sag	01/09/1983	12:13	Ari	05/08/1983	17:15
Vir	09/15/1982	13:57	Cap	01/12/1983	00:25	Tau	05/11/1983	00:34
Lib	09/17/1982	17:02	Aqu	01/14/1983	13:25	Gem	05/13/1983	05:02
Sco	09/19/1982	22:33	Pis	01/17/1983	02:01	Can	05/15/1983	07:47
Sag	09/22/1982	07:30	Ari	01/19/1983	13:06	Leo	05/17/1983	10:00
Cap	09/24/1982	19:30	Tau	01/21/1983	21:34	Vir	05/19/1983	12:36
Aqu	09/27/1982	08:20	Gem	01/24/1983	02:38	Lib	05/21/1983	16:11
Pis	09/29/1982	19:17	Can	01/26/1983	04:27	Sco	05/23/1983	21:17
Ari	10/02/1982	03:04	Leo	01/28/1983	04:09	Sag	05/26/1983	04:27
Tau	10/04/1982	08:07	Vir	01/30/1983	03:34	Cap	05/28/1983	14:06
Gem	10/06/1982	11:37	Lib	02/01/1983	04:46	Aqu	05/31/1983	01:59
Can	10/08/1982	14:38	Sco	02/03/1983	09:32	Pis	06/02/1983	14:40
Leo	10/10/1982	17:43	Sag	02/05/1983	18:28	Ari	06/05/1983	01:57
Vir	10/12/1982	21:08	Cap	02/08/1983	06:33	Tau	06/07/1983	10:02
Lib	10/15/1982	01:22	Aqu	02/10/1983	19:40	Gem	06/09/1983	14:35
Sco	10/17/1982	07:20	Pis	02/13/1983	08:00	Can	06/11/1983	16:31
Sag	10/19/1982	16:02	Ari	02/15/1983	18:45	Leo	06/13/1983	17:20
Cap	10/22/1982	03:37	Tau	02/18/1983	03:29	Vir	06/15/1983	18:37
Aqu	10/24/1982	16:34	Gem	02/20/1983	09:50	Lib	06/17/1983	21:36
Pis	10/27/1982	04:11	Can	02/22/1983	13:29	Sco	06/20/1983	02:59
Ari	10/29/1982	12:23	Leo	02/24/1983	14:45	Sag	06/22/1983	10:55
Tau	10/31/1982	17:02	Vir	02/26/1983	14:48	Cap	06/24/1983	21:08

Aqu	06/27/1983	09:06	Gem	10/24/1983	04:09	Lib	02/18/1984	22:39
Pis	06/29/1983	21:50	Can	10/26/1983	09:45	Sco	02/20/1984	23:45
Ari	07/02/1983	09:46	Leo	10/28/1983	13:49	Sag	02/23/1984	04:22
Tau	07/04/1983	19:04	Vir	10/30/1983	16:32	Cap	02/25/1984	12:49
Gem	07/07/1983	00:39	Lib	11/01/1983	18:30	Aqu	02/28/1984	00:02
Can	07/09/1983	02:49	Sco	11/03/1983	20:53	Pis	03/01/1984	12:28
Leo	07/11/1983	02:53	Sag	11/06/1983	01:09	Ari	03/04/1984	01:06
Vir	07/13/1983	02:42	Cap	11/08/1983	08:31	Tau	03/06/1984	13:07
Lib	07/15/1983	04:10	Aqu	11/10/1983	19:10	Gem	03/08/1984	23:27
Sco	07/17/1983	08:38	Pis	11/13/1983	07:39	Can	03/11/1984	06:47
Sag	07/19/1983	16:31	Ari	11/15/1983	19:35	Leo	03/13/1984	10:19
Cap	07/22/1983	03:10	Tau	11/18/1983	05:05	Vir	03/15/1984	10:45
Aqu	07/24/1983	15:26	Gem	11/20/1983	11:43	Lib	03/17/1984	09:51
Pis	07/27/1983	04:10	Can	11/22/1983	16:09	Sco	03/19/1984	09:49
Ari	07/29/1983	16:19	Leo	11/24/1983	19:18	Sag	03/21/1984	12:42
Tau	08/01/1983	02:35	Vir	11/26/1983	22:01	Cap	03/23/1984	19:36
Gem	08/03/1983	09:41	Lib	11/29/1983	00:56	Aqu	03/26/1984	06:08
Can	08/05/1983	13:07	Sco	12/01/1983	04:40	Pis	03/28/1984	18:36
Leo	08/07/1983	13:35	Sag	12/03/1983	09:56	Ari	03/31/1984	07:13
Vir	08/09/1983	12:48	Cap	12/05/1983	17:27	Tau	04/02/1984	18:54
Lib	08/11/1983	12:52	Aqu	12/08/1983	03:39	Gem	04/05/1984	05:03
Sco	08/13/1983	15:44	Pis	12/10/1983	15:52	Can	04/07/1984	12:57
Sag	08/15/1983	22:34	Ari	12/13/1983	04:15	Leo	04/09/1984	18:00
Cap	08/18/1983	08:59	Tau	12/15/1983	14:31	Vir	04/11/1984	20:09
Aqu	08/20/1983	21:25	Gem	12/17/1983	21:22	Lib	04/13/1984	20:28
Pis	08/23/1983	10:08	Can	12/20/1983	01:01	Sco	04/15/1984	20:41
Ari	08/25/1983	22:07	Leo	12/22/1983	02:43	Sag	04/17/1984	22:44
Tau	08/28/1983	08:36	Vir	12/24/1983	04:01	Cap	04/20/1984	04:10
Gem	08/30/1983	16:47	Lib	12/26/1983	06:17	Aqu	04/22/1984	13:27
Can	09/01/1983	21:51	Sco	12/28/1983	10:26	Pis	04/25/1984	01:25
Leo	09/03/1983	23:45	Sag	12/30/1983	16:43	Ari	04/27/1984	14:01
Vir	09/05/1983	23:35	Cap	01/02/1984	01:07	Tau	04/30/1984	01:29
Lib	09/07/1983	23:13	Aqu	01/04/1984	11:30	Gem	05/02/1984	11:00
Sco	09/10/1983	00:49	Pis	01/06/1984	23:33	Can	05/04/1984	18:25
Sag	09/12/1983	06:07	Ari	01/09/1984	12:14	Leo	05/06/1984	23:41
Cap	09/14/1983	15:33	Tau	01/11/1984	23:34	Vir	05/09/1984	03:00
Aqu	09/17/1983	03:44	Gem	01/14/1984	07:39	Lib	05/11/1984	04:53
Pis	09/19/1983	16:29	Can	01/16/1984	11:45	Sco	05/13/1984	06:21
Ari	09/22/1983	04:09	Leo	01/18/1984	12:48	Sag	05/15/1984	08:49
Tau	09/24/1983	14:11	Vir	01/20/1984	12:35	Cap	05/17/1984	13:43
Gem	09/26/1983	22:23	Lib	01/22/1984	13:07	Aqu	05/19/1984	21:55
Can	09/29/1983	04:23	Sco	01/24/1984	16:04	Pis	05/22/1984	09:08
Leo	10/01/1983	07:53	Sag	01/26/1984	22:12	Ari	05/24/1984	21:38
Vir	10/03/1983	09:14	Cap	01/29/1984	07:12	Tau	05/27/1984	09:12
Lib	10/05/1983	09:41	Aqu	01/31/1984	18:10	Gem	05/29/1984	18:22
Sco	10/07/1983	11:06	Pis	02/03/1984	06:21	Can	06/01/1984	00:52
Sag	10/09/1983	15:21	Ari	02/05/1984	19:03	Leo	06/03/1984	05:18
Cap	10/11/1983	23:30	Tau	02/08/1984	07:04	Vir	06/05/1984	08:26
Aqu	10/14/1983	10:59	Gem	02/10/1984	16:38	Lib	06/07/1984	11:02
Pis	10/16/1983	23:40	Can	02/12/1984	22:18	Sco	06/09/1984	13:48
Ari	10/19/1983	11:17	Leo	02/15/1984	00:07	Sag	06/11/1984	17:25
Tau	10/21/1983	20:46	Vir	02/16/1984	23:31	Cap	06/13/1984	22:48

Aqu	06/16/1984	06:40	Gem	10/13/1984	09:12	Lib	02/08/1985	09:10
Pis	06/18/1984	17:17	Can	10/15/1984	18:59	Sco	02/10/1985	10:49
Ari	06/21/1984	05:39	Leo	10/18/1984	01:39	Sag	02/12/1985	14:08
Tau	06/23/1984	17:37	Vir	10/20/1984	04:54	Cap	02/14/1985	19:26
Gem	06/26/1984	03:02	Lib	10/22/1984	05:31	Aqu	02/17/1985	02:36
Can	06/28/1984	09:07	Sco	10/24/1984	05:07	Pis	02/19/1985	11:38
Leo	06/30/1984	12:28	Sag	10/26/1984	05:42	Ari	02/21/1985	22:42
Vir	07/02/1984	14:26	Cap	10/28/1984	09:05	Tau	02/24/1985	11:26
Lib	07/04/1984	16:26	Aqu	10/30/1984	16:13	Gem	02/27/1985	00:09
Sco	07/06/1984	19:28	Pis	11/02/1984	02:49	Can	03/01/1985	10:21
Sag	07/09/1984	00:03	Ari	11/04/1984	15:19	Leo	03/03/1985	16:27
Cap	07/11/1984	06:22	Tau	11/07/1984	03:52	Vir	03/05/1985	18:41
Aqu	07/13/1984	14:41	Gem	11/09/1984	15:09	Lib	03/07/1985	18:46
Pis	07/16/1984	01:10	Can	11/12/1984	00:29	Sco	03/09/1985	18:46
Ari	07/18/1984	13:25	Leo	11/14/1984	07:32	Sag	03/11/1985	20:29
Tau	07/21/1984	01:51	Vir	11/16/1984	12:06	Cap	03/14/1985	00:55
Gem	07/23/1984	12:08	Lib	11/18/1984	14:28	Aqu	03/16/1985	08:10
Can	07/25/1984	18:43	Sco	11/20/1984	15:30	Pis	03/18/1985	17:49
Leo	07/27/1984	21:40	Sag	11/22/1984	16:33	Ari	03/21/1985	05:19
Vir	07/29/1984	22:28	Cap	11/24/1984	19:17	Tau	03/23/1985	18:05
Lib	07/31/1984	23:02	Aqu	11/27/1984	01:06	Gem	03/26/1985	07:01
Sco	08/03/1984	01:04	Pis	11/29/1984	10:33	Can	03/28/1985	18:12
Sag	08/05/1984	05:29	Ari	12/01/1984	22:41	Leo	03/31/1985	01:49
Cap	08/07/1984	12:24	Tau	12/04/1984	11:19	Vir	04/02/1985	05:24
Aqu	08/09/1984	21:25	Gem	12/06/1984	22:22	Lib	04/04/1985	05:53
Pis	08/12/1984	08:12	Can	12/09/1984	06:55	Sco	04/06/1985	05:09
Ari	08/14/1984	20:27	Leo	12/11/1984	13:07	Sag	04/08/1985	05:17
Tau	08/17/1984	09:12	Vir	12/13/1984	17:34	Cap	04/10/1985	07:57
Gem	08/19/1984	20:30	Lib	12/15/1984	20:51	Aqu	04/12/1985	14:04
Can	08/22/1984	04:19	Sco	12/17/1984	23:26	Pis	04/14/1985	23:30
Leo	08/24/1984	07:58	Sag	12/20/1984	01:58	Ari	04/17/1985	11:18
Vir	08/26/1984	08:31	Cap	12/22/1984	05:20	Tau	04/20/1985	00:11
Lib	08/28/1984	07:56	Aqu	12/24/1984	10:47	Gem	04/22/1985	12:59
Sco	08/30/1984	08:23	Pis	12/26/1984	19:18	Can	04/25/1985	00:24
Sag	09/01/1984	11:30	Ari	12/29/1984	06:49	Leo	04/27/1985	09:08
Cap	09/03/1984	17:54	Tau	12/31/1984	19:35	Vir	04/29/1985	14:22
Aqu	09/06/1984	03:11	Gem	01/03/1985	06:59	Lib	05/01/1985	16:20
Pis	09/08/1984	14:24	Can	01/05/1985	15:16	Sco	05/03/1985	16:16
Ari	09/11/1984	02:46	Leo	01/07/1985	20:27	Sag	05/05/1985	15:55
Tau	09/13/1984	15:32	Vir	01/09/1985	23:38	Cap	05/07/1985	17:11
Gem	09/16/1984	03:24	Lib	01/12/1985	02:13	Aqu	05/09/1985	21:38
Can	09/18/1984	12:33	Sco	01/14/1985	05:07	Pis	05/12/1985	05:55
Leo	09/20/1984	17:48	Sag	01/16/1985	08:47	Ari	05/14/1985	17:25
Vir	09/22/1984	19:18	Cap	01/18/1985	13:29	Tau	05/17/1985	06:22
Lib	09/24/1984	18:40	Aqu	01/20/1985	19:38	Gem	05/19/1985	19:00
Sco	09/26/1984	18:03	Pis	01/23/1985	04:02	Can	05/22/1985	06:04
Sag	09/28/1984	19:31	Ari	01/25/1985	15:05	Leo	05/24/1985	14:52
Cap	10/01/1984	00:28	Tau	01/28/1985	03:52	Vir	05/26/1985	21:05
Aqu	10/03/1984	09:03	Gem	01/30/1985	15:59	Lib	05/29/1985	00:39
Pis	10/05/1984	20:18	Can	02/02/1985	00:57	Sco	05/31/1985	02:06
Ari	10/08/1984	08:50	Leo	02/04/1985	06:01	Sag	06/02/1985	02:33
Tau	10/10/1984	21:27	Vir	02/06/1985	08:08	Cap	06/04/1985	03:33

Aqu	06/06/1985	06:51	Gem	10/03/1985	08:35	Lib	01/29/1986	21:09
Pis	06/08/1985	13:47	Can	10/05/1985	20:58	Sco	02/01/1986	01:18
Ari	06/11/1985	00:24	Leo	10/08/1985	06:32	Sag	02/03/1986	04:31
Tau	06/13/1985	13:10	Vir	10/10/1985	12:07	Cap	02/05/1986	07:01
Gem	06/16/1985	01:44	Lib	10/12/1985	14:10	Aqu	02/07/1986	09:35
Can	06/18/1985	12:20	Sco	10/14/1985	14:12	Pis	02/09/1986	13:33
Leo	06/20/1985	20:31	Sag	10/16/1985	14:05	Ari	02/11/1986	20:21
Vir	06/23/1985	02:31	Cap	10/18/1985	15:35	Tau	02/14/1986	06:38
Lib	06/25/1985	06:46	Aqu	10/20/1985	19:54	Gem	02/16/1986	19:16
Sco	06/27/1985	09:36	Pis	10/23/1985	03:27	Can	02/19/1986	07:38
Sag	06/29/1985	11:29	Ari	10/25/1985	13:47	Leo	02/21/1986	17:24
Cap	07/01/1985	13:22	Tau	10/28/1985	01:59	Vir	02/23/1986	23:56
Aqu	07/03/1985	16:35	Gem	10/30/1985	14:58	Lib	02/26/1986	04:06
Pis	07/05/1985	22:40	Can	11/02/1985	03:30	Sco	02/28/1986	07:05
Ari	07/08/1985	08:20	Leo	11/04/1985	14:02	Sag	03/02/1986	09:51
Tau	07/10/1985	20:43	Vir	11/06/1985	21:16	Cap	03/04/1986	12:55
Gem	07/13/1985	09:22	Lib	11/09/1985	00:50	Aqu	03/06/1986	16:42
Can	07/15/1985	19:53	Sco	11/11/1985	01:29	Pis	03/08/1986	21:48
Leo	07/18/1985	03:24	Sag	11/13/1985	00:52	Ari	03/11/1986	05:03
Vir	07/20/1985	08:28	Cap	11/15/1985	00:53	Tau	03/13/1986	15:04
Lib	07/22/1985	12:09	Aqu	11/17/1985	03:25	Gem	03/16/1986	03:22
Sco	07/24/1985	15:15	Pis	11/19/1985	09:43	Can	03/18/1986	16:03
Sag	07/26/1985	18:12	Ari	11/21/1985	19:42	Leo	03/21/1986	02:37
Cap	07/28/1985	21:20	Tau	11/24/1985	08:06	Vir	03/23/1986	09:38
Aqu	07/31/1985	01:25	Gem	11/26/1985	21:07	Lib	03/25/1986	13:21
Pis	08/02/1985	07:33	Can	11/29/1985	09:22	Sco	03/27/1986	15:04
Ari	08/04/1985	16:42	Leo	12/01/1985	19:58	Sag	03/29/1986	16:20
Tau	08/07/1985	04:40	Vir	12/04/1985	04:13	Cap	03/31/1986	18:25
Gem	08/09/1985	17:31	Lib	12/06/1985	09:32	Aqu	04/02/1986	22:11
Can	08/12/1985	04:27	Sco	12/08/1985	11:55	Pis	04/05/1986	04:03
Leo	08/14/1985	11:55	Sag	12/10/1985	12:12	Ari	04/07/1986	12:12
Vir	08/16/1985	16:14	Cap	12/12/1985	11:59	Tau	04/09/1986	22:36
Lib	08/18/1985	18:43	Aqu	12/14/1985	13:15	Gem	04/12/1986	10:50
Sco	08/20/1985	20:50	Pis	12/16/1985	17:49	Can	04/14/1986	23:41
Sag	08/22/1985	23:36	Ari	12/19/1985	02:37	Leo	04/17/1986	11:08
Cap	08/25/1985	03:24	Tau	12/21/1985	14:40	Vir	04/19/1986	19:23
Aqu	08/27/1985	08:31	Gem	12/24/1985	03:44	Lib	04/21/1986	23:48
Pis	08/29/1985	15:25	Can	12/26/1985	15:43	Sco	04/24/1986	01:14
Ari	09/01/1985	00:42	Leo	12/29/1985	01:43	Sag	04/26/1986	01:16
Tau	09/03/1985	12:27	Vir	12/31/1985	09:42	Cap	04/28/1986	01:41
Gem	09/06/1985	01:26	Lib	01/02/1986	15:44	Aqu	04/30/1986	04:06
Can	09/08/1985	13:08	Sco	01/04/1986	19:43	Pis	05/02/1986	09:30
Leo	09/10/1985	21:25	Sag	01/06/1986	21:46	Ari	05/04/1986	18:00
Vir	09/13/1985	01:50	Cap	01/08/1986	22:41	Tau	05/07/1986	04:58
Lib	09/15/1985	03:32	Aqu	01/11/1986	00:02	Gem	05/09/1986	17:25
Sco	09/17/1985	04:16	Pis	01/13/1986	03:39	Can	05/12/1986	06:17
Sag	09/19/1985	05:39	Ari	01/15/1986	11:04	Leo	05/14/1986	18:14
Cap	09/21/1985	08:49	Tau	01/17/1986	22:13	Vir	05/17/1986	03:43
Aqu	09/23/1985	14:11	Gem	01/20/1986	11:11	Lib	05/19/1986	09:39
Pis	09/25/1985	21:50	Can	01/22/1986	23:13	Sco	05/21/1986	12:00
Ari	09/28/1985	07:42	Leo	01/25/1986	08:46	Sag	05/23/1986	11:56
Tau	09/30/1985	19:34	Vir	01/27/1986	15:50	Cap	05/25/1986	11:15

Aqu	05/27/1986	12:00	Gem	09/23/1986	04:13	Lib	01/20/1987	06:08
Pis	05/29/1986	15:54	Can	09/25/1986	16:44	Sco	01/22/1987	13:29
Ari	05/31/1986	23:43	Leo	09/28/1986	04:38	Sag	01/24/1987	17:35
Tau	06/03/1986	10:45	Vir	09/30/1986	13:56	Cap	01/26/1987	18:41
Gem	06/05/1986	23:26	Lib	10/02/1986	20:01	Aqu	01/28/1987	18:16
Can	06/08/1986	12:15	Sco	10/04/1986	23:34	Pis	01/30/1987	18:24
Leo	06/11/1986	00:10	Sag	10/07/1986	01:47	Ari	02/01/1987	21:10
Vir	06/13/1986	10:16	Cap	10/09/1986	03:52	Tau	02/04/1987	03:53
Lib	06/15/1986	17:37	Aqu	10/11/1986	06:45	Gem	02/06/1987	14:23
Sco	06/17/1986	21:34	Pis	10/13/1986	11:03	Can	02/09/1987	02:54
Sag	06/19/1986	22:34	Ari	10/15/1986	17:13	Leo	02/11/1987	15:20
Cap	06/21/1986	21:59	Tau	10/18/1986	01:35	Vir	02/14/1987	02:25
Aqu	06/23/1986	21:50	Gem	10/20/1986	12:15	Lib	02/16/1987	11:43
Pis	06/26/1986	00:13	Can	10/23/1986	00:37	Sco	02/18/1987	19:03
Ari	06/28/1986	06:34	Leo	10/25/1986	13:01	Sag	02/21/1987	00:08
Tau	06/30/1986	16:54	Vir	10/27/1986	23:18	Cap	02/23/1987	02:56
Gem	07/03/1986	05:31	Lib	10/30/1986	06:04	Aqu	02/25/1987	04:08
Can	07/05/1986	18:19	Sco	11/01/1986	09:18	Pis	02/27/1987	05:06
Leo	07/08/1986	05:55	Sag	11/03/1986	10:18	Ari	03/01/1987	07:37
Vir	07/10/1986	15:49	Cap	11/05/1986	10:48	Tau	03/03/1987	13:12
Lib	07/12/1986	23:38	Aqu	11/07/1986	12:29	Gem	03/05/1987	22:27
Sco	07/15/1986	04:57	Pis	11/09/1986	16:29	Can	03/08/1987	10:24
Sag	07/17/1986	07:33	Ari	11/11/1986	23:14	Leo	03/10/1987	22:53
Cap	07/19/1986	08:09	Tau	11/14/1986	08:24	Vir	03/13/1987	09:54
Aqu	07/21/1986	08:17	Gem	11/16/1986	19:26	Lib	03/15/1987	18:33
Pis	07/23/1986	09:59	Can	11/19/1986	07:45	Sco	03/18/1987	00:56
Ari	07/25/1986	15:03	Leo	11/21/1986	20:24	Sag	03/20/1987	05:31
Tau	07/28/1986	00:11	Vir	11/24/1986	07:45	Cap	03/22/1987	08:47
Gem	07/30/1986	12:18	Lib	11/26/1986	15:57	Aqu	03/24/1987	11:17
Can	08/02/1986	01:03	Sco	11/28/1986	20:12	Pis	03/26/1987	13:45
Leo	08/04/1986	12:25	Sag	11/30/1986	21:07	Ari	03/28/1987	17:12
Vir	08/06/1986	21:43	Cap	12/02/1986	20:28	Tau	03/30/1987	22:46
Lib	08/09/1986	05:04	Aqu	12/04/1986	20:23	Gem	04/02/1987	07:16
Sco	08/11/1986	10:34	Pis	12/06/1986	22:49	Can	04/04/1987	18:33
Sag	08/13/1986	14:16	Ari	12/09/1986	04:49	Leo	04/07/1987	07:03
Cap	08/15/1986	16:22	Tau	12/11/1986	14:10	Vir	04/09/1987	18:27
Aqu	08/17/1986	17:44	Gem	12/14/1986	01:41	Lib	04/12/1987	03:04
Pis	08/19/1986	19:52	Can	12/16/1986	14:09	Sco	04/14/1987	08:39
Ari	08/22/1986	00:28	Leo	12/19/1986	02:43	Sag	04/16/1987	12:00
Tau	08/24/1986	08:37	Vir	12/21/1986	14:29	Cap	04/18/1987	14:20
Gem	08/26/1986	20:00	Lib	12/24/1986	00:03	Aqu	04/20/1987	16:45
Can	08/29/1986	08:39	Sco	12/26/1986	06:06	Pis	04/22/1987	20:01
Leo	08/31/1986	20:07	Sag	12/28/1986	08:18	Ari	04/25/1987	00:41
Vir	09/03/1986	05:05	Cap	12/30/1986	07:53	Tau	04/27/1987	07:05
Lib	09/05/1986	11:32	Aqu	01/01/1987	06:53	Gem	04/29/1987	15:43
Sco	09/07/1986	16:11	Pis	01/03/1987	07:36	Can	05/02/1987	02:39
Sag	09/09/1986	19:40	Ari	01/05/1987	11:52	Leo	05/04/1987	15:06
Cap	09/11/1986	22:27	Tau	01/07/1987	20:13	Vir	05/07/1987	03:06
Aqu	09/14/1986	01:07	Gem	01/10/1987	07:39	Lib	05/09/1987	12:27
Pis	09/16/1986	04:27	Can	01/12/1987	20:18	Sco	05/11/1987	18:09
Ari	09/18/1986	09:34	Leo	01/15/1987	08:44	Sag	05/13/1987	20:40
Tau	09/20/1986	17:25	Vir	01/17/1987	20:14	Cap	05/15/1987	21:36

Aqu	05/17/1987	22:43	Gem	09/13/1987	00:55	Lib	01/10/1988	08:16
Pis	05/20/1987	01:24	Can	09/15/1987	11:22	Sco	01/12/1988	18:38
Ari	05/22/1987	06:22	Leo	09/17/1987	23:50	Sag	01/15/1988	00:56
Tau	05/24/1987	13:39	Vir	09/20/1987	12:12	Cap	01/17/1988	03:14
Gem	05/26/1987	22:55	Lib	09/22/1987	22:57	Aqu	01/19/1988	03:01
Can	05/29/1987	09:59	Sco	09/25/1987	07:29	Pis	01/21/1988	02:27
Leo	05/31/1987	22:25	Sag	09/27/1987	13:48	Ari	01/23/1988	03:31
Vir	06/03/1987	10:55	Cap	09/29/1987	18:08	Tau	01/25/1988	07:36
Lib	06/05/1987	21:22	Aqu	10/01/1987	20:50	Gem	01/27/1988	15:02
Sco	06/08/1987	04:05	Pis	10/03/1987	22:39	Can	01/30/1988	01:11
Sag	06/10/1987	06:52	Ari	10/06/1987	00:35	Leo	02/01/1988	13:06
Cap	06/12/1987	07:04	Tau	10/08/1987	03:57	Vir	02/04/1988	01:54
Aqu	06/14/1987	06:44	Gem	10/10/1987	10:04	Lib	02/06/1988	14:35
Pis	06/16/1987	07:54	Can	10/12/1987	19:30	Sco	02/09/1988	01:40
Ari	06/18/1987	11:57	Leo	10/15/1987	07:34	Sag	02/11/1988	09:34
Tau	06/20/1987	19:08	Vir	10/17/1987	20:05	Cap	02/13/1988	13:35
Gem	06/23/1987	04:54	Lib	10/20/1987	06:49	Aqu	02/15/1988	14:24
Can	06/25/1987	16:22	Sco	10/22/1987	14:40	Pis	02/17/1988	13:43
Leo	06/28/1987	04:51	Sag	10/24/1987	19:56	Ari	02/19/1988	13:35
Vir	06/30/1987	17:33	Cap	10/26/1987	23:32	Tau	02/21/1988	15:51
Lib	07/03/1987	04:54	Aqu	10/29/1987	02:26	Gem	02/23/1988	21:43
Sco	07/05/1987	13:01	Pis	10/31/1987	05:19	Can	02/26/1988	07:12
Sag	07/07/1987	17:04	Ari	11/02/1987	08:40	Leo	02/28/1988	19:12
Cap	07/09/1987	17:43	Tau	11/04/1987	13:02	Vir	03/02/1988	08:06
Aqu	07/11/1987	16:49	Gem	11/06/1987	19:16	Lib	03/04/1988	20:31
Pis	07/13/1987	16:36	Can	11/09/1987	04:10	Sco	03/07/1988	07:26
Ari	07/15/1987	19:00	Leo	11/11/1987	15:45	Sag	03/09/1988	15:58
Tau	07/18/1987	01:05	Vir	11/14/1987	04:29	Cap	03/11/1988	21:30
Gem	07/20/1987	10:33	Lib	11/16/1987	15:47	Aqu	03/14/1988	00:06
Can	07/22/1987	22:13	Sco	11/18/1987	23:45	Pis	03/16/1988	00:41
Leo	07/25/1987	10:49	Sag	11/21/1987	04:15	Ari	03/18/1988	00:45
Vir	07/27/1987	23:25	Cap	11/23/1987	06:31	Tau	03/20/1988	02:06
Lib	07/30/1987	10:58	Aqu	11/25/1987	08:12	Gem	03/22/1988	06:21
Sco	08/01/1987	20:08	Pis	11/27/1987	10:41	Can	03/24/1988	14:28
Sag	08/04/1987	01:45	Ari	11/29/1987	14:36	Leo	03/27/1988	01:54
Cap	08/06/1987	03:50	Tau	12/01/1987	20:05	Vir	03/29/1988	14:48
Aqu	08/08/1987	03:36	Gem	12/04/1987	03:13	Lib	04/01/1988	03:04
Pis	08/10/1987	03:01	Can	12/06/1987	12:20	Sco	04/03/1988	13:24
Ari	08/12/1987	04:09	Leo	12/08/1987	23:40	Sag	04/05/1988	21:27
Tau	08/14/1987	08:39	Vir	12/11/1987	12:29	Cap	04/08/1988	03:18
Gem	08/16/1987	16:58	Lib	12/14/1987	00:38	Aqu	04/10/1988	07:10
Can	08/19/1987	04:19	Sco	12/16/1987	09:39	Pis	04/12/1988	09:24
Leo	08/21/1987	16:57	Sag	12/18/1987	14:31	Ari	04/14/1988	10:46
Vir	08/24/1987	05:23	Cap	12/20/1987	16:07	Tau	04/16/1988	12:32
Lib	08/26/1987	16:35	Aqu	12/22/1987	16:20	Gem	04/18/1988	16:10
Sco	08/29/1987	01:48	Pis	12/24/1987	17:10	Can	04/20/1988	23:05
Sag	08/31/1987	08:23	Ari	12/26/1987	20:05	Leo	04/23/1988	09:34
Cap	09/02/1987	12:02	Tau	12/29/1987	01:37	Vir	04/25/1988	22:15
Aqu	09/04/1987	13:21	Gem	12/31/1987	09:29	Lib	04/28/1988	10:36
Pis	09/06/1987	13:36	Can	01/02/1988	19:16	Sco	04/30/1988	20:38
Ari	09/08/1987	14:34	Leo	01/05/1988	06:47	Sag	05/03/1988	03:51
Tau	09/10/1987	17:57	Vir	01/07/1988	19:35	Cap	05/05/1988	08:53

Aqu	05/07/1988	12:36	Gem	09/02/1988	03:12	Lib	12/30/1988	04:09
Pis	05/09/1988	15:38	Can	09/04/1988	10:38	Sco	01/01/1989	16:33
Ari	05/11/1988	18:23	Leo	09/06/1988	21:14	Sag	01/04/1989	02:10
Tau	05/13/1988	21:22	Vir	09/09/1988	09:48	Cap	01/06/1989	08:13
Gem	05/16/1988	01:32	Lib	09/11/1988	22:51	Aqu	01/08/1989	11:30
Can	05/18/1988	08:05	Sco	09/14/1988	11:06	Pis	01/10/1989	13:30
Leo	05/20/1988	17:51	Sag	09/16/1988	21:24	Ari	01/12/1989	15:36
Vir	05/23/1988	06:12	Cap	09/19/1988	04:44	Tau	01/14/1989	18:36
Lib	05/25/1988	18:49	Aqu	09/21/1988	08:42	Gem	01/16/1989	22:57
Sco	05/28/1988	05:05	Pis	09/23/1988	09:50	Can	01/19/1989	04:57
Sag	05/30/1988	11:56	Ari	09/25/1988	09:29	Leo	01/21/1989	13:03
Cap	06/01/1988	15:58	Tau	09/27/1988	09:29	Vir	01/23/1989	23:33
Aqu	06/03/1988	18:33	Gem	09/29/1988	11:44	Lib	01/26/1989	12:01
Pis	06/05/1988	21:00	Can	10/01/1988	17:38	Sco	01/29/1989	00:48
Ari	06/08/1988	00:04	Leo	10/04/1988	03:31	Sag	01/31/1989	11:29
Tau	06/10/1988	04:02	Vir	10/06/1988	16:01	Cap	02/02/1989	18:29
Gem	06/12/1988	09:14	Lib	10/09/1988	05:03	Aqu	02/04/1989	21:50
Can	06/14/1988	16:19	Sco	10/11/1988	16:57	Pis	02/06/1989	22:51
Leo	06/17/1988	01:57	Sag	10/14/1988	02:57	Ari	02/08/1989	23:18
Vir	06/19/1988	14:03	Cap	10/16/1988	10:43	Tau	02/11/1989	00:45
Lib	06/22/1988	02:56	Aqu	10/18/1988	16:04	Gem	02/13/1989	04:22
Sco	06/24/1988	13:57	Pis	10/20/1988	18:58	Can	02/15/1989	10:41
Sag	06/26/1988	21:16	Ari	10/22/1988	19:58	Leo	02/17/1989	19:33
Cap	06/29/1988	00:58	Tau	10/24/1988	20:22	Vir	02/20/1989	06:34
Aqu	07/01/1988	02:29	Gem	10/26/1988	21:56	Lib	02/22/1989	19:05
Pis	07/03/1988	03:33	Can	10/29/1988	02:29	Sco	02/25/1989	07:56
Ari	07/05/1988	05:37	Leo	10/31/1988	11:04	Sag	02/27/1989	19:28
Tau	07/07/1988	09:27	Vir	11/02/1988	23:01	Cap	03/02/1989	03:57
Gem	07/09/1988	15:16	Lib	11/05/1988	12:03	Aqu	03/04/1989	08:35
Can	07/11/1988	23:09	Sco	11/07/1988	23:45	Pis	03/06/1989	09:58
Leo	07/14/1988	09:11	Sag	11/10/1988	09:05	Ari	03/08/1989	09:36
Vir	07/16/1988	21:17	Cap	11/12/1988	16:12	Tau	03/10/1989	09:26
Lib	07/19/1988	10:21	Aqu	11/14/1988	21:36	Gem	03/12/1989	11:17
Sco	07/21/1988	22:12	Pis	11/17/1988	01:33	Can	03/14/1989	16:28
Sag	07/24/1988	06:41	Ari	11/19/1988	04:12	Leo	03/17/1989	01:13
Cap	07/26/1988	11:05	Tau	11/21/1988	06:02	Vir	03/19/1989	12:40
Aqu	07/28/1988	12:24	Gem	11/23/1988	08:12	Lib	03/22/1989	01:24
Pis	07/30/1988	12:23	Can	11/25/1988	12:20	Sco	03/24/1989	14:10
Ari	08/01/1988	12:54	Leo	11/27/1988	19:52	Sag	03/27/1989	01:53
Tau	08/03/1988	15:24	Vir	11/30/1988	06:59	Cap	03/29/1989	11:24
Gem	08/05/1988	20:43	Lib	12/02/1988	19:55	Aqu	03/31/1989	17:44
Can	08/08/1988	04:52	Sco	12/05/1988	07:50	Pis	04/02/1989	20:36
Leo	08/10/1988	15:26	Sag	12/07/1988	16:55	Ari	04/04/1989	20:50
Vir	08/13/1988	03:45	Cap	12/09/1988	23:06	Tau	04/06/1989	20:07
Lib	08/15/1988	16:51	Aqu	12/12/1988	03:25	Gem	04/08/1989	20:32
Sco	08/18/1988	05:11	Pis	12/14/1988	06:53	Can	04/10/1989	23:59
Sag	08/20/1988	14:53	Ari	12/16/1988	10:03	Leo	04/13/1989	07:31
Cap	08/22/1988	20:48	Tau	12/18/1988	13:11	Vir	04/15/1989	18:39
Aqu	08/24/1988	23:03	Gem	12/20/1988	16:43	Lib	04/18/1989	07:31
Pis	08/26/1988	23:00	Can	12/22/1988	21:35	Sco	04/20/1989	20:13
Ari	08/28/1988	22:29	Leo	12/25/1988	04:57	Sag	04/23/1989	07:38
Tau	08/30/1988	23:23	Vir	12/27/1988	15:28	Cap	04/25/1989	17:15

Aqu	04/28/1989	00:32	Gem	08/23/1989	12:39	Lib	12/19/1989	22:46
Pis	04/30/1989	05:03	Can	08/25/1989	17:13	Sco	12/22/1989	11:18
Ari	05/02/1989	06:50	Leo	08/28/1989	00:12	Sag	12/24/1989	23:36
Tau	05/04/1989	06:55	Vir	08/30/1989	09:30	Cap	12/27/1989	10:09
Gem	05/06/1989	07:03	Lib	09/01/1989	20:48	Aqu	12/29/1989	18:37
Can	05/08/1989	09:20	Sco	09/04/1989	09:23	Pis	01/01/1990	01:09
Leo	05/10/1989	15:24	Sag	09/06/1989	21:50	Ari	01/03/1990	05:56
Vir	05/13/1989	01:31	Cap	09/09/1989	08:12	Tau	01/05/1990	09:03
Lib	05/15/1989	14:07	Aqu	09/11/1989	15:00	Gem	01/07/1990	11:01
Sco	05/18/1989	02:47	Pis	09/13/1989	18:07	Can	01/09/1990	12:52
Sag	05/20/1989	13:51	Ari	09/15/1989	18:38	Leo	01/11/1990	16:03
Cap	05/22/1989	22:53	Tau	09/17/1989	18:22	Vir	01/13/1990	21:58
Aqu	05/25/1989	06:01	Gem	09/19/1989	19:16	Lib	01/16/1990	07:18
Pis	05/27/1989	11:12	Can	09/21/1989	22:51	Sco	01/18/1990	19:16
Ari	05/29/1989	14:25	Leo	09/24/1989	05:44	Sag	01/21/1990	07:43
Tau	05/31/1989	15:59	Vir	09/26/1989	15:32	Cap	01/23/1990	18:27
Gem	06/02/1989	17:02	Lib	09/29/1989	03:15	Aqu	01/26/1990	02:24
Can	06/04/1989	19:17	Sco	10/01/1989	15:53	Pis	01/28/1990	07:50
Leo	06/07/1989	00:29	Sag	10/04/1989	04:29	Ari	01/30/1990	11:34
Vir	06/09/1989	09:30	Cap	10/06/1989	15:44	Tau	02/01/1990	14:27
Lib	06/11/1989	21:31	Aqu	10/09/1989	00:05	Gem	02/03/1990	17:12
Sco	06/14/1989	10:10	Pis	10/11/1989	04:37	Can	02/05/1990	20:27
Sag	06/16/1989	21:11	Ari	10/13/1989	05:41	Leo	02/08/1990	00:52
Cap	06/19/1989	05:41	Tau	10/15/1989	04:52	Vir	02/10/1990	07:13
Aqu	06/21/1989	11:56	Gem	10/17/1989	04:20	Lib	02/12/1990	16:10
Pis	06/23/1989	16:36	Can	10/19/1989	06:09	Sco	02/15/1990	03:34
Ari	06/25/1989	20:06	Leo	10/21/1989	11:49	Sag	02/17/1990	16:07
Tau	06/27/1989	22:45	Vir	10/23/1989	21:15	Cap	02/20/1990	03:29
Gem	06/30/1989	01:08	Lib	10/26/1989	09:11	Aqu	02/22/1990	11:51
Can	07/02/1989	04:19	Sco	10/28/1989	21:56	Pis	02/24/1990	16:49
Leo	07/04/1989	09:38	Sag	10/31/1989	10:22	Ari	02/26/1990	19:16
Vir	07/06/1989	18:04	Cap	11/02/1989	21:46	Tau	02/28/1990	20:43
Lib	07/09/1989	05:30	Aqu	11/05/1989	07:08	Gem	03/02/1990	22:38
Sco	07/11/1989	18:09	Pis	11/07/1989	13:23	Can	03/05/1990	02:03
Sag	07/14/1989	05:31	Ari	11/09/1989	16:07	Leo	03/07/1990	07:25
Cap	07/16/1989	14:00	Tau	11/11/1989	16:09	Vir	03/09/1990	14:47
Aqu	07/18/1989	19:35	Gem	11/13/1989	15:19	Lib	03/12/1990	00:09
Pis	07/20/1989	23:06	Can	11/15/1989	15:52	Sco	03/14/1990	11:25
Ari	07/23/1989	01:40	Leo	11/17/1989	19:46	Sag	03/16/1990	23:56
Tau	07/25/1989	04:10	Vir	11/20/1989	03:55	Cap	03/19/1990	12:00
Gem	07/27/1989	07:15	Lib	11/22/1989	15:25	Aqu	03/21/1990	21:30
Can	07/29/1989	11:32	Sco	11/25/1989	04:13	Pis	03/24/1990	03:08
Leo	07/31/1989	17:41	Sag	11/27/1989	16:29	Ari	03/26/1990	05:15
Vir	08/03/1989	02:20	Cap	11/30/1989	03:26	Tau	03/28/1990	05:26
Lib	08/05/1989	13:28	Aqu	12/02/1989	12:41	Gem	03/30/1990	05:42
Sco	08/08/1989	02:05	Pis	12/04/1989	19:47	Can	04/01/1990	07:50
Sag	08/10/1989	14:02	Ari	12/07/1989	00:10	Leo	04/03/1990	12:51
Cap	08/12/1989	23:15	Tau	12/09/1989	01:58	Vir	04/05/1990	20:42
Aqu	08/15/1989	04:58	Gem	12/11/1989	02:15	Lib	04/08/1990	06:44
Pis	08/17/1989	07:45	Can	12/13/1989	02:50	Sco	04/10/1990	18:18
Ari	08/19/1989	08:59	Leo	12/15/1989	05:41	Sag	04/13/1990	06:48
Tau	08/21/1989	10:11	Vir	12/17/1989	12:20	Cap	04/15/1990	19:14

Aqu	04/18/1990	05:52	Gem	08/14/1990	02:41	Lib	12/09/1990	22:01
Pis	04/20/1990	12:55	Can	08/16/1990	05:12	Sco	12/12/1990	08:28
Ari	04/22/1990	15:57	Leo	08/18/1990	08:11	Sag	12/14/1990	20:44
Tau	04/24/1990	16:02	Vir	08/20/1990	12:34	Cap	12/17/1990	09:34
Gem	04/26/1990	15:12	Lib	08/22/1990	19:17	Aqu	12/19/1990	21:58
Can	04/28/1990	15:40	Sco	08/25/1990	04:56	Pis	12/22/1990	08:47
Leo	04/30/1990	19:09	Sag	08/27/1990	16:57	Ari	12/24/1990	16:44
Vir	05/03/1990	02:19	Cap	08/30/1990	05:23	Tau	12/26/1990	21:08
Lib	05/05/1990	12:29	Aqu	09/01/1990	15:50	Gem	12/28/1990	22:25
Sco	05/08/1990	00:22	Pis	09/03/1990	23:04	Can	12/30/1990	22:02
Sag	05/10/1990	12:56	Ari	09/06/1990	03:22	Leo	01/01/1991	21:55
Cap	05/13/1990	01:20	Tau	09/08/1990	05:55	Vir	01/03/1991	23:58
Aqu	05/15/1990	12:29	Gem	09/10/1990	08:05	Lib	01/06/1991	05:33
Pis	05/17/1990	20:53	Can	09/12/1990	10:53	Sco	01/08/1991	15:00
Ari	05/20/1990	01:30	Leo	09/14/1990	14:52	Sag	01/11/1991	03:06
Tau	05/22/1990	02:41	Vir	09/16/1990	20:19	Cap	01/13/1991	16:00
Gem	05/24/1990	02:00	Lib	09/19/1990	03:34	Aqu	01/16/1991	04:04
Can	05/26/1990	01:35	Sco	09/21/1990	13:06	Pis	01/18/1991	14:23
Leo	05/28/1990	03:30	Sag	09/24/1990	00:52	Ari	01/20/1991	22:27
Vir	05/30/1990	09:09	Cap	09/26/1990	13:36	Tau	01/23/1991	04:00
Lib	06/01/1990	18:31	Aqu	09/29/1990	00:52	Gem	01/25/1991	07:06
Sco	06/04/1990	06:21	Pis	10/01/1990	08:41	Can	01/27/1991	08:23
Sag	06/06/1990	18:59	Ari	10/03/1990	12:40	Leo	01/29/1991	09:04
Cap	06/09/1990	07:11	Tau	10/05/1990	14:05	Vir	01/31/1991	10:45
Aqu	06/11/1990	18:09	Gem	10/07/1990	14:47	Lib	02/02/1991	15:03
Pis	06/14/1990	02:59	Can	10/09/1990	16:30	Sco	02/04/1991	23:02
Ari	06/16/1990	08:54	Leo	10/11/1990	20:17	Sag	02/07/1991	10:24
Tau	06/18/1990	11:42	Vir	10/14/1990	02:21	Cap	02/09/1991	23:15
Gem	06/20/1990	12:14	Lib	10/16/1990	10:27	Aqu	02/12/1991	11:16
Can	06/22/1990	12:10	Sco	10/18/1990	20:24	Pis	02/14/1991	20:58
Leo	06/24/1990	13:26	Sag	10/21/1990	08:09	Ari	02/17/1991	04:11
Vir	06/26/1990	17:42	Cap	10/23/1990	21:02	Tau	02/19/1991	09:24
Lib	06/29/1990	01:48	Aqu	10/26/1990	09:13	Gem	02/21/1991	13:10
Sco	07/01/1990	13:01	Pis	10/28/1990	18:21	Can	02/23/1991	15:56
Sag	07/04/1990	01:35	Ari	10/30/1990	23:13	Leo	02/25/1991	18:13
Cap	07/06/1990	13:39	Tau	11/02/1990	00:31	Vir	02/27/1991	20:51
Aqu	07/09/1990	00:06	Gem	11/04/1990	00:06	Lib	03/02/1991	01:04
Pis	07/11/1990	08:29	Can	11/06/1990	00:08	Sco	03/04/1991	08:09
Ari	07/13/1990	14:36	Leo	11/08/1990	02:25	Sag	03/06/1991	18:35
Tau	07/15/1990	18:28	Vir	11/10/1990	07:49	Cap	03/09/1991	07:14
Gem	07/17/1990	20:31	Lib	11/12/1990	16:09	Aqu	03/11/1991	19:30
Can	07/19/1990	21:44	Sco	11/15/1990	02:39	Pis	03/14/1991	05:10
Leo	07/21/1990	23:29	Sag	11/17/1990	14:39	Ari	03/16/1991	11:37
Vir	07/24/1990	03:18	Cap	11/20/1990	03:31	Tau	03/18/1991	15:40
Lib	07/26/1990	10:20	Aqu	11/22/1990	16:06	Gem	03/20/1991	18:37
Sco	07/28/1990	20:39	Pis	11/25/1990	02:30	Can	03/22/1991	21:27
Sag	07/31/1990	09:00	Ari	11/27/1990	09:05	Leo	03/25/1991	00:44
Cap	08/02/1990	21:08	Tau	11/29/1990	11:36	Vir	03/27/1991	04:41
Aqu	08/05/1990	07:19	Gem	12/01/1990	11:22	Lib	03/29/1991	09:50
Pis	08/07/1990	14:53	Can	12/03/1990	10:28	Sco	03/31/1991	17:01
Ari	08/09/1990	20:12	Leo	12/05/1990	11:01	Sag	04/03/1991	02:59
Tau	08/11/1990	23:54	Vir	12/07/1990	14:40	Cap	04/05/1991	15:20

Aqu	04/08/1991	03:59	Gem	08/04/1991	15:54	Lib	11/30/1991	04:47
Pis	04/10/1991	14:16	Can	08/06/1991	17:47	Sco	12/02/1991	11:34
Ari	04/12/1991	20:49	Leo	08/08/1991	18:09	Sag	12/04/1991	20:33
Tau	04/15/1991	00:05	Vir	08/10/1991	18:35	Cap	12/07/1991	07:41
Gem	04/17/1991	01:41	Lib	08/12/1991	20:53	Aqu	12/09/1991	20:26
Can	04/19/1991	03:18	Sco	08/15/1991	02:35	Pis	12/12/1991	09:18
Leo	04/21/1991	06:04	Sag	08/17/1991	12:12	Ari	12/14/1991	20:06
Vir	04/23/1991	10:30	Cap	08/20/1991	00:34	Tau	12/17/1991	03:09
Lib	04/25/1991	16:36	Aqu	08/22/1991	13:26	Gem	12/19/1991	06:21
Sco	04/28/1991	00:34	Pis	08/25/1991	00:50	Can	12/21/1991	06:55
Sag	04/30/1991	10:43	Ari	08/27/1991	10:00	Leo	12/23/1991	06:39
Cap	05/02/1991	22:55	Tau	08/29/1991	16:59	Vir	12/25/1991	07:24
Aqu	05/05/1991	11:50	Gem	08/31/1991	22:02	Lib	12/27/1991	10:39
Pis	05/07/1991	23:03	Can	09/03/1991	01:19	Sco	12/29/1991	17:03
Ari	05/10/1991	06:34	Leo	09/05/1991	03:13	Sag	01/01/1992	02:31
Tau	05/12/1991	10:06	Vir	09/07/1991	04:35	Cap	01/03/1992	14:09
Gem	05/14/1991	11:02	Lib	09/09/1991	06:52	Aqu	01/06/1992	02:59
Can	05/16/1991	11:14	Sco	09/11/1991	11:43	Pis	01/08/1992	15:52
Leo	05/18/1991	12:31	Sag	09/13/1991	20:15	Ari	01/11/1992	03:22
Vir	05/20/1991	16:01	Cap	09/16/1991	08:04	Tau	01/13/1992	11:59
Lib	05/22/1991	22:08	Aqu	09/18/1991	20:57	Gem	01/15/1992	16:54
Sco	05/25/1991	06:41	Pis	09/21/1991	08:20	Can	01/17/1992	18:26
Sag	05/27/1991	17:21	Ari	09/23/1991	16:55	Leo	01/19/1992	17:57
Cap	05/30/1991	05:40	Tau	09/25/1991	22:58	Vir	01/21/1992	17:22
Aqu	06/01/1991	18:41	Gem	09/28/1991	03:25	Lib	01/23/1992	18:42
Pis	06/04/1991	06:36	Can	09/30/1991	06:58	Sco	01/25/1992	23:33
Ari	06/06/1991	15:24	Leo	10/02/1991	09:58	Sag	01/28/1992	08:20
Tau	06/08/1991	20:12	Vir	10/04/1991	12:45	Cap	01/30/1992	20:08
Gem	06/10/1991	21:36	Lib	10/06/1991	16:01	Aqu	02/02/1992	09:09
Can	06/12/1991	21:17	Sco	10/08/1991	21:01	Pis	02/04/1992	21:50
Leo	06/14/1991	21:11	Sag	10/11/1991	04:58	Ari	02/07/1992	09:14
Vir	06/16/1991	23:04	Cap	10/13/1991	16:10	Tau	02/09/1992	18:35
Lib	06/19/1991	04:02	Aqu	10/16/1991	05:04	Gem	02/12/1992	01:07
Sco	06/21/1991	12:19	Pis	10/18/1991	16:52	Can	02/14/1992	04:30
Sag	06/23/1991	23:17	Ari	10/21/1991	01:32	Leo	02/16/1992	05:15
Cap	06/26/1991	11:49	Tau	10/23/1991	06:55	Vir	02/18/1992	04:46
Aqu	06/29/1991	00:47	Gem	10/25/1991	10:08	Lib	02/20/1992	05:05
Pis	07/01/1991	12:50	Can	10/27/1991	12:37	Sco	02/22/1992	08:12
Ari	07/03/1991	22:32	Leo	10/29/1991	15:20	Sag	02/24/1992	15:27
Tau	07/06/1991	04:51	Vir	10/31/1991	18:47	Cap	02/27/1992	02:34
Gem	07/08/1991	07:41	Lib	11/02/1991	23:13	Aqu	02/29/1992	15:34
Can	07/10/1991	08:02	Sco	11/05/1991	05:09	Pis	03/03/1992	04:11
Leo	07/12/1991	07:35	Sag	11/07/1991	13:22	Ari	03/05/1992	15:06
Vir	07/14/1991	08:12	Cap	11/10/1991	00:17	Tau	03/08/1992	00:04
Lib	07/16/1991	11:35	Aqu	11/12/1991	13:06	Gem	03/10/1992	07:03
Sco	07/18/1991	18:41	Pis	11/15/1991	01:32	Can	03/12/1992	11:49
Sag	07/21/1991	05:17	Ari	11/17/1991	11:06	Leo	03/14/1992	14:20
Cap	07/23/1991	17:55	Tau	11/19/1991	16:49	Vir	03/16/1992	15:13
Aqu	07/26/1991	06:49	Gem	11/21/1991	19:22	Lib	03/18/1992	15:55
Pis	07/28/1991	18:34	Can	11/23/1991	20:25	Sco	03/20/1992	18:20
Ari	07/31/1991	04:20	Leo	11/25/1991	21:38	Sag	03/23/1992	00:14
Tau	08/02/1991	11:31	Vir	11/28/1991	00:13	Cap	03/25/1992	10:09

Aqu	03/27/1992	22:44	Gem	07/24/1992	23:43	Lib	11/19/1992	17:02
Pis	03/30/1992	11:22	Can	07/27/1992	03:07	Sco	11/21/1992	19:52
Ari	04/01/1992	22:03	Leo	07/29/1992	03:39	Sag	11/24/1992	00:02
Tau	04/04/1992	06:18	Vir	07/31/1992	03:01	Cap	11/26/1992	06:38
Gem	04/06/1992	12:32	Lib	08/02/1992	03:18	Aqu	11/28/1992	16:19
Can	04/08/1992	17:18	Sco	08/04/1992	06:16	Pis	12/01/1992	04:23
Leo	04/10/1992	20:46	Sag	08/06/1992	12:58	Ari	12/03/1992	16:48
Vir	04/12/1992	23:09	Cap	08/08/1992	23:01	Tau	12/06/1992	03:16
Lib	04/15/1992	01:11	Aqu	08/11/1992	11:07	Gem	12/08/1992	10:36
Sco	04/17/1992	04:10	Pis	08/13/1992	23:51	Can	12/10/1992	15:05
Sag	04/19/1992	09:41	Ari	08/16/1992	12:11	Leo	12/12/1992	17:47
Cap	04/21/1992	18:41	Tau	08/18/1992	23:09	Vir	12/14/1992	19:56
Aqu	04/24/1992	06:38	Gem	08/21/1992	07:36	Lib	12/16/1992	22:33
Pis	04/26/1992	19:19	Can	08/23/1992	12:35	Sco	12/19/1992	02:20
Ari	04/29/1992	06:13	Leo	08/25/1992	14:14	Sag	12/21/1992	07:43
Tau	05/01/1992	14:08	Vir	08/27/1992	13:46	Cap	12/23/1992	15:05
Gem	05/03/1992	19:28	Lib	08/29/1992	13:11	Aqu	12/26/1992	00:44
Can	05/05/1992	23:09	Sco	08/31/1992	14:39	Pis	12/28/1992	12:28
Leo	05/08/1992	02:07	Sag	09/02/1992	19:51	Ari	12/31/1992	01:06
Vir	05/10/1992	04:56	Cap	09/05/1992	05:06	Tau	01/02/1993	12:29
Lib	05/12/1992	08:05	Aqu	09/07/1992	17:08	Gem	01/04/1993	20:41
Sco	05/14/1992	12:16	Pis	09/10/1992	05:56	Can	01/07/1993	01:09
Sag	05/16/1992	18:22	Ari	09/12/1992	18:02	Leo	01/09/1993	02:49
Cap	05/19/1992	03:13	Tau	09/15/1992	04:47	Vir	01/11/1993	03:21
Aqu	05/21/1992	14:44	Gem	09/17/1992	13:39	Lib	01/13/1993	04:31
Pis	05/24/1992	03:25	Can	09/19/1992	19:58	Sco	01/15/1993	07:42
Ari	05/26/1992	14:52	Leo	09/21/1992	23:18	Sag	01/17/1993	13:31
Tau	05/28/1992	23:15	Vir	09/24/1992	00:07	Cap	01/19/1993	21:47
Gem	05/31/1992	04:19	Lib	09/25/1992	23:56	Aqu	01/22/1993	08:01
Can	06/02/1992	06:58	Sco	09/28/1992	00:45	Pis	01/24/1993	19:47
Leo	06/04/1992	08:35	Sag	09/30/1992	04:34	Ari	01/27/1993	08:28
Vir	06/06/1992	10:28	Cap	10/02/1992	12:30	Tau	01/29/1993	20:36
Lib	06/08/1992	13:34	Aqu	10/04/1992	23:53	Gem	02/01/1993	06:14
Sco	06/10/1992	18:27	Pis	10/07/1992	12:37	Can	02/03/1993	11:55
Sag	06/13/1992	01:30	Ari	10/10/1992	00:35	Leo	02/05/1993	13:50
Cap	06/15/1992	10:50	Tau	10/12/1992	10:48	Vir	02/07/1993	13:29
Aqu	06/17/1992	22:19	Gem	10/14/1992	19:08	Lib	02/09/1993	12:59
Pis	06/20/1992	11:00	Can	10/17/1992	01:35	Sco	02/11/1993	14:25
Ari	06/22/1992	23:02	Leo	10/19/1992	06:01	Sag	02/13/1993	19:08
Tau	06/25/1992	08:28	Vir	10/21/1992	08:27	Cap	02/16/1993	03:21
Gem	06/27/1992	14:13	Lib	10/23/1992	09:39	Aqu	02/18/1993	14:06
Can	06/29/1992	16:42	Sco	10/25/1992	11:05	Pis	02/21/1993	02:12
Leo	07/01/1992	17:15	Sag	10/27/1992	14:30	Ari	02/23/1993	14:50
Vir	07/03/1992	17:37	Cap	10/29/1992	21:19	Tau	02/26/1993	03:11
Lib	07/05/1992	19:28	Aqu	11/01/1992	07:43	Gem	02/28/1993	13:51
Sco	07/07/1992	23:55	Pis	11/03/1992	20:12	Can	03/02/1993	21:15
Sag	07/10/1992	07:18	Ari	11/06/1992	08:19	Leo	03/05/1993	00:39
Cap	07/12/1992	17:16	Tau	11/08/1992	18:19	Vir	03/07/1993	00:51
Aqu	07/15/1992	05:03	Gem	11/11/1992	01:49	Lib	03/08/1993	23:46
Pis	07/17/1992	17:44	Can	11/13/1992	07:19	Sco	03/10/1993	23:41
Ari	07/20/1992	06:07	Leo	11/15/1992	11:23	Sag	03/13/1993	02:35
Tau	07/22/1992	16:35	Vir	11/17/1992	14:28	Cap	03/15/1993	09:29

Aqu	03/17/1993	19:53	Gem	07/15/1993	01:05	Lib	11/10/1993	05:42
Pis	03/20/1993	08:11	Can	07/17/1993	08:07	Sco	11/12/1993	05:59
Ari	03/22/1993	20:51	Leo	07/19/1993	11:46	Sag	11/14/1993	06:20
Tau	03/25/1993	08:59	Vir	07/21/1993	13:24	Cap	11/16/1993	08:35
Gem	03/27/1993	19:47	Lib	07/23/1993	14:40	Aqu	11/18/1993	14:09
Can	03/30/1993	04:13	Sco	07/25/1993	17:00	Pis	11/20/1993	23:28
Leo	04/01/1993	09:20	Sag	07/27/1993	21:13	Ari	11/23/1993	11:30
Vir	04/03/1993	11:09	Cap	07/30/1993	03:27	Tau	11/26/1993	00:13
Lib	04/05/1993	10:54	Aqu	08/01/1993	11:37	Gem	11/28/1993	11:47
Sco	04/07/1993	10:33	Pis	08/03/1993	21:44	Can	11/30/1993	21:16
Sag	04/09/1993	12:11	Ari	08/06/1993	09:39	Leo	12/03/1993	04:32
Cap	04/11/1993	17:24	Tau	08/08/1993	22:22	Vir	12/05/1993	09:42
Aqu	04/14/1993	02:36	Gem	08/11/1993	09:46	Lib	12/07/1993	13:03
Pis	04/16/1993	14:33	Can	08/13/1993	17:46	Sco	12/09/1993	15:04
Ari	04/19/1993	03:14	Leo	08/15/1993	21:42	Sag	12/11/1993	16:39
Tau	04/21/1993	15:07	Vir	08/17/1993	22:40	Cap	12/13/1993	19:06
Gem	04/24/1993	01:26	Lib	08/19/1993	22:35	Aqu	12/15/1993	23:52
Can	04/26/1993	09:45	Sco	08/21/1993	23:28	Pis	12/18/1993	07:59
Leo	04/28/1993	15:39	Sag	08/24/1993	02:46	Ari	12/20/1993	19:19
Vir	04/30/1993	18:59	Cap	08/26/1993	08:58	Tau	12/23/1993	08:04
Lib	05/02/1993	20:20	Aqu	08/28/1993	17:41	Gem	12/25/1993	19:45
Sco	05/04/1993	20:57	Pis	08/31/1993	04:19	Can	12/28/1993	04:46
Sag	05/06/1993	22:35	Ari	09/02/1993	16:21	Leo	12/30/1993	10:58
Cap	05/09/1993	02:52	Tau	09/05/1993	05:09	Vir	01/01/1994	15:14
Aqu	05/11/1993	10:45	Gem	09/07/1993	17:16	Lib	01/03/1994	18:31
Pis	05/13/1993	21:51	Can	09/10/1993	02:35	Sco	01/05/1994	21:29
Ari	05/16/1993	10:24	Leo	09/12/1993	07:50	Sag	01/08/1994	00:34
Tau	05/18/1993	22:15	Vir	09/14/1993	09:19	Cap	01/10/1994	04:16
Gem	05/21/1993	08:07	Lib	09/16/1993	08:44	Aqu	01/12/1994	09:26
Can	05/23/1993	15:38	Sco	09/18/1993	08:15	Pis	01/14/1994	17:04
Leo	05/25/1993	21:03	Sag	09/20/1993	09:54	Ari	01/17/1994	03:42
Vir	05/28/1993	00:46	Cap	09/22/1993	14:55	Tau	01/19/1994	16:22
Lib	05/30/1993	03:18	Aqu	09/24/1993	23:19	Gem	01/22/1994	04:34
Sco	06/01/1993	05:22	Pis	09/27/1993	10:13	Can	01/24/1994	13:54
Sag	06/03/1993	08:01	Ari	09/29/1993	22:29	Leo	01/26/1994	19:37
Cap	06/05/1993	12:27	Tau	10/02/1993	11:13	Vir	01/28/1994	22:38
Aqu	06/07/1993	19:40	Gem	10/04/1993	23:26	Lib	01/31/1994	00:34
Pis	06/10/1993	05:56	Can	10/07/1993	09:41	Sco	02/02/1994	02:50
Ari	06/12/1993	18:14	Leo	10/09/1993	16:33	Sag	02/04/1994	06:14
Tau	06/15/1993	06:19	Vir	10/11/1993	19:35	Cap	02/06/1994	11:02
Gem	06/17/1993	16:11	Lib	10/13/1993	19:47	Aqu	02/08/1994	17:17
Can	06/19/1993	23:04	Sco	10/15/1993	19:01	Pis	02/11/1994	01:23
Leo	06/22/1993	03:26	Sag	10/17/1993	19:23	Ari	02/13/1994	11:50
Vir	06/24/1993	06:18	Cap	10/19/1993	22:43	Tau	02/16/1994	00:20
Lib	06/26/1993	08:46	Aqu	10/22/1993	05:49	Gem	02/18/1994	13:05
Sco	06/28/1993	11:38	Pis	10/24/1993	16:17	Can	02/20/1994	23:26
Sag	06/30/1993	15:28	Ari	10/27/1993	04:39	Leo	02/23/1994	05:48
Cap	07/02/1993	20:49	Tau	10/29/1993	17:20	Vir	02/25/1994	08:26
Aqu	07/05/1993	04:14	Gem	11/01/1993	05:12	Lib	02/27/1994	09:06
Pis	07/07/1993	14:10	Can	11/03/1993	15:24	Sco	03/01/1994	09:44
Ari	07/10/1993	02:11	Leo	11/05/1993	23:05	Sag	03/03/1994	11:54
Tau	07/12/1993	14:37	Vir	11/08/1993	03:46	Cap	03/05/1994	16:24

Aqu	03/07/1994	23:15	Gem	07/04/1994	22:12	Lib	10/31/1994	14:45
Pis	03/10/1994	08:10	Can	07/07/1994	09:17	Sco	11/02/1994	15:19
Ari	03/12/1994	18:59	Leo	07/09/1994	17:43	Sag	11/04/1994	14:46
Tau	03/15/1994	07:27	Vir	07/11/1994	23:48	Cap	11/06/1994	15:02
Gem	03/17/1994	20:28	Lib	07/14/1994	04:14	Aqu	11/08/1994	17:48
Can	03/20/1994	07:53	Sco	07/16/1994	07:34	Pis	11/11/1994	00:05
Leo	03/22/1994	15:38	Sag	07/18/1994	10:09	Ari	11/13/1994	09:44
Vir	03/24/1994	19:13	Cap	07/20/1994	12:30	Tau	11/15/1994	21:44
Lib	03/26/1994	19:46	Aqu	07/22/1994	15:39	Gem	11/18/1994	10:41
Sco	03/28/1994	19:15	Pis	07/24/1994	20:57	Can	11/20/1994	23:20
Sag	03/30/1994	19:41	Ari	07/27/1994	05:30	Leo	11/23/1994	10:32
Cap	04/01/1994	22:39	Tau	07/29/1994	17:13	Vir	11/25/1994	19:08
Aqu	04/04/1994	04:46	Gem	08/01/1994	06:05	Lib	11/28/1994	00:21
Pis	04/06/1994	13:51	Can	08/03/1994	17:22	Sco	11/30/1994	02:20
Ari	04/09/1994	01:09	Leo	08/06/1994	01:30	Sag	12/02/1994	02:12
Tau	04/11/1994	13:47	Vir	08/08/1994	06:42	Cap	12/04/1994	01:43
Gem	04/14/1994	02:47	Lib	08/10/1994	10:06	Aqu	12/06/1994	02:52
Can	04/16/1994	14:40	Sco	08/12/1994	12:56	Pis	12/08/1994	07:24
Leo	04/18/1994	23:43	Sag	08/14/1994	15:53	Ari	12/10/1994	16:04
Vir	04/21/1994	04:57	Cap	08/16/1994	19:18	Tau	12/13/1994	03:56
Lib	04/23/1994	06:40	Aqu	08/18/1994	23:34	Gem	12/15/1994	17:00
Sco	04/25/1994	06:18	Pis	08/21/1994	05:27	Can	12/18/1994	05:24
Sag	04/27/1994	05:48	Ari	08/23/1994	13:55	Leo	12/20/1994	16:13
Cap	04/29/1994	07:05	Tau	08/26/1994	01:14	Vir	12/23/1994	01:00
Aqu	05/01/1994	11:36	Gem	08/28/1994	14:07	Lib	12/25/1994	07:27
Pis	05/03/1994	19:47	Can	08/31/1994	01:59	Sco	12/27/1994	11:16
Ari	05/06/1994	07:01	Leo	09/02/1994	10:36	Sag	12/29/1994	12:45
Tau	05/08/1994	19:50	Vir	09/04/1994	15:33	Cap	12/31/1994	12:57
Gem	05/11/1994	08:43	Lib	09/06/1994	17:56	Aqu	01/02/1995	13:40
Can	05/13/1994	20:26	Sco	09/08/1994	19:25	Pis	01/04/1995	16:49
Leo	05/16/1994	05:58	Sag	09/10/1994	21:25	Ari	01/06/1995	23:58
Vir	05/18/1994	12:29	Cap	09/13/1994	00:45	Tau	01/09/1995	10:58
Lib	05/20/1994	15:54	Aqu	09/15/1994	05:42	Gem	01/11/1995	23:57
Sco	05/22/1994	16:50	Pis	09/17/1994	12:32	Can	01/14/1995	12:19
Sag	05/24/1994	16:43	Ari	09/19/1994	21:30	Leo	01/16/1995	22:36
Cap	05/26/1994	17:17	Tau	09/22/1994	08:48	Vir	01/19/1995	06:39
Aqu	05/28/1994	20:20	Gem	09/24/1994	21:41	Lib	01/21/1995	12:53
Pis	05/31/1994	03:04	Can	09/27/1994	10:11	Sco	01/23/1995	17:32
Ari	06/02/1994	13:32	Leo	09/29/1994	19:54	Sag	01/25/1995	20:36
Tau	06/05/1994	02:14	Vir	10/02/1994	01:38	Cap	01/27/1995	22:26
Gem	06/07/1994	15:03	Lib	10/04/1994	03:55	Aqu	01/30/1995	00:03
Can	06/10/1994	02:21	Sco	10/06/1994	04:21	Pis	02/01/1995	03:06
Leo	06/12/1994	11:28	Sag	10/08/1994	04:47	Ari	02/03/1995	09:13
Vir	06/14/1994	18:16	Cap	10/10/1994	06:44	Tau	02/05/1995	19:09
Lib	06/16/1994	22:47	Aqu	10/12/1994	11:10	Gem	02/08/1995	07:43
Sco	06/19/1994	01:19	Pis	10/14/1994	18:18	Can	02/10/1995	20:16
Sag	06/21/1994	02:32	Ari	10/17/1994	03:56	Leo	02/13/1995	06:31
Cap	06/23/1994	03:37	Tau	10/19/1994	15:34	Vir	02/15/1995	13:51
Aqu	06/25/1994	06:09	Gem	10/22/1994	04:27	Lib	02/17/1995	19:00
Pis	06/27/1994	11:45	Can	10/24/1994	17:15	Sco	02/19/1995	22:55
Ari	06/29/1994	21:07	Leo	10/27/1994	04:04	Sag	02/22/1995	02:12
Tau	07/02/1994	09:23	Vir	10/29/1994	11:20	Cap	02/24/1995	05:10

Aqu	02/26/1995	08:14	Gem	06/24/1995	19:02	Lib	10/21/1995	19:14
Pis	02/28/1995	12:16	Can	06/27/1995	07:56	Sco	10/23/1995	23:05
Ari	03/02/1995	18:30	Leo	06/29/1995	20:01	Sag	10/26/1995	00:56
Tau	03/05/1995	03:51	Vir	07/02/1995	06:35	Cap	10/28/1995	02:15
Gem	03/07/1995	15:55	Lib	07/04/1995	14:54	Aqu	10/30/1995	04:23
Can	03/10/1995	04:40	Sco	07/06/1995	20:18	Pis	11/01/1995	08:18
Leo	03/12/1995	15:27	Sag	07/08/1995	22:36	Ari	11/03/1995	14:21
Vir	03/14/1995	22:53	Cap	07/10/1995	22:43	Tau	11/05/1995	22:35
Lib	03/17/1995	03:17	Aqu	07/12/1995	22:21	Gem	11/08/1995	08:55
Sco	03/19/1995	05:52	Pis	07/14/1995	23:38	Can	11/10/1995	20:56
Sag	03/21/1995	07:57	Ari	07/17/1995	04:23	Leo	11/13/1995	09:37
Cap	03/23/1995	10:32	Tau	07/19/1995	13:21	Vir	11/15/1995	21:01
Aqu	03/25/1995	14:10	Gem	07/22/1995	01:23	Lib	11/18/1995	05:17
Pis	03/27/1995	19:18	Can	07/24/1995	14:15	Sco	11/20/1995	09:39
Ari	03/30/1995	02:26	Leo	07/27/1995	02:06	Sag	11/22/1995	10:55
Tau	04/01/1995	11:59	Vir	07/29/1995	12:11	Cap	11/24/1995	10:48
Gem	04/03/1995	23:49	Lib	07/31/1995	20:23	Aqu	11/26/1995	11:16
Can	04/06/1995	12:39	Sco	08/03/1995	02:28	Pis	11/28/1995	14:00
Leo	04/09/1995	00:14	Sag	08/05/1995	06:14	Ari	11/30/1995	19:51
Vir	04/11/1995	08:38	Cap	08/07/1995	07:51	Tau	12/03/1995	04:40
Lib	04/13/1995	13:19	Aqu	08/09/1995	08:28	Gem	12/05/1995	15:34
Sco	04/15/1995	15:12	Pis	08/11/1995	09:47	Can	12/08/1995	03:44
Sag	04/17/1995	15:51	Ari	08/13/1995	13:42	Leo	12/10/1995	16:24
Cap	04/19/1995	16:53	Tau	08/15/1995	21:26	Vir	12/13/1995	04:26
Aqu	04/21/1995	19:38	Gem	08/18/1995	08:40	Lib	12/15/1995	14:08
Pis	04/24/1995	00:51	Can	08/20/1995	21:23	Sco	12/17/1995	20:06
Ari	04/26/1995	08:41	Leo	08/23/1995	09:12	Sag	12/19/1995	22:12
Tau	04/28/1995	18:53	Vir	08/25/1995	18:50	Cap	12/21/1995	21:46
Gem	05/01/1995	06:53	Lib	08/28/1995	02:14	Aqu	12/23/1995	20:52
Can	05/03/1995	19:44	Sco	08/30/1995	07:51	Pis	12/25/1995	21:46
Leo	05/06/1995	07:54	Sag	09/01/1995	11:56	Ari	12/28/1995	02:07
Vir	05/08/1995	17:33	Cap	09/03/1995	14:44	Tau	12/30/1995	10:21
Lib	05/10/1995	23:28	Aqu	09/05/1995	16:47	Gem	01/01/1996	21:29
Sco	05/13/1995	01:52	Pis	09/07/1995	19:08	Can	01/04/1996	09:56
Sag	05/15/1995	01:58	Ari	09/09/1995	23:15	Leo	01/06/1996	22:30
Cap	05/17/1995	01:36	Tau	09/12/1995	06:21	Vir	01/09/1996	10:29
Aqu	05/19/1995	02:40	Gem	09/14/1995	16:48	Lib	01/11/1996	20:54
Pis	05/21/1995	06:40	Can	09/17/1995	05:15	Sco	01/14/1996	04:29
Ari	05/23/1995	14:14	Leo	09/19/1995	17:19	Sag	01/16/1996	08:24
Tau	05/26/1995	00:47	Vir	09/22/1995	03:00	Cap	01/18/1996	09:06
Gem	05/28/1995	13:07	Lib	09/24/1995	09:49	Aqu	01/20/1996	08:14
Can	05/31/1995	01:59	Sco	09/26/1995	14:19	Pis	01/22/1996	08:02
Leo	06/02/1995	14:16	Sag	09/28/1995	17:30	Ari	01/24/1996	10:38
Vir	06/05/1995	00:45	Cap	09/30/1995	20:10	Tau	01/26/1996	17:16
Lib	06/07/1995	08:12	Aqu	10/02/1995	23:00	Gem	01/29/1996	03:42
Sco	06/09/1995	12:02	Pis	10/05/1995	02:35	Can	01/31/1996	16:10
Sag	06/11/1995	12:49	Ari	10/07/1995	07:42	Leo	02/03/1996	04:45
Cap	06/13/1995	12:05	Tau	10/09/1995	15:05	Vir	02/05/1996	16:22
Aqu	06/15/1995	11:53	Gem	10/12/1995	01:10	Lib	02/08/1996	02:29
Pis	06/17/1995	14:14	Can	10/14/1995	13:20	Sco	02/10/1996	10:34
Ari	06/19/1995	20:30	Leo	10/17/1995	01:46	Sag	02/12/1996	15:57
Tau	06/22/1995	06:35	Vir	10/19/1995	12:10	Cap	02/14/1996	18:29

Aqu	02/16/1996	18:59	Gem	06/13/1996	19:15	Lib	10/10/1996	19:59
Pis	02/18/1996	19:09	Can	06/16/1996	06:08	Sco	10/13/1996	04:45
Ari	02/20/1996	20:59	Leo	06/18/1996	18:21	Sag	10/15/1996	11:06
Tau	02/23/1996	02:09	Vir	06/21/1996	07:06	Cap	10/17/1996	15:36
Gem	02/25/1996	11:14	Lib	06/23/1996	18:37	Aqu	10/19/1996	18:50
Can	02/27/1996	23:10	Sco	06/26/1996	02:52	Pis	10/21/1996	21:22
Leo	03/01/1996	11:46	Sag	06/28/1996	07:00	Ari	10/23/1996	23:50
Vir	03/03/1996	23:12	Cap	06/30/1996	07:46	Tau	10/26/1996	03:11
Lib	03/06/1996	08:40	Aqu	07/02/1996	07:05	Gem	10/28/1996	08:35
Sco	03/08/1996	16:05	Pis	07/04/1996	07:07	Can	10/30/1996	16:56
Sag	03/10/1996	21:31	Ari	07/06/1996	09:42	Leo	11/02/1996	04:16
Cap	03/13/1996	01:07	Tau	07/08/1996	15:44	Vir	11/04/1996	16:57
Aqu	03/15/1996	03:14	Gem	07/11/1996	00:53	Lib	11/07/1996	04:28
Pis	03/17/1996	04:50	Can	07/13/1996	12:08	Sco	11/09/1996	13:00
Ari	03/19/1996	07:15	Leo	07/16/1996	00:31	Sag	11/11/1996	18:26
Tau	03/21/1996	12:00	Vir	07/18/1996	13:16	Cap	11/13/1996	21:43
Gem	03/23/1996	20:00	Lib	07/21/1996	01:13	Aqu	11/16/1996	00:14
Can	03/26/1996	07:05	Sco	07/23/1996	10:41	Pis	11/18/1996	03:00
Leo	03/28/1996	19:36	Sag	07/25/1996	16:23	Ari	11/20/1996	06:33
Vir	03/31/1996	07:14	Cap	07/27/1996	18:17	Tau	11/22/1996	11:12
Lib	04/02/1996	16:26	Aqu	07/29/1996	17:47	Gem	11/24/1996	17:19
Sco	04/04/1996	22:56	Pis	07/31/1996	17:01	Can	11/27/1996	01:38
Sag	04/07/1996	03:20	Ari	08/02/1996	18:04	Leo	11/29/1996	12:30
Cap	04/09/1996	06:30	Tau	08/04/1996	22:34	Vir	12/02/1996	01:10
Aqu	04/11/1996	09:09	Gem	08/07/1996	06:49	Lib	12/04/1996	13:22
Pis	04/13/1996	12:00	Can	08/09/1996	17:57	Sco	12/06/1996	22:37
Ari	04/15/1996	15:43	Leo	08/12/1996	06:29	Sag	12/09/1996	03:57
Tau	04/17/1996	21:06	Vir	08/14/1996	19:07	Cap	12/11/1996	06:14
Gem	04/20/1996	04:54	Lib	08/17/1996	06:55	Aqu	12/13/1996	07:13
Can	04/22/1996	15:25	Sco	08/19/1996	16:50	Pis	12/15/1996	08:44
Leo	04/25/1996	03:44	Sag	08/21/1996	23:46	Ari	12/17/1996	11:56
Vir	04/27/1996	15:48	Cap	08/24/1996	03:21	Tau	12/19/1996	17:09
Lib	04/30/1996	01:25	Aqu	08/26/1996	04:10	Gem	12/22/1996	00:17
Sco	05/02/1996	07:42	Pis	08/28/1996	03:48	Can	12/24/1996	09:14
Sag	05/04/1996	11:03	Ari	08/30/1996	04:15	Leo	12/26/1996	20:09
Cap	05/06/1996	12:53	Tau	09/01/1996	07:20	Vir	12/29/1996	08:44
Aqu	05/08/1996	14:39	Gem	09/03/1996	14:09	Lib	12/31/1996	21:31
Pis	05/10/1996	17:28	Can	09/06/1996	00:30	Sco	01/03/1997	08:00
Ari	05/12/1996	22:00	Leo	09/08/1996	12:54	Sag	01/05/1997	14:26
Tau	05/15/1996	04:24	Vir	09/11/1996	01:28	Cap	01/07/1997	16:54
Gem	05/17/1996	12:48	Lib	09/13/1996	12:50	Aqu	01/09/1997	16:59
Can	05/19/1996	23:16	Sco	09/15/1996	22:19	Pis	01/11/1997	16:50
Leo	05/22/1996	11:28	Sag	09/18/1996	05:30	Ari	01/13/1997	18:21
Vir	05/24/1996	23:58	Cap	09/20/1996	10:11	Tau	01/15/1997	22:40
Lib	05/27/1996	10:32	Aqu	09/22/1996	12:38	Gem	01/18/1997	05:53
Sco	05/29/1996	17:30	Pis	09/24/1996	13:43	Can	01/20/1997	15:28
Sag	05/31/1996	20:42	Ari	09/26/1996	14:46	Leo	01/23/1997	02:50
Cap	06/02/1996	21:28	Tau	09/28/1996	17:23	Vir	01/25/1997	15:26
Aqu	06/04/1996	21:45	Gem	09/30/1996	23:02	Lib	01/28/1997	04:21
Pis	06/06/1996	23:20	Can	10/03/1996	08:14	Sco	01/30/1997	15:47
Ari	06/09/1996	03:23	Leo	10/05/1996	20:11	Sag	02/01/1997	23:49
Tau	06/11/1996	10:11	Vir	10/08/1996	08:48	Cap	02/04/1997	03:43

Aqu	02/06/1997	04:20	Gem	06/03/1997	23:55	Lib	09/30/1997	18:32
Pis	02/08/1997	03:33	Can	06/06/1997	06:01	Sco	10/03/1997	06:57
Ari	02/10/1997	03:29	Leo	06/08/1997	14:58	Sag	10/05/1997	17:42
Tau	02/12/1997	05:56	Vir	06/11/1997	02:43	Cap	10/08/1997	02:02
Gem	02/14/1997	11:54	Lib	06/13/1997	15:35	Aqu	10/10/1997	07:28
Can	02/16/1997	21:12	Sco	06/16/1997	02:50	Pis	10/12/1997	09:58
Leo	02/19/1997	08:52	Sag	06/18/1997	10:37	Ari	10/14/1997	10:24
Vir	02/21/1997	21:38	Cap	06/20/1997	15:01	Tau	10/16/1997	10:16
Lib	02/24/1997	10:22	Aqu	06/22/1997	17:20	Gem	10/18/1997	11:27
Sco	02/26/1997	21:55	Pis	06/24/1997	19:08	Can	10/20/1997	15:45
Sag	03/01/1997	07:00	Ari	06/26/1997	21:38	Leo	10/23/1997	00:10
Cap	03/03/1997	12:37	Tau	06/29/1997	01:23	Vir	10/25/1997	11:59
Aqu	03/05/1997	14:53	Gem	07/01/1997	06:35	Lib	10/28/1997	01:04
Pis	03/07/1997	14:56	Can	07/03/1997	13:33	Sco	10/30/1997	13:14
Ari	03/09/1997	14:32	Leo	07/05/1997	22:45	Sag	11/01/1997	23:25
Tau	03/11/1997	15:38	Vir	07/08/1997	10:22	Cap	11/04/1997	07:30
Gem	03/13/1997	19:49	Lib	07/10/1997	23:20	Aqu	11/06/1997	13:32
Can	03/16/1997	03:51	Sco	07/13/1997	11:19	Pis	11/08/1997	17:34
Leo	03/18/1997	15:08	Sag	07/15/1997	20:01	Ari	11/10/1997	19:43
Vir	03/21/1997	03:59	Cap	07/18/1997	00:44	Tau	11/12/1997	20:45
Lib	03/23/1997	16:34	Aqu	07/20/1997	02:28	Gem	11/14/1997	22:05
Sco	03/26/1997	03:41	Pis	07/22/1997	02:59	Can	11/17/1997	01:33
Sag	03/28/1997	12:38	Ari	07/24/1997	04:03	Leo	11/19/1997	08:38
Cap	03/30/1997	19:06	Tau	07/26/1997	06:53	Vir	11/21/1997	19:32
Aqu	04/01/1997	22:57	Gem	07/28/1997	12:04	Lib	11/24/1997	08:29
Pis	04/04/1997	00:41	Can	07/30/1997	19:38	Sco	11/26/1997	20:42
Ari	04/06/1997	01:19	Leo	08/02/1997	05:26	Sag	11/29/1997	06:28
Tau	04/08/1997	02:21	Vir	08/04/1997	17:15	Cap	12/01/1997	13:37
Gem	04/10/1997	05:27	Lib	08/07/1997	06:16	Aqu	12/03/1997	18:57
Can	04/12/1997	12:04	Sco	08/09/1997	18:49	Pis	12/05/1997	23:06
Leo	04/14/1997	22:22	Sag	08/12/1997	04:44	Ari	12/08/1997	02:23
Vir	04/17/1997	11:00	Cap	08/14/1997	10:40	Tau	12/10/1997	04:59
Lib	04/19/1997	23:35	Aqu	08/16/1997	12:57	Gem	12/12/1997	07:35
Sco	04/22/1997	10:17	Pis	08/18/1997	13:00	Can	12/14/1997	11:25
Sag	04/24/1997	18:31	Ari	08/20/1997	12:45	Leo	12/16/1997	17:57
Cap	04/27/1997	00:31	Tau	08/22/1997	13:58	Vir	12/19/1997	03:59
Aqu	04/29/1997	04:49	Gem	08/24/1997	17:56	Lib	12/21/1997	16:34
Pis	05/01/1997	07:49	Can	08/27/1997	01:11	Sco	12/24/1997	05:06
Ari	05/03/1997	09:59	Leo	08/29/1997	11:19	Sag	12/26/1997	15:06
Tau	05/05/1997	12:04	Vir	08/31/1997	23:27	Cap	12/28/1997	21:47
Gem	05/07/1997	15:21	Lib	09/03/1997	12:29	Aqu	12/31/1997	01:57
Can	05/09/1997	21:13	Sco	09/06/1997	01:08	Pis	01/02/1998	04:55
Leo	05/12/1997	06:32	Sag	09/08/1997	11:53	Ari	01/04/1998	07:43
Vir	05/14/1997	18:43	Cap	09/10/1997	19:22	Tau	01/06/1998	10:52
Lib	05/17/1997	07:26	Aqu	09/12/1997	23:08	Gem	01/08/1998	14:42
Sco	05/19/1997	18:11	Pis	09/14/1997	23:58	Can	01/10/1998	19:43
Sag	05/22/1997	01:49	Ari	09/16/1997	23:25	Leo	01/13/1998	02:45
Cap	05/24/1997	06:50	Tau	09/18/1997	23:22	Vir	01/15/1998	12:31
Aqu	05/26/1997	10:19	Gem	09/21/1997	01:39	Lib	01/18/1998	00:44
Pis	05/28/1997	13:17	Can	09/23/1997	07:33	Sco	01/20/1998	13:33
Ari	05/30/1997	16:17	Leo	09/25/1997	17:12	Sag	01/23/1998	00:23
Tau	06/01/1997	19:39	Vir	09/28/1997	05:27	Cap	01/25/1998	07:38

Aqu	01/27/1998	11:25	Gem	05/25/1998	07:25	Lib	09/20/1998	16:57
Pis	01/29/1998	13:07	Can	05/27/1998	08:59	Sco	09/23/1998	05:21
Ari	01/31/1998	14:21	Leo	05/29/1998	13:39	Sag	09/25/1998	18:04
Tau	02/02/1998	16:24	Vir	05/31/1998	22:21	Cap	09/28/1998	05:29
Gem	02/04/1998	20:09	Lib	06/03/1998	10:16	Aqu	09/30/1998	13:51
Can	02/07/1998	01:57	Sco	06/05/1998	23:04	Pis	10/02/1998	18:22
Leo	02/09/1998	09:57	Sag	06/08/1998	10:33	Ari	10/04/1998	19:31
Vir	02/11/1998	20:09	Cap	06/10/1998	19:49	Tau	10/06/1998	18:57
Lib	02/14/1998	08:17	Aqu	06/13/1998	03:02	Gem	10/08/1998	18:43
Sco	02/16/1998	21:12	Pis	06/15/1998	08:30	Can	10/10/1998	20:49
Sag	02/19/1998	08:55	Ari	06/17/1998	12:22	Leo	10/13/1998	02:25
Cap	02/21/1998	17:29	Tau	06/19/1998	14:47	Vir	10/15/1998	11:32
Aqu	02/23/1998	22:08	Gem	06/21/1998	16:26	Lib	10/17/1998	23:02
Pis	02/25/1998	23:41	Can	06/23/1998	18:38	Sco	10/20/1998	11:36
Ari	02/27/1998	23:42	Leo	06/25/1998	23:04	Sag	10/23/1998	00:15
Tau	03/02/1998	00:01	Vir	06/28/1998	06:54	Cap	10/25/1998	12:03
Gem	03/04/1998	02:15	Lib	06/30/1998	18:04	Aqu	10/27/1998	21:42
Can	03/06/1998	07:26	Sco	07/03/1998	06:45	Pis	10/30/1998	03:57
Leo	03/08/1998	15:45	Sag	07/05/1998	18:23	Ari	11/01/1998	06:26
Vir	03/11/1998	02:35	Cap	07/08/1998	03:26	Tau	11/03/1998	06:11
Lib	03/13/1998	14:57	Aqu	07/10/1998	09:51	Gem	11/05/1998	05:10
Sco	03/16/1998	03:50	Pis	07/12/1998	14:21	Can	11/07/1998	05:39
Sag	03/18/1998	15:55	Ari	07/14/1998	17:44	Leo	11/09/1998	09:33
Cap	03/21/1998	01:41	Tau	07/16/1998	20:33	Vir	11/11/1998	17:36
Aqu	03/23/1998	08:00	Gem	07/18/1998	23:18	Lib	11/14/1998	04:57
Pis	03/25/1998	10:41	Can	07/21/1998	02:43	Sco	11/16/1998	17:40
Ari	03/27/1998	10:48	Leo	07/23/1998	07:48	Sag	11/19/1998	06:12
Tau	03/29/1998	10:06	Vir	07/25/1998	15:34	Cap	11/21/1998	17:44
Gem	03/31/1998	10:38	Lib	07/28/1998	02:14	Aqu	11/24/1998	03:42
Can	04/02/1998	14:10	Sco	07/30/1998	14:44	Pis	11/26/1998	11:12
Leo	04/04/1998	21:36	Sag	08/02/1998	02:47	Ari	11/28/1998	15:32
Vir	04/07/1998	08:25	Cap	08/04/1998	12:16	Tau	11/30/1998	16:51
Lib	04/09/1998	21:04	Aqu	08/06/1998	18:30	Gem	12/02/1998	16:29
Sco	04/12/1998	09:55	Pis	08/08/1998	22:03	Can	12/04/1998	16:27
Sag	04/14/1998	21:51	Ari	08/11/1998	00:09	Leo	12/06/1998	18:55
Cap	04/17/1998	08:04	Tau	08/13/1998	02:04	Vir	12/09/1998	01:22
Aqu	04/19/1998	15:40	Gem	08/15/1998	04:45	Lib	12/11/1998	11:43
Pis	04/21/1998	20:04	Can	08/17/1998	08:55	Sco	12/14/1998	00:16
Ari	04/23/1998	21:29	Leo	08/19/1998	15:00	Sag	12/16/1998	12:46
Tau	04/25/1998	21:08	Vir	08/21/1998	23:21	Cap	12/18/1998	23:54
Gem	04/27/1998	20:55	Lib	08/24/1998	10:02	Aqu	12/21/1998	09:15
Can	04/29/1998	22:58	Sco	08/26/1998	22:25	Pis	12/23/1998	16:44
Leo	05/02/1998	04:49	Sag	08/29/1998	10:54	Ari	12/25/1998	22:02
Vir	05/04/1998	14:47	Cap	08/31/1998	21:21	Tau	12/28/1998	01:03
Lib	05/07/1998	03:18	Aqu	09/03/1998	04:19	Gem	12/30/1998	02:21
Sco	05/09/1998	16:09	Pis	09/05/1998	07:46	Can	01/01/1999	03:15
Sag	05/12/1998	03:47	Ari	09/07/1998	08:52	Leo	01/03/1999	05:30
Cap	05/14/1998	13:37	Tau	09/09/1998	09:16	Vir	01/05/1999	10:50
Aqu	05/16/1998	21:29	Gem	09/11/1998	10:40	Lib	01/07/1999	19:52
Pis	05/19/1998	03:02	Can	09/13/1998	14:20	Sco	01/10/1999	07:48
Ari	05/21/1998	06:05	Leo	09/15/1998	20:48	Sag	01/12/1999	20:22
Tau	05/23/1998	07:05	Vir	09/18/1998	05:51	Cap	01/15/1999	07:27

Aqu	01/17/1999	16:10	Gem	05/15/1999	16:07	Lib	09/10/1999	17:15
Pis	01/19/1999	22:39	Can	05/17/1999	15:39	Sco	09/13/1999	02:08
Ari	01/22/1999	03:24	Leo	05/19/1999	17:36	Sag	09/15/1999	13:34
Tau	01/24/1999	06:51	Vir	05/21/1999	23:16	Cap	09/18/1999	02:12
Gem	01/26/1999	09:28	Lib	05/24/1999	08:29	Aqu	09/20/1999	13:36
Can	01/28/1999	11:56	Sco	05/26/1999	20:04	Pis	09/22/1999	21:49
Leo	01/30/1999	15:16	Sag	05/29/1999	08:36	Ari	09/25/1999	02:32
Vir	02/01/1999	20:37	Cap	05/31/1999	21:04	Tau	09/27/1999	04:49
Lib	02/04/1999	04:55	Aqu	06/03/1999	08:35	Gem	09/29/1999	06:20
Sco	02/06/1999	16:06	Pis	06/05/1999	18:01	Can	10/01/1999	08:31
Sag	02/09/1999	04:37	Ari	06/08/1999	00:06	Leo	10/03/1999	12:13
Cap	02/11/1999	16:09	Tau	06/10/1999	02:42	Vir	10/05/1999	17:39
Aqu	02/14/1999	00:55	Gem	06/12/1999	02:47	Lib	10/08/1999	00:51
Pis	02/16/1999	06:39	Can	06/14/1999	02:14	Sco	10/10/1999	10:01
Ari	02/18/1999	10:05	Leo	06/16/1999	03:07	Sag	10/12/1999	21:18
Tau	02/20/1999	12:28	Vir	06/18/1999	07:12	Cap	10/15/1999	10:02
Gem	02/22/1999	14:53	Lib	06/20/1999	15:10	Aqu	10/17/1999	22:15
Can	02/24/1999	18:08	Sco	06/23/1999	02:17	Pis	10/20/1999	07:31
Leo	02/26/1999	22:44	Sag	06/25/1999	14:50	Ari	10/22/1999	12:39
Vir	03/01/1999	05:04	Cap	06/28/1999	03:10	Tau	10/24/1999	14:24
Lib	03/03/1999	13:34	Aqu	06/30/1999	14:18	Gem	10/26/1999	14:33
Sco	03/06/1999	00:22	Pis	07/02/1999	23:33	Can	10/28/1999	15:09
Sag	03/08/1999	12:45	Ari	07/05/1999	06:20	Leo	10/30/1999	17:46
Cap	03/11/1999	00:52	Tau	07/07/1999	10:20	Vir	11/01/1999	23:07
Aqu	03/13/1999	10:30	Gem	07/09/1999	11:58	Lib	11/04/1999	06:56
Pis	03/15/1999	16:29	Can	07/11/1999	12:27	Sco	11/06/1999	16:45
Ari	03/17/1999	19:12	Leo	07/13/1999	13:26	Sag	11/09/1999	04:14
Tau	03/19/1999	20:08	Vir	07/15/1999	16:38	Cap	11/11/1999	16:59
Gem	03/21/1999	21:05	Lib	07/17/1999	23:20	Aqu	11/14/1999	05:44
Can	03/23/1999	23:34	Sco	07/20/1999	09:30	Pis	11/16/1999	16:19
Leo	03/26/1999	04:22	Sag	07/22/1999	21:47	Ari	11/18/1999	22:55
Vir	03/28/1999	11:34	Cap	07/25/1999	10:07	Tau	11/21/1999	01:24
Lib	03/30/1999	20:49	Aqu	07/27/1999	20:53	Gem	11/23/1999	01:13
Sco	04/02/1999	07:48	Pis	07/30/1999	05:26	Can	11/25/1999	00:29
Sag	04/04/1999	20:07	Ari	08/01/1999	11:45	Leo	11/27/1999	01:19
Cap	04/07/1999	08:38	Tau	08/03/1999	16:07	Vir	11/29/1999	05:10
Aqu	04/09/1999	19:23	Gem	08/05/1999	18:56	Lib	12/01/1999	12:29
Pis	04/12/1999	02:33	Can	08/07/1999	20:52	Sco	12/03/1999	22:35
Ari	04/14/1999	05:45	Leo	08/09/1999	22:55	Sag	12/06/1999	10:27
Tau	04/16/1999	06:06	Vir	08/12/1999	02:21	Cap	12/08/1999	23:12
Gem	04/18/1999	05:38	Lib	08/14/1999	08:24	Aqu	12/11/1999	11:57
Can	04/20/1999	06:27	Sco	08/16/1999	17:39	Pis	12/13/1999	23:15
Leo	04/22/1999	10:06	Sag	08/19/1999	05:31	Ari	12/16/1999	07:28
Vir	04/24/1999	17:03	Cap	08/21/1999	17:59	Tau	12/18/1999	11:43
Lib	04/27/1999	02:46	Aqu	08/24/1999	04:48	Gem	12/20/1999	12:37
Sco	04/29/1999	14:12	Pis	08/26/1999	12:48	Can	12/22/1999	11:52
Sag	05/02/1999	02:35	Ari	08/28/1999	18:08	Leo	12/24/1999	11:32
Cap	05/04/1999	15:11	Tau	08/30/1999	21:39	Vir	12/26/1999	13:34
Aqu	05/07/1999	02:39	Gem	09/02/1999	00:24	Lib	12/28/1999	19:14
Pis	05/09/1999	11:14	Can	09/04/1999	03:09	Sco	12/31/1999	04:36
Ari	05/11/1999	15:51	Leo	09/06/1999	06:28	Sag	01/02/2000	16:31
Tau	05/13/1999	16:55	Vir	09/08/1999	10:56	Cap	01/05/2000	05:23

Aqu	01/07/2000	17:52	Gem	05/05/2000	01:22	Lib	08/30/2000	20:33
Pis	01/10/2000	04:58	Can	05/07/2000	02:13	Sco	09/02/2000	00:56
Ari	01/12/2000	13:46	Leo	05/09/2000	04:01	Sag	09/04/2000	09:08
Tau	01/14/2000	19:36	Vir	05/11/2000	07:40	Cap	09/06/2000	20:46
Gem	01/16/2000	22:23	Lib	05/13/2000	13:27	Aqu	09/09/2000	09:43
Can	01/18/2000	23:00	Sco	05/15/2000	21:16	Pis	09/11/2000	21:32
Leo	01/20/2000	22:58	Sag	05/18/2000	07:09	Ari	09/14/2000	06:59
Vir	01/23/2000	00:07	Cap	05/20/2000	19:00	Tau	09/16/2000	14:04
Lib	01/25/2000	04:09	Aqu	05/23/2000	07:59	Gem	09/18/2000	19:21
Sco	01/27/2000	12:01	Pis	05/25/2000	20:06	Can	09/20/2000	23:14
Sag	01/29/2000	23:17	Ari	05/28/2000	05:06	Leo	09/23/2000	01:59
Cap	02/01/2000	12:09	Tau	05/30/2000	10:00	Vir	09/25/2000	04:01
Aqu	02/04/2000	00:30	Gem	06/01/2000	11:33	Lib	09/27/2000	06:21
Pis	02/06/2000	11:00	Can	06/03/2000	11:29	Sco	09/29/2000	10:30
Ari	02/08/2000	19:16	Leo	06/05/2000	11:45	Sag	10/01/2000	17:49
Tau	02/11/2000	01:19	Vir	06/07/2000	13:57	Cap	10/04/2000	04:42
Gem	02/13/2000	05:22	Lib	06/09/2000	18:58	Aqu	10/06/2000	17:32
Can	02/15/2000	07:44	Sco	06/12/2000	02:55	Pis	10/09/2000	05:35
Leo	02/17/2000	09:11	Sag	06/14/2000	13:18	Ari	10/11/2000	14:49
Vir	02/19/2000	10:53	Cap	06/17/2000	01:26	Tau	10/13/2000	21:04
Lib	02/21/2000	14:21	Aqu	06/19/2000	14:25	Gem	10/16/2000	01:17
Sco	02/23/2000	20:58	Pis	06/22/2000	02:50	Can	10/18/2000	04:36
Sag	02/26/2000	07:09	Ari	06/24/2000	12:53	Leo	10/20/2000	07:41
Cap	02/28/2000	19:44	Tau	06/26/2000	19:17	Vir	10/22/2000	10:52
Aqu	03/02/2000	08:13	Gem	06/28/2000	21:57	Lib	10/24/2000	14:29
Pis	03/04/2000	18:29	Can	06/30/2000	22:08	Sco	10/26/2000	19:23
Ari	03/07/2000	01:52	Leo	07/02/2000	21:37	Sag	10/29/2000	02:40
Tau	03/09/2000	07:00	Vir	07/04/2000	22:19	Cap	10/31/2000	13:01
Gem	03/11/2000	10:44	Lib	07/07/2000	01:47	Aqu	11/03/2000	01:39
Can	03/13/2000	13:50	Sco	07/09/2000	08:48	Pis	11/05/2000	14:11
Leo	03/15/2000	16:42	Sag	07/11/2000	19:05	Ari	11/08/2000	00:00
Vir	03/17/2000	19:48	Cap	07/14/2000	07:27	Tau	11/10/2000	06:11
Lib	03/19/2000	23:57	Aqu	07/16/2000	20:25	Gem	11/12/2000	09:26
Sco	03/22/2000	06:17	Pis	07/19/2000	08:42	Can	11/14/2000	11:20
Sag	03/24/2000	15:42	Ari	07/21/2000	19:08	Leo	11/16/2000	13:18
Cap	03/27/2000	03:50	Tau	07/24/2000	02:42	Vir	11/18/2000	16:15
Aqu	03/29/2000	16:33	Gem	07/26/2000	07:00	Lib	11/20/2000	20:34
Pis	04/01/2000	03:10	Can	07/28/2000	08:28	Sco	11/23/2000	02:32
Ari	04/03/2000	10:20	Leo	07/30/2000	08:23	Sag	11/25/2000	10:32
Tau	04/05/2000	14:27	Vir	08/01/2000	08:27	Cap	11/27/2000	20:56
Gem	04/07/2000	16:57	Lib	08/03/2000	10:32	Aqu	11/30/2000	09:25
Can	04/09/2000	19:15	Sco	08/05/2000	16:04	Pis	12/02/2000	22:21
Leo	04/11/2000	22:15	Sag	08/08/2000	01:30	Ari	12/05/2000	09:15
Vir	04/14/2000	02:18	Cap	08/10/2000	13:43	Tau	12/07/2000	16:25
Lib	04/16/2000	07:35	Aqu	08/13/2000	02:42	Gem	12/09/2000	19:49
Sco	04/18/2000	14:35	Pis	08/15/2000	14:40	Can	12/11/2000	20:47
Sag	04/20/2000	23:57	Ari	08/18/2000	00:42	Leo	12/13/2000	21:08
Cap	04/23/2000	11:46	Tau	08/20/2000	08:29	Vir	12/15/2000	22:30
Aqu	04/26/2000	00:40	Gem	08/22/2000	13:53	Lib	12/18/2000	02:01
Pis	04/28/2000	12:04	Can	08/24/2000	16:58	Sco	12/20/2000	08:11
Ari	04/30/2000	19:53	Leo	08/26/2000	18:16	Sag	12/22/2000	16:56
Tau	05/02/2000	23:52	Vir	08/28/2000	18:54	Cap	12/25/2000	03:53

Aqu	12/27/2000	16:24	Gem	04/25/2001	10:10	Lib	08/21/2001	03:18
Pis	12/30/2000	05:26	Can	04/27/2001	14:48	Sco	08/23/2001	04:49
Ari	01/01/2001	17:13	Leo	04/29/2001	18:24	Sag	08/25/2001	09:59
Tau	01/04/2001	01:54	Vir	05/01/2001	21:15	Cap	08/27/2001	19:01
Gem	01/06/2001	06:43	Lib	05/03/2001	23:49	Aqu	08/30/2001	06:46
Can	01/08/2001	08:07	Sco	05/06/2001	03:00	Pis	09/01/2001	19:31
Leo	01/10/2001	07:43	Sag	05/08/2001	08:05	Ari	09/04/2001	07:57
Vir	01/12/2001	07:25	Cap	05/10/2001	16:09	Tau	09/06/2001	19:16
Lib	01/14/2001	09:05	Aqu	05/13/2001	03:19	Gem	09/09/2001	04:39
Sco	01/16/2001	14:03	Pis	05/15/2001	16:00	Can	09/11/2001	11:07
Sag	01/18/2001	22:36	Ari	05/18/2001	03:39	Leo	09/13/2001	14:14
Cap	01/21/2001	09:56	Tau	05/20/2001	12:27	Vir	09/15/2001	14:38
Aqu	01/23/2001	22:42	Gem	05/22/2001	18:11	Lib	09/17/2001	13:59
Pis	01/26/2001	11:37	Can	05/24/2001	21:41	Sco	09/19/2001	14:27
Ari	01/28/2001	23:33	Leo	05/27/2001	00:11	Sag	09/21/2001	18:01
Tau	01/31/2001	09:19	Vir	05/29/2001	02:37	Cap	09/24/2001	01:48
Gem	02/02/2001	15:54	Lib	05/31/2001	05:40	Aqu	09/26/2001	13:04
Can	02/04/2001	18:59	Sco	06/02/2001	09:56	Pis	09/29/2001	01:49
Leo	02/06/2001	19:20	Sag	06/04/2001	15:57	Ari	10/01/2001	14:06
Vir	02/08/2001	18:34	Cap	06/07/2001	00:23	Tau	10/04/2001	00:59
Lib	02/10/2001	18:45	Aqu	06/09/2001	11:19	Gem	10/06/2001	10:10
Sco	02/12/2001	21:52	Pis	06/11/2001	23:52	Can	10/08/2001	17:18
Sag	02/15/2001	05:02	Ari	06/14/2001	12:01	Leo	10/10/2001	21:52
Cap	02/17/2001	15:58	Tau	06/16/2001	21:37	Vir	10/12/2001	23:56
Aqu	02/20/2001	04:53	Gem	06/19/2001	03:40	Lib	10/15/2001	00:25
Pis	02/22/2001	17:44	Can	06/21/2001	06:40	Sco	10/17/2001	01:02
Ari	02/25/2001	05:19	Leo	06/23/2001	07:54	Sag	10/19/2001	03:47
Tau	02/27/2001	15:04	Vir	06/25/2001	08:57	Cap	10/21/2001	10:12
Gem	03/01/2001	22:34	Lib	06/27/2001	11:10	Aqu	10/23/2001	20:26
Can	03/04/2001	03:23	Sco	06/29/2001	15:28	Pis	10/26/2001	08:54
Leo	03/06/2001	05:29	Sag	07/01/2001	22:13	Ari	10/28/2001	21:13
Vir	03/08/2001	05:43	Cap	07/04/2001	07:21	Tau	10/31/2001	07:46
Lib	03/10/2001	05:46	Aqu	07/06/2001	18:32	Gem	11/02/2001	16:11
Sco	03/12/2001	07:42	Pis	07/09/2001	07:04	Can	11/04/2001	22:42
Sag	03/14/2001	13:17	Ari	07/11/2001	19:34	Leo	11/07/2001	03:32
Cap	03/16/2001	23:02	Tau	07/14/2001	06:12	Vir	11/09/2001	06:48
Aqu	03/19/2001	11:35	Gem	07/16/2001	13:23	Lib	11/11/2001	08:52
Pis	03/22/2001	00:27	Can	07/18/2001	16:55	Sco	11/13/2001	10:44
Ari	03/24/2001	11:42	Leo	07/20/2001	17:42	Sag	11/15/2001	13:51
Tau	03/26/2001	20:49	Vir	07/22/2001	17:28	Cap	11/17/2001	19:39
Gem	03/29/2001	04:00	Lib	07/24/2001	18:07	Aqu	11/20/2001	04:54
Can	03/31/2001	09:21	Sco	07/26/2001	21:17	Pis	11/22/2001	16:51
Leo	04/02/2001	12:52	Sag	07/29/2001	03:44	Ari	11/25/2001	05:20
Vir	04/04/2001	14:45	Cap	07/31/2001	13:16	Tau	11/27/2001	16:04
Lib	04/06/2001	15:56	Aqu	08/03/2001	00:52	Gem	11/30/2001	00:02
Sco	04/08/2001	18:00	Pis	08/05/2001	13:29	Can	12/02/2001	05:29
Sag	04/10/2001	22:47	Ari	08/08/2001	02:03	Leo	12/04/2001	09:14
Cap	04/13/2001	07:20	Tau	08/10/2001	13:21	Vir	12/06/2001	12:10
Aqu	04/15/2001	19:10	Gem	08/12/2001	21:56	Lib	12/08/2001	14:56
Pis	04/18/2001	07:59	Can	08/15/2001	02:53	Sco	12/10/2001	18:08
Ari	04/20/2001	19:16	Leo	08/17/2001	04:24	Sag	12/12/2001	22:29
Tau	04/23/2001	03:54	Vir	08/19/2001	03:52	Cap	12/15/2001	04:47

Aqu	12/17/2001	13:43	Gem	04/15/2002	15:55	Lib	08/11/2002	13:37
Pis	12/20/2001	01:09	Can	04/18/2002	00:59	Sco	08/13/2002	15:00
Ari	12/22/2001	13:44	Leo	04/20/2002	07:19	Sag	08/15/2002	18:24
Tau	12/25/2001	01:10	Vir	04/22/2002	10:33	Cap	08/18/2002	00:15
Gem	12/27/2001	09:37	Lib	04/24/2002	11:20	Aqu	08/20/2002	08:16
Can	12/29/2001	14:38	Sco	04/26/2002	11:15	Pis	08/22/2002	18:10
Leo	12/31/2001	17:08	Sag	04/28/2002	12:13	Ari	08/25/2002	05:46
Vir	01/02/2002	18:33	Cap	04/30/2002	16:02	Tau	08/27/2002	18:30
Lib	01/04/2002	20:23	Aqu	05/02/2002	23:44	Gem	08/30/2002	06:44
Sco	01/06/2002	23:41	Pis	05/05/2002	10:45	Can	09/01/2002	16:12
Sag	01/09/2002	04:57	Ari	05/07/2002	23:21	Leo	09/03/2002	21:34
Cap	01/11/2002	12:18	Tau	05/10/2002	11:30	Vir	09/05/2002	23:14
Aqu	01/13/2002	21:41	Gem	05/12/2002	22:03	Lib	09/07/2002	22:56
Pis	01/16/2002	08:59	Can	05/15/2002	06:32	Sco	09/09/2002	22:48
Ari	01/18/2002	21:34	Leo	05/17/2002	12:50	Sag	09/12/2002	00:44
Tau	01/21/2002	09:45	Vir	05/19/2002	16:59	Cap	09/14/2002	05:47
Gem	01/23/2002	19:26	Lib	05/21/2002	19:17	Aqu	09/16/2002	13:54
Can	01/26/2002	01:15	Sco	05/23/2002	20:37	Pis	09/19/2002	00:17
Leo	01/28/2002	03:29	Sag	05/25/2002	22:19	Ari	09/21/2002	12:10
Vir	01/30/2002	03:39	Cap	05/28/2002	01:54	Tau	09/24/2002	00:53
Lib	02/01/2002	03:44	Aqu	05/30/2002	08:34	Gem	09/26/2002	13:25
Sco	02/03/2002	05:34	Pis	06/01/2002	18:36	Can	09/28/2002	23:59
Sag	02/05/2002	10:21	Ari	06/04/2002	06:50	Leo	10/01/2002	06:57
Cap	02/07/2002	18:07	Tau	06/06/2002	19:05	Vir	10/03/2002	09:50
Aqu	02/10/2002	04:14	Gem	06/09/2002	05:28	Lib	10/05/2002	09:50
Pis	02/12/2002	15:52	Can	06/11/2002	13:13	Sco	10/07/2002	08:57
Ari	02/15/2002	04:24	Leo	06/13/2002	18:38	Sag	10/09/2002	09:21
Tau	02/17/2002	16:57	Vir	06/15/2002	22:22	Cap	10/11/2002	12:45
Gem	02/20/2002	03:48	Lib	06/18/2002	01:10	Aqu	10/13/2002	19:51
Can	02/22/2002	11:13	Sco	06/20/2002	03:41	Pis	10/16/2002	06:06
Leo	02/24/2002	14:34	Sag	06/22/2002	06:41	Ari	10/18/2002	18:12
Vir	02/26/2002	14:45	Cap	06/24/2002	11:01	Tau	10/21/2002	06:55
Lib	02/28/2002	13:46	Aqu	06/26/2002	17:35	Gem	10/23/2002	19:16
Sco	03/02/2002	13:52	Pis	06/29/2002	03:00	Can	10/26/2002	06:09
Sag	03/04/2002	16:54	Ari	07/01/2002	14:48	Leo	10/28/2002	14:18
Cap	03/06/2002	23:48	Tau	07/04/2002	03:15	Vir	10/30/2002	18:58
Aqu	03/09/2002	09:56	Gem	07/06/2002	13:58	Lib	11/01/2002	20:27
Pis	03/11/2002	21:56	Can	07/08/2002	21:34	Sco	11/03/2002	20:09
Ari	03/14/2002	10:33	Leo	07/11/2002	02:06	Sag	11/05/2002	20:01
Tau	03/16/2002	22:59	Vir	07/13/2002	04:39	Cap	11/07/2002	21:59
Gem	03/19/2002	10:18	Lib	07/15/2002	06:38	Aqu	11/10/2002	03:27
Can	03/21/2002	19:05	Sco	07/17/2002	09:12	Pis	11/12/2002	12:41
Leo	03/24/2002	00:10	Sag	07/19/2002	13:02	Ari	11/15/2002	00:37
Vir	03/26/2002	01:42	Cap	07/21/2002	18:25	Tau	11/17/2002	13:22
Lib	03/28/2002	01:03	Aqu	07/24/2002	01:39	Gem	11/20/2002	01:23
Sco	03/30/2002	00:21	Pis	07/26/2002	11:04	Can	11/22/2002	11:46
Sag	04/01/2002	01:49	Ari	07/28/2002	22:38	Leo	11/24/2002	19:58
Cap	04/03/2002	06:58	Tau	07/31/2002	11:15	Vir	11/27/2002	01:40
Aqu	04/05/2002	16:06	Gem	08/02/2002	22:44	Lib	11/29/2002	04:53
Pis	04/08/2002	03:57	Can	08/05/2002	07:00	Sco	12/01/2002	06:14
Ari	04/10/2002	16:39	Leo	08/07/2002	11:25	Sag	12/03/2002	06:57
Tau	04/13/2002	04:54	Vir	08/09/2002	13:02	Cap	12/05/2002	08:38

Aqu	12/07/2002	12:54	Gem	04/05/2003	16:23	Lib	08/02/2003	01:46
Pis	12/09/2002	20:46	Can	04/08/2003	04:35	Sco	08/04/2003	05:11
Ari	12/12/2002	07:57	Leo	04/10/2003	13:51	Sag	08/06/2003	08:10
Tau	12/14/2002	20:42	Vir	04/12/2003	19:05	Cap	08/08/2003	11:02
Gem	12/17/2002	08:41	Lib	04/14/2003	20:40	Aqu	08/10/2003	14:23
Can	12/19/2002	18:29	Sco	04/16/2003	20:15	Pis	08/12/2003	19:18
Leo	12/22/2002	01:47	Sag	04/18/2003	19:51	Ari	08/15/2003	03:00
Vir	12/24/2002	07:04	Cap	04/20/2003	21:20	Tau	08/17/2003	13:52
Lib	12/26/2002	10:52	Aqu	04/23/2003	01:58	Gem	08/20/2003	02:40
Sco	12/28/2002	13:40	Pis	04/25/2003	10:02	Can	08/22/2003	14:43
Sag	12/30/2002	16:00	Ari	04/27/2003	20:54	Leo	08/24/2003	23:46
Cap	01/01/2003	18:42	Tau	04/30/2003	09:25	Vir	08/27/2003	05:25
Aqu	01/03/2003	22:57	Gem	05/02/2003	22:26	Lib	08/29/2003	08:40
Pis	01/06/2003	05:56	Can	05/05/2003	10:40	Sco	08/31/2003	10:59
Ari	01/08/2003	16:14	Leo	05/07/2003	20:44	Sag	09/02/2003	13:31
Tau	01/11/2003	04:47	Vir	05/10/2003	03:29	Cap	09/04/2003	16:50
Gem	01/13/2003	17:06	Lib	05/12/2003	06:41	Aqu	09/06/2003	21:14
Can	01/16/2003	02:54	Sco	05/14/2003	07:12	Pis	09/09/2003	03:06
Leo	01/18/2003	09:27	Sag	05/16/2003	06:42	Ari	09/11/2003	11:09
Vir	01/20/2003	13:30	Cap	05/18/2003	07:03	Tau	09/13/2003	21:49
Lib	01/22/2003	16:22	Aqu	05/20/2003	10:01	Gem	09/16/2003	10:31
Sco	01/24/2003	19:08	Pis	05/22/2003	16:40	Can	09/18/2003	23:06
Sag	01/26/2003	22:25	Ari	05/25/2003	02:58	Leo	09/21/2003	09:01
Cap	01/29/2003	02:29	Tau	05/27/2003	15:31	Vir	09/23/2003	15:02
Aqu	01/31/2003	07:44	Gem	05/30/2003	04:30	Lib	09/25/2003	17:48
Pis	02/02/2003	14:54	Can	06/01/2003	16:26	Sco	09/27/2003	18:51
Ari	02/05/2003	00:44	Leo	06/04/2003	02:23	Sag	09/29/2003	19:56
Tau	02/07/2003	12:58	Vir	06/06/2003	09:49	Cap	10/01/2003	22:21
Gem	02/10/2003	01:44	Lib	06/08/2003	14:28	Aqu	10/04/2003	02:45
Can	02/12/2003	12:17	Sco	06/10/2003	16:37	Pis	10/06/2003	09:20
Leo	02/14/2003	19:03	Sag	06/12/2003	17:11	Ari	10/08/2003	18:07
Vir	02/16/2003	22:21	Cap	06/14/2003	17:37	Tau	10/11/2003	05:04
Lib	02/18/2003	23:47	Aqu	06/16/2003	19:41	Gem	10/13/2003	17:44
Sco	02/21/2003	01:09	Pis	06/19/2003	00:57	Can	10/16/2003	06:40
Sag	02/23/2003	03:45	Ari	06/21/2003	10:05	Leo	10/18/2003	17:40
Cap	02/25/2003	08:10	Tau	06/23/2003	22:14	Vir	10/21/2003	00:59
Aqu	02/27/2003	14:24	Gem	06/26/2003	11:11	Lib	10/23/2003	04:25
Pis	03/01/2003	22:25	Can	06/28/2003	22:50	Sco	10/25/2003	05:07
Ari	03/04/2003	08:29	Leo	07/01/2003	08:12	Sag	10/27/2003	04:54
Tau	03/06/2003	20:35	Vir	07/03/2003	15:14	Cap	10/29/2003	05:36
Gem	03/09/2003	09:36	Lib	07/05/2003	20:19	Aqu	10/31/2003	08:41
Can	03/11/2003	21:10	Sco	07/07/2003	23:42	Pis	11/02/2003	14:52
Leo	03/14/2003	05:05	Sag	07/10/2003	01:47	Ari	11/05/2003	00:02
Vir	03/16/2003	08:51	Cap	07/12/2003	03:20	Tau	11/07/2003	11:28
Lib	03/18/2003	09:42	Aqu	07/14/2003	05:37	Gem	11/10/2003	00:13
Sco	03/20/2003	09:37	Pis	07/16/2003	10:14	Can	11/12/2003	13:09
Sag	03/22/2003	10:33	Ari	07/18/2003	18:18	Leo	11/15/2003	00:46
Cap	03/24/2003	13:48	Tau	07/21/2003	05:47	Vir	11/17/2003	09:34
Aqu	03/26/2003	19:50	Gem	07/23/2003	18:41	Lib	11/19/2003	14:40
Pis	03/29/2003	04:25	Can	07/26/2003	06:22	Sco	11/21/2003	16:22
Ari	03/31/2003	15:04	Leo	07/28/2003	15:15	Sag	11/23/2003	16:02
Tau	04/03/2003	03:19	Vir	07/30/2003	21:25	Cap	11/25/2003	15:31

Aqu	11/27/2003	16:48	Gem	03/25/2004	12:34	Lib	07/22/2004	11:37
Pis	11/29/2003	21:26	Can	03/28/2004	01:22	Sco	07/24/2004	18:07
Ari	12/02/2003	05:55	Leo	03/30/2004	13:05	Sag	07/26/2004	21:46
Tau	12/04/2003	17:29	Vir	04/01/2004	21:43	Cap	07/28/2004	22:56
Gem	12/07/2003	06:25	Lib	04/04/2004	02:50	Aqu	07/30/2004	22:54
Can	12/09/2003	19:10	Sco	04/06/2004	05:23	Pis	08/01/2004	23:35
Leo	12/12/2003	06:39	Sag	04/08/2004	06:49	Ari	08/04/2004	03:00
Vir	12/14/2003	16:05	Cap	04/10/2004	08:33	Tau	08/06/2004	10:26
Lib	12/16/2003	22:44	Aqu	04/12/2004	11:33	Gem	08/08/2004	21:32
Sco	12/19/2003	02:18	Pis	04/14/2004	16:23	Can	08/11/2004	10:19
Sag	12/21/2003	03:14	Ari	04/16/2004	23:24	Leo	08/13/2004	22:28
Cap	12/23/2003	02:55	Tau	04/19/2004	08:42	Vir	08/16/2004	08:48
Aqu	12/25/2003	03:13	Gem	04/21/2004	20:09	Lib	08/18/2004	17:08
Pis	12/27/2003	06:09	Can	04/24/2004	08:55	Sco	08/20/2004	23:35
Ari	12/29/2003	13:09	Leo	04/26/2004	21:13	Sag	08/23/2004	04:07
Tau	01/01/2004	00:01	Vir	04/29/2004	06:59	Cap	08/25/2004	06:46
Gem	01/03/2004	12:57	Lib	05/01/2004	13:00	Aqu	08/27/2004	08:07
Can	01/06/2004	01:37	Sco	05/03/2004	15:37	Pis	08/29/2004	09:33
Leo	01/08/2004	12:37	Sag	05/05/2004	16:07	Ari	08/31/2004	12:46
Vir	01/10/2004	21:36	Cap	05/07/2004	16:16	Tau	09/02/2004	19:15
Lib	01/13/2004	04:37	Aqu	05/09/2004	17:45	Gem	09/05/2004	05:24
Sco	01/15/2004	09:31	Pis	05/11/2004	21:52	Can	09/07/2004	17:49
Sag	01/17/2004	12:16	Ari	05/14/2004	05:02	Leo	09/10/2004	06:05
Cap	01/19/2004	13:23	Tau	05/16/2004	14:56	Vir	09/12/2004	16:15
Aqu	01/21/2004	14:10	Gem	05/19/2004	02:46	Lib	09/14/2004	23:52
Pis	01/23/2004	16:28	Can	05/21/2004	15:34	Sco	09/17/2004	05:24
Ari	01/25/2004	22:06	Leo	05/24/2004	04:06	Sag	09/19/2004	09:28
Tau	01/28/2004	07:46	Vir	05/26/2004	14:50	Cap	09/21/2004	12:34
Gem	01/30/2004	20:17	Lib	05/28/2004	22:20	Aqu	09/23/2004	15:09
Can	02/02/2004	09:02	Sco	05/31/2004	02:06	Pis	09/25/2004	17:55
Leo	02/04/2004	19:49	Sag	06/02/2004	02:51	Ari	09/27/2004	21:57
Vir	02/07/2004	04:01	Cap	06/04/2004	02:12	Tau	09/30/2004	04:23
Lib	02/09/2004	10:11	Aqu	06/06/2004	02:10	Gem	10/02/2004	13:55
Sco	02/11/2004	14:56	Pis	06/08/2004	04:38	Can	10/05/2004	01:53
Sag	02/13/2004	18:34	Ari	06/10/2004	10:50	Leo	10/07/2004	14:22
Cap	02/15/2004	21:13	Tau	06/12/2004	20:36	Vir	10/10/2004	00:58
Aqu	02/17/2004	23:27	Gem	06/15/2004	08:43	Lib	10/12/2004	08:30
Pis	02/20/2004	02:27	Can	06/17/2004	21:36	Sco	10/14/2004	13:09
Ari	02/22/2004	07:45	Leo	06/20/2004	10:03	Sag	10/16/2004	15:57
Tau	02/24/2004	16:30	Vir	06/22/2004	21:08	Cap	10/18/2004	18:06
Gem	02/27/2004	04:22	Lib	06/25/2004	05:49	Aqu	10/20/2004	20:37
Can	02/29/2004	17:11	Sco	06/27/2004	11:10	Pis	10/23/2004	00:13
Leo	03/03/2004	04:16	Sag	06/29/2004	13:14	Ari	10/25/2004	05:24
Vir	03/05/2004	12:16	Cap	07/01/2004	13:00	Tau	10/27/2004	12:37
Lib	03/07/2004	17:30	Aqu	07/03/2004	12:22	Gem	10/29/2004	22:11
Sco	03/09/2004	21:02	Pis	07/05/2004	13:27	Can	11/01/2004	09:52
Sag	03/11/2004	23:56	Ari	07/07/2004	18:02	Leo	11/03/2004	22:31
Cap	03/14/2004	02:51	Tau	07/10/2004	02:50	Vir	11/06/2004	09:58
Aqu	03/16/2004	06:09	Gem	07/12/2004	14:44	Lib	11/08/2004	18:22
Pis	03/18/2004	10:26	Can	07/15/2004	03:40	Sco	11/10/2004	23:03
Ari	03/20/2004	16:28	Leo	07/17/2004	15:55	Sag	11/13/2004	00:55
Tau	03/23/2004	01:09	Vir	07/20/2004	02:43	Cap	11/15/2004	01:32

Aqu	11/17/2004	02:39	Gem	03/15/2005	08:44	Lib	07/12/2005	15:08
Pis	11/19/2004	05:37	Can	03/17/2005	19:43	Sco	07/15/2005	00:49
Ari	11/21/2004	11:11	Leo	03/20/2005	08:16	Sag	07/17/2005	06:34
Tau	11/23/2004	19:15	Vir	03/22/2005	20:09	Cap	07/19/2005	08:25
Gem	11/26/2004	05:24	Lib	03/25/2005	05:59	Aqu	07/21/2005	07:54
Can	11/28/2004	17:10	Sco	03/27/2005	13:27	Pis	07/23/2005	07:11
Leo	12/01/2004	05:49	Sag	03/29/2005	18:55	Ari	07/25/2005	08:23
Vir	12/03/2004	17:59	Cap	03/31/2005	22:47	Tau	07/27/2005	12:55
Lib	12/06/2004	03:45	Aqu	04/03/2005	01:30	Gem	07/29/2005	21:02
Sco	12/08/2004	09:41	Pis	04/05/2005	03:45	Can	08/01/2005	07:52
Sag	12/10/2004	11:52	Ari	04/07/2005	06:27	Leo	08/03/2005	20:09
Cap	12/12/2004	11:41	Tau	04/09/2005	10:50	Vir	08/06/2005	08:53
Aqu	12/14/2004	11:10	Gem	04/11/2005	17:54	Lib	08/08/2005	21:07
Pis	12/16/2004	12:24	Can	04/14/2005	04:03	Sco	08/11/2005	07:33
Ari	12/18/2004	16:52	Leo	04/16/2005	16:16	Sag	08/13/2005	14:45
Tau	12/21/2004	00:52	Vir	04/19/2005	04:26	Cap	08/15/2005	18:12
Gem	12/23/2004	11:32	Lib	04/21/2005	14:25	Aqu	08/17/2005	18:38
Can	12/25/2004	23:37	Sco	04/23/2005	21:24	Pis	08/19/2005	17:52
Leo	12/28/2004	12:13	Sag	04/26/2005	01:44	Ari	08/21/2005	18:00
Vir	12/31/2004	00:32	Cap	04/28/2005	04:32	Tau	08/23/2005	20:58
Lib	01/02/2005	11:18	Aqu	04/30/2005	06:53	Gem	08/26/2005	03:43
Sco	01/04/2005	18:58	Pis	05/02/2005	09:42	Can	08/28/2005	13:57
Sag	01/06/2005	22:42	Ari	05/04/2005	13:36	Leo	08/31/2005	02:14
Cap	01/08/2005	23:09	Tau	05/06/2005	19:01	Vir	09/02/2005	14:55
Aqu	01/10/2005	22:07	Gem	05/09/2005	02:28	Lib	09/05/2005	02:51
Pis	01/12/2005	21:51	Can	05/11/2005	12:20	Sco	09/07/2005	13:09
Ari	01/15/2005	00:27	Leo	05/14/2005	00:16	Sag	09/09/2005	21:01
Tau	01/17/2005	07:06	Vir	05/16/2005	12:45	Cap	09/12/2005	01:55
Gem	01/19/2005	17:23	Lib	05/18/2005	23:28	Aqu	09/14/2005	04:01
Can	01/22/2005	05:41	Sco	05/21/2005	06:47	Pis	09/16/2005	04:24
Leo	01/24/2005	18:20	Sag	05/23/2005	10:36	Ari	09/18/2005	04:42
Vir	01/27/2005	06:23	Cap	05/25/2005	12:10	Tau	09/20/2005	06:47
Lib	01/29/2005	17:12	Aqu	05/27/2005	13:09	Gem	09/22/2005	12:07
Sco	02/01/2005	01:49	Pis	05/29/2005	15:09	Can	09/24/2005	21:10
Sag	02/03/2005	07:20	Ari	05/31/2005	19:07	Leo	09/27/2005	09:02
Cap	02/05/2005	09:30	Tau	06/03/2005	01:19	Vir	09/29/2005	21:43
Aqu	02/07/2005	09:25	Gem	06/05/2005	09:35	Lib	10/02/2005	09:23
Pis	02/09/2005	08:59	Can	06/07/2005	19:46	Sco	10/04/2005	19:02
Ari	02/11/2005	10:22	Leo	06/10/2005	07:39	Sag	10/07/2005	02:27
Tau	02/13/2005	15:18	Vir	06/12/2005	20:21	Cap	10/09/2005	07:42
Gem	02/16/2005	00:18	Lib	06/15/2005	07:57	Aqu	10/11/2005	11:04
Can	02/18/2005	12:12	Sco	06/17/2005	16:22	Pis	10/13/2005	13:04
Leo	02/21/2005	00:53	Sag	06/19/2005	20:43	Ari	10/15/2005	14:39
Vir	02/23/2005	12:43	Cap	06/21/2005	21:51	Tau	10/17/2005	17:04
Lib	02/25/2005	22:57	Aqu	06/23/2005	21:36	Gem	10/19/2005	21:44
Sco	02/28/2005	07:19	Pis	06/25/2005	22:03	Can	10/22/2005	05:40
Sag	03/02/2005	13:28	Ari	06/28/2005	00:52	Leo	10/24/2005	16:48
Cap	03/04/2005	17:11	Tau	06/30/2005	06:44	Vir	10/27/2005	05:27
Aqu	03/06/2005	18:48	Gem	07/02/2005	15:25	Lib	10/29/2005	17:14
Pis	03/08/2005	19:32	Can	07/05/2005	02:07	Sco	11/01/2005	02:27
Ari	03/10/2005	21:03	Leo	07/07/2005	14:10	Sag	11/03/2005	08:54
Tau	03/13/2005	01:06	Vir	07/10/2005	02:56	Cap	11/05/2005	13:16

Aqu	11/07/2005	16:30	Lib	11/26/2005	01:56	Gem	12/13/2005	14:59
Pis	11/09/2005	19:22	Sco	11/28/2005	11:31	Can	12/15/2005	23:01
Ari	11/11/2005	22:22	Sag	11/30/2005	17:31	Leo	12/18/2005	09:18
Tau	11/14/2005	02:02	Cap	12/02/2005	20:41	Vir	12/20/2005	21:38
Gem	11/16/2005	07:09	Aqu	12/04/2005	22:36	Lib	12/23/2005	10:25
Can	11/18/2005	14:42	Pis	12/07/2005	00:44	Sco	12/25/2005	21:02
Leo	11/21/2005	01:10	Ari	12/09/2005	04:02	Sag	12/28/2005	03:42
Vir	11/23/2005	13:41	Tau	12/11/2005	08:46	Cap	12/30/2005	06:34